THE CLOUDS STILL HANG

Episodes from inside a life

A Biographical Trilogy

by

Patrick C Notchtree

First published 2012 by Limebury Books
www.limebury.com

ISBN 978-0-9572361-2-7

@pcnotchtree

Copyright © Patrick C. Notchtree & Limebury Books

Formatted and set by Limebury Books

The first part of this trilogy, "The Book of Daniel", was previously published under the trilogy title "The Secret Catamite".

This book is sold subject to the condition that it shall not, by way of trade or otherwise, be lent, resold, hired out or otherwise circulated without the publisher's prior consent in any form, binding or cover other than that in which it is published and without a similar condition including this condition being imposed on the subsequent purchaser.

Foreword

This is a work of fiction. It is an account of one person's struggle with the demons within, and not always successfully. It was originally written as a form of therapy. If others wish to read it, perhaps they too may gain something from it. They may condemn it and the characters within. That in a free society is their privilege. But one thing the author has learned is not to rush to judgement, heeding the advice of St Matthew, "Judge not, that ye be not judged" (Matthew 7.1), and also the sound advice of Islam, "Good deeds annul evil deeds." (Qur'an, 11:114).

Inevitably it draws upon the life experiences of the author and of others but should not taken as a factual autobiography of the author. The names used are also fictitious and where they coincide with real people, those real people have no connection whatsoever with the fictional characters of this novel.

"Let us have the honesty to see things as they are,
since to see things as they ought to be is to miss them entirely."
Fernando Pessoa (1888-1935)

For my dear wife,
for whom my love knows no bounds,
for her devotion and forgiveness;
and my family,
the greatest blessing a man can have.

Also for my special friend
Stephen
whose tragic life could so easily have been
my own.

&

For 'Daniel'

Book One – The Book of Daniel

1. *1949 First Memory*

Simon felt the increasing panic well up in him. He knew that he was not going to make it in time. He ran up the stairs, nearly tripping over a loose stair rod that was failing to keep the worn, rough, red stair carpet in place. The bathroom door was closed, and Simon reached up for the handle struggling to turn it. Perhaps it was the way his small body had to stretch up, but he knew then that he had lost. As he stood inside the bathroom, his body could contain its load no longer and he felt the wet warmth as it slithered out of his little shorts and down the back of his left thigh on to the linoleum floor.

"Mummy!" Simon cried out in despair. And then the tears started to flow. Mummy appeared, and calmly set to clearing up the mess.

"I couldn't wait," wailed Simon through his sobbing.

"Why don't you go earlier?" asked Mummy irritably, as she carefully deposited the smelly lump into the pan which had been its intended destination.

"I didn't know I wanted to," explained Simon, now wracked with guilt at having let Mummy down and caused all this upset.

Steadily, Mummy removed the stained clothing, dropping it into the bath which stood on its little iron feet next to the pan. While the tears subsided, Mummy wiped her son down with a warm wet flannel, removing the evidence of his failure.

"Are you cross with me?" asked Simon, pleading for her not to be.

Mummy regarded the three year old, and her love for him watered her eyes.

"Of course not," she replied, and she took him into her arms. There, on the bathroom floor, mother and son re-affirmed their love and mutual dependence. She looked at her son, as ever worried about him. Since his very difficult birth which had nearly killed her, he had been a cause of concern, born blue, his slow development leading to him being labelled in the terminology of the day as Mentally Deficient, a crippled spastic. But now he was walking and talking, even if he had not yet mastered bowel control. She hugged him again and his sobbing subsided.

Later, Daddy came home, and was cross with him for making a mess. To Simon, Daddy was a part of his life. Some of the other, older children in the street said he was bad because he had been divorced from another woman so wasn't properly married to Mummy and they would go to hell, but Simon could not understand that. Going to hell was something to do with God, and that was far too remote for him to deal with. Perhaps the older children had met God; after all, Mummy said that when people were old, they did go to meet God.

Maybe some of the biguns already had. Simon kept away from the biguns as much as he could. They made him cry by calling him names, and some of their mummies said that they were not to play with him because his Daddy swore, and that it was all very wrong. Sometimes, when he went out to play in the street, in his pedal car or on his battered old green tricycle, the nasty ones would shout names at him like "Simple Simon". When it wasn't that it was "Little bastard!" One or two had started calling him this, and it had taken hold and was a regular taunt. Simon knew from the tone in which it was said, or often shouted, that it was not nice, whatever it meant. He asked his older sister, Frances, what names she got called. She didn't seem to know what he was talking about. But Frances was five years older and rarely played with Simon. She had her best friend, Jennifer, with whom she spent lots of time.

Once, when a little older, Simon asked Mummy what a bastard was, and she started to cry. So he did not ask the question again, but he felt sure that it was something about him that the biguns knew, that he did not. The mystery remained unsolved in Simon's mind, and the situation became one of the accepted factors of his existence. The problem did not go away and with each hurtful name-calling, it was again brought to the fore. But he never mentioned it to Mummy in case that made her cry, and when Mummy cried, Simon could not bear it.

Simon had to bear it though, because Mummy seemed to cry sometimes for no obvious reason, and would not tell him why. Frances would not tell him why either, and told him not to worry. Mummy sometimes said it was the war, but Simon did know that the war had ended just before he was born. And anyway, he knew Daddy had got a medal for flying in the war and that was supposed to be good. So Simon cried too, and he and Mummy would cling to each other, sharing their joint misery, hers caused by the natural injustice of the lottery of life, perhaps for her precipitate wartime marriage, his for no better reason than Mummy was unhappy. Simon could never discover what he had done to make Mummy cry, and although she always said it was not his fault, he knew that it must be. What he did not know of were the tears shed in the loneliness of the nights after his bedtime when Daddy came home very late, or not at all.

As he grew older, Simon started to be frightened of Daddy. He often came home in a very bad temper, and would shout at Mummy and him for no real reason that Simon could see. If he was really in a bad temper, he would make Simon bend over a chair and hit him with one of his old black, leather soled slippers. Mummy would protest sometimes that he was being too hard, and that the offence that Simon had committed did not merit such treatment. Daddy's response was always either one of two.

"Spare the rod and spoil the child!" or,

"My father used to beat me when I did something wrong, and it never did me any harm!"

Simon used to wonder how it was that anyone could be beaten and it not hurt them. He found a way of coping with this by pretending it was someone else. It was as though he was outside his body, watching Simon being beaten as though in a film. But it hurt and after the punishment, he would go upstairs to his bedroom and cry, while the raised voices of argument could be heard from below.

Yet Daddy could be loving. He took Simon aged almost five to London to see the Festival of Britain, which Simon found exciting and stimulating, the image of the delicate Skylon apparently magically suspended in mid air remained fixed in his mind. Daddy also took him the Battersea Fun Fair associated with the festival. Simon knew Daddy was important because when they went to get a meal first in a restaurant, suddenly Daddy said, "Stop eating."

Simon stopped eating.

"I've come out without my wallet," said Daddy. "I can't pay for the meal."

Daddy called the waiter over and explained. The manager came over and Daddy explained again.

"I'm sorry, sir," said the manager. "Perhaps if you had some form of identification?"

Daddy looked in his pockets and found some small white cards with printing on, his business card. The manager looked impressed.

"Certainly, sir. Send us a cheque. Please finish your meal." The manager paused. "Were you planning to take the boy on the funfair?"

"Yes, I was actually."

The Manager reached into his pocket and took a note out of his wallet, and gave it to Daddy.

"Please allow me to lend you this, sir, and I hope your son enjoys the fair."

"Thank you very much," said Daddy. "That is extremely kind of you. I will send a cheque as soon as I get home. Come on, son. Eat up!" Daddy smiled at Simon, who was thinking how special Daddy must be, ate heartily. And then he enjoyed the funfair.

2. *1951 Starting school, Daniel*

Starting school was an upset for Simon. Firstly, he had to leave Mummy, and he worried about whether she would be even more unhappy. Secondly, he was frightened of how he would be received by the other children.

He liked his teacher, Mrs. Hastings, because she was a bit like Mummy, except that she did not cry. He did not like Miss Harvey, the headmistress, because she never smiled and used to get cross with the children. She had a bamboo cane that she would hit children with. The girls were hit across the palm of the hand, but Miss Harvey made the boys bend over while she caned their bottoms. Simon did his best to keep out of her way.

His sense of isolation did not diminish at school. The other children called him names still, and so he retreated into the security of his own company, clutching his teddy bear at night for comfort. One solace to which an isolated Simon clung was that he could meet Frances at playtime in the school yard. The juniors were supposed to play in a different area from the infants, but she would come to meet him. Simon liked the reassurance, but he knew that soon Frances would be leaving the juniors and then he would be friendless again.

The exception was Daniel. He was almost two years older than Simon, and therefore not in the same class, but he did live near Simon, in the next street. He could see Daniel's house from his bedroom window. He had become aware of Daniel not long after starting school and his quiet self-confidence attracted Simon. He was good at school and at sports, and, with his dark hair, kind face and deep blue eyes, the girls said he was he was dishy. Simon thought so too.

The two started to travel to school together, either by bus from the main road or in good weather, a long walk. Although at first Daniel sometimes joined the others at school in baiting him, he always came back afterwards and was his friend. Simon never asked why he appeared so fickle, it was a fact of the universe, like the sun and moon and stars. He didn't question, they just were! But soon, as the two boys became firm friends, Daniel would instead defend Simon rather than join in the taunts.

Simon's problems were compounded by the difficulty he had at school. He could not remember what all the letters meant, and he found writing hard to grasp. Numbers seemed totally meaningless. Soon he was sent for some of the time to see Miss Brown for extra help. Her room was next to the balcony which ran across one end of the hall. Simon liked being up there, climbing the stone staircase with its brown glazed brick walls, emerging high up on the balcony from where he could look down into the hall, and even into some of the classrooms through their hall side windows. Up there with Miss Brown and the small group she helped, he felt away from the hurly burly of the school and his large class of over forty children. He was safe for a while. He was to remain a part of that extra help group until the end of his junior school. Of course this added force to those who wanted to taunt him, giving "Simple Simon" added veracity, and Simon less defence against it.

3. *1952/2 Death of the King*

He slowly became more aware of the wider world. Daniel, being older, knew much more of course, but Mummy would talk to him about things and Simon became increasingly curious. One day, he was at home with some illness, sitting in bed while Mummy tried to explain to him about the war in Korea.

There was much of it he didn't understand, but he was worried by the Communists, and if the war would come into his life.

"Daddy won't have to go and fight again, will he?" asked Simon anxiously.

"No, dear," said Mummy.

"But wasn't he good or something, with his medal. They want good fighters don't they?" Simon was in no doubt that Daddy would be a good fighter, he knew how strong he was, although how this fitted in with being in an aeroplane he put to one side.

"Daddy won't be going to fight again, he's done all that. And the DFC was for the last war, it doesn't mean he'll have to go again."

"Will I have to go and fight when I grow up?" asked Simon.

"Oh, I hope not," said Mummy, and gave him a hug. "I'll get you a drink."

Mummy went downstairs and he heard the reassuring sound of the wireless. It was talking because Mummy often listened to the Home Service. Suddenly Mummy gave a little cry, and Simon wondered if she had dropped something. It was a while before Mummy came back up, carrying a tray with his drink and some bread and dripping on it.

"The King's dead!" she said, and then started to cry, spilling the drink.

Simon was aware that this was momentous news, he knew the King was head of the country, and he felt the loss too in some way he didn't understand. And Mummy was crying so he cried too.

"Who will be King now?"

Mummy smiled though her tears, and wiped both her eyes and his.

"We don't have a King now," she said. "We have a Queen, a new young Queen, Queen Elizabeth the second."

"Oh," said Simon, not quite understanding but glad that the matter had been settled and that there was continuity.

"Eat your sandwich," said Mummy, and she sat on the edge of the bed while Simon ate.

4. 1952/3 *Miss Harvey*

Then there was the day that Mrs. Hastings was away from school. When the whistle went, Simon went into the line, next to the high, red bricked wall round the playground where the younger classes lined up. Beside him in the next line was Daniel. Simon smiled at him, but one of the biguns was watching so Daniel paid no attention. Then Miss Harvey came out into the yard and total silence fell on the children, each individual petrified that the icy stare might alight arbitrarily on themselves. Miss Harvey came over to Simon's line.

"Stand up, Class two!" she snapped. Class two did their best to comply from a standing position already. As they were led in, Simon realised that Mrs. Hastings was not about, and that he was to be subject to Miss Harvey's iron rule all day. His fears were confirmed when they were sat in the classroom.

"Mrs. Hastings is unwell today," Miss Harvey announced, "so I shall have to put up with you. I expect you all to behave yourselves. Any disobedience I will deal with in the proper manner."

Simon knew what the proper manner was, and had no intention of bringing himself to her attention. He tried to slide down a bit behind the desk.

"That boy, sit up!"

Simon looked up to find the icy blue eyes fixed upon him. Miss Harvey was a tall, thin woman with silver hair and small, steel-rimmed, rectangular spectacles. She always wore a black dress that added to the sinister appearance. Simon sat up.

"I shall be watching you today, boy," said Miss Harvey. Simon felt he had failed at the first hurdle, and dreaded the rest of the day.

After assembly, Miss Harvey gave them all a sheet of paper. The children started to write their names at the top. Simon was very proud because he had now learned to write his name without copying from the card that Mrs. Hastings had written out for each child. Miss Brown said his writing was coming on well. He thought that this would be a good opportunity to regain his status in Miss Harvey's eyes by demonstrating this feat. With unerring certainty, Miss Harvey's eyes found the one desk on which there was no name card. She strode down the aisle between the rows of forward facing double desks until she was standing over Simon.

"Where is your name card?"

Simon's resolve left him faced with Miss Harvey at close quarters. Shaking, he explained.

"I can write my name without it now, please Miss."

Miss Harvey looked at Simon's paper. He had got as far as the first three letters.

"Sim!" Miss Harvey exclaimed. "Sim!" she repeated, equally dramatically. Simon cowered. "Is your name Sim?" she demanded.

"No, Miss," said Simon, barely audible.

"No? Then why have you written 'Sim', boy?"

Simon instinctively knew that it would be unwise to explain to Miss Harvey that this was just the beginning of the word 'Simon', and wondered what it was about some grown ups that made them forget such obvious things, yet were ready to blame children for forgetting quite difficult things.

"Dumb insolence now," was Miss Harvey's response to Simon's reticence. "What makes you think you are different from everybody else?" she demanded.

Somehow, Miss Harvey had hit upon the great unresolved problem of Simon's life. It did serve though to reinforce the knowledge that he was somehow different from ordinary boys. Simon had no answer for himself, let alone Miss Harvey, and so he remained silent. This enraged an already fearsome Miss Harvey. She took hold of Simon's ear, and twisting it and pulling, forced

Simon out of his seat, down the aisle to the front of the class. Miss Harvey turned to face the class.

"Now you will see what I think of disobedient children who are very rude as well," she said. Simon looked miserably at the class. The sea of faces intimidated him a bit. All those eyes! He could see that most of the children were clearly nervous, some of the girls looked upset. One or two of the boys, like Barry Spence, were obviously going to enjoy watching Simon, their favourite target for both verbal and physical bullying, suffering at Miss Harvey's hands also. A strange alliance, Barry Spence and Miss Harvey.

"Bend over, boy!" came the inevitable command. Simon tried hard not to cry as the bamboo cut across his buttocks, but the pain of six successive strokes, even through his grey flannel shorts and pants was too much, he didn't even have time to go out of himself to protect himself by letting it happen to his other self and he returned to his seat with tears running down his small face to the sniggers of the Spence gang and the frightened, averted gaze of most of the others. Still crying, he got out his name card, with Mrs. Hastings' beautiful italic script on it, and completed writing his name.

There was no respite for Simon the next day, either. Mrs. Hasting was still absent and Miss Harvey was taking the class again. Her irritation at this was plain. Simon's next crisis came at lunchtime. It was salad for school dinner. This meant an assortment of grated lettuce, grated tomato, grated carrot and worst of all, grated cheese. Simon could not stand the smell of cheese, and the taste made him feel desperately sick. He forced down the various grated components of this meal, except the cheese, which he tried to distribute over the surface of the plate so that its presence would be less noticeable. He placed his knife and fork together as Mummy had taught him, signifying that he had finished. Barry Spence saw his chance. Thick blond hair and sharp blue eyes, his angelic face bathed in righteous indignation, he put up his hand to attract one of the kitchen ladies.

"Please Miss, Simon hasn't eaten his cheese."

"Barry, you're rotten," whispered Cynthia Jackson.

"Shut up, cow," snarled Barry Spence, "or I'll bash you in."

Cynthia Jackson shut up.

"Why have you not eaten your cheese?" demanded the figure in the yellow overall coat.

"Please Miss, I don't like it," said Simon.

"Miss Harvey, this boy won't eat his dinner," called yellow overall across the dining hall. With sinking heart, Simon heard Miss Harvey's footsteps coming across to his table. In the hush, he was aware of the black dress next him, and of Miss Harvey's powerful presence.

"It's you!" proclaimed Miss Harvey to the rest of the school. Simon wondered how he could ever not be him. Miss Harvey lowered her voice, but without any loss of threatening power.

"Eat your meal," she demanded. Simon knew that resistance was pointless. Miss Harvey would never understand the effect that cheese had on him. Slowly he started to force the abhorrent gratings into his mouth, and down his throat. With each swallow, his bile rose even more, and the tears started down his face again.

"It's no good just playing with it," said Miss Harvey. "Good men died to bring us food in the war. I'm going to stand here until it's all gone."

Simon knew that she would, and tried to hurry up to shorten his ordeal. Suddenly, he could contain it no longer. He felt the uncontrollable rush into his throat, opening from within. Unthinking, he turned to the side and vomited all down Miss Harvey's black dress.

"You vile little boy!" she shrieked. "You did that deliberately, you wicked child!" Miss Harvey seized a cloth from yellow overall, and frantically wiped at her dress. Boiling with rage, she then seized Simon and dragged him to the front of the dining hall. Simon stood shaking, the taste of vomit still in his mouth, still feeling sick through cheese and fear.

"Bend over, you nasty little boy," demanded Miss Harvey. Simon bent. The force behind the strokes seemed far greater than the earlier beating and for Simon, whose counting was not the best anyway, there seemed to be more than the earlier six.

Simon spent the afternoon standing in the corner of the classroom, because Miss Harvey said she could not bear his face. For Simon this was a blessing because he did not want to have to sit, and while he was standing in the corner, he could not get into trouble about his work. It was probably the safest place to be, only returning to his place at the end of the day to put his chair up and say the prayer.

5. 1952/3 Going home

On the way home, Daniel asked Simon about the beatings. Simon tried to explain what had happened, and how Miss Harvey had beat him because he was different. The two boys took a short cut home through the wood. In fact, it was slightly longer than going by the road route, but it was more fun.

"Did she hit you hard?" asked Daniel as they walked through the trees.

"Yes," said Simon, "very hard." He knew that his face still showed the signs of his tears.

"What will your Mum say," asked Daniel, still curious.

"Don't know," replied Simon.

"Did it hurt?" asked Daniel.

"It was horrible," answered Simon, the memory starting to bring back his tears. Cross with Daniel's incessant questioning, he said, "Look."

Simon stopped, and looking along the path to see if anyone was coming, he dropped his gabardine mac to the ground, pulled his shirt out of his shorts, and slackening the front fastening, eased his shorts down sufficiently to expose much of his buttocks. Looking over his shoulder, Simon could see from the expression on Daniel's face that there were marks in plenty.

Daniel gently lifted Simon's shirt a bit more with one hand, and with the other, tugged Simon's shorts down to reveal his bottom completely. Simon felt reassured by the tenderness of his friend's touch and so allowed this. Simon felt his gentle hand run smoothly and lightly over his hips and buttocks, but did not resist his friend's advance. Daniel broke the brief spell of the moment.

"She didn't half whack you," he said. Simon nodded, pulling up his shorts. "I'm glad I'm not different, if that's what you get," said Daniel, thankfully.

When Simon got home, he started to tell Mummy about it, oblivious of her warning glances. Daddy came into the room, and Simon realised his mistake.

"What have you done?" demanded Daddy sternly.

"Leave him, he'll be alright," said Mummy.

"He must have done something," said Daddy, then, glaring at Simon, "Well, what was it?"

Simon didn't answer, unsure of what response any answer would bring. Daddy insisted on examining the marks on Simon's bottom. Simon did not like this, but was no position to refuse. In the end he got away with being sent to bed early.

6. *1952/3 Daniel in the Den*

A few days later, at the weekend, when Simon and Daniel were discussing what had happened, Daniel thought it was unfair.

"It's not your fault," he said. "Did old Harvey really hit you because you were different?"

"I think so," said Simon, "But I don't know how I am. I don't look much different to anyone else do I?"

"Not really," said Daniel, "but you are a bit odd sometimes."

"I'm the only one the biguns call 'bastard'," said Simon, "but I think I'm the same as everyone else, like you."

"Don't know," said Daniel, "let's have a look at you, and I'll see if we are different."

It was decided that they should both compare themselves. They set off into the small wood, known as the Spinney, that lay beyond the allotments at the end of the street. Simon felt an unexplained thrill of anticipation as they searched together for a suitably hidden place.

"I know a place," said Daniel, "Come on." Simon followed as Daniel led the way across a bombsite and through the trees, and down into an overgrown depression that was hard to see unless one knew it was there. The warm sunlight cast speckled green shadows over the two boys' faces as they sat in a small clear area, almost totally concealed by the bushes from any casual passer-by.

"It's my den," announced Daniel, looking at Simon with the pride of one who has shared a great secret, and yet seeking Simon's approval. Simon beamed back at him, and looked around the den.

"It's a super den," said Simon.

"Our secret den," said Daniel.

"Yes," said Simon simply.

For a few moments, the two boys sat in the warmth of the den and each other's company, the communion of their eyes saying more to each other than their limited vocabulary could ever have done.

"We could be soldiers in the war," suggested Daniel.

"A secret base against the Germans," added Simon. Neither boy was exactly sure who the Germans were, but both knew that they were to be feared, even though they had been beaten in the war. Simon knew about the war, because Daddy had been in it, and had shown Simon some photographs of him in uniform. Daddy's RAF uniform still hung in the wardrobe and the medal was in the top drawer. Sometimes, some men would come to the house, and they and Daddy would drink a lot of beer and then start talking and laughing about what they had done in the war together. Simon thought the war must have been great fun, even though the Germans had obviously tried to spoil it. Maybe that's why we fought them, to stop them spoiling the war.

Daniel suddenly threw himself onto his stomach, holding an imaginary rifle.

"Quiet, men!" he commanded. "The Germans are close."

Simon lay next to Daniel, and both boys stared out through the leaves and trees to where the houses could be seen beyond the allotments. One or two men could be seen digging in their allotment patches, but in the minds of the two boys, these were the real Germans, out to kill them.

The Germans made no attempt to advance and do battle, in fact they seemed unaware of the British soldiers lying concealed in the wood. The boys lay increasingly uneasily, each waiting for the other to admit first that the game had lost its sparkle. Daniel eventually gave way.

"What shall we do now?" he asked, tacitly admitting the lack of co-operation afforded by the allotment diggers.

"We could light a fire," suggested Simon in a moment of inspiration. He had watched Mummy light the fire at home, using paper and sticks to get the coal burning, but it occurred to him that he had no paper, sticks, coal or matches.

"You burn wood," said Daniel, looking around the den.

"We haven't got any matches." said Simon finally.

He remembered then why they had come here, and asked Daniel The Question.

"What's a bastard?" asked Simon. Daniel thought for a moment.

"Don't know," he said. "Why?"

"I asked Mummy, but she didn't tell me."

"I'll ask mine," offered Daniel, "and then I'll tell you. Why do the biguns call you that?"

"Don't know," said Simon. "I don't know what it is."

"Why are you different?" persisted Daniel. Simon thought about this. He was always aware that he was somehow different from the others, that they knew this. They laughed at some of the ideas he came up with, at the way he talked, at Mummy and Daddy, and at him because of the 'Bastard'. Now Daniel too knew that he was different, and Daniel was his friend. He was older, and knew lots of things. Sometimes he even played with the biguns.

"Don't know. I don't want to be. I've looked in the mirror, and I can't see what's wrong," said Simon.

"Let's have a look," said Daniel, assuming an air of authority that Simon found somehow exciting, yet feeling compelled to oblige. He looked around the wood from the concealed den to check that no-one was about. Daniel stood up.

"It's all right," he said. Simon started to undo the buttons of his shorts. Watching him, Daniel felt his dominance over his younger friend growing, and felt he had to assert it.

"Take everything off," he commanded. Simon stripped off, conscious of Daniel watching him, and felt a stirring of excitement at what they were doing.

"Socks as well," said Daniel, and Simon obeyed. He sat naked on the soft grass in the hollow, arms round his drawn up knees, buttocks feeling the warm grass. It felt good. Daniel knelt beside him and gently pushed Simon so that he was lying down, face up, looking at the overhead canopy of green, with the blue sky peeping through here and there. Daniel looked over Simon's body. He gently ran his hand over Simon's skin, and as his friend made no move, established mastery of the relationship by caressing Simon's most intimate parts.

"I think I know what it is," he said. "It's your cock."

Simon lifted up onto his elbows and looked at his penis.

"What about it?" he asked.

"It's different," said Daniel. "Look." Daniel quickly undid his shorts and pulled them and his pants down. Slipping them off and his T-shirt, he lay next to Simon on the grass. Simon could see the difference. The end was different from Daniel's. Simon looked at his circumcision and wondered. He looked at Daniel frightened and puzzled.

"How do they know?" he asked.

"Who?" asked Daniel.

"The biguns and Miss Harvey and all them."

"Don't know, but I won't tell", said Daniel. "Are your marks still there?"

Simon rolled over and Daniel examined the fading bruises. He again ran his hand round Simon's body, over his buttocks and through his legs. Simon felt the softness of his touch and was glad for it. He felt the warmth of Daniel's body close to him and felt something of the comfort he got from Mummy.

Simon was glad he had a friend who knew how he was different, and still wanted him. Simon was happy.

They lay there for a while, as the day cooled, then dressed and went home, Daniel for a piano lesson, Simon for tea, each happy with their time in the den, each for their own reasons.

7. 1953/6 Coronation

The Coronation was a memorable event for Simon. It was going to be on television! Daddy had always said television was a waste of money and radio was much better. But then it said that the Coronation would be on television. Daniel's family were going to get one, a point raised one day when all four were at home having tea.

"Daniel's Daddy's getting a television," announced Simon. He had no real hope that this would produce a 'yes, let's get one too' moment, but felt compelled to say it.

"Maybe Daniel's father can afford one," said Daddy, sharply.

"I think Jennifer's going to get one too," said Frances. "She says I can go and watch the Coronation at hers if I want."

"Can I come?" asked Simon quickly.

"Definitely not," said Frances curtly.

"I'll go to Daniel's then," said Simon.

"Good, at least you won't be bothering me," retorted his sister.

"Children, stop it," said Mummy. "Frances, you must wait to be asked by Jennifer's mother, not just by Jennifer. Same goes for you Simon. Wait to be asked properly."

"I'll get Jennifer to ask her," said Frances.

"And I'll get Daniel to ask," said Simon not wishing to be outdone.

"For heaven's sake, stop it," said Daddy crossly, glaring at Simon. Was it just because he had been the last to speak, or was because Frances was older. Whatever, Simon fell quiet.

"I expect it'll be on the radio," said Mummy brightly.

"Help Mummy clear the table," said Daddy, getting up and leaving the dining room.

"That meant you," said Frances to Simon, also getting up.

"Ask to leave the table properly," said Mummy. Frances sat down again, but tensed ready to get up again.

"Please may I leave the table?"

"Yes dear," said Mummy.

"Why isn't she going to help clear up?" demanded Simon indignantly.

"Yes," said Mummy to Frances, "you can help."

"Mum!" whined Frances, "I'm going to Jennifer's and I've got to get ready and I'll be late if I don't get ready now."

Simon often wondered why Frances took so long to 'get ready'. This was some feminine ritual that was completely incomprehensible. She would disappear for ages and then come out again, looking to Simon's eyes pretty much as she had when she went in. Simon would just get up and go out, it saved a lot of time. But Mummy fell for it. She spent a lot of time 'getting ready' too.

"Well, you do it next time," said Mummy.

"Thanks Mummy," said Frances, already half way out of the dining room door.

Simon looked at Mummy crossly. "It's not fair," he said. "I bet she doesn't do it next time."

"Come on, love," she coaxed, "we'll do it together, you and me."

It was the Wednesday tea time before the Tuesday of Coronation Day when the van came to the house.

There was a knock at the door.

"Ah," said Daddy, who had come home early for some unexplained reason. He got up, smiling broadly. Mummy was smiling too.

Simon and Frances exchanged glances, they were suspicious of these parental conspiracies.

Daddy opened the door to a man in overalls.

"Mr Scott?" said the man.

"Yes," said Daddy, turning to smile at the two puzzled and curious children behind him.

The man in overalls went away to return with another overall man, and they were carrying a television!

"Is that ours?" said Frances.

"Yes, princess," said Daddy.

The men carried the television through to the sitting room. Mummy and Daddy moved the table out of the corner to make room.

"Will there do?" said Daddy.

The man looked round and then out of the window for some reason.

"Fine, sir," he said. "OK if we go round the back?"

"Of course," said Mummy.

Simon followed to see what they were doing.

"Don't get in the way, love," called Mummy.

"He's OK," said the man.

They took ladders off the van and took them round to the back garden. Then a big roll of round wire and of course! The aerial.

Simon watched as they climbed up onto the roof of the house. The large 'H' shaped aerial was strapped to the chimney and the wire fixed to the wall, in through the window frame to the television set.

"You're a lucky young fellow," said the man to Simon.

"Why?" said Simon.

"Why!" repeated the man. "Do you know what the waiting list is for these things? There's going to be a lot of disappointed people on Tuesday."

"Will we see the Coronation on it?" asked Simon.

"I expect so," said the man, laughing. "I expect it helps when your Dad works for the BBC."

Simon knew Daddy worked for the BBC and that this was important. Daniel thought so anyway. He said it was because Daddy had done well in the war. But Daniel's Daddy was a policeman and a high up one too, and Simon thought that was pretty important.

The two men, one up by the aerial and the other looking at an instrument on the ground, spent some time talking about something called alignment, then they seemed happy.

"What's that for?" asked Simon.

"The aerial's got to be lined up with the transmitter," explained the man. Simon liked the sound of 'transmitter'. It sounded mysterious and powerful.

Simon looked out across the garden and the allotments to see if he could see the transmitter.

"No, son," said the man, chuckling, "you won't see it from here. It's at Sutton Coldfield." Simon had never heard of Sutton Coldfield, so he let that pass.

The men went into the sitting room. They connected up the wires and the plug. Time to turn it on.

Nothing happened at first and then there was a noise from the set, a steady hum. The men seemed pleased, then the picture appeared. Simon was disappointed. He thought it would perhaps be cowboys or something interesting. Instead it was a load of black, white and grey patterns.

"That's the test card," said the man to Daddy and Mummy. "It's looking good."

"Thank you," said Daddy and went out with the men. Simon and Frances stayed, looking at the unchanging test card, with its thin lines, squares and the big circle in the middle with more lines inside. But it was magic. A picture coming through the air.

Daddy came back in. The two jumped up.

"Thanks Daddy," said Frances, and they hugged Daddy. Daddy smiled down at his children. Mummy was smiling too.

"You've got a telly," said Daniel when the two met up.

"How'd you know?" asked Simon, annoyed that his surprise had been spoiled.

"There's a damn great aerial on your roof, idiot!" said Daniel, laughing.

"Oh," said Simon, deflated. He had forgotten that. Daniel could see his house from his bedroom window. They had tried to set up a signalling system from their bedroom windows, but it had proved too complicated to devise a code with sufficient variety of meaning. Then it occurred to him that there was no aerial on Daniel's house.

"When's yours coming?" said Simon.

"Dunno," said Daniel, glumly. "Might not get it in time."

Simon remembered what the man had said about waiting lists.

"Well, there's a long waiting list for them, you know," said Simon knowledgeably.

"So how'd you get yours then?" demanded Daniel crossly. Again Simon remembered the man's comments.

"My Dad works for the BBC."

"Well, my Dad's important too, he's a high up policeman."

"I know," said Simon, suddenly aware of his friend's hurt feelings. It mattered to Daniel to be in the lead, in their friendship, in everything. He hated being second.

"You can come and watch it on ours if you like," offered Simon, generously.

"Can I?" said Daniel, smiling back now. Simon's soul warmed to that smile, as always. He nodded happily.

A very similar conversation, with a similar outcome was taking place not far away at Jennifer's, with Frances being equally expansive. So it was at tea, the usual place for family conversations, that the diplomacy began.

Sitting round the dining room table, the burning question was on Simon's mind. He was committed, he had asked Daniel, but now he had to make sure it was OK. But of course, Frances got in first.

"Mummy, is it all right if Jennifer comes to watch the Coronation? Their television hasn't come yet, so I said she could."

"I think that'll be all right," said Mummy. Daddy just nodded.

"Can Daniel come? His telly hasn't come yet," said Simon, hoping that the recently established precedent would work in his favour.

"Television," said Daddy. Daddy hated 'telly'. He said it was slovenly language.

"We can't have everybody," said Mummy, a bit worried.

"I've asked Jennifer already," said Frances.

"That was naughty of you, dear," said Mummy.

"You should ask first, Frances," said Daddy.

Frances looked at her parents, waiting for the decision. Simon waited, wondering what to do for the best.

"I expect it'll be all right," said Mummy. Frances smiled, and turned to Simon with a look of triumph.

"I've asked Daniel," said Simon.

"For God's sake! This isn't a public house!" said Daddy, getting angry.

Simon was taken aback by the sudden change and Daddy's anger. He got frightened when Daddy was angry. It showed.

"It's all right, Simon," said Mummy. "Harry, it is a special occasion. And you have done well to get a set in time."

Simon looked hopefully at Daddy.

"Oh very well," said Daddy, "In for a penny, in for a pound."

Simon and Frances cheered.

By the time Tuesday came, the small sitting room was full. Some friends of Daddy's and Mummy's were there, Jennifer and her brother and both parents, Daniel and his Mummy. His sister Louise was watching it somewhere else, and his Daddy was at work. They had brought some extra chairs round from Daniel's, the two boys struggling round the corner with them. Mummy had made some sandwiches and some jam tarts. Mummy's pastry was lovely. There were cups of tea and pop for the children out of their coronation mugs.

They watched, the end of Westminster Abbey used as a filler shot becoming very familiar, but there was the Queen, actually getting crowned. And it was happening at the same time as they were watching it. The children all had their special souvenir programmes, and it was a great occasion.

Simon and Daniel sat together in one chair as there were still not enough chairs to go round. But they enjoyed the close physical contact this afforded and when, to make more room of course, Daniel boldly put his arm round Simon, nobody seemed to care. So it stayed there. The two boys unified by the common bond of friendship, Daddy in his chair, revelling in being the generous host, who just happened to be the only person in the road with a television. Of course, certain people had not been invited, the nasty ones, and serve them right too! Simon rested his head on Daniel's shoulder, and was happy.

8.   *1953/8 Westward Ho!*

A major event each year was the annual family holiday. The week before this was always one of chaos and stress, mixed with excitement and anticipation. The packing of The Trunk was the centre of all this from Simon's point of view. The Trunk was a large brown case, easily big enough for Simon to climb inside, into which all the family's needs for two weeks away in the boarding house would be packed. There were lists, and lists of lists.

Simon looked forward to this. Things seemed different somehow when they were away. Mummy seemed happier, Daddy didn't get so cross with him and Frances played with him.

The journey itself was an adventure. The alarm clock would be set early so everybody would be up in good time. They now had a telephone, which Daddy had for his work, and not many people had telephones, although Daniel did because his Daddy was a policeman. The phone would ring in the small hours of the morning and Daddy or Mummy would go downstairs to answer and speak to the operator. This was safer than just using the alarm clock because sometimes you could go back to sleep.

To Simon, the world seemed strange and exciting at three or four o'clock in the morning. Outside there was a strange quiet, unlike the darkness of the evening, this morning darkness was somehow peaceful, the family's activity seeming out of place and a disturbance. Breakfast, prepared the night before, would be eaten, although Simon and Frances were usually too excited eat much, and then the taxi would come. Daddy always said the taxi had to big enough to take The Trunk, so it was usually a big car that came. It took Daddy and the taxi driver to carry The Trunk out. Then they went down to the station to catch the train to London.

Simon liked trains, they were big, powerful and exciting. The train would arrive on its journey south, everything would be loaded on board and off they would go. Sometimes it was a corridor train which Simon liked because he and Frances would explore the train, although Simon was always nervous about crossing the wobbly bits where the coaches joined. They tried to go from the very front to the back where the guard's van was, and among everything else, The Trunk would be there. The guard was usually friendly and didn't mind them looking in. When he went out along the train for something, he locked it. Then they would go back along, looking for their own compartment where Mummy and Daddy would be sitting. Sometimes they got the wrong coach and a moment of panic would set in, but Frances always knew which way to go.

Simon was always fascinated by the stations in London. Every other station he knew of the trains came in at one end and went out the other. But in London, the line stopped! When they got off, he would run to the front of the train where the huge locomotive was now at rest, hissing and steaming, say hello to the driver in his mucky overalls and battered cap and then look at the giant buffers with the front of the locomotive just a few feet away.

But the best part of this journey from Simon's point of view was yet to come. The Devon Belle!

This took them from London to Devon and their holiday. He loved the ornate Pullman coaches, the slab sided look of the powerful locomotive and especially the observation coach at the rear of the train with windows all round and armchair seating. Simon liked to sit right at the back of the train, looking out through the rear facing window, watching the track speeding out from under him and the wreaths of smoke from the locomotive many coaches ahead of him writhing away in the train's slipstream.

It was teatime before they arrived at Barnstaple, and from there to Bideford for the last leg of their journey, another adventure, by pony and trap to the boarding house at Westward Ho!

Mrs Thorne – there never seemed to be a Mr Thorne in this world of widows – ran the boarding house and Simon liked her because she was kind and gave him extra biscuits. Mummy and Daddy used to grumble about her rules though, but that was grown-ups' stuff.

In the morning after breakfast, they would fill bags with buckets, spades and walk down to the beach where the Atlantic rollers would come crashing when the weather was rough, but often there would be waves just right for Simon to jump around in, making Mummy and Daddy laugh. And then of course there was the pebble ridge. This long mound of stones, seemingly endless to Simon, was a source of fascination. He would lift the stones and find crabs, search for barnacles and pull out long strands of seaweed. There was a metal track laid over the ridge and he would watch tanks come over this, going where to and from he didn't know, and when they came, he had to watch from a distance.

But this was the last year of the Devon Belle, and Simon would never ride it again. A death and a legacy meant the end of holidays in Westward Ho! and a new horizon opening for Simon.

9. 1954/8 Swimming Lesson

"Why don't you come?" Daniel looked at his friend and could not understand Simon's hesitation.

"I can't swim," said Simon dully.

"That's OK, I'll teach you," said Daniel confidently. Daniel had found swimming to add to his love of music and piano, and what's more found that he loved it just as much. He loved the feel of his healthy young body coursing through the water, the almost weightless agility it gave him to twist and turn, somersault and dive, and move in a way that was simply impossible on dry land. He looked at Simon, who although younger of course, was just as fit. "You'll love it," he continued encouragingly.

Simon looked at Daniel whom he trusted absolutely and nodded.

"Go get your trunks then," Daniel advised, adding helpfully, "You'll need a towel as well, and a shilling."

Simon ran off home. Mummy was at work but Frances was in.

"What's the matter?" she asked as Simon entered like a tornado.

"Need my swimming trunks!" shouted Simon back as he ran up the stairs. He found the rarely used trunks at the bottom of his drawer and bounded down again. Frances was in the sitting room.

"Which towel shall I take?" Simon asked his big sister.

"Any," said Frances, uninterested. But then, "You can't swim," she added, puzzled.

"Daniel's going to teach me at the lido," said Simon.

"Might have guessed."

"I need a shilling, Daniel says," said Simon hopefully.

"Well, don't look at me," responded Frances tersely. Then, seeing Simon's crestfallen face, added, "Wait a moment." Frances disappeared upstairs while Simon paced around impatiently.

"Here you are," said Frances returning with the prized shilling. "you owe me that."

"I'll tell Mummy," shouted back Simon, who was already half way out of the house.

Daniel was waiting at the corner.

"Shall I get my bike?" asked Simon.

"No," said Daniel, "We'll walk. They might get pinched."

Simon nodded agreement. The Lido wasn't far away and the noise of the bathers could clearly be heard.

"Race you," said Simon, impishly. He might not be able to swim yet, but at almost eight years old Simon was a fast runner and could hold his own against the older and slightly taller Daniel.

"One, two, three!" said Daniel, setting off immediately.

"Hey, that's not fair!" shouted Simon, taken unaware by the quick start. But soon he was off, hard on Daniel's heels. The two boys raced down the hill, along past the Parade and arrived at the Lido entrance, both panting out of breath in the summer heat.

"I won," said Daniel.

"Only coz you set off first," complained Simon, then punching Daniel playfully. Daniel punched back equally playfully. "Come on then," he said. "Got your money?"

Simon nodded.

They paid their ninepence entry fee. "The thruppence change, we can get some sherbet," Daniel pointed out. They were each given a locker key.

Then they were through the turnstile and the shimmering pool lay before them. It was semicircular, the straight side was the deep part below the diving boards, that looked horribly high to Simon. In the middle was an island platform. On the grass and paved area around the pool, people lay in the sunshine. The pool had quite a lot of people in it.

"Come on," said Daniel. The two boys moved around the semicircular building that followed the shape of the pool looking for an empty cubicle. They squeezed into one together. As they were only wearing a few summer things, there weren't many clothes to cope with. They got undressed, each comfortable with the other in their familiar nakedness and then wriggled into their trunks.

"Wrap your clothes in your towel," said Daniel. Opening the door, he led the way out into the sunshine and along to a bank of lockers. They were next to each other luckily with consecutive numbers, and they put their things in and locked the doors, wrapping the key bands round their wrists. They turned and looked at the blue pool, its little wavelets catching the sun in a dazzling display that made the boys squint. Then Daniel ran forward and jumped into the water creating a large splash, some of which landed on Simon.

"What are you waiting for?" shouted Daniel happily as he surfaced and looked around for Simon. "It's OK, it's not deep," he said unnecessarily as he was standing up and the water was just above his waist. Simon ventured forward and jumped. The water was colder than he had expected and he gasped as the splashing subsided. Daniel was laughing, water streaming off his face and body.

"Right," said Daniel, "just do what I do." He launched himself forward into the water, burying his face and with a kick of his legs and strong arm strokes set off in a rapid front crawl away from Simon, who tried to follow but ended up floundering in the water and putting his feet down again after a couple of breathless attempts. Daniel swam back to his friend.

"Let me support you. Lie flat on my hands," said Daniel, extending his arms to make a platform. Simon leaned forward and lay trustingly across them. Daniel lifted Simon up in the water until he was lying along the surface.

"Now kick your legs." The result was a wild cascade of water as Simon obeyed, his legs flailing about in and out of the water.

"Keep them under the water if you can and sort of wave them."

Simon obeyed to some effect.

"Now pull over with your arms like I did." Simon made the front crawl arm movements, twisting his head to keep it clear of the water.

"You have to keep kicking as well, idiot!" said Daniel. Simon realised that in the effort to get the arm movement right, the kicking had stopped. As he did both together, Daniel stepped sideways to absorb the slight forward motion that Simon was creating.

"That's right!" exclaimed Daniel, and let go of Simon, who promptly started to sink and had to put his feet down. They tried again, with the same result.

"You're not doing it right," said Daniel crossly.

"I'm doing my best," argued Simon.

"You've got to put your face down so your back's straighter," diagnosed Daniel. So Simon tried but could not synchronise the arms, legs and breathing successfully. He managed a few independent strokes by holding his breath, but his eyes filled up with water so he could not see. But this small progress seemed to satisfy Daniel who was growing weary of his teaching role and wanted to show his friend his own swimming skills. He swam round Simon who stood up to his chest in the water, while Daniel tried to swim under water and between Simon's legs. Simon felt him wriggling through and then Daniel surfaced just in front him, smiling.

"Follow me!" said Daniel, climbing out of the pool. The two ran round to the straight side of the pool.

"Watch this!" said Daniel and started up the diving board steps. Simon, still obeying the 'follow me' instruction, followed. Up they went, behind a tanned looking man with a crew cut. He ran along the high board and just vanished! Then Daniel went out without looking behind, reached up with his arms and dived off into the water seemingly far below. Simon watched from the end of the board as his friend's body curved deep under water. It looked so easy. Then, with the same blind trust that Simon always had for Daniel, he did the same. But instead of entering the water smoothly like Daniel, he landed awkwardly, the water, much more resistant that he had thought, knocking the breath out of him. He was underwater, his eyes open in surprise. He could see the side of the pool wall, pale blue. Near the bottom there were some drain type holes. He was in an upright sitting position, almost foetal – and sinking. He settled on the bottom, twenty feet down, and stopped. A brief moment of serenity.

But he had no idea what to do next and fear gripped him. He couldn't breathe! Simon panicked, sure he was going to die. A shape appeared in front of him, dark hair floating free in the water, those blue eyes like beacons of hope. Daniel grabbed Simon's arms and pulled up. Thinking again, Simon pushed hard with his legs, using the last of his energy to propel himself upwards. Daniel was pushing him now, upwards and towards the pool wall. Simon felt as though he were going to burst. He opened his mouth and swallowed pool water in desperation for breath. After an eternity, Simon grabbed the lip that ran round the edge of the pool and broke surface. Air! Air! Simon gasped. His eyes were waterlogged again and he could not see, but he could feel Daniel next to him, holding him up. All he wanted to do was breathe. Spluttering, he took one hand from the tiled lip and tried to wipe the water from his eyes. He was shaking and frightened.

"I thought I was going to drown," he gasped, as he made out Daniel's face next to him, still trying to clear his vision. He hated the water in his eyes, he wanted to see and it made him feel still closed in.

"Not while I'm around," said Daniel, who was holding the lip with one hand while he trod water and supported Simon with the other. "What did you do that for, you idiot?"

"What?" answered Simon, still rubbing his eyes. If only just one of them would clear!

"Dive in!" said Daniel's voice. "You were supposed to watch me from the side."

"You said follow," explained Simon, "and when you did it, it looked so good, I wanted to as well." His eyes cleared a bit now and blinking, he could see Daniel next to him, his strong legs still treading water, supporting them both.

"Idiot!" said Daniel again. "Come on, let's get out."

Simon again realised he was hanging onto a tiled lip and to Daniel, with his body suspended above twenty feet of water, the deepest part of the Lido beneath the high boards. Occasionally there was a splash a few feet away as someone entered the water from the boards. He nodded and tried to pull himself out of the pool, but all his strength had gone. Daniel pushed him, Simon finding time to wonder briefly what Daniel was pushing against, but then he had enough grip as Daniel's push left his upper body flat on the paving. Ungainly, he scrambled forwards to pull his legs out and sat on the slabs. Daniel seemed to bob back into the pool and then in one swift movement, lifted himself clear of the water and onto the paving next to Simon.

"You OK now?" Daniel asked. He had been scared when he realised that Simon had jumped off after him and was only aware when he broke surface and could not see him, but felt the shockwave of Simon's entry not far away. He had looked down and seen Simon, a blank expression on his face, sinking to the bottom. He had surfaced again, taken a deep breath and pushed hard down to where Simon was now sitting unmoving on the bottom. His fear initially had been of retribution if anything had happened to Simon, but then he realised that he didn't want anything to happen to Simon. Simon meant so much to him, idiot though he was sometimes. He was his closest friend whom he knew would never let him down.

He looked at Simon sitting, still breathing hard, rubbing his eyes and nodding his answer to the question. He looked at Simon's body and knew how much he would miss his friend. He patted his shoulder, wanting to do more, but conscious of people around.

"Let's get some sherbet," he said.

Dipping their wet fingers into the little conical paper sherbet bags, and licking it off, they sat on the grass, resting.

"Do you want to try again?" said Daniel. "In the shallow side," he added quickly.

"Next time," said Simon.

"Mind if I go in again?"

Simon shook his head. Daniel jumped up and was in the water, powering along with his front crawl, occasionally turning for back stroke, weaving in and out of other swimmers, completely at home in the water in a way that made Simon envious yet proud of his talented friend. With a shout for Simon to watch – unnecessary as Simon's eyes followed Daniel's every move – Daniel went up to the highest board and dived off, his lithe body entering the water like an arrow, and then he surfaced, grinning at Simon, who waved and grinned back. He swam over to Simon and climbed out.

"I've got to go," said Daniel. "I've a piano lesson later."

"That's OK," said Simon, quietly pleased that this removed any threat of being lured back into the water.

Back in a cubicle, the two boys dried down together.

"Thought I'd lost you then," said Daniel.

"I really thought I was going to drown," said Simon, the memory of that fear real again. "But you saved my life." He looked at Daniel, emotion in his eyes.

"Had to, didn't I?" Then the two boys held each other close and hugged tightly, feeling their bodies together and safe.

Daniel looked at his friend. "You're just too pretty," he said smiling.

"Pretty?" said Simon, unsure of this use of the word to describe a boy.

"Yes, it's those long eyelashes of yours, they hold the water. That's why you can't see."

"Well, I'm not going to pull them out just so I can swim."

"No, never do that," said Daniel simply. The boys got dressed.

Once out of the Lido, the boys ran home, the race was on again, with Simon just edging the win to the corner.

"You're fast!" said Daniel, panting. Simon grinned, happy to have regained some status after the failure in the water.

"Don't tell what happened will you?" asked Daniel. "I might get into trouble."

"Course not," said Simon, "you know I can keep a secret." He laughed and Daniel laughed too, the context not needing to be spoken. Simon looked at Daniel, now serious.

"I'll never forget what you did today," said Simon.

He never did.

10. 1954/9 Bike ride & Autumn Radio

"I've made you a card," said Simon, "but it's not very good." It was September again, and they would be moving up classes. Daniel, because his birthday was so early in September, so early in fact that it often was in the school holidays as this time, was the oldest in his class. With his late August birthday, Simon was always the youngest in his. Their birthdays were exactly a week apart. The two boys were out on their bikes and as they had got older, they had become more adventurous, leaving the city behind and heading out into the countryside.

So this day they were out among the green fields, winding country lanes and little villages. They had stopped at the top of a hill from where a good view all round could be had. They needed a rest and were sharing a bottle of lemonade that clever Daniel had thoughtfully brought along, sitting on the grass near their bikes and were talking birthdays. This was the one week in the year when their ages were just one year different. Simon now eight and Daniel still, just, nine.

"Made a card yourself?" said Daniel. "Where is it?"

"Home," said Simon, "but it's not very good."

"Bet it is," said Daniel. Then thinking of something his mother had said, he continued, "Anybody can go and buy a card, but sitting down and making one, takes time and thought, so it's much better than a bought one. And I'm sure it'll be very good."

Simon smiled at his friend's encouragement. "I'll get it when we get back in case I don't see you tomorrow. Know what you're getting?"

"I 'xpect you will," replied Daniel. "I think so, but I'm not supposed to say."

"Go on," pleaded Simon. Daniel grinned, and shook his head.

"But you can be the first to see, I promise. So you bring your super card tomorrow."

"OK. Hey! Don't drink all the pop!"

"I carried it here," said Daniel.

"Well, I'll carry it back," said Simon.

"Empty. It's a lot lighter when it's empty, " argued Daniel.

"Well then, you can get the money back on the bottle," offered Simon.

"I will. It's my bottle to start with," Daniel reminded Simon, who knew when he was defeated, and he slumped back from his pose of indignation. Daniel laughed and thrust the bottle at Simon.

"I've had enough, you finish it off." Simon took the bottle and gratefully drank off the last few mouthfuls. "You're carrying it back though," said Daniel. 'Glug' said Simon.

"Thanks," said Simon, removing the glass bottle from his lips and wiping them on his bare forearm. Shorts and T Shirts were the order of the day. Putting the bottle in his bag, he turned and threw himself on the unsuspecting Daniel. Quickly Simon had the advantage through surprise and was on top, pinning Daniel down. This did not last long though as the older and stronger Daniel managed to get Simon off and then the two were wrestling on the grass, panting and laughing. For a moment, Simon regained dominance, but Daniel played the trump card.

"Hey, no tickling!" shrieked Simon as he writhed in response to Daniel's probing fingers.

"All's fair in love and war – and fun fights," said Daniel. "And anyway, you started it." But he stopped tickling and was now sitting astride Simon, pinning his arms back. Simon knew it would end like this, it always did. Daniel was stronger than he was.

"You're a bully," he said to Daniel. "I'm a year younger than you."

"Two years," corrected Daniel.

"Not this week," said Simon defiantly.

"You're an idiot," said Daniel, threatening to tickle Simon again. "I'll always be two years older than you. You can't change that now."

"OK, but not quite two years."

"Right, one year and fifty-one weeks, if it makes you feel better." Daniel rolled off Simon and lay next to him panting. Then, propping himself up, he looked around. "There's a little wood over there. No houses round." He looked meaningfully at Simon, who just after the physical closeness of their fun fight, understood perfectly. He nodded and they rode their bikes a short distance along the lane to the wood. It was unlike the spinney at home because there were no worn paths created by many cycling children or more sedate walkers. It was wild, cool and quiet. They wheeled their bikes into the wood.

"This'll do," said Daniel. He had chosen well, they were shielded by undergrowth but would hear any approach, and were some distance into the wood from the lane. As he removed his T shirt and shorts, Simon copied and the two stood naked, facing each other.

"We've got nothing to lie on," said Simon. "There might be prickles in the grass."

"We've laid on the grass before," said Daniel. He knelt down and felt all around. "It's fine, no prickles." He lay down himself and beckoned Simon downward. Simon looked quickly round and obeyed. The two explored each other with tender hands, each caressing the now familiar contours of the other.

"Yours is almost as big as mine," said Daniel.

Simon looked at that part which fascinates boys about their bodies more than any other. "Is that good?" he asked.

"Suppose so. Dunno really," said Daniel. "Maybe it's because it's different. Probably be OK."

The two lay together in the woods, listening for any danger, but relaxed in each other's company. Daniel propped himself up on his elbows and reached across pulling Simon toward him, holding him. Simon looked up at his friend's face. He knew he could always trust Daniel. He had saved his life in the Lido just a couple of weeks before, although each time he mentioned it, Daniel just said it was OK and to stop going on about it. But Simon kept thinking about it.

"Do you like doing this?" asked Daniel. There was a hint of nervousness in his voice.

"Bike rides?"

"No, idiot. Like this. Stripping off together and sort of, stroking and all that."

Simon thought how he could express his feelings of safety and security when he was with Daniel, and especially when he was being held in their shared nakedness. "I love it," he said simply.

"Me too," said Daniel relieved, and ran his hand slowly down Simon's back from the nape of his neck, down his spine and on, staying a bit longer on his buttocks and then to the backs of his thighs, a move he knew Simon loved. Simon gently sighed, and then responded equally. Their eyes met but neither had the words or dared, so the bond remained unspoken.

"We'd better get back," said Daniel after a while. "Must be getting on for tea time. Piano practice." The boys got dressed and wheeled their bikes back to the lane.

They raced down the hill on their bikes, passing the thirty mile an hour sign with a laugh as they cycled through the village at top speed, imagining themselves to be space rockets breaking the sound barrier. More carefully when they reached the main road and saw their first cars again since they had left it earlier. Cycling on the paths, they were soon back on their own quiet streets.

"See you tomorrow," said Daniel at the corner.

"Yes. Happy birthday," said Simon. "Oh, I was going to get the card. Will you be in later?"

"Not sure," said Daniel. "We might be going out. So I'll have to see you tomorrow." They parted with a wave.

The next morning, after rushing his breakfast of bread and pork dripping, Simon looked out of his bedroom window to see if he could see Daniel, but his bedroom window showed nothing. Simon thought of Daniel's family, his Daddy, wishing him a happy birthday. Simon often wished his Daddy was more like Daniel's. He sat looking out across the allotments towards the spinney, and where their den was, although that could not be seen of course. Something attracted his eye and he looked back at Daniel's house. He was there at his window, waving at Simon. Then Daniel opened his bedroom window and was shouting something. Simon opened his window, however it opened towards Daniel's house and so was still between them, but he could hear Daniel's voice, although not what he was saying. But the beckoning motion he was making was clear enough. Simon waved and closed the window, running downstairs, just remembering to pick up the homemade card. It was beside the bought one Daniel had given him last week.

"Going round Daniel's, Mummy," he shouted.

"Oh, OK love," came Mummy's voice form the sitting room. "Oh, say Happy Birthday from me. It is today isn't it?" But she got no reply as by that time Simon was running along the path to the corner and then round to Daniel's house. As usual he went straight to the back door and there was Daniel, waiting.

"Come in Simon," said Mrs. Gray.

Simon stepped in, looking at Daniel, glad he was there. He held out the homemade card.

"Happy Birthday, Daniel," he said.

Daniel looked at the card, with his name on it and pictures Simon had drawn of the two of them on their bikes and Daniel playing his piano, and then turned to the message of friendship inside. Simon looked anxiously for Daniel's reaction.

"Thanks," said Daniel. "It's super."

"Did you make that yourself, Simon," asked Mrs Gray, coming over to have a look. Simon nodded. She took the card from Daniel and opened it. Simon instantly regretted his message inside, thinking maybe it was too much. And then she read it out.

"'Happy Birthday to Daniel, my very best friend forever and always.' That's really nice, Simon. Taking the time and trouble to make a card yourself."

Relieved, Simon beamed with pleasure at Daniel and his mother.

"Come upstairs, I've something to show you," said Daniel. The two went upstairs to Daniel's bedroom. Daniel stood expectantly while Simon looked round for anything different.

"What?" said Simon. "Oh! Gosh!" This was what Daniel wanted him to see. It was his very own wireless, an Ever Ready.

"Let's turn it on," said Simon. Daniel turned it on. Soon the speaker was blaring music.

"Once I had a secret love
That lived within the heart of me
All too soon my secret love
Became impatient to be free"

The two joined in, adding their raucous voices to Doris Day's.

"Try something else," said Simon. Daniel turned the tuning knob and the two boys listened as strange voices came from the wireless.

"That's German," said Daniel with the authority of a new ten year old. Simon thought it could be, because he knew what French sounded like a bit. "It's got four valves and of course it's battery powered so we can take it out if we want."

"Will your Mummy let you?" asked Simon.

"Probably," said Daniel. And then a new thought came to him. "Did you know *'Journey into Space'* is coming back?"

"What's that?" said Simon.

"It's excellent, " said Daniel, "it was all about spaceships and that, and going to the moon. But in the new one they are going to Mars. We can listen to it together."

Simon nodded enthusiastically. He liked space. Daniel liked Dan Dare and so did Simon, so *'Journey into Space'* sounded very good.

11. 1954/9 A Death and a Car

Simon came home from school to find Mummy already home from her part time journalism. But Mummy was, or just had been, crying.

"Mummy, what's the matter?" he asked nervously. "Is Daddy in?" When Mummy was crying, it was usually something to do with Daddy. But Mummy shook her head.

"No, darling." She paused, and drew her lips tight, trying to find the words to say. "Grandpa's died."

Simon's grandparents were on the periphery of his life. Both pairs lived an hour's bus ride away but in opposite directions, and sometimes the family – well, Mummy, Frances and Simon – would go and see Grandpa and Nana Drummond, Daddy only went sometimes, but all went to see Grandpa and Grandma Scott. Of course.

"Grandpa Drummond?" said Simon, although he was sure by Mummy's tears it was her Daddy. Mummy nodded. Simon moved to where Mummy was sitting and put his arms around her and he started to cry too. Because he knew he would never see Grandpa again, but mainly because Mummy was crying. A thought occurred to him.

"Is Nana all right?"

Mummy nodded. At that moment the back door opened and shut and the whirlwind that was Frances came through the kitchen.

"I'm home," she called cheerfully to whoever might be listening, dropped her bag in the hall and was gone upstairs to the bathroom. Mummy disentangled herself from Simon's grasp and dried her face with a handkerchief just as Frances reappeared. Mummy and Simon turned to face her.

"What?" said Frances, seeing that all was not as it should be. "Mummy, what's the matter?" she added now tuning in to Mummy's distress. Again that tightening of the lips. Simon intervened to save her the pain of having to say yet again.

"Grandpa Drummond's died," he said.

"Oh Mummy!" shrieked Frances, grief on her face and she flung her arms around Mummy. "When? What happened?" For Grandpa Drummond, although seeming old to Simon, was not that old.

"Earlier today," said Mummy. "Lilian phoned. She's with Nana now. Heart attack." And Mummy cried again.

"Does Daddy know?" asked the sensible Frances, recovering and moving into command mode with all the force of her thirteen years.

Mummy nodded. "He's coming home as soon as he can."

About an hour later, they were in the dining room trying to eat the small tea Frances had prepared when the front door opened. Daddy was home. Mummy got up and went into the hall, followed by Frances. Simon hung back, fearful of Daddy's reaction to this unique circumstance.

"Oh Kate," was Daddy's voice. Simon ventured into the hall to see Daddy hugging Mummy tightly, his face upset and drawn. Then Frances started to cry again and joined in the hug. Soon all four were hugging, united by the shock of the news. It was a moment of rare family togetherness that Simon would long remember, and not just for the event that engendered it.

Mummy went over to see Nana the next day in the village out in the country where they lived. Daddy had to go back to work and of course, Simon and Frances were at school. The funeral was held in the village a few days later, but this was held to be too upsetting for Simon to attend, although Frances went. So Simon went to school as usual, and by the time he came home, Mummy, Frances and Daddy were back home. Simon had wanted to go. He knew Grandpa Drummond as a kindly man who would take Simon down his large garden and pick blackcurrants for Nana to make a pie. He also kept hens and they would gather the eggs and check the fence was secure against foxes.

Grandpa Drummond's death led to a major change in the family's lifestyle. Grandpa Drummond's pride and joy was his Wolseley Series III, but Nana couldn't drive. Neither could Mummy's sister, Auntie Rose who lived down near London anyway. But Mummy could drive. Grandpa Drummond had taught his older daughter even before she had met Daddy, or in that phrase with which Simon was so familiar, 'before the war'. So it was, that one day when Simon was walking home from school, he and Daniel came up the hill from the main road to the corner.

"You've got visitors," said Daniel. Simon looked along from the junction to his house. Outside was a big black car. In Simon's road, only Mr. Searle had a car, an old Rover and it was always in bits. Sometimes Simon had gone to watch and was fascinated by the engine parts, laid out on the floor. How was it that this jumble of metal of all sorts of shapes, could when properly assembled, come alive with power, energy and motion? At the far end of the road, Mr Millward had a Morris 8. So a car parked outside a house was noteworthy. It took a moment for Simon to register.

"It's my Grandpa's car."

"The one that's died?" queried Daniel. Simon nodded. He was puzzled, and hesitated. He wasn't sure what to do. Daniel sensed his friend's uncertainty and he was also very curious.

"I'll come with you if you want," he offered. Simon nodded and the two boys went round to the back door and in through the kitchen. Mummy was in the dining room, getting tea ready.

"Oh, hello Daniel," said Mummy.

"Hello Mrs Scott," said Daniel respectfully, but nudging Simon at the same time. Taking the hint, Simon asked the burning question.

"What's Grandpa's car here for?"

"Well, Nana can't drive, so until things are sorted out, I'm using it."

"You mean it's ours?" exclaimed Simon gleefully.

"Just for the time being," said Mummy, and her further explanation about settling the estate was lost in whoops of joy from Simon, with Daniel joining in.

"Can we go out in it?" said Simon.

"Don't be silly, Simon," said Mummy. "Frances will be home soon and I'm getting tea ready."

Faced with two boys' faces looking disappointed, she continued, "Maybe after tea just for a short run."

"Can Daniel come?" asked Simon.

"I expect so," said Mummy. "Daniel, would you like some tea?"

Daniel hesitated. He was cautious about getting trapped at Simon's house for he too shared Simon's apprehension of his father, but the prospect of a ride in the luxurious Wolseley proved too much.

"Yes please," he said, and noted Simon's pleasure at his acceptance. He rarely did and it was far more common for Simon to go to Daniel's for tea than the other way round.

"You'd better tell your mother then," said Mummy.

"OK, back in a minute!" and Daniel fled, keen to get back as quickly as possible in case the car vanished while he was away.

Annoyingly, his mother insisted on him putting his school things away and getting properly washed before going back round the corner to Simon's. He needn't have worried. He ran round the corner and the car was still exactly where it had been an age earlier.

"That was quick," said Mummy when Daniel reappeared panting in the back doorway. "Come on in."

Frances now arrived and much of the scene was repeated.

"Mummy's taking us out for a ride after tea," announced Simon. Frances shot a questioning look at Mummy, who simply nodded as she put the last tea things on the table.

"I'm sitting in the front, then," said Frances, with a look that challenged Simon, or Mummy for that matter, to deny it. But Simon was not taken aback by this.

"OK," he said. "Daniel and I will be in the back."

"Won't **you** be in the front, Mrs Scott," asked Daniel puzzled. His father could drive, and there had been talk of buying a car, but his mother couldn't drive as far as Daniel knew anyway.

"I hope so," replied Mummy, laughing. "It's hard to drive from anywhere else."

Daniel's face flushed with his mistake. "I'm sorry, Mrs Scott, I just thought Mr Scott..." His voice tailed off.

"That's all right, Daniel," said Mummy. "I can drive. I learned before the war. Simon's Daddy can't drive." And with that, for some reason neither Simon nor Daniel could fathom, she burst out laughing. Soon everybody had the giggles.

"But Daddy can fly a plane," said Simon, loyally.

"So can I!" said Mummy, with another burst of laughter.

"You're a pilot?" asked an astounded Daniel.

"I learned to fly before the war," said Mummy. "I had a friend at the local flying club."

"Did you fly Spitfires?" asked Simon, equally amazed by these revelations.

"I wish I had," said Mummy. "I wanted to, as a ferry pilot, but I'm not tall enough. I would love to have flown a Spitfire."

"What planes did you fly, Mrs Scott," asked Daniel, a little more composed, while Simon wondered how one could fly a ferry.

"Just one," said Mummy. "Tiger Moth. Lovely little aeroplane."

Mummy continued to talk of her pre-war flying days and the light mood lasted through tea, eaten rather hurriedly so as to hasten the car ride.

Simon and Daniel climbed into the back seat and sprawled on the brown leather. It had a posh smell, thought Simon. Of course he had ridden in the car once or twice before when Grandpa drove it, but this was special. Mummy was going to drive and Daniel was with him. Simon was pleased that he had a car before Daniel, but also pleased that his friend was there to share the moment.

"Sit properly," said Mummy.

"Boys," remarked Frances scornfully from her front seat status.

Mummy pulled out the choke, turned the ignition key and pressed the starter button to start the engine and they were off. Simon revelled in the car, he had chosen the nearside, hoping to be seen by as many people as possible while they drove around. As the car swept down the hill to the main road, they passed a couple of boys they knew, but sadly they barely gave the passing Wolseley a glance. Still, nothing should detract from the joy of this moment.

"Let's pretend this is *Discovery*," said Simon.

"I'm Jet Morgan then," said Daniel, instantly understanding the reference to '*Journey into Space*' that had both boys, and the country, enthralled.

"The other cars can be the freighters," said Simon. Then Daniel pulled a strange face and holding his arms in front of him intoning, "I'm Whitaker from freighter number six." He then moved closer to Simon in a scary way.

Simon pushed him off.

"Will you sit still please boys," said Mummy. "It's very distracting and I'm still getting used to the car."

So the boys fell silent for a time as the game hadn't been such a good idea after all. But soon they were chatting again. Simon from his seat could see Mummy driving, the movement of her hands and feet creating a sort of poetic ballet that translated into the speed and power of the Wolseley.

The drive lasted about half an hour and took them out into the countryside that in those days was so close to the city. Going along the country roads familiar to both boys from their bike rides, it seemed so quick compared to the effort involved in pedalling so far. All too soon they were back.

"Thank you for taking me," said Daniel dutifully.

"No trouble Daniel," said Mummy, "glad you enjoyed it." Lovely manners, that boy, she thought.

Duty done, Daniel poked Simon and said loudly, "Coming round mine?"

Simon looked at Mummy, who simply said, "Don't be late."

"Race yer!" shouted Daniel, and the two boys ran off, Simon overhauling Daniel to beat him round the corner to Daniel's house.

"You're faster than Roger Bannister," panted Daniel. Now the roles were reversed in terms of decorum.

"I'm back Mummy," shouted Daniel. "We went for ride in Simon's new car."

"New car?" said Daniel's father, looking up from a book, suddenly interested.

"Hello, Mr Gray, Mrs Gray," said Simon. "It's not new, it was my Grandpa's car but he died."

"Yes, Daniel told us about that. I'm sorry," said Mrs Gray. Simon was puzzled for a moment until it dawned on him she was sorry about Grandpa, not the car.

"It's like a police car, only a lot posher," said Daniel by way of explanation to his father.

"Ah, I saw it when I came home," said Mr Gray. "I wondered about that."

"Can we get a car, Daddy?" said Daniel. His father was often collected and brought home in a car, and sometimes he drove one, but he had never felt the need for one of his own.

"Maybe, just maybe," he said, ruffling Daniel's dark hair, and smiling.

"When did this happen?" asked Mrs Gray.

"I wasn't going to say anything until it was certain, but it looks like I've got the promotion," Mr Gray smiled.

"Darling, that's wonderful," said Mrs Gray, beaming with delight.

"Yes!" shouted Daniel leaping up and down. He looked at Simon expectantly, waiting for enthusiasm. Simon responded with as vigorous a nodding as he could muster.

"You won't have to move, will you?" asked Mrs Gray suddenly. Everybody froze for a moment. Move? Away? Simon and Daniel exchanged worried looks.

"No, right here in the city," said Mr Gray, looking pleased.

"What'll that make you, Daddy?" asked Daniel.

"Chief Superintendent, Daniel," said Mr Gray, still grinning. "But it has to be confirmed."

"And can we get a car then?" persisted Daniel.

"Maybe, Daniel, maybe," said his father.

"You might be Chief Constable one day," said Mrs Gray. "It's true that some are now being promoted from the ranks instead of this daft idea of bringing in these ex army colonels and the like."

"Sir Malcolm is an excellent Chief Constable," replied Mr Gray loyally. "But he can't go on forever either," he added mischievously with a grin just like Daniel's.

At that point Daniel's older sister Louise arrived, and the whole scene had to be rerun.

Daniel soon afterwards gave Simon the news that the promotion was confirmed. A few weeks later a small Ford car appeared on the driveway of Daniel's house. Not as posh as the Wolseley, but as Simon quickly pointed out in compensation, the Wolseley didn't really belong to his family.

Mr Harrison two doors along from Simon got a Ford Prefect soon after. The motor age was arriving.

12. 1955/8 Lakes in the Wolseley

The monotonous hum of the windscreen wipers, back and forth, back and forth. Everywhere seemed so wet. It was the end of a long journey from home to the Lake District. Simon looked through the trees across the broad lake and to the mountains. Having the Wolseley meant his horizons had been opened up with drives to the Peak District, more frequent visits to both grandmothers and a variety of days out. It had helped Mummy too because she had been able to take on more work, and was on the radio now as well as in the newspaper. But it meant she was away from home sometimes at the weekends making the radio programmes at different places. Then, Daddy would be at home all the time, but thankfully he was often busy and left Simon pretty much to own devices. Simon went out with Daniel most of the time. But now they were here. The trips to Westward Ho were over and this, making use of their temporary windfall, was the summer holiday.

"Are we nearly there yet, Mummy?" asked Simon, yet again.

"Almost, darling," she replied. "I think it's just along here." Suddenly the trees cleared and there was a view right across the lake. There was a wooden boat with people on it in the distance, and the rain seemed to be stopping. The sun was just over the tops of the mountains opposite.

"Yes, I think this is it," said Mummy, and steered the big car off the road and through a gateway.

Daddy drew in his breath sharply. "Careful Kate, you nearly hit the gatepost."

"There was plenty of room," she snapped. Simon thought Mummy was an expert driver and now she was really used to the Wolseley she handled it well, just like her Tiger Moth she said. But Mummy's tone of voice showed Simon and Frances that she was tired. The car went up a long drive with a field on one side, and a large white building up ahead with a few cars parked in front of it. Mummy brought the big car to a stop on the gravel and turned off the engine. The rain had stopped and there was evening sunshine.

"Everybody help get the stuff in," said Daddy. The two children were out of the car and busy hauling cases out of the boot. Simon felt suddenly excited, all tiredness gone. Spread before him was the large field in front of the hotel, beyond that the lake and mountains, the sun now settling behind them, their flanks in shadow. Over to the right a large mountain was still catching the sun on its upper slopes. Simon thought it was beautiful.

"Come on, Simon, help with the luggage!" Daddy's urging brought Simon out of his reverie and he picked up a suitcase and struggling, took it to the door of the hotel, following Frances. A young woman came and took it from him.

"Please. I must help you," she said. She was dressed in a maid's uniform, and Simon thought she spoke in a funny way. That must be how they speak here, he thought. But then Mummy was talking to a man behind the large, polished wooden counter in the hallway.

"Scott," he said, turning the pages of a large book. "Ah yes, here we are. Scott," he repeated, in quite a normal voice, Simon thought. "Zelda, rooms fourteen and fifteen."

"Fourteen and fifteen," the maid repeated in her precise tones. "Feartsayn, foonftsayn." Simon wondered what that meant.

Zelda led the way up the large carpeted staircase with panelled walls, with the family following behind, Simon now with a smaller bag, Zelda still carrying Simon's. Daddy said something to Zelda he couldn't understand, sounding like 'zindsee doitch.' but Zelda nodded and said "Yar." Simon thought this a peculiar Lake District custom that Daddy knew about.

"She's German," said Daddy to Mummy.

"I gathered that," said Mummy, her tiredness still apparent. They put the bags in the rooms and Daddy said something to Zelda who said 'Bitter' back and smiled. She winked at Simon as she left the room. Frances lost no time.

"This is my bed," she said, using the authority of her fourteen years to bag the bed near the window.

"We're just next door, children," said Mummy.

"Who's for a walk before dinner?" said Daddy brightly.

"I'm going to have a lie down," said Mummy. "I've driven all that way, and I'm tired."

"You've just been sitting down all the time, how can you be tired?" said Daddy. Mummy looked furious.

"Well, weren't you just sitting down all the time you flew to Berlin and back or wherever? You got tired."

"That's completely different, that was the war."

Frances grabbed Simon. "Come on, let's explore the hotel," she said quickly and practically dragged Simon out of the room. "Let's leave them to it," she said. They heard the raised voices as they ran down the passage way, Simon running his hands along the panelling. He wondered if there were any secret passages. Lots of old buildings had them he knew, and this must be pretty old. He and Frances had once gone with Mummy on one of her radio weekends and had stayed at an old hotel in Ludlow. That had secret passages, and Simon was certain that this hotel was bound to have at least one.

"Hello, children." It was Zelda again. "Are you the hotel exploring?" Simon stopped, knowing now she was German and wondering what to say.

"Yes, that's right," said Frances. "We always do when we get to a hotel."

"If you go out to the back there gives there a waterfall, but you must promise to be careful, please, children."

"We will," they shouted, finding their way out and exploring the garden and climbing the paths through the woods next to the waterfall. Simon thought it was magical. He fell in love with the place instantly.

The days passed by. They went for walks, rides in the car, and climbed some of the closer mountains. Daddy said they were just hills really, although they seemed like mountains to Simon. But then Daddy had been climbing in the Alps before the war. That's how he knew German, he said.

One day at breakfast, Daddy looked at Simon. "Today, I'm going to teach you to row, son." Simon grinned happily. He had seen people rowing boats on the lake and now he was going to as well.

"Don't I get a chance?" said Frances.

"Of course, Princess," said Daddy, "everybody will." So soon they were on the launch going along the lake to the town. They decided to leave the car at the hotel and use the motor launch because you could catch it just at the end of the hotel drive. From out on the lake, the scenery seemed even more wonderful but soon they arrived at the landing stages and Daddy ordered a rowing boat big enough for them all. They put their bags in and a boatman pushed them off. Simon thought the boatman was good because he could drive the motor launch as well. Simon wanted to drive the motor launch. But Daddy was rowing now, Mummy sitting at the back, Frances up at the front, trailing her hand in the water. Simon was watching Daddy, pulling back on the oars, making the boat go. The lake seemed so much bigger than from the motor launch.

"How deep is it, Daddy?" he asked.

"Not very, I don't think. About seventy feet in the middle. It's not the deepest lake."

Simon gulped. Seventy feet sounded very deep to him. He remembered the Lido from last year and sat away from the edge of the boat. Daddy stopped rowing, the boat rocking gently out on the lake.

"Come on then, son." Carefully they changed places, the boat now rocking precariously.

"Careful, Harry," said Mummy.

"I'm fine," said Daddy.

"It was Simon I was thinking of," she said.

"Now son, take hold of the oars, make sure they don't slip back through the rowlocks."

"The what?"

"Those, like an upside down horseshoe," said Daddy. "Keep the collar inside the rowlock." Each oar had a large leather collar that was to stop it sliding through into the lake. "Lean forward, drop the oars into the water, brace your feet and pull back."

Simon did as he was told, but the oars were heavy. As he pulled back, one came high out of the water, catching him unawares, so that he let go of the other. It slid away, but the collar stopped it. The oar he still had hold of had jumped out of the rowlock and was suddenly very heavy, trying to slide away over the side. Making the boat rock violently, Daddy jumped forward and grabbed the oar slipping out of Simon's grasp. Simon looked at Daddy nervously. He knew he had got it wrong, and he didn't want Daddy to be cross. But the cross look on Daddy's face faded.

"Right son, try again, but make sure you keep the oars in the water when you pull them back, and lift them when you come forwards again."

Patiently, Daddy taught his son to row, and Simon, now more relaxed because Daddy wasn't cross, soon picked it up and found a rhythm. He liked the steady repeated motion. Push down, go forward, lift the oar handles, holding the blades vertical into the water, brace the feet and pull back. The boat moved. Again and again, forward and pulling, forward and pulling. Simon found the rhythm of his rocking body soothing, coupled with a sense of achievement. He rowed along the lake, straining and panting but not stopping. They passed the hotel, looking strange from this viewpoint.

"Do you want to have a go, Frances?" Daddy asked at one point.

"No, another time maybe," she replied. "Let him keep going." And she continued to trail her fingers in the water, lost in her own thoughts. Slowly they entered the flat lands around where the river entered the lake. Simon rowed up the narrowing river, reeds and grass either side. The water was now clear, and Simon realised with horror and fear that he could see the bottom, gravel and even a couple of fish. It looked so deep to his young eyes. In his mind he was under the water at the Lido and panic set in. Shaking he stopped rowing.

"I want to go back," he said.

"What for?" said Daddy.

"It's deep." Simon was visibly shaking now, and tears of panic were starting.

"Don't be silly, boy," said Daddy. "It's not as deep as the water you've been rowing along quite happily."

Simon knew it would be no good pointing out that now he could see the bottom, that made it worse. The actual depth didn't matter.

"Harry, can't you see he's frightened," said Mummy.

"I'll row then," said Daddy. So Daddy rowed the boat quickly back out onto the main lake. Simon later rowed again, feeling safer in his mind because the dark water of the lake hid its depth. But he knew that in some way he had let Daddy down, that Daddy was disappointed in him.

It was another day. There was the usual discussion over breakfast of the plans for the day.

"The weather forecast is good," said Mummy. "A good day for the tops."

"You mean another mountain?" said Frances with a distinct lack of enthusiasm.

"A real one this time," said Daddy. "Great Gable."

Simon felt a pang of disquiet at this. The very name seemed somehow full of foreboding. He wondered if at eight years old - OK, almost nine - he was capable of climbing a mountain with such a name.

"It's quite a lot for the children, Simon especially," said Mummy.

"We'll take the car to Honister top – if that's all right with you?"

"Yes, OK then," agreed Mummy.

So it was decided. Boots, anoraks, sandwiches, flasks, chocolate all gathered together for the expedition, and then into the car. Along the valley past some farms and buildings, through a little village, and then Mummy had a real job. The hill was the steepest Simon had ever seen. Mummy was working the gears to get the Wolseley up the hill. Luckily it was a reasonably powerful car. They overtook a small Morris stopped with steam belching from its engine. But Mummy's skill got them to the top. They parked by some buildings where they got slate down from the mountain. There were mounds of it all round. Simon looked round. This was supposed to be the easier route, but everyway up looked steep.

"Which one is Great Gable, Daddy?"

Daddy laughed. "You can't see it from here, but that's our route." He pointed to the steepest path around, it went straight up the side of a hill and disappeared through a gap over the top.

The climb had Simon panting. Daddy was in front, Mummy and Frances behind, talking. He was in his own little world, putting one foot in front of the other, plodding on and up. He kept having to stop for breath, but when he turned round he realised how far up he had come. The car was a little toy car next to some little toy buildings. He trudged up, thinking about home, wondering what Daniel was doing while he was away, remembering that Daniel was away on holiday too. He wished Daniel was here. After going through a little rocky gap, the path levelled out a bit and the going got easier. Daddy was up ahead along the dead straight path, and soon they came to a stone ramp where Daddy stopped.

"Daddy, did there used to be trains up here?" asked Simon. He had noticed what looked like railway sleepers on the path, and it occurred to him that the straightness of the path was like a railway line.

"Not bad, son. Not trains in that sense, but they used to take the slate down in wagons drawn up and down by a big steam engine. Not a locomotive, but a big drum that wound a cable round it attached to the wagons."

"Where was the big drum?"

"Here. This is what used to be the Drum House, pulling the wagons up the slope. Clever boy."

Simon felt pleased to have drawn praise from Daddy, and sat contented to wait for Mummy and Frances. It seemed so wild and quiet. Some other people came past and said hello.

"Do you know them, Daddy?" asked Simon when they had gone past.

"No, but people often say hello to each other on the fells, even when at home they would pass in the street without a word."

After Mummy and Frances caught up and had got their breath, the family set out away from the Drum House following a path that would take them to Great Gable. Soon the great, forbidding dome, black against the sky with wisps of cloud brushing across it, was in view.

"Are we climbing **that**?" asked Frances. Simon concurred with her concern.

"Soon be there," said Daddy. They marched on, the path going up and down, past some small pools until they started the steep climb to the top of Great Gable's little companion, Green Gable. Little in this case of course being a relative term. But Simon now felt he had the measure of this and simply kept going until they were all at the top, looking up at the mass of Great Gable. Simon was first off down into the gap between the two, Windy Gap, which justified its name when Mummy's woolly hat blew off as the wind is funnelled between the peaks. But Simon ran after it and recovered it. He was enjoying being so high, looking down on the mountains and down into the valleys below. Soon he was scrambling up the path to the top of Great Gable. It took quite a while, and Daddy kept saying not to go too far ahead, but now Simon had the bit between his teeth and like a mountain goat as Mummy said, he sprang from rock to rock until it levelled out into a broad rocky top. But where was the top of the mountain? Clouds kept brushing past and then he could see a mound of rocks, a stick sticking up and people gathered round it. Alone now, he set off towards it. Sometimes it was lost in the cloud, as was he, but he kept going and then the clouds swept away, there was sunshine and he was there, at the very top. He clambered past some other people who were sitting round, some eating sandwiches, and stood on the very top. Only in one direction was the view blocked by other mountains. Otherwise he could see now for miles and miles. He could see the sea, so far away. And faintly in the distance beyond the sea, he could make out the grey shapes of other mountains. It was an exhilaration of a kind Simon had never known before. He had conquered the mountain, he could conquer the world! Looking round, he could see Mummy's blue anorak as a dot coming towards him, along with Daddy's less visible brown one and Frances. But he was there first. He let out a whoop of sheer delight, which startled the sandwich eaters, not that Simon cared. Even when the others arrived he refused to get down from his perch at the highest point. He was going to savour this for as long as he could!

"Come and get your sandwiches, Simon," called Mummy, who was producing food and a flask from her rucksack. With some regret, Simon succumbed to the call of food and climbed down.

"This is fantastic," he said. "Everybody should do this."

And in the years to come, he certainly tried his best to offer that same elation to as many others as he could.

All too soon the holiday was over, and Mummy drove the Wolseley back home. It was not the only holiday Simon was to have in the Lake District as a child, but it was the most memorable, and the most influential. Here were the seeds sown of later triumphs and disaster. Simon spent much of the homeward journey thinking of Daniel and hoping he would be home. Now that the holiday was over, all he wanted was his friend's company, to feel his comforting touch. He knew that when they got home, Mummy and Daddy would be arguing again.

Within a few days, it was as though the holiday had never been. Things were back to normal and Simon sought refuge with his friend. Daniel listened patiently while Simon told him all about the mountains and the conquering of Great Gable. He seemed to take on some of Simon's enthusiasm. Daniel told Simon of his family's seaside holiday, of swimming in the sea, a prospect that would worry Simon.

"I had a snorkel," said Daniel.

"What's that?"

"It's a tube and you can keep your head underwater and still breathe. You saw people with them at the lido last summer."

"Don't remind me," said Simon ruefully. "I didn't know that's what they were called."

"I could see fish and crabs and all the rocks under the water," enthused Daniel.

"Is it safe?" asked Simon with a note of concern.

"Course it is," said Daniel robustly. "I'm an excellent swimmer."

And Simon knew that to be true. The two boys resumed their friendship for the remainder of the summer holidays, riding their bikes, sharing their time, their joys and their intimacy once more. Simon was happy.

13. 1955/9 *Should never have been born*

It was Barry Spence, of course, who asked the question. Miss Day was talking to the class of nine year olds about swearing. Simon liked Miss Day, and he was now third year juniors. Daniel was in Mr West's class in fourth year, getting ready for the eleven plus exams. But now Miss Day had brought up about swearing. Simon was fearful of this subject, as the years had not diminished Daddy's propensity for raw language. Some of the children had been glancing at Simon all through the lesson, many aware of his situation, and wondering how he was feeling. Susan James and Cynthia Jackson tried to smile at him, their natural empathy stirred by Simon's plight. Simon liked both of them, they were the best girls in the class. Daniel had kissed Cynthia, but he was older. Simon liked Susan, and he thought that she liked him. Simon was sitting at his double desk next to his friend Peter Holman but at the moment though, all he wanted was Daniel to be near him, Daniel on whom he could always rely, Daniel who had protected him over the years from the biguns, and even though

Simon was now in the third year juniors himself, Daniel continued to protect him and provide comfort.

"Now children," droned Miss Day cheerfully, "we all know that there are some words we should never use, don't we, even though we may hear others say them."

"Yes, Miss," replied one or two, losing hope that Miss Day was going to provide actual examples. The response seemed to satisfy Miss Day, however.

"Sometimes people use them out of bad temper, or because they know no better," she continued, oblivious to the distress Simon was being caused by this. He looked up and saw the Spence gang smirking at him, waiting to see how they could exploit the situation to hurt Simon more.

"It's usually because of poor upbringing that people swear for no good reason, that is, supposing that there could ever be a good reason," Miss Day went on. Sidney Forth too was enjoying Simon's embarrassment. Simon hated Sidney Forth. Simon was doing well now with English and reading and was one of the better ones in the class. His stories got top marks. But arithmetic was still a closed book to Simon. The numbers just seemed to go round and round and get jumbled up. Sidney Forth was clever, he could read well, write and he knew ALL his tables, right up to twelve twelves, straight away, without having to say up the table first! But that was not the real reason Simon hated Forth; it was because Forth despised Simon because he could not do these things. He was supremely contemptuous of any who could not match his abilities. He was not one of the Spence gang, in fact at times he was just as much their victim as was Simon. Forth had his wit to protect him, and that stayed with him all the time. Simon had come to rely on Daniel, but he was not always there.

"Now, when is the only time we should use a word?" asked Miss Day, and looked expectantly round the class. Many of the children were caught out by the fact that she had suddenly stopped talking, and that something was expected of them. Roused from their reverie, they glanced anxiously around. What was the question?

Cynthia Jackson raised her hand.

"Yes, Cynthia," said Miss Day.

"When we mean what we say, Miss," answered Cynthia.

"Good, Cynthia, but what about the words we use, when should we use them?"

Sidney Forth put up his hand. Miss Day nodded at him.

"When we know what the words mean, Miss," said Sidney Forth.

"That's right, Sidney, good boy," she beamed. "I'm glad that somebody was listening," she remarked tartly to rest of the class.

The rest of the class tried to look as if they had been listening all along, but had suffered a purely momentary lapse of memory.

"Please, Miss, do all the bad words have meanings?" asked Frank Hinds.

"Well, err.., yes they do," replied Miss Day, a little uncertainly, unsure of where this might lead. Inspiration came to her rescue. "But of course we don't need them because there are other perfectly good words that we can use instead of these awful words."

"What are they, Miss?" persisted Frank.

"Well, err.., we don't need to go into that right now," said Miss Day, glancing at her wristwatch hopefully. Almost playtime. Simon too hoped this lesson would end soon.

"Please Miss, what's a bastard?"

Simon went rigid, his pulse racing, every sense in his body suddenly at fever pitch. It had been Barry Spence's voice asking the question. Simon saw Spence and his cronies watching him.

Miss Day was taken aback by the question too. Another glance at the time. Surely the bell was late? I wish I had never started this discussion, she thought.

"Well, er... Barry, that's not er.. a nice word to use about anyone, is it?"

Simon felt now that everyone was looking at him. They all knew that he was the one they called bastard, and Simon was still unsure what it really meant.

Miss Day searched for a way out.

"It's when someone is illegitimate, Barry," she said relieved, hoping that would suffice. It didn't.

"Illy-what, Miss?" posed Barry Spence, putting his innocent looking expression to good use.

"It means, well, er.. I suppose that the person should never have been born, in a way." She paused for a moment's thought. "When someone......"

The bell rang shrilly in the corridor outside the classroom, and Miss Day stopped, relieved.

"Put your things away and go out to play," she said, and, picking up her handbag, hastened out to the staffroom, hoping the kettle was boiled ready for a cup of tea. Thank God that lesson was over. Never do that again.

In the classroom, Simon sat still, the devastating import of that casual sentence sinking in. Should never have been born. Should never have been born.

"Outside, bastard," leered Spence right in Simon's face, arousing him from his thoughts. Simon looked up, frightened by Spence. Did this mean he was a sort of outlaw, like Robin Hood, who could be got by anybody? Robin Hood had his Merry Men, Simon had ... Simon had Daniel. Daniel! Find Daniel and tell him, and also get away from Barry Spence. Simon quickly ran out into the yard, looking for Daniel.

Daniel was with some boys from his class on the other side of the yard. Simon ran over, his desperation conquering his usual nervousness of Daniel's fourth year friends.

"Hiya, Simon," said Daniel, "what's the matter?"

"I've got something to tell you," whispered Simon, urgently.

"Not now, on the way home," said Daniel, sensing his friend's mood.

The Spence gang were playing football and were taking little notice of Simon now as they followed the battered tennis ball round the school yard, a swarm each anxious to get a kick. But Simon remained near Daniel for the rest of playtime, puzzled and upset by what Miss Day had said and impatient for Daniel's opinion on the way home.

14. 1955/9 Two Talking

Unfortunately, Daniel was not of much help to Simon. As the two walked home that evening, they both pondered the significance of Miss Day's pronouncement.

"Does she know that's what some of the others call you?" asked Daniel.

Simon shook his head. "Dunno," he said.

"Why don't you go and ask her what it really means?" suggested Daniel.

Simon thought about this for a moment. What would she say? Then he realised the danger of such a move.

"Can't do that," he said, "coz then she will know that I'm one, and if I never should've been born, she might report me or something, and then I might get taken off to a camp or something."

Simon felt the old sadness grow inside him as he thought of this possibility, and the effect this would have on Mummy, never mind what might happen to him at a Camp. He had heard terrible stories about Concentration Camps, and he supposed that the same sort of things would apply in whatever Camp was reserved for people like him. At this prospect, tears started gently to flow down his cheek, and he wiped them with the sleeve of his coat.

Daniel too contemplated the idea of his friend being taken off, like in the films from Germany. It at once excited and frightened him. Simon was a continuing puzzle to Daniel, and he was aware of the faith that Simon placed in him. Daniel thought of Simon's slim, soft body that he now knew so well, and what might happen to it in one of those places. He felt his own body stir at the thought, and decided he would ask Simon to the den with him on the way home.

The two had continued to visit their secret den over the years since that first time, as well finding other opportunities, out on bike rides, sometimes in Daniel's room when the coast was clear. The pretence was maintained that Daniel was looking after Simon and keeping a check on him since the discovery of the Great Difference. Daniel by this time was aware that circumcision was not out of the ordinary having seen other boys at the swimming baths, and wondered if Simon really knew. Neither said anything though, and each wished to continue to have the excuse for their intimate sessions together. Daniel found his friend's willing compliance with his demands intensely exciting, and gained considerable satisfaction from the feeling of mastery it gave him. Simon too looked forward to their sessions. For him they were times of real happiness. He trusted Daniel totally and derived from their friendship the masculine love and protection he missed so much, and which Daddy did not provide. In his submission to Daniel, he too experienced excitement, and felt that in allowing Daniel intimate knowledge of his body, the bond between them was strengthened.

This evening though, as they walked home together, Simon's self-esteem as low as it could sink, his thoughts were more on the sensitive side of their friendship than the sensual.

"I'm glad I've got you," said Simon, again wiping his tears on his sleeve.

Daniel turned to look at Simon, and saw the distress he was in. His heart went out to his friend, and his thoughts of the den were put aside. Daniel knew that it was not the time. Instead he put the arm of solace across Simon's shoulders.

"You know I'll be your friend, Simon," he comforted, "we always have been, haven't we?"

Simon nodded and sniffed his agreement.

Daniel continued. "I'll not tell. Best not to say anything to Day. She'll probably not understand anyway."

"Promise you'll not tell, anyone, anyone ever?" pleaded Simon.

"'Course not," assured Daniel. "Look, neither of us has ever told anyone about our secrets, you know, the den and all that, have we?"

Simon shook his head. Daniel was not reassured by this however.

"You haven't, have you?" he demanded, worried.

"No," said Simon. He certainly had not, and moreover would not. The closeness of his friendship with Daniel was a precious secret to share between the two of them. He did not want anyone else to share it. Also he knew that if the adult world found out, there would be condemnation, Daddy would beat him unmercifully, but worse, far worse than all that, he would be stopped from ever seeing Daniel again. At that thought, tears flowed anew.

Daniel saw the renewal of crying, and was alarmed by this.

"What's the matter?" he asked anxiously. "You've not told anyone, have you? Honest?"

"No," said Simon, realising his friend's misinterpretation of his tears. "No, I couldn't ever do that. If people found out, we couldn't be friends anymore. I'd hate that."

"Me too," said Daniel, relieved. "I'd hate that too."

Each felt the love for one another that had become the value of their relationship, and each shrank from uttering the word. It wasn't done. Love was silly and soft, for girls. But each instinctively knew of the love of the other. They parted at the end of the street, with a wave and a casual "See ya!", and both went home, warmed within by the further sealing of their love for each other.

15. 1955/9 Daniel asks the Question

Daniel entered the house, dropping his bag in the hall.

"I'm home," he shouted to the house in general, cocking his ear for an answer. After a pause, his mother answered from the direction of the kitchen.

"Hello, love, come and get your hands washed, tea's almost ready."

Daniel went through to the kitchen, and quickly rinsed his hands under the cold tap.

"Dad home yet?" he asked.

"He's upstairs, getting changed. He's got to go back later. Don't forget your piano practice, will you?"

"No, Mum. I want to learn that new piece."

"Good boy. Here, put these on the table, will you," said his mother, handing Daniel jam and butter.

Daniel put them on the table, and turned to see his Dad enter the kitchen.

"Hello, son," his Dad said, roughing Daniel's hair with his hand. "Had a good day?"

"O.K.," replied Daniel, with his stock response to queries about the boredom of school. Then he remembered.

"Miss Day talked to Simon's class about swearing today," he said. "Simon got a bit upset, but Miss Day didn't notice."

"Poor Simon," said his mother, "that boy leads an awful life. Did you walk home with him?"

Daniel nodded.

"He's a funny little kid, though Daniel," said his Dad, "I don't know what you see in him, really."

Daniel felt the conversation was getting onto to dangerous ground.

"He's O.K. He's a good friend," Daniel fended, then, sensing the chance to earn credit, he continued, "Anyway, he hasn't many friends, so I like to keep an eye on him." Only as he said the words did Daniel realise just how appropriate they were.

"That's very thoughtful, Daniel," said his Mum, as she put the last items on the table. "I know you and he get on well. Always have done. Come on then, sit down."

She turned to the hall, and raised her voice. "Louise, tea's ready!"

From upstairs came the muffled reply from Daniel's fifteen year old sister. It seemed to satisfy Mum.

As they started to eat, Daniel thought about the events of the day, and aware that his sister was coming decided to capitalise on his earlier discussion of school immediately.

"Mum?" he opened.

"Yes, dear," said Mum," don't talk with your mouth full."

Pushing aside this irrelevance, Daniel swallowed his piece of scrambled egg.

"What's a bastard?"

"You are!" said Louise, pulling a face at her brother as she entered the large kitchen.

"Don't start, Louise," said Dad, sharply.

"Sorry," said Louise, without grace.

"Did Simon ask you?" queried Mum of Daniel.

"Sort of," replied Daniel, "he said that Miss Day was talking about swearing in his class, and Barry Spence asked what a bastard is."

"Now he **is** one," interjected Louise.

"Be quiet, Louise," said Mum. "Go on, Daniel."

"Well, Simon said that Miss Day said that it was someone who should never have been born, and Simon got upset about it coz that's what they all call him."

"Because", emphasised Dad.

"Mm?" Daniel frowned, puzzled at the interruption.

"Because, not coz, Daniel," said Dad, "I keep telling you to speak properly. It is important."

"Yes, Dad," said Daniel, "but I was talking about Simon."

"So talk about him using proper language then, please."

"O.K. Dad," said Daniel, who felt this opportunity of enlightenment slipping away. "What I mean is, when Simon asked me about it I wasn't really sure what to say to him." Daniel sensed the chance to earn credit, and added, "He was really upset and I wanted to try and help him."

"Saint Daniel!" mocked Louise.

Trust her to spoil it, thought Daniel. I wish she weren't here.

"That's very good of you, love," said Mum, approvingly, "but it's a difficult problem really."

Daniel looked expectantly at Mum, and Mum looked expectantly at Dad. Dad was suddenly engrossed in the difficulties of spreading butter carefully right into the corners of the bread. Mum sighed to herself and continued.

"All it means, Daniel," she said, "is that someone's mother and father are not married when they are born. I don't think Miss Day can have meant that he shouldn't have been born. That's a terrible thing to say about a child. And as far as I know, his parents are married. I know Kate, er, Simon's mother, reasonably well. Simon probably didn't hear properly."

"He's a bit dim, that kid," said Louise.

"Louise, if you can't think of anything helpful to say, then keep quiet," snapped Mum. "Can we just get on with our meal, please."

"Sorry I spoke," pouted Louise.

Daniel grinned at her discomfort, despite his annoyance at the curtailing of the conversation. He wanted the information to maintain his ascendancy over Simon.

"Don't crow over your minor victories, Daniel," said Dad, "they may be short-lived. I seem to remember it's your turn to help wash up tonight. And you've your piano practice to do."

It was Louise's turn to grin.

Later, as Daniel was putting the dishes away with his Mum, he broached the subject again.

"Is Simon one of those?" he asked her.

She regarded her son quizzically. "You are persistent, aren't you? Almost certainly not. His parents are married I'm sure. But they say his Dad was married before the war and they got divorced. Some people think that divorce is wrong and a later marriage doesn't count."

"So what about any children then?"

"Oh, I see what you mean. Look, Simon's parents got married before he was born so he is not illegitimate, neither is his sister – what's her name?"

"Frances," supplied Daniel, eager to maintain the momentum.

"Oh, yes," continued Mum, "but there are some silly people who can't accept that because his father was married before. At least, that's what people say. Maybe someone said something like that and that's how all this silly name calling started."

Daniel digested this for a moment. "Is he really his Dad?"

"Oh yes, I'm sure," said Mum, "they were married during the war. I shouldn't be saying this to you, Daniel. Don't you go repeating what I've said."

"No, Mum," said Daniel automatically, while he thought how to ask the next, vital question.

"Pass me the big plates," said Mum.

"Does it show?" asked Daniel, holding up the dinner plates.

"Show?" said Mum, puzzled. "What do you mean? Where's the salt and pepper?"

Daniel looked for the salt and pepper, and passed them over to Mum who put them in the kitchen cabinet.

"On you," said Daniel, searching for words, "I mean, can you tell from looking?"

Mum laughed. "Of course not. Simon doesn't look any different from any other boy, does he? He's just an ordinary little boy, like any other. Nobody can be blamed for who their parents are, Daniel. I think his father had a hard time in the war. People should try to be a bit more understanding. He got a medal, you know. His Mum seems very nice. Fetch me the teapot, please."

Breathing quickly with the tension of the situation, Daniel handed over the teapot. This was getting close, but maybe too close. What could he say?

"Oh Daniel," said Mum, "you forgot the teapot lid."

"Even undressed?" asked Daniel, as casually as he could.

Mum stopped rinsing the teapot out, and turned to Daniel. "What do you mean? How can it?"

Daniel suddenly had a brainwave. "You know before when we went to the baths coz Simon wanted me to teach him how to swim?"

"Because!" corrected Mum. "Yes, I remember. Not very successfully, as I recall."

"Well, when we were in the changing cubicle, I couldn't help noticing that the end" - Daniel sought the correct word for cock - "of his penis was different, and he thought, I mean I thought..."

Mum was laughing. "O dear, Daniel," she laughed. "You mean he's circumcised." She laughed again. "Lots of boys are. Sometimes their religion demands it, like the Jews, other times the foreskin is too tight and has to be removed. It's nothing to do with being illegitimate; that's the proper word for a bastard. You are funny."

Daniel did not think this was especially funny, as a new aspect struck him. "But they sent the Jews away to camps and gassed them, didn't they?"

Mum was still amused at Daniel's naivety, failed to catch the solemnity of her son's question.

"Yes dear, but that was because Hitler hated the Jews because they were Jews, not because they were circumcised. Now run along, there's a good boy. I want to hear that piece, note perfect."

Pleased with his new information, Daniel went into the back room, specially extended, where the large Bösendorfer grand piano stood, and started his practice. After a few scales, he started on his new piece, and soon was lost in the magical pattern of the notes, revelling in the way his hands running across the keyboard could stir this big machine into making wonderful music. In the kitchen, Mrs Gray, herself a skilled pianist, nodded approvingly.

16. 1955/10 Onward Christian Soldiers

The confrontation came at morning playtime, but it started earlier. In Assembly, Miss Harvey stopped the singing of "Onward Christian Soldiers" to complain about the singing.

Onward, Christian soldiers, marching as to war,
With the cross of Jesus going on before.
Christ, the royal Master, leads against the foe;
Forward into battle see His banners go!
Onward, Christian soldiers, marching as to war,
With the cross of Jesus going on before.

Just as the children were singing the chorus for the second time, Miss Harvey banged on the lectern that stood at the front of the hall during assemblies. Miss Smith, the young teacher who played the piano visibly startled, played one disharmonious chord and stopped, turning to Miss Harvey with a fearful expression on her face.

"Thank you, Miss Smith," said Miss Harvey, somehow managing to convey menace in that simple statement, also the fact that she did not feel thankful at all; it was a mere formality.

Miss Harvey turned her attention to the assembled school. The singing had tailed off and the children now stood in their lines, regarding the headmistress with some apprehension. The teachers, stood at each side of the hall, glared at the children.

"Marching!" declaimed Miss Harvey. "Marching!"

Simon saw one or two of the teachers exchange glances, but when he looked again, their faces were completely expressionless.

"Not Mar Chin!" continued Miss Harvey, "It has I-N-G on the end. MarchING! I don't want to hear anyone singing Mar Chin! Miss Smith!"

Miss Smith jumped again, and looked questioningly at Miss Harvey.

"Carry on, Miss Smith, please," commanded Miss Harvey.

"We'll start verse two again," said Miss Smith to the school, watching Miss Harvey out of the corner of her eye. Miss Harvey appeared content with that, so Miss Smith struck the note to give the children the key, paused and then the repeat of verse two got underway.

"*Like a mighty army moves the church of God...*" sang the children. As the verse ended, and the chorus began, Miss Harvey craned forward slightly, listening intently to the words.

"*Onward Christian soldiers,*
Marching as to war,"

Simon distinctly heard Barry Spence, standing just behind him say "MAR CHIN" with just enough clarity for it to be heard, yet not enough for the culprit to be obvious to those not as close as Simon.

"With the cross....."

Miss Harvey straightened, banged furiously on the lectern and brought the singing to a halt. She turned and glared straight at Simon. He felt himself redden, and despite his best efforts, he literally started to quake in his shoes. Simon knew he was looking guilty, and that knowledge only compounded the circumstances and led to further appearance of guilt.

"Simon Scott!" shouted Miss Harvey. "You deliberately disobeyed me."

Simon sensed that this was the command to confess his guilt in front of the whole school. But he could not do that. Simon knew who was responsible, but dared not look round at Barry Spence. Instead he looked at Miss Harvey and was aware of the younger classes who were stood in front, between Simon and Miss Harvey, turning round to view the object of Miss Harvey's accusation, the sea of silent faces making him even more confused and frightened.

"Miss, it wasn't me," said Simon.

"Do you deny it?" demanded Miss Harvey, angrily. "What is it that wasn't you?"

"Please Miss, it wasn't me that sang Mar Chin."

Miss Harvey lifted her head in triumph.

"I did not say in what way you had disobeyed me, boy. You have just admitted your guilt in front of the whole school, haven't you?"

Simon knew when he was beaten, and just stayed silent, head down, looking at the grey socks of the second year boy standing in front him, and finding time to notice the two green hoops around the tops, and the line of his thigh muscles as his legs disappeared into his grey school short trousers. Then Simon heard Miss Day's voice.

"It was someone here, Miss Harvey, but I'm not sure if it was Simon."

Simon's hopes rose as he heard Miss Day speak up for him, only for them to crash as he heard his enemy's scornful retort.

"Well, Miss Day, I have just heard the boy admit he knew what he had done. We all heard it, didn't we?" she demanded of the school en masse.

"Yes Miss," replied the school dutifully en masse.

Simon looked up to see Miss Harvey's triumphant face, and Miss Day's embarrassed face, downcast. Simon felt grateful for her intervention, but he knew that it was to no avail. For some reason, he knew that it was his role in life to take the blame, and nothing could stop the inevitability of that, not Day, not Daniel, not Mummy.

Miss Harvey picked up her cane, that was never far away and flexed it with both hands.

"Simon Scott, we will deal with you at the end of assembly. Thank you, Miss Smith, verse two again."

The singing started, and Simon noticed that Barry Spence sang MARCHING this time.

The assembly seemed to last an age to Simon. Each time he raised his eyes, Miss Harvey seemed to be watching him. Simon started to cry, the tears rolling down his cheeks in a slow procession.

At the end, after the prayers, in which Miss Harvey called upon the children to love each other for the sake of Lord Jesus, who loved each and every one of them, the dreaded moment arrived.

"Scott! Come out here!"

Simon willed his feet out of their place in the line facing the front of the hall and walked to the side of the hall and slowly down to the front, to stand in front of Miss Harvey. His head hung, looking sideways he could see the children looking at him.

Then Miss Harvey thought of a new way to extend Simon's torment.

"Mrs. Hastings, I think the infants should return to their classes before I administer the punishment."

Simon turned and for a moment his eyes met with those of Mrs. Hastings. Somehow, she managed to convey to him a message of warmth in that brief instant, before she turned and led the infants with their teachers out of the hall.

"Now then, junior school," said Miss Harvey, "it is my unpleasant duty to demonstrate that obedience is the first lesson that must be learnt. Watch and learn yourselves."

Like some spectre of death, the headmistress turned to Simon.

"What have go to say for yourself, boy?"

"Please Miss, it wasn't me," Simon replied, so quietly through his tears that only Miss Harvey could have heard him. Simon wondered as he said it how he got the courage to maintain his defence, despite the overwhelming evidence against him; or was it just desperation to avoid the pain to come? Simon knew she hated him, and there was nothing he could do about it. Certainly, Simon's temerity in maintaining his innocence fired her up now.

"How dare you!" she snapped. "Bend over!"

At the front of the hall, in front of all the juniors, Simon slowly leant forward, feeling the pressure of Miss Harvey's hand on his back until he reached an acceptable angle. He saw Barry Spence smirking and behind his own class, the fourth years, some of them laughing quietly. He sought Daniel's face in vain. If only he could find Daniel, it wouldn't be so bad. He was aware of himself on the stage, in front of the school, as though watching himself. He tried to pretend it was a film.

The first stroke smashed across Simon's bottom, and the pain seared through him. He winced and cried out. One of the little first year girls started to cry. Then Simon saw Daniel at the back, his face impassively rigid as he watched his friend's agony. Simon tried to meet his eyes, but Miss Harvey put paid to that.

"Face down boy!"

Simon turned his head down, shut his eyes and somehow survived the rest of his punishment. As the sixth and final blow fell, he felt dizzy and nearly toppled forward, just managing to stop himself. Slowly he stood up, tears streaming down his face, chest heaving and sobbing, his disgrace for all the junior school to see.

"Let that be a lesson to you, Simon Scott. I assure you that you will tire of your disobedience before I ever tire of trying to reform you. Return to your class."

Simon walked back to where his class were waiting, and then with them back to classroom. As they passed the door to Mr. West's room, he and Miss Day were in conversation.

"The woman's quite mad, you know," Mr. West was saying.

"As the proverbial Hatter," agreed Miss Day, "and as for reform, what a hope! She should try a bit of loving sympathy. She's always had it in for that boy."

Simon did not hear Mr. West's next comment, and he wondered vaguely who they were talking about, but his preoccupation with his pain and disgrace was not conducive to sustained thought on the matter. The conversation between the two teachers did have one effect which was only eventually to worsen matters for Simon. Whilst they were each venting their frustration at Miss Harvey's iron rule on each other, Simon arrived back in his classroom unsupervised, along with the rest of his class.

Cynthia came up to Simon, genuine concern on her face.

"Are you alright, Simon?" she asked.

Simon, touched by the sympathy, felt a further tear roll down his face.

"Softy!" shouted Barry Spence, hoping to provoke further distress in Simon, amid more catcalls from his followers.

Sidney Forth joined in at this point, swept along on the wave of victimisation of Simon.

"Proves he should never have been born, just like Miss Day said," yelled Forth to the class. A roar of approval greeted this announcement, and Forth grinned at his triumph.

Simon, unable to respond to the Spence gang, was suddenly overwhelmed by his anger and frustration. Forth he could respond to, Forth he could attack, and all Simon's fury was streaming up through his body, filling his consciousness, his mind aware only of Forth, and oblivious to all other inputs. He launched himself at Forth, whose idiotic grin of triumph transformed into alarm as he saw the projectile that was Simon coming at him, hatred all over his face.

Simon hit Forth with such force that both boys were carried across the top of Forth's desk, knocking it over, the lid opening as it toppled, smashing off as it hit the ground, ink from the inkwell trickling out onto Forth's strewn books. Simon landed on top of Forth and started hitting him about the face and head as hard as he could, uncaring of the pain caused to his own hands. Blood started to ooze from Forth's face as the boy tried to protect his head from the onslaught as best he could.

Something in Simon sensed that he had done enough, but the anger still needed a further outlet. He turned and saw Forth's books scattered about. His rage returning, Simon picked up an exercise book and ripped it in two, flinging the parts in opposite directions, and stamping and trampling as best he could on the rest of Forth's possessions.

One of the halves of the exercise book landed at the feet of Miss Day, who, hearing the commotion, had hurried from her talk with Mr. West to see what was going on.

"Simon!" she shouted, "what do you think you are doing?" Then she saw Forth's inert form on the floor.

"Sidney, are you all right? Let me look at you," said Miss Day, hurrying over and kneeling by Forth's side.

"I think so, Miss," said Forth, sitting, and then slowly standing up.

"Good heavens!" exclaimed Miss Day, as she started to see the mess created by the fracas, "What has been going on?"

"Miss, he just attacked me," said Forth.

"That's right, Miss," said Spence, and the gang chorused agreement.

"Miss, they were calling Simon names and things," said Cynthia, and Susan and Pamela chimed in with similar comments. Suddenly there was commotion again as the children argued, putting their case.

The silence came quickly, children stopping in mid sentence, as they became aware of another presence in the room. Standing in the doorway, like the personification of evil, was Miss Harvey, still carrying the cane. She spoke with ominous quietness.

"Just what is going on in here, may I ask?"

Miss Day started to speak. "There seems to have been an accident ...."

"Simon Scott attacked Sidney Forth...", chimed in a voice.

Then there were others.

"..and just kept hitting him...made him bleed....they called him names, Miss...smashed the desk...ripped up the books...the others started it...poured ink on his things..."

"Quiet!" snapped Miss Harvey. There was quiet. "Simon Scott, are you responsible for this assault and the damage school property and to Sidney's books?"

Simon remained silent, not daring to say anything. It was all so unfair, so unjust. How is that Spence's lot can get away with anything, but I get caught straight away? She didn't come in when they were being nasty to me, did she?

"Your silence speaks more than your feeble lies and excuses ever could, boy," said Miss Harvey. "As you have just received punishment for disobedience, I shall not cane you again this morning. Instead, you will come to me at playtime this afternoon for punishment. Perhaps in the interim, you might reflect on your future in this school."

Miss Harvey turned and swept out of the room. Most of the class looked at Simon with awe, and fear for what he was due to suffer again so soon. Simon saw Spence looking at him in new way, that Simon could not interpret. Forth was glaring, indignant at his physical defeat, gloating at the prospect of his assailant's torture to come.

Miss Day again spoke. "Come on, now, boys. Pick up the desk. Girls, help Sidney to tidy up his things. Simon, come here please."

Simon went to Miss Day's desk, while the rest of the class busied themselves clearing the debris.

"What happened, Simon?" asked Miss Day, gently.

He knew that she was being sympathetic, sensed too that she disagreed with Miss Harvey in some way, but intuitively knew that she was powerless to help, and the effort of trying to justify his actions to her would change nothing, and was not worth the attempt. He shrugged, and remained silent.

Miss Day knew too that Simon was somehow aware of her impotence in the matter, and that he was ready to talk, if he ever would be. Poor boy, he really got dealt a raw deal in life.

"Go back to your place then Simon," she said, "and maybe we'll talk later." But she knew that they would not. There was no way across the abyss to reach that boy and offer help, even if she knew what help to give. And there was always Miss Harvey, who would never approve.

Simon went back to his seat, among the glances of his classmates, who were looking at him in a new light. Even Barry Spence regarded him with a slightly puzzled face. But Simon could not quell the anger within him. Somehow the outburst had failed to satisfy this new need to lash out, his soul remained unsatiated, the thirst of his frustration unquenched. All the years of insults, taunts and jibes flowed through his mind, fuelling the resentment he felt against Spence, Forth, Miss Harvey and even Miss Day for her inability to help. As the morning's lessons went on, Simon mechanically went through the motions of taking out books, putting books away and so on, but his mind was elsewhere, seething with emotion.

By midday, the desire to escape had become overwhelming. Fear of the caning to come at afternoon playtime drove his feelings upward. There was no hope here, no justice, no protection from persecution. The only way was out.

So Simon took his coat from the peg and instead of joining the dinner line, walked out into the yard and through the gate with the children going home for lunch. Mr. Ashby on the gate made as though to speak to him, but Simon was simply walking with the rest, and he decided that really he had no cause to question Simon. After all, the poor kid had probably had enough, and the last thing he wanted to do was to get him into further trouble with Miss Harvey.

Once in the street, Simon faced a decision. Where to go? Automatically, he headed towards home, and Mummy. But Daddy might be at home, and he would most likely hit Simon for leaving school. For some time, Simon wandered round the streets, past the time when he should have returned to school. No going back now!

17. 1955/10 Truancy and Theft

Simon found himself at a bombsite. Some had now been built on, but this one still had piles of bricks and wood, the remains of someone's home. He wondered if anybody had been killed. He sat for a while, trying to hide among the rubble, but there wasn't enough. Some had been removed. He wandered down to where there were bombed out houses. Some windows still had dirty glass in them. Simon picked up a half brick from the rubble and launched it at a window. The resulting smash was very satisfying and he spent a few minutes throwing stones and smashing in an orgy of broken glass, venting his frustration in the destruction until a man shouted at him. He ran off as fast as he could.

Simon realised that he was hungry. He wandered further and came to the shopping parade, which was fairly busy. Unfortunately, Simon didn't have any money. The newsagent and sweetshop was a natural target for a hungry boy, and Simon went in. Mr. Cole was serving behind the counter, but there were racks of sweets and chocolates on display. Lots of shops were doing that now, so you could choose what you wanted and then take it to the counter to pay for them, instead of having to queue and let Mr. Cole get you what you wanted, item by item. A lady was having some kind of argument with Mr. Cole, and then a man came in and waited impatiently. As the argument about a paper bill progressed, the man got more and more cross. At last he interrupted.

"Could I have a little service round here, please?" he said abruptly.

"Excuse me," said the lady, "but I was here first."

"The way you're going on, you'll be here when the bomb drops, too," replied the man.

"Wait a moment," said Mr. Cole, "there's no need to go off the deep end."

And suddenly the three of them were arguing like mad. Acting on instinct, Simon quickly scooped two Mars Bars and a packet of Refreshers and ran out of the shop back onto the parade. He broke into a run and turned the corner at the end. Heart pounding, he kept running, through the quiet streets, past the allotments. The den! Safety! He ran and lay panting on the soft grass of the den. The passing years had not diminished the importance of the den to Simon. It was not quite the secret place it had once been, because sometimes it was obvious that other people had been there, but Simon was now realistic enough to know that this was only to be expected. It did not reduce the significance it had as the place where he could relax with Daniel, and feel a whole person, accepted for what he was by the one person in the world (apart from Mummy) who he felt treated him with love and care.

Simon lay there elated. Then he started on a Mars Bar. It had been so easy! Just pick it up and run. Simon was sure that Mr. Cole didn't know who he was, and would probably never miss a few sweets from all those others anyway. As he ate, his hunger seemed to grow, and the second bar went the way of the first. Wait till Barry Spence finds out what I've done, thought Simon. That would make him think differently about me. But the impracticality of telling Spence, even if he were believed, tarnished that particular daydream.

Simon peered out from the den. Others may come here, but once in, one was hidden from view, yet had plenty of warning of anybody coming. Ideal place. There was nobody around, nobody in the allotments. Spurred on by his success, Simon climbed from the den and walked down to the allotments. There were one or two small sheds dotted about, mostly rather old and broken down. Simon looked in through the dirty windows at bags of unknown materials, gardening tools, old pairs of gloves and jars of unknown liquids. Coming upon a shed with an unlocked door (many had padlocks) Simon went in. There was the usual assortment of gardening apparatus, and a small bench. Curious, Simon pulled open the drawer set beneath this. Inside was a book about cabbages or something, all soiled from being handled, some cutters, but screwed up beside them was a brown ten shilling note. Ten shillings! Simon could not remember the last time he had held a ten bob note. He thought of what that could buy, and stuffed it into his pocket. Cautiously, he looked round the allotments before quickly leaving the shed and hurrying back to the den.

His heart thumping, Simon felt that same feeling of elation that he had felt earlier. Somehow, the fear itself was exciting, and justified by the success of the venture. The elation and excitement drove out the emotions of anger and frustration, and the success drove away the feelings of inadequacy and helplessness.

After a while, sucking on a Refresher and holding the ten shilling note in his hand he noticed some children on the road at the other side of the allotments. It must be home time. This brought Simon down to earth again. He would have to go home at some time. What would Mummy say about the sweet shop and the ten bob note? He knew of course that he could not tell her. She would not approve and he felt a little ashamed at the betrayal of trust to come. But if Daddy knew, Simon would be well beaten. He never needed much excuse to hit Simon, so with an excuse like stealing (and Simon knew what he had done) the severity of the beating would be limitless. Simon had had enough beating, and the thought reminded him of his own soreness. Looking out again, Simon's heart leapt. Joy of joys! Daniel was walking across the allotments straight towards the den. Simon watched his friend approach with pleasure and happiness driving out the anxiety he had felt as earlier elation and triumph had driven out anger and fear.

"Hiya," greeted Daniel as he clambered into the den, "Thought you'd probably be here. Harvey was steaming when you didn't turn up. When d'you walk out?"

"Dinner time," said Simon, as he tried to put aside thoughts of facing a steaming Miss Harvey. "Have a Refresher."

Daniel took the top one of the pastel coloured sweets from the packet.

"Where'd you get these?" asked Daniel, surprised. Simon rarely if ever had money.

"Parade," said Simon. "I took them, and two Mars bars. But I've eaten them. Dint have any dinner."

"You mean you pinched 'em?" asked an astounded Daniel.

Simon nodded. "And that's not all." Simon held out the ten shilling note.

"D'you pinch that from the shop an'all?" Daniel's jaw literally dropped at this.

"No," said Simon, "from a shed on the allotments. We could have a good time with this."

"I dunno, Simon," said Daniel frowning, "I didn't think you pinched things."

Anxiously, Simon asked, "Not done it before. Are you gonna tell? You wouldn't tell would you?"

"No, course not. Let's have another Refresher." Daniel sat and thought for a moment. "Simon?"

"What?"

"Please don't ever do that again."

"What?"

"Pinch things."

"OK," said Simon lightly.

"No, really. Promise. I mean it."

Simon looked at Daniel. His face was serious, concerned. It reminded him of Mummy's face when she was worried about him. His blue eyes seemed to search his soul, they could see right into him. He knew that this was really important to Daniel.

"OK, I promise," said Simon solemnly.

"Scout's honour?" Daniel had recently joined the scouts and as with everything he did, had thrown himself wholeheartedly into it.

"I'm not in the scouts," countered Simon.

Daniel suddenly seized Simon, glaring at him, angry in a way that Simon hadn't seen before. "That doesn't matter, and you will be when I take you," he shouted, right in Simon's face. "So promise, now! You will never ever pinch things again. Scout's honour!"

Simon was frightened by the strength of Daniel's feeling, by his evident anger, and yet felt the deep concern for him that had evoked it.

"I'm sorry, Daniel. I promise. Scout's honour."

This seemed to satisfy Daniel and the mood lightened.

So the two boys sat together eating sweets, and talking about how to spend the huge sum of ten shillings. Daniel was slightly perturbed by this show of initiative on Simon's part, feeling a little insecure that his dominance over his friend might be slipping. He had no need to fear. As soon as he put his arm round Simon, he felt the other relax into the safe haven of his arms, and they lay in the den, as so often before, Daniel enjoying the power over his friend's body he achieved, Simon gladly submitting to his friend's closeness. This, after his triumphs, was true contentment.

18. 1955/10 Retribution at Home

"Good luck," said Daniel outside his house.

"Maybe they won't know," said Simon, optimistically. He waved to Daniel and set off round the corner to his house. With every step his optimism drained away and the fear grew. He opened the side gate as quietly as he could and trod lightly down the side of the house to the back door. He eased it open. He could hear the radio, the Light Programme by the sound of it so probably just Mummy. Relief. He went into the sitting room. Mummy was there.

"Simon! Where have you been?"

Simon said nothing.

"Well? Miss Harvey telephoned and said you had left school at lunchtime. She was worried. Where have you been?"

Simon took a moment to reflect on the idea of Miss Harvey being worried about him. Two faced cow!

"The woods."

"Simon, what on earth is going on? Miss Harvey said you attacked another boy and created havoc in the classroom."

"Well, they're always picking on me. I hate it."

"But Miss Harvey said she can't understand it. The boy you attacked was not like that."

Simon could hardly explain that he had attacked Sidney Forth because he was too scared to attack Barry Spence. He could see now that there was no logic in it, not one that grown ups would understand anyway, not even Mummy. So he turned onto the attack.

"Just shut up about Miss Harvey! I hate her!" And he stormed out of the sitting room and went up to his room, and threw himself on to the bed and buried his face in his hands. He heard a sound and Mummy was there.

"Tell me what happened, darling," said Mummy's worried voice. Simon said nothing, kept his face hidden, but moved his body slightly to show he had heard. He felt Mummy's hand on his shoulder.

"What's the matter?" pursued Mummy. Simon thought, how could he say it? How could he explain how he felt? He couldn't. It was something a grown up just wouldn't understand.

"Please tell me. I want to help."

Help is what he wanted, but Mummy couldn't give the kind of help he needed. Murdering Barry Spence would be a good start.

"I was worried about you," said Mummy. Simon felt a pang of guilt about that, but he stayed still.

"I'll have to tell Daddy." What! No! Simon turned round and sat up, revealing his tearstained face to Mummy.

"No, Mummy. Please," said Simon, desperation growing his voice.

"Well, tell me about it," said Mummy entirely reasonably, "and then I can explain to Daddy."

"You wouldn't understand," said Simon.

"Try me," said Mummy with encouragement. But Simon did not know where to begin, let alone end. He just shrugged.

Simon was in bed when Daddy came home late, as so often. He heard Mummy come into the hall.

"Harry, I need to have a word about Simon."

"Why? Now? I'm tired," said Daddy's voice. Daddy often was in a bad temper when he came home late, perhaps too much to drink, perhaps guilt, or a combination. There was a constant feeling in the house of treading on eggshells.

Whatever, it was a cocktail that Simon feared. He lay in bed, his room illuminated gently by light seeping up the stairs from the hall. Their voices disappeared into the sitting room and became muffled. Mummy's voice in a long explanation, rising to placatory tone as she stopped speaking.

"What!" shouted Daddy. That was quite clear. More muffled conversation, and them Daddy's footsteps coming up the stairs.

"Go back to bed, Frances," he ordered. It was likely she was coming out to intervene, but Simon thought she would be sticking her nose out to watch the fun. Then Daddy came into his bedroom, turning on the light, making Simon screw his eyes up against the bright light. But he could see Daddy had the slipper in his hand.

"Is this true?" demanded Daddy loudly. Simon said nothing for fear of saying the wrong thing. But nothing was also the wrong thing.

"Well?" insisted Daddy. Simon kept quiet, squinting as his eyes got used to the light.

"Did you attack this other boy and ruin all his work and then run away from school?"

Simon felt he had to speak.

"Yes, but ..."

"Never mind 'but'. Out of bed!" Simon knew what was coming and climbed out of bed, resigned to his fate. It seemed that this was somehow his fate and Simon must endure it.

"Bend!" Simon bent. The pain of the leather soled slipper through just his pyjama trousers was intense. Did Daddy know he had already been beaten at school? Would he care? He stepped out of his body and watched himself being hit. It was not him, it was a character in some story; his usual way of coping with unpleasant things. But he cried out in sheer pain, something he rarely did when Daddy beat him because he felt that by keeping quiet, he was in some way winning and denying Daddy his victory. But this was just too much. Daddy stopped, and Simon collapsed to the floor next to his bed, sobbing and heaving.

Daddy, as always failing completely to understand his son, said, "Yes, I should think you are ashamed of yourself. You need to think hard, my lad, about yourself. You'll never amount to anything if you go on like this."

The light went out and the door closed, leaving Simon alone in the dark. After a few moments he walked to the window and pushed the curtains aside to look out. The darkness of the allotments was ringed by lights from the houses, and the dark outline of the spinney could be seen against the night sky. He turned and looked at Daniel's house. His bedroom curtains were drawn but Simon could tell there was a light on. He had a vision of Daniel lying peacefully in his big bed, perhaps reading a book. He so wanted to be in that big bed with him so they could be close and feel Daniel's warmth.

Simon heard his bedroom being slowly opened. He turned, frightened because he was out of bed. But it was Frances, her face peering round the edge of the door. She saw Simon standing by the window and then came in.

"Are you all right?"

Simon realised he wasn't all right. "It hurts." he said and despite all his efforts not to cry in front of his sister, the tears flowed.

"Sssh!" hissed Frances. "What happened?"

"Miss Harvey hates me."

"She hates everybody," muttered Frances, who remembered Miss Harvey well from her time in the juniors.

"She picked on me again and caned me for something Barry Spence did and I got angry and went mad in the classroom" he took a breath "and then she came in and found it all and the others all told her it was me and so she said she was going to cane me again in the afternoon" another breath "and I was fed up and scared so I ran out at dinnertime but of course she phoned Mummy and told her and now she's told Daddy and now this." Simon stopped at last.

"You know Daddy," said Frances. "It's done now, he'll be better in the morning."

"It's all right for you," said Simon. "He never hits you."

"Let him bloody try!" said Frances vehemently.

"He calls you 'Princess'," said Simon.

"Well, it would be odd if he called you that," said Frances, brightly, hugging her little brother. Despite himself, Simon smiled at that.

"See you in the morning," said Frances. Simon nodded, as Frances tiptoed to the door and crept out along the landing to her small room. Simon returned to the window and looked again at Daniel's, trying to penetrate the curtains, imagining that room he knew well, thinking of Daniel. How long he stood there, thinking of his friend, he could not remember, but he realised Daniel's light was out and found himself falling asleep, so he crawled back into bed and back into his own private world. Simon had learnt quickly that life is hard and to retreat into a world of his own construction, using imagination to build a fantasy where he was safe and could express himself without fear of put down. In those days there were no ready made fantasy worlds available on-line or in an electronic box, children had only their imagination to fall back on with whatever tools or toys were to hand.

19. 1955/11 Daddy learns to drive

The Wolseley sadly had gone, although Simon had been a bit puzzled when he and Daniel were in the city with a group of Daniel's friends.

"Stop!" shouted Simon. "Look!" He was looking at a garage with cars for sale in the large windows.

"What's he want?" asked one of the group. They were happy for Simon to tag along, he was no trouble. Often it seemed as if it were a case of no Simon, no Daniel. So Simon came. Simon was pointing at the window.

"Is that the same one?" asked Daniel, suddenly understanding Simon's shout.

"Yes," said Simon. "Look at the number." There in the window was Grandpa Drummond's beautiful Wolseley, freshly polished and gleaming.

"It's his Grandpa's old car," Daniel said to the group in general, who nodded and moved on.

"I'll tell Mummy and maybe she can get it back," said Simon.

"I think she probably already knows," said Daniel. "I remember her saying ages back that it would have to be sold."

"Just seems unfair that somebody else should have it."

"But you've got another car now and your Dad's learning to drive."

"Yes," said Simon with feeling. "More arguments."

"Come on," said Daniel, "let's catch up."

With a last look at the Wolseley, Simon ran after Daniel to rejoin the group.

"Mummy, Mummy!" Simon ran into the house.

"What's the matter?" said Mummy.

"I know where Grandpa's car is. The Wolseley. We can get it back!"

"What's he talking about?" said Daddy.

"He's seen the Wolseley in the garage I think," said Mummy. Simon nodded – and then thought.

"You already knew?"

"It had to be sold, son," said Daddy. "It was never really ours, and we couldn't afford to keep it."

"That's right, love," said Mummy. "But we've got the Austin now."

"Good thing too," remarked Daddy, "that Wolseley was a big car to drive."

"You never drove it," said Mummy.

"It's hardly my fault that you could drive and I couldn't, is it," retorted Daddy crossly.

"Hardly my fault either, Harry," Mummy came back.

Simon and Frances exchanged looks. They both knew the warning signs. Simon went up to his bedroom to ride out the storm. It actually subsided more quickly than usual. But driving had become a sore point. Daddy was learning to drive. At first Mummy had tried to teach him but they had argued too much so Daddy had gone to get lessons. It didn't help when Daddy tried to reverse the Austin Somerset off the drive by himself, and had gone backwards straight across the road and through Mr Harrop's garden fence into his pond. The car had had to be fixed, as well as the fence and the pond. The new section of fence opposite the drive was a constant reminder. But Daddy still wanted Mummy to go out with him in the Austin so he could practise.

"I'm sorry, Kate," said Daddy. Simon and Frances peered over the landing banister rail, checking on the state of the quarrel. "Can we go out for a drive, I've another lesson tomorrow?"

"No. What about the children?" said Mummy.

"They'll be all right for half an hour. Frances can look after Simon."

"We'll be OK, Mummy," called Frances unexpectedly.

"There you are," said Daddy.

"Half an hour then," said Mummy. "Be good, children!"

"We will," chorused Frances and Simon. They went downstairs while Daddy tied on the red 'L' plates.

"Why do you always take these off?" said Daddy irritably to Mummy.

"I don't like them on when I'm driving," said Mummy. "and anyway, it's against the law."

"Other people do," said Daddy going to the back of the Austin to tie on the other one.

"I'm not other people," retorted Mummy quickly. At this point Frances nudged Simon, and nodded towards the other side of the road. Mr Harrop was watching the 'L' plates go on warily from over his fence. Frances put her hand up to quash her giggles. Simon tried to suppress his laughter.

"I'll reverse the car off the drive," said Mummy. Mr Harrop's sigh of relief was almost audible the other side of the road. Daddy made no objection and soon the Austin was on the road and Daddy was slowly and cautiously driving off, Mummy, as the law demanded, sitting beside him. Simon ran to the gate to see Daddy make the trafficator arm come out at the corner as he was turning right. He would go past Daniel's house.

"We won't get the Wolseley back, Simon," said Frances kindly.

"It was much bigger and nicer than the Austin."

"Yes, but we have a car now. Most people don't. Maybe if we'd never had Grandpa's car, Daddy would never have bought one."

"Yes, money doesn't grow on trees," said Simon, wearily, but smiling.

Laughing, brother and sister went back into the house.

20. *1956/2 Gramophone*

"Jennifer's got a new radiogram."

Frances came in and deposited this news like a lead brick dropped into custard. Simon looked at Mummy, then Daddy, then Mummy again. Mummy wanted to play some records. She liked Frankie Vaughan, and had met him because of her job at the paper. She said he did lots of good for boys' clubs, although Simon wasn't quite sure what they were.

Daddy put down his paper.

"Waste of money," he announced. "Doesn't compare with going to concerts and getting the real sound of the orchestra."

"But you can get pop records to play as well," said Frances, refusing to let the thought of a radiogram out of her head.

"Pop records?" exclaimed Daddy. "Rubbish. Call that noise music?"

Frances realised her tactics had been wrong. "You can buy proper music records too, Daddy," she smiled at him.

Daddy smiled back. He called Frances his little princess.

"Yes, darling, but we already have a radio and there's the Third Programme. And of you want to hear that awful noise that you like, you can hear it on the Light programme." Daddy picked up his paper.

Simon thought it was time to help. "Daniel's got a new bike for passing his eleven plus. He's going to go to Henrys. If I pass, can we have a radiogram then, Daddy?"

"What Daniel gets is up to his parents. It's nothing to do with what goes on here," retorted Daddy sharply from behind the newspaper.

Frances glared at Simon for his unhelpful intervention. "Daddy. Please!" Frances tried again. The paper was lowered.

"No. We can't afford it. Money doesn't grow on trees."

How often had we heard that. Mummy wanted a new sofa, but money doesn't grow on trees. The sitting room needed a new carpet, but money doesn't grow on trees. The stair carpet actually had holes it – but money doesn't grow on trees.

"You always say that," said Frances crossly. Simon looked in awe, waiting for the explosion that would surely follow this backchat, as Daddy called it. But Frances could get away with it, she always did. There was no explosion. Daddy simply got up and left the room. Both Simon and Frances looked at Mummy. She had said nothing during this exchange.

"Don't worry, loves," she said, "I've an idea."

The idea matured a couple of weeks later. Daddy was going to be late, as usual, and Mummy came home with a large black box. She set it down on the table, and then produced another bag. The black box had a catch on the side and a lid. It also had a hole in the side with a square thing in it.

"What is it?" Frances asked. Mummy smiled, and undid the catch, and lifted the lid.

"A radiogram!" shouted Simon.

"Don't be silly," said Frances. "Radiograms are big. It's a gramophone."

It was undeniably a gramophone. There was a turntable and a needle arm and a big hole where the sound would come out. The function of the hole on the side now became clear. It was to wind it up.

Simon was jumping and down, excited. "Come on then, let's play it. How do you play it?"

"I thought you might ask that," said Mummy smiling even more at her children's happiness. She reached for the other bag and took out some records. There were some twelve inch records of *Eine kleine Nachtmusik* and a couple of ten inch records – Frankie Vaughan! Soon the music was basting out.

There's an old piano and they play it hot behind the green door!

Mummy grabbed Simon and Frances by the hands and they danced round the room, hand in hand in a small circle, filling the sitting room.

Soon Simon was swaggering round the room, mimicking Frankie Vaughan from the television,

Give Me The Moonlight Give Me The Girl, and leave rest, ho ho ho, to me.

Mummy and Frances were laughing at Simon's impersonation. Mummy, Frances and Simon, happy together, forgetting the outside world. Mummy was smiling, so Simon kept on clowning. They played *Green Door* again and Simon was kicking his legs up in imitation of Frankie Vaughan. Mummy was laughing now. Simon wanted to keep the moment going forever.

"I think we'd better pack it way now, darlings," said Mummy. "Daddy will be home soon," she added by way of explanation. No further explanation was needed. Simon knew that Daddy would think it was a waste of money, even though Mummy had bought it herself from her job with the newspaper and radio. But nobody wanted the confrontation that would ensue. So the gramophone was packed away.

Slowly the record collection built up, and Simon would listen to the records, sometimes alone, as long he remembered to change the needle every two records. They came in small tin boxes of a hundred. Simon even got to listen to the Mozart and grew to like it. Apart from the music Daniel played for him on the piano, it was his first introduction to classical music, a taste which lasted a lifetime. But Noël Coward (*Señorita Nina, from Argentina*) and Phil Harris (*Dark Town Poker Club* and *Woodman Spare that Tree*) were favourites.

There were a couple of close calls. One evening they were all four sitting watching the television. Suddenly Daddy said, "What's that?" He was looking at the worn carpet. Simon followed the direction of the look. There, catching the light, was a gramophone needle. Daddy started to get up, but quick as a flash, Frances jumped up and picked it up.

"It's mine," she said. "It's from my needlework set," she added, thinking quickly to forestall the inevitable question. Daddy sat down again and looked again at the television. Simon, Frances and Mummy exchanged glances. Mummy winked at Frances, Frances glared at Simon, who in her mind almost certainly had dropped the needle.

Daddy very often stayed out late, ostensibly late at work. Mummy used to cry sometimes and Simon hated it when Mummy cried. Frances got upset sometimes too and tried to comfort Mummy. Only later did Simon find out what they both already knew, that Daddy wasn't working late, but playing late, with a series of lady friends. He must have cut a dash, the minor war hero, good looking, a prestigious job. Any job with the BBC was prestigious but Simon gathered Daddy was some kind of boss. This of course, as he later found, was the cause of the diversion of so much of his ample salary, and of Mummy's developing drive for financial independence.

They were playing the gramophone one winter evening, it was only eight o'clock when suddenly Mummy lifted the needle.

"Sshh!" she commanded.

They listened, and heard the sound of the side gates being opened and the car engine running. Panic set in.

"Quick!" said Mummy. Hastily, they started packing up the records.

"Simon, the needle box! Frances, put the television on."

Simon grabbed the box and put it in its place under the lid. The television started to warm up. The car moved down the side of the house. Frances was packing up the records, Mummy closed the lid on the gramophone. She heaved it off the table and rushed to the cupboard where it hid behind mundane stuff.

The back door opened. Frances pushed the records behind the settee. Would the television warm up in time? Please, hurry up! Daddy was in the hall, taking off his coat. The sound was now coming from the television, but the picture wasn't there yet. Footsteps, but going up the stairs. While they heard the toilet flush and the taps run, the picture came on. They sat back in their accustomed seats to watch it. Daddy came in.

"Hello, darling," said Mummy brightly. "Finished earlier than expected?"

"Yes," said Daddy. "McLaren has to go to London early in the morning to see the DG."

The DG came up occasionally in conversation, and was usually spoken about in reverent terms. Simon's DG was Daniel Gray of course, but he wasn't sure who this DG was, but Daddy knew and had met the DG, who he was sure was a Very Important Man. So this was obviously a good reason for the meeting to finish early.

Daddy sat down as Mummy got up.

"I'll get us some supper then," she said. The crisis had passed.

21. *1956/5 Daniel's new potency*

It was a fine Spring Saturday afternoon, Daniel was back from swimming club and the two were out walking, going nowhere in particular, but heading for the Parade. Daniel jumped onto a wall and started to walk along the top in typical daredevil fashion, his feet now level with Simon's shoulders, who ever cautious had stayed safely on the ground.

"Careful. You'll fall off and break your neck," said Simon.

"Like Bert Trautmann. He played in the Cup Final with a broken neck."

"Only the last bit though, wasn't it?" said Simon, who didn't follow sports as closely as Daniel, mainly because he wasn't any good at sports, and Daniel was.

"That's enough though," said Daniel. "He was a paratrooper and you have to be brave to do that. Won medals."

"Yes, but that was for the Germans."

"So? Still got to be brave, haven't you?"

"S'pose so," admitted Simon, who thought Daniel was brave.

Daniel had now reached the end of the wall and contemplated how to get down. Simon stopped. "How're you going to get down?" he asked.

"Jump," said Daniel. And he did, landing next to Simon, laughing. They came to the Parade.

"Got any money?" asked Daniel. Simon shook his head. "I've got a bit, come on," Daniel continued, heading for the newsagent and sweetshop. Simon hung back.

"What if Cole's in there?"

"He probably will be, it's his shop," said Daniel. Then remembering why Simon was cautious, he went on, "It'll be OK. It was months ago. He won't even remember you, even if he noticed at the time."

Simon moved reluctantly forward.

"Come on, I'll be with you," urged Daniel. Reassured by that confirmation, Simon walked into Cole's shop behind Daniel. They looked at the sweet display, which brought back uncomfortable memories for Simon. He felt Mr Cole looking at him intently, although in fact Mr Cole was busy helping a man settle his paper bill. Only when that was done did Mr Cole turn to the boys; without a trace of recognition, he smiled at them.

"Well boys, what are you after?" he said in a friendly manner, which made Simon feel even more guilty about having stolen from him six months earlier.

"Refreshers or Spangles?" asked Daniel of Simon.

"Refreshers."

Daniel bought a packet of refreshers and they left the shop, to Simon's relief.

"See, it was OK. I bet he never noticed the stuff you pinched, or that it was you if he did."

"S'pose so," said Simon, "I've stayed out since."

"Well, now you can go in again. Come on, let's try the den. I've got something to tell you."

"What? Is it about school?" Simon knew that Daniel, being clever, had passed his eleven plus exam and in September would not be at the juniors with him but at the posh grammar school, King Henry VII Grammar School for Boys, but known locally as the Hooray Henrys, a nickname originally given by those who had failed to attend, but now adopted by the Henrys kids themselves. There was a technical grammar school in the city, but Hooray Henrys was the elite.

"No, I'll tell you in the den. It's that kind of thing," said Daniel mysteriously. The two boys made their way to the den, approaching carefully in case anybody else was around. They pushed their way in through the bushes to find the den empty. They sat down on the grass and looked out, nobody was around. Daniel carefully broke the Refresher packet in half and gave one part to Simon.

"Thanks," said Simon. "So, what is it then?"

"I can come," said Daniel, looking to gauge Simon's reaction.

"Where to?" said Simon.

"No," said Daniel, "I mean come off, get spunk."

"How do you know?" asked Simon, stupidly.

"How do you think, idiot?" But Daniel was smiling. Simon flushed at his silliness.

"When did it happen?"

"Thursday. I was going to tell you yesterday, but never got the chance at school and I was at Scouts last night."

"What's it like?" asked Simon, his curiosity about this new facet of Daniel's body enlivening him.

"Scouts? It's good," said Daniel.

"No, now you're the idiot. I mean what's it feel like?"

"It feels fantastic. It's like this great feeling goes right down your cock and round your body, and the spunk comes up."

Simon looked in awe at his friend, aware that at nearly twelve this was a new phase in Daniel's life.

Daniel put his arm round Simon. "I was thinking about you, and that made it come," he said.

"About me?" said Simon, surprised.

"Who else? I was thinking about us, what we do and that."

Simon felt pleased that he had been a part of Daniel's feat, and that, coupled with his present closeness, spurred him on. "Do you want to now?" he asked.

Daniel nodded, and checked their surroundings again. "All clear," he said, and they quickly took off their clothes.

As they started to feel each other's warm bodies, Simon noticed Daniel's arousal and took it in his hand.

"I love doing this with you, Simon," said Daniel.

"Me too," said Simon, thinking of the warmth and comfort it gave him, tempered now a bit by nervousness at this new development that Daniel had revealed.

Daniel responded in kind to Simon's touch, and they continued to caress and stimulate.

Then Daniel stopped stroking Simon but said, "Don't stop now, Simon."

Simon carried on, he could feel the mounting tension in Daniel, his hardness increasing until suddenly, with a sigh, the precious liquid was there, Daniel's moist blue eyes looking into Simon's. Daniel's tension subsided, Simon let go.

"It's better when you do it," said Daniel, using his hanky to wipe himself with.

"I'll do it again, if you like," said Simon.

"Not now," said Daniel. "It takes time to make some more. But you can next time."

"Why is it better?"

"Coz you're there, doing it, I s'pose," said Daniel. "It's like – " He tried to find the words – "like a fire, a fire down below that spreads all over."

Simon started to sing a sea shanty he knew from school.

"Fire! fire! fire down below;
Fetch a bucket of water, boys, There's fire down below! "

Daniel laughed, and joined in. The two stayed for a while, talking, lying close. Simon now aware of something new in Daniel's body, a new power that intrigued and fascinated him, for he knew that he too in time would undergo this transformation. But for the time being he revelled in the new potency of his friend and wondered what it might mean for their friendship.

They heard the voices of some kids in the spinney. To be on the safe side, they got dressed and left the den, walking back across the allotments.

"You won't tell anyone, will you," said Daniel.

"I never have."

"I mean about me, now. Spunk and that."

"Course not. They might ask how I know."

"Good. Come on then." Daniel burst into song, sheer exuberance and happiness radiating from him. Simon joined in, their singing loud and clear in the sunshine.

"Fire! fire! fire down below;
Fetch a bucket of water, boys, There's fire down below!
There's fire in the fore-top, fire in the main,
Fire in the windlass and fire in the chain
Fire! fire! fire down below;
Fetch a bucket of water, boys, There's fire down below! "

22. *1956/6 Church Parade 17/6/56*

"Will you come? Please?" Daniel looked at Simon sitting on his big bed, hoping for the answer he wanted. Daniel had been going to Scouts on Friday nights for some time and often would talk to Simon at the weekend about it, as well as his triumphs – usually – at the swimming club on Saturday morning, also demonstrating his growing prowess at the piano. Simon had nothing similar about which to tell Daniel, but it didn't seem to matter. But now Daniel was asking him to go to Church the next day, because the scouts were having a church parade and he was carrying the Union Flag when they marched into church and when they marched out. Daniel wanted his best friend there.

"I'm carrying the Union Flag. It's an honour to be picked, you know." Since joining scouts, Daniel had never referred to the Union Jack and corrected Simon if he did. Simon was unsure.

"Well, make sure it's the right way up then," joked Simon. He had never thought about there being a right way and wrong way up for the flag until Daniel had pointed it out. Now, when out in the city or on their bikes, if they saw one flying upside down, they would go and point this out to the owners, who were often disbelieving.

"Course it will be. Well? My parents are going, maybe Louise. You can sit with them if yours aren't going."

The prospect of his parents going together to church struck Simon as odd. Mummy he knew didn't like the church because of something that had happened before he was born, Daddy just said he had seen enough in the war to know there was no God. Simon found that disturbing because he was sure deep down that God was real, and anyway Daniel said he was.

"OK then," said Simon, smiling. Daniel returned the smile and gave Simon a hug.

"Mummy, I'm going to church in the morning."

"Oh? What's brought this on?" asked Mummy.

"The Scouts are having a parade and Daniel is carrying the Union Flag."

Frances looked up from her tea. "For a moment I thought my little brother had found Jesus. But it's just Daniel after all."

Simon chose to ignore that. "Can I, Mummy?"

"I expect so, I'd better make sure you've got clean clothes. You don't want me to come with you, do you?" At this Frances looked up sharply.

But Simon recoiled from the idea. "No, it's OK, Mummy. Daniel's Mummy and Daddy are going, so I can sit with them I expect." Frances resumed her tea.

"Fine then, dear. You had better wear a shirt and tie."

Simon accepted this as the price of going, and anyway he wasn't sure what one wore at church, so he was prepared to be guided by Mummy on this one.

"Are you going to come with me? We've got to meet half an hour before, but you could watch," asked Daniel. Simon, spruced up, had gone round to Daniel's in good time.

"Do that if you want to, Simon," said Mrs Gray. "We'll come down a bit later."

"OK then," said Simon, whose eyes were firmly on Daniel, dressed in his scout uniform. Simon had seen Daniel in uniform before, but somehow today, freshly ironed, it seemed to invest him with a new authority, somehow emphasising Daniel's new potency.

"Super!" said Daniel, and went through to the hall mirror to make final adjustments to his uniform, making sure the neckerchief was even and positioning his beret correctly. He turned back to Simon. "How do I look?"

"Perfect," said Simon, wishing he too could look as good. But Daniel had a natural poise that meant he looked good in the scruffiest clothes. In his uniform to Simon the effect was stunning.

"I was supposed to get my hair cut, so I hope Skip isn't cross," said Daniel. In the heyday of short back and sides, Daniel had his hair a bit longer. It brushed his ears and just reached down to his collar, thick and dark. Simon thought Daniel's hair was good, and wished he could let his grow a bit more. Daniel took pains with his appearance, and Simon knew there was no way he would ever have a short back and sides.

The two walked down over the footbridge to the church. Simon felt a bit nervous because there were several other scouts there, all bigger boys, but they knew Daniel.

"Hiya Daniel. Who's this?" asked a bigger boy who had two white bars on his shirt pocket.

"Simon. He's my friend and he's going to join when he's old enough."

Daniel had said this before and Simon knew it was true. The day he was eleven, he would join and follow in Daniel's footsteps. So he just nodded.

"You'll be very welcome. We'll have you in Harriers if we can," said the boy moving off to talk to some others.

"That's Miles Evans, my Patrol Leader," said Daniel, proudly, "and Harriers is my patrol. He's at Henrys, where I'm going. Be good if we could be in the same patrol."

"Troop, fall in!" came a shouted command. Simon looked round to see more scouts now, and two men also in scout uniform. But the order had come from a big boy, who Simon noticed had three bars on his shirt pocket, the middle one went under his scout badge.

"That's John Riley, the troop leader. I'm going to be troop leader one day, just you wait. Watch me, won't you?" said Daniel as he left.

"Bearers, over here?" called the Troop Leader. Most of the scouts were getting into lines, each patrol together but Daniel and another boy went over to the Troop Leader and were given leather straps to wear over their shoulders with a little pocket hanging in front. Then the two flags were brought out, a large green flag with the scout badge and the name and number of the scout troop on it, and a large Union Flag. Daniel took the latter and raised it into the air and dropped the end of the pole into the leather pocket, the strap taking the weight. Daniel and the other flag bearer took up position in front of the whole scout troop. Simon, along with a crowd that had now gathered, watched bewitched by the sight of the boys all lined up, silent now, disciplined and waiting for instructions. Simon wished he were eleven already. The only sound was the fluttering of the two flags in the breeze, until they were startled by the church bells pealing out. But the boys all held ranks and then listened as final instructions were given out by one of the scoutmasters. The scouts all came to attention, then stood at ease again.

"Hello, Simon, shall we go in?" It was Mrs Gray, Mr Gray with her. Simon nodded and they went into the church. They found a seat a few rows back and waited. Simon was given a hymn book.

Then everybody stood and the cross entered followed by the choir and the vicar. But then came the Scouts, led by the two flag bearers, holding their flags up at matching angles as they moved between the pews. Daniel was looking straight ahead, head held high. He looked glorious. The flags were placed at the altar as the scouts filed into the pews reserved for them, and Daniel took his seat at the front. Only then did he permit himself to look round for his parents and Simon. Their eyes met and they smiled at each other, then Daniel turned back.

The service didn't mean a lot to Simon, the hymns weren't ones he knew from school, but he followed it, overawed by the sense of occasion and the majesty of the ceremony in this ancient building. There was a moment of embarrassment for Simon as the collection plate was passed round and he had no money, but Mrs Gray said it was all right.

There was a pause, and then the choir came out and knelt along the altar rail. The Vicar gave each one something, and Simon was close enough to hear the words. "The body of Christ keep you in eternal life". Another person followed with a silver cup, from which each one drank to the words, "The blood of Christ keep you in eternal life." It seemed magical to Simon. Then Daniel was on his feet and with the other flag bearer, leading the scouts to kneel at the altar rail. Simon strained to watch and listen. Daniel was not offered the bread or wine, but bowed his head. The vicar placed his hand on Daniel's dark hair, saying, "Daniel, The Lord bless you and keep you. The Lord make his face to shine upon you and be gracious to you. The Lord lift up his countenance upon you and give you peace."

Simon heard Daniel say "Amen." The vicar knew Daniel's name! Daniel stood up and turned. He looked so serious, thought Simon. And so special. Simon looked at Mrs Gray next to him. She was smiling with pleasure and when she saw Simon looking at her, she smiled again. "He's done well, hasn't he?" she whispered. Simon just nodded, not trusting himself further.

But now the scouts were leaving the rail, one or two receiving the bread and wine, most having received a blessing, although few by name like Daniel. The organ was now playing and the rest of the people were now going out and it was their row's turn.

"Are you coming out with me, Simon?" said Mrs Gray. Simon's first reaction was to stay where he was, but something made him say yes. "Just keep your hands by your side when the priest gets to you," she advised.

They knelt at the altar rail, Simon next to Mrs Gray, Mr Gray beyond her. The priest came along the line, placing the wafer on the hands of each person, with the same words, "The body of Christ keep you in eternal life". It was Mrs Gray's turn and Simon tried to watch without turning his head, but also aware of Daniel sitting back in his front pew, not far behind him. He knew Daniel would be watching him and didn't want to let him down.

The vicar stood before Simon, hesitated slightly but Simon, copying Daniel, kept his head bowed and his hands by his side. He felt the vicar's hand on his head, as it had been on Daniel's.

"The Lord bless you and keep you. The Lord make his face to shine upon you and be gracious to you. The Lord lift up his countenance upon you and give you peace," said the vicar, then raising his hand moved on. Simon felt a delicious tingle of warmth spread from his head down his body. He stayed still, drinking in the strange feeling of contentment that this had given him.

"The blood of Christ keep you in eternal life." Mrs Gray was sipping from the cup, so Simon kept his head bowed and the person passed by to the grown up next to him on the other side. After a moment, Mrs Gray gently nudged him, and they stood up to go back to their pew. There was Daniel, smiling at them. Simon smiled back, pleased.

After a further hymn, one Simon did know and which he sang out loud feeling happy inside, it was the end of the service. Solemnly, Daniel and the other flag bearer approached the altar and the flags were placed in their holders. The two scouts turned to face the congregation, and marched back through the church, the scouts falling in behind them as they passed the end of each scout filled pew. Then the choir and the vicar left and the people started going out, Simon among them. The scouts were outside in their silent ordered ranks, the two flag bearers in front. The Troop Leader shouted commands and the Scouts all turned left. Then they set off marching now two abreast round the church yard, led by the flags.

"Left. Left. Left right left," called John Riley rhythmically every so often to keep the whole troop in step. Simon watched, his eyes fixed on Daniel, the breeze whipping the flags out straight. The Scout flag bearer had a slight problem with the wind, but Daniel managed to keep the Union Flag rock steady, although Simon could see his right arm tensed with the effort. The troop moved away round the other side of the church.

"Where are they going?" he asked Mrs Gray.

"They always take the flags right round the church," she said. Simon didn't question why, ritual was a part of the whole occasion. He ran round the church the other way to meet them. There was the troop, marching in disciplined order towards him along the gravel path, the two flags at the head. Daniel looked very serious again, immersed in his duty to carry the Union Flag as best he could. Simon kept pace, along with some other kids, as the troop marched back to the starting point.

"Troop ..... Halt!" called the Troop Leader. All the scouts stopped, almost as one.

"Troop .....Right turn!" All the scouts turned right so that instead of being in two long columns, they were now in two rows, facing John Riley and the Scoutmasters.

"Troop, stand at ...ease!" ordered the Troop Leader. The scouts stood legs astride, hands behind their backs, except Daniel and the other boy who had to keep hold of their flags. The scoutmaster spoke to them, saying how well they had done and that they were a credit to the troop, to scouting and to the country. After that he nodded to John Riley.

"Troop atten ... SHUN!" The scouts came to attention.

"Troop, Dismiss!" The scouts turned right, paused and then scattered, each looking for his own family or friend. The two flag bearers took out the flags, furling them carefully and removed the leather belt. The scoutmaster took the flags and put them in the back of his estate car.

"Well done, you two," he said. "Very good, especially you Daniel, your first time."

"Thanks Skip," said Daniel. He then turned to his parents and Simon.

"Glad that went OK," he said. "I was scared stiff of dropping it or going the wrong way."

"Well, it didn't show," said Simon. He wanted to say more, but was aware of Daniel's parents.

"Well done Daniel, you really looked the part, I'm proud of you" said Mr Gray.

"Thanks Dad," said Daniel warmly.

They walked back home, but the two boys hung back to talk.

"What did you think, Simon?" asked Daniel. It occurred to Simon that it really mattered to Daniel what he thought. He need not worry.

"You were super. The best there. And I am going to join as soon as I can."

"Thanks, Simon," said Daniel with as much warmth as he had thanked his Dad a few minutes before. "And when you join, I'll promise to get Skip to put you in the same patrol as me."

Fourteen months later, Daniel kept that promise.

23. *1956/8 One way train ride*

Simon ran round the corner to Daniel's. He was later than usual, so he had an idea. He had brought all his pocket money with him and a bar of chocolate.

"I'm sorry, Simon," said Mrs Gray at the back door, "Daniel's out. Some boys came for him about half an hour ago."

"Oh," said a crestfallen Simon. "Do you know where they've gone?"

"I don't, I'm afraid. They may have gone to the swimming baths, but I'll tell him you called."

"Thank you, Mrs Gray," said Simon politely. He turned away disconsolately. He had no desire to follow Daniel to the swimming baths. Daniel was a brilliant swimmer and won races and that, but Simon knew his own limitations. He walked slowly out onto the pavement again, wondering what to do now. He felt cross he had been late, really just through not getting a move on. And now Daniel had gone off with some other friends. Well, decided Simon, that would not stop him. He was going anyway. Simon was interested in trains and the latest thing was diesel trains. The new two carriage, DMUs, or Diesel Multiple Units were now running on local lines and Simon had wanted he and Daniel to try one out. He had even bought a new Ian Allan Railway book. So, Daniel would have to miss it.

With renewed determination, he set off down the hill to the main road. He crossed the road carefully to the bus stop. It was not long before a bus came and naturally he ran to get an upstairs seat. He often wondered why, with so many people upstairs, especially in the mornings going to school, and so few downstairs, the bus didn't topple over. Automatically he paid the conductor and stuffed the little square ticket into his pocket. He let the school bus stop pass and the bus carried on to the city centre. At the Railway station he got off.

The station was big and busy, but not strange to Simon. He wandered along the platforms, looking for a DMU train that would leaving soon. Coulton-in-the-Bottom. What a funny name for a place. It must be very strange to live in Coulton-in-the-Bottom. He imagined a conversation:

"And where to you live?"

"Coulton-in-the-Bottom."

"Oh dear, that must be very uncomfortable."

Simon was curious about Coulton-in-the-Bottom and there seemed to be a train leaving soon that would call there. He ran to the ticket office and asked how much it was to Coulton-in-the-Bottom. Luckily he just had enough. Clutching the precious little card in his hand, he went back to the platform and ran towards the waiting DMU.

"Hold on there, son!" Simon realised that meant him. He turned to where the ticket inspector was standing by the gate he had just run through. "Have you got a platform ticket? You need one to be train spotting."

"No," said Simon, pleased, "I've got a proper ticket." He held out the little piece of stiff card that was the valued ticket. The inspector took it and punched a funny shaped hole in it.

"Mind how you go, son," said the inspector, mollified.

Simon ran to the train, keen to get a seat up front. There were few people on the train. Perhaps nobody wanted to go to Coulton-in-the-Bottom thought Simon. But he got a seat right at the front and sat to the right. The driver would be sitting to the left in his cab in front, but Simon would have a clear view through the windows. He waited impatiently.

At last the driver came in and seemed to Simon to take an age to get ready. But then he started the engines. Simon could feel the power somewhere beneath his feet. With a hoot from its siren, the train started to move. Simon was thrilled. He could see everything the driver could see, the track ahead, the points and signals as the train navigated its way out of the station and on to its chosen track. Through the city it went. Simon wondered why cities always looked so ugly from the railway lines. They took care to make the roads into the city look nice, why not the view from the train?

Then out of the city and into the countryside, the train hurrying along, under bridges, the occasional level crossing, mostly with nobody waiting, but at one there was a long queue of cars and lorries. Simon felt exalted as he whisked past, they all waiting for his train. Simon watched fascinated as a station came into view and the train slowed. He had never seen a train coming into a station from the driver's view before. Suddenly there was the platform alongside and the train stopped. It was a village station and a few people got on, one or two got off. Then the stationmaster's whistle and they were off again, the green fields and woods rushing past. The village stop was repeated a couple of times before the train started to come into a larger town. This, Simon knew, was Coulton-in-the-Bottom. He watched as the train came into the station, waiting as long as he could before leaving his seat, so as not to get caught on the train when it continued its journey.

"On your own, son?" asked the ticket inspector at the barrier.

"Yes," said Simon, showing his ticket. Then he went out to experience the strangeness of Coulton-in-the-Bottom.

The thrill of anticipation waned as Simon walked around the town. It all seemed so ordinary. Ordinary buildings. Ordinary people doing ordinary things. A bit disappointed that Coulton-in-the-Bottom was not rather less ordinary, Simon sat on a seat in the Market Square that seemed to be the centre of Coulton-in-the-Bottom and ate his chocolate bar. He had intended to share it with Daniel, but as he wasn't there, he ate the whole bar himself.

At last, Simon had to admit to himself that Coulton-in-the-Bottom had lost whatever aura of mystery it may once have held. Time to go home.

At this, a sudden fear gripped Simon. He didn't have enough money! In his rush to get to Coulton-in-the-Bottom and delve into its secrets, he had completely overlooked the need to have enough fare for both ways. Panic started to set in and he felt lost and alone. What to do? He sat for a moment and then an idea came to him. Mummy always said that the policeman was his friend, that if ever he was in trouble, to find a policeman. Simon had a great respect for policemen, although the only one he knew personally was Daniel's Daddy. And that could be useful now, thought Simon.

He looked around. Not a policeman in sight. A lady walking a dog came past his seat.

"Excuse me," chimed Simon, "Please can you tell me where the police station is?"

"You see the church over there? Well, the police station is just round the corner. Are you all right, little boy?" said the lady. Simon resented the 'little boy' part, but remembered to be polite.

"I'm fine, thank you, and thank you for telling me the way." With renewed confidence, Simon set off in the direction indicated. Sure enough, there was the police station, a red brick building with stone steps and the usual blue lamp outside. He marched in.

Once at the counter inside, with a large policeman looking down at him, Simon's confidence started to ebb.

"Excuse me, but I haven't got enough money to get home." Under questioning from the sergeant, the story came out. The sergeant started laughing, and two other policemen came to join in, once they had been told the story.

"Well now, young lad," we'll have to see what to do with you."

"A night in the cells for being silly, do you think, Sarge?" said one of the policeman. Simon gulped, but then realised this was a tease. He plucked up courage to play his ace.

"I know a policeman at home," he said. "He's a high up one." Simon struggled to remember the rank. "He's a Chief something," he ended lamely.

"Chief Constable no doubt," said the sergeant, not very impressed with Simon's failed name dropping.

"Chief Super, maybe?" guessed the other policeman.

"Yes, that's it."

"And who might that be then?" asked the sergeant. It dawned on Simon he didn't know Daniel's Daddy's first name.

"Mr Gray," he said.

"Ah, Chief Superintendent Gray, city division," said the sergeant. Simon was satisfied that the connection had been made. "Come on then, young lad, I expect you're hungry." He lifted up part of the counter and took Simon through. "Better let your mother know where you are. You say you're on the phone at home?"

Simon nodded and gave the number. Ponderously, the sergeant dialled the operator and then asked for the city number that was Simon's. He heard Mummy's voice and felt really stupid while the sergeant explained what had happened. He was handed the phone.

"Simon? Are you all right?"

"Yes, Mummy. I'm at the police station but I've not been locked up or anything, but you always said if I was in trouble to go to the police so I did – "

"It's all right darling," Mummy said, "Now that I know you're safe."

"OK, Mummy. Here's the sergeant again." He gave the receiver back to the sergeant.

"Mrs Scott? ... yes of course ... We've a car coming to the city shortly, so it's no trouble ... Good bye."

Simon was given a sandwich and a drink of orange squash. Soon it was time to go. A policeman he had not met yet, wearing a cap, not a helmet, gave him a box of papers to carry.

"Follow me, Simon," he said cheerily. "We're going for a ride." They went out of the back of the police station to a yard where a couple of police cars were parked. Simon put the box of papers on the back seat of one, as instructed, and the policeman put several more there. Then, Simon in the front next to the policeman, they set off.

"Can we make the bells ring?" asked Simon

"Only if we have to chase some robbers," said the policeman, so Simon started to look for robbers, until it occurred to him the policeman was joking.

They chatted a bit as the car drove back to the city. Simon thought being in a police car was great fun. One or two people looked. Simon felt important.

"I think I'll take you home first," said the driver. "I expect your mother will be worrying about you."

As the car turned off the main road, Simon looked out for any boys he knew, anxious for his status to be recognised, best of all Daniel. But nobody was about.

"Here you are, Mrs Scott," said the policeman, "one errant child delivered."

"Thank you so much," said Mummy.

Once the policeman had gone, Mummy turned to Simon.

"What did you think you were doing, Simon?"

"I wanted to ride on one of the new diesel trains, and I wanted to go to Coulton-in-the-Bottom. Just to see what it's like."

"Well, now you know. I don't know what your father will say." Simon was gripped by fear.

"Please Mummy, don't tell Daddy. He'll be cross."

"I'll see what mood he's in when he comes home." Simon had to accept that.

"Can I go round to see if Daniel's in?"

"Oh yes, he called round about an hour ago. But don't be long. Tea will be ready soon."

Simon ran round and knocked on Daniel's back door. To his surprise, Mr Gray opened it. He was wearing his police uniform.

"Ah, the intrepid explorer," he said, smiling. "Come in. Daniel's upstairs I think."

Simon went to Daniel's bedroom. His friend was there.

"What happened?"

Simon explained the whole story, Daniel listened, chuckling. When Simon said he felt important in the police car, Daniel pointed out that people would probably think he was a bad boy who had been arrested.

"Simon, you're such an idiot," he said, and then gave him a hug. But Simon was happy.

24. 1956/9 School without Daniel

It was the last Saturday morning of the school summer holidays, September already, and it was raining. Simon was reading in his bedroom trying to take his mind off school next week. He would be fourth year so that meant he would be in one of the oldest classes, but Daniel would not be there anymore. The prospect of facing up to the Spence gang without Daniel, never mind Miss Harvey whose dislike of Simon remained tangible, was frightening. Daniel had of course passed his eleven plus exam, which meant he was going to the Hooray

Henrys grammar school. Most of the other kids who didn't pass went to Victoria Road Secondary Modern School. As Simon was still struggling at school and getting extra help, especially with arithmetic, he was trying to face up to the fact that he would too, and despite Daniel's confidence that he would follow him to Hooray Henrys, Simon knew in his heart he would fail and have to go to Victoria Road, probably with all the Spence gang. Simon's stomach churned at the thought of his future schooling from this point on.

He was looking forward to the afternoon when Daniel would be back from his swimming club. So he carried on reading. One thing that had improved a lot was his reading, and he was devouring the *Famous Five* books. They were derided by many, but Simon loved them. He so wanted to be like them, a group of friends and he also wanted a dog, like Timmy, but Daddy said No. They cost too much and would need too much looking after.

Simon suddenly felt the presence of somebody. He turned to look and for a moment could not take in what he saw. It was Daniel in his bedroom doorway, leaning against the side, looking somehow taller and elegant, one leg straight, the other crossing at the ankle with a natural grace, smiling at him. But it was what he was wearing that had the most effect. Daniel was wearing his brand new Hooray Henrys school uniform, the green blazer with the colourful embroidered coat of arms on the pocket, the white shirt with the school tie, and long, dark grey trousers. All crisp and new. And long school trousers! Suddenly Daniel looked so much older than the twelve years old he would be on Monday. Simon was awestruck.

"What do you think?" Daniel stood up and advanced into the bedroom, stopped and twirled around, facing Simon again.

"You look fantastic!" said Simon, admiring his friend.

Daniel smiled happily. "I had to beg Mum to let me come round with it on to show you. But you had to be the first to see."

Simon's feelings were mixed, pleasure that Daniel had thought of him when trying his new uniform ready for next week, sadness because it symbolised their parting at school forever. This must have shown because Daniel's face became one of concern.

"Simon, what's the matter? Don't you like it?"

"I think it's super. It's just that I'll never wear it and I'm back with Spence and them and Miss Harvey next week without you." At this vocalisation of his fears, a tear rolled out of Simon's eye. Daniel came and sat on the bed next to Simon, comforting him with a hug. Simon felt better for the warmth and strength of Daniel's touch, the scent of his body mingled with the crisp new smell of his clothes.

Daniel's heart went out to his sad friend with his uncontrollable emotions. "You'll be fine. You've got Peter thingummy you're friends with. You don't need me to stick up for you with Spence. I know you can do that. You've just got to be strong."

"Peter Holman," corrected Simon, "I can be when you're there, but not without you."

"Well, I **will** be there," said Daniel.

"How?" said Simon. "You'll be at Henrys."

Daniel tapped Simon's chest twice. "But I'll be in there, all the time. Whenever you need me, just think of me being there, and I will be."

"Really?" said Simon hopefully.

"Really. I sometimes think of you and it's like you're with me. I like to think of you when I'm in bed at night, specially if I'm having a wank. I always think of you then."

"Do you? Honest?", said Simon. To Daniel's nod, he continued, "I think of you too a lot, and specially in bed. I try to wank and make it come like you, but nothing happens."

"It will. I'm two years older than you, remember. But I like it that you think of me when you try," said Daniel, smiling. "Aren't I sort of there with you then?" Simon nodded. "So there you are then," said Daniel. "It'll be like that at school, I'll be there."

Simon smiled, trying hard to believe it. "But we'll never be at school together again. I won't be able to go to Henrys, I'll end up at Victoria Road."

"Why? You're going to pass the eleven plus. If I could, then you can."

"I'm stupid. I'm no good at school."

"Yes you are. You showed me your report, remember? It said your English was good. Sums a bit dodgy though. But we can work on that."

"We?"

"I'll help you. Don't want you going with the morons to Victoria Road."

"They're not all morons," said Simon indignantly.

"That's true. There are some Vicks at scouts, and they're OK. But there's a lot of morons too. And it's pretty rough."

"You'll really help me with arithmetic?"

"Of course. A scout has to help other people at all times, and be loyal. Who better to help and be loyal to than you?" said Daniel, tightening his hug, "We're best friends, aren't we."

Real hope started to fill Simon. If Daniel said it was possible, then it was possible.

"Thanks, Daniel."

"I'd better get back, or I'll be in trouble," said Daniel, releasing Simon and standing up. "I said I would just come and show you the uniform and then get straight back."

"I'm glad you did. How was swimming?"

"Good. There's this new kid, Layton. He's almost as fast as me, but he's older."

"So you're still the best then?"

"Of course. You coming back with me?"

"Yes," said Simon, leaping up off the bed. They went downstairs, Simon calling out to Mummy where he was going. They ran round the corner in the wet, Daniel anxious not to get his new uniform soaked. Simon was hoping that somehow they would be able to use Daniel's bedroom, as many times before, to be alone and intimate together. The two boys came in through the back door at top speed.

"Slow down," said Mrs Gray at the arrival of this whirlwind. "Hello Simon."

Mr Gray came into the kitchen at this point.

"Hello Mrs Gray, Mr Gray," said Simon politely.

"Daniel, I hope you've not got that uniform wet. Go and take it off," said Mr Gray.

"OK Dad," said Daniel. "Come on." This last to Simon, and they ran up the stairs.

"Very smart, bruvver," said Louise as they reached the landing. She was just going into her room.

"I look good, don't I?" said Daniel.

"You sure that cap will fit over your big head?" jibed Louise, closing her bedroom door.

Daniel threw the green cap with gold piping onto his bed, and closed the door. He stood in front of the mirror and adjusted his tie. Simon sat on the bed and watched. Daniel's pride in his King Henry VII Grammar School for Boys place and uniform was evident. Simon now had a glimmer of hope that he too might achieve this.

Daniel turned away from the mirror. "Better hang this lot up," he said, and started to undress, carefully hanging the blazer, trousers and shirt up in his wardrobe. "I've got a hard on now," he said unnecessarily, because Simon had already noticed the effect on Daniel's underpants. "That's coz you're here," he added looking at Simon, with a grin.

Simon looked at the closed bedroom door, which was not lost on Daniel.

"Better not," Daniel said. "Everybody's at home. Too risky."

"I don't mind," said Simon, feeling reckless.

"I do. It would spoil everything we've got, and we've managed lots of times in the holidays," replied Daniel, pulling on some denim jeans. Simon wanted some denim jeans like Daniel but Daddy said he was not old enough for long trousers. Daniel pulled on his favourite red socks he liked to wear when not at school. Simon wanted red socks but Daddy said they were too flashy.

"Come and listen to my new piece," said Daniel. He led the way downstairs to the back room. Daniel opened the keyboard of the piano, and stroked the keys lovingly, before setting up his music and then starting to play. Simon watched, spellbound, as Daniel's hands caressed the keys, bringing the piano alive with sound. Once or twice, Daniel frowned, hesitated and repeated a section when he made a mistake. Afterwards, he started again and played the whole piece through without error. Simon liked the music, but it was the sight of his friend, in command of this complex mechanism, his power and skill in converting the lines and dots on the page into sound, that he loved.

"Did you like it?" said Daniel.

"It was good," said Simon. He had asked Daddy and Mummy for a piano, just a little one, not a grand like this, would do. But nothing had happened.

"Beethoven. It's called *Für Elise*, but I'm going to call it *For Simon*, because I played it for you," said Daniel. "Let's play the note game."

The two had developed a game on the piano, one which intrigued Daniel. Simon had to turn his back on the piano and Daniel would play a single note. Then Simon had to press the same key on the keyboard. He nearly always got it right. When it was Daniel's turn, despite his musical talent, he often got the wrong note. At the succession of single notes, Mrs Gray came in, curious.

"What are you doing?" she inquired.

"We play this game, Mum," said Daniel. "Watch this." The game was demonstrated to Mrs Gray, herself a skilful pianist. Time and again Simon hit the right note.

"Fascinating," she said. "Simon, have you ever thought of music lessons?"

"I would like to learn how to play the piano, but I've asked."

"Simon can play some tunes by ear, and he can often repeat chords as well," said Daniel. "He plays tunes and puts in the chords, just triads, but they match. Play Greensleeves," he said, turning to Simon.

"I'm useless, it's not proper playing, like you," said Simon, embarrassed at playing the piano in front of Mrs Gray.

"I'd like to hear it, Simon, if you would," said Mrs Gray encouragingly. Daniel was nodding.

Nervously Simon sat at the keyboard of the big piano. He placed his fingers on the keys and started to play, watching the keys, his brain somehow telling him which notes to press next, a single line melody with the right hand and matching three note chords with the left. Once started he felt at ease, and completed the piece.

"Very good, Simon," said Mrs Gray. "Your fingering is pretty much correct, much better than I was expecting. You're a natural."

"He can tell straight away when I play a wrong note, just a semitone out," said Daniel.

"I'm not surprised," said Mrs Gray. "He obviously has a musical ear, and quite likely perfect pitch. Well, Simon, I hope you get the chance to learn sometime," said Mrs Gray. She sighed and left the pair to it.

So the two boys spent the wet afternoon playing on the piano, talking, playing with Daniel's toys and sharing his books.

The first day of school arrived. Simon left home to get the bus to the juniors, to find Daniel waiting at the corner, as usual, but now wearing his

Henrys uniform. "I thought," he said, "We can still get the bus in the morning, just you get off before me now." Simon remembered that there had always been some Henrys boys on the bus.

"Good," said Simon, happy for the time being as they walked down the hill to the bus stop on the main road. "Aren't you scared? Starting at Hooray Henrys I mean."

"I suppose, a bit, but Evans said he'd meet me and look out for me."

"Who's that?"

"Miles Evans. You've met him, He's my Patrol Leader."

Simon remembered the big, kind boy who had spoken to him at the church parade a few months ago. "I'm still a bit scared of going back, but I'll try to remember what you said on Saturday." And he tapped his chest twice.

Daniel laughed. "You'll be OK as well. I bet it's a lot better once you get there than you think now."

It was hard getting off the bus without Daniel, and Simon watched it as it went on into the city along the busy main road. He walked alone up the street to the juniors.

"Hiya, Simon!" came a chirpy voice next to him. It was Peter Holman. Simon was glad to see him. They had sat together and were friends in school, but never met outside as they lived too far apart.

"Hiya Peter, you sound happy."

"So should you be, haven't you heard?"

"Bout what?"

"Harvey. She's not coming back," said Peter.

Simon stopped dead. "What!"

"She's ill or something, but anyway, she won't be there."

Simon could have hugged Peter Holman right there and then. He felt a weight lift from his body. But wait, perhaps Peter was wrong.

"You sure?"

"We'll find out, won't we," said the chirpy Peter. "Come on." The boys ran the rest of the way and into the juniors' yard. Many of the kids were talking about the rumours concerning Miss Harvey, but nobody seemed to know for certain.

Simon and Peter were confronted with Barry Spence plus hangers on, a triumphant smirk on his face as he looked hard at Simon. Simon thought how different his blue eyes were from Daniel's.

"Piss off, Holman," said Spence, without even looking at Peter. Peter nervously backed away. "So where's Gray then?" mocked Spence.

"You know where he is. Henrys," said Simon. By mentioning Daniel, Barry Spence had in fact helped Simon. He tapped his chest twice.

"Heart trouble?" scoffed Spence, and pushed Simon hard back against the wall. Forth was there, waiting for the fun. Simon reached out and pushed Spence back. The hangers on gasped. Nobody pushed Barry Spence!

"Fight!" the cry went up and the nearer kids started to gather to watch. Barry Spence came forward again, aiming a punch at Simon. But Simon dodged it, and his mind full of Daniel, he launched a straight punch with all his strength at Spence's unprepared face. Spence received the blow on his nose which started to bleed. He staggered and then fell over, and was lying on the ground, crying and holding his hands to his face. The crowd looked on, astonished, gone quiet.

"Any of you lot want the same?" Simon glared at the hangers on who were trying to melt back into the gathering crowds.

"What's going on?" The kids parted as Miss Day came through.

There was a chorus of responses. "Miss, Barry Spence started it ... Hit Simon first ... self defence, Miss." Simon noticed that some of these comments were coming from the Spence gang! Miss Day helped Barry Spence to his feet.

"I'll get you, Scott," he snarled.

"No you won't!" said Simon and Miss Day, almost in unison, which surprised both of them. "Come along, Simon," she ordered. Simon followed, wishing he was still in Miss Day's class, instead of Mr West's. Daniel said Mr West was good, so maybe it would be OK. But then the whistle went and the children lined up.

"I'll see you later instead, Simon," said Miss Day, "I've Barry to see to now."

So Simon joined his class line, the others making space for him, with a new respect.

"Well done, Simon," said Peter, who had rejoined him. "He's had that coming for a long time."

"My hero," said Cynthia Jackson.

Simon felt tall, but was still a bit worried about Miss Harvey. But it would be worth getting the cane to have beaten Spence.

"Hang your coats up and go straight into the hall," the teachers were saying.

The children filed into the hall, Simon's class now at the back, being the oldest. Where Daniel used to stand. Simon wondered how he was getting on at Henrys.

The door at the side of the stage opened and Miss Harvey – wait. It wasn't Miss Harvey! It was Mr West. The school went quiet, waiting. Mr West stood at the lectern.

"Before we start the new school year," Mr West began, "I have some sad news. Miss Harvey was taken seriously ill during the summer holiday with what's called a stroke. She was with a friend in France at the time I understand. She is back in England, and is being treated in hospital in the city. I am sure you hope that she will soon be well again." There was a murmur of assent. "However, what is certain is that she will never be well enough to return to work here. So we will need a new head teacher. But in the meantime, the Board of Managers and the Education Committee have asked me to take on the job."

There was a buzz of excitement round the school hall. Mr West held up his hand, the noise died down. "This does mean that there are some changes to your classes." He went on to read out a list of classes and teachers. "And Junior 4W, that would have been my class this year, will now be Junior 4D, and will remain with Miss Day."

Simon heard that with amazement. Miss Day was taking them up. There was happy whispering along the line.

Then it was a normal assembly, except for a special prayer for Miss Harvey. At the end, Mr West picked up a piece of paper from the lectern.

"I want to see the following children immediately after assembly outside Miss .. outside the head teacher's room." He read out a list of about a dozen names, Barry Spence, some of his gang and Simon Scott among them.

The crowd gathered outside the head's room. Miss Brown was there to keep order while one by one the children went in to speak to Mr West.

"It's about the fight," one said as she came out

"That's enough, no talking," said Miss Brown. Simon liked Miss Brown, he went to her for extra help, but she seemed stern today. At last there was only Barry Spence and Simon left, waiting as far apart as they could.

"Barry Spence!" called Mr West's voice. Barry Spence went in and pushed the door behind him, but this time it didn't quite close. Parts of the conversation could be heard. Mr West sounded very cross. "Got away with far too much for far too long ... the end of the line of you, young lad ... better change your ways". Spence came out and managed a scowl at Simon, but said nothing.

"Simon Scott! And you can get back to your room now, Miss Brown, thank you."

Simon went into the hated office as Miss Brown left, giving Simon a smile. Simon stood in front of that desk, with Mr West sitting behind it now.

"Not a very good start to the new school year, Simon?"

"No, sir," said Simon, looking down but glancing round for the cane.

"Are you planning any more fights?"

Simon looked up, taken unawares by the unexpected question. "No, sir."

"I'm glad to hear it. After that fracas last year with Sidney Forth, and your demolition job on Barry Spence this morning, don't you think you've done enough?"

"Yes, sir," said Simon, puzzled about how this was going. He still could not see the cane.

"I'll be straight with you, old chap," said Mr West, his tone softening. "I don't think you've always had a fair deal, so I want to draw a line under the past and start from scratch. Starting from now. The rest is up to you. Do you understand?"

Simon was not sure if he did, but he understood 'start from scratch'. "Yes, sir."

"Any problem at all with Barry Spence, tell Miss Day – she knows about this – or come and see me."

"Yes, sir." Simon's mind was in a whirl. He couldn't grasp the change and what was happening, but he knew it was good.

"Good lad. Now we've a bargain, so don't let me down."

"Yes, sir. I mean, no sir. I mean ..." Simon stopped, confused. "I won't, sir."

"That's the ticket! Fresh start, as from now. Off you go."

"Thank you, sir," said Simon, and he left the room, feeling light and happy. As he walked along the corridor he stopped as a thought came to him. Daniel's words echoed in his mind. 'I bet it's a lot better once you get there than you think now.' How did Daniel know? He is amazing. Simon tapped his chest twice and walking tall, crossed the hall and went into his classroom without a trace of fear.

Simon soon settled into fourth year. The pace was hard, with the eleven plus coming up after Christmas, but with renewed confidence, Simon worked hard and slowly made progress with arithmetic. His reading and writing had already come on to the point where Miss Brown stopped working on that and concentrated on sums. She gave him papers to do at home, and if he got stuck, Daniel patiently sat with him and they worked through it together.

Once or twice, Simon was the object of taunts, his detractors pointing out that Daniel Gray was not around any more. Simon would tap his chest twice and think, 'yes he is'. Simon grew closer to Peter Holman at school, but still looked forward to the evenings and weekends when he could be with Daniel, and Simon was happy.

One event that stood out for Simon was related to the church. Daniel was being confirmed, and he asked Simon to be there. Simon was not sure what that meant, but he knew it was important to Daniel, and it seemed important to him that Simon was there. So there he was, sitting once more with Mr and Mrs Gray who had come to see this special service. The vicar was there that Simon had seen before, but also, dressed in a gold embroidered cloak was the Bishop. Simon had seen his picture in the local newspaper a couple of times. Daniel was wearing his long, grey school trousers, neatly ironed, along with a white shirt. He looked so smart. There were some other people, not all kids, who were being confirmed as well, and they were wearing white, but Simon's eyes were fixed on Daniel as he knelt before the Bishop.

"Daniel, God has called you by name and made you his own."

The Bishop then placed his hands on Daniel's head saying, "Confirm, O Lord, your servant Daniel with your Holy Spirit."

"Amen," said Daniel clearly.

Simon felt so proud of his friend, addressed by name by the Bishop. Then Daniel, along with the other new communicants, took the bread and wine.

Simon was again moved by the service and as the rest of the congregation took communion, he accompanied Mr and Mrs Gray to the rail as before, and received the same blessing, followed by the warm glow he had felt before.

Afterwards, he was asking Daniel about it.

"What's it mean now?"

"I can take communion now, and receive the bread and wine. It means I am a full member of the Church of England."

Simon wanted to be a full member of the Church of England too, but instead he asked, "What's the wine like?"

Daniel grinned. "It's good stuff. It's a shame they only let you have a little sip."

Daniel didn't go to church every Sunday, sometime he was involved in Scouts or swimming events. When he could, Simon went along to the latter to be with Daniel and offer him support, the true friend that he was.

25. 1956/10 Accident in the Spinney

That warm summer had gone, the nights had closed in and perforce Simon and Daniel could no longer play outdoors as much. The den was often wet so they would meet up and hang around the shopping parade. Sometimes they could still go to the wood beyond the allotments. The earth paths though the spinney had been compacted by the wheels of many children's bicycles for this was a regular circuit. The two friends would cycle down there and speed round the spinney, flying over roots and taking off from small bumps. Often there would be crowds of local children there, racing round without a care for their own safety, or anyone else's. It was fast, exhilarating and the elements of risk added to rather than detracted from the excitement. The risk was real.

One day in the half term holiday, Gavin Strong, who was Daniel's age and a Hooray Henry, was going very fast, took off over a makeshift ramp and lost control. His bike, with him on it, hit a tree. Gavin was hurt and bleeding as he lay on ground entangled in his bicycle, howling. Some of the children ran off and Simon was moving in this direction also.

"Where're you going?" asked Daniel with a note of surprise.

"Dunno, just away," said Simon, worried that he might somehow get the blame by association for Gavin's injuries. He wasn't sure what Mummy would say about him being in the woods, rough riding.

"We can't just leave him," said Daniel. "He needs some help."

The remaining kids hung back, watching, uncertain, content to let Daniel take charge. So there were just the two of them to help, and of course the howling Gavin, whose cries had subsided a little.

Daniel moved over to where Gavin lay, and Simon followed. Gavin looked up at the pair, pain on his face but also expectation, now that help was at hand.

"I can't get up, I'm stuck," said Gavin.

"Here, Simon, give me a hand," commanded Daniel, taking hold of the bicycle. Together they carefully lifted the bike, allowing Gavin to extract his legs that had somehow become locked in it.

"Hold the bike," said Daniel, so Simon held the bike, and Daniel went to the still prone Gavin.

"Where's it hurt?" asked Daniel.

"All over," replied Gavin.

"Do you think you've broken anything?" continued Daniel.

Gavin shook his head. He was a chubby lad, and Daniel put his arms around Gavin to help him up. Simon felt suddenly and stupidly jealous. Gavin was now standing, leaning on Daniel. His face was cut, his leg was bleeding and he looked very muddy.

"You wheel your bike and his," said Daniel to Simon, "I'll take mine."

Simon, quiet now, said nothing but wheeled Gavin's bike over to his own, lying on its side, and with one hand on the centre of each handlebar, stood with a bike either side of him. Daniel picked up his own bike and wheeled that, with his left hand, supporting Gavin on his right. They set off, Simon following behind.

"You'll be OK," said Daniel. "It's not far, is it?"

"No," said Gavin, "just round the block."

"Come on then," said Daniel, encouragingly.

"Thanks for the help, Daniel," said Gavin. "You're a mate."

"S'OK," said Daniel.

"Well, the others all ran off, but you stopped."

Hearing the two classmates chatting did nothing to calm Simon's feelings of insecurity. Of course he knew Daniel had other friends, lots actually, he was popular in a way that Simon could only dream of, and that made him all the more wonderful in Simon's eyes. It was illogical to doubt Daniel's loyalty to him, knowing all that Daniel did for him, especially with regard to arithmetic. But seeing and hearing Daniel and Gavin together, his sensibilities in this regard were heightened. But then Daniel replied.

"Simon stopped to help as well." Simon's heart leapt. Hearing Daniel talk about him to his friends was a real pick up.

"Yeah, thanks Simon," said Gavin, trying to turn his neck to look back, but failing and wincing with sudden pain. "Ow!" He turned back.

"Lives near you, doesn't he?" Gavin asked Daniel.

"Yes."

"You friends?"

"Yes," said Daniel, "he's my best friend. He'll be at Henrys next year."

Swiftly from suspicion to soaring the heights, Simon's mood took off, and he followed behind, happy once more, Daniel oblivious to the smile now on Simon's face. The small matter of first having to pass the eleven plus went unnoticed.

They entered Gavin's short driveway and limped round the side of the house to the back door.

"Mum!" shouted Gavin as they opened it. They leaned the bikes against the wall of the house and while Gavin stepped gingerly into the kitchen, Daniel and Simon stood outside, not entering uninvited. Mrs Strong appeared.

"Gavin, what happened to you?" she asked, worriedly.

"Came off me bike," explained Gavin. "These two helped me home."

"Hello, Daniel," said Mrs Strong. Simon wondered how well Daniel knew Gavin. His mother obviously knew him. But then he remembered what Daniel had said and felt better.

"And who's this other little hero?" asked Mrs Strong of Gavin, looking at Simon.

"That's Simon. He's Daniel's best friend."

Mrs Strong beamed at Simon, Simon beamed back, happy in the confirmation of his status from Gavin, as a representative of Daniel's peers.

She now had a wet flannel and was wiping Gavin's wounds with it. They looked a lot less serious with all the blood and muck removed.

"Come in, boys." he said, and Daniel went into the kitchen, Simon following. Gavin seemed a lot happier now, and smiled at the two.

"Thanks for helping," he said. Then to his mother, "The rest all ran off, only these helped."

"Where was this?" asked Mrs Strong.

"In the spinney," said Simon, feeling more confident.

"Gavin, what have I told you about riding your bike in there?" Mrs Strong said sharply. Gavin shot Simon a cross look. Daniel moved very slightly so as to be slightly more between Simon and Gavin and his mother. But both boys remained silent, Simon now feeling stupid.

Mrs Strong went on, "Still, it was very good of you both to help Gavin. I'll see what I can find." She finished applying a sticking plaster to Gavin's knee and then disappeared into the house.

"Simon didn't know you weren't supposed to be there," whispered Daniel to Gavin.

Gavin's look softened a bit. "Never mind," he said.

Mrs Strong returned with three boxes of jelly babies. "Here we are," she said brightly, handing each of them a box. "One for a brave boy and one for two good helpers each."

"Thank you," said Simon and Daniel in unison.

"We'd better go now," said Daniel.

The two set off, riding their bikes again now, weaving slowly along the street.

"Let's go to mine," said Daniel.

So they rode to Daniel's house. He let himself in. Daniel had his own key for the house.

"Where's your Mum and Dad?" asked Simon.

"Work." They dumped their coats and shoes and Daniel led the way to his bedroom. It was much bigger than Simon's, the house was bigger. It had a toilet downstairs as well as upstairs. Daniel had a double bed in his room, and Simon thought that was very special. The two usually played in Daniel's room rather Simon's because it was heated, a major reason in the winter. Simon sat on the bed and watched him tidy away some things on the floor. Daniel turned to Simon.

"You OK?" he asked. Simon nodded, his gaze fixed on his friend. Daniel came over and sat next to Simon.

"Did you mean that, what you said?" asked Simon, clumsily.

"What?"

"When you told Gavin I was your best friend."

"Of course. You are." Daniel put his arm round Simon's slim shoulders. "You know you are," he said, grinning, and he put his other hand on Simon's thigh. Simon responded by doing the same. He felt excited.

"We've got lots of time," said Daniel. "Let's undress."

Simon nodded, ready as always to comply, excited at the prospect without really knowing why, anxious to lay to rest the doubts he had felt earlier and to re-affirm his standing with Daniel. Daniel too had felt his friend's uncertainty and while he enjoyed the feeling of ascendancy he got when close to Simon, he began to feel it was more than that. He looked forward to their times alone together, to seeing and in a way possessing Simon's body, running his hands over his smooth flesh, revelling in that Simon allowed the most personal caressing, and even more so in the knowledge that Simon knew his own body so well and that he would respond in kind, bringing him to climax even though he could not yet achieve that himself. Daniel was aware now that this was sexual in a way that his younger friend was not yet. He was not sure how to handle this new dimension in his head, but felt he had to be careful and not upset Simon, whom he knew, looked up to him. He reflected on what he had said to Gavin, and it was true. Simon was his best friend, there was nobody he was closer to and he knew that Simon would never betray their secret.

In the glowing aftermath of his sexual release, he looked at Simon lying beside him, and he felt new emotion and hugged Simon tightly.

"What was that for?" said Simon, slightly surprised at this sudden squeeze.

"For you," said Daniel, happily.

The afternoon ended happily for Simon too as the two boys relaxed in their sensual intimacy and comfort of each other's touch, they lay on the big bed, eating jelly babies and talking about the huge American aircraft carrier that was the cutaway in the middle of Daniel's *Eagle* comic until it was time to get dressed.

Lying in bed that night with the wind rattling around outside, Simon felt safe and warm under the blankets and eiderdown, while the gales, like the troubles of his world, raged on, but for the time being could not get to him. He did not have to be concerned with lost roof slates and damaged fences so he snuggled down and listened to the tempest outside, content with his day. He knew that a few hundred yards away, Daniel would be doing the same, and felt the closeness again.

26. 1956/11 Long Division

Miss Brown had worked through it patiently with him, and he understood it then, or so he thought, but now on a cold November Saturday morning, it had all gone. Long division of money. Simon didn't know where to start. That feeling of cold panic and helplessness came over him as he thought of having to spend the next five years at Victoria Road with Barry Spence. It was true that Spence had kept his distance since being felled spectacularly in the school yard by a single punch from Simon, and he was shorn of most of his hangers on by constant pressure from Miss Day and Mr West, but Simon knew it wouldn't last. Spence had said as much. "Wait till you get to Vicks, Scott. I've got friends there who are going to beat you up every day." Simon had no reason to doubt the truth of this and was frightened.

Daniel was backing him, helping him with these 11 plus papers he was given for practice, and he knew that Daniel had turned down chances to go out with his other friends from Hooray Henrys in order to help him with his maths. But Daniel would not be there at the juniors when the exam had to be taken. Simon shook with fear and a tear came. Daniel had told him that in one place they were going to abolish the 11 plus. That had sounded a good idea to Simon until Daniel said that it meant all the children would go to one school. So that would not help his predicament, and anyway, Daniel was against it. All right for him, he was clever and had got to Hooray Henrys.

He folded up the test paper and went downstairs. The fire was lit in the sitting room and he went in to get warm. He sat on the settee, not the broken end, and looked again at the test paper. If only he could understand it. The numbers just seemed to dance in front of his eyes. He looked into the fire, seeing patterns in the red hot coals. He closed the test paper and picked up his book. He liked reading and was now one of the best readers in the class. And that had improved his spelling too. So he tried to shut his mind to the future and lose himself in the story about space ships and mining the asteroids.

Mummy put her head round the door. "Lunch is ready." Mummy always called it lunch, although everybody else he knew called it dinner. He sat at the dining table and started to eat.

"Frances, how do you do division of money?"

Frances thought for a moment. "Well, you start by dividing the pounds and transfer the remainder to the shillings, add it on and then divide that, and do the same for pennies," she said helpfully. Mummy and Daddy nodded approval. Simon was left none the wiser. But what did that **mean**?

"I'll teach you to use a slide rule when you're older," said Daddy.

"Thanks Daddy, "said Simon, wise enough not to add that it would not help him now when he needed it.

"Can I go round to Daniel's after dinner, Mummy," he requested.

"I expect so, darling," said Mummy, but with a glance at Daddy, who just shrugged.

Simon ate the rest of his dinner and as soon as he could, took the hated paper, put on his coat and went round the corner to Daniel's. Would he be back from swimming? Maybe he was going out with some Henrys. He knocked on the back door, which opened.

"Oh, come in, Simon, it's freezing out there."

Simon stepped into the warm kitchen. The Aga kept it warm. Mummy wanted an Aga, but Daddy said money doesn't grow on trees. Anyway, there was nowhere to put it.

"Is Daniel home please, Mrs Gray?" asked Simon.

"Yes, he's about somewhere," she answered. "Daniel!"

Daniel came in from the sitting room. He was wearing his denim jeans. Simon felt a bit silly in his short trousers.

"Hiya Simon. Let's go up."

Simon followed Daniel upstairs, hanging his coat in the hall on the way.

"How was swimming this morning?" asked Simon.

"Cold," said Daniel with feeling. "but it went OK. Coach said I was really good."

Simon thought that was obvious. "What about Layton?"

"He's OK. I like him, but I like beating him better."

"Did you?" asked Simon as they went into Daniel's bedroom.

"Yeah, in front crawl of course, and breaststroke, just. But he well beat me in backstroke and butterfly. What's that? Another eleven plus paper?"

Simon nodded. "You don't mind, do you?" he asked anxiously. He saw Daniel's green Henrys blazer and his long school trousers on a hanger on the edge of his wardrobe door. Simon wondered if he would ever have a Henrys uniform. It occurred to Simon he didn't even have his own wardrobe. Daniel had lots of clothes.

"No, of course not. 'Help other people at all times', remember? And 'Be Prepared'. You might not be a scout yet, but you're going to be as prepared for the eleven plus as you can be."

"Thanks, Daniel. You're tops."

"I want you at Henrys. I know you're clever enough, and I won't have you going to Vicks. I just won't," said Daniel vehemently.

Simon didn't know what to say to that. The two years in age between them sometimes seemed so much to Simon, although he was only one school year behind Daniel because of how their birthdays fell.

"Pull up the stool and let's have a look," said Daniel.

The two boys sat at the desk. Daniel looked at the test paper thoughtfully. Simon admired Daniel in many ways, not least because he was so clever. So now he looked at him and waited.

"Long division of money?" asked Daniel.

"Yes, I just can't do it."

"Won't have defeatist talk here," said Daniel crossly. Simon could be a bit nervous of Daniel when he was in this mood. "Come on, let's look at this one. Fifty eight pounds, six shillings and threepence divided by fifteen. Write it out." Daniel pushed pad and pencil to Simon, who copied the sum down.

"What do we do first?" Daniel demanded.

"Divide the pounds?"

"Good, what's fifty eight divided by fifteen?"

Simon stalled.

"How many fifteens are there in fifty eight?" tried Daniel.

"Dunno," said Simon glumly.

"What's two fifteens?"

"Thirty?"

"Good, now what's three fifteens?"

"Er, forty five?"

"OK, what's four fifteens?"

"Sixty. Oh, that's too much. So it goes three times, remainder ... um ...thirteen."

"Yes. You see, you can do it. Put down the three."

Simon wrote 3 under the pounds, and started to write the 13 under the shillings.

"Wait," said Daniel. "That thirteen remainder. Thirteen what?"

Simon looked puzzled.

"Well, what did we just divide?"

"Oh, pounds. Thirteen pounds," said Simon.

"Good. But you can't put thirteen pounds just like that in the shillings. It's not thirteen shillings, is it?"

"No," said Simon, understanding starting to form. "You've got to change the thirteen pounds into shillings first."

"You mean **you** have," said Daniel. "How do you do that?"

"Twenty shillings in a pound, so times by twenty?"

"That's right. So what's thirteen times twenty?"

Simon scribbled at the side of the sheet. "Two hundred and sixty?"

"Good. What next?"

"Carry it to the shillings column and add it to the six shillings there. Two hundred and sixty six."

"OK, so now we have two hundred and sixty six shillings to divide by fifteen. Ordinary long division I think, a bit high to keep adding fifteens like we did for the pounds."

Daniel watched as Simon did the division of 266 by 15 at the side.

"Seventeen remainder eleven," announced Simon.

"That's what I get too," said Daniel, pleased. "So far we've got the answer three pounds and seventeen shillings, now to divide the pennies. What's your remainder from the shillings?"

"Eleven. But that's eleven shillings, it's got to be changed into pennies," said Simon, as the darkness lifted to reveal understanding at last of how this worked.

"You're getting it," said Daniel, smiling. "So, twelve pennies make a shilling; what's eleven shillings in pennies. Twelve times table."

Simon thought for a moment. He had been working hard on learning his tables. "One hundred and thirty two."

"Right. So carry that to the pennies column."

"Add that to the thrupence, is one hundred and thirty five." said Simon.

"OK, so now divide that by fifteen."

Once again, Simon did the long division sum at the side. "Nine, and no remainder."

"Good. So put the nine in the pennies column, and that's it."

"That's it?" repeated Simon. "You mean I've done it?"

"You have, Simon. What is fifty eight pounds, six shillings and thrupence divided by fifteen?" grinned Daniel.

Simon looked at the sum. "Three pounds, seventeen shillings and ninepence. Yes! It's the changing the remainders I didn't understand, but I do now. Thanks to you."

"You did it," Daniel reminded him. "I didn't do a single calculation for you in all that."

"You're the best friend anybody could have," said Simon.

"So are you," said Daniel. "And I mean that."

Under Daniel's watchful eye, Simon worked through more examples until Daniel was sure Simon really had grasped it. Some involved ha'pennies and farthings, but now Simon had the concept in his head, he coped with those too. Daniel watched with pleasure at Simon's happiness as he gained confidence.

Daniel spent many such sessions with Simon that autumn and winter. He knew his emotional and vulnerable friend would go under if he had to go to Vicks, and he was determined that would not happen.

27. 1957/1 Sledging Accident

Simon lay on his bed, wrapped in his pyjamas and dressing gown. It had been a good day and he had even been able to forget the approaching eleven plus for a few hours. All the local kids had been on the hill with their sledges, careering down, getting faster and faster as the snow became more compacted from their passage, as well as the very occasional car that moved cautiously along. As soon as it was gone, the hordes returned, vying for the best run. Simon's sledge was sought after as it was long enough for two, three with a squeeze, and some of the kids, boys and girls, who hadn't got their own sledges would ask for, and get a ride down with Simon. But best of all of course was when he and Daniel would go flying down together at top speed, often falling off in a heap together at the bottom of the hill, and then trudging back up again hauling the sledge, dodging the others as they came flying down.

Only encroaching cold darkness in the late afternoon had called a halt and slowly the children had drifted away homewards for tea. Simon and Daniel had parted at the corner with a quick "See ya!", each off to their own home. Simon lay, happily savouring the fun of the day just gone, reliving it in his mind. He should really be in bed, asleep, but excitement had kept him up.

He was aware of the sound of the car engine running and side gates opening. Then Daddy opening the garage doors. Suddenly there was a stream of swearing and Simon knew with abrupt certainty what the cause was. He had forgotten to put the sledge away and it was left outside the back door, in the way of the car. Quietly, Simon got up and looked out of his bedroom window, peering down to see the open garage doors, and Daddy, lifting up the sledge high over his head (and it was a heavy sledge) and hurling it across the small patio area, it crashing into the side of the coalhouse, smashing into pieces as it did so. Simon watched shocked and helpless, tears coming to his eyes as the device of so much joy that day was quickly and ruthlessly destroyed. He watched unseen as Daddy stood a moment looking at what was now a broken mess of wood and metal runners, and then turned away. The headlights came on illuminating the garage and the car passed slowly into view as it came down the side of the house and then out of view as it went into the garage. Simon looked down at his ruined sledge. He could see that repair would be difficult, if not impossible. He got into bed and cried, half fearing his father's wrath and more for failing to put the sledge away. But Daddy never came and he fell asleep, his happy memories now expunged by the loss of his sledge.

The next morning, Simon was wary indeed. He looked out of his bedroom window. It had not snowed again, but yesterday's was still lying. No good now. The wreckage of the sledge had been moved from by the coalhouse to near the garage, footprints across the patio. He could see now by the white, winter morning light that the damage was considerable. He could hear the Home Service from the radio downstairs.

Mummy's voice called up. "Frances! Simon! 'Lift up your hearts'!"

Simon heard Frances reply and shouted and OK from him too. This was a reminder of the time, as 'Lift up your hearts' was on the wireless at ten to eight each morning. He finished dressing and went downstairs to the dining room, warmed by the electric fire.

"You left your sledge out last night, Simon," said Daddy, stating a fact. Simon felt it best to say nothing, wondering which way this would go. He sat down and picked up a piece of toast.

Daddy continued, in mollifying tones, "I'm sorry, son, but when I put the car away, I didn't see it and the car hit it. It's broken I'm afraid." Daddy looked at Simon, smiling, wholly unaware that this deception, this attempted softening of the blow, had already been scooped by Simon's own witness. Simon felt empty inside, astonished at this version of what he had seen. He wanted to shout out that he had seen what had happened, he knew that it wasn't true! But at ten years and four months he dare not, in case his challenge of the new orthodoxy would lead to a further release of temper and retribution. Feeling cold inside like the snow outside, Simon simply nodded and bit his toast. As Daddy got up to leave for work, he patted Simon on the head as he went past.

"I'm getting the bus into the studio today," he said. "I'm trying to get some extra petrol coupons though. Bloody Nasser."

"Maybe it won't last long," said Mummy. "We're out of Egypt and perhaps Macmillan will sort something out."

"I doubt it, Kate. Bye love," he was saying to Mummy in the hall. "I may be late tonight," he added.

"So what's new?" muttered Frances more to herself than Simon, as the front door closed.

"I saw it," said Simon, now tearful.

"What?" said Frances, puzzled by her little brother's upset. "It'll be OK, it's only a sledge."

"It's not that," said Simon, "Daddy smashed it on purpose."

"What for?" asked Frances. "You mean he drove into it on purpose."

"He didn't drive into it," explained Simon. "I saw from my bedroom. It was in the way so he picked it up and threw it against the coalhouse. That's when it smashed."

"I thought I heard something," said Mummy, who had come in from the kitchen and caught the tail end of this. Simon turned, he had been oblivious to Mummy's return. "I thought it was from next door," Mummy continued. "I'm sure Daddy didn't mean it," she added hopefully.

"Mummy!" shouted Frances indignant, who then got up and stormed out.

Mummy looked at Simon, knowing that her attempt to gloss over the issue had been fruitless.

"Never mind, darling," she said. "We'll see what we can do."

Simon dawdled round the corner to Daniel's, disconsolate, wondering what to say to his friend. And there he was, smiling, wrapped in his dark blue duffel coat, the dear face peering out from the hood.

"I was just coming for you," he said. Then, seeing Simon's downcast mood, "What's the matter?"

Simon recounted the whole episode. Daniel listened saying nothing, allowing Simon to relate the whole thing.

"Sorry, Simon," he said, with the comforting arm round his shoulders. He knew what Simon's Daddy was like. Then an idea!

"Come on, Simon!" Daniel led the way to his house and round into the garden. There was a large, slightly dilapidated shed into which Daniel disappeared.

"Help me shift this lot," he said, indicating piles of miscellaneous stuff that meant little to Simon. But when they had moved stuff, there was revealed – a sledge! Simon looked at Daniel, eyes hopeful.

Daniel laughed at Simon's expression. "It's my sister's old one," he said dragging it out. It looked old, too. the runners were rusty and a lot of paint was missing. But it was a sledge. The two boys dragged it out where it stuck in the snow. They dragged the unwilling sledge to the back door, leaving long brown, rusty marks in the snow.

"Mummy," called Daniel, only to be stopped by a poke from Simon.

"Don't tell, please," implored Simon quietly.

"Course not, silly." Then again, "Mummy!"

"Yes, Daniel?" said Mrs Gray, coming into the kitchen. "Oh, hello Simon. Shut the door, you're letting the heat out."

The two boys stepped in and closed the door. Daniel's kitchen was much bigger than Simon's, and there was a table where they had breakfast. There was the Aga too that kept the house warm.

"Mummy, Simon's sledge got broken. Can he have Louise's old one?"

"Heavens, have we still got that?"

"It was in the shed," supplied Daniel.

"I expect so," said Mrs Gray. "I doubt if Louise will want it again. Certainly he can use it in the meantime."

"Thank you, Mrs Gray," said Simon happily.

The two boys took the rusty sledge to the hill where some others had already gathered. After a few slow runs, held back by the rust, the sledge started to pick up speed, and now side by side, Daniel and Simon would race the others down the hill. By the end of the morning, the runners were shiny and polished, and the sledge as fast as any other. Simon was content. He looked at Daniel.

"Thanks for getting me the sledge," he said to his rescuer.

"S'OK," said Daniel. "Race yer!" And off down the hill again.

28. 1957/1 Eleven Plus

Miss Day and Miss Brown could not help him now. Not even Daniel could help him now. It was January and the last eleven plus day. Arithmetic day. Simon and Daniel sat together on the bus that morning as usual. Simon was actually shaking with fear, which Daniel noticed, and surreptitiously held his hand to calm him. Simon felt his friend's strength, and yet the green Henrys blazer under Daniel's gabardine mac only served to taunt him. The Vicks kids on the bus were as rowdy as ever.

"You'll be fine. You said the English and Reasoning went OK," said Daniel.

"Yes, but I'm going to fail the arithmetic, and you have to pass them all," said Simon, close to tears.

"You will pass, I know it. Look at all the work you've done."

"**We've** done," said Simon, gloomily.

"I've only helped as much as I could. You've got to pass, for me," said Daniel. "And anyway, you're young in your year. They add marks on if you're young, so that will help."

"What about you then? You didn't get any marks added on, then."

"No, but I'm brainy. And so are you. You **will** be at Henrys. I know it."

"Here's my stop," said Simon, "See you tonight." Daniel moved to let Simon away from the window seat, and Simon, his legs feeling so heavy, got up into the aisle.

"Simon," called Daniel after him, as he moved to the top of stairs. Simon looked back and Daniel tapped his chest twice. Simon nodded and went down the stairs. Daniel slid back to the window and wiping the condensation off the window, looked down to try to see Simon. There were crowds of junior kids about and he couldn't pick him out soon enough before the bus moved off into the city centre. Daniel sat and thought about Simon's stress these past few months. Seeing his young friend's torment had been an eye opener for Daniel. He had not found the eleven plus that hard, and had been confident of a pass, and not just a place at the grammar tech, but a high pass, getting a coveted place at King Henrys. Seeing what it cost Simon, and presumably so many other kids, was changing Daniel's mind about the whole process. There had to be a better way, it was so unfair on kids like Simon. All he could do now was cross his fingers and hope. Even a tech grammar place would be better than Victoria Road.

Simon waited to cross the road, watching the bus bearing Daniel into the city and to Hooray Henrys.

"Hello Simon," said a bright voice at his side.

"Hiya Peter," said Simon. "Let's go in together."

So Simon and Peter Holman walked up to the juniors.

"You scared?" asked Simon, tentatively.

"A bit," said Peter, "but I'm not expecting much. My Dad says that if I get to the grammar tech I'll have done well. What did your Dad and Mum say?"

"Just said do your best. But I know they'll be disappointed when I go to Vicks."

"We might get to the tech together. That would be good," said Peter, optimistically.

Simon wondered why Peter was always so cheerful. But that's the way he was. He liked Peter and this year was his best friend at the juniors now Daniel had left, but he was irritating at times. Mainly because he wasn't Daniel. Today Simon was glad of the friendship and company. But he was worried. He knew Mummy was annoyed that Mr West wasn't taking the fourth years. He had a good record with the eleven plus passes, had got Frances and Daniel through, and this was Miss Day's first time with the fourth years. Not good for confidence.

"Maybe," said Simon.

There was no assembly at all this week because all the desks were set out in the hall for the fourth years to take the eleven plus exams. The children all filed in and sat at their allocated desks. This was the day Simon had been dreading. A fatalism overcame him and he seemed to accept his future. Victoria Road. It seemed that this was somehow his fate and he must endure it. In a strange way that seemed to calm him. At the command from Mr West, he opened the exam booklet, like so many he had worked through with Miss Brown and Daniel. They were hard, and Simon struggled to remember everything he had learned. He plodded on. He noticed Sidney Forth working rapidly and confidently, evidently finishing in good time, going back to check his work. Forget Forth, concentrate! Simon was still on the last page when the command came to stop. He hadn't even finished! A feeling of desperation overcame him. He wanted to cry but could not.

They went out to play, just the fourth years as the rest of the school had already had playtime. Simon, unconsciously perhaps, leaned on the schoolyard wall at the point where he had knocked Spence over in September. Peter came with him.

"How'd you get on?" asked Peter.

"Didn't even finish," said Simon, miserably, watching Spence playing football as if this day were like any other. "Did you?"

"Yes of course," said Peter, unthinkingly, and then, trying to soften the blow, added, "But only with a few minutes to spare."

That did not help Simon.

That night, shunning the company of the bus he walked home in the darkness and through a thick smoke laden fog. At times he had to use his torch to be sure he was in the right place in the well known route. The weather matched his mood. He was lost within as well as at risk of it from without.

Later he poured his heart out to Daniel, and sobbed on his shoulder, while Daniel, unable to help further, just kept his arm round him to give what comfort he could. Nobody should have to go through this, thought Daniel.

The next few weeks dragged slowly. Simon could not find any zest for life at all. He went through the motions, spending what time he could with Daniel, often just lying on his big bed watching while Daniel did his Henrys homework at his desk or listening while Daniel played the piano. If Daniel had the lid up, he watched the intricate patterns the elaborate mechanism made as the hammers rippled along the strings obedient to Daniel's fingers, reflecting in movement the patterns of the sound. Just being with Daniel was comforting, and Daniel didn't mind Simon being there while he did his homework.

Six weeks later Mr West came into the classroom just before home time.
"Excuse me, Miss Day. I have these for the children to take home."
A dead silence fell in the room. Every child knew exactly what those letters were. While Miss Day gave out the sealed envelopes, Mr West continued, "These letters are addressed to your parents. You are not to open them yourselves. If I find that any letter has been opened before it's given to your parents, or those looking after you, I am very serious when I say that this might be one occasion when I find Miss Harvey's cane and use it, girls or boys."

The look on his face told everybody that this was no joke. Miss Day dropped Simon's envelope onto his desk, and Peter's next to him. The two boys looked at each other, fearfully. Simon noticed, without understanding, that his envelope and Peter's were white, many others, including Susan James's and Barry Spence's, were brown. Sidney Forth's and Cynthia Jackson's were white too. But Simon was not concerned about that. As home time came, and he and Peter walked to the main road to get their separate buses, Peter was chattering away as usual, while Simon replied in grunts, his mind focused on what would happen when he got home. He hoped that Daddy would not be at home, because he knew that while he might not get hit for failing, there would be that look that he had failed in Daddy's eyes.

He went in the back door without his usual "I'm home!" and went into the sitting room. Mummy was there on the settee, Daddy was not at home. Without a word, he gave the envelope to Mummy and went to take his coat off. He lingered in the hall, scared to go back in, listening for any reaction. None came and unable to stand the suspense any longer, he went and stood in the doorway. Mummy was holding the open letter in her hands, she looked up at him, there were tears in her eyes. Simon's heart sank.

"Come here, Simon," she said, holding out her arms, "Come here, my darling." Simon went and sat next to her, she hugged him. "I am so proud of you, my son. You've passed."

Simon felt dizzy. Passed? Him? Waves of feeling raced through him. He was lightheaded. Passed?

"Me?" was all he could manage.

"Look," said Mummy, "not only passed, but enough for a place at King Henrys!" She showed the letter to Simon. It was his letter all right. It was printed, but there were gaps where someone had typed in parts that applied to him. Simon Scott, it said, his birthday and then about a very high score in English and Reasoning, a pass in mathematics, the mean score (Simon didn't understand how it could be a mean score if he had passed) entitling him to a place at either City Technical Grammar School or King Henry VII Grammar School for Boys. There was something about it being a direct grant grammar school with places allocated to boys from county junior schools. Simon didn't understand that. He lived in the city for a start.

"Does that mean I can go to Henrys, not Vicks?" asked Simon, not yet ready to believe.

"Unless you would rather go to the grammar tech?" said Mummy, but in a tone which made it obvious she was joking.

Then Simon was up, dancing round the room. He felt he could fly, the feeling of relief, of liberation was indescribable. He started to cry from sheer relief, a huge burden of fear lifted from his ten year old body. Mother and son hugged and cheered. A thought came to Simon as he started to calm down.

"Mummy, can I go round to Daniel's?"

"What about tea?"

"Please. He helped me."

"All right. Come back for tea."

Simon looked at the clock before running out, forgetting his coat in the late February cold. Daniel would probably not be home yet as he got a later bus at home time.

"Hello, Mrs Gray, is Daniel home yet," said Simon after knocking on the back door.

"Not yet, Simon, but he shouldn't be long." And then noticing Simon's agitation, "Is something the matter?"

"No, thank you," shouted Simon cheerfully as he ran back round the house and to the corner. Just in his short school trousers, shirt and pullover, but unfeeling of the cold, he could not bear to wait at the corner but ran down the hill toward the main road. There was the unmistakeable figure of Daniel, green cap with gold piping, gabardine mac, walking up the hill. Simon was shouting, and Daniel looked up, saw his friend running towards him. He too started to run, and as they got closer, Simon was yelling, "I've passed, I've passed!"

Relief surged through Daniel, no Vicks then. Simon would at least be safe. Then they were together, Simon was gripping Daniel, twirling him round, oblivious of any passers by or other kids about on their way home.

"I've passed, Daniel, I've passed."

"I gather that," said Daniel, disentangling himself. "I'm glad, really glad." Daniel paused. "Grammar Tech, then?"

"No! Henrys! I'm going to Hooray Henrys with you!"

"Henrys?" repeated Daniel, "Henrys! Simon, what did I tell you? Didn't I always say you would be going to Henrys?"

"Yes, and now I am," said Simon gleefully, his happiness knew no bounds. He wanted to hug Daniel there and then. But the two ran up the hill to Daniel's house and into the warm kitchen. Only then did Simon realise how cold he had been outside.

"Calm down you two," said Mrs Gray, "what's going on?"

"Mum, Simon's passed and is going to Henrys!" shouted Daniel excitedly.

"That's wonderful Simon. Well done," said Mrs Gray.

Simon beamed. "Thank you Mrs Gray," he said. And then a realisation came to him. "I couldn't have done it without Daniel."

"Well, that's very kind of you to say so, Simon," said Mrs Gray, thinking back to the long autumn evenings that Daniel had spent working with Simon, often she had wondered, at the expense of his own homework. Not to mention a Christmas dominated by Simon's arithmetic.

"Come on," said Daniel, leading the way to his room, hanging his coat in the hall. In his bedroom, he hung up his green blazer, with the embroidered coat of arms, a blazer that now Simon would be wearing, took off his Henrys tie, and turned to Simon, white shirt now open at the neck, long school trousers, a vision of salvation.

"Come here," he said, holding out his arms. The two hugged tightly until emotion overcame them both, blinking back the tears. Joy, relief, release of tension, shared happiness. They sat down on the bed.

"I meant what I said, Daniel. I know that without you I would be going to Vicks."

"Well, you did it," said Daniel.

Simon looked directly into Daniel's blue eyes. "Only with your help. I will never, ever forget this, Daniel. I just don't know what to say."

"Just thank you would do," said Daniel, smiling at Simon's seriousness.

"Thank you, Daniel, from the bottom of my heart," said Simon solemnly. Daniel laughed and hugged him again, and then the comprehension of what had happened hit them once more, the two were dancing round the room, whooping and yelling with jubilation.

The significance of the white and brown envelopes became apparent over the next few days. Passes had white envelopes, and failures had brown. Mummy was disgusted when that was pointed out to her, saying it was wrong to show children up in that way. She wrote a piece about it in her newspaper column. Some people said it was only because her son had failed, until they were told, that shut them up. Mummy and Daddy asked what present he would like for passing; Simon said a radio like Daniel's. In fact he got an even better one, the latest Roberts portable. On hearing that Simon was going to Henrys, Barry Spence, bound for Victoria Road, simply ignored him from that time on, which suited Simon. Barry Spence was now irrelevant. To his undying amazement, for once lost for words, Peter Holman had also qualified for a place at Hooray Henrys. Sidney Forth too had passed, but was going to the grammar tech. "It's a more modern education," he said sourly. But Simon didn't care. In the cold winter, the sun was shining for Simon.

29. 1957/6 Bike rides

Winter turned to Spring and for Simon and Daniel it was a renaissance. Only when the burden of the eleven plus was lifted did they realise what a weight it had been, Daniel almost as much as Simon. Both boys became more carefree and more relaxed. When Daniel was out with some of his friends, Simon was more accepted now, perhaps as a Hooray Henry in waiting. But the pair also spent much time together, riding their bikes out into the countryside, a favourite place being the airfield where the flying club was based. Both boys were interested in aeroplanes, and liked to watch the small aircraft, mainly Austers, the occasional biplane and rarely some more exotic types, landing and taking off.

"I might be a pilot when I grow up," said Daniel. "Either that or a policeman like Dad."

"Me too," said Simon, "or I might be a journalist like Mummy."

"Need good exam results," said Daniel.

"To be a journalist?"

"Maybe. But I meant to be a pilot. I'll get them at Hooray Henrys."

The conversation turned to life at Hooray Henrys, Simon attentively listening to Daniel's descriptions of grammar school life, soaking in every detail so as to be better prepared for September. Daniel had kept Simon up to date on an almost daily basis, and Simon felt as if he knew almost as much about Henrys as he did. The initiation ritual worried Simon a bit, but that was for the future.

Near the airfield on a low hilltop was a copse of trees, fringed by long grass, which they had taken to visiting while out on their rides as it offered the seclusion they wanted together. Apart from a drink and something to eat, Daniel's groundsheet was always in his pack as well now. They pushed their bikes across the field, following the hedgerow up the hill. On the edge of the copse, they had a view of the airfield in the distance, the runway at right angles to them so that the aircraft didn't fly over the hill when landing or taking off.

Lying together on the groundsheet in the long grass, they let the heat of the summer sun warm their bare skin as they enjoyed each other's companionship, nudity and sensual pleasure. After Simon had brought Daniel off, they lay close in the summer sun.

"I wish I could do it for you," said Daniel. "You get so close sometimes, I think."

"It's OK," said Simon. "I like it when you come off."

"No," said Daniel firmly. "Sex is about giving, and I feel as if I'm doing all the taking."

"You wait," smiled Simon, "I'll make up for it, and then you can pay me back."

"You're on," said Daniel, laughing.

They wrestled with each other on the groundsheet, perspiring with the effort until either they both gave up with the exertion or Daniel had Simon pinned down, bringing the bout to an end.

As they lay, a familiar but wonderful sound filled the air. Both boys recognised the distinctive song of a Merlin engine immediately and looked at each other, eyes full of anticipation and wonderment before searching the sky. And there it was, its gull wings clear against the sky – a Spitfire! It came over the hill and flew low across the airfield below them before climbing away again and heading off into the distance. It capped a perfect afternoon for the two boys.

On one occasion, they were lying together in the sun on the groundsheet, when Daniel gripped Simon tightly. "Don't move, Simon" he said. There was fear in Daniel's voice.

"What's the matter? Someone coming?"

"No," whispered Daniel. "A snake, right behind you. An adder." Daniel watched as the snake, its zigzag markings identifying it as England's only poisonous snake, moved slowly from the long grass onto the edge of the groundsheet.

"Where is it?" asked Simon in a whisper, lying frozen on his side facing Daniel.

Daniel, looking over Simon's shoulder, could see the reptile. "About four inches from your bum. Keep still." Terrified, Simon lay still in Daniel's grasp. "It's going," said Daniel again, as the snake slid back into the long grass and disappeared. "Gone," said Daniel, relieved.

"Isn't it safe here?" asked Simon.

"Course it is," said Daniel. "They're quite rare, and it's only coz we were lying still it came, I'm sure. Probably was as surprised to see us as we were to see it."

"I'm glad it didn't bite me."

"Would've been a job explaining how a snake bit your bare bum," said Daniel, and they both laughed, tension gone.

30. *1957/8 Salcombe*

As every summer, the two friends were parted and there was a gap in their times together when their families went off on their annual holiday. The middle two weeks of August were favoured by both families, but when they did not coincide exactly, both boys felt at a loose end waiting for the other to return. There was always one week away in common so the most one would be at home without the other would be a week. They usually went in opposite directions with both households now having cars, the Grays often heading for Scotland, while the Scotts retained their affiliation with Devon. Not to Westward Ho anymore but to Salcombe, in the far south of that county.

For Simon, the adventure started before that, as he had become the family's navigator. Bitter experience had taught the family to avoid the Exeter by-pass where traffic came to a halt on holiday Saturdays with miles of queuing cars funnelling into the county from far and wide. Simon would study the maps and find new ways to reach Salcombe without hitting the jams. From a predawn start, his route took them down the Fosseway through Moreton-in-Marsh, Stow-on-the-Wold, Bourton-on-the-Water and then across country via Shepton Mallet towards Honiton, but then no further, as often the queues from the Exeter By pass could stretch that far. Simon would navigate across country, keeping the car moving through leafy Devon lanes with their high hedges past Crediton, Tedburn St Mary and eventually to Totnes and then south to Salcombe. There was always a competition for who would be the first to see the sea.

The hotel was just south of the town, with gardens reaching down to the shore and its own moorings in the shelter of the large inlet known as the estuary. It was these moorings that were the source of Simon's delight at being in Salcombe. The hotel had its own little open motor boat, *Invention*, which was hired for him for the two weeks each year. Despite remaining a total non swimmer, Simon became adept at boat handling and found a role as a ferryman for his family and the others with whom they met up each year. Simon would ferry people across to the beaches and up to the town jetty by the Ferry Inn. He had a chart of the estuary and his boat was often seen exploring the creeks, and when the tide was right, as far as Kingsbridge.

Simon developed a technique of running the boat's bow onto the beach and digging the boathook into the sand to stop *Invention* being pushed broadside on to the beach, which would have stranded it, possibly damaging the propeller and it would have been a disaster. This worked well at the relatively sheltered Mill Bay and Telegraph Bay which were favourites, but Sunny Cove had much rougher waves as a rule and Simon could only hold the boat for so long, so people had to be quick on and off. He would then push the lever for full astern and as *Invention* backed off the sand, grab the boathook in one deft movement. If he was staying on the beach, he took *Invention* out into three or four feet of water, tested by the boathook, anchored it securely and then dropped over the side and waded ashore. He kept a check on the state of the tide and would periodically move the boat, away if the tide was going out, closer if it were coming in, so that he could always wade out and haul himself aboard again.

So for two weeks each August, Simon was on top of the world. They met up with the same families each year and together formed a friendly group, Simon friends with boys around his own age whom he would ride around with in the motor boat. Mum and Dad didn't argue, Frances made friends with some older boys who had their own sailing boat, a National 12 foot, in which they competed in the annual regatta. Simon too learned to sail and developed a love of being on the water, if not in it.

A particular friend was Jack Griffin, who was from London and whom they met up with each year. He was a few months younger than Simon, blond, blue eyed. He was keen on sailing and would help crew his parents' Enterprise dinghy. Over the years a regular routine developed whereby the two boys would get up early and meet at the moorings, row the pram dinghy out to *Invention's* mooring buoy and set off up the estuary to pick up a can of fuel from a boatyard which opened up at seven o'clock near the Ferry Inn. Often the boys were there waiting for it to be opened. *Invention* was known of course and the fuel was charged to the hotel's account.

There was the time on this early morning run that they got into trouble. Carefree and happy together, as *Invention* chugged up the estuary, they burst into song.

"*Volare, oh oh*
E contare, oh oh oh oh
Nel blu, dipinto di blu
Felice di stare lassu ..."

In the quiet of the early morning when only hotel staff were up preparing the many breakfasts to be served in Salcombe that morning, two young voices echoing across the town and up the sides of the estuary raised a barrage of complaints which of course came straight back to the hotel, as the boat's ownership was recognised. But they managed to retain the use of the boat, sworn to early morning silence. They remained friends and when it came to depart, it was always,

"See you next year, Jack?"

"Yes, see you then, Simon."

The two weeks seemed to last for ever to Simon while he was in Salcombe, but when it came to an end, it seemed to have lasted no time at all. The journey home was always more subdued, Simon with very mixed feelings, worried each time about the new school year, knowing that once away from the magical world away from the world that was Salcombe each year, everything at home would be back the way it was; yet keen to see Daniel, hoping that all would be well and that in the fortnight away from him, somehow things hadn't changed. One of Simon's first tasks he set himself when he got back home was to construct a calendar on which he could count down the days until the family would be setting off again to their escape from reality. That hope and his friendship with Daniel were his anchors in his troubled life.

With regard to Daniel, he need never have worried. As soon as the two were back together, recounting their various holiday adventures, it was as though they had never been apart, and they resumed their routine.

On one of their visits to the aerodrome hill as the summer holiday drew to an end, Simon voiced a worry he had about Hooray Henrys to Daniel. One aspect that worried Simon was the ritual that the new boys, called fags, would be chased by groups of older boys and their trousers and pants pulled down, known as debagging.

"All the fags get it done to them," said Daniel.

"Even you?"

"Yes, you know. I told you last year."

The thought of his dear friend being set upon, overpowered and humiliated upset Simon.

"It's OK," said Daniel, noticing. "It happens to everyone and then it's done."

"I thought that friend of yours from Scouts ..."

"Evans?"

"Yes, Evans. I thought he was going to look after you. Couldn't he stop them?"

"Yes, he could have I suppose, but that would have been the worst thing he could've done. It's like a way of showing that you can take it, and if you can't, nobody will be your friend. They'll think you're soft."

"So what do you do?"

"When the second years catch you, it's best to put up a bit of a fight to show you can, but they're bound to get you coz there'll be so many. Main thing is not to cry, whatever you do. It's quite quick really."

"Do they do anything else? I mean, like this, us?"

"Oh no. As soon as they've pulled 'em down and seen your cock, they're off to get the next fag. And that reminds me, whatever you do, don't get a hard on. A kid in my class did that and they call him a queer now."

"How do you stop yourself if it wants to?"

"Do what I did. I was saying my times tables to myself in my head."

"Don't the teachers stop it?"

"Teachers never come out on the field, which is where it happens, they leave it to the prefects and they all had it done when they were fags and did to the new fags when they were second years."

"You'll be a second year when I start."

Daniel grinned. "That's true."

"So just stay off the field then?"

"No. They'll know you're hiding and then it's worse. A kid in my year tried and some got him in the toilets, stripped him completely and shoved his head down the toilet. I heard they pissed on him. He's never been the same since. Mind you, I don't know what he was like before. He's not in my class. Best just go down to the field and get it over with. Make sure you've got clean underpants on too. You'll be OK, I promise. Scout's honour."

Simon knew that when Daniel said that, he really meant it, and felt a little reassured.

31. 1957/9 Off to Hooray Henrys

That summer was Simon's last with his few friends from his neighbourhood. He was the only one to go to Henrys, a couple of other boys went to the Grammar Tech, most went to Vicks. Their lives gradually separated, drawing him even closer to Daniel if that were possible.

But that first day came, and as arranged, they met at the corner as usual, Simon now proudly wearing the coveted green blazer and long grey trousers like Daniel but at just eleven years old, anxious about what lay ahead. On the bus there were some other new Henrys kids and a lot of scared looking young kids in new Victoria Road uniforms.

"Remember what I said, you have to let them get you in the end, don't cry, and say your tables in your head," smiled Daniel. "Don't want any unexpected standing to attention."

Simon had to smile despite his nerves. He watched as the junior kids got off, one or two saying hello to Simon and Daniel, and the bus continued its journey.

Off the bus, they walked towards the gates of King Henry VII Grammar School for Boys. Just inside the gates, there was a large group of green blazers, all looking very new, fags gathered together like fish in a shoal, seeking protection from sharks.

"When will it happen?"

"Maybe now, but most probably morning break or dinner time. Look, I have to go. I can't stay with you, it's not done. See that group of trees over there?" Daniel pointed across the school field.

"Yes," said Simon.

"At morning break, get down there as quickly as you can and stay there."

"Why?"

"You'll see," said Daniel, and left, pushing Simon toward the shoal.

Simon went over to the sea of strange faces, most looking as scared as he felt.

"Hey, Simon!" came a familiar cheery voice. Peter. Never was Simon so glad to see Peter Holman.

"Hiya Peter."

Peter came close. "Is it true they pull your pants down?"

Simon nodded. "Whatever you do don't cry, and don't get a hard on."

Peter looked surprised at this, but nodded. "OK. I'll remember. You're a pal, Simon."

At the top of the drive, another group of boys was standing, watching the shoal. Simon knew that they were the predators. He thought for a moment of leaving the shoal and inviting the ordeal, getting it over with, but he didn't want to be the first and he remembered what Daniel had said about the trees at morning break. With a start he saw Daniel, in among the predators, laughing and joking, watching the shoal like the rest.

But a teacher came and led all the fags into the school hall, a large impressive place, with high beams, dark panelling, old paintings in heavy gilt frames. They were divided into their first year classes. Simon and Peter were in the same class, and they managed to sit together.

"Like the juniors," said Peter, happily. Books were given out, a timetable to be copied down. Their form tutor, Mr Andrews, seemed nice, but of course he would not be teaching them all the time. His subject was French.

Then it was break. Daniel had warned him never to call it playtime like at the juniors.

"Come with me, Peter," said Simon, urgently. He led the way quickly down the field to the trees. He saw some fags being taken unawares and dropped to the grass by groups of second years. Peter watched and gulped. "So it's true then," he said.

They stood by the trees, Simon wondering about the meaning behind Daniel's instruction. Was this a sanctuary? They watched as chases developed across the field, all with the inevitable result. At the top of a grassy bank, two much older boys were watching and laughing, with cups of tea in their hands, their green blazers edged in gold. Sixth form prefects.

"There's two more!" came the shout. A group of perhaps twenty predators was fast coming towards them.

"Remember what I said," urged Simon to Peter. "Run!" They ran, splitting up to divide the approaching sharks. Simon ran as fast as he could, outrunning the pack.

He heard them shouting behind him. "You get that one, we'll get this one." Daniel's voice! Now understanding Daniel's intention, he slowed and swerved back towards the trees, a move deliberately designed to look like he was still avoiding but in fact to allow capture by Daniel's group. Then they were all around him. He couldn't see Peter. He was pushed to the ground, his arms and legs pinned.

"I know this one, he was at my juniors. My turn." Daniel getting in quickly, speaking with authority.

"Go on then, Gray, debag 'im."

Daniel knelt down beside Simon in the circle of boys and quickly undid Simon's long school trousers, pulling them down to his knees, and then his pants.

"His shirt, Gray," shouted one of the boys. Daniel lifted up Simon's shirt front to complete the exposure. Simon was trying to say his twelve times table, but all he could think of was Daniel and all these boys. Oh no, please no! But then one said, "He's OK, he'll do," and the predators were leaving for their next victim.

Daniel dropped Simon's shirt down again. "That was OK," he said.

"Thanks, Daniel," said Simon. "I'm glad it was you."

"That was the plan," said Daniel, with a grin. "Nobody else was gonna do that to **you**. If it had to be done, it was going to be me. Give me your hand." Daniel was scrawling 'DG 2A' on the back of Simon's hand. "Shows you've been done and who by. You won't get done again. Get dressed quick, you've got a hard on now. That's why I did it as quick as I could, I know you. Gotta go, see you tonight." And he was gone.

Simon recovered himself and pulled up his pants and trousers. He saw Peter coming towards him, shirt hanging out, obviously upset.

"Don't cry, Peter, for Christ's sake, don't cry."

"I'll be OK," said Peter, but he was close to tears.

"They got you?" asked Simon. "But you didn't cry then, did you?"

"No," said Peter, "but remember what you said about a, you know, a hard on? I felt it was going to happen to me. I was scared."

"Did they say anything?"

"They said 'He's passed muster'. What does that mean?"

"It means you're OK. You passed the test, Peter," said Simon relieved. He saw 'TH 2B' on Peter's hand.

"Oh good," said Peter. "Did you get done?"

"Yes, Daniel Gray did me." He showed Peter his hand with Daniel's mark on it.

"Daniel Gray? Yes, he's here, isn't he. I'm surprised, I thought he used to be your friend."

"He still is," said Simon. "That's why **he** did it to me instead of letting anybody else."

"I get it," said Peter, understanding dawning. "I'm glad I didn't actually get that hard on."

"Me too," said Simon, omitting that it was touch and go because it had been Daniel, his protective predator on that day, that had almost given rise to it and that he had succumbed when Daniel was talking to him afterwards.

Simon gradually settled in at Henrys, absorbing the ethos of the place, its traditions and rituals, aping the great British public schools. A lot of famous people were 'old boys' and the school's foundation dated back to Henry VII – it was made clear a lot was expected. But Daniel was there and although there was less opportunity for them to be together at school – friendships outside one's own year group were discouraged – Simon felt better knowing that contact could be made if needed, usually in the school's own tuck shop at dinner break.

32. *1957/9 Simon catches up*

Much changed for Simon in that September. Fitting in at Hooray Henrys as best he could, coping with the demands of a new range of subjects to study, finding maths hard once again, doing well in English, French and History, less certain with Latin, physics, chemistry (especially) and biology.

On the sporting front, Simon quickly found that he hated rugby football. This was the winter game at Henrys, and Simon knew that Daniel liked it, sporty as always. Daddy also was a great follower of rugby, rugger as he called it. Daddy had taken him to one or two games where the city team, one of the top ones in the country, had usually won. Daddy had played rugger as fly half at school and for his county down south, and was sure Simon would be a great rugger player. But Simon found there was a great difference between watching from the stands and being down in the mud, which is where he inevitably finished up. It always seemed to rain on games day. Lots of the boys had played rugger already at their prep schools, and Simon was taken unaware by the violence of the game. Already his speed was recognised, and they tried him on the wing, but he lacked the ball handing ability required.

After a particularly brutal game, he came home dirty, bruised and battered and then recounted what had happened and his feelings about rugger at tea, unhappily when Daddy was there. The disappointment in Daddy's face was obvious. Simon knew he had failed again in his father's eyes, but by now was getting used to it. Daddy just got up and left the table. Simon found he didn't care.

But Mr Atherstone, the school athletics coach, had noticed this speedy eleven year old with his quick acceleration, and pulled him to one side.

"What's your name, son?"

"Scott, sir."

"Not very keen on rugby football, are you?"

"It's OK, sir," said Simon, warily.

"Don't try to kid me, Scott. You detest it, that's obvious."

Simon nodded, fearing he was in trouble for not liking rugger, for being no good at rugger.

"I thought as much," said Mr Atherstone. "How would you like to run instead?"

"Run, sir?"

"Yes, on the track. You look to have makings of a sprinter. Depends on your stamina."

"Did you say 'instead', sir?"

Mr Atherstone smiled. "Yes, Scott, I did. I assume that means you would like to try? I understand, even if perhaps some other people don't, that rugby is not every boy's cup of tea."

"Yes, please, sir," said Simon with enthusiasm, smiling now.

"It will be hard work, make no mistake," said Mr Atherstone. "A lot of training and fitness work, as well as technique. I'll talk to Mr Russell. Next games lesson, report to me in the gym. Standard PE kit."

"Yes sir. Thank you sir."

So began a new interest for Simon. He had always been a fast runner, even Daniel had said that more than once, so perhaps this was something he could be good at. Maybe Daddy would approve after all. And he was spared the ignominy of the ritual of team picking where he was left last, publicly unwanted, pushed into the team with last pick unwillingly and unwelcome. Unlike some, at least he had a way out, his speed.

It was hard work, a lot of gym training and hours running round the track, but at least from there he could see his classmates getting muddy and bashed about on the rugby pitch. He also liked the other boys Mr Atherstone had recruited too. And then Peter Holman came along as well.

"I didn't really like rugger," said Peter. This was an understatement. Peter had always been a bit smaller than Simon, and he had got crushed a few times playing rugger, but that understatement was typical of Peter's positive way of saying things. "Mr Atherstone thinks I might be able to do distance running."

So Simon had a companion in his training and running. Gradually his body grew fitter and stronger and filled out, a fact not lost on Daniel in the coming months.

Also that September, Daniel took Simon to scouts. Not quite on the day he was eleven therefore, but not long afterwards.

"It'll be OK," said Daniel. "I've talked to Evans and he says he's spoken to Skip. I think you'll be in my patrol". This use of the possessive was partly justified for Daniel's shirt now sported a single white bar. He was Second in the Harriers patrol. Daniel had explained his promotion over other scouts by pointing out that he was the best one for the job. "The other kids are OK, but not the brightest." Simon wondered how he would fit into this hierarchy that Daniel described. But his prediction came true.

"Welcome to Harriers Patrol, Simon," said Evans. "Daniel has told me all about you."

Simon had a moment of worry at that, but realised that Daniel would not have divulged their secret. Simon developed a keen interest in Scouts, he loved the ethos, the competitive yet friendly and supportive company of the other boys. He soon made his mark as a promising scout, and worked hard for his tenderfoot. Mum was always finding bits of rope tied to the backs of the dining chairs as knots were practised. He was to achieve his tenderfoot in only a few sessions, took the oath of the Scout Promise and could then sew the scout badge to the centre of his shirt pocket, and was a proper scout.

In term time it was harder for them to be alone together as Daniel's mother was at home at weekends, and if she went out and his Dad was at work, Louise might be around. There was the den of course, but if they could they preferred the even greater security and seclusion of the hilltop near the airfield. It took almost an hour of cycling to get there, but the aircraft provided a valid reason to go, and as the summer's fine weather by and large extended into September, they would go as they had earlier that summer.

Lying together in the cooler early autumn sunshine on a Saturday afternoon, feeling the gentle breeze play across their skin, they enjoyed again the touch and warmth of each other. On the groundsheet in the long grass, they were close, naked and both aroused. Daniel came, sighing with the release but Simon was still aroused. Daniel noticed this and perhaps recognising something in Simon, drew him close, putting his left arm round his shoulders, drawing his head to his shoulder, his right hand working on Simon. Simon started to experience a new feeling, beyond arousal. His body trembled as he felt the mounting exquisite tension.

"You're ready, Simon, I know it," said Daniel. "Come on."

Simon simply nodded, his whole body tensing like a huge spring within. He was rigid as his muscles tightened.

"It's OK, Simon, just relax, let it come."

Simon did. It felt like nothing he had ever felt before. His body was wrapped in warm fire, shooting down through his groin, from his buttocks up his back and round his body, licking his neck and throat, at the same time enveloping his thighs, wrapping round above his knees sending tingles right down to his toes. Each ejaculatory pulse from his groin sent a further wave of fiery pleasure shuddering through his young body while Daniel continued to extract the last ounce of orgasmic ecstasy for him. Simon let out a deep, panting sigh. He looked up at Daniel's smiling face as the waves subsided, feeling the sensual warmth of Daniel's body close to his.

"Fire down below?" said Daniel, grinning now at his friend's reaction to his first full orgasm.

"Wow. Fire all over, I think," said Simon, now shaking with emotion, and tears started to come. Daniel wiped him, pulled him onto his side, facing him and continued to stroke him, down his back, his buttocks, running his fingers lightly over his tummy. Simon's body trembled still under his touch.

"Idiot, why're you crying?" Daniel asked gently.

"I don't know," said Simon. He wanted to say so much to Daniel, how much he felt towards him, but could not find the words. Daniel just held him close, making no demands.

After a while, as Simon recovered both physically and mentally from this fundamental change in himself, he started to sing, *"Fire in the foretop, fire in the main, it's fetch a bucket of water boys, there's fire down below."* And Daniel joined in.

Autumn turned to winter amid the excitement of the Sputnik and there were as usual fewer opportunities for sex as it became too wet and cold to visit the den, and as the darker nights closed in, bike rides ceased. But at half term, again in some of the Christmas holidays and in the miserable half term in winter, they made use of Daniel's room whenever they could. Otherwise they would just enjoy being together, knowing each other so well, doing homework in Daniel's room straight after school most nights ("Get's it over with," said Daniel. Simon agreed.) and playing on the piano. Simon's ability to pick out tunes by ear improved, but of course this was nothing compared to Daniel's increasing mastery of that great machine. He had passed all his piano exams so far with flying colours.

"Can you come to church this Sunday?" Daniel's eyes begged for a yes.

"It's not a Church Parade is it?" asked Simon, puzzled.

"No, but I'm going to be Altar Boy. It's a great honour and I want you to see me."

Simon had seen these robed priest's helpers on his visits to church before, but now Daniel was going to be one!

"Course I will. Wouldn't miss it for anything. Don't drop the wine though," he smiled. "Or have a sly swig."

Daniel's reply was a sharp dig in the ribs. "My parents will be there so you can sit with them again if you want."

On that Sunday, Simon, dressed in school long grey trousers and white shirt, watched entranced as Daniel who was wearing a long white robe – Daniel said it was called an alb – prepared the communion and the altar. During the service Simon kept looking at his friend, sitting at one side behind the altar rail on that sacred ground, imbued in his mind with the reflected majesty of the priesthood and of the Eucharist.

After the communion prayers Daniel received the bread and wine directly from the Vicar even before the choir. Then with the congregation, Simon went up to the rail and knelt for the Vicar's blessing. He saw that Daniel was taking the wine, which the altar boy sometimes did. He was aware of Daniel's closeness as he followed the Vicar along the rail with the chalice. The vicar reached Simon, and placing his hand on Simon's bowed head, said "The Lord bless you and keep you. The Lord make his face to shine upon you and be gracious to you. The Lord lift up his countenance upon you and give you peace" and then moved on. Simon felt that warm glow of peace he always did. He saw Daniel's white robe stop in front of him and looked up into Daniel's eyes.

"The blood of Christ keep you in eternal life," said Daniel, pleading on his face and offering Simon the chalice. By this time the Vicar was about four people further along. Simon put his lips to the rim of the silver chalice and sipped the wine. It was strong and dark tasting, and sent a warm glow through him. Daniel smiled, wiped the edge of the chalice with his cloth and moved on. Simon stayed at the rail, savouring the moment, his friend's closeness and new status. Mrs Gray nudged Simon so he had to leave. Back in the pew he watched Daniel as he continued to follow the Vicar offering the wine.

"Daniel shouldn't really have offered you the wine," whispered Mrs Gray. "It's not like him to forget that."

Simon knew perfectly well that it had been no error on Daniel's part.

After the service, he waited for Daniel, who had to clear the altar and put things away.

"Why did you do that?" asked Simon as they walked home.

"The wine?"

"Yes. Your Mum said you weren't supposed to because I'm not confirmed."

"I know, but I so wanted to give you the wine. I told the Vicar I had got muddled because it was my first time."

"Were you in trouble?"

"Not really, he just said I should be more observant next time."

"I'm glad there'll be a next time, then. You've not been banned?"

"No, it's OK. I won't be able to get away with it again though."

"I'm glad you did this time. It felt so special to me with it being you holding the cup."

"That was the plan," laughed Daniel. "I knew you'd like it. I wanted to say the words to you."

"I wish it had been you giving me the blessing," joked Simon.

"Kneel down," said Daniel. They were in the grassy area near the footbridge over the stream. Simon knelt on the grass.

Placing his hand on Simon's head, Daniel said solemnly, "Simon, The Lord bless you and keep you. The Lord make his face to shine upon you and be gracious to you. The Lord lift up his countenance upon you and give you peace."

"Amen," replied Simon, tears of overwhelming emotion in his eyes, and looked at Daniel's face.

Daniel smiled. "Come on, idiot," he said as Simon stood up. "I can see that meant a lot to you."

Simon could only nod his head.

"To me too, Simon," said Daniel, risking a quick hug as they walked on.

Over forty years later when Simon was offered the chance to perform the same function at church, to be a server, he jumped at the chance.

33. *1958/4 Fielding*

Simon covered his ears. He could not bear the shouting. Mum and Dad were arguing again, and Frances with all the righteousness of her sixteen years, was joining in. Simon didn't know what the argument was about this time, and it didn't really matter. It was always the same. He stayed in his room, wondering if he could get out of the house without being spotted and possibly drawn in.

The shouting subsided and he heard footsteps on the stairs. Simon was suddenly fearful that it would be Dad, but when his bedroom door opened, it was Frances.

"Are you all right?" she asked. She looked kindly at her little brother. He seemed younger than his eleven years and she could see he was upset.

"Yes, I suppose so," said Simon. "Is it safe to go down yet?"

"I would just stay here, if I were you," said Frances.

"Not doing that," said Simon, "I just want to get out."

"I'll come down with you, then."

Brother and sister went out on to the landing. Frances peered over the banister. The noise had subsided. Frances led the way down the stairs. Just as they got to the bottom, Dad came out of the dining room, red faced and angry looking.

"What have you two been up to," he snapped.

"Just talking," said Frances, defensively, a nuance that did not escape Dad.

"Talking? Talking about what?" Dad demanded irritably.

"Just things," said Simon, wanting to support his sister.

"Answer me properly, Simon," barked Dad, grabbing Simon by the arm. "What kind of things?"

Simon turned to Frances for support. He thought this was the prelude to a beating.

"Dad, it's nothing," she said

"I'll decide whether it's nothing or something."

"Harry, what's going on?" came Mum's voice as she entered the hallway.

"This boy's being cheeky again, answering back," said Dad, and shook Simon who put up his hand to defend a possible blow.

"What!" shouted Dad. "You would try to strike me?" He roughly pulled Simon round the better to aim a retaliation against the strike that never was.

"Harry! Stop it!" snapped Mum.

"It really isn't fair, Dad," said Frances. "He's not done anything."

Faced with this from his wife and teenage daughter, not to mention Simon's growing size and strength, Dad released his grip on Simon.

"You had better be very careful, my lad," said Dad, and he turned back into the dining room.

"You all right, love?" said Mum.

Simon nodded, shaken, and breathing quickly with subsiding fear.

"I'm going out," he said. He grabbed his jacket off the hall pegs and went back through the kitchen and out of the back door. He wasn't sure where he was going. He thought of getting his bike out but decided on a quick getaway. Unthinkingly, he walked round the corner to Daniel's house, his refuge in times of trouble. Daniel knew about the rows at home. There had been one occasion with huge embarrassment when Daniel on one of his rare visits to Simon's home witnessed a family row. Simon was so ashamed that Daniel saw it and he rushed off to escape. Daniel followed and was so understanding.

As he walked along beside the privet hedge, he heard Daniel's voice. But when he reached the gates, he saw Daniel on his driveway talking to two other boys, Fielding and Richardson, who were standing astride their bicycles. Simon hated them. They were both at Victoria Road, and they hated Hooray Henrys. Fielding especially was a bully, and Richardson was his sidekick. But Daniel knew them, they were a bit older than him. Simon stood for a moment at the gate, wondering why Daniel was talking to them and hesitating now to go in. The three became conscious of his presence.

"Fuck off, you," said Fielding.

Before anything else could be said, Simon turned and walked on, past Daniel's house. He went into the allotments. There was nobody about. He was at a loose end now, he had wanted to be with Daniel to find some feeling of comfort after the row at home, but Fielding had put paid to that. He sat for a few moments, wondering where he might go. The Parade? But he had no money. For want of anything better, he got up and started down the allotments towards the den.

"Simple Simon!" came the catcall. Simon turned to see Fielding and Richardson coming up on their bikes along the allotment path. Before Simon could think of evasive action, they were there.

"What do you want?" said Simon. Fielding thrust his face towards Simon. His face always seemed dirty, thought Simon. He had a scar on his left cheek which Simon supposed was from a fight. The two had dropped their bikes.

"This!" said Fielding, as he suddenly punched Simon in the gut, catching him unawares.

"Ah! What was that for?"

"We're going to beat you up," said Fielding.

"What for?" groaned Simon, still partly doubled up.

"Because we can," gloated Richardson.

"I don't like kids who listen to my conversations," said Fielding.

"I wasn't listening," Simon tried to explain.

"Fibbing as well. I'm going to knock your block off," said Fielding. Then the two were punching Simon, raining blows on his body. He tried to move out of the way, but to no effect. Simon's face exploded with pain as his nose took a hard punch from Fielding and there was blood streaming down his face, onto his jacket. Suddenly Fielding jerked backwards and was spun round. Daniel stood facing Fielding, his stance displaying complete readiness to take him on, even though Fielding was perhaps a good inch or more taller.

"Leave him alone, Fielding," said Daniel resolutely. But Daniel had that inner steadfastness that Simon admired so much and that Fielding and Richardson, like all bullies, feared. Fielding knew that if he took on Daniel, he and Richardson against Daniel and Simon, they might well win, but the cost would be too great.

"Yeah, well. He's had his lesson now," said Fielding, unconsciously but revealingly taking a step back.

"Just go then," said Daniel, unmoving.

"Just coz your Dad's a copper," said Fielding. "Come on, let's go," he added to Richardson.

"That's nothing to do with it," said Daniel, "and you know it!"

The two bullies moved off as Daniel came to where Simon was now sitting on the grass next to the path.

"Look after your little friend!" called Fielding sarcastically from a safer distance.

"What does he mean by that?" asked Simon, worried that their precious secret might be out.

Daniel of course understood. "Nothing like that," he said reassuringly. "Come on, I'll take you home."

"No," said Simon. "They've been shouting and arguing again."

"OK," said Daniel, "I'll take you to mine."

The two friends moved off back along the path having first made sure that Fielding and Richardson were gone.

"Why were they beating you up?" asked Daniel.

"Does Fielding need a reason?" replied Simon bitterly. "They said I had been listening to you talking to them."

"That's rubbish," said Daniel.

"Why were you talking to them anyway?" asked Simon. "They're not your friends are they?"

"No. It's sort of complicated."

When they got back to Daniel's house, they went to the kitchen.

"Sit down," said Daniel, as he turned on the tap. He went to the cupboard and came back with cotton wool. Simon's nose was still bleeding a bit and his face and front were blood streaked.

"What happened to you?" said Louise, Daniel's sister, coming into the kitchen and seeing Simon.

"Fielding," explained Daniel, gently wiping Simon's face with damp cotton wool.

"That oik," said Louise, "Really Daniel, I don't know why you bother helping him. Can you manage?"

"Yes," said Daniel, "Basic first aid."

"Regular Boy Scout," said Louise as she left the kitchen. Daniel finished cleaning Simon's face.

"There, all looks normal again," said Daniel, smiling. Simon didn't think it felt normal, His nose still hurt.

"Is my nose swollen?" he asked. Daniel looked and considered for a moment.

"No," he said, laughing, "you're just as ugly as usual."

Simon grinned back. Daniel cupped Simon's jaw in his hands and moved close so his forehead rested against Simon's. For a few seconds, the two remained still, in unspoken communion. Daniel stood back.

"How are you helping Fielding?" asked Simon, baffled. Then a disturbing thought occurred to him. "You're not… It's not like with him, like with us, is it?"

"Bloody hell! Definitely not!" said Daniel, pulling a face of disgust. "That's just you and me," he continued, "nobody else."

"Me too," said Simon quickly. "So what is it with Fielding then?"

"Tell you later," said Daniel.

But the moment passed, and he never did.

34. 1958/5 *First Kiss*

As Spring moved toward summer, the boys' horizons widened. Scout activities moved more outdoors, the athletics could get back out on the track in earnest and the bike rides began again. They would return to the vantage point overlooking the aerodrome, with sandwiches, drinks and the groundsheet. Since Simon's first climax, the boys' relationship in that sense had become reciprocal, and both enjoyed it more.

Relaxing on the groundsheet after their mutual release, they were allowing the sun to bathe their bodies once more.

"I like it much better now that you come as well," said Daniel.

"How?" said Simon, looking up at the fluffy clouds dotted across the blue early summer sky.

"Because we're more equal. I always thought it was unfair before, and I didn't like that. It's much better now."

"I like it better, too," said Simon.

Daniel laughed. "Well, obviously. You're such an idiot."

Simon knew that this was just an expression Daniel used, and was not at all upset by it. Feeling Daniel's hand stroke his body, he lay back and closed his eyes. He could hear the noise of the countryside, some insects, birds, a tractor in the distance. He could feel Daniel next to him, hear his breathing. He sensed Daniel's face close to his. He felt the touch, Daniel's lips against his. Surprised, he opened his eyes, Daniel drew back, and was looking down at him, framed against the blue sky, uncertainty on his face, the question ready to be spoken.

"I'm sorry, Simon. I didn't mean to .. I mean ... " Daniel stopped, wondering what Simon would say to his clumsy attempt to kiss him. What if it was a step too far? Sometimes that two year gap was too much.

Simon looked up at his friend. He had been surprised, the feel of another person's lips against his own was new to him. But now, seeing the anxiety on Daniel's face, he saw the moist tenderness of Daniel's lips afresh. He wanted to feel it again. Without speaking, he reached up and drew Daniel to him again, and they kissed, lips exploring lips, tongues touching, the effects reaching through each boy's body to fresh arousal. This was new to both of them, neither had realised the erogenous consequence of such kissing. They drew apart.

"Was that OK?" asked Simon.

"Super. Fantastic. I'm so glad you liked it. I was worried you might not've and that I'd spoiled things."

"You could never spoil things. I liked it too. Really did. You've done it before, though."

"I haven't, Simon. You're the first. Who with?"

"Everybody knows you kissed Cynthia Jackson at the juniors."

"You can't count that," said Daniel, indignant. "It was just – " and he leaned over and briefly touched his closed lips against Simon's " – like that. Not a proper kiss."

"So was that a proper kiss then, what we just did?"

"You bet." And Daniel kissed Simon again, as they embraced, rolling on the groundsheet, their bare skin warm in the sun and against each other.

Simon had always thought of Daniel's hair as black, but now, running his hands through it, stroking it in the sunlight, he could see a host of colours, shades of deep, dark brown as well as black. This variation seemed to reflect the complexity of his lover's nature. Somehow, the closer he got to Daniel, the more there was to know. It was an adventure that would go on forever.

The following week when they arrived together at Scouts, their Patrol Leader, Miles Evans, met them.

"Daniel, Simon, I've got some news for you. I'm leaving scouts. In fact, I'm leaving altogether. My Dad's got a new job and we're moving to London."

"I'm sorry about that, Miles," said Daniel. "When are you going?"

"Next week. All a bit sudden I'm afraid. Leaving Henrys too. Bit of a blow. My Dad's hoping I can get a place at Westminster."

"Top notch," said Daniel. Simon wasn't sure what that meant, so he just waited.

"Might not happen," said Miles Evans. "But in the meantime, Harriers will get a new Patrol Leader. I know Skip was thinking of Colley, but I put in a good case for you Daniel. You've been a very good second."

"When will we find out?" asked Simon.

"That's up to Skip, Simon. Don't build your hopes up Daniel, Colley may not have been Second of Falcons as long as you've been my Second, but you're still thirteen and he is older than you."

Both Simon and Daniel knew Nigel Colley as a keen scout, very good at the practical aspects of scouting. He was at the Grammar Tech. Daniel knew that this was perhaps his best chance at being a Patrol Leader, but Colley was a serious rival.

"I know I'd be good, Miles, and the patrol know me," said Daniel. Simon nodded encouragingly.

"As I say, I did my best for you, Daniel. You deserve it, but then so does Nigel. But I think you have more of something than Colley, and I put that case to Skip and Jeremy."

Jeremy was the assistant Scoutmaster, and his view was very important also.

"What's that? First Class badge?" asked Daniel.

Evans grinned. "No, but that does give you a big advantage. Colley's not quite there yet. I'll tell you what I meant if you get it."

As the troop paraded for the start of the session, Skip made the announcement that Miles Evans was leaving. He said what a valuable contribution he had made to the troop and to his patrol. Miles Evans would be missed, but all the scouts wished him well. Skip said that in the appointment of a new Patrol Leader for Harriers, he had looked carefully at all the patrols' Seconds. He had to take account of who already had their First Class, strongly recommended in P.O.R. for PL status, also the needs of the troop. He had discussed this with John Riley the Troop Leader and the Patrol Leaders in the Court of Honour and they had reached a decision on who would be the next Patrol Leader of Harriers. Daniel Gray.

Daniel flushed with pleasure and pride, while the Harriers made their approval known in whispers.

"Quiet, Harriers," said Miles Evans.

"We also listened carefully to what others had to say, especially Miles, on the question of who would replace Daniel as Second of the Harriers," continued Skip. "The chosen Scout has proved his worth, has already achieved Second Class badge and we know he is respected by the scouts of Harriers Patrol. Simon Scott."

For a moment, Simon couldn't take it in. There were other kids who had been in scouts a lot longer, and some had their second class badge too. But Daniel was now grinning twice as broadly. It was true. Daniel would get his second bar as PL and he, Simon, would get his single bar as his Second. Simon looked across to where Falcons patrol stood in line. Nigel Colley's face was expressionless. He felt sorry for him for a moment, but his happiness at his and Daniel's promotion swept that away.

Later, they discussed this with Miles Evans.

"You said you would tell me something if I got it," said Daniel.

"I did, yes. In fact you've both got it, although perhaps you don't realise it. I thought you were in with a good chance, Daniel. I was less sure about you Simon because of your age, although I hoped so."

"Yes, but what is it?" repeated Daniel, agitated.

"Leadership. Pure and simple. And John Riley agreed with me and backed you both in the Court of Honour."

Both Daniel and Simon weren't sure what to make of this, although Simon already knew that Daniel had it in abundance. But him?

"I felt sorry for Colley though," said Simon. "What about him? He deserved it as well."

"See what I mean?" joked Evans to Daniel. "That's the sort of thing I meant. Don't worry about Colley. Tim Perrett is leaving for Ventures soon, so that will mean a vacancy as Falcons PL. Not a word, but the job's his. So it all works out rather nicely."

Daniel and Simon, sworn to secrecy, just had to agree.

35. 1958/6 Clothing

"Got much homework?" asked Daniel. They were walking up the hill from the bus stop, hot under their Henrys blazers in the June heat, school satchels full of books.

"French, Latin and maths," said Simon.

"Bring it round mine," said Daniel decisively. And with a knowing look at Simon, said, "I think I'm in on my own tonight. I know Dad and Mum are out till late.

"Where are they going?"

"Some police do. They usually get back about midnight from those."

Simon felt a thrill of anticipation, but said, "What about Louise?"

"I think she's going out. Mum asked this morning if I would be OK on my own. 'Course I am old enough and can look after myself. I said you'd be coming round to do homework."

"I'll ask. It'll be OK." By this time they were at the corner.

"See you after tea then," said Daniel.

"See ya!"

Daniel went in though the back door into the kitchen. "I'm home!" he called.

"In here, love," came his mother's voice from the sitting room. Daniel went in and gave his Mum a hug. "Much homework?"

"Algebra, Geography and science," said Daniel. "Is it OK if Simon comes round with his. We can do it together."

"Yes love, of course. He often does anyway. Be company for you, while we're out."

"What time will you be back?"

"Late I expect. Eleven at the earliest, probably a bit later. I don't know what time Louise will be back."

"Where's she going?"

"She's already gone out with Graham. I don't know where he's taking her. She said don't wait up." Graham was Louise's nineteen year old boyfriend. Daniel quite liked him, but he treated Daniel like a kid sometimes. Daniel felt excited at the prospect of he and Simon having the house to themselves. This happened a lot in the school holidays now when both his Dad and Mum were at work, and Louise was at her holiday job at the insurance office. They had taken full advantage of it. But in term time it was more difficult.

"Go and get changed, I'll make you some tea. Dad and I are eating out of course."

Daniel went upstairs and hung up his Henry's uniform. In the bathroom he washed himself down as he felt sweaty and wanted to be clean for Simon. He chose a T shirt and put on his red socks and blue denim jeans. Feeling cleaner and cooler, he went downstairs to eat his tea. His Dad had arrived home.

"Hello son," he said, patting Daniel's shoulder. "How was school?"

"Good," said Daniel, munching. "Simon's coming round later with his homework."

"Well, don't spend all your time helping Simon at the expense of your own work, will you?"

"No, Dad. Anyway, Simon can do his homework OK."

His Dad nodded and went to take his own uniform off. Taking his tea things from the kitchen table to the sink, Daniel rinsed them off, dried them and put them away, while his parents struggled with evening dress and dinner jacket.

Simon was late. Daniel went upstairs and cleaned his teeth. He would normally wait until bedtime, but after his tea, he wanted to be fresh when Simon came. Since he had taken the risk of kissing Simon a few weeks earlier, they had both willingly explored this new aspect of their friendship. He brushed his hair and decided to make a start on his homework, tackling the algebra first. He worked steadily on at his desk, engrossed in the magical way the equations would resolve themselves.

"Simon's here!" called his mother, "and we're off now. Don't stay up too late. Lock up when you go to bed but leave the bolt off, and make sure the television's unplugged. Oh, and don't forget the Aga."

"Yes, OK. Bye!," called back Daniel. "Send him up, and have a good time."

Simon came into the room, dressed now like Daniel in jeans, but retaining his white Henrys shirt. Daniel knew immediately that all was not well. Simon put down his satchel and sat on the bed, looking unhappy.

"What's the matter?"

"They were arguing again. I hate it when my Dad's at home at teatime."

"What about?"

"Dunno. But they were shouting and Frances tried to stop them, so I did. But then Dad started on me, so I did what you showed me ages ago and tapped my chest twice for you, and I told him to stop shouting at me coz I'd done nothing wrong. But he got madder and said he was going to slipper me, so I just said I was coming here to do my homework and walked out. Here I am."

"Does he still slipper you?"

"No. Well, he hasn't for ages now, but he sometimes says he will."

Daniel left his desk and sat next to Simon, putting his arm round his troubled friend.

"I'm sorry, Simon," he said. To Daniel, his own Dad was someone he was proud of. He didn't have a high up medal like Simon's Dad, he had spent the war in the military police, but he was high up in the ordinary police now and Daniel loved him.

"It's OK," said Simon, "I'm used to it. And I've got you."

"You've always got me," said Daniel, and leaned toward Simon's face, who responded by meeting his lips.

"Now?" said Simon, "While everybody's out?"

"That's just to keep you going," said Daniel happily. "I've just had a pee, and you know it takes time after that. We've got all evening, and anyway, homework first."

"OK," said Simon, accepting Daniel's lead. "But I mustn't be too late back."

Daniel shifted his things along his desk to make room for Simon to work on the end, sitting on a stool. The two boys worked on, in unspoken unity, Daniel with his geography and science, Simon with Latin and French translation and maths.

"Can I borrow your French dictionary?"

"What word?" said Daniel.

"That one," Simon pointed.

Daniel looked across. "Jusqu'à. It means 'up to' or 'until'." Daniel read the French sentence. "Best there would be, 'as far as'."

They worked on. Daniel finished to see Simon working on his maths. But he was stopped, looking blankly at the page.

"You stuck?"

Simon nodded. "Can you help me?" Daniel knew that Simon found mathematics hard, ever since he had helped him get ready for the eleven plus. Patiently he sat and talked Simon through the problems, trying to show him the reasoning, not just do it for him. It was done, and with relief, Simon put his books in his satchel.

"Thanks, Daniel. I'd be lost without you."

"Me too, without you. That's school, now it's our time,"

They lay on the bed, holding and kissing, feeling each other.

"You're ready, aren't you," said Daniel, smiling.

"So are you," replied Simon, starting to undo Daniel's jeans.

"Wait," said Daniel, and gently moved Simon onto his back, lying face up. Slowly, Daniel unbuttoned Simons' white shirt, and pulling it out of his jeans, pushed it aside, and stroked Simon's chest and tummy. Simon sighed at the touch.

"What do you want me to do?" asked Simon.

"Nothing. I've been thinking about undressing you like this for ages, ever since your first day at Henrys when I was the one to debag you. Just lie still."

Simon lay still, content to hand over control and responsibility to Daniel. Daniel removed Simon's socks and then ran his hands up Simon's jeans, teasing his hardness, but carrying on to Simon's shoulders, kissing him again. He then eased Simon's arms out of his shirt, and lifting Simon slightly, pulled the shirt away. Daniel smiled at Simon's erotic response to this caressing. He moved his hand down Simon's tummy, sliding under the jeans to the warmth of Simon's groin. Simon stirred, his eyes meeting Daniel's in mutual sensuality. Daniel undid the jeans and slid them and his pants past Simon's bottom, Simon's eyes closed in ecstasy as Daniel's hands guided his clothes over his buttocks and down his thighs, legs and off his feet.

Daniel, still fully dressed, stood up and looked at his friend, lying nude on the bed and now very aroused. Daniel again felt that satisfaction he gained when Simon surrendered control to him. A sense of power certainly, but also a strong feeling toward Simon. He wanted to protect Simon, look after him, make everything right for him. He felt Simon's unhappiness and it made him unhappy. Conversely, when Simon was happy - and Daniel knew he was a major source of happiness to Simon – then he was happy too.

Simon looked up from the bed at Daniel, standing, smiling down at him. Simon as always felt overawed by Daniel's physical presence and yet in no way intimidated. As he had for many years now, he trusted Daniel implicitly and was ready, wanting, to please him; in this, at scouts, at school, on the running track.

"Your body is just super," said Daniel.

"Mine? What about yours? It's fabulous."

"It's all that running, you're really fit now."

"Then it's all that swimming. But you've always been super fit."

"That's true," said Daniel in a matter of fact way. "You feeling better now, after the shouting and all that?"

Simon nodded. "I feel really good now."

Daniel quickly undressed and lay next to Simon. "Did you like that, me undressing you?"

"I loved it."

"So I can do it again?"

"Yes. Every time." Simon thrust his hand down to Daniel's groin, stroking his scrotum, aware of the potency within. He knew Daniel liked that.

Daniel squeezed Simon tightly. "Let's get in." They climbed into the bed, already warmed by their body heat. They kissed and hugged, enjoying each other, admiring the other's body, but the older, bigger Daniel dominant. Then Simon was lying on his front, Daniel running his hands up and down him. Simon felt Daniel lie on top, felt the shaft of his arousal, hard and male, pushing down between his thighs. Simon didn't move, wondering what Daniel was going to do. Daniel was moving himself against Simon's groin, holding his shoulders, kissing his neck.

Then Daniel stopped. "This doesn't feel right," he said.

"Are you going to stick it in?" asked Simon, nervously.

"You mean fuck you?" said Daniel, surprise in his voice. Simon, still on his front with Daniel poised above him, nodded. Daniel pulled Simon over onto his back, now facing Daniel. His face was serious.

"Simon, I wasn't going do that to you. You're my best friend. Why did you think that I would? You trust me don't you?"

Simon was relieved but felt a bit ashamed that he had misjudged Daniel, after all these years. He felt tears coming, but fought them back.

"Course I do. More than anybody, ever. It's just that when you said it didn't feel right, I thought you wanted more."

"Would you have let me?"

"I think so, I think I want you to. It's just I'm not sure."

"Oh, you are an idiot. Did you like it when I was between your legs?"

"Yes, that was good. It's like you were sort of extra close to me."

"Well, when I said it doesn't feel right, I meant that that it was wrong for you. It was all me. I felt like you were being used and that made me feel horrible inside."

"It's OK," said Simon.

"No it's not," said Daniel firmly. "You are a wonderful kid, with a super body too. You're the best friend I've ever had and ever will have. I know I'm two years older than you but that just means I have look after you, not be a bully."

"Daniel, you could never be a bully. You stand up to bullies, like Fielding. I wish I could."

"You can. Remember Barry Spence?"

"Oh yes," said Simon, pleased. He tapped his chest twice. "Coz you were there."

Daniel smiled. "You've had no real problems like that at Henrys, have you?"

"No," conceded Simon.

"So there you are." Daniel gave Simon a squeeze. Both boys' arousal had faded during this discussion, but quickly returned.

"Try again if you want, but this way," said Simon. "I did like the closeness. And if you want to put it in, you can."

"Maybe later, when you're ready and feel absolutely sure." Daniel put his arms round Simon, lying beneath him. Simon felt enveloped by the male power and strength of Daniel, yet safe as always, his desperate inner insecurity assuaged by Daniel's strong, warm, masculine presence. They kissed again as Daniel placed himself between Simon's thighs.

"No, keep your legs together," Daniel said, as he moved up and down, the two now holding each other, pulling closer. Simon knew Daniel well enough to know when he was getting close and squeezed his legs more and moved his body to help, which served to bring him close too. Then Daniel buried his head on Simon's shoulder, his body shuddering and arching as Simon felt against his groin the thrusting pulses of Daniel's climax, instantly transporting Simon to the same heights of orgasm.

For a moment they just lay, recovering. Daniel lifted his head and kissed Simon gently. "We came off together. Brilliant.

"Fire! fire! fire down below;
Fetch a bucket of water, boys, There's fire down below! "

Daniel pushed the bedclothes back and rolled off Simon, reaching down for a box of Kleenex for Men next to the bed.

"Here, let me clean you up," said Daniel. "You've got mine as well as yours. 'Stays strong when wet', they say. I bet this is what they really mean."

Simon let Daniel wipe him clean with the tissues, his tummy and between his legs.

"Some of mine's on the sheet. Wait a minute." Daniel got up with the tissues he had used and went into the bathroom, flushing the tissues away. He came back with a towel which he put on the sheet and the two lay on that.

"We'll use a towel or something next time," said Daniel, pulling the bedcovers over them. Simon snuggled up to Daniel, resting his head on Daniel's shoulder.

"What about your Mum?" asked Simon. "The extra towel, I mean."

"Oh, she's always saying I don't change my towel often enough. That'll be OK."

They lay together in silence for a few moments.

Then Simon spoke. "Is it wrong?"

"What?"

"Us. Like this. Sex."

"Does it feel wrong to you?"

"No. The opposite. Sex with you feels so right. It's fantastic. But just coz it feels right – does it mean it is right?"

"Oh, we both know that lots of people anyway would think it's wrong, but I don't care about them. I care about us."

"Doesn't it say in the Bible it's wrong?" persisted Simon.

"It says lots of things in the Bible, some of it's well out of date. Look, God gave us our bodies. He gave us sex. So it can't be wrong to enjoy it."

"But sex is supposed to be for having children. We can't have children."

"Speak for yourself. I will when I'm grown up. I bet you do. I'm going to have two boys and two girls. And I bet God doesn't want us to be having kids at our age, but we've still got sex. So let's enjoy it while we're young. Having kids is for later, if we're all still here, so we'll still be doing what God wants."

"I suppose you're right."

"Course I am," said Daniel. He leaned over and kissed Simon. Simon felt Daniel's lips against his and all doubt was swept away.

"We're only young once," said Simon, "and the bomb might drop tomorrow." He turned and pulled Daniel down onto him and kissed him again, his hands in Daniel's hair, sliding over Daniel's back, following the smooth contours of his fit body. It had been a marvellous evening after all. That night Simon dreamt of Daniel as he had seen him, playing cricket at school, the sunlight on his cricket whites making him seem like a vision from heaven.

36. *1958/7 Defining the roles*

Both boys were now involved in and supporting each other in their sporting activity, Daniel of course mainly for swimming and for Simon, running. Whether it was the physical training or natural maturation and growth, or more likely a combination, each noted and took delight in the way each other became more muscular, filled out and of course the growth of underarm and pubic hair. This transition towards manhood was a journey they made together, inevitably with Daniel some two years ahead with Simon approaching twelve and Daniel towards fourteen, but this also helped Simon become aware of his own progress, by watching and learning from Daniel's experience.

Simon grew in confidence, boosted by Daniel's regard for him, and the success he gained as a runner added to this. His talent was recognised as a short sprinter, the ability to accelerate quickly and maintain high speed over short distance gave him success, especially at 100 yards events, where he first represented his house year at school, and then Hooray Henrys in local interschool events. Longer distance, and especially cross country running, a favourite at Henrys, was anathema to him. The smaller and lighter Peter Holman did well at this, and would encourage Simon when his body wanted to stop on the compulsory cross country runs, which sometimes included the local sewage works, often at the expense of Peter's own placing.

Such was the boys' increasing fitness and growth that the once hour-long bike ride to the aerodrome hill was now accomplished in forty minutes or so. Having found a place where they felt safe, adders apart (and they never saw another one), they stayed with it, and the aircraft provided both a reason and some entertainment from their vantage point.

Lying in the long grass on a warm, sunny July day, they were relaxing in the familiar comfort of each other. As arousal took hold of both of them, Daniel surprised Simon.

"Simon, why don't you go on top?"

"Don't you mind? You sure?" asked Simon, uncertainly.

"Yeah, come on. Try it," replied Daniel, turning face up and drawing Simon to him. So Simon did. Pushing himself in to the warmth of Daniel's loins, he found it arousing but within he was in some way uncomfortable. He found the same when they kissed, with Daniel beneath him, and also the friction was starting to hurt him, so after a while he just stopped.

"What the matter?" asked Daniel gently, holding him.

"It's not right," Simon said, easing himself off, lying next to Daniel. His insecurity returned and he felt unsettled. Daniel moved so they were on their sides, facing each other, a more familiar situation for Simon.

"Why not? There's no rule that says it has to be me on top," said Daniel, stroking Simon's short hair.

"Well, you're older than me."

"So what? We're friends, aren't we? It doesn't matter who's older or younger."

"It just didn't feel right, me on you. I mean, you've always been ahead of me. At school, scouts as well as this."

"Now you're being an idiot. That's only coz I'm older. You're just as good as me. You're as fit as me. Look at you." With that, Daniel pushed Simon slowly onto his back and ran his hands over his friend. "No, I mean I want you to look at your body."

Simon lifted his head and looked, following Daniel's hand as it brushed over his skin in a light, sensuous touch.

"I think your body is beautiful," said Daniel, "you're fit as hell, easily as fit as me now, your cock's as big as mine already, so you've nothing to be ashamed of."

Simon felt better in the warmth of Daniel's praise. "But anyway, it was starting to hurt a bit, the rubbing I mean," he said.

Daniel thought for a moment. "I think that's because you're circumcised, so it rubs straight onto my skin."

"Doesn't it for you?"

"No. I think because I'm not circumcised that I can make it rub mostly inside, in my foreskin, so it doesn't hurt. The very opposite!" Daniel smiled.

"I wish I wasn't circumcised," said Simon. "I hate it. I know you've got more feeling there than I have."

"Doesn't stop you coming, though," said Daniel. "Don't worry so much. You're super."

"How d'you mean?" said Simon, still wanting reassurance.

"You're clever, funny."

"Funny?"

"Yeah, I don't mean silly funny. Clever funny, witty and that."

"Telling jokes?"

"Not just that. It's the way you see things. You come out with some really witty things at times, from nowhere. It makes me laugh, you know it does. You just seem to see things from a different angle to most other kids. Ones I know, anyway."

"You're clever too."

"I know. But your cleverness is one of the things I like about you. I can talk to you better than other kid I know, ones in my own year too. And I know you're a real friend. Never let me down."

"I would never do that, Daniel. You've never let me down. Ever. Just think about eleven plus, never mind scouts and everything."

"I'm just a kid, you know, like you. A bit older, that's all. I love you being my friend, Simon. You make me feel good. It's sort of ... where I get my strength from."

"From me?" exclaimed an astonished Simon.

"Don't sound so surprised. Of course from you. There's nobody else like you. So don't worry about not liking being on top. You're such an emotional kid, more than any I know. But if it's not fun for both of us, what's the point? Be honest, d'you like it when I'm on top?"

"Yes, you know I do. It feels right to me. I just feel ... sort of ... safe. And you know that when I know you're coming, it usually makes me too."

"Good. I like that. And you are. Safe, I mean. We don't have to do it that way every time anyway."

"But we can now, if you want," said Simon. Daniel's actions were his answer.

Satisfied, lying together in the sunshine, Simon felt content. He knew that Daniel would never demand of him anything he didn't want to give, and in return he was happy to give Daniel all he wanted. He thought about what Daniel had said about how he made him feel good. His feeling of self worth returned. It was true what Daniel had said about his emotions. They were volatile and Simon sometimes could not control how he felt, especially where Daniel was concerned. But Daniel's confirmation of his value, his fitness, his friendship meant more than anything else because Daniel really knew him. There was no pretence, no false front, no attempt to impress, just Simon, his body and soul open to Daniel who knew and saw all, and yet still was his best friend. They lay together, testing each other from Daniel's *Flags of the World* book.

Simon followed Daniel in another respect too. He was chosen to carry the flag at church parade. What surprised Simon was that Mum and Dad came as well. To see him carry the Union Flag. Simon was glad it was the Union Flag he was given because that was the one Daniel had carried. George Morrison, PL of Eagles, was carrying the Scout Flag. The two stood outside with the troop lined up behind them, flags in their holders, fluttering in the breeze. Simon felt Daniel's gaze behind him. He had to do this well. He had of course been to most of the church parades so he knew the routine, unchanged since that first time he had come along to watch Daniel.

John Riley, the Troop Leader, gave the commands and they marched off, Simon concentrating hard on keeping in step, back erect, holding the flag high. It was heavy and the breeze kept wanting it to sway it to one side and then the other. When it was time to enter the church, he dipped the flag as it went through the porch, being careful it did not touch the stone flagged floor. He controlled his nervousness as he saw how full the church was. He noticed Mum and Dad, there to support him, but deliberately avoided eye contact. He must keep focused; Daniel had stressed how important that was. Holding their flags high, with George on his left, arms level, right elbows out at shoulder height as trained, they walked down the nave of the church toward the altar, the congregation watching the regular ritual. Suddenly with a loud crack, Simon's right elbow caught a wooden staff with a small cross on top slotted in on the end of a pew. It twanged back and forth noisily like a ruler flipped on a desk edge. Simon felt himself flush with embarrassment but kept his steady step alongside George and reached the altar rail. The flags were taken and laid by the altar and Simon and George went to their position in the front pew. The rest of the troop filed into their places. Luckily the post wasn't broken and was now still again, but Simon's elbow was sore.

The service was now more familiar to Simon, and he followed it. From his front pew he was able to watch as the sacraments were prepared, and at the time of communion as the vicar took the bread and wine followed by the choir; then it was Simon's turn. As before, Simon knelt at the rail and kept his head bowed and hands by his side. He felt the priest's hand on his head.

"The Lord bless you and keep you. The Lord make his face to shine upon you and be gracious to you. The Lord lift up his countenance upon you and give you peace."

Simon felt that same warm tingling suffuse his body as he had the first time and every time since. He felt at ease in some way he could not explain.

"The body of Christ keep you in eternal life."

Simon realised that George was taking Communion. He risked a sidelong glance, and saw him take the wafer, and then sip the wine. Simon waited until he had done that and then moved back to his seat, past the line of waiting scouts. Daniel gave him a quiet dig in the side as he passed.

Back in his seat, Simon watched as Daniel knelt among the scouts at the rail and received the wafer – "The body of Christ keep you in eternal life " – and then sipping from the silver chalice - "The blood of Christ keep you in eternal life" – and remained kneeling while other scouts received either the sacraments or a blessing as Simon had. Since his confirmation, Simon had seen Daniel take communion at Church Parades before, and he wondered if he ever would. If Daniel was going to get eternal life, Simon wanted to be there too with him. He turned round to see Mum and Dad sitting further back. He caught their eye and smiled.

At the end it was time to take the flag out again, Simon this time careful where his elbow was. He and George led the troop, under the orders of the Troop Leader, for the parade round the church, watched by many of the congregation. Many of course were family of the scouts, but many were not.

The double column came to halt and turned to form two rows as usual. After dismiss, Simon and George took the flags to Skip's estate car. Simon was nervous about what might be said about the wooden staff. He decided to speak first.

"Skip, I'm sorry about hitting that pole thing."

"Made me jump out of my skin," commented George.

"It's called a churchwarden's wand, Simon. You both did very well," said Skip. "And Simon, forget about hitting the wand. You did extremely well not to panic, you kept your head and simply carried on without missing a step. Excellent. Both of you did us proud today. Is your elbow all right, Simon?"

"Yes, it's OK, Skip."

"Good. Off you go then."

Simon saw Mum and Dad waiting for him. He looked round for Daniel, and saw him with his parents.

"Is your arm hurting, Simon?" asked Mum.

"No, it's fine."

"You hit that pole with an awful clatter," said Dad. "But you just carried on as though nothing had happened. Great presence of mind, Simon. Well done."

Simon smiled at this praise from Dad.

"What do you have to do now?" asked Mum. "Only I should go and get the lunch ready or it will be teatime by the time we get it."

"No, we're finished now," said Simon. They walked from the churchyard, over the footbridge and up the hill. Daniel with his parents was several yards in front of them.

"Daniel!" shouted Simon.

Daniel stopped and waited, Simon ran ahead, and they walked up together, between the parents.

"What happened with that post thingy? It made a hell of a racket," asked Daniel.

"I just clipped it with my elbow, made it twang. It's called a wand."

"I thought it was never going to stop. Didn't you see it?"

"I suppose so, just didn't realise it was so close."

Daniel punched Simon playfully and shook his head. "Simon, you're such an idiot. But you did really well not to drop the flag or something. Super Second."

"Perfect PL," responded Simon, happy with this praise from his Patrol Leader and best friend.

Through that Summer, the boys made a real effort to improve their fitness. They devised a programme of exercises; sit ups, lifting using various household objects, and Daniel's bedroom became a makeshift fitness room. His mother had to keep retrieving the 2lb bags of sugar from the bedroom. They went out running, the bike rides continued and of course Daniel's swimming club kept his body perfectly toned.

But it wasn't just the physical that improved. Daniel had watched Simon get narrowly beaten in the 100 yards at school, and he knew why.

"It's like swimming, Simon. You've not just got to be fast, you have to concentrate. He beat you because he got a better start."

Simon nodded, the memory of the defeat still vexed him. "I went as soon as I heard the gun."

"You didn't. I was watching. You went when the others went."

"That's the same thing, isn't it?"

"No. If you wait to see them move there's a split second delay that puts you behind."

"But I don't want to be disqualified."

"Thought so. Forget the others. Look, I was the same when I started racing at swimming. You're scared of going too soon so you wait too long. When I'm waiting for a race, I don't think about anything else. You have to really focus your mind on the gun, or when the swimmer touches if it's a relay. Nothing else matters in the world. When I'm like that, the bomb could drop and it wouldn't make a difference."

Simon knew what Daniel meant, he knew that ability of Daniel's for fierce concentration, not just at swimming galas, but in his piano playing, his work. Everything. Simon wished he had it. "Yes, you're good at that," he said.

"So can you be. You've got to want to win so much you don't care about anything else at that time. I'm going to teach you to get a good start."

In Daniel's garden, in the street, Simon did start after start, Daniel acting as starter, using two wooden blocks he had found to simulate the crack of the starting pistol. Simon learned to train his mind to exclude all else, his whole being concentrated on the starter's orders, and the loud crack that meant 'Go!'

Daniel cheered at the next house races, when Simon made a perfect start and won the 100 yards by several yards, beating a boy from Daniel's house. Daniel got some comments about cheering a boy from another house, but he didn't care. He could see the change in Simon's start. He knew he had helped and felt proud of that. For Daniel, it was a success by proxy, and Simon's happiness made him happy too.

37. *1959/3 Nearly caught*

Simon decided to wait for the next bus. He was at the main road, waiting to meet Daniel back from his Saturday morning swimming club, and he had not arrived on the expected bus. It was a chilly March day, but Simon was wearing a warm coat with scarf and hat. He stomped up and down by the bus stop, stepping back when a bus arrived to indicate he did not want to get on, even though it was not a request stop. At last another bus that might be carrying Daniel arrived, and there was his friend, getting off the bus. But he didn't look especially pleased to see Simon.

"Hiya, Daniel," said Simon hesitantly, catching his friend's mood.

"Hiya," said Daniel curtly.

"What's the matter?"

"Layton, that's what's the matter, if you want to know," came Daniel's gruff response. "Come on, let's go."

As the two walked up the hill, Simon wondered what had happened to upset Daniel. He could guess, because Daniel had talked of Layton before, and indeed when Simon had gone to watch and cheer Daniel on at swimming galas, he had seen the boy in question, undoubtedly a big and strong swimmer.

"He is older than you, though, isn't he?" offered Simon in consolation.

"Not the point, I'm better than him." Daniel hated not being first.

"But it was just a practice, though?"

"Again, not the point. And it is for the county team."

They walked on in silence until they got to the corner.

"See you later?" said Simon cautiously.

Daniel stopped. "I'm sorry, Simon, it's not your fault. You were waiting for me and all I've done is be bad tempered with you. Come in with me. Please?"

"'Course I will," said Simon, gratified. So they went to Daniel's house and entered through the back door into the kitchen. Mrs Gray was there, putting things in her handbag.

"Hello, darling, how did you get on?"

"Don't ask," said Daniel, dropping his bag and taking off his coat. Mrs Gray looked questioningly at Simon.

"That Layton again, I think, Mrs Gray," said Simon.

"Oh darling, what happened?" she said to her morose fourteen year old son.

"I came second in backstroke AND butterfly," grumbled Daniel.

"Front crawl?"

"Oh I won that of course, by miles. But I wanted to beat Layton in backstroke especially."

"Well, you can't win everything, Daniel. What about the county? You are in the team?"

"Yes," said Daniel, "first two go through."

"You mean you're on the team for all three strokes?" said Simon, wondering why in that case Daniel was so upset.

"Yes," said Daniel, a bit defensively now. "It's just that I really wanted to beat Layton in something other than crawl. And the county gala is in two weeks. Easter Saturday."

"Well," said Mrs Gray, "nobody can question that you're the best when it comes to the crawl, and you're in the team for the others as well. You've done very well."

"Oh, I suppose so. I took it out on Simon a bit too," he admitted, mellowing somewhat now.

"It's OK," said Simon. "You stink of chlorine, anyway." And it was true. The chlorine of the swimming pool was now evident in the warm kitchen.

"Oh," said Daniel, "yes, there was a lot in the water today."

"Well, anyway boys," said Mrs Gray, "I'm going into town for a couple of hours, will you try not to burn the house down?"

"Where's Dad and Louise?" asked Daniel quickly.

"Dad won't be home until this evening, Louise probably won't be back until late. She went out with Sarah and that lot. I think she's seeing Graham later. You'd better do something about that chlorine." With that, Mrs Gray took up her handbag, put on her coat and left to get the bus.

"Better take your coat off," said Daniel to Simon once the two were alone. Simon did so.

"Back room," Daniel commanded. Simon knew what was coming. When Daniel felt frustrated, he would play the piano, venting his frustration into the music.

"Rachmaninoff, I think," said Daniel, rummaging among the music books. "Sit," he ordered Simon, patting the piano stool. Simon sat next to Daniel. To him, the mass of tightly packed notes meant nothing, except that the tune went higher when the notes went up. But when Daniel said "Turn", Simon's job was to turn the page.

Daniel paused, and then with a burst of sound began to play. The three dark opening chords matching his mood. Simon loved the Russian music, its emotion, its soaring drive and rhythms, its complexity, but especially he loved it because Daniel loved it and played it. He watched Daniel's hands, those large, strong but somehow delicate hands, sweeping across the keys, his legs as he pedalled, raising and lowering allowing the sound to crescendo, killing it when he wanted. His passion and feeling, even anger, going into the poignant chords as the piece reached its climax, and then subsiding, its work done. Simon watched with a mixture of admiration and envy, turning the pages on command. Daniel's face expressing the feeling in the music. The piece ended. Daniel stopped, panting slightly.

"That's better," he said. "Did you like it? I played that for you."

"Of course I did."

"Good. The prelude in C sharp minor, Opus 3, number 2."

"I do recognise the prelude," Simon said. "Quite apart from it saying at the top of the page. Why do you like Rachmaninoff so much?"

"It matches my mood. He's an amazing composer, especially for piano. And it's very challenging, hard to play. When I was younger my hands were too small but Mum adapted his music for me, but my hands are bigger now. So I like to master it. There's a part of that where there is so much fingering, he used double staves to fit all the notes in. That took me ages to learn. But listen to this one," he said, thumbing the music book, "It's a bit more cheerful, now I'm feeling better."

The next piece was different in tone, but Simon could see that it was a hard piece, *Prelude Op. 23 No. 5*, according to the book. The music danced, Simon almost felt like clapping along with it, and this time Daniel was smiling slightly as he played it, glancing at Simon to see his reaction. Simon knew this was being played for him too.

"Do you like that one?" asked Daniel as he finished.

"Yes, it's a bit more cheerful than the C sharp one."

"C sharp minor," corrected Daniel. "I have to work on that last one, I made a couple of mistakes. Can you still smell the chlorine?"

"I didn't notice any mistakes," said Simon, but he knew how Daniel always strove for perfection. "And you do reek a bit."

Daniel sniffed. "Suppose I do a bit." He went into the kitchen and checked the Aga. "I'll have a bath." Turning to Simon, he added mischievously, "Want to come and wash my back?"

Simon smiled and nodded, followed Daniel upstairs, where he started to run the bath. Simon sat on Daniel's big bed and watched as his friend undressed, completely unselfconscious with Simon. In Simon's eyes, he was the most beautiful creature walking on God's Earth. In the bathroom, Daniel tested the water and then climbed in and sat down.

"That's good," he said, and lay back, allowing the hot water to swirl around him and over his chest. Simon perched on the side of the bath. Daniel lay further back and submerged his head, his hair floating out, momentarily reminding Simon of the lido when they were younger. Daniel blew bubbles up at Simon and then surfaced, pushing his now wet hair back, and lay back again.

"I can't do your back with you lying on it," Simon pointed out.

"You get in," said Daniel.

"There's not room."

"I'll make room. Come on. They're all out. Let's have a bath together."

At that, Simon quickly undressed, watched by Daniel, both boys now becoming aroused with the anticipation of this novel arena. Daniel sat up and Simon got in, facing Daniel, their legs overlapping each other.

"Ah!" exclaimed Simon as the cold tap touched his back. "I've got the tap end. It's cold."

"Well, don't lean on it then, idiot," said Daniel, with that wide grin on his face for the first time since getting off the bus. He reached forward and pulled Simon close, their hands exploring each other. Simon reached round and started to rub Daniel's back.

"Simon, what are you doing?"

"Washing your back. Or trying to. It's a bit awkward. Turn round."

With some splashing and difficulty in the confines of the bathtub, Daniel turned and sat, knees drawn up, with Simon behind him, his legs either side of Daniel. But Simon was pushed back against the cold tap again.

"This is too awkward," he complained.

"They manage in the films," said Daniel.

"Have you seen the size of the baths they have, though?" countered Simon. He kissed the wet nape of Daniel's neck, who responded by running his hand up the inside of Simon's thigh.

"You're right," said Daniel, "I think the chlorine will have washed off now anyway. Let's get dried off."

They both climbed out, and stood together, dripping. Daniel took up a bath towel and started to dry himself down.

"What towel can I use?" asked Simon.

"Better share this one. Too many wet towels might look odd."

So they dried themselves and each other, using the ends of the large towel. Daniel hung it on the towel rail. "Come on, bring your clothes." Daniel led the way into his bedroom, closing the door. Simon dumped his clothes by Daniel's heap on the floor. Daniel lay on the bed and beckoned him.

"Come on, then. After this morning, I need this."

Simon joined Daniel and they lay arms round each other.

"Let's get in," said Daniel. They both climbed under the sheet and blankets. It was warmer and Simon always loved being in Daniel's big bed with him. It was warm, safe and like a loving cocoon.

Daniel propped up on one elbow, looked down at Simon's head on the pillow, put his arm round the back of Simon's neck and leaning down, kissed him, their lips exploring each other, Simon's hands in Daniel's now almost dry hair, arousal heightening, Daniel running his hand down Simon's back to his thighs, Simon responding.

They used their bodies to pleasure the other, the joy each found in the other's body ending with mutual climax, each drinking the fruit of the other's loins. And as so often, they sang the chorus of what they had come to think of as their private song, certainly in this sense, in celebration of their shared joy.

Fire! fire! fire down below;
Fetch a bucket of water, boys, There's fire down below!

As they lay together afterwards, Daniel said, "You always make me feel better. I know I get too tense sometimes. You're good for me."

"And you for me," said Simon.

"You do like doing this?"

"Yes, you know I do. Why are you asking about that again?"

"I feel a bit guilty I suppose."

"Guilty? What about?" asked Simon, puzzled.

"Ages ago, when we first started, going to the den and that, one reason why I liked it was because ..." Daniel stopped.

"What?"

"I was the boss, telling you what to do, it made me feel kind of powerful."

"That's all right."

"No, Simon, it's not. It's almost like I was using you, and I'm really sorry. You're worth more than that."

"Honest Daniel, it's OK. I never felt used. Just safe and looked after. Maybe I was using you in my own way. You've always been there for me and you've never let me down, ever. No apology required."

"If you ever do feel like that, used I mean, tell me, won't you?"

"OK, but I know you never would. You're just not like that, and this proves it."

"Well, I was a bit worried about it," continued Daniel, "especially now I am sometimes going into you. If you're not happy about it, I would feel as though I was using you."

"No," reiterated Simon. "It's super. It feels right and you know I sometimes come just from the way you are in me. I like it when you come there as well. I know I've got you for longer in a kind of way." Simon had never heard of the prostate but was very aware of its highly erogenous effect when stimulated! He turned and kissed Daniel. "No more apologies, right?"

"Right. Thank you, Simon. You're an amazing friend to have. Do I still smell of chlorine?"

Simon moved closer and drew in breath on Daniel's shoulder. There was no chlorine, all Simon could smell was the masculine scent of him that he found so exciting. But all he said was, "No. You smell normal now."

"Good," said Daniel, "so do you."

"I didn't smell of chlorine in the first place."

"So? You still smell normal."

Simon laughed, but it was cut short by a shout from downstairs.

"Daniel? Are you in?"

"It's Louise, shhh," said Daniel. They heard Louise coming up the stairs. Simon instinctively clung closer to Daniel's warm body. Louise seemed to stop outside the door.

"I didn't lock the door," whispered Daniel anxiously, fearful that his eighteen year old sister would just come in.

"Daniel, are you in there?" came from the other side of the door. Daniel knew he would have to answer.

"Yes. Got back from swimming."

"D'you make the team? Silly question."

"Yes, three events."

"Three? Good," Louise said. "Simon in there with you?"

For a moment Daniel wondered what to say, just in time remembering Simon's coat on the chair in the kitchen.

"Yeah. We're OK," he called back from the bed, praying Louise would not open the door.

"I'm sure you are," answered Louise. "I've just come back for some things. I'm off out again. Mum in town?"

"Yes," said Daniel, he and Simon still locked in unmoving embrace.

"OK bruvver." They heard Louise go to her room. A few minutes of movement during the which the two boys didn't stir, and then footsteps on the landing outside the door.

"I'm off then. See you later."

"Bye!" called Daniel.

"Bye!" Louise paused. "Bye Simon!"

Daniel nudged Simon, nodding.

"Bye!" shouted Simon, hoping the nervousness in his voice wouldn't show. They heard Louise going downstairs and a few moments later, the front door closing. Both boys exhaled and relaxed their grip on each other.

"That was close," said Simon.

"You can say that again!"

"That was close," said Simon, smiling now, and then getting poked by Daniel for deliberately taking him literally. The two remained in that warm cocoon for an hour longer, relaxing in their closeness and talking, of the county swimming gala - "Of course I'll be there!" said Simon – of Simon's athletics – "I bet you win the 100 yards again," said Daniel. "I will if you're watching," said Simon. "Try and stop me," said Daniel – of school and plans for the coming Easter holiday, including more time like this. Holidays, when both Daniel's parents were at work, presented the best chance for the two to use Daniel's bed. When Daniel said his mother might be back soon, they reluctantly relinquished their warm nest and got dressed.

Simon watched Daniel with Mr and Mrs Gray and Louise from the spectator seats as he sped through the water to win the county front crawl well in front of the next boy, Daniel waving up at them as he climbed out of the pool. He came second again in the backstroke and butterfly heats, losing the final place to Layton, but he went on to star in the four length relay. His team were in third place after three lengths, and Daniel was to swim the final part. Simon watched as Daniel, face set in determination and concentration, was poised on the edge, waiting for his teammate to touch, risking disqualification if he dived too early. As soon as the boy touched, Daniel dived over the boy's head, but well behind the leader who was already powering away. Simon looked on agitated with excitement and anxiety, as Daniel's powerful, lithe body cut through the water leaving barely a ripple, the muscles on his back, arms and legs working hard to make up the deficit, his skin glistening as the water coursed across it. Simon couldn't see Daniel's face as his breathing side was away from him, but he could visualise the look of resolve he knew so well. By half the length Daniel had pulled almost level, the leader seeing this redoubling his efforts, but it was neck and neck as they neared the end. Everybody was now on their feet yelling. Simon was shouting "Come on Daniel!" at the top of his voice. In the last yards, Daniel eased in front to touch an arm's length ahead. The crowd roared at the excitement of the race and the home club's victory. After a pause in the water while other swimmers finished, Daniel leapt out of the water and stood on the pool edge. He waved at his family and Simon, exhilarated. He hadn't won all his races, but he had helped his team win the county gala overall. Daniel was pleased, and so was Simon.

38. *1959/6 Scouts*

That Spring there were further changes at Scouts. The Troop Leader John Riley was now old enough for Venture Scouts and moved on. Daniel was convinced that either Nigel Colley, Patrol Leader of the Falcons or Christopher Gerrard of the Kestrels would be promoted. It turned out that Christopher Gerrard was only four months away from leaving for Ventures anyway, but still Colley was a bit older than Daniel but had not been a PL for as long. Daniel said that Gerrard had been offered it for the four months, but had said it would be added disruption for the troop to have another change so quickly and he wanted to spend those months with his beloved Kestrels. As with promotion to Patrol Leader, Daniel again beat Nigel Colley to the prize, his prophesy of three years earlier that he would be Troop Leader one day coming true.

Simon sat with Daniel in his bedroom while he unpicked the scout badge from his uniform shirt pocket so that he could sew on the third white stripe in the centre. The badge was then sewn on again over the top so that the stripe went underneath it.

"I told you I'd be Troop Leader one day," said a confident Daniel. "Remember? That first time I carried the flag and you came along to watch?"

"Yes," said Simon. "What about Colley though? He's older than you but now you outrank him."

"He'll be OK. He's a good scout. I can manage that OK as well."

"I expect you will," said Simon, poking Daniel. "I feel sorry for him though, with all those spots." Nigel Colley was cursed by acne. One or two of the scouts were suffering this teenage pain, but Colley was the worst afflicted.

"Must be rotten," said Daniel. "I've never said anything and I don't think anyone else has. I expect he's very self conscious about it."

"I'm glad we haven't got spots. I'd hate to be all spotty."

"Some kids get them like Colley, others get hardly any. My Dad says it runs in families, but he didn't have it so maybe that's why I don't."

"You've got really nice skin," said Simon. "I'll have to ask my Dad if he had them."

"So have you. Some kids in my year need a shave already," said Daniel, rubbing his still smooth chin. "I suppose that will happen one day."

"Me too, I suppose. Does Colley shave? It must be dead awkward with spots."

"I hope not for his sake. Anyway, I've got other things to think about now. My next job now I'm Troop Leader is to get you made PL of Harriers."

Simon, as Second of Harriers was now acting Patrol Leader after Daniel's promotion. "How can you do that? It's up to Skip, isn't it?"

"Yes, but the Court of Honour has a big say, and I'm in charge of it now."

"But I'm in that now," said Simon. The Court of Honour was a meeting of the Troop Leader and Patrol Leaders which formed a governing committee of the troop under the guidance of the Scoutmasters.

"Yes, as acting PL. And when it gets discussed, you would have to leave."

A few weeks later, the Court of Honour was meeting.

"The first item on the agenda is the permanent appointment of a new PL for Harriers," said Daniel, now comfortable in his authority as TL. "I'm sorry, Simon, but you have to leave the meeting for this section."

Skip nodded. Simon, as ordered, got up and left the meeting.

"Before I say anything, I would like to hear what ideas the Patrol Leaders have about this?" said Daniel.

The other PLs spoke, two, including Nigel Colley, making a case for their own Seconds to get promoted, but two, whose Seconds were relatively new, spoke in favour of Simon. Faced with this result, Daniel said he felt Simon should be promoted.

"Patrol Leaders should really have their First Class," said Skip.

"He's done a good job though as Second, and acting PL," said Daniel. "Who else is there?"

"That's a problem," said Skip. "None of the other Seconds have First Class either, but some are older than Simon, who is what, twelve and a half, Daniel? Jeremy?"

Jeremy, assistant Scoutmaster, thought for a moment. "It's hard. We can't leave Harriers without a proper Patrol Leader much longer, and it would be difficult to put someone in over Simon now he's been acting PL. And I tend to think he's probably the best one for it, despite the fact he's young. He would be the youngest PL, am I right? And then younger than some of the Seconds, not to mention other scouts?"

"Yes," said Skip. "How far towards First Class is he, Daniel?"

"He's doing well, Skip. He's much closer than any other Second."

"Are you sure your judgement is not clouded by the fact that he's your friend, Daniel?" posed Jeremy. Nigel Colley smiled to himself at this.

"It's true we're good friends, have been for years. But that's why I know he'd be good for the job. He was a really good second for me when I was Harriers' PL, and I think he's doing a good job leading Harriers now, as acting PL instead of PL."

"How will he cope with any problems from some of the older Seconds. They might feel they've been unfairly passed over?" asked Colley.

Daniel considered this. "I don't think there would be a problem, and if there was, Simon would deal with it OK. There's only Tim Lawson anything like ready for PL apart Simon, and Tim's only just got his Second Class. He was made Second before he'd got it, so there's a .. you know, when it's been done before."

"Precedent?" said Skip.

"Yes, that's the word I was looking for. And Gareth's doing OK as acting Second of Harriers as well. I think that .."

Skip held up his hand to stop Daniel. "A moment please Daniel. Let **me** think." Skip closed his eyes and covered his face with hands in thought for a few moments. "Jeremy, I am inclined to go along with what Daniel and the majority of the Court says. Make them both up. Simon to substantive Patrol Leader and Gareth to Second. Unless you feel differently?"

"I agree," said Jeremy. "It's a risk, but Simon's a bright lad. And it is the decision of the Court of Honour. Yes, I'm in favour."

"OK, that's it then," pronounced Skip. "Daniel, all I can say is you're very persuasive. But as Troop Leader, it's up to you make it work. And Simon's got to go flat out for First Class."

"I guarantee it, Skip," said Daniel.

"Better call Simon back in then."

Daniel opened the door and saw Simon in Harriers' patrol corner. Simon looked up at Daniel at the top of the wooden steps.

"Come back now, please, Simon," called Daniel.

Simon walked back and up the steps. He looked at Daniel for some clue, but Daniel did not make eye contact and said nothing. Tim Lawson then, thought Simon. He took his seat at the table, Daniel resumed his at the head.

"The Court of Honour has reached a decision on the new Patrol Leader for Harriers," said Daniel impassively. And then he pushed a strip of white tape across the table to Simon, and smiled that wonderful smile.

"Congratulations, Simon," said Nigel Colley, the first to say so. The others joined in and there was general chatter. Daniel rapped his knuckles on the table. Silence fell immediately.

"The Court of Honour also thinks Gareth should be promoted to be your Second, but we would like to hear your views before making a final decision," said Daniel.

Skip and Jeremy glanced at each other, slight smiles on their lips.

Still recovering, and fingering the second white stripe that would soon adorn his shirt pocket to balance the single Second's stripe, Simon thought. "Yes, he's good and learning fast. I agree with the Court, I mean the rest of the Court."

"That's it then," smiled Daniel. "Gareth Smart to be full Second of Harriers."

Later that night in Daniel's bed taking advantage of an empty house, something occurred to Simon. "Colley was the first to say congratulations. That was good."

"I told you he's a good Scout. He didn't vote for you, but he accepts the Court's decision. He's OK."

"I'm glad the Court decided to have me."

Daniel laughed, and shook his head. "Idiot, I knew it would."

"How?"

"I knew that Colley for one wouldn't back you, so I had a word with Tom Rawlinson and Ladislas Balázs coz their Seconds just weren't in it. I got them to back you. I am Troop Leader you know."

"What did Colley say about that?"

"No, idiot, before the meeting I mean. A quiet word, you know? My Dad says that all important decisions are really made before the actual meeting."

"But you looked so serious and wouldn't look at me when I went back in. I thought it was Lawson."

"I know. Rotten, aren't I?" laughed Daniel. He leaned over and kissed Simon, stifling any reply.

"Again?" said Simon when he could, so anxious to feel Daniel within him once more, to receive him. Daniel smiled and reached down for the Vaseline.

The whole troop, or most of them anyway, went away on an annual week long camp to a large scout camp; everything, including the scouts, carried on the back of a large lorry for the two hour drive. Each patrol had its own tent, and the leaders had theirs. Previously Simon and Daniel had been in the same tent with the Harriers as Patrol Leader and Second, but Riley had slept in the tent with the Scoutmasters. They were worried that they would be separated this time, but need not have.

"Daniel, do you want to come in with Jeremy and me?" offered Skip.

"I'd like to kip in with my old patrol, Harriers, if that's OK," said Daniel.

"Of course, catch up on old times. But it's Simon's call. If he says no, which I doubt, come back."

"Yes Skip," Daniel replied, knowing full well that Simon had not only agreed, but had asked Daniel to share the Harriers' tent in the first place.

So it was that the two boys spent the week together at camp, lucky with the weather, by day each carrying out the roles of their ranks; by night, lying in their sleeping bags next to each other, falling asleep with the other's face the last thing seen, each waking in the morning, the first thing seen was again the face of his friend. This was real happiness.

39. 1959/9 Head Injury

It was a warm September Friday evening, and being a Friday, Scout night. As normal, Simon and Daniel walked together, over the footbridge, past the stream and the church and along the lane to the Church Hall, behind which was the Scout hut.

"You don't mind coming early?" asked Daniel. As Troop Leader he had to arrive before the rest of the Scouts to help Skip prepare the evening.

"No," said Simon. "I would rather be with you and anyway, I find out what's happening before the other Patrol Leaders, so my lot get a head start."

Daniel laughed. "I bet that's not in P.O.R. Got to keep the Harriers ahead, haven't we?"

"You're not supposed to take sides now," said Simon.

"Moi? Take sides? Favour my old patrol over the others? Of course not. Anyway, I don't need to. They've got the best Patrol Leader."

"But I'm the youngest PL, and Nigel Colley never lets me forget it," said Simon ruefully.

"That's because he mistakenly thinks the Falcons are the best patrol, and he thinks he should have been Troop Leader."

"He wouldn't be half as good as you. Does he hate you for it?"

"No, we get on fine. I only know that because he told me to my face, and then shook hands. I respect him for that. He's a good Scout, you know that. And I know he really thinks you're a good PL too."

There came a shout from behind them. "Off to tie your little knots?"

Simon and Daniel turned to see Fielding's little brother, as nasty as his older sibling, catcalling from a safe distance. Dressed in their full Scout uniforms, the two were conspicuous. Simon tried to think of a stinging reply, but Daniel forestalled him.

"You should come along," Daniel called back. "You would learn a lot."

Nonplussed by this placatory answer, Fielding Jnr. just stuck two fingers up and turned away.

"Like where his brains are," added Daniel quietly, and they both laughed. They arrived at the Scout hut and went in. Colley was there already rummaging through his Patrol Box.

"Hiya Daniel, hiya Simon, he said.

"Hiya, Nigel," they both said back, and Daniel nudged Simon and nodded, as if to say, I told you.

"See you soon," said Daniel to Simon, and went up the wooden stairs to the office. He knocked and went in. Simon heard Skip's voice say, "Oh, hello Daniel" as the door closed.

Simon set about checking his Patrol box, making sure the subs book was there. He had a new Scout still doing Tenderfoot so he made a note to go over the Scout Law with him, and he still couldn't tie a sheepshank. Other scouts started to arrive and were milling around outside, although there was some time before the meeting was due to start.

"Shall we sort that lot out?" said Simon to Nigel Colley, heartened by what Daniel had told him.

"Yeah, set 'em up with something," said Colley, "I'll be out in a minute."

Simon went outside, and seeing a Patrol Leader, the scouts gathered round, waiting for instructions. Simon quickly set up a small wide game based round the Scout hut and Church hall grounds. The Scouts scattered to take part. It soon became a chase, with the boys running around at full speed, Simon included. He noticed his new boy and to make him feel included, gave chase. The Scout took the hint and set off with Simon in full pursuit. With Simon's speed he was soon catching him up, but at the front of the church hall, the eleven year old boy leapt the small wall that formed the boundary with the pavement, and Simon followed. But he missed his footing, his feet slid back, but his momentum carried him onward, he was falling uncontrollably forward, too late to put his hands out he saw the pavement coming up to meet him, there was an explosion of white light in his head and -.

Daniel had come down from the office and gone out to join in the fun when several scouts came running up to him, all talking at once.

"Daniel, it's Simon ... Dead ... fallen over .. not breathing .. over the wall."

Daniel felt his heart go cold with fear. Not Simon. Please, no. But he must function.

"Michael, go and get Skip. Now! Right you lot, show me, quickly." He ran round after the scouts to the front of the church hall. A couple of scouts were standing there, including the new kid from Simon's patrol, he noted. But what he saw froze his heart. Simon was lying face on the ground and head down over the wall, his legs still sticking up in the air against the wall, arms crashed out at his side. There was blood pulsing from his forehead. At least that means his heart is beating, Daniel thought. He took command, as his three Troop Leader bars required.

"You and you, help me lift him. You take his legs, you, his body," he ordered. Daniel took Simon's shoulders and head himself and the three scouts, watched now by a gathering crowd, lifted Simon, turning him. "Lean him against the wall. Gently." Simon was carefully propped up against the wall, legs in front of him. Daniel used his hanky to wipe the blood away, and then kept pressure on the cut.

"Here, keep that pressed on firmly," he said to the new scout, whose uniform shirt pocket was still bereft of the coveted Tenderfoot badge.

"He's my PL," said the boy. Daniel didn't answer, he was too busy checking to see if Simon was breathing. With relief he felt Simon's breath. He looked under Simon's eyelids. His eyes were looking up and unseeing. Daniel felt a pang of strong emotion, grief, anxiety.

"Is he going to be all right?" asked a scout.

"Yes, of course he is," replied Daniel. "We'll sort him out OK."

When Daniel said something could be done, all the boys believed it. Simon of course knew that already and that was why he was Troop Leader.

Then Skip was there, next to Daniel. Discipline and training took over.

"Skip, there's a cut on the forehead that this scout is compressing, he's breathing and he's unconscious, his eyes are turned up a bit. He was upside down when I got here, but we sat him up."

"Any sign of him being sick?"

"No, Skip."

"Well done, Daniel. I think we should move him as little as possible." Skip carefully felt Simon's legs and arms. "Nothing seems broken, he's breathing OK. Will you stay with him? I need to phone an ambulance. Shout if anything changes, even the smallest thing. Any sign of retching, turn him."

"Yes Skip."

Skip left, leaving Daniel and the Scouts.

"I need a couple of you to wait with me, in case I need messengers," said Daniel.

"We'll wait," said a few voices, but all the Scouts stayed. Daniel now noticed that all the Harriers were there, with worried looks on their faces as they saw their unconscious Patrol Leader. They started to talk, later arrivals being updated by the others. Daniel sat next to Simon on the pavement, carefully putting his arm round him and putting his own head close to Simon's so he could detect his breathing by the slight movement of his chest. Daniel felt a pang of pain at the feel of Simon's completely inert body, almost dead instead of the fit, healthy boy he knew so well. The new boy was still holding the handkerchief.

"Here, let me," said Daniel, placing his hand on the hanky and carefully removing the pressure. The hanky was red with Simon's precious blood, but Daniel noticed that the bleeding was now just oozing lightly. He remembered his role.

"Well done," he said to the new scout. "You controlled the bleeding. What's your name again?"

"Arthur, sir .. I mean TL, er Daniel." He stuttered to a stop, pleasure at the compliment from his Troop Leader mixed with confusion as to how he should address such an important personage directly. One or two of the scouts laughed, but kindly.

"Carry on then, Arthur. Gentle but firm pressure. Find a clean part though."

Arthur refolded the hanky and carefully put it back on the cut. Daniel turned back to Simon's motionless body. He fought back tears. No way could he possibly allow tears in front of the Scouts. But the emotion must have shown.

"You OK, Daniel?" Daniel looked up. It was Colley. Daniel just nodded, not risking speech until he had control of his emotions.

"They're best friends out of Scouts," one of the Scouts was saying. And in Scouts too, thought Daniel. He looked, it was Neil Smith, Second of Kestrel Patrol. He lived at the end of Daniel's road. Daniel turned his attention back to Simon, holding his friend close, tenderly, probing with his finger past Simon's lips. Tongue still flat, airway clear.

Soon Skip came back. "Any change?"

"No Skip. Breathing and pulse still OK. No sign of consciousness though. No retching, mouth still clear."

"Good. An ambulance is coming, and I managed to get his mother on the phone. Good job they've got a phone."

Daniel nodded. "Have to send runners otherwise," he said, and then remembered Arthur. "Arthur's doing a grand job here, Skip. He'll do OK I think."

Arthur beamed with pleasure.

"Good lad, Arthur," said Skip.

"He's my PL, Skip," said Arthur, now emboldened.

"I know that," said Skip. "So now you can help look after him as he looks after you." Arthur nodded and focused on the hanky.

A clanging bell could be heard in the distance. It was coming closer. The ambulance swung round the corner and came to a halt by the group of Scouts, the bell stopped. The two crew got out. One came for Simon, the scouts parting to make way, falling back to allow room, the other went to the back of the ambulance, and started to pull out a stretcher. A couple of the scouts went to help.

"Simon!" There was an anguished shout. Looking up, Daniel saw that the Scotts' Austin Cambridge was now parked behind the ambulance. Again the scouts parted for Simon's mother.

"What happened?" she asked.

Skip answered. "It seems he missed his footing jumping over the wall and fell head first onto the path."

At that point Daniel felt Simon move.

"He's waking up, I think," Daniel announced, turning back to examine Simon's face. The ambulance man was crouching down, looking at Simon, Mrs Scott standing just behind.

"Daniel? Mum?" Simon's eyes slowly opened and focused. Relief swept through Daniel's body. He gently squeezed Simon.

"Are you all right, darling," said Mum.

"My head hurts," said Simon.

"What' your name, son?" asked the ambulance man.

"Simon, Simon Scott."

"Can you hear me OK? Both ears?"

"Yes."

"How old are you?"

"Thirteen."

"Where are you?"

"Scouts. We were playing a game and Arthur was in front of me and..." Simon became aware of Arthur, pressing the hanky onto his head. "Arthur, not so hard. It hurts. Is it bleeding?"

"A bit," said Daniel. Simon managed to look at Daniel without causing Arthur a problem. Daniel was there, cradling him, as always. And Mum was there. But the ambulance man was still speaking.

"What's the day?"

"Friday," said Simon, and then gathering that these questions were to test if his brain was still working, added "September 11th, 1959."

"Thank God," said Mum.

"Any bleeding from the nose or ears?" asked the ambulance man. He looked at Skip. Skip looked at Daniel.

"No, none," said Daniel decisively.

"Good. Can you stand up, Simon," asked the ambulance man.

"I think so," said Simon. Carefully, helped by Daniel and Skip, he stood up. Slowly he was walked round to the back of the ambulance, bypassing the maroon stretcher laid out on the pavement, with Arthur managing to keep station. Simon now too remembered his two Patrol Leader bars.

"Thanks Arthur. We'll have to do the sheepshank next week, I think."

Arthur grinned happily that his PL recognised his efforts and where he was up to with his Tenderfoot badge, and with relief that his PL was OK. He relinquished his first aid job to a lint pad provided by the ambulance man. Simon sat in the back while his forehead was dressed, Mum on one side, holding his hand, Daniel close by on the other.

"I think we need to take him to get checked over by the Casualty doctor," said the ambulance man to Mum. "Do you want to ride with him?" Mum hesitated for a second.

"I will, Mrs Scott, if you want to follow in the car," offered Daniel, sensing the reason for her hesitation. "If you will give us both a lift home later," he added with a grin. "That OK Skip?"

"Yes, fine, Daniel. I expect we'll manage without you," he said, tongue in cheek.

So the ambulance set off for casualty, Simon, Daniel and one of the crew in the back.

Simon called through to the driver, "What no bells?"

The crewman chuckled. "Not much wrong with you, son."

"Is there blood on my uniform?" asked Simon worried.

"Not a drop," said Daniel. "Blame Arthur."

Simon was taken down for X-ray and then there was a long wait before the doctor announced that Simon's skull was very thick and was not fractured. But because he had been unconscious for quite a long time, he was to be kept in, "for observation". Mum agreed.

"Always said you had a thick skull," said Daniel as they parted from Simon in his hospital borrowed pyjamas.

"You'll be OK. Don't be nuisance for the nurses, and I'll see you in the morning," said Mum, giving him a kiss on the unbandaged portion of his forehead.

"How will Daniel get home?" asked Simon.

"I'll take him in the car. He phoned home while you were in X-ray."

And they left with a wave. Simon spent the night in hospital, making friends with the other patients. Every so often a nurse would come and tap him to get a reflex reaction. They seemed happy. He was discharged the next day, and went home, but Mum made him stay in bed all weekend. Unfair! It would be the weekend. But Daniel came round and sat with him on Saturday after his swimming club, again on Sunday, and the two friends talked, Daniel making a rare visit to his friend's home. Simon went through everything that had happened, right up to when he hit the concrete.

"It felt like straight away when you and Mum were there, though," he said.

"It was a lot longer than that," said Daniel. "I was scared stiff you were going to die."

"Mum said Skip said you were fabulous. Did everything right."

"Did Skip say that? Cor!"

"I think I'll stay away from that wall in future," said Simon with feeling.

Daniel hugged Simon. "I would if I were you. You're such an idiot." They both laughed. Simon was happy.

40. 1959/11 A bogie wagon

When Simon was thirteen, he went one winter evening with his parents to a village near the city to visit friends. This was an ex RAF wartime friend of his father's, Wing Commander Bob O'Hanlon. He was still in the RAF. While the grown ups talked, Simon went with the four O'Hanlon sons, Matthew, Martin, Michael and Melvin - Simon was about the same age as their second son - across to a railway yard next to the station over the road from the house. There were heaps of coal and sidings with some trucks on them. This was a regular haunt for the O'Hanlon boys. As it got dark, they played in the railway yard with their torches lighting their way.

"Over here!" shouted Michael. He had found a flat top bogie wagon, the type one can make go using levers.

"Come on, lets have a ride," urged Martin. So the five boys jumped on board. It was heavy but together they had enough muscle power to get it moving. They played with this up and down the track a few times, but as they tired, they lost control of it. The siding was slightly higher than the main line that ran past and through the station. The bogie got past the tipping point and started to move downhill.

"Harder!" shouted Matthew, as the heavy wagon slipped out of their control. The boys all strained to control the wagon, but despite their efforts, it trundled down where it stopped as the points on the main line were set against it. There it remained, half overhanging the main Central line. They heard a bell from the signal box at the far end of the yard.

"Let's push it, " suggested Melvin, but it was a hopeless task. It was simply too heavy.

"What are we going to do?" asked Simon.

"You can do what you want, but we're not staying here," said Matthew. "Come on, we're off."

The brothers ran off, realising that this meant trouble, and Simon followed but then slowed. He could see that if a train hit the bogie in the dark, there would be a crash, possibly a high speed derailment (most trains sped straight through the village station) and injury or worse. Simon had the image of the giant steam locomotive, off the tracks hurtling into the trucks, pulling its coaches of people behind. Simon knew in his soul what he must do. Torn between fear of retribution and fear of disaster, he stood unmoving, unable to leave yet unable to do what had to be done. He needed courage. Then he tapped himself on the chest twice, and filled with sudden resolve, he ran along the yard to the signal box. He knew there would be a reckoning, but as often at such times, he felt himself simply to be an actor in his own life, watching from without.

He climbed the steps and could see through the door windows into the lit interior of the box where the signalman was drinking from an enamel mug, tea Simon assumed, and looking at a newspaper. Simon's courage started to fail him, so he tapped his chest twice and then the door twice. The signalman looked up, and seeing a teenage kid at the door, waved him away. Simon knocked again, harder. He was committed now. The signal man got up and opened the door.

"Go away, son," said the signalman. "You shouldn't be here."

"There's going to be an accident," said Simon. Something about his determined tenor and confident steadfastness struck a chord with the signalman.

"Come in, and tell me what it's about."

Simon went in and, heart in his mouth, told the signalman what had happened.

"Christ Almighty!" said the signalman. "The express!" He leapt across to the long row of levers and threw several of them, some points, some signals. Then he was on the phone, winding the handle and talking to someone. Bells were clanging in the signal box, and the signalman made some more ring. It was all pretty meaningless to Simon but the storm of frantic activity from the previous calm made him feel that he had done the right thing, whatever the consequences. At least there would be no train crash.

"You're a lucky lad," said the signalman after the storm subsided. "A few more minutes and there could have been a disaster. Now show me."

They walked quickly back along the yard to where the bogie wagon was stuck.

"Bloody kids! What the hell did you think you were playing at? This isn't a bloody playground."

Simon said nothing. What could he say?

"Come on, back to the box. You're staying with me."

Simon followed him back to the signal box. As they did a police car came into the yard, and his heart sank.

Of course the police came to the house too and the four boys got a beating from their father. Simon was terrified that he would too, but instead, all he got was a severe telling off. Looking back, perhaps there was a little parental pride that Simon had gone to the signal box and had averted a possible tragedy.

41. 1960/3 *New decade*

The first Spring of a new decade went well for Simon. He was doing well in the top stream at Hooray Henrys, but never matching Daniel's record, who was never lower than third and very often top in his class. It was, as ever, his Maths that held him back.

Then there was King Henry's attempt at sex education. Daniel had warned Simon about this, saying it was pretty useless, and saying that perhaps he and Simon should run the class. To Simon's shocked look, he added hastily he was only joking.

The sessions were taken by the Divinity teacher, nicknamed 'God's Partner' probably from his surname Pardiner, and seemed centred round establishing marriage as the one and only situation where sex could legitimately take place. Mr Pardiner stumbled along until one day when he was talking incomprehensibly to the class of boys about God's purpose for seed, abuse of the body and the sin of wastage. The class of boys looked at each other, puzzled, the unspoken question, "What's he on about?".

Then Thomas English from the back of the class saw the light.

"Oh, sir. You mean wanking!" he blurted out before he could stop himself. Laughter and uproar ensued, bringing the lesson, and the only formal sex education Simon was ever to receive, to an abrupt end. Mr Pardiner stuck to Divinity after that. Thomas English became a hero for a while, and when he was told about it Daniel thought it was hilarious. He said it just showed how little they really understood their teenage pupils.

Simon's self esteem was boosted by the regard his own scout patrol seemed to have for him. He would spent summer weekends and holidays off on day hikes with them in the Midlands shire countryside, cooking over an open fire. Simon had developed a method of cooking the sausages by setting fire to the fat in the billy can! They cooked quickly and evenly! They made 'dampers' and 'twisters', flour and water baked in front of the campfire, and simply had fun. The other scouts were always wanting to go again. Arthur now regarded Simon as a firm friend, he had completed his tenderfoot and was working hard for the second class badge. And he had done the first aid badge! Sometimes, but not always, Daniel would also come along on these hikes. Daniel did not want to upstage Simon, such as one day when Simon asked Daniel to come on a Harriers Patrol hike.

"I'm going to see my Grandma," said Daniel. "And anyway, I shouldn't come really. I'm not Harriers' PL anymore."

"But you're Troop Leader."

"Which means I can't favour one patrol, even my old one. And they have to see you as Patrol Leader, capable of commanding them without me there."

"They do, I'm sure of it. They think I'm good for persuading you to come along. But you know I've taken them out lots of times without you."

"And that's good, but me being there should be the exception."

"When they call round, whose house do they come to now? They don't call at yours anymore, they come to mine."

"Which proves what I said. They look to you now, and I don't want to spoil that for you. It's your hike, and if I'm there, there just might be doubt in their minds about who is in charge. I do outrank you, remember," he ended, smiling at Simon to draw any sting from that last part. Not that it was needed, their mutual trust and closeness ensured it was simply a statement of fact to help the argument.

"Don't you like coming along, then?" persisted Simon.

"Of course I do. I love it, but yours are the only ones I've been on, and if I keep coming on Harriers' hikes, I'll have to go with other patrols as well, and there's not the time."

"Other patrols don't do their own hikes at weekends," said Simon.

"Maybe not. Well, Eagles did last year but they got washed out. But suppose they did? You'll find out what it's like when you're Troop Leader."

"Me?"

"Of course. You'll be Troop Leader after me. And then you'll have to take all the patrols on hikes," laughed Daniel.

"OK, I give in," said Simon, and then grabbed Daniel and wrestled him to the ground, the fun fight resolving any tension from their discussion. Daniel won of course, as usual. Simon liked it that Daniel played it straight and never let him win on purpose. He knew that Daniel recognised that it would be demeaning for Simon to be allowed a victory and it would render meaningless those times when Simon did actually manage to better Daniel.

A wet weekday summer afternoon, and the boys retired to Daniel's bedroom to quench their needs together. Daniel tenderly running his hands across Simon's willing body, kissing and stimulating, gently entering. Simon welcoming Daniel, his arousal rising rapidly with Daniel's action. Simon was then unaware of the erogenous nature of the prostate but was highly responsive to its effects as together they reached climax, holding close, the fire sweeping through their young bodies, uniting them in unspoken love.

Their lovemaking completed, they lay as one on the bed talking. The conversation covered scouts, school and Francis Chichester's solo Atlantic crossing among other things.

Then Simon asked, "Do you ever think about girls?"

"Yes, sometimes, do you?"

"Sometimes, yes."

"Any girl in particular?" asked Daniel, curious about what had prompted this at this moment as they cuddled naked on the bed.

"No, it's just a sort of general feeling. What about you?"

"Same really. Well, there is one girl, Janice, at the swimming club. She's nice and I talk to her sometimes."

"Is she good looking?"

"I suppose so. She's got short brown hair and brown eyes, and she's really fit. One thing about swimming is you can get a better idea of a girl's figure."

Simon grinned. "So you fancy her, then?"

"Sort of," said Daniel, uneasy about being put on the spot. "But I've got my GCEs to think about this next year and I'm going to get all A grades, so I can't afford to start thinking more about that. And anyway, I've got you."

That raised a spectre in Simon's mind. "But after that? I mean if you start going out with her later on, what about us?"

Simon's apprehensive tone registered with Daniel. "Simon, nothing could affect us, I promise. You're such an idiot."

"You always say that. Do you really think I'm an idiot?"

Daniel looked shocked. "No, absolutely not. If you really were an idiot, I would never hurt you by saying it. I mean, look at some of the scouts. Not all the brightest penny in the shilling, but they are all scouts, they try their best. I try to help them, not show them up."

"Yes, you're good at that. No wonder they all think you're fantastic. I do too. So you like being my friend?"

"Of course I do, Simon, more than anything. Remember something else, too. I know the patrol think you're fantastic. You're a better PL than I was, you do loads more for them. I'm proud to be your friend. You're my best friend."

"I sometimes think I'm not as good as you."

"Why d'you say that? Course you are. They think you are. Remember, you are what other kids say you are. You're fun to be with, you make me laugh more than anyone I know, you're clever – "

"Not as clever as you."

"Oh stop it. I bet you are, just a couple of years younger, that's all. I wish I had your way with words, you're brilliant there. I once told you that you gave me my strength, remember? That's still true. You're so good for me. And you would never let me down, I know that. It's really good having a friend like you, that I know would stand by me whatever."

"Well, you would me, I know that, too."

"That's coz we're friends. And we know each other so well, in **every** way," Daniel smiled, taking intimate hold of Simon to make the point. "I know I can talk to you about anything, anything at all," he continued. "You know me better than anyone else, even Dad and Mum. I love that about you."

"I love that about you, too. It's not just sex," said Simon.

"Of course not. Although that's really good too. Having a friend I can trust enough to have sex with and be completely relaxed with is just super. I love it that you know me in every possible way. Don't you?"

"Yes, you're right," said Simon. "I feel just like that too."

"So don't ask if I like being your friend again. Idiot!" he laughed, punching Simon playfully. Simon punched back and their fun fight on the bed released the tension and emotion of their talk, reawakening their arousal.

The summer passed with the friends spending much time together. Daniel did accompany Harriers Patrol on one hike, but Simon led the remainder himself. They were apart as always for the middle two weeks of August, with the Scott family making the annual trip to Salcombe. Simon renewed his friendship with Jack Griffin and his role as ferryman for the group of families using the inboard motor boat *Invention*. Once more, away from the pressures and possibly temptations at home, Simon's parents did not argue and one could perhaps see why they had got married in 1940. Frances was involved with sailing and spent time with her friends who again were racing the National 12 foot. Simon was happy, his role with *Invention* providing him with a pivotal role in the group's affairs. He and Jack spent time together, but Simon sometimes missed Daniel, perhaps this year more than before. Jack was a great pal, but just that; there was not the closeness there was with Daniel. But this did not spoil Simon's happiness, and he knew that he would see Daniel again soon.

As always, once back in the tempest that often was his home life, Simon made the countdown calendar to mark off the three hundred and fifty days until the next holiday to Salcombe. And he and Daniel would pick up where they left off, talking about their holidays.

In the new term it was Simon's turn to be a hero. He had been selected to represent the school's athletics club in the 100 yards at the Midland Counties meeting in September. This really marked the climax of the season. Daniel had Simon running and working out in their homemade fitness room, in other words Daniel's room, as well as working on the all important start. The benefits from this training were already evident in his selection, but Simon was determined to make the most of this opportunity and he was strengthened by Daniel's unwavering support.

"Thanks for helping me, Daniel," said Simon, as he sat on the floor after doing press ups.

"You support me at swimming," countered Daniel.

"But you come running with me, and I don't go swimming with you."

Daniel smiled. "I seem to remember we tried that once before. I think you're better on dry land."

Simon grinned ruefully back, remembering that day at the lido. "OK. But I must do my best ever time for this. All the top kids will be there. And some of them will be almost a year older than me. I hate being young in my year."

"You're as good as any of them," said Daniel, encouragingly.

"There's a kid my age group in Sussex who's done a hundred yards in ten and a half seconds. Must have very long legs."

"Well, let's hope he and his long legs stay in Sussex then. Right! I want to see those stomach muscles working. Sit ups!"

Simon obediently commenced sit ups.

On the Saturday of the meeting, they travelled in Mum's old little Ford she had bought to help her travel for work. Mum was driving, but Simon chose to sit in the back next to Daniel, rather than be separate. He felt nervous and wanted the support that Daniel's proximity gave him. On arrival, he had to find the others of his team and Mr Atherstone.

"Don't look for us, we'll be watching, remember, concentrate!" urged Daniel.

Mum gave Simon a hug. "Good luck, son. Just do your best."

Simon left to find his team and then the long wait until his event, under fifteens 100 yards. Check kit, get changed. Luckily the weather was fine but not too hot, especially as there was little wind.

When it came time to go out and line up for his heat he looked into the crowd but could not find Mum or Daniel. So stop looking and concentrate. He looked at his competitors. They all looked so confident and fit. One or two familiar faces from previous meetings, but nobody he really knew. He nodded to them, they nodded back, each boy concentrating on the inner person. Simon saw a tall fair boy in the colours of a club unknown to him watching him. He looked familiar, perhaps from a previous meeting. Loosening up, moving around. Keep loose. Not the time to talk.

Line up. Lane but one furthest from the crowd. Good. He glanced sideways. The tall fair boy in the next but one lane was still looking at him. Simon felt uneasy. The boy smirked at Simon. Barry Spence! Christ! Simon looked away quickly. Stay focused. His heart was racing with the shock. Simon looked down the lane at the finish exactly a hundred yards away. Focus on that.

"Set!"

Simons hands lay exactly along the line. All else blotted out now, waiting for the gun.

Crack! And Simon went. He knew immediately it was an excellent start. His heart pounding, his legs driving him forward, Simon felt on top form, no sign of running out, aware of a boy on his left, but just behind. The crowd cheering something. Simon crossed the line first! He had won his heat and would be in the final later. Now he looked for Mum and Daniel, and still could not see them, but he knew they would have been cheering. They had been cheering his race of course. Simon noticed with satisfaction that Barry Spence had not qualified, and now he could not see him. Good.

"Well done, Scott. Brilliant run," said Mr Atherstone. "Get a drink, but not too much. Do you know that was equal to your previous best?"

Simon drank some Lucozade. "No sir. That's good though isn't it. I'd love to crack that eleven second barrier though. So near, again."

"Don't worry too much about times, it's the race that's important. Now Scott, next time you are up against the very best, King Henrys is relying on you to produce your best, and I know you can. So now rest a bit, but do your stretches and keep loose."

Again Simon had to wait.

"Good run, Scott," said some of the other boys. One asked, "Tell me where you get the invisible wings from. You were flying!"

Time for the 100 yards under fifteens final. Simon felt confident. He could do this. He had flown in his heat, his body had recovered, he was ready! No Spence this time. Up to the line, under starter's orders. He glanced into the crowd, straight into Daniel's face. **There** he was. Simon felt his already buoyant confidence soar. But now focus.

"Set!"

Simon was totally focused on the gun. So much so that when the line moved for a false start before the gun had even gone off, he was the only one that didn't move, so much had he cut out the others. He didn't know or care who had moved first. They moved about to reduce the tension. Daniel was still there. Now he saw Mum too. Then they lined up again.

"Set!"

Simon was calm, confident.

Crack! Simon again knew at once he had made the perfect start. He was flying and he knew it. Oblivious to the crowd's noise he put all his might, all his effort, all that training into running the race of his young life. He felt as if he could keep running forever but it was he who burst the tape to win the final. He had done it! He slowed and felt the others come in behind him, some patting his shoulder and saying words of congratulations between their panting. Simon could not find the breath to reply as he sucked in the oxygen.

He heard the Tannoy announcing the results. "The winner of the under fifteen one hundred yards is Simon Scott of King Henry VII Grammar School Athletics Club in 10.9 seconds, a new under fifteens county record!"

Simon gasped. He had done it. He had broken the eleven second barrier. Sussex watch out! People were suddenly round him congratulating him. He was King of the World!

"Scott, that was fantastic!" said Mr Atherstone. "Henrys will be very proud of you."

"Thank you, sir."

"No more for you today, go and shower and change. I've still got Tomkinson in the 800 to see to yet. Well done."

Mum and Daniel were by the changing rooms. "Well done, Simon," said Mum, hugging him, against Simon's will as there were other kids about.

"You were simply super," said Daniel. Simon just grinned back. He was on top of the world, as he was later at the presentations which closed the meeting.

On the way home in the back of the car, the boys talked.

"You saw him, didn't you?" said Daniel.

"Spence?"

"Yeah. I saw him watching you for a while before you noticed him. It took me a time to remember who it was, then it came to me. I was hoping you wouldn't recognise him."

"Nearly didn't," said Simon. "I only realised who it was when he gave me that evil, cocky grin of his. Upset me a bit."

"Who's Spence?" asked Mum from the driving seat.

"Just a stupid kid we knew at the juniors," said Simon.

"Well, it didn't show, you upset, I mean," said Daniel. "Anyway you left him standing. Serves him right. And I thought it was brilliant when you were the only one who didn't move on the false start."

King Henrys always made a fuss about sports, and rewarded successful sportsmen with a ritual standing ovation in assembly. Daniel had received it once for swimming, mainly because he had chosen to stay with his swimming club rather than compete all the time for Hooray Henrys. And of course he played the piano in school concerts, Rachmaninoff a favourite. Simon had never dreamt that he, the clumsy kid who couldn't catch a ball, would ever be on the stage in the great panelled hall receiving the plaudits of the entire school, from the new fags up to the Prefects, and teachers. It felt wonderful!

The two continued to do their homework together, usually straight after school at Daniel's house. Now that Louise was working and at college, and Simon's mother was, and Frances now working, both boys were 'latch key kids', coming back to empty houses. But they both went to Daniel's, which they both preferred. Daniel rarely visited Simon's house. They both knew why, but neither said it. It had always been so. Knowing they had perhaps an hour and a half before they would be interrupted, they would release the stress of the day in the big bed. Pressed close against each other, stroking, kissing, legs entwined, hands caressing the other's admired body, often just that closeness and sensuality would be enough for one to reach orgasm, causing the other to follow rapidly, sometimes achieving this together, their teenage bodies pulsing with desire. Sometimes they would slake their passion for each other in the union of their bodies, Simon happy in his role as catamite to Daniel, Ganymedes to his Zeus, and then they would relax in each other's arms, talking before getting dressed again. The hungry teenage boys would often then descend to the kitchen where Daniel would make bacon sandwiches.

"Do you want me to help?" offered Simon.

"Not likely!" said Daniel. "You set the whole pan on fire."

"That's for sausages and out of doors," argued Simon, knowing full well that Daniel knew that too. So he would watch while Daniel flipped the bacon over with the casual competence about him that Simon envied. Then back to the room for food and homework. In the run up to GCEs, Daniel worked with a fierce intensity that Simon could only wonder at, the piano being his counterbalancing outlet, the Rachmaninoff *Prelude in C Sharp Minor Opus 3 No.2* a favourite for permitting his pent up energy to be spent, especially when his mood matched it. And yet he never refused to help Simon if he needed it, especially with Mathematics.

Simon glanced over to Daniel's work, curious about the equations he was working on.

"What's that lot?"

"I'm writing up a physics experiment," said Daniel.

"Which one?"

"To test Boyle's Law, it's about gases."

"What about them?"

"Well, at a given temperature, the absolute pressure and the volume of a gas are inversely proportional. In a closed system of course. We can use it to predict the changes in either the pressure of a gas if the volume changes, or the volume if the pressure changes. You see, the equation ..."

"OK, stop there! Why would we need to?"

"If you're a scientist, working on pressures, or maybe you work for the gas board and are installing new pipes, or something like that," said Daniel.

"OK, I believe you. I can see that, I mean how the pressure and volume have a relationship, it's just the maths that gets me, as always. I like physics until the maths starts."

"Can't be good at everything."

"You are," said Simon. "But perhaps I can interest you in the causes of the French Revolution?" he added with a smile.

"Would that be an increasing middle class who were excluded by the privilege of the nobility from any power," started Daniel, grinning, "coupled with France's inability to feed the poor despite having a large agricultural economy? And then there's the ..."

"Daniel Gray, there are times when I hate you," laughed Simon, bringing Daniel's historical discourse to a halt with a thump. "But what about the massive government debt? And the King's support for the American Revolutionaries which made it worse, the rise in anti-clericalism as a reaction to the church's opulence and its taxes on agriculture which made the price of bread even higher, and..."

"OK, OK," said Daniel. "I know you know much more about history than I do. That's why I pick your brains on history as well as English and things like that."

So Simon was able to repay the favour sometimes, helping with English essays, and in history, where Simon's extra reading often covered areas that he would study in the future and that Daniel was studying now. He would throw ideas at Daniel about history who would eagerly take every morsel Simon could give. So there was reciprocity and balance in their friendship which made it grow even deeper and stronger.

When they had finished, Daniel said, "Come down and listen to my new piece I'm working on."

So they went down to the back room where the Bösendorfer piano awaited them.

"More Rachmaninoff?" asked Simon, while Daniel looked for the music.

"No, Beethoven. Sonata number eight, the Pathetique."

"Why's it called the Pathetique?" asked Simon.

"Never mind. Sit there and turn when I say."

Daniel started to play. Simon recognised the tune but wisely kept silent, aware of the look of intense concentration on Daniel's face. It seemed a hard piece and Daniel frowned once or twice, but to Simon it was an excellent performance.

Daniel stopped, and turned to Simon, seeking his approval. "That's just the first part. What do you think?" he asked anxiously. He really cared what Simon thought.

"Brilliant, as always," said Simon. He looked at his friend in admiration and love, although he would never have expressed it as such.

Peter and Simon were lying on the grass of the school field on a warm autumn day. Fourth years now, around whom the younger boys trod warily. As they themselves did of the prefects, sixth formers and fifth formers, bar one in Simon's case. Both boys were now stars in the eyes of the other boys, Simon for his record run, Peter had found a niche in the school's drama club and had taken to acting like a duck to water. He now wanted this to be his career.

"You've always been a such a pal to me, Simon," said Peter. Simon looked at his friend, aware that something was troubling him. He wasn't the usual chirpy Peter.

"Well, you have been to me."

"You're my best friend, Simon."

Simon felt a little guilty about that. How could he respond in kind? He liked Peter, always had, but he was not Simon's number one. He knew little of Peter's life out of school. He was saved when Peter continued, "Oh, I know Gray's your best friend, always has been, I know that. But you do like me, don't you?"

"Yes of course I do, Peter," said Simon, relieved at not having either to lie or let Peter down. "What's the matter? You don't seem right lately."

"If I tell you something, promise you won't tell anyone? Anyone at all."

"Yes, OK."

"No, I really mean it. I just know I can talk to you, you're the sort of person people can talk to. But you have to promise."

"I promise. What is it?" said Simon, curious yet concerned at Peter's evident upset.

"Not even Gray. In fact, especially not Daniel Gray."

"Why especially? He's very understanding too, you know."

"Not about this. Promise. Not even Daniel Gray."

"OK, Peter. I promise. Not a soul, not even Daniel."

"Good. Thank you." Peter fell silent.

"Well?"

"It's difficult. I **more** than like you, Simon. You understand?" He reached out and placed his hand on Simon's upper thigh. As close as he dared? But his face said it all.

Now Simon understood perfectly. "You mean sex? You want to have sex with me?"

Peter nodded, he was close to tears. What could Simon say? He'd had no idea. He knew though that he must not reveal his true friendship with Daniel. He played a straight bat.

"Peter, are you telling me that you're a queer?" he said in as sympathetic a tone as he could manage.

"Yes, I had to tell someone, and you're the one. I've liked you that way for ages. I see you when we're in the showers and it makes me ... well, you know. Please don't be angry. I would hate that." He withdrew his hand.

"I'm not angry, Peter. Just surprised. I had no idea you were like that, or that you felt that way about me." At least that part was true.

"I know you're not one, Simon, but can we still be friends? Please? I haven't spoilt it have I? It's just I had to say. It's been burning me up for ages."

Poor kid, thought Simon. Would I be in that hidden anguish were it not for Daniel?

"Of course we're still friends. Just like we always have been. I'm not going to drop you because of that. You're still the Peter I've known for years." He reached out and patted Peter's shoulder.

Peter's face was one of sheer relief and pleasure. "Thank you Simon. I knew in my heart that you'd be OK. I couldn't keep it bottled up any longer. I've been wanting to tell you for ages."

"Honestly, Peter, it's fine," said Simon. He looked at Peter anew, and briefly wondered what sex with him would be like. But no, put that out of your mind. "Why were you so worried about Daniel?"

"Daniel Gray! Are you joking? You know him. A homo is the last thing he is. He's good at sports, music, dead brainy and all that, like you. I can see why you're friends. But please don't tell. You promised."

"OK, I promised. I'll keep my promise. But he's a very kind person, and he would not condemn you. He's not a bigot like so many of them here."

"Bigot?" muttered Peter. "Oh yes, bigot. I know what you mean. So we're friends still?"

"Of course, Peter. We always have been, always will be. Don't worry, your secret's safe."

"I know you're friends with Gray, so maybe I shouldn't say this," said Peter.

"What?" said Simon, suddenly anxious.

"Well, as I seem to be telling you everything, it's just about Daniel Gray."

Simon's head was spinning. Was there something about Daniel that despite their closeness, he didn't know? Hideous doubt crept into Simon's mind.

"What, Peter?" he said, his impatience showing.

"Well, some of the boys say he's ..." Peter's voice tailed off.

What was he going to say? That they thought Daniel was queer, a homo? He felt panic. Had they been found out?

"Peter, what is it?" he demanded.

"Well, they say he's a bit too big for his boots, big headed sometimes. But they might not say that to you coz you're his friend."

Relief surged through Simon. "Is that all, Peter?" he said, relaxing. "I wondered what the hell you were going to say. Like he was a murderer or something."

"Did you know?"

"Don't worry, Peter. I can see how he comes across that way, and yes, he is a little bit sometimes. I tell him off for it."

"So you don't mind me telling you?"

"Of course not."

"And you really won't tell him what I've just told you? About me, I mean."

"No, Peter, I won't. I promised, didn't I?"

Simon kept his promise. He and Peter talked more about it, Peter happy to have someone he could trust and be open with. Simon knew how that felt and was happy for Peter, and knowing how Peter felt about him, being attracted to him, made him feel flattered. Daniel was never told, even though Simon knew he could be trusted. He had promised Peter.

As the nights drew in and it got cooler, the pressure of school work mounted and the scout hikes stopped. Scout activities became more indoor oriented, concentrating on badge work for Simon, as well as helping his patrol with their mainstream work, another new tenderfoot and the second class course for most. Gareth was a good Second and almost had his First Class. Definitely a future Patrol Leader. Daniel had his eye on him for promotion. Scout nights often ended with games such as British Bulldog or Hot Rice, and then perhaps camp fire songs such as *Coming Round the Mountain* and *Quartermaster's*

Stores and of course the Scout 'anthem' Ralph Reader's *Riding Along on the Crest of a Wave.*

"*We're riding along on the crest of a wave, and the sun is in the sky.*
All of our eyes on the distant horizon,
Look out for passers by.
We'll do the hailing,
When all the ships are round us sailing,
We're riding along on the crest of a wave,
And the world is ours!"

One evening Daniel said, "Who knows *Fire Down Below*?"

Simon looked across at Daniel, startled. Daniel refused to make eye contact but was aware of Simon, a slight smile playing round his lips. Simon knew he was being privately teased, in public! About half the boys put up their hands.

"We did that one at school," said one and others nodded.

"Right," said Daniel. "I'll start, you all join in and the ones that don't know it, join in the chorus."

Daniel launched into the sea shanty, with the boys joining in. Their raucous singing of that song took Simon by surprise and for a moment he didn't sing. Then Daniel caught his eye, smiled through his singing and gave him a wink. Simon grinned back and joined in as loudly as any other.

When the shanty ended, Daniel held up his hand, and the troop fell silent. Daniel gestured they get up, and the scouts got to their feet, all eyes on their Troop Leader.

"Troop! 'Shun!" commanded Daniel.

Thirty-seven boys came to attention and waited. All that could be heard was the breathing after the singing and quick standing and coming to attention. Simon knew that this was a way Daniel had of allowing the boys' exuberance to ebb, to calm the troop down before the prayers that would close the meeting.

"Simon, tell Skip we're ready," ordered Daniel.

Obediently Simon stepped out from his Patrol's line and up the steps to Skip's little office.

"Troop! At ease!" Daniel barked. The scouts placed their feet apart and their hands behind their backs, right hand in left, thumbs crossed as Daniel had taught them.

Skip came out of the office just as Simon appeared through the glass.

"Thank you, Simon," said Skip, and followed him down the steps. When Skip entered the circle of boys next to Daniel, the Troop Leader again brought the troop smartly to attention.

"Troop! 'Shun!" commanded Daniel. Turning to Skip and saluting, "Troop ready, Skip."

"Thank you Daniel," said Skip.

"Troop, stand at ease. Stand easy," said Skip. The scouts stood relaxed as the notices and reminders were given out and with the prayers, another scout night was ended.

42. 1960/10 Separation

Simon woke up. Something was wrong. He switched on his bedside lamp and looked at his watch, it was just after midnight. Then he heard what had woken him It was Mum in the bedroom next door, arguing with Dad. With mounting horror, he realised what was going on.

"No, Harry, not now. I don't want it."

Then Dad's voice, but lower, the words indistinct. But Simon could hear the bed creaking.

"Get off me, you brute!" shouted Mum. But the steady hammering of the bed could still be heard. Simon's heart was pounding, he felt sick, frightened, angry, powerless. He lay there, listening to his father forcing himself on his mother in the next bedroom.

"Oh God!" he heard Mum cry. But his mother's protests went unheeded and Simon was overwhelmed with helplessness because he could not, dare not, intervene. He wanted to cover his ears but yet was compelled to listen, to share Mum's suffering. At last the hideous creaking stopped. There was silence, broken only by the sound of Mum crying through the wall. Simon turned out his light and lay in bed, weeping through that October night.

In the morning, Dad was not at breakfast.

"Where's Dad?" asked Frances.

"He's left already, early this morning," said Mum, subdued. Simon looked at Frances. Had she slept through it? In which case, how did he tell her? She seemed not to notice Mum's quiet manner that morning. Outwardly, all seemed relatively normal, but Simon knew the truth. Alone with Mum for a moment, he asked, "Mum?"

"Yes, Simon."

"Are you all right?"

"Yes of course, darling," Mum replied, forcing a smile. Simon knew then that she would not confide in her fourteen year old son. How could he say it? What could he say? And what difference would it make if he did? Simon saw that revealing his knowledge would only upset her further. Mum was trying to protect him.

He put on his green blazer and his coat. It was cool outside, but not cold.

"See you tonight, Mum."

"Yes love, have a good day."

"I love you, Mum."

"And I love you too, Simon. Never doubt that," Mum said giving him a hug. Simon, now taller than Mum, hugged her back. He turned and went out before the tears he felt would show.

He waited at the corner. Daniel appeared, carrying his heavy satchel. This was his GCE year and he seemed to have more books than ever.

"Hi Simon," he said.

On seeing Daniel, Simon could contain himself no longer. On the corner he burst out in tears, sobbing, unable to speak.

"What's the matter? What's wrong? They been arguing again?"

"Worse, far worse," sobbed Simon. "I can't go to school today, I just can't."

"You'll get detention or even worse if you don't," said Daniel.

"I don't fucking care," snapped Simon, angrily. Seeing Daniel's hurt expression, "I'm sorry, Daniel. It's not your fault. Can I tell you about it?"

"You can tell me anything, you know that," said Daniel gently. Simon knew he could. But not here, on the corner. Daniel continued, "Get through the day, we'll talk tonight. We have to get the bus now."

Simon knew the sense of what Daniel said, with the wisdom of his sixteen years. Comforted by Daniel's support, he walked down with him and got the bus to school. How Simon got through that day, he could never remember. It was a blur. Peter knew there was something wrong, but Simon could not tell Peter. Not even Peter who had trusted him with his darkest secret.

At home time, Simon was walking down the school drive to the gates past the field. Peter was with him, but in response to Simon's downcast mood, uncharacteristically quiet.

Then Daniel was beside them. "Sorry, Peter. I'm taking him now." Without waiting for Peter's reply, Daniel took Simon's arm and steered him away. "Come on, I'm with you now," he said to Simon, ignoring Peter's puzzled look.

They spoke little on the bus, and walking up the hill, Daniel said, "Come straight to mine. We can talk there."

Simon nodded. Daniel let himself in, and Simon followed. They hung up their coats. The house was quiet.

"Must check the Aga," said Daniel. Simon waited. Daniel led the way to his room. He hung up his blazer, Simon put his over Daniel's chair and stood, feeling helpless, not knowing where to begin

Daniel sat on the bed. "Come on, sit with me."

Simon sat next to Daniel. "I don't know how to say it."

"Just say what's wrong. What happened? Something last night? You seemed OK when you left here."

Simon nodded.

"So? Something about your Mum and Dad? You can tell me, but only if you want to."

"I want to, it's just I don't know how to."

"Simon, we've known other each practically all our lives. We've no secrets, none at all. We trust each other, don't we." A statement, not a question.

Simon nodded again and slowly the painful events of the previous night came out. Daniel listened, stony faced, horrified by what he heard. Simon's anguish and fear manifested as he collapsed in sobs at the end, relief at having someone in whom to confide. His true friend, Daniel. In tears himself now, Daniel took Simon into his arms and rested his head on his shoulder and just held him tight, allowing the tears to flow. Daniel was outraged, and felt the same protective care he had always felt for Simon, his closest friend, his lover. But he knew he could not change what had happened and was angry at his own impotence in this matter. But the important thing now was Simon.

"I'm so sorry, Simon. What can I say? What can I do?"

"Just be there. Please?"

"Always. You know that."

"Sex with a woman isn't supposed to be like that, is it, Daniel?"

"Well, *I* don't think so. I'm sorry, Simon, I know it's your parents, but it sounds wrong to me."

"Me too," said Simon, sadly. "It's not like that with us, is it?"

"Of course not," replied Daniel. A ghastly thought came into Daniel's mind. "Simon, tell me honestly. You've never done anything with me you didn't want to, have you? I mean, tell me now if you've ever felt forced at all."

"No, Daniel. Never. You would never do that anyway. You're just not like that."

"Thanks, Simon. I couldn't bear it if I thought I'd done that."

"I never want to do that!" said Simon with feeling.

"Do what?"

"Do that, to a girl. It's horrible."

"Like that, yes," said Daniel, all concern. "But it doesn't have to be like that. I do it to you, after all."

"Yes, but that's different. That's you, and you're .... I love it when you're in me, you're just special, that's all." Simon felt the emotion of his feelings for Daniel welling up inside him. Daniel saw this and his own emotions, his love for Simon, seeing his lover's distress, overtook him and he shed a tear.

"Simon, trust me, you'll feel differently when you're older."

Simon nodded again against Daniel's shirt, damp with his tears, wiping his eyes. "I do trust you, you know that. I'll never have a better friend than you, Daniel."

"Same here, Simon, same here."

Back home, Mum simply said over tea that Dad would not be home for a while. This came as no real surprise to either Simon or Frances. They just accepted it and resumed life in as normal a way as possible.

A few days later, Simon was in bed late at night but not asleep. He heard the front door open and voices in the hallway. Mum and Dad! He got out of bed and went onto the landing, to find Frances arriving there too.

"Dad?" she said.

Mum and Dad looked up to see the faces of their two children peering over the banister rail.

"It's all right," said Mum. "Dad and I have some talking to do."

"I'll come up and see you soon," said Dad. To Simon, Dad seemed sad and drawn. The brother and sister exchanged glances as Mum and Dad went into the sitting room.

"Is Dad coming home again?" asked Simon.

"No," said Frances. "I don't want you to get upset, Simon, but I think they're talking about getting a divorce. It's not been right between them for years, has it?"

Simon shook his head. "What will happen?"

"I don't know. We'll have to wait and see. But we'll be together, won't we?"

Simon looked at his big sister. Frances had always been there, taken for granted perhaps. The age and gender difference combined meant that they had not been playmates. But Simon knew that he could count on her.

She in turn looked at her younger brother. She knew so much more than she could tell him, yet anyway. She had tried to protect him from so much. She knew of Mum's wartime misery, of her younger baby sister that died (accounting in part for the big age gap between herself and Simon), of how Mum had gone to the church, the Mothers Union, for help and been rejected because she had married a divorced man. Mum had been left to bear that grief alone with a young daughter to care for in the dark days in the middle of the war. And later of Simon's own harrowing birth just after the war, how Mum had nearly died in childbirth and Simon, born blue, had been labelled subnormal, retarded, mentally deficient, and of Dad's deep disappointment that his first and only son was not what he had hoped for. The rift had opened then and had simply got wider. But she could not tell him these things. Not now. If ever.

"I'm going back to bed," said Simon.

He lay in bed, his room being over the sitting room, he could hear the low voices of Mum and Dad talking. They weren't arguing, that was one thing. But the tones weren't happy ones either. There was no laughter or joking, as there sometimes once had been. Then the sitting room door opened and Dad's footsteps were coming up the stairs. Simon looked at his watch. Ten past midnight. Dad went along the landing to see Frances. Simon heard them talking for a while, Dad and his now grown up princess. Once or twice he thought he heard his name. Her bedroom door opened.

"Good night, darling," Dad said.

"Night, Dad," said Frances.

Then a knock on Simon's half open door. A knock!

"Dad?" said Simon, sitting up in bed.

Dad came in. He sat on the end of the bed. Simon waited. Dad seemed so quiet, miserable even.

"I've just come to say, Simon, how much you mean to me, son. I want you to know that whatever happens, it's not your fault, or Mummy's. Everything that might happen now is my fault, old son. Do you understand that?"

Simon simply nodded, wondering what all this meant. He looked at this man almost apologising to his son, a man who should have been a tower of strength to him, a model to emulate but who instead had been inconsistent, capricious, feared. Simon felt anger and resentment amid his uncertainty, and yet this was his Dad. He didn't want to lose him.

"Are you and Mum getting divorced?"

"Yes, I think so," said Dad. "But you must remember that as far as you and Frances are concerned, we will always be your father and mother. Mummy and I are completely agreed about that. We both want the best for the pair of you. Of course Frances is a lot older, almost grown up, but we still need to take care of you, Simon."

Simon said nothing, unsure, confused, frightened by the now uncertain future. He was aware that his world was changing. The stability of his life was breaking apart.

Dad said, "I'm sorry, Simon. I may not be with you, but Mummy and I will always love you and take care of you."

Simon nodded, not knowing what to say. He felt a leaden weight in his heart.

"I have to go now, son. It's very late." Dad leaned and kissed Simon on his forehead, and then got up and went to the door.

"Dad."

"Yes, Simon?"

"I love you, Dad."

"I love you too, son. Remember that." And then he was gone. There were voices in the hall and the front door. Simon heard the Austin start up, and leave the quiet road. It was nearly one o'clock.

"They're getting a divorce." Simon was in Daniel's bedroom after school recounting the nocturnal visit and voicing his fears for the future.

"So your Dad's left for good then?" asked Daniel.

"I think so. I don't know. I hope we don't move. That would wreck everything."

"Would you have to leave Henrys?"

"I don't know. That would mean losing Atherstone for athletics, but more, it would mean moving away from you. I can't do that. I just can't do that."

"I hope not, Simon, I really do."

"What can we do?"

"Just wait and see, I suppose. They never ask kids what they want or need."

"I can't bear it if we can't be close again. I don't know what I would do."

"Well it might not happen, so let's make the most of the present."

Simon found solace and comfort from his fears with Daniel.

It was a few days later that Mum said she was going away for a couple of days.

"I've got to go up north to sort some things out," said Mum over tea.

"What sort of things?" asked Frances.

"Work. I need to find a job, loves," replied Mum.

"Where are you going?" asked Simon, worried.

"Bilthaven."

"That's miles away!" exclaimed Frances.

"Look, it's just to see. Things have changed. I'm sorry but I have to find a proper job. The part time work isn't steady enough and it doesn't pay enough. It's only for a night or two."

"Why there?" asked Simon.

"I know people there. You remember Ken Thompson, used to be on the paper here? Well, he's in Bilthaven and he thinks there is work I can do there."

Simon remembered the tall, fair journalist who had visited the house a couple of times. "Is Dad coming back to look after us?" he asked.

"No. Frances is old enough not to need it. She can look after you, Simon. Or maybe I could ask Daniel's parents if you could stay a night or two."

"Daniel won't mind," said Simon, hastily.

"It's up to his mother, Simon, not Daniel. I'll have a word. Would you stay here or with Jennifer, Frances?"

"I'll ask Jennifer, if Simon's staying at Daniel's. Yes, I suppose so."

"That's settled then," said Mum with an air of finality.

Later the two talked about this development.

"Looks like we might be moving, bro," said Frances.

"I don't want to move," said Simon. "I'm happy here. What about school?"

"Don't worry," said his big sister, "These things take ages to sort out. Nothing will happen in a hurry."

Simon knew he was approaching his GCEs and this would be his trump card. He just could not move now, and certainly not next year when he would be fifth year. He felt reassured, and relayed this to Daniel.

Mrs Gray said she would be happy to have Simon to stay. She could put a camp bed in Daniel's room, if that was all right. Of course it was. Frances went to stay with Jennifer. So when the day came, Simon and Frances said good bye to Mum that morning, knowing she would soon be setting off on the long train journey north.

"You'll be OK, both of you, won't you?"

"Yes, of course Mum," said Frances.

"Be on your best behaviour Simon, won't you," said Mum.

"Of course I will," said Simon indignantly.

"And you've both got keys in case you need anything, but make sure you lock up again afterwards."

"Yes, Mum," replied both together.

Simon was used to going straight to Daniel's after school to spend time with him and do homework. But this night it had a special sweetness. They would be together all night! Daniel let them both in, and as usual his first job was to check the Aga, and then they went up to Daniel's room. There was a camp bed made up next to Daniel's big bed. They hung up their school uniforms together, two green blazers, two pairs of grey trousers.

"Do you want it now, or shall we wait until tonight?" asked Simon.

"Do you want to wait?"

"No," said Simon. "I just thought ... I'm not sure what I thought, what with me staying here."

"Both then," said Daniel, and he kissed Simon, they hugged and rolled over on to the bed, each pulling the remaining clothes off the other and making love, lost in their union, enveloped in mutual ecstacy.

Simon had already left some more casual clothes to change into so they got dressed, and started the homework. Later Mrs Gray came home, and they were called down for tea.

"I remembered you don't eat cheese, Simon, so I hope this is all right."

"It's fine, thank you. It's very good of you to remember things like that," said Simon with genuine feeling.

"It's no trouble at all, Simon," she said, thinking what nice manners he had.

After tea, Daniel announced, "We've both got rather a lot of homework, so as soon as I've done piano, we'll just go back up if that's OK."

"Of course, love," said Mrs Gray. "I'll clear away, Dad and Louise will be back later anyway."

Daniel motioned Simon to follow and led the way to the back room and the piano.

"Rachmaninoff prelude?" suggested Simon.

"Something more cheerful tonight, I think," said Daniel smiling. "Chopin maybe, but first some exercises."

Daniel played a series of scales, each more complex than the last, encompassing almost the whole keyboard with both hands. He then moved on to play a series of pieces with Simon turning for him, some Chopin, but of course some Rachmaninoff after all, but not the dark *Prelude in C sharp minor*. Instead his *Prelude in G minor, Op 23 No. 5* and unusually for Daniel, Mozart, the *Piano Sonata no, 15 in C Major*. Simon knew this because he was turning the pages and it was helpfully printed at the top of the first page.

Simon watched as Daniel's hands, those strong yet sensitive hands, swept across the keyboard, at times so fast Simon found it hard to see individual fingering, especially in the G minor. He had watched Daniel's skill grow over the years to the point where he could now tackle even the most demanding of pieces.

After the Mozart, Daniel stopped and turned to Simon.

"You see how different the Mozart is from the Rachmaninoff?" he said.

"Yes, there seems somehow less of it. Less full in a way."

"Pianos in Mozart's day were much lighter than modern pianos, so I suppose that's why the music has a lighter feel. Good though."

"But you like Rachmaninoff better?"

"Yes, he's my favourite. I've got something to tell you."

"What?"

"I've passed my grade 8 piano exam." Daniel sat looking for Simon's reaction. Simon had heard of these grades before, and so assumed that this was good news.

"That's good, is it?" he asked cautiously.

"It's more than good, Simon. Not many kids my age get grade 8!"

"For once, he's not boasting," said Mrs Gray passing the door with pride in her voice. "I was in my twenties before I reached that kind of standard. It **is** very good, Simon."

Daniel beamed with pleasure. Simon wanted to reach out and hug him, but contented himself with a pat on the shoulder.

"Well done, Daniel. I've always said you were good."

"Thanks, Simon," said Daniel, pleased. Then to Simon's astonishment he suddenly launched into a piano version of "*Only the Lonely*", Roy Orbison's number one hit. Laughing, Simon joined in with Daniel's left hand.

"*Dum-dum-dum-dumdy-doo-wah*"

"There. What did you think of that?" asked Daniel, amused by Simon's surprise.

"Brilliant, as always. I wish I could play the piano, properly, I mean."

"You do OK," said Daniel. "Come on, homework."

They went back up to Daniel's room and worked together on Daniel's desk as so many times before. His father put his head round the door to say hello.

"Are you two all right?"

"Hello, Dad," responded Daniel, eagerly, and got up from his chair to give his Dad a hug, genuinely pleased to see him. Simon watched this, the contrast not lost on him.

"OK, I'll leave you two to your homework then," said Mr Gray, and left.

When they finished, Daniel said, "Do you want to go downstairs and watch TV, or just stay up here?"

"Up to you," said Simon, but really wanting to stay so he had Daniel's company to himself.

"Let's stay here then," said Daniel, glad that Simon hadn't opted to go downstairs, as he wanted Simon's company to himself.

So they stayed and talked, risking the occasional (fully dressed) hug and kiss. Just being together in deep companionship.

A call came from downstairs. "Supper, boys!"

They went downstairs to the big kitchen, Simon thinking how warm the house was, the kitchen especially because of the Aga. There was a coal fire burning in the sitting room, but Simon wondered if that was really needed. Louise came in and said hello, and then went out again. After their light supper, they said good night and went back to the bedroom.

"You go to the bathroom first," said Daniel, so Simon did, returning to find Daniel in pyjamas.

"I'll go now. Better get in the camp bed," he said.

A bit disappointed, Simon climbed into the camp bed. Not the most comfortable he had ever slept in. Daniel came back from the bathroom, and laughed.

"You really did! Idiot," he smiled. But then he had a thought. "Actually, better stay there for the moment." He climbed into his own big bed.

Soon, there was a knock at the door. "Are you two all right in there?" asked Mrs Gray.

"It's OK Mum, come in," said Daniel.

Mrs Gray's head appeared round the door. "Are you comfortable, Simon?"

"Yes, thank you, it's fine," said Simon politely.

"Good night, then," said Mrs Gray.

The door closed. Daniel wriggled about in the bed and then dropped his pyjama trousers on Simon's head. Simon grinned back, and in response to Daniel's beckoning, slipped into the big bed with him. Daniel removed his own pyjama top and then Simon's pyjamas.

"I can't believe we can spend the whole night like this together," said Daniel. "I've wanted to for ages."

"It's super, isn't it," agreed Simon.

Unhurried, and wary of noise, they held each other, kissed and made love until they fell asleep, still in each other's arms.

Simon woke first, in the dim light he could see Daniel's sleeping face close to his, feel his gentle breathing, the warmth, the scent of his body. Simon just watched, enraptured, savouring the moment. He could not ever remember being so happy.

In the event, Mum was away three nights on her visit to Bilthaven. Three wonderful nights of unbelievable sensuality, closeness and happiness. The spectre of any move forgotten for the time being. But it came to an end. Mum returned from Bilthaven and he returned home. Simon had learned a bit about Bilthaven in history. The industrial revolution, a place of big factories, heavy industry. A seaport. He put it out of his mind.

An air of gloom hung over the household, from which Simon escaped to Daniel at every opportunity. Mum was quiet, but it seemed as though a move to Bilthaven looked more likely. But Simon felt secure in that Mum would not move him before his GCEs, they were too important. That was over a year away, and beyond that Simon could not think. Just concentrate on the next year or so. This November morning Mum was still in bed, while Simon was up and getting his breakfast. He grabbed his blazer, and went back upstairs to say goodbye to Mum.

"I'm off, Mum," he said, standing in Mum's bedroom doorway.

"All right love, see you tonight, " said Mum, dully.

On impulse, Simon asked, "Do you know when we're moving? Only I would need time to sort things out at school, there are records and that sort of thing."

Mum was quiet for a moment. Then, "Yes, I suppose you do. Two weeks today. We go two weeks today."

Simon was rooted to the spot, in shock. Two weeks! Just two weeks! His heart raced, this was horrible. Unbelievable. Daniel!

"What about my GCEs?" he asked shakily.

"I'm sorry if it's come as a shock," said Mum. "They have good schools there. You'll be all right."

"I won't! I won't be all right!" he shouted.

Simon turned and ran downstairs, slamming the front door behind him. Daniel was waiting on the corner.

"Come on, slowcoach," he said, cheerily. "We'll miss the bus."

"Two weeks, Daniel. We're moving in two weeks!"

The shock registered on Daniel's face. "O Jesus, Simon! Just two weeks? What will we do?"

"Have a bloody good time in the next two weeks, that's one thing. Every night!" said Simon angrily.

"You bet," said Daniel. "But then what?"

"I don't know, Daniel. Come on, we'll be late."

The two boys spent every possible moment together for the rest of that November, expressing their as yet unspoken but deeply felt love in physical, sexual, emotional ways. Their lovemaking was the more frequent, varied and passionate, borne of desperation. There were tears on both sides as each tried to come to terms with their impending separation.

43. 1960/11 North!

The day before departure, so many things had been packed away, ready for the van to come. Only those things needed for overnight, which would be carried in the car, and the items being left behind for Dad when he returned to live alone in the house, were not being packed away. Simon's bed was ready for the van, but he would use his sleeping bag that last night. To his annoyance, he was sent to school on that day, so Mum could concentrate on getting ready. But at least it was another journey to and from school with Daniel.

The last night in their old house arrived too quickly, the house where Simon had lived for the first fourteen years and three months of his life. He came home to find the removal van had been, their stuff was already on its way to Bilthaven.

"I'm going back round to see Daniel," said Simon after bolting down his tea and dumping his school uniform, it occurred to him for the last time.

"OK love," said Mum. "Try not to be too late back, we want to make an early start." Simon left without another word, feelings of fear, uncertainty and anger running through him. He ran round to Daniel's in the November drizzle. Please be in! He knocked on the back door.

"Come in, Simon," said Mrs Gray, cheerily. "Daniel thought you'd be round. He's in his room I think. Daniel! Simon's here!"

"Send him up," came Daniel's voice. To Mrs Gray's nod, Simon went through to the hall and hung up his damp jacket.

"Hello Simon," said Louise. "Tomorrow's the big day then?"

"Yes, 'fraid so," said Simon, glumly.

"I hope it goes OK. Daniel's waiting for you I think," she said, with a smile. Simon ran up the stairs to Daniel's room. He was at his desk, but got up when Simon came in.

"Shut the door," he said. Simon did, and there they stood for a moment facing each other. Simon felt the emotion welling up in him, which of course Daniel noticed. He came to Simon and put his arms round him and they hugged tightly.

"It's so unfair," said Simon.

"I know, I know."

"Why do I have to go? It's rotten."

"I suppose they couldn't work things out together."

"But why so far away?"

"You can come and stay in the holidays and that. Perhaps I can come and visit the frozen north too."

"Yes, please do. I'd love that. I may be coming back to see my Dad as well."

And so the two friends sat and talked, Simon making sure Daniel had his new address, but the unspoken undercurrent was there, waiting to surface. In the end it was Simon.

"I want it. I want us to do it again before I go."

"I know. Me too. But where? How can we?" wondered Daniel.

"It's too cold and wet outside, and where could we go anyway?"

"And my Mum and Louise are in."

"Where's your Dad?"

"Working late. Some case or other." Daniel sat on the edge of the big bed and pulled Simon down next to him.

"OK, now," said Daniel. "What the hell, I don't care." He got up and opened his bedroom door.

"Mum, we're talking for a while," he called down.

"Right Daniel," Simon heard her reply from downstairs. "I expect you've a lot to get sorted out."

Daniel closed the door and turned the lock.

"What if she comes up?" asked Simon, anxiously.

"She's watching telly. Lie down, you. I want you," said Daniel, smiling. Simon did so, arousal coursing through his body. Gently, lovingly, Daniel removed Simon's clothing, Simon feeling his nakedness coming and the eroticism of being undressed, and when Simon tried to respond, Daniel shook his head.

"No, I'll do it," he said and quickly undressed, dropping his clothes on the floor until he too was naked, standing looking at Simon, each taking in the other's admired form. He joined Simon on the bed, and they kissed, tentatively at first, then with sudden passion as they explored and probed each other's well-known body, forgetful of all else, their surroundings, time passing and the parting to come. Over the years, they had learned each other's most erotic stimuli, experts on the erogenous needs of the teenage male, so they were entwined, locked, fused, flesh against warm flesh, using all their bodies, hands, mouths, thighs, a writhing decapod, until both were spent, each at the doing of the other. Breathless, they lay together, Simon refusing to allow Daniel to withdraw, holding fast, frightened to let go in case they would never touch again.

"What time are you going?" asked Daniel eventually.

"Not sure. An early start Mum said."

"I'll come and see you off."

"Thanks." And then there seemed little left to say. So they just remained, holding, trying to make the precious time last just a little longer.

"I want to lie like this with you forever," said Simon, trying to imprint on his mind the warm strength of Daniel next to him so that he would never forget how it felt.

"Me too. But it might be a bit awkward, food and that, never mind missing school," Daniel joked, but tightening his hold on Simon, he too trying to store the memory.

After some time, Simon reached forward and kissed Daniel gently. "Again, please, again. Can you?"

"You bet," said Daniel. "This?" he asked, holding the Vaseline jar. Simon nodded.

"How, this time?" asked Daniel.

"I want to see you," said Simon.

So Daniel lifted Simon's legs to his shoulders and pulled Simon's lips into his fiercely, and gripping his younger friend, their lovemaking the second time was if anything stronger and more ferocious than before. All the violent but largely unspoken feelings for each other finding expression now in the fusion of their beings, reckless love determined by the deadline of the morrow, Daniel now arched over his lover as so many times before until once more exhausted, his precious seed within Simon, both used up, they lay panting.

"I don't know what I'll do," said Simon, remembering the next day.

"You'll be OK, you'll make friends," comforted Daniel.

"Not like you. You know me better than anyone in the world."

"You know **me** better than anyone. And you'll still have me," said Daniel, tapping Simon's chest twice. "There's trains I assume? Unless it's still all pony and trap stuff up there!"

Simon had to smile.

But then there was the sound of the door handle, followed by a knock on the door.

"Daniel, are you all right? What's going on?" It was Mrs Gray. Simon's heart pounded, Daniel froze. But then recovered.

"It's OK, Mum, Simon and I were just mucking about."

"Why is your door locked?"

"Mum, I **am** sixteen," countered Daniel, looking at Simon's scared face. Listening for a reaction the other side of the door.

"Well, Simon's fourteen. And I think perhaps it's getting a bit late. He will need to be up early."

"OK, Mum, we'll be down soon."

"Are you going to open this door or not?"

"No, Mum," said Daniel, firmly. Strong Daniel.

"Why not?"

"Jesus!" whispered Daniel quietly. And then louder, "Because we're both stark naked in bed."

Simon gasped, his body now racing at fever pitch. Outside the door, there was a pause, and then the sense of Mrs Gray moving away and going downstairs.

"Why did you say that?" asked Simon, sitting up on the bed.

"I think she'd guessed anyway. We probably made too much noise. What difference can it make now? You'll be gone tomorrow."

"But what about you?"

"I'll be OK. You know I will." And somehow, Simon knew he would be. "Come on, get dressed. Let's go down and tell them," said Daniel.

"How can we? What will they think? And isn't two boys, I mean, it's against the law or something isn't it?"

"We've always known that, so nothing new there."

"Yes, but not when just we knew."

"Get dressed."

"A minute," said Simon. "I want to remember you." He reached out and ran his hands over Daniel's smooth, athletic body, memories flooding back, times in the den, out on their bike rides, scout camps, being pulled from the lido, in this very bed. So much, so long. Tears rolled down Simon's face, and then Daniel too, so uncharacteristically, was in tears too. They held each other for a last time, and then silently, the two boys got dressed.

"Come on then, let's go and face the world," said Daniel, brave Daniel, and unlocked the door. He led the way down. Simon was all for grabbing his jacket from the hall and going, but Daniel took Simon's hand and they went into the sitting room. Mrs Gray stood up, expressions running across her face in rapid succession as thoughts raced through her mind. Louise sat in the chair, looking at Daniel, with a quizzical gaze.

"Here we are, Mum," said Daniel.

"I don't know what to say, to either of you," said Mrs Gray. "You were both naked? I don't understand."

"Oh Mum," said Louise, despairingly. "They've been at it for years."

"What!" said Daniel, turning to his sister. For once, Daniel was lost for words.

"Well, look at you, it's obvious you two are in love, and knowing boys, the rest was pretty obvious too."

Simon flushed red and shook, looking down at the floor. But Daniel continued to hold his hand tightly.

"You mean Daniel's a ... and Simon too?" Mrs Gray said, but looking at her son, standing quietly and defiantly before her. "What will your father say?"

"If he doesn't know now, don't tell him," suggested Louise, pragmatically. "And Simon goes north tomorrow, so what's the point?"

"Is there anybody else?" Mrs Gray abruptly demanded of Daniel. "Now or in the past? Am I going to get more surprises?"

"No," said Daniel. "Simon has only ever been the one, and only ever will be. He's so special."

"That's what you call it, special. I think it's..." and then Mrs Gray stopped, unable to say how she felt; to voice the feelings would be to commit, and she didn't want to commit. "Simon, have you anything to say?"

But Daniel spoke first. "Mum, leave Simon out of it. It's not his fault and anyway, as Louise says, what's the point now?"

"I'm sorry ... "began Simon, unable to meet Mrs Gray's eyes, but Daniel cut in.

"Simon, don't be sorry," he said turning to his friend. "You've nothing to be sorry about and I'm not sorry," he finished with emphasis, turning back to his mother and sister.

"I just don't feel I can just leave it at that, Daniel. We need to sort this out. We have to talk," said Mrs Gray.

"Not now, Mum. Not tonight of all nights. Tomorrow. Please," Daniel pleaded.

Mrs Gray hesitated, looked at Louise who was nodding.

"Very well, but I think it's time for Simon to leave."

"Come on," said Daniel, drawing Simon away.

"Good bye," said Simon, "Thank ..." He was going automatically to say 'Thank you for having me', but somehow, he just could not.

"Come on," said Daniel again, and the two went out into the hallway.

"Simon!" Mrs Gray was calling after him. "I hope it works out for you all up there." Simon turned and just nodded. Louise was smiling and nodding also. Then they turned and closed the sitting room door, leaving the two alone in the hall.

"Your jacket," said Daniel, helping Simon on with it.

"Why did it have to end like this?" said Simon, bitterly.

"What did you want? 'They all lived happily ever after'? You're such an idiot," said Daniel, smiling through the tears in his eyes. "Louise is right. I love you. I have loved you for as many years as I can remember. I don't regret a single thing and I never will. Remember that Doris Day song?

Once I had a secret love
That lived within the heart of me

Maybe one day this bloody country will wake up to the truth."

Simon looked at Daniel, waves of emotion released. "Oh God. I love you too. I don't regret it either. I'm going to miss you. I love you so much."

"We'll meet again."

"In all the old familiar places?"

"Different song, idiot. But I expect so," said Daniel, managing a smile, "just don't know where, don't know when."

"Promise? Scout's Honour?"

"Promise. Scout's Honour."

In that hallway, the two hugged tightly and kissed, a kiss that summed up all the years of closeness, of shared childhood and youth, of sexual exploration, passion and deep, abiding love. They drew apart, and Daniel opened the front door to the cold, wet late November night.

"Write," said Simon. Daniel nodded. And Simon left, stopping at the gate to look back at Daniel, silhouetted against the light from the hallway. Then he turned and ran home.

He ran in through the back door, and hung up his wet jacket. Mum called from the sitting room.

"That you Simon? Say goodbye to Daniel?" The word – goodbye – cut Simon deep inside. He didn't answer. "Are you all right, love?" called Mum.

"No, not really," said Simon. "I'm going to bed. 'Night."

"Leave him, Mum," he heard Frances say. "He'll be OK. It must be hard, he and Daniel have been friends for years. It's like me saying goodbye to Jennifer."

But by then he was upstairs in his room, lying on the temporary airbed, weeping uncontrollably. Mourning the loss of all he knew, his whole world, but specially, hugely and overwhelmingly, the loss of Daniel. Why had it taken so long for them to say it? Why wait until now to say just how much they loved each other? Why did it take Louise of all people? What is wrong with this bloody world? The love that dare not speak its name. Well, it had now, but it was Daniel who would bear the brunt of it.

The next morning was cold, now December, and showing it. But it was dry. Mum had got them up early, it was a long way to go. Bilthaven. Simon had this image of a grim and grimy place, heavy industry. A long way. It was a Thursday, but no school now for Simon. After breakfast, still dark outside, they packed their last things and put them in the little Ford. It was crammed and Simon was to share the back seat with an assortment of effects that had not gone on ahead. A last look at his room, a few things remaining, and round the house. Would Dad be OK when he came back, he wondered.

As it grew light, it was time to go. They climbed in the car. Mum was pale and quiet, determination and resolve on her face, Frances quiet too, lost in her thoughts. They backed out of the drive for the last time and turned towards the corner.

There he was, leaning with his consuming elegance in Hooray Henrys uniform against the corner fence. Seeing the car, Daniel stood up.

"Oh, there's Daniel, Simon," said Mum. "That's nice." Simon looked at his love as the car drew level. Their eyes met, those wonderful blue eyes. Mum looked and then the car moved round the corner, turning away from Daniel.

"I love you, Simon!" shouted Daniel.

"What did he say?" asked Mum. Nobody replied. Simon looked out of the back window as the car went down the hill to the main road until Daniel was gone from sight. Gone.

Book Two – The Sixties, the dark decade

1. *1960/12 Bilthaven*

The long journey north took the whole day. Simon sat in the back, quiet, trying to close his mind to both the past because of the pain of losing it and to the future because of his fear of facing it. It was dark when at last they drove into Bilthaven. Simon watched as this strange big city passed before him, its bright lights, the river from which the city took its name, busy streets. Would he ever find his way round this place? But it seemed to have a certain atmosphere and excitement about it that stirred Simon, even through his misery and fatigue. They came to the area called Swiford, just outside the city centre, and their new home.

Mum's colleague in her new job on the *Bilthaven Mail*, Ken Thompson, was waiting.

"Hello, Kate," he said. "Long journey, I expect."

"Gruesome, Ken," Mum replied. "Did the van arrive OK?"

"Yes, everything's in. I had to use my best judgement about where you would want stuff, but of course you can change it."

"Thanks, Ken. You're very kind," said Mum. "Come on, kids, this is it."

The flat was part of a house in an affluent area, the owner lived downstairs, they had the next floor. They went in the hallway and up the stairs to their new home. There was a lounge, kitchen, bathroom and just two bedrooms.

"Mum, there's only two bedrooms!" said Frances, "I'm **not** sharing with Simon!"

"No love, it's OK.," said Mum. "I will sleep on this divan bed in the lounge. Your things should be in the big bedroom, is that right, Ken? And Simon's in the smaller room."

"Why do I get the small room?" said Simon, feeling very uncooperative.

"It's not that small, is it Ken? Perhaps not quite as big as your old room, but everything should be in there."

"Yes, it's all there, as you said, Kate," said Ken. "There's bread, milk in the fridge and some food in the kitchen cupboards. I ought to be going. I'll see you tomorrow. Bye Frances, Simon."

"Bye," they mumbled unenthusiastically. The flat had a fridge. That was something anyway. The old house hadn't had one. Daniel had one though.

Frances and Simon went to find their rooms while Mum saw Ken out. Simon's room was long and narrow, but his own bed was there, and his desk, chest of drawers, his bedside table and his portable Roberts Radio. His books were piled up on the floor and there were boxes. But grudgingly Simon had to admit that Ken had done well on that score. Frances also found all her possessions in place, the downside for her was that Mum's clothes were in the built in wardrobes as well as her own. Mum would sleep in the lounge, but would need to dress and keep her clothes in the big bedroom. Simon had his room to himself. He thought now he had the better bargain.

Mum managed to drum up some supper, and then they fell into bed, exhausted, listening to the strange sounds of a new place, but at least this night Simon was in his own familiar bed again.

Simon woke with a start in the morning, and found himself in this new room, new life. No school today, even though it was a Friday. He looked at his watch. It was the time he would normally be meeting Daniel on the corner. A stab of pain went through him, he pulled the blankets over his head and cried. He wanted to go home.

There was a knock at the door. "Simon? I thought I heard something," said Mum, with her head round the door. "Time to get up, I want to sort out a school for you if I can today, because I start work on Monday."

Simon had to face the reality of his position. He got up. He dressed in his school shirt and trousers, but not the green blazer.

Bilthaven's Royal Grammar School was the city's equivalent of Hooray Henrys. Mum had the documentation from Henrys and they were called in to see the headmaster. The interview did not go as expected.

"Mrs Scott, I don't think I can help you. There is no grant for Simon."

"But he was at King Henrys," said Mum. "He's a bright boy."

"I can see that, Mrs Scott, indeed yes. And I know King Henrys is an excellent school. I have met the headmaster a number of times. But you must understand this school is in a different education authority from King Henrys, and I am afraid there is no guarantee that Simon would be grant aided here."

"You mean you don't have a place for him?" said Mum, dumbfounded.

"Oh dear," said the headmaster. "It's not a question of the place, but of the funding. Might you be in a position for Simon to be a fee paying boy?"

"Fee paying? How much?" said Mum.

The headmaster gently pushed a brochure across his desk. "The fee structure is there," he said, indicating a table of figures.

Mum stopped and looked at the table. Simon could see from her face that she was disappointed. She shook her head.

"I'm sorry. I can't manage that. In my new circumstances it's simply out of my reach."

"You're living in Swiford, I believe?" said the headmaster, kindly.

Mum nodded.

"The grammar school there, it's a full state school of course, is very well thought of."

"Thank you. Come on, Simon."

They left the school and headed back to Swiford. Back in the flat, there was an air of gloom. Frances had returned from an unsuccessful job hunt. Mum phoned Swiford Grammar School. Another hammer blow. There were no fourth year places. She should ring the education office.

Simon listened, helpless, a piece of flotsam, as his future was decided by others. The conversation did not seem to be going too well.

"But we are living in Swiford. Surely there should be a place for him at Swiford Grammar?" ... "Where's that?" ... "Where? Cermerton School? How far is that?" .... "What! How far?" .... "A bus. I see."

It turned out that Swiford Grammar was always heavily oversubscribed but the council had built a new school campus on the edge of the city at Cermerton some miles away. There was a college, a grammar school and a secondary modern school on the same site. There was a school bus provided from Swiford across the city to Cermerton. Mum made an appointment that afternoon to see the headmaster of the grammar school.

Lunch was a drink and a sandwich. ("I need to find the shops and get some shopping in," said Mum.) But Simon didn't feel hungry anyway.

Armed with an A to Z, Simon navigated Mum in the old Ford to Cermerton. As they drove into the gates, they were confronted with a range of modern 1950s buildings, looking as though they had been built from giant kits. Signs directed them to the grammar school. The headmaster saw them coming and came out to greet them.

"Mrs Scott? Simon?" He shook hands with Mum and then with Simon. That was a first, he thought. They went into the office. He introduced himself as George Catterall. Simon had never known the Headmaster's first name at Henrys. He was very friendly and explained that the grammar and secondary modern schools wore the same uniform and shared many facilities, but of course academically the grammar school was more geared to GCEs. That sounded reassuring. The uniform was designed to be inexpensive, and Simon already had shirts and trousers. The blazer was plain black, obtainable quite reasonably in many Bilthaven shops and the badges and ties could be bought here at the school. No, caps were not worn. It was agreed that Simon could join the fourth year top class, based on the information from King Henrys, starting after Christmas. But Simon should come to the Christmas party. Arrangements were made for Simon to catch the school bus that left Swiford at 8:25, from the cross roads about a ten minute walk from the flat. As they shook hands again, young voices could be heard outside the office. It was home time. They stepped out into the entrance lobby and Simon stopped, rooted to the spot. Perhaps it had been so obvious it hadn't been mentioned, but to Simon it came as a complete surprise. There were girls. Lots of them. It was a mixed school!

That evening, Simon sat at his desk in his room, warmed by a small electric fire, to write to Daniel. He had never written to him before. He wanted to put 'To my beloved Daniel' or 'Darling Daniel' or 'Dearest Daniel'; in the end he just put 'Dear Daniel'. He put his feelings about Bilthaven so far into the letter and of course about the new school, girls and all.

On Saturday, he and Mum found shops not far away along Swiford High Street, and the post office, so off went the letter to Daniel. Of course there were bigger shops in the city centre, just a bus ride away. Trolley buses humming along, Simon noted with fascination. He would have to tell Daniel about those.

His new uniform was quickly obtained and the school badge sewn on the blazer pocket, unlike the embroidered complete pocket on a Henrys blazer. Mum started the new job, and Frances found a job in the city. For December, Simon was left to explore his surroundings, riding the trolley bus into the city. An imposing place, centred on Victoria Square, with grand buildings, the main route leading out over the river across an impressive bridge, with an equally impressive railway bridge not far away. From Victoria Square, which Simon learned was in what was called the new town, a steep hill, Port Road, led down to the harbour area and the older part of the city known appropriately as The Port and the port area itself. This was an exciting area for Simon, with the ships tied up, unloading cargo, with all the hustle and bustle, there were fishing boats and out beyond the harbour piers, the sea! Blue and brilliant in this December sunshine, but cold no doubt. Simon felt an affinity with this place, his love of the sea reawakened from its hibernation between Salcombe visits. There was a Royal Navy warship tied up on the opposite bank, and it seems there was a small naval base. One of Simon's great excitements at Salcombe was the occasional visits by small naval vessels.

Much of the time he was on his own in the flat. His mood would dip, and then he would hate the place and everything about it. He stayed in bed until late for want of anything better to do, and as fourteen year old boys are wont to do, sought solace in the pleasures of the body, amid thoughts and memories of Daniel. The sound of the postman downstairs would rouse him and he would put on his dressing gown and run down to collect the hoped for letter. The mail was mostly for Russell Deverill, the local businessman who owned the house and now divorced, lived downstairs; there were some for Mum, occasionally one for Frances, but none for him. He left Russell's letters on the hall table and dropped the rest on the table in the lounge. His mood would darken with disappointment.

Mum had told him to keep out of Russell's way, but they soon became acquainted, as he allowed Simon to keep his bike in the large garage which opened onto a back lane. The garage had been extended to accommodate his two cars, a red Triumph TR3A and a workhorse Morris estate car. Mum's old car was parked in the back street. But there was also a workbench and plenty of space for Simon's bike. Russell loved the Triumph and Simon would use the excuse of fiddling with his bike to cross the small yard to the garage when he knew Russell was there so he could look more closely at the Triumph.

Eventually his persistence paid off and he was given a ride in the sports car, at some speed through Bilthaven and into the surrounding countryside.

Cermerton Grammar School's Christmas Party and Dance was a new experience for Simon. He was put in the charge of Alan Croft, a boy in his class. He seemed friendly and keen to put Simon at ease. The boys and girls knew the various dances, such as the Barn Dance, which were new to Simon. Dancing in close proximity with a girl was new as well. He did his best but felt as though he had two left feet, but did manage not to tread on anyone's toes, in itself an accomplishment.

"Were there no girls at all at your last school?" asked Alan, incredulously.

"No, it was a posh, all boys grammar school."

"So what did you do about girls and that, then?"

Simon wasn't sure how to answer this without losing vast quantities of 'face', so he shrugged, smiled and just said, "We had our moments."

"You randy sod," said Alan, grinning.

So his answer seemed to suffice. Many of his class were already fifteen and most of the boys seemed to have girlfriends and if their own statements were anything to go by, were all leading very active sex lives. Both boys and girls quizzed him about Hooray Henrys – they thought the nickname hilarious – and why he had moved to Bilthaven. Most seemed to regard moving to Bilthaven as an act of folly, describing the city as a dump. Simon nervously said his parents were getting divorced, which surprisingly seemed to raise his status. This went up even more when he said his mother was now working at the *Bilthaven Mail*. But the question of girls and sex kept coming up, and Simon's reticence on this matter earned him the reputation of being a bit of a dark horse, no doubt with a string of girlfriends left behind weeping. Simon thought it best to allow this reputation to persist. He was sure that if they found out about him and Daniel, life could get very unpleasant. All in all, the party was a success. He had met many if not most of his new classmates of both sexes and made at least one friend in Alan, who alas lived nowhere near Swiford.

Christmas was a strange one. Simon was saddened by the lack of reply from Daniel, despite the fact that he had written each week. There was not even a Christmas card. Mum took him and Frances, along with Ken, who was a constant source of help, out for Christmas Lunch at a posh hotel. It was organised by the newspaper and several important people were there. Dad sent him a large cheque, and Mum bought him some new clothes. Simon had sent Daniel a book about swimming, but nothing came back. He buried the heartache and tried to get on with life. But he missed Daniel so much and he wept silently in the night.

The new year, a new school – a new world! Simon, now dressed in the black blazer under his coat, satchel over his shoulder, walked along Swiford

High Street that January morning to where the bus would be waiting. It wasn't, but a crowd of kids in Cermerton uniform were. Simon approached cautiously.

"Hello," said a boy. "Are you new?"

"Yes," said Simon.

"Which school are you at?"

"Cermerton," answered Simon, puzzled.

"Well, obviously, but which one?"

"Oh, the grammar school. I'm in fourth year."

"Thought so, by the satchel. I'd get rid of that if I were you. I'm fourth year at the grammar too. Which class?"

"I'm not sure what it's called, but Alan Croft is in my class."

"Oh, top stream," said the boy. "I'm in the class below. You must be brainy then?"

"Everybody at the grammar school is supposed to be aren't they?"

The boy laughed. "Dunno where you've come from, but that's not true here. And then there's the kids from the sec mod. Some of them are Neanderthals."

"My name's Simon Scott," he offered.

"Martin Passmore," said the boy. "You talk posh."

But before Simon could make any response, a motor coach pulled up beside the crowd of children. They got on and found seats.

"Can I sit anywhere?" asked Simon, in case there were regular seats.

"Yes, but leave the back seat."

"Who for?"

"Neanderthals," said Martin, knowingly.

Simon sat on a comfortable window seat, noting the luxury coach was only half full. Plenty of seats for all, he thought. He noticed that all the kids carried haversacks. How would he ever learn all the new ground rules for this place?

The bus radio was on, playing pop music. Then there was a two minute news summary at half past eight.

As the bus drove along unfamiliar streets through Bilthaven suburbs, it stopped and more Cermerton pupils got on each time. After one such stop, with the bus now almost full except for the back seat, a boy about his own age stopped in the aisle and looked at Simon.

"Who are you?" he said, aggressively.

"Simon Scott. I'm just starting at Cermerton." Oh no, thought Simon, a Barry Spence type.

"Oh, posh are you?" sneered the boy, mimicking Simon's different accent, honed at Henrys into the Queen's English. "Hey Bruce, got a new posh kid here."

Another boy behind him peered over to see. Simon looked at him and instantly felt uneasy. He had light brown hair but it was the eyes! Cold and calculating, hard grey eyes, with the feel of a malevolent intelligence behind them. This Bruce looked Simon up and down dismissively.

"Grammar school kid?" he demanded.

Simon nodded.

"Thought so." He came close to Simon. "Keep out of my way. Understand?"

The menace was obvious. Simon thought he had no intention of getting in his way, he was unpredictable and no doubt violent.

"Come on, Nev," he said to the first boy. "Time for sport later."

The first boy, Nev, smiled and obeyed but waved his finger in Simon's face and said, "Later." They moved down the bus and took the back seat, along with another fair haired boy.

Simon was inwardly shaking and trying hard not to show it. He knew that other kids had been watching this exchange and wondered how his stock had fared. He saw Martin looking at him, but there was nothing to read in his face. O God, how he missed Daniel!

Had Simon known what the future held in store for him with regard to this Bruce, his friend Nev and the fair haired boy with them, he would have never travelled on that bus again and never set foot near Cermerton again.

Simon settled into his new class. He found himself sitting near the front which he preferred. He had used this as a device at Henrys to force him to concentrate on the lesson and there were fewer problems with the inevitable back row distractions. Now he needed to concentrate more than ever because the continuity of his GCE studies had been broken. Alan Croft was sitting near him but next to him on one side was a tall, red haired girl called Marjorie Wilson, on the other side was a quiet, studious boy called Stuart Miller. That first day was spent for Simon getting used to the new building with its many staircases and classrooms that all looked the same, the routine at breaks and dinner time, new teachers. He saw and spoke briefly to Martin Passmore at dinner time, who asked Simon how it was going.

One change was that there was no Latin taught at the school. Simon did not mourn this particularly because with the logic of youth, he had wondered when he might meet a Roman with whom to converse. One of the alternatives he was offered instead was German, which he accepted, having been interested in European history at Henrys, German history especially. Simon could see how these two might tie in at a later stage. But he would have to work hard to catch up the rest of the German group in time for the GCE next year. Alan looked after him and made sure he knew where to go. Simon tried hard to remember because he knew it would only be a matter of time before Alan would weary of his nursemaid role. Alan was very friendly and used his first name rather than his surname, the only person to do so. He also noted that Alan and Stuart were not friends, but did not know why. However, Stuart was quite happy to talk to Simon.

This was also the first time since leaving the juniors that he had women teachers. Simon especially liked the history teacher, a charismatic woman who Simon was to find brought the subject alive to him and was to be a major influence on his studies later.

But at the end of the day, Simon had to leave the security of his grammar school class and walk down to the bus circle inside the main gates where a series of buses and coaches were waiting to take children home from the whole campus. Simon realised he had no idea which bus would take him to Swiford. He saw a couple of faces he recognised and then Martin Passmore, so he followed him and climbed onto the bus. It was already fairly full, but he found a seat and sat with his satchel on his lap. A younger boy sat next to him.

As the bus moved off, looking out of the window, he felt the younger boy get up and someone else sit next to him. It was the boy, Bruce.

"Enjoy your first day, then?" he said.

"Yes, it was OK," answered Simon.

"Well then, posh," Bruce continued, "What things do you learn in the grammar school?"

"Just ordinary subjects," said Simon, wondering what they learned in the secondary modern school. Was it like Vicks, he thought.

Bruce then grabbed Simon's satchel before he could react.

"Give that back," said Simon.

"I'm just having a look to see what you lot get up to," said Bruce cockily, all pretence of a friendly tone now gone. Simon made to grab the satchel but Bruce pulled it away, and thrusting his face into Simon's, those hard grey eyes looking straight into his, said, "Don't do that." There was such force in the way he quietly said those three words that Simon let go of the strap. Bruce got up and took Simon's satchel toward the back of the bus, Simon got up as well, but was pushed back into his seat by the one called Nev who remained blocking Simon's way. Bruce sat on the back seat and he and the fair haired boy emptied out his satchel, providing a sarcastic running commentary about Simon's books. Each time Simon tried to get away from the seat, Nev blocked him, punching him so he sat down again. Simon looked around for any sign of help from the other kids on board, but most seemed either to be enjoying the show, mainly Simon thought the sec mod kids, while those that Simon knew were from the grammar school seemed either much younger or unwilling to get involved. One or two of the girls were positively enjoying Simon's discomfort. Nev was now standing in Simon's way but watching the events on the back seat as the satchel was dismembered. Tapping himself on the chest twice, Simon resolved to act and raised his fist to hit Nev, but then caught sight of Martin Passmore, who seeing this, shook his head slowly in silent warning. So Simon's resolve melted.

At last the stop came when these three got off. They came down the aisle of the bus past Simon.

"Where's my bag?" demanded Simon.

"Speak when you're spoken to, and only then," snarled Bruce, with a cruelty in his face that Barry Spence would have truly envied.

"Back seat, you have my permission to get it now," said the fair haired young boy, with a superior snigger.

As the bus moved away from that stop, Simon went to the back seat. The contents of his satchel were strewn about, some books were ripped, his pens were missing, but the leather satchel had long slashing cuts in it. It was ruined. The strap was cut right through and useless. Simon started to gather the remnants into the tattered remains of the satchel. Another pair of hands came to help, Simon looked, it was Martin Passmore. Once they had picked everything up, Martin sat next to Simon.

"Meet the Neanderthals," he said.

"Who **are** they?" asked Simon.

"Bruce Watson, he's the leader. He's nasty and vicious. Don't get the wrong side of him."

"I think I am already."

"They might let it go at that, if you're lucky and keep out of their way."

"What if I don't?" asked Simon.

"They carry knives," said Martin. "What do you think cut up your satchel? It takes a very sharp knife to cut through thick leather like that. We do that for harnesses sometimes. So I know."

"Harnesses?"

"Yes, we used to have working horses on the farm where I live, but now my Dad keeps a couple for show."

"Oh. Who are the other two?"

"Bruce is in our year, but at the sec mod of course. The younger one, the fair one, is David Watson, Bruce's kid brother and almost as nasty. I think he's just second year, but he acts as though he's older, never far from his big brother. The other one is Neville Carter, he's always with them. He's as bad as Bruce Watson. He's our year too."

"How do they get away with it?"

"Are you going to stop them?" asked Martin.

"I could try."

"Only if you wanted a load of stitches across your face from their knives."

"They wouldn't do that," said Simon incredulously.

"They already have," replied Martin. "Believe me, keep out of their way. Oh, we're here."

The bus had arrived back in Swiford.

"Where's the farm then?" asked Simon curious in these urban surroundings.

"A couple of miles away I suppose, just outside Swiford. I get an ordinary bus from here."

The remaining children got off and dispersed. Simon was clutching his ruined bag under his arm.

"See ya tomorrow, Simon," said Martin.

"Yeah, see ya," replied Simon, taken slightly off guard by the use of his first name. At Henrys unless one was particularly friendly, it had always been surnames, except for friends like himself and Peter Holman and of course Daniel. That was perhaps a good sign, thought Simon. Like Alan Croft. A friend on that bus was badly needed.

He walked back along Swiford High Street. He noted a shop selling haversacks but did not have enough money. He stopped at a baker's shop and bought a small apple pie which he ate. Back at the house, he found the front door open, and Russell Deverill in the hall.

"Hello, young man," said Russell. "How was the first day?"

"OK," said Simon.

"So what happened to the satchel?"

"Some Neanderthals on the school bus."

"Oh dear, so you need a new bag then."

"Yes. They all carry haversacks, so I suppose a satchel stood out a bit."

"Yes, made you a marked man, Simon."

"There's a shop on the High Street selling haversacks, but I'll have to wait until Mum gets home. The shop might be shut by then." Then realising that this might sound as though he were fishing for some money, he added quickly. "Sorry, I didn't mean that to sound as though I were asking..."

"Of course not. But we can't have you going in with a brand new haversack anyway. Mark you out again. I expect all their haversacks are decorated."

"Yes, they all seemed to have drawn all over them."

"Thought so. Come with me."

Russell led Simon through the hallway and out across the small yard to the garage. The Triumph and the estate car were there, the former gleaming as always, the latter dirty and neglected looking, as always.

"Let's have a look what I've got," Russell said, rummaging in some drawers. As that drew a blank, he took some boxes down from some high shelves and put them on the heavy workbench. In the third such box, he found what he was looking for.

"Here we are. Just the job, I think."

He pulled out a battered, grubby looking haversack, with a series of patterns in faded biro of different colours covering most of it.

"Was that yours?" asked Simon.

"Heavens no, it was my son's."

"Oh," said Simon, who hadn't given Russell Deverill's family life any thought. Then remembering, "Thank you for the haversack."

"Got to merge with the mob sometimes, young man," said Russell. "There's a time to stand out and a time to merge. You're in a merge time at the moment."

Simon took his satchel and the haversack up to his room. Inside the haversack wasn't too bad. He wiped it out with a cloth from the kitchen and sorted out his books. He taped up most of the damage, and found some new pens from his desk. Next down to the yard to dump the shredded satchel in the bin. Then Homework. He sat down at his desk and started working. And then stopped. Was Daniel at this very moment doing exactly the same? Was he sitting in that familiar room at that desk they had so often shared? Was he missing Simon? He wiped back a tear and carried on with his work.

Next day, Martin Passmore approved of the haversack.

"Where'd you get that?"

"From the man that owns the house we live in."

"A landlord?"

"I suppose so. It's a flat, he lives downstairs and we live upstairs."

There followed a conversation about where Simon was living, and also about the farm where Martin lived. They had cows as well as growing crops. The bus came and Martin this time sat next to Simon to carry on the conversation.

"When do the sports clubs and that kind of thing meet?" asked Simon, thinking about his running.

"Sports Clubs?"

"Yes, isn't there a school athletics club?"

"What for?" asked Martin.

"For running, track and field stuff, like that."

Martin shook his head. "Nothing like that at Cermerton. Is that what you had at your last school?"

"Yes, there were lots of clubs. I was in the athletics club and we used to compete against other clubs at meetings and such."

"No, nothing like that. We get Games lesson once a week, and gym. Do you like football?"

Simon knew that this was not about rugger but about association football. He was aware that Bilthaven FC was one of the country's top clubs, but that was about as far as it went.

"Not much. Never had much to do with it. What happens in Games lessons?"

"Football."

Simon's heart sank. Memories of enforced rugger came back to him. But then the bus was at the bus stop where the Neanderthals got on. The Watson brothers and Nev Carter got on. Bruce Watson stopped on his way to the vacant back seat alongside Simon and Martin.

"Friends with Passmore now, Scott?"

Simon made no reply, partly because he wasn't sure if he counted Martin Passmore as a friend or if he counted Simon as one. "We're just talking," he said in the end.

"You better not be talking about me," said Bruce Watson.

"Believe it or not, we hadn't given you a second thought," retorted Simon, managing to tap his chest twice.

"Don't you fucking cheek me, you posh cunt," said Watson, reaching across Martin and grabbing Simon's lapel. "Where's your bag?"

"Let go," said Simon.

"His bag's there," said Martin, nervously, pointing to the floor beside Simon's feet.

"Come on Bruce," said Nev Carter, "leave him for later." The bus was moving and lurching along a bit through traffic.

"I can see you're going to be trouble, Scott," said Bruce Watson. "Have to deal with you." He moved on, followed by Nev Carter and David Watson, both of whom managed a sinister grin at Simon as they passed.

"Why did you do that?" asked Martin.

"What?"

"Backchat them. It's asking for trouble."

"I've met their sort before," said Simon confidently.

"Not like them you haven't," said Martin. "They use those knives. They gave a kid a real beating last year and he had to have stitches across his cheek. Probably be scarred for life."

"What about the police?"

"Are you mad? Getting them involved would be asking for it. No, they just keep getting away with it. Probably kill someone one day."

"That would be the end of them."

"No consolation if it's you they get hung for."

"Hanged," said Simon, unthinkingly.

"What?"

"Things get hung, people get hanged," explained Simon.

"Oh clever sod, aren't you," said Martin, getting up to move to another seat.

"I'm sorry," said Simon, taking hold of Martin's arm. "It's just hard trying to fit in. It's all so different here."

Martin sat down again. "Apology accepted. I think you're right actually. People get hanged."

Simon was tactful enough not to point out that he knew he was right.

2. 1961/1 *Farmhouse tea*

Gradually Simon adjusted to life at Cermerton Grammar. Winter turned to Spring. Simon's lack of prowess at football was soon apparent, but his running record stood him in good stead. He was allowed to train and run in Games lessons, which kept him fit and as he was the only one, it afforded him time to think. Soon the games teacher realised it was not just a way of doing nothing. Simon prepared a programme for himself based on Mr Atherstone's training, which was approved, and then to a large extent he was left alone. The other kids accepted this as just another southern eccentricity. But there was no competitive running and Simon knew he was losing his edge.

The daily bus journeys remained a trial, with harassment on each journey from the Watsons and Carter, sometime just verbal, sometimes a swipe at his head as they passed. Simon grew to hate them. One day a red haired boy annoyed him and in retaliation, Simon called him carrot top from then on. The more Simon was harassed by the Watsons, the more Simon called the red haired boy. This went on for some weeks until one day, the boy sat next to Simon on the bus.

"Will you stop calling me names? Why are you doing it? Don't you think we all have enough of it from that lot without some stuck up southern kid coming and throwing his weight about?"

Simon was completely taken aback by the frankness of this approach. He realised that he had simply been trying to compensate for his own being bullied by bullying this boy.

"Yes, OK then," said Simon, abashed. The red haired boy got up and moved to his usual seat. Martin Passmore had seen this and came to Simon's seat.

"You had that coming," he said, and then went to sit elsewhere, leaving Simon alone and feeling stupid as well as miserable. Of course the boy and Martin Passmore were right. He had been a fool, and now stood to lose whatever gains he had made since starting to use the bus.

"On your own today, Scotty?" It was Bruce Watson, going down towards the back seat. Simon wondered what would happen next. Bruce Watson hit him. Then Nev Carter hit him.

"Your turn, Davey, hit him," said Bruce.

Simon suffered the indignity of being hit by this boy two years younger than him, who could do so with impunity because of who he was. The red haired boy was watching this unexpected payback with satisfaction. Then they moved to the back seat, their sport over; for the time being. Simon looked out of the window at the city suburbs. He was very glad he was not at the sec mod with the Neanderthals. Was Vicks like that? He thought of all the work Daniel had done with him to get him to the grammar school. Oh, Daniel! He tried to pretend it was unreal, he was watching someone else, but was brought back from his make believe.

"Why do you think you're better than everyone else?"

Simon turned back from the window, it was Martin who now sat next to him.

"I don't," he said.

"It's the way you act. You make sarky comments, you talk posh. You've got to try and fit in."

"I am trying. It's OK at school, it's just this confounded bus."

"There you go again! Confounded bus. What's that mean?"

Simon suppressed a remark that it was just the Queen's English. Instead he said, "Sorry. Didn't mean it."

"You're a funny one. Are they all like you down south?"

"I don't know," said Simon. "It's just different, that's all."

"Why don't you come for tea one night?" said Martin, unexpectedly.

"To the farm where you live?"

"Of course. I'll ask my Mam."

"Thanks, Martin. That would be really topper."

"Topper? Who says topper?"

"Sorry again," said Simon. "There I go, can't get out of it."

"Southerner," jibed Martin, but he was grinning as he said it. Simon felt a bit of happiness for the first time since arriving in Bilthaven.

That evening, he was walking back along Swiford High Street in good spirits with his individual apple pie. The shop staff had got so used to him coming in for it that now they kept one back for him; which made Simon feel obliged to call for it every night.

He let himself in and picked up his copy of *Navy News*. He was now having this delivered, as his interest in the Royal Navy increased. He was still doing his homework in his room when he heard Mum come in. Ken was with her, as he often was.

"Hello, love," Mum called from the landing. "Everything all right?"

"Yes, Mum, fine," he called back from his desk.

He heard Mum go into the lounge, and then her call. "Didn't you see your letter?"

Letter!! At last!! Simon ran across the landing into the lounge.

"Where? Where's the letter?"

"I left it propped up on the mantelpiece for you. Look," said Mum, smiling.

Simon practically flew to the mantelpiece, but as soon as he saw the envelope, he knew it was not the longed for letter from Daniel. It was Dad's handwriting. Mum was still smiling in expectation of her son's pleasure at getting a letter from his father. How could she know the depth of his disappointment, the raised hope suddenly crushed?

"It's from Dad," he said.

"Yes, I expect he wants to tell you something."

"Usual reason for writing a letter," said Simon, grumpily.

"There's no need to be like that, Simon," said Mum, crossly.

"Sorry," said Simon automatically and took the letter to his bedroom. He read it sitting on his bed. It was a surprise. Dad had booked the hotel in Salcombe, and *Invention*, for the same two weeks, if he would like to go. Like to go? Of course he would like to go! He had thought the separation and the move north had killed Salcombe for him, but here was Dad offering to take him! The fact that Dad had left their old home, their old city and moved to Nottingham, escaped him at first.

"Mum! Dad's taking me to Salcombe again this year!" he shouted down the landing.

"Well, that's changed your mood," said Mum, smiling now. "You'd better write back and tell him you want to go."

So Simon sat down and wrote straight back, accepting and saying how much he was looking forward to it. Salcombe! Yes!

With his letter writing stuff out, he toyed with writing yet another letter to Daniel. In the months since coming to Bilthaven, the stream of letters he had written had gradually come to a halt, and it was now some weeks since the last attempt. But Simon knew in his heart there would be no reply. He did not know why, and it hurt. To write again, to raise his hopes, to be again watching the post, rushing in from school to see if there was a letter for him among those on the mat, or if Russell had picked them up, on the hall table; all that would just be too painful to start again. With sadness, Simon put the writing case away, and wiped a single tear from his eye. But he was going to Salcombe!

"Why has Dad moved to Nottingham?" he asked Mum over tea.

"He's changed jobs, I think," replied Mum.

"Has he left the BBC then?"

"No, just a new job, a better one I expect."

"What about our old house?"

"That's up for sale, and I could do with my share."

"Will you get some money?"

"I'd bloody better," said Mum with feeling.

"I'm sure Harry will treat you fairly," said Ken.

"It's about time he did," said Mum. "Oh, I'm sorry Simon, I know he's still your Dad."

Simon thought back to that night last October – was it only last October? – that he heard those dreadful sounds from their bedroom. "It's OK, Mum. I understand." He got up to return to his room to continue his homework.

"I sometimes think that boy knows more about what's gone on than we think," he heard Ken say when he was on the landing.

"No, that's one thing Harry and I were agreed upon. Simon must be protected."

Simon smiled a wry smile, and returned to his desk.

It was a few days later that Simon was to go the farm. Mum had said it was fine, glad that Simon was making friends at last. Martin's Mam had also agreed. They sat together on the bus home, nervous as always until the stop about halfway when the Neanderthals got off, and then joined in the inaudible but very real sigh of relief that went round the bus.

Martin visibly relaxed. "That's better. Can't wait for their stop on a night time."

"And dread getting to it in the morning," added Simon.

Martin nodded vigorously.

"Who will be there then?" asked Simon.

"Me, you, my Dad, my Mam. Maybe my cousin."

"Is your cousin coming? How old is he?"

"No, she's not coming, she lives on the farm too. About our age."

"Why doesn't she come to Cermerton then?"

"My uncle, her Dad, sent her to a girls' school. He doesn't like Cermerton."

"A man with taste then," quipped Simon.

Martin looked uncertainly at Simon for a moment, then realised it was meant as a joke and smiled.

As they got off the bus at Swiford, Simon felt a pang of guilt. His apple pie!

"How long before the bus to the farm?" he asked.

"About ten minutes," answered Martin, looking at his watch.

"Come on then, something to do," said Simon, and set off at a run along the High Street, Martin following.

"Where're we going?" asked Martin, breathlessly.

"Food!" said Simon.

They ran into the baker's shop.

"Oh, hello, pet. Oh, two of you tonight."

"Yes," said Simon. "Have you got two left?"

"We've got yours," said the assistant, reaching under the counter and producing an apple pie. "I'll have a look." She scanned the almost empty display cabinets. Her voice changed to a piercing shriek.

"Doris! Have we got any more small apple pies? That lad's come in but he's got a pal with him!"

From somewhere in the depths of the shop a muffled reply came, presumably from Doris.

"Hang on, I'll 'ave a look." There was a pause while the assistant smiled at the two boys. Doris appeared from the recesses of the shop bearing an apple pie.

"You're in luck, pet. There was still one on the tray."

"Thanks," said Simon, paying for both pies.

They left the shop, Simon handing Martin one of the pies in its paper bag.

"What's that for?" said Martin.

"To eat," said Simon.

"I know that, but why did you buy one for me? And why do they keep one for you? Do they keep one every night?"

"I bought it for you, isn't that good enough? Thought you would like it. And they keep one for me every night because my Mum doesn't get in until later and they've got used to me coming in. I didn't want not to turn up when I knew they would be keeping it. Sort of lets them down."

"We **are** going to have some tea," said Martin bluntly. "My Mam's baking."

Simon now saw how his apple pies could be construed. "I didn't mean anything like that," said Simon, hurriedly. "I know we are, but I didn't want to let them down, and I thought we could eat them on the bus."

"OK then," said Martin, "talking of which, we'd better hurry."

They went upstairs on the bus, a motor bus on this route as the trolley buses evidently didn't go out into the countryside where the farm would be. They munched their apple pies.

"Thanks, Simon," said Martin. "Sorry if I sounded ungrateful. It's just that it's ... Well, you're unusual. Different. I wasn't expecting it."

Simon thought for a moment. Was he ever going to get away from being 'different'? At least nobody in Bilthaven called him a bastard. Maybe because it had its fair share of bastards anyway, both in terms of Neanderthals and judging from what he had gleaned, a significant proportion of kids from single parent families. Oh, I'm now one of those, he thought.

"That's OK. If you're giving me tea, at least I can buy you an apple pie. Lucky they had an extra one."

"Yes. They're good, aren't they?" said Martin, munching. "If I get hungry, I usually make myself a bacon sandwich. We've got an Aga, do you know what they are?"

Simon's mind was suddenly full of Daniel, standing by the Aga, deftly flipping the bacon over with the casual competence about him that Simon had so envied. He managed a nod, but he felt the grief welling up in him.

"You OK?" asked Martin.

"Yes, I'm fine," said Simon. "Just brought back some memories, and yes, I do know what an Aga is."

Simon saw that the bus was now out of the city. It had followed a route through a part of Swiford that Simon didn't know and now had fields on both sides.

"Come on," said Martin, getting up. The road was quite undulating which made it hard to move along the top deck and down the stairs. Martin pressed the bell as they went. They stood on the open platform at the back of the bus, holding the pole as it slowed to a stop by a farm. The farm. The boys jumped off and the bus moved away. It was suddenly very quiet.

"Have you got your own personal bus stop?" asked Simon, impressed, looking at the bus stop sign outside the farm entrance.

"How else would we get the bus to stop?" replied Martin.

Simon looked around. It dawned on him that this was the first time he had been out in the countryside since; since the last bike ride with Daniel. There was a collection of farm buildings, and some stone houses with slate roofs. There was now the sound of mooing coming from one of the farm buildings and machine noises.

Martin led the way to one of the houses. "Not used to the countryside, then?"

"Yes, I used to go for bike rides into the country from where we lived, but I've not been on a farm before. What's the noise?"

"Cows," said Martin. Then seeing that more explanation was needed, added, "Milking time."

Mrs Passmore made them welcome. She had prepared what can only be described, aptly in this case, as a real farmhouse tea. It was mouth watering to look at. But they would have to wait until Mr Passmore came back from milking.

"Can we go and see?" asked Simon.

"What for?" said Martin. "It's just cows getting milked. And anyway, not in those clothes."

"Oh, I see," said Simon disappointed.

"Mam, can I take Simon to my room?"

"Yes love."

The boys went up an old, wide stairway that turned twice before coming out onto a large landing. Through the window at the end, Simon could see the edge of Bilthaven in the distance, Swiford he assumed.

Martin noticed.

"When I was little, you couldn't see any houses from here. They built those in the last few years. But we got a lot of money for the land, so I suppose we shouldn't complain."

Simon hadn't thought about ownership until now. "Do you own all this farm and all the land?"

"My Granda does, but my Dad and Uncle part own it as well. Not sure of the details."

"Will you own it one day?" asked Simon, now in awe of Martin's apparent wealth.

"Maybe, but I don't want to be a farmer. Definitely not. Not dairy anyway."

Simon let that pass as they went into Martin's room. It was quite large, perhaps about the same size as Daniel's, but very different in feel. There was a desk, a chest of drawers, a large wardrobe, a heavy Ottoman chest; all the furniture was old fashioned, solid stuff. Martin's bed, a single bed, stood along one wall and the window looked out over fields to woods beyond. How different from his own bedroom window in Swiford, thought Simon. On one side there was a record player which Martin was now opening.

"Do you like Elvis?" he asked Simon.

"Yeah, he's OK."

Soon the record player was blasting out.

"We only got mains electric a few years ago," said Martin over the music. "Was part of the land deal."

"What did you do before that?" asked Simon, wondering how anybody could live without electricity.

"We had a generator, still got it for emergencies. And we used oil lamps upstairs. We only got the wires upstairs when we got mains in."

There was a shout from downstairs which Martin could make out but Simon could not.

"My cousin's here," said Martin, turning off the record player. "Come on." He led the way downstairs. Two girls about Simon's age were in the kitchen, a large farmhouse kitchen, with the Aga, that reminded Simon so much of Daniel's. But far more cluttered and busy seeming. A working kitchen. There was the smell of fresh baking. But Simon's eye was immediately caught by the girls. One was fair haired with blue eyes and the family likeness to Martin was clearly discernable. That must be the cousin then. But other the girl was the one who attracted Simon's attention. Smaller, slim with long shoulder length, dark brown hair and deep brown eyes. And she was smiling at Simon too. He felt something stir within him. He wanted to get to know this girl. He smiled at her. Yes! There was no quick looking away, no rejection. She smiled back, warmly.

"Simon, this is Edith my cousin, and her friend, Diane. This is Simon, we're at school together," Martin was saying. Simon pulled himself out of his reverie to recover his manners.

"How do you do," he said formally, wondering if he should shake hands.

"Hi," said Edith.

"Hi Simon," said Diane. She said my name! thought Simon, elated.

Martin was explaining that Simon was a southerner recently arrived in Bilthaven, he lived in Swiford and his Mam worked for the *Bilthaven Mail* and was in the paper. He was in the class above Martin, and so must be a brain box. But Simon could not keep his eyes off Diane. He said something deprecatory about not being that brainy.

Then Martin's Dad appeared. "You must be Simon, Martin's told us all about you."

"How do you do," he repeated.

They all sat down to eat the tea of fresh ham sandwiches ("Our own pork," said Mr Passmore.), freshly baked cakes, scones with all the trimmings.

"What do you think of the farm, Simon," Edith asked.

"I haven't seen much of it."

"We'll show you around next time you come," said Mr Passmore. "Getting a bit late now." And indeed, it was dusk.

"That would be very nice, thank you."

"Do you like the countryside, Simon?" It was Diane, sitting opposite him who had asked the question!

"Yes, I was in the Scouts before we moved, so we got out into the countryside a lot. And I went for bike rides with my friend."

"Not in the Scouts now?" asked Mrs Passmore.

"No. I wouldn't have long before I would have to move up to Venture Scouts, and I didn't feel like starting again. I was a Patrol Leader, but obviously I couldn't be if I joined a scout troop here."

"Very wise," said Mr Passmore. "Never go backwards, move forwards."

"And I've got a lot of work catching up for my GCEs. Some of the subjects are different."

So the conversation progressed, the family curious about life 'down south', Hooray Henrys, his family troubles and his Mum working for the paper.

"I always read her page," said Mrs Passmore. "I never knew that Kate Drummond was your Mam."

"That was her maiden name," explained Simon. "She always uses that for work."

Later the four teenagers went through to the lounge, referred to as The Room, which it was apparently a privilege for them to use. They sat and talked. Simon and Diane were sitting next to each other on a settee, they called it a sofa. He wanted to reach out and touch her hair, the closeness of her exciting him in an unfamiliar way. Not the way he found Daniel's closeness exciting, here he felt protective and wanting to take the lead with this girl. Daniel and he had been so close, so familiar, but this was new, strange. She wasn't like the girls at school, many of whom were just catty beyond belief. She seemed sensible and kind. He knew he wanted to meet her again. He found his hand touching hers. While the conversation carried on, he gently increased the contact to gauge her reaction. She didn't move her hand! Then he saw Martin was watching. Suddenly nervous he moved his hand away.

It was time for the bus. Simon said his goodbyes, thanked Martin's parents for the tea and with his haversack and coat, walked with Martin up the driveway to the road. It was very dark and the sky was full of stars.

"You liked Diane, didn't you?" said Martin. In the dark, Simon could not judge Martin's feeling behind this. Was it hostile? Resentful? Teasing? He shone his borrowed torch towards Martin. He was smiling slightly.

"Yes, she's not your girlfriend or anything is she?" he asked, worried.

"No, we did go out for a while, though, but not now."

"I'm sorry," said Simon as they crossed the road to stand opposite the bus stop.

"Don't be," said Martin. "I could tell she liked you. Really did."

"Honest?" said Simon.

"Why not, you're good looking, posh, talk posh too. Your Mam works for the paper."

"All the things you've told me not to be!" laughed Simon.

"At school, yes," said Martin flatly. "Otherwise, be yourself. Especially if Diane likes it."

The lights of the bus could be seen in the distance. As it approached, Martin stood at the edge of the road and waved his torch slowly back and forth, and the noise of the bus's engine changed as it started to slow down. It came to a stop next to them, big and brightly lit in the darkness. Simon got on. The conductor rang the bell and the bus started to move.

"Thanks, Martin," he called.

"She's always here to see Edith on a Saturday," shouted Martin as the bus moved away.

"Come on son, can't stand here," said the conductor, urging Simon to leave the exposed platform. He climbed the stairs, looking back he saw the pinprick of light that was Martin's torch crossing the road, and the lights of the farmhouses. He sat down upstairs, pondering the import of Martin's last comment A very good evening, he thought, as the bus entered the built up Bilthaven suburb of Swiford.

The following day Martin said that he had been right, Diane did like Simon. It was arranged that Simon should come to the farm on Saturday. Now Simon knew the route, he could cycle it in half an hour, which would save the bus fare.

That evening, Simon lay on his bed reading *Navy News*. He noticed an item that caught his eye, for scholarships at Dartmouth Royal Naval College for officer training for the Royal Navy. The more Simon thought about this, the more it appealed to him. He was interested in the sea, and in naval matters, naval history. He took the magazine through to the lounge, where Mum and Frances were watching television.

"Mum, what do you think of this?"

Mum read the item.

"It says they are looking to recruit more officers from grammar schools, instead of the public schools. Is it what you want, Simon?"

"Yes, I've been thinking about it for a while, and then seeing this has made me realise that it really is."

"Very well then, write off for the application forms and information and see what you get."

Simon wrote a letter in his best handwriting that evening, and sent it off the next day.

On Saturday, Simon rode his bicycle to the farm, dressed, as advised, in his older clothes. They made a foursome, Martin, Edith, Diane and Simon. Martin seemed quite relaxed in Diane's company, even though they had previously dated. Simon wanted to see Diane more, but was nervous. He toyed with the idea of telling Martin that he hadn't actually been out with a girl before, but he knew he had a reputation now based on his ambiguous comments when he first arrived at Cermerton, so that was a closed option. He wondered 'how far' Martin had gone with Diane.

But first he was shown round the farm, its byre, the dairy, the machinery and the barns. There were three tractors, two large blue Fordson Majors, and a smaller grey Ferguson. Other machinery was brought over from the other farm when needed, Martin explained.

"What other farm?" asked Simon, surprised.

"We've another farm which my other uncle runs. It's about five miles away. There's more stuff there which both farms share."

Simon tried to take in this sudden extension of Martin's already large wealth. He said nothing about that, but as for the moment they were away from the two girls, he asked, as casually as he could manage, "How long did you go out with Diane for?"

"A few months, not long."

"Why did it stop?"

"I don't know. I suppose she's Edith's best friend, and with her being my cousin, it just seemed awkward. Neither of us finished with the other, it just kind of stopped."

Simon wondered how to ask the question most on his mind. He found himself tapping his chest twice as he asked, "How far did things go between you, then?"

"Nosey boy, aren't you?" said Martin. Simon flushed, but he saw Martin was smiling. "Must be all that sailor stuff you do, you want to plot your course before you even set out. Where's your spirit of adventure?"

"Well, any sailor likes to know where the rocks are and where the deep, safe water is before he sets sail," said Simon, continuing Martin's metaphor.

"We kissed, we snogged. A bit of downstairs stuff if you get my meaning, but we didn't have sex. Intercourse I mean."

"I'm sorry, Martin. I do like her and I'm just a bit nervous."

"After all those girls you had down south?" said Martin. So Martin's bought into the Casanova legend as well.

"Diane's different, she's special I think," said Simon, a reply which had the benefit of truth and explained his attitude he hoped. It seemed to suffice.

"I still like Diane, as a friend," said Martin. "Just don't hurt her, that's all."

"Last thing I want to do, Martin," said Simon with feeling.

At that moment the girls found them.

"Come on, let's go and look at the horses," said Diane to Simon. And she took him by the hand, leading him to where the former work horses, large shire horses, were stabled. Simon caught Martin's eye as he was pulled away; Martin was smiling to himself, it seemed.

So the afternoon was a success from Simon's point of view. He felt he had developed his friendship with Martin, become accepted by the Passmores but most of all, his friendship with Diane had grown. Over the coming weeks it would continue to flourish as Simon spent most weekends at the farm, treading the fine line between being a guest and a burden. But he made himself useful, putting his fit young body to use around the farm, learning about milking, how to handle the cattle, and later, he was trusted to drive the Fordsons, but for some reason, never the Ferguson. To Martin's bemusement, he was happy spending a few hours sitting on the tractor, ploughing or harrowing, getting filthy from the exhaust which simply stuck straight up from the engine, much of the diesel exhaust blowing past him on the open driving seat, blackening his face. But it gave Simon a purpose, and a focus to life in Bilthaven, a chance to think, to grieve even, and come to terms with his new life. And of course, there was Diane!

Simon's naval ambitions took a step further when he was asked to attend an interview in Edinburgh. Scotland! Simon had not been to Scotland before, so that was an adventure in itself. He made the early morning train journey from Bilthaven to Edinburgh and then following his instructions, to the naval base at Granton. This was a preliminary screening involving some academic tests and a series of interviews, rather daunting in front of a panel of naval officers in uniform. But he was able to answer all their questions and it turned out that one of the officers, a Commander, had been to Hooray Henrys! An old boy! Perhaps that did Simon some good. Then late at night, back home to Bilthaven to await the result. This came quite quickly and having passed the first hurdle, Simon was asked to attend a three day assessment at HMS Sultan in Portsmouth, if he wished. Of course he wished!

Gradually it became accepted that Simon came to the farm to see Diane as much as Martin, and they would walk across the fields, through the woods that the farm included. It was on one such early summer's day walk, alone together that they sat on a fallen tree in the wood, talking. There came a natural lull in the conversation. Simon put his arm around Diane, drawing her close. She looked up at him, there seemed an expectancy about her. Simon leaned forward and kissed her gently on the lips. She responded by running her hands round his neck and shoulders, through his hair and kissing him again. For Simon, this first kiss with a girl made him feel excited and aroused, it was different to Daniel because the whole relationship was different. Did she guess this was his first kiss with a girl?

When they pulled apart, she laughed and said, "You've done that before, haven't you?"

Simon was unsure what to say, so just smiled.

"It's OK, I don't mind," she said. "Martin's told me about you, and anyway, it's not my first time, of course. You know Martin and I went out for a while?"

"Yes, he told me. I was a bit worried about that, in case he didn't like us being together."

"Martin's OK," said Diane. "He doesn't say much though, does he? What the word I want?"

"Laconic?" suggested Simon. "Yes, he is a bit. But I like him. My first friend here in Bilthaven, that I see outside school I mean. Until you."

"I'm glad you met him then, otherwise we wouldn't be here now, doing this." With that she kissed Simon again, with a passion that took him by surprise. He allowed his hand to fall to her shoulder, wanting to explore her breast. She made no attempt to stop him, as she ran her hands down his back, feeling his body through his shirt. His hand felt her breast, cupping it and enjoying its firm and yet soft texture. She smiled at him and her hand brushed his denim jeans, briefly touching his hardness.

"You're a big boy," she said, playfully.

"Had no complaints," replied Simon, wondering where this was leading.

"Mmm. I bet not," she said, this time pressing more firmly, feeling the outline through his jeans. She was teasing him he knew, but Simon sensed it was kindly, inviting even, desire in her eyes also. But then she pulled away.

"We'd better get back," she said.

"Oh, all right," said Simon.

She saw the look on his face. "Don't worry, we can do this again. If you want, of course."

"Yes, I want to. Very much," said Simon. That evoked a smile from Diane, she took his hand and they walked back to the farm, talking about Yuri Gagarin and Soviet achievements in space.

3. 1961/6 Seeing the future

Frances had never taken to Bilthaven, so it came as no real surprise when she announced she was leaving. She had got a job in London, working for the BBC in radio and had found a flat she was going to share.

"Will you be OK?" asked Simon. He was thinking how Frances had always been a part of his life, there in the background, his big sister. He remembered the times she had comforted him when he was little, when Dad was in one of his moods, of the times she had crept into his room to talk late at night.

"Of course I will. I am more worried about you, little bro. But Mum will take care of you, and you've got this navy thing now. I hope that goes OK. You'll let me know."

"Course. You know I'm going to Salcombe with Dad. It'll be odd being there without you and Mum."

"The sea is in your blood. More than mine. I like sailing, but not to spend my life at sea. But if it's what you want."

"You know what they say," said Simon, "We joined the navy to see the world, and what did we see? We saw the sea! But it's what I want to do."

"You'll be OK in Salcombe. Is Jack whatsisname going to be there?"

"Griffin. I'm not sure, I hope so. I'll ask Dad if the Griffins are going."

"Try not to judge Dad too harshly. I know he's been pretty rough with you, but I think he loves you in his own way."

"Maybe," said Simon, unconvinced. "I'll try."

She was gone. Off to her new life in London and away from the dull life she had found in the north. It had lasted only a few months, but she was a lot older than Simon. Another part of his life changed. No Frances. Only when she had gone did he really start to miss her. It seemed as though everything in his life was in turmoil. Nothing any longer could be taken for granted. The flat seemed empty without her. Mum left the divan bed in the lounge and moved into the big front bedroom, which made things a lot easier.

Parker's Field on the edge of the city centre was the site each year for a large travelling fair to visit Bilthaven. Simon met up there with Diane. Martin and Edith came too and they wandered around, going on some of the rides. At one side of the fair were some fortune tellers' caravans. 'The Original Gypsy Rose Lee' proclaimed one.

"Shall I go in?" Simon asked Diane, joking. He had no belief in such things but was curious about what 'Gypsy Rose Lee' might say.

"It's your money," remarked Martin.

"Go on then," said Diane. "I'll come too."

"We'll see you by the waltzer," said Martin as he and Edith made off through the crowds in the summer sunshine.

Simon and Diane climbed the steps.

"Just one at a time, dears," said Gypsy Rose Lee.

"You go, Simon," said Diane. So he stepped into the small caravan. It was heavily draped but there was a small round table on which was a glass ball in a stand and a chair either side of the table. Gypsy Rose Lee sat in one and indicated the other to Simon, having first pulled a curtain across the door. She looked about fifty, Simon thought.

"Cross my palm with silver," she commanded in the cool gloom.

Simon was unsure what she meant, and the uncertainly showed on his face.

"I need some money, dear," she explained.

Simon offered half a crown and this was acceptable. She sat and looked intently at Simon for what seemed liked several minutes, he looked rather uncomfortably back. She cupped her hands round around the glass ball.

"The crystal is speaking to me," she said. "The young lady, she's special to you."

Pretty obvious, thought Simon, so he just nodded. He realised he should give as few clues as possible.

"I can see animals," she said. "Large animals, not pets." She looked at Simon for some response.

"Cows?"

"Yes, that's right, there's a farm I see. But it's not yours, or hers."

Simon was surprised and was forced to nod, then was annoyed with himself for giving away information.

"But you love another. You pine for another you've left behind."

Simon felt the shock. How could she know that? The pain that brought must have shown on his face and she moved quickly on.

"You've a yen to wear a uniform," she continued, and then stopped, seeming puzzled. She frowned and stared into the glass ball. "You won't."

That's what you think, thought Simon, relieved to have found a flaw in Gypsy Rose Lee.

But she carried on. "Well, you will, but it won't be for your work. And you'll work for the state, but you won't wear a uniform for that," she said in a hesitant tone.

By this time Simon was feeling very sceptical. She had obviously no idea.

"Will I be rich?" he asked.

"No," she said, "you'll never be rich. But you won't be poor either."

Then she seemed to stop abruptly, her tone changing. "I can't see beyond the age of sixty," she said. Simon had the distinct impression she could but didn't want to say.

"That's all I can see," she concluded.

"Thank you," said Simon. He got up to leave. As he drew back the curtain, she called to him.

"Young man," she said, with some emotion on her face. "Beware of three."

"Three what?" said Simon.

But she shook her head and waved him out. He climbed down the steps into the bright sunshine.

"What did she say?" asked Diane. "Shall I go in?"

"I wouldn't bother," said Simon. "She said I liked you which was fairly obvious by the way we went in together. And she guessed about the farm. But she got it hopelessly wrong about me joining the navy."

"Come on then, let's go to the waltzer and meet the others," said Diane.

So they wandered off, and Gypsy Rose Lee was largely forgotten, a bit of harmless fun.

4. 1961/7 Testing times

The day came for the trip south to HMS Sultan. Another adventure for Simon. Portsmouth was a long way, and it would take most of the day. He would travel alone to London, cross the capital and then get a train to Portsmouth. This was on a ticket provided by the Royal Navy and he was to meet other boys who would travel that last part together and they would be met at Portsmouth station by the navy.

Mum was at work so Simon got the trolley bus to the station, armed with his naval ticket and his bag, containing enough for three days as well as PE kit and swimming trunks as instructed. It had been a while since he had travelled by train. He waited on the platform for the London train. On time, it pulled into the station on its southward journey, the steam locomotive seeming so huge, powerful, strong and invincible. As it approached drawing its slender train behind, Simon watched the rods connecting the wheels moving back and forth along their oiled way in and out of the cylinder block, slowing as their work was done, and as the huge beast came to rest its final energy was dissipated in a sudden noisy jet of white steam from the boiler and then it was still, panting quietly as it gathered its strength for the next stage of its journey. Simon stood for a moment in awe of the potency of this huge and rugged machine and then went to find a seat.

As he walked down the corridor, he realised he was not going to find an empty compartment, but he did find one with just one man in, which meant Simon could sit at the window seat. The journey passed unremarkably, Simon dipping into his packed food and drink. He was excited at the arrival in London, and felt very grown up as he consulted the tube map to find his route to Waterloo station. He arrived in good time for his train to Portsmouth which he noticed looking again at the travel documents was Portsmouth Harbour.

This station was by the sea, as might be expected. He got out and looked around for some likely sign of the reception. He saw two sailors in navy uniform, one was holding a sign that read HMS Sultan, and there were two boys about his own age standing with them. That must be it. Simon walked over.

"Hello, I think I'm supposed to be with you."

One of the sailors, a Petty Officer Simon noted, produced some papers. "What's your name?"

"Simon Scott." Should he have said 'Sir'? Not to a Petty Officer, he thought.

"Yes, Mr Scott, you're in the right place."

Mr Scott! Simon could not remember being called Mr Scott before. Quickly a few more boys arrived until the sailor was satisfied. The group was led out to a waiting blue minibus. This set off and soon was on a ferry crossing over the water. Simon realised they were going across to Gosport. Then through the town until they arrived at HMS Sultan, which seemed a large place. The boys were talking throughout the journey, getting to know each other and inevitably sizing up each other, the competition. Simon quickly realised he was the only one to be attending a standard state grammar school. He wished he were still at Hooray Henrys, at least that would have had some cachet. But they seemed a good bunch. Most had more sailing and naval experience than he had, some had their own yachts and their wealth was evident. Simon started to feel distinctly disadvantaged. The boys were curious about Cermerton Grammar School, and regarded Simon as a bit of an oddity. Would he ever fit in?

They were put in a dormitory room, Simon took a bottom bunk, and a Scottish lad known as Jock of course took the top one above him.

"It's all right," he said, "I gave up wetting the bed last year."

The others all laughed, and Simon was not sure whether they were laughing **at** him or not.

In the evening after eating, they were shown round and given a timetable for the next two days. These were spent in a variety of activities, individual interviews, physical drills and what Simon had been dreading, swimming.

When the swimming session came, Simon had fortunately already earned some credit by beating everybody over a 100 yard race by a good margin. The Petty Officer had tersely announced to everybody that he would have been surprised if he had not won, given his county record breaking run. How did they know about that? thought Simon. But it raised his creditworthiness in what Simon now was finding the most competitive situation he had ever been in, far more than Henrys athletics. Just as at school, he was the youngest in the group too. Only he and one other boy were still fourteen, and that one was a very big, strong boy for fourteen.

So when they were taken to the pool, Simon had to tell the instructor. Tapping his chest twice for courage, he approached the sailor, a Leading Seaman, he thought.

"Excuse me, but I can't swim."

The sailor looked at Simon, plainly surprised. "Can't swim? And you want to be an officer in Her Majesty's Navy?"

"I'm afraid so. I would learn before starting at Dartmouth," said Simon. He saw the others looking curiously at him, but not unkindly.

"Wait there please, Mr Scott," said the sailor. He went away and returned with the Chief Petty Officer who was in charge of the group. The sailor then turned to the others and got them into the water, swimming lengths. Simon felt stupid.

"Willis tells me you can't swim, Mr Scott," said the CPO.

"Yes, I had an incident when young learning to swim and never really went back to it."

"What kind of incident?"

"In a swimming pool, an outdoor one, and I got into trouble and had to be pulled from the bottom of the pool. I suppose it's put me off a bit."

"You were lucky there was a lifeguard, then."

"It was my friend who pulled me out, but yes, I was lucky."

"Well, it's no good being 'put off'. We can't have the future leaders of the Royal Navy being 'put off', can we?"

"No. I understand that, I will be learning to swim."

"You go sailing, don't you? Isn't it dangerous being unable to swim?"

"I usually wear a life jacket," answered Simon.

"Can you manage today with a float?"

"Yes, I expect so."

So Simon paddled along the pool, keeping close to the side, using a cork float for support, feeling very uneasy when he knew he was out of his depth. The session lasted over two hours, but it felt like two days to Simon.

In the changing room, Simon kept himself to one side, unsure what to say. None of the others said anything to him about it, until Jock.

"How do you expect to be an officer in the Royal Navy if you can't swim, Scott?"

"I expect they have ships," replied Simon. He knew the joke was an old one, but it was enough to get a laugh and break the ice. "And I will be able to swim by the time we all start at Dartmouth."

Simon liked the 'we all'; he thought it was an olive branch to the group. It worked, because the others started talking to him again, and he felt re-accepted.

He managed to hold his own in the gym despite being the youngest and he was conscious that he was also one of the smallest. But his fitness matched the others, if his coordination with ball games didn't. The individual sessions went better, usually with officers, wide ranging discussions on various topics, including history, where Simon felt he did really well. He was able to talk knowledgably about Nelson's tactics at Trafalgar, and impressed when he described how Admiral Yamamoto had taken on board the Royal Navy's victory at Taranto, proving what he had advocated for some time, that aircraft carriers were rendering the battleships obsolete.

They got on as a group, the various characters coming out. Jock was always last out of bed, having to be roused by the Petty Officer that came in to get them up.

But the afternoon of the last day went badly. The group were in the gym again, and were each given a problem to solve using only the equipment to hand, taking it in turns to command the group, watched by the CPO, some officers and others.

The boys were able quickly to assess the situation and allocate tasks to group members to achieve the task in hand. Simon was third to go in command. His task was to get the whole group across a 'river', a gap between floor mats, using some beams, ropes and other sundry items. Simon's mind froze. He just could not see how he could achieve this. The others were waiting for his orders, the assessors were watching. He could not see a workable solution. He felt the pressure mounting. He did this sort of thing at scouts, why not now? He started to talk, but he knew it wasn't making a lot of sense. He felt as though he were watching himself making such a mess of it. But the other boys started to carry out his orders, asking him questions, rallying round, but it was quite apparent they were asking him whether to do what they thought would work, rather than Simon's own inept plan. So Simon agreed and the group eventually got across. But he felt humiliated, and spent the rest of the time carrying out the orders as each boy took his turn, none of whom made such a mess of it as he had.

Back in the changing room, the boys were chatting away, Simon was quiet.

Fernley-Smythe came over to him. "Don't worry Scott, we all have bad days. You got us across in the end."

Simon felt grateful for the encouragement but knew he didn't deserve it.

"No, you lot got us across. Thanks for helping out though."

"You'll be OK," said Fernley-Smythe, to the nods of the others. "We have to be a team, don't we?"

After supper, the boys had individual sessions. Simon was interviewed by a small man in a grey suit. He looked a bit scruffy Simon thought.

"Home tomorrow then," said the man.

"Yes, it's quite a long journey."

"How do you feel about the two days?"

"OK. The boys are all very good. It's been interesting."

"You are well read when it comes to naval history."

"History generally. I think it's important to understand that naval power is used as an extension of politics, so you have to understand what's going on and the reasons behind any naval or military action being taken."

"Suppose you, as a naval commander, disagree with the policy of the government, and don't feel the ordered action is right?"

"I don't think that's a problem in a democracy. And even Yamamoto, who disagreed with his government's policy, carried out his orders to the best of his ability."

"If you thought the action was doomed to failure?"

"The naval officers should advise the government on the naval aspects of any plan, but not against the policy behind it."

"Hmm. Good. How did you feel about this afternoon's command exercise?"

This was the question Simon had been dreading. "I think everybody did well, we all achieved the task given." He knew this was a weak answer.

"You seemed all at sixes and sevens out there, not sure what to do when faced with the challenge."

"It took a bit of time to get organised," Simon hedged.

"But it was the others that did the organising, was it not? You were supposed to be in command."

Faced with this direct confrontation of his failure, Simon could hedge no longer. "Yes, that's right. I just couldn't see how to do it."

"Yet the others could. Why was that, do you think?"

"I could see it once they got started. I just panicked a bit."

"How effective do you think a naval officer would be in the eyes of his men if he just panicked a bit when faced with an emergency?"

"Not very good."

"No good at all, wouldn't you agree?"

Simon could not answer, he just nodded.

"Well, that was a low point, but we do take the whole course into account. Have a safe journey home, Mr Scott."

Simon found it hard to join in the jollities of the last evening. The others tried to cheer him up, but Simon was glad for lights out.

In the morning he was relieved to be going home. He got out of bed and got ready, noticing that Jock, once again, was still in his top bunk.

"Jock, time to get up," said Simon.

"Go away," said a sleepy Jock from beneath the covers. At that moment the Petty Officer came in to check they were all up and ready. He marched over to Jock, shaking him.

"Why is it always you in the morning?" he demanded.

Jock peeped out from beneath the covers at the Petty Officer.

"Ach, and why is it always you in the morning?" he asked in his Scots accent.

Everybody laughed, Jock's Scottishness somehow adding to the humour of his reply. Jock was persuaded out of bed, and the ice had been broken.

The boys travelled together to London, except one who went off in a different direction. This helped keep the mood buoyant as they talked about the assessment, and looking forward to all meeting up again at Dartmouth in a few years.

But Simon's train journey north to Bilthaven was not a happy one for him. He knew he had not shown himself at his best. He travelled home disappointed. He sat on the train, watching the regular, swooping rise and fall of the telegraph wires, sometimes wreathed in steamy smoke, their undulating rhythm marking off the miles away from HMS Sultan and toward home, Cermerton School, and Diane. The prospect of seeing her again raised his spirits, but he knew she would be asking how he got on. He would cross that bridge when he reached it.

Over the next weeks, Simon's relationship with Diane advanced. They always met at the farm, Simon's questions about her home were avoided. She hinted that things at home were not well, one reason why she spent so much time with Edith. Simon knew exactly what she meant, seeking refuge with a friend from problems at home. Martin and Edith didn't seem to mind this, in fact from Simon's point of view at least, Martin appeared more than happy with it, encouraging it even. He said Simon was good for Diane, that she was coming out of herself. He didn't elaborate, Martin was always taciturn, and used as few words as possible.

Simon still felt obliged to work at the farm, his favourite being driving the tractors, but he was a regular helper at Saturday afternoon milking. As each cow was due to be milked, he would tip her feed into the trough at the front of her stall and then bring the milking machine, connect it to the overhead feed, start the cow by hand milking and checking for anything unusual on the four teats that might indicate disease and then placing the four cups onto them to draw out the milk. He also set up the cooler in the dairy, ensuring that the cooling water was running through, and then after each cow was milked, carry the urn along to the dairy, tip it into the top of the cooler and allow it run down over the cooled part and into the large churn underneath. Each time he went along he checked the churn to prevent it overflowing, putting the stopper in the cooler tray while he changed the now heavy churn for an empty one. It was hard, physical work, but he liked the feel of his body working and he was fit enough for it. Martin was faintly amused by this, but was quite happy for Simon to do it.

Simon and Mr Passmore, Martin's father, had several long conversations about the new idea of milking parlours where instead of the cows being in stalls in a long byre, they came through a milking station in conveyor belt fashion and the milk would be taken away through pipes to the dairy. But nothing ever came of it, in Simon's time there anyway.

Otherwise, he and Diane would go off for walks, the same fallen tree in the wood being a favourite spot to stop. Another favoured place, especially if the weather wasn't as good, was the upper floor of one of the barns where there was some hay they lay on to talk and explore each other's bodies. They had plenty of warning if anybody came in because the door was really squeaky and then there was a ladder to climb. So they felt secure there, as Simon found out.

"It's a good place, this," said Simon. "Safe, I mean."

"Am I safe when you're here?" joked Diane.

"Not if you play your cards right," replied Simon, kissing Diane, then kissing and stroking her bare breasts.

"We're safe enough here. Martin and I used to come here, and we were never interrupted."

Simon found the image of Diane and Martin, up here, doing what they were doing together, a bit off putting. It must have shown.

"Don't worry, he won't come if he thinks this is where we are," said Diane. Simon did not find that particularly reassuring, knowing that Martin knew where they were and probably what they were doing. "Oh, that didn't help, did it?" added Diane.

"Well, it's a bit odd, knowing he knows."

"What he tell you about what we did? I bet he said something."

"Yes, but not much, just said you snogged and that."

"Is that all?" said Diane, surprised.

"Well, he said you and he hadn't had intercourse, but there was some 'downstairs action' or something like that. You're not mad at him, or me, for him saying are you? Don't tell him I told you."

"Course I won't. I like 'downstairs action' though. Is that what he said?"

"Something like that."

"I wonder if this is what he meant?" said Diane, and started to undo Simon's belt, pulling down the zip of his jeans, and taking hold of his now very erect penis. She eased his jeans and pants down, while overcome by arousal, Simon kissed her breasts again and sent his hand to explore her most intimate parts. But she put out a hand to stop him.

"Not this week, Simon, maybe next week." He recoiled quickly as her meaning became clear to him.

"Sorry, I didn't know it was that time."

"That's OK, why should you? But that shouldn't stop you having fun, should it? Lie back, big boy." She took Simon in hand and slowly and gently brought him to climax, his first with another since Daniel, since that dreadful last evening. The waves of pleasure swept over his body and subsided. Diane was looking at him, smiling.

"What are you singing?"

Simon had been unaware he was singing, quietly to himself. *Fire, fire, fire down below*.

"It's just a song I used to sing with my last, er, girlfriend. We thought it suited it, *Fire down below* and all that." Simon thought it wiser not to mention it had in fact been his boyfriend.

"I like that, it fits, I suppose," said Diane. "I'll use that myself. It's a sea shanty, isn't it?"

"Yes, we used to it sing at scouts too."

"What, you and your girlfriend?" she said laughing.

"Well no, obviously not," said Simon, reaching for tissues from his jeans pocket.

"Did you like it then?"

"Of course, it was super," said Simon. "I'm sure most girls would just rush it to get a boy off as quickly as possible, but you made it last. It was brilliant."

"You can thank Martin for that, then. I made that mistake at first, but he told me to take it slowly."

"You're very open about what you and Martin did, aren't you?"

"Why not? It's not a state secret. And who knows, if the bomb drops tomorrow, I'd hate to have missed out just by not saying what I meant and what I wanted."

"What **do** you want?" asked Simon, wondering at the back of his mind, or more to the front really, if she was wanting to go 'all the way'."

"Next week you can do for me what I just did for you," she said teasingly.

Simon felt a moment of panic. How would he do that? Surely now his inexperience with girls would be exposed.

"It's the very least I can do," he smiled, hiding his doubts.

Back home, he took advantage of Mum and Ken going to the pub to rummage in some of the still unpacked boxes in Mum's room. He felt guilty about this, but he had to find out. There was a book, *Ideal Marriage* or something like that, he had once seen at their old home, but it had been hidden away from him. Now he needed it because he knew it would have the information he required. He went meticulously through the boxes, finding nothing. Lots of books, but not that one. Suppose they had left it, and Dad now had it in Nottingham? Disaster. Not that Dad needed it if what he had heard was right! Sadly he turned around, and saw another box by the window. There it was! Swiftly he took the book into his room and lay on his bed and started reading. He had a lot of catching up to do where the opposite sex was concerned.

With a mixture of nervousness and anticipation, Simon cycled to the farm the next Saturday, despite rain that made the journey a miserable one. He was now armed with at least some more knowledge about girls and what they might like. He felt it was important that he could give pleasure to Diane, because sex was about giving, and last week he had done all the taking. As he pedalled along, out of the town and toward the farm in the rain, he went over in his head how events might develop once he and Diane were able to be alone in the barn. He wanted to give certainly, but as a teenage boy, he was also hoping that Diane would again bring him slowly and sensually to orgasm.

He parked his bike against the house. Martin answered the door.

"Hi Simon. Diane's here I think, probably with Edith in her house."

"OK," said Simon. "What are you doing this afternoon?"

"Not much. I was going to shoot, but I'm not now."

Simon knew that Martin sometimes took a shotgun out onto the farm to shoot rats, rabbits, pigeons and crows and the like, a fox too if he saw one. He said this was because they were pests that damaged the crops.

"Why are you not now?"

"Rain."

"Of course," said Simon, matching Martin's laconic replies.

"I might go later if it clears up a bit," said Martin. "Want to come if I do?"

"Oh, yes please," said Simon, wondering if he would be allowed to handle the shotgun.

"Unless you're busy with Diane, of course," said Martin.

"I'd better go and find her."

"See you later then," said Martin.

Simon walked across to Edith's house, eager to see Diane. As soon as he saw her he knew she was glad to see him. She smiled and he smiled back as he stood in the doorway. She picked up her coat and came out to him.

"Doesn't Edith mind you just leaving?" asked Simon.

"It's fine," said Diane. "She was expecting that when you arrived."

"Where shall we go? Everywhere's wet."

"Come on, silly," she replied, leading the way towards the farm buildings. In the top barn, they kissed and talked.

"I've a favour to repay," said Simon.

"Plenty of time for that," said Diane. "There's no rush, is there?"

"No, of course not. It's up to you." Simon was fearful of moving too quickly, perhaps asking more of her than she was wanting to give. He remembered how considerate Daniel had been with him, taking their relationship slowly, always waiting until Simon was ready, allowing their sexual relationship to reach its fullness without haste.

"What's the matter? You looked really sad then."

"Sorry, I was just thinking of something in the past."

"You still miss her, don't you?"

"Who?" said Simon, puzzled.

"Well, I don't know. Whoever she was, the person you were just thinking about."

"I'm sorry, I don't want to spoil anything by rushing in. What we do, or don't do, is entirely up to you."

"You're sweet. Most boys would be just after as much as they could get as quickly as they could get it. Are they all like you where you come from?"

Simon thought of Daniel, but also of Barry Spence. "Some are, some aren't. Like here I suppose. I mean, Martin's not like that, is he?"

"No, he's not. He's really nice. I can see why you two hit it off."

"You two are still friends, then?" asked Simon.

"Oh yes. I think we always will be. I like Martin a lot," she answered. "But I like you too," Diane added, allowing her hand to explore his jeans, Simon gasping at her touch. She smiled at the surge of desire in him that her intimate contact produced. She undid his belt and zip, but when Simon tried to respond, she pushed his hand away.

"Lots of time," she said, and then again caressed Simon, stroking him and easing his trousers down to get fuller access. A bit puzzled by her apparent change of mind, he allowed her to gently handle him.

"Is that what circumcised is like?" she suddenly asked.

Simon looked at his erection, held tenderly in her hand. "I have been circumcised, if that's what you mean."

"Why?"

"I don't know, I wasn't consulted," said Simon with a trace of bitterness. "I wish I hadn't been."

"Why? It's nice."

"It's not as sensitive. I suppose because there's no foreskin to protect it."

"Does that matter? It doesn't seem to if last time and now are anything to go by."

"It takes longer to come sometimes."

"How do you know, do you have races?" she laughed.

Simon realised he had been almost indiscrete. How could he say that he knew Daniel had been more sensitive there and that he had always been able to come more easily than Simon? He knew Daniel had sometimes deliberately delayed orgasm; Simon had never had that problem. He changed tack.

"So I guess Martin is not circumcised then," he said.

"No. I thought boys talked about things like that among themselves."

"Some do maybe. Boys at school talk about sex a lot, but Martin doesn't. I don't actually see Martin a lot at school, he's not in my class. It's mainly on the bus."

"I've heard about that. The ones he calls Neanderthals?"

"They're horrible. They've got everybody scared of them. With good reason if what Martin says is right."

"I'd just stay away from them then. Hey, are you going off me?" she smiled. Simon realised that despite her hand still holding him, his hardness was waning.

"No," he said quickly. "It's just talking about other things."

Without a word she increased Simon's arousal and again brought him off.

"What about you?" asked Simon, thinking about all his research in preparation for today.

"Don't be in such a rush," she said, and kissed him. Simon was happy that she was content with that, and of course pleased with his own sexual release.

Simon went across to the byre to help with the milking. Diane came with him, watching.

"You like doing this, don't you?" she asked as he heaved the milking urn up to the top of the cooler, tipping in the still warm milk.

"Yes. And it gives me a reason to come here so I can see you as well."

"You're quite strong, aren't you," she said as Simon manhandled the heavy full milk churn from beneath the cooler, replacing it with an empty one. She reached out and ran her hand her over his shirt, feeling the fitness of his teenage body.

"I suppose so," said Simon, and turned and kissed her in the dairy, she running her hands across his body, he fondling her neck and long hair, as their lips explored each other again. Simon broke away. "I must get back to the byre, the milking doesn't just stop."

She followed him back as he continued to help both Mr Passmores with the milking.

He didn't go shooting with Martin that day, but it had gone well and he was happy riding home again having said goodbye to both Martin and Diane.

Over the next few weeks, matters stayed much the same. Simon would go to the farm, see Diane and spent time together, but the barn was being cleared out so their refuge was denied them. When the weather was good, the pair would wander into the woodland that occupied some of the farm, often their favourite log, and talk and kiss, getting to know each other. As for further sexual exploration, neither felt inclined to risk more intimate contact in the open, although the chances of being disturbed were not great, as the wood was on private land.

Simon and Martin did go shooting sometimes, and Simon learned how to handle the shotgun and proved a good shot, learning that quiet and patience were the primary skills required. He bagged a few rabbits, about which he felt a few pangs of conscience, and more than a few rats, about which he felt none. Martin was the master at bagging moving targets such as pigeons and crows, Simon found the offset hard to gauge and Martin decided that to avoid the expense of too many cartridges used up in vain, he would go for the birds.

The school year drew to a close, with Simon doing well in the fourth year exams, doing more than enough to retain his place in the top class for the fifth year. Apart from his increasing closeness with Diane, he also drew closer to the quiet and serious Stuart Miller, and became less involved with Alan Croft. The two remained friends but gradually spent less time together as Alan's interest in Bilthaven FC and more easy-going attitude to his studies conflicted more with Simon's lack of interest in football and his own desire to achieve as well as he could. This was more matched by Stuart's determination to do his best and his contempt for those he considered timewasters which, Simon gathered, included Alan Croft.

5. 1961/8 Rescue at sea

The summer holidays brought both pleasure and disappointment for Simon. The pleasure was his holiday once again to Salcombe. It was strange going down to Dad's in Nottingham and then just the two of them driving off down the familiar road to Devon. In an effort to beat the traffic jams, they travelled down on the Friday, having booked an overnight stay at a bed and breakfast on a farm just outside Kingsbridge, just a few miles from Salcombe. This worked well and they arrived at the hotel in Salcombe on the Saturday before anyone else and feeling refreshed. Dad had booked *Invention* for Simon once again and quickly Simon was at the reception desk.

"Hello again, Simon," said the owner. "Are you going to take care of *Invention* again?"

"I hope so," said Simon happily. "Are the Griffins coming?"

"Yes, they should be here later today."

Simon's feelings surged with happiness that not only would he have *Invention* as his personal boat but that he would have Jack to share it with.

"Thanks. What rooms have they got?"

"Same as before, like you I think. With all your group of families each year at the same time, this fortnight is one of the easier ones to manage; I just copy the accommodation arrangements from last year," said the owner, smiling. "But I haven't forgotten your singing exploits with young Jack."

"That was years ago!" complained Simon, indignantly. "We were both kids then."

"Yes, of course," came the reply with a wink at Dad.

But Simon was too happy to be back in Salcombe, waiting for Jack, to take umbrage at the implication that they still were kids, now aged fourteen.

Jack was equally as happy when they arrived, tired after their drive from London, to see Simon.

"Hi Simon!" he grinned. "Got *Invention*?"

Simon nodded and the two went straight down to the moorings in the dusk to check 'their' boat. *Invention* was riding out on her mooring buoy and the two rowed out in a pram dinghy to carry out an inspection.

"It's been painted," noted Simon, fingering the new white paint and maroon gunwales and trims. A rope fender had also been fitted right round the boat to protect the new paint.

"Must have guessed you were coming," joked Jack in a dig at Simon's boat handling ability. But he knew that Simon could handle the boat and it was unlikely that the rope fender was to protect the boat from any mishandling on Simon's part. Presumably by this time many other people had been using the boat since its winter refit, not all as used to the sea as Simon.

"Shall we take her out?" suggested Jack hopefully.

"It's a bit late now, and anyway, we need to get changed for dinner," said Simon, using his few months age advantage over Jack to take charge. So they rowed back to the mooring steps and lashed the pram dinghy to the rope, and climbed the steps to the hotel.

Simon was once again in his element for the next two weeks, he and Jack acting as ferrymen for the group of families, but often leaving them on the beach and going off in the boat around the estuary with instructions to return at a prearranged time to ferry the group back to the hotel. Occasionally the group would decide on North or South Sands, and then some would go by car, which meant that the car users would take all the group back to the hotel as those beaches were on the same side of the estuary as the town, allowing the boys to venture further without fear of missing the deadline. They would aim to get all the way up to Kingsbridge, but this called for a careful watch on the tides and even more careful navigation as there was just a single channel to keep to otherwise *Invention* could get stuck on the mud. Neither relished the thought of trying to pole the boat off the mud in The Bag or higher up, or even worse, having to go over the side deep into the mud to try and push the boat off.

On one occasion they came across a family who had done exactly that in their day hired motor boat, very similar to *Invention*. The two boys used the chart carefully to keep to the channel and saw the stricken boat, and the even more stricken family, stuck on the mud not far from the deeper water. The father was desperately trying to push the boat off with the boathook, but that just kept sinking into the mud just below the surface, his wife kept churning up the mud with the engine and two frightened children sat upset and quiet.

Simon carefully approached the stranded boat.

"Jack, watch the depth with the boathook," ordered Simon. Jack took the boathook and as Simon crept the boat forward, Jack probed the water with the boathook to test the depth under her keel, calling out the results to Simon. A few feet from the other boat, Jack called, "Stop!"

Simon put *Invention* to slow astern and brought the boat to a halt. Four hopeful faces watched as the two boys stopped close. The father was not one, in this situation at least, to allow pride to get in the way of possible rescue, even if by two teenage boys.

"Can you help us?" he called.

"Throw us the painter," said Jack, reaching out from the bow.

"The what?" said the man, clearly not familiar with nautical terminology.

"The rope at the front of the boat you tie it up with," explained Jack.

While Simon kept *Invention* steady, Jack reached out to catch the rope, but it kept falling short. It simply wasn't long enough.

"Can't you come closer?" called the man.

Simon looked at Jack, who shook his head. "Sorry," said Simon, "if we do, we could get stuck too."

"What about using the boathooks, linked together?" suggested the man. Jack looked at Simon, who this time shook his head. He could see that the inherent unsteadiness of that idea, coupled with the unknown ability of the man to retain the grasp under the strain and the possible loss of both boathooks made that idea impractical.

Jack looked up, smiling. From under the front thwart or seat of *Invention* he produced a coil of rope.

"Brilliant, Jack!" exclaimed Simon. "Make it fast." But Jack was already lashing the rope round the front thwart. Jack then threw the longer rope across to the other boat, where it was grabbed by the small girl who handed it to her father.

"Tie it on," said Jack.

"A good knot," called Simon, "round turn and two half hitches or something."

"What's that?" said the man, holding the rope, looking lost.

"I know," said his young son, aged about eleven, and seizing the rope from his father, started to tie it round the tiller post.

"No, not there," called Jack, "or it might get ripped off. Somewhere stronger."

The boy looked for a moment and then started to tie the rope round the stern thwart. Jack watching the knot, turned and nodded approval to Simon. The boy knew his knots.

"OK," said Simon, "we'll pull you off stern first. When the rope goes tight and is out of the water, put it full astern."

"He means reverse, Daddy," said the boy, enjoying his superior knowledge.

Simon eased *Invention* astern until rope was taut and then put on full astern, nodding at the man. The water frothed at the stern of both boats, mud spewing up from the stranded one.

"Use the boathook to push from the bow at the same time," shouted Simon.

The woman took their boathook and with a punting action, added that small thrust to the joint effort. The boat seemed to move a bit. Simon pushed his engine from neutral to full astern repeatedly, causing the rope to slacken and then jerk tight again, giving the marooned boat repeated tugs. Suddenly it moved smartly backwards as both boats shot back into deeper water.

"OK, go into neutral," shouted Simon, worried that the slack rope might foul their propeller. With both boats in neutral in the deep channel, they pulled on the rope to bring both boats together.

"I want to thank you two lads, " said the man, to the nods of his wife and children.

"Good thing your boy knows his knots," said Jack. The boy beamed with pleasure at this recognition from someone he no doubt regarded as a seasoned sailor.

"Are you local?" said the man.

"No, we meet up each year on holiday. I'm from London, Simon's from Bilthaven now," said Jack.

"That's a long way," said the man. So they chatted awhile, about holidays and hotels, and Simon gave them information to enable them to return safely to Salcombe. In the event, they decided to follow Simon and Jack back down the estuary along the safe channel to Salcombe. As they reached the town near the Ferry Inn, they veered off to the boatyard where they had hired the boat, waving and shouting thanks once again, as Jack, now at the tiller, steered *Invention* back down past the town to their hotel.

"Our good turn for the day," said Jack.

"Dead right there," agreed Simon, the significance of Jack's choice of words lost on him, and not to be revealed until the following year.

While the families were at dinner that evening, the boys scrubbed and in shirt and tie, the owner came into the dining room and asked for attention.

"I've just had a visit from a gentleman concerning two boys staying this hotel and their use of the motor boat *Invention*," he said with a serious look.

Dad shot Simon a cross look, and Mrs Griffin said to Jack, "You've not been singing again, have you?"

Jack and Simon's worried eyes met across the dining room, and all the guests' eyes were on them.

"No, Mrs Griffin, it's not about singing. It seems we have two young heroes," he said, now smiling.

Simon screwed his face up in embarrassment, Jack covered his face in his hands. The owner continued, "It seems that Simon and Jack were exploring today near Kingsbridge, off Gerston Point when they found a family whose boat had become stuck on the mud on the ebbing tide. With great skill and initiative they managed to tow the boat free with *Invention* and then escort the family in their boat back down safe channels to Salcombe."

At this point, the guests started clapping, most of whom were the families from their annual group. Dad was now smiling at Simon, as were Jack's parents at him. His little sister was hugging him. Simon and Jack were beckoned out of their seats. Flushed red with being the centre of attention, the two boys went out to the owner.

"The gentleman concerned wanted to show his appreciation and has left me these to give to Simon and Jack." He handed the boys an envelope each, who then went back to their seats. The meal resumed, while nearby guests looked across to see what was in the envelope. Both Simon and Jack were opening them, and Jack looked across at Simon with a thumbs up sign. They each had a record token from the man they had helped.

It was another good holiday in Salcombe and on the journey back to Nottingham in the Austin, Simon and Dad talked. Simon was still wary of his father, but he was older and bigger, and when they chatted, Simon just wished it had always been like this. Maybe if it had, he and Mum would not have moved and he would still be with Daniel. That made him feel angry and resentful again, which Dad just put down to teenage moodiness.

Simon stayed a few days in Nottingham with Dad and met Phoebe Ellis, a new friend of Dad's. It was obvious to Simon that they were close and he wondered where the relationship was going. Not that it concerned him, he told himself.

The disappointment of the summer was waiting when Simon got home to Bilthaven. There was a letter from the Royal Navy to say that Simon had not qualified for a Dartmouth scholarship. It did however say that a reserved cadetship was available for him after he had done his A levels, subject to further assessment. Simon was disappointed not have made the scholarship level, but he now knew that to fulfil his ambition of a naval career he would have to work hard and get good 'O' levels at GCE and good 'A' levels too. All was not lost.

Diane was sympathetic when he told her about his naval setback, but being Diane, was positive as well, reminding him that the door had not closed. Simon suddenly realised that her open and positive nature reminded him of Peter Holman. How incongruous! He wondered how Peter was.

The barn had been cleaned and there was the new summer hay being stored ready to feed the animals through the winter. The small bales for the horses were stored on the upper level, and Simon and Diane made use of the bedding as the summer drew to a close. Simon was at last able to test his knowledge gained some time before. He had kept the book hidden in the bedroom and had read it right through. It had not been missed.

He and Diane would kiss, cuddle and their hands explored each other's bodies, stroking, gripping, tantalising. He was determined to give Diane maximum pleasure and as they lay half dressed on the hay, he put his research into action.

"Why did you do that? You often do that," she asked.

"What?" replied Simon, stopping, wondering what he had done wrong.

"You just gave yourself that funny little tap on your chest twice. I've seen you do that before."

Simon felt embarrassed. He hadn't realised it had become a mannerism worthy of comment. How could he explain it?

"Just a thing I do when I'm a bit nervous, I suppose."

"Nervous? Of me?"

"Not **of** you, but of letting you down," admitted Simon shyly.

"No need to be nervous, Simon," Diane reassured him, and seizing his wrist, guided his hand between her legs. Simon was able to return the favour and he loved it when Diane's body close to his was lost in ecstasy at his touch.

"That's amazing," she said, panting after an intense orgasm.

Simon smiled, pleased he was able to give her such pleasure. But he added, "Just the same as before though?"

"What do you mean, before?"

"With Martin, I suppose. I mean you said there had been 'downstairs action'," said Simon, worried about bringing Martin into the conversation. Was that too personal? He need not have worried.

"Yes there was. Don't get me wrong, Martin was great, but you seem to know exactly what to do. You done it before, I can tell," she smiled.

"Are you jealous?"

"No, of course not. But she must have been a lucky girl."

Simon felt really good that Diane thought so well of him, and that his inexperience and doubts had been put aside. He had nothing to fear now, he thought.

"Are you jealous of Martin?" asked Diane.

Simon, fresh in his new found self confidence, replied, "Not at all. I'm lucky to have you."

She laughed. "Come on then, your turn." Simon relaxed and was lost in the pleasure she gave him.

Summer turned to autumn, and the weather made the barn less inviting. Simon was now in the run up to his 'O' level GCEs and was working hard, his mind fixed on Dartmouth and the ground he felt he had lost and would need to make up to gain entry at 18. He also thought about swimming, but for the moment, the academic side took precedence.

The Watsons and Carter were still on the bus and still sometimes subjected Simon to taunts, mocking his 'southern' ways and his evident commitment to his own education, as well as occasional blows. But he and Martin would often sit together and talk, sometimes about Diane but also about school and the farm. Sometimes Martin would sit with other kids from his own class, often to talk about football, which he knew Simon had little interest in.

The autumn brought two other changes. Ken moved in, leaving his shared bachelor flat off Port Road in the city centre to take the small room at the top of the house where Russell's maid had once lived. But the facilities were rudimentary and it was not a self contained bedsit even. So Ken became more or less resident and Simon could see the strong bond growing between Ken and Mum. He had mixed feelings about this. There was still at some level a feeling of loyalty to Dad, even though Dad and Mum were now divorced, also he had enjoyed being in the flat with Mum, just the two of them, especially since Frances had left. But Simon put these feelings aside. He wanted Mum to be happy and he was immersed in his own studies, the farm and of course, Diane.

The other change was the departure of Russell's Triumph and its replacement by a new, white, Jaguar E-type coupé, with a 3.8 litre engine, red leather upholstery and an engine note to die for. This beast was now Russell's pride and joy, and he would often just sit in it, when he wasn't cleaning the already immaculate car, that is. Simon sat in the driving seat and took in the smell of the leather and the newness of it, looking out over the long bonnet beneath which lay the gleaming engine capable of taking the car up to 150 miles per hour with acceleration to match.

6. 1961/10 Showdown

The conflict was bound to happen, all that remained would be when and on what pretext. It came over the chair.

Simon was at home, listening to music on the record player. He had put a stack of 45s on the autochanger and was therefore sitting in the big armchair next to the record player.

Perhaps one or two records had played when he heard Mum and Ken coming home from work. They were late as so often. Probably been to the pub after work. Mum went straight on to the bedroom, but Ken came into the lounge. He glanced at Simon as he went through to the kitchen.

Soon he returned and stood in front of Simon, expectantly. Simon knew what he wanted, but he felt stubborn and remained in the armchair.

"I want to sit down," said Ken.

"I'm sitting here," replied Simon.

"Listen, I've been at work all day and now I'm home I want to sit down and relax."

"Well, I've been at school," countered Simon, "and I'm pretty tired too."

Simon was aware of Ken's mounting anger, as on both sides a simmering resentment was coming to the boil. Ken from the point of view of an adult with little experience of children being thwarted by this teenager who was in his chair. Simon felt angry inside. Who was Ken? He had come into their lives and perhaps for the first time in his life, he felt that there was a threat to his relationship with Mum. They had found a kind of bond when faced with the common adversary that so often had been Dad, now there was just Mum and him – and even Frances was now off the scene. Then suddenly, here was this interloper not just living with them but in some way taking Mum away just when the two had been close, alone together.

But Ken was speaking again, his anger evident now.

"Don't be so bloody cheeky. Who do you think you are?"

"I live here, with Mum!" Simon shouted.

"Are you going to get up?" bellowed Ken.

"Why should I?"

"Right!" said Ken, and leant down and grabbed Simon by the arms, dragging him out of the armchair. Simon fought back, punching Ken about the body as best he could with his restrained arms.

"What the hell is going on?" Mum had entered the room.

"I was sitting in the chair first," said Simon, as Ken let go of his arms, and he sat down again.

"This is ridiculous," said Ken. "This boy needs to learn his manners. It's not been an easy day and now when I just want to sit down, I get this."

"Darling," said Mum, "let Ken have his seat. We're both tired and can do without this."

Simon looked at Mum. He had lost. He was now in second place and this was the proof. He got up and with tears welling up, he walked past her and into his room. He slammed the door and threw himself down on the bed and wept. For the loss of the argument, for his loss of position in some domestic pecking order but mainly and deeply for the loss of Mum. Just at a time when he had lost so much, his old home, old life, old friends; and Daniel, Daniel, Daniel. Now his mainstay and anchor in all this time of trial, Mum, was lost to him too. Moving north had been her route to happiness, he thought bitterly, but at the cost of his own. Some part of him felt he would never forgive her for that. Despite his friendship with Diane, he suddenly felt more alone than he had ever been, and felt desperate and wretched.

7.   *1962/3-5 End of the Affair*

Simon continued to see Diane as the winter nights drew in but their opportunities for intimacy were reduced as the barn became too cold, and there was nowhere else. They started to meet up in Bilthaven in the evenings when the homework load was less, as Diane was also preparing for 'O' levels. It was only when this was apparent that Simon realised Diane was in fact slightly older than him. Not that it made any difference. But she shared his interest in the world at large, and they had both followed the Eichmann trial and were pleased at the verdict. Diane liked to dance and although this was something Simon was not keen on, did go with her to the dance hall in Bilthaven. At least he could do the twist, as it seemed to require little coordination, just fitness and energy, and he had both of those. Simon secretly gave thanks for Chubby Checker!

At Christmas he went to Nottingham to stay with Dad for a few days, travelling by train. He had to change trains and the journey took much of the day.

Dad was glad to see him, and Phoebe was there too. It was now more than a year since Mum had taken him to Bilthaven, and it was plain that the relationship between Dad and Phoebe was serious. But then Mum and Ken were too. Simon felt duty bound to stay a few days but he wanted to get back to Bilthaven – that in itself was a sea change – and of course to Diane, as well as do some work for his 'O' level exams in the summer.

The new term was hard work, the bus journey became more of a trial as the Neanderthals ruled the roost by fear and intimidation. They spent much of their time having 'sport' as they termed it with some younger boys. Simon felt very angry about it but was restrained by Martin's pragmatic approach.

"They'll leave at the end of this year, then there'll just be the young one, and he'll be quiet without the other two."

"I wish they would leave right now," said Simon. He got his wish in part as the weeks went on, as there were an increasing number of days when they weren't on the bus, truanting or 'dolling off' as they called it. Nobody on the bus was in a hurry for them to return to education, but in the end they did, for a time.

As the Spring warmth returned, he and Diane resumed their walks and visits to the barn. Both were now in the throes of their 'O' level GCEs but the talk was rarely of the exams. They wanted to escape with each other for a time. They lay in the barn, discussing the dramatic escape of a group of East Germans under the Berlin Wall

"Just one of the things that's so good about you is the way you're interested in things, like what's on the news."

"And that's just one of the things that's good about you, too," she said, amused.

That warm May afternoon, they lay in the barn, coat spread on the hay, talking and kissing, putting exam pressure away for a few hours. Simon felt desire rising in him, and Diane, noticing the physical evidence of this, started removing Simon's clothes. Quickly he responded and soon, for the first time they were both completely naked together, passion eating them up, their joint arousal reaching new heights. Simon thought he had not felt arousal like this for months, his whole body burning with desire for consummation.

He buried his face between her firm breasts, she put her leg around his and rolled onto her back, pulling him with her. She ran her hands down Simon's back to his buttocks in the move so familiar to him. He lifted his face and kissed her, his hardness pressing against her as she opened to him.

"Are you sure?" he whispered. She simply nodded frantically and pulled him down. He felt the entry, taut and warm. Slowly and carefully he pressed in, watching her face for any sign of distress, there was none. He was now in as deep as he could go, moving gently while Diane trembled with each slow movement. So Simon continued, adapting the skills he had learned over many years to his new situation. The words 'sex is about giving' kept running through his mind. He felt Diane's arousal mounting and then rapidly, their bodies combining their movements for the greatest stimulation, lost in an erotic trance as their bodies raced together towards the finale. As Diane's body climaxed beneath him he could let his own orgasm come, their two bodies united in simultaneous pleasure. Simon felt jubilant, confident, rampant, triumphant. They lay panting together, bodies still fused, Diane's body gripping his softening penis, trying to hold on to the bliss as long as possible.

Still lying above her he whispered gently in her ear, *"Fire, Fire, fire down below. Fetch a bucket of water boys, there's fire down below."* She smiled, running her hands up and down his back.

He withdrew and lay beside her, then reaching over, he kissed her gently.

"You're fantastic," he said simply.

"So are you, but you've had practice," she smiled back, her soft eyes looking back at him.

"Haven't you?" he hedged.

"No. You're my first, all the way that is," she said.

"Oh God, I'm sorry," said Simon, the thought of having stolen her virginity disturbing him.

"Why are you sorry? I'm not. It was super. I knew you'd done it before so I knew it would be good."

What could he say? "Can I tell you something?"

"Of course you can, what?"

Simon hesitated. "That was my first time too." He nearly added 'with a girl' but bit his lip in time. And of course it had been Daniel who was the leader in their affair.

"Really? You're not just saying that to make me feel better or something?"

"Really. Honest. I know people think I'm some of kind Casanova, but I'm not."

"I know Martin thinks you are, he warned me about you."

"When?"

"Ages ago. Really true? You were a virgin too?" Simon nodded. She reached up and kissed him. "You're sweet, you really are," she said.

"I suppose we could get into trouble. We're both still fifteen," said Simon.

"How? You going to get your Mam to put it in the *Bilthaven Mail*?"

They laughed and got dressed, and arms around each other, walked back to the farm houses. They met Martin, shotgun on his arm.

"Hi."

"Get anything?" asked Simon.

"Rats," said Martin, and then seeing that more was required, added, "By the stream." He joined them walking along. "You OK, Diane?" he asked unexpectedly, looking at strands of hay clinging to their clothing.

Diane nodded and looked up at Simon, he smiled back. There was an indefinable electricity between them.

Martin gave them a searching look, and smiled to himself, nodding slightly. He knows! thought Simon.

Later he said as much to Diane, while in the dairy changing the churn.

"So?" she said. "He can only be guessing, and even if he does, it doesn't matter."

Riding home, it occurred to Simon that at fifteen he had lost his virginity at a younger age than Daniel, with a girl, anyway. Had he had sex with a girl by now? What was her name? The girl at the swimming club he talked about? Janice, that was it. And then, did losing one's virginity have only to be with the opposite sex? Had Daniel lost his virginity with him, Simon, already? Simon mused on this as he rode back to the flat in Swiford, and decided it didn't matter anyway. He was feeling very pleased with himself.

Simon's evenings were spent in revision, his life revolving around the exam timetable. At school, he now spent most free time with Stuart Miller and the group of friends more concerned with exam success. But Stuart lived in Cermerton and so travel to his home would not be easy. Most of their lessons at school were given over to revision and the teacher's best guesses of what questions would turn up this year, based on their experience. They were on the whole fairly accurate, none more so than the history teacher, the charismatic Miss Black. Simon knew he had done well in History. He knew too that English Language and Literature had gone well, also Geography. French was good and even the German he had come late to went well. The three sciences went better than expected, and in the Physics, that Simon had been fearing because of the Maths, he had a stroke of luck. The practical experiment he was given was to do with the refraction of light, one he knew well. But his biggest fear, as always was the Maths. He revised as best he could but the numbers just seemed to dance in front of his eyes and holding some of the concepts in his head proved so hard. Once again, Daniel came into his mind, wishing his friend were there to help. But that was the past. He went in, gritted his teeth and did his best.

May turned to June and the exams drew to a close. There were fewer children travelling on the bus now. The sixth formers had long since stopped going, and many of the fifth years had decided they'd had enough. Most of the time this included the Neanderthals, including the younger one, David, who evidently decided that if his brother wasn't going to school, there was no reason for him to.

There was one day, when they were there. It was a homeward journey, the bus was hot and so were the pupils. Tempers were short. A younger boy, Simon thought a third year, got in the way of Bruce Watson, whose reply was give the boy a punch across the back of the neck which felled him into the gangway. Watson then kicked the boy and was about to jump on him when Simon could stand it no longer. He leapt up, slipping out of Martin's attempt to haul him back, and punched Bruce Watson with all his strength on his left ear, the nearest available point.

"That's enough, Watson!" shouted Simon, red hot with anger now. Watson reeled from the blow, but then Simon felt a sharp pain in his side and saw Carter had leaned over the seat with a knife. Simon drew back quickly, as the bus shuddered to a halt. The driver, Ted Johnson, who had always tried to get on with the driving and ignore what was happening behind him, came up the gangway. The knife disappeared from view.

"What do you lot think you're up to? I'm bloody sick of this. What's the matter with him?" he asked, looking at the boy still lying in the gangway.

"Watson hit him," said Simon, "and then kicked him."

"He would have jumped on him if Scott hadn't stopped him," offered one of the girls.

"It's true," said Martin, "Watson was going to jump on him."

"Right," said Ted. "You two. Off!" He indicated Bruce Watson and Neville Carter. "Now!"

"You've got to take us to our stop," said Watson, his arrogance showing his contempt for anybody else's opinion of his actions.

"No I don't. Not any more. I've got to the end of line where you two are concerned. Don't think I don't know what's been going on. If you two don't get off this bus right now, I'll drive straight to the police station and they can deal with you and what you've done to this lad." The driver was adamant, and stood his ground.

Slowly, gaining in volume, the chant started from the pupils on the bus. "Off! Off! Off! Off! Off!"

Bruce Watson turned to Simon, those hard grey eyes looking unflinchingly at him. "You're dead meat, Scott. You're going to die." It wasn't said with anger, just flatly in a matter of fact way, that gave it all the more force. Simon found himself tapping his chest twice as he said, "Piss off, Watson. Nobody wants you here."

The chanting continued. Slowly, resentfully, Watson and Carter started to move back down the bus. David Watson followed.

"You can stay, son, as long as you behave," said Ted Johnson.

"Him off as well," came a voice from somewhere, and this produced a cheer. Red faced, beckoned by his brother, David Watson too left the bus. The driver slammed the door, and left them on the footpath a mile or two from their stop, the three defiantly putting two fingers up at the bus.

As the coach pulled away, there were cheers, and Simon, now shaking with reaction, found himself a hero. He sat down, trembling with the realisation of what he had done. Others helped up the bruised third year who complained of aches and pains. Martin sat next to Simon.

"You OK, Simon?"

"Not sure, to be truthful. Carter had a knife," said Simon. "He actually tried to stab me with it."

"Here, let's see," said Martin. Simon slipped off his blazer, and pulled the side of shirt up. The shirt had a small hole and there was small cut in Simon's side with a drop of blood.

"You were lucky," said Martin. "I've told you loads of times not to interfere with them."

Simon examined his blazer and found a slit at the top of the right side pocket. "Not too bad," he said.

"For your blazer maybe," said Martin. "Not sure about you. I just hope they don't catch up with you."

Simon felt fear grip his stomach. What had he done? What a fool! He knew he was in danger. What could he do now?

"Thanks, Scott," said a voice in his left ear. It was the third year. "Are you OK? That was really brave."

Me, brave? thought Simon. An idiot, more like. But the boy's grateful face justified it in his mind. "Yes, it's OK. Just a scratch. What about you?"

"It hurts a bit, but I'm all right. Thanks again, Scott."

The next morning, Simon got on the bus, frightened of what might happen, but determined not to be cowed. Martin sat next to him this day, but said even less than usual. Simon remembered his 11 plus arithmetic day when Daniel had held his hand on the bus going to school. But it wasn't Daniel next to him, it was Martin, and so he kept his hand away. The coach reached the Watsons' bus stop. They weren't there. Others got on.

"Where are they," asked someone.

"They'll not be on this bus again," said the driver, overhearing. "My boss has banned them and told the school what happened." The sigh of relief turned to a cheer, and Simon felt relief surge through him, fear lifted.

They heard later that all three had been expelled from Cermerton, and that there had been an incident in their school in which a boy had been either stabbed or threatened with it. But as Bruce Watson and Nev Carter were leaving school anyway, it made little difference to them. Nobody knew or cared about David Watson's future education. But Simon's intervention was to have a consequence that would change his life utterly.

Diane too had found the exams gruelling, but they met at the farm as always. Martin of course had told the family, and Diane, about his 'heroic' intervention. Simon just said he had lost his temper and he didn't feel particularly heroic. But Diane thought it was super of him, and Simon was content with that of course. They met up in town sometimes, walking, sometimes going to the cinema or a coffee bar.

The farm was busy, with much hay making still to do, which Simon helped with, often driving one of the Fordsons, Diane perched next to him sometimes. They occasionally worked as a pair, with Martin driving the other Fordson. But when they could, he and Diane returned to the barn, each wanted to feel the other again, to experience the union of their bodies afresh. Simon found his mind thinking about Diane, making love to Diane. He felt good because he knew Diane felt the same about him. Both were so wrapped up in their sensuous needs that little thought went to the possible consequences.

It was early July when Simon went to the farm, exams now over, feeling relaxed. Martin met him as he cycled down the short track from the road to the houses.

"Hi Martin."

"Hi. She's not here."

"Diane?"

"Diane."

"Do you know why? Is she OK?" asked Simon, leaning his bike on the wall, and walking beside Martin to the farm buildings.

"As far as I know. But I don't think she'll be coming back."

Simon felt as though he had been punched in the gut. "Not coming back? Ever?"

"Don't think so."

"Why not, Martin. There must be a reason!"

"Well, I don't know it. You could ask Edith."

"Right," said Simon, turning back to the houses.

"You're not coming over?" said Martin, referring to the farm buildings.

"Later. See you over there," shouted Simon as he ran back to Edith's house. His conversation with Edith produced nothing new. She was upset about Diane, and thought there was trouble at home, but she didn't know what. She also seemed cool toward Simon which he found worrying. Had he in some way precipitated this crisis? Maybe it was just because she was upset.

He found Martin in the byre, helping his Dad get ready for the afternoon milking.

"Well?" said Martin.

"Nothing," said Simon. "She doesn't know."

"I'll see what I can find out," said Martin.

"Will you tell me, when you do? On the bus?"

"If I find out in time," said Martin.

"What do you mean?"

"I'm not staying on, so I'll probably not be on the bus much more."

Simon was dumbfounded. It was a given that he would be staying to do A levels and he had simply assumed Martin would be too.

Martin saw his puzzled look. "We're not all clever clogs, you know." It was said in a not altogether friendly way. Simon had thought in the months they had been friends that such things had been forgotten. He was now unsure of where he stood, what was the real situation here? He carried out his usual duties but later after the briefest good bye, left and rode home, his thoughts in turmoil with all the changes in one afternoon.

The following Monday turned out to be Martin's last time on the bus. He spoke to Simon to say he had heard nothing new about Diane, but then sat with his own classmates that remained on the bus. That evening, his haversack was full, he explained he had emptied his desk and didn't have any reason to see out the term. He would go to college instead next term, but if his 'O' levels weren't that good, get a job.

As they got off the bus at Swiford, he said with a finality in his tone, "Good bye, Simon." He turned and walked off to get his service bus. Simon watched, upset. He knew somehow it was a final goodbye, the closing of a chapter and he didn't know why. He blinked back tears and walked along the High Street, upset, confused and angry. Eating his apple pie, he was lost in his thoughts. Did Martin know something he did not? He was puzzled by Martin but upset about Diane. He had really liked her. Did he love her? Perhaps. But then he remembered what deep love really felt like, and he knew he didn't, however much he had liked her and enjoyed the sex with her. It wasn't the same. Would he ever feel like that again?

8. *1962/8 Salcombe*

The end of the school year arrived. It did not so much end as wither away, as many fifth years stopped coming after the exams. Simon too saw little point in attending once the exams were over and fell in with Ed Baker, a relative newcomer like himself to Bilthaven. He and Ed started to meet up in Bilthaven and go to an underground coffee bar close to Victoria Square. He was still smarting from the sudden break with Diane and his visits to the farm, but part of him knew that this dependency had been in large part a compensation for his feelings of loneliness since arriving in Bilthaven. He needed to widen his friendships, and concentrate on the important A levels. Now with Stuart and Ed as friends at school, both of whom would be there in the autumn, his optimism helped ameliorate the loss of Diane. But first there was the summer and the wait for the 'O' level results.

He travelled by train to stay with Dad and Phoebe. Dad had once again booked the hotel in Salcombe and Simon was counting the days. He got to know Phoebe better. She was unused to children, even less a fifteen year old boy, but she made the effort. She was an expert cook and a former stage actress of some note. But her career had been brought short by tuberculosis, and had it not been for the then new drug streptomycin, she would not have survived. This did not stop her smoking heavily though.

Simon spent some time with Dad at the studio, learning some broadcasting skills, such as how to edit tape using the high quality Ferrograph tape machines, including music editing which is much harder than speech because of the need to keep the beat exact. Dad did not teach Simon these things, but the studio engineer Nathan Harrison.

But the main event of the summer was of course the holiday to Salcombe. They said goodbye to Phoebe and made the long drive south, stopping again at the farmhouse bed and breakfast just outside Kingsbridge on the Friday night.

Their regular group was diminishing as the Broomfields did not come, but Simon was happy the Griffins were again there, and he and Jack renewed their friendship. *Invention* was again booked for Simon and the two boys more or less resumed from where they had left off the previous year, ferrying the group about and then going off on their own to enjoy the boat and their companionship.

On one occasion, for which Simon and Jack got into trouble, they took the little inboard motor boat out over the Bar and into Starehole Bay to see the wreck of *Herzogin Cecilie*. Simon still felt uneasy about being over clear, deep water, especially looking down at the dark shape of the shipwreck, but he was older and told himself that he was being illogical. But out over the Bar, the small boat was subject to the Atlantic rollers coming in and even in the fearlessness of youth, Simon felt some nervousness as *Invention* was lifted and dropped by the large waves. But he trusted his seamanship. Both he and Jack were wearing life jackets whenever they were on the water but neither was anxious to put them to the test. However now the sea was getting bigger, the rollers coming in higher than when they had come out and some were breaking at the top.

"I think we should go back," said Simon.

"Yes, let's," said Jack with relief.

Carefully, Simon pushed the tiller to turn *Invention* to the waves, and they made their way, rising and falling several feet over the rollers out of the bay, keeping well away from the rocks under Sharpitor. They were bounding around on the waves as Simon sought to turn the boat round Sharpitor to re-enter the estuary and find safety. Both boys were inwardly afraid but neither wanted the other to know. The turn had to be done, but it meant that for a time *Invention* was beam on to the sea, the most dangerous state, especially for a little boat that really should not have gone further than the Bar at most. At the top of a roller, Simon looked up sea to choose the best opportunity.

"When are you going to turn, Simon?" asked Jack. "At this rate we'll be in France."

Simon did not laugh at the joke, his mind was entirely concentrated on judging the right moment to push the tiller over to bring *Invention* round.

"When I'm ready," he said. "It's got to be right or we'll capsize."

The little boat dropped into a huge trough, Jack went quiet. He was a competent sailor and his family had their own Enterprise dinghy, but he was not usually allowed to take it out on his own. And although he understood the sea, he also knew that Simon was more used to handling *Invention*. The two had known each other for some years, and he had confidence in Simon. Also Simon at almost sixteen was a few months older. So he sat, held on, and hoped.

As *Invention* reached the crest of a roller, Simon chose his moment and pushed the tiller hard to starboard to bring the boat round to port. At the top of the roller, *Invention* turned and now stern to the sea, raced down into the trough.

"Yippee!" they shouted at the sudden acceleration, relieved at having made the dangerous turn successfully. Now riding the rollers towards the Bar, they felt more relaxed and could enjoy the exhilaration of their adventure.

Then the engine stopped.

Without steerage way, they were in serious danger.

"What are we going to do?" asked Jack, nervously.

"Here, take the tiller. Try to keep us stern on," said Simon, reaching for the tools. He was praying that he knew what the trouble was. The little water cooled two stroke was prone to plug whiskers, a deposit of carbon that built up on the sparking plug, killing the spark and causing the engine to stop.

Jack was doing his best but *Invention* was now at the mercy of the waves. Being intended for inshore work inside the estuary, there was no flare or similar aboard, and as they looked around, there were no boats near enough to attract attention. They shouted at some people high above on Sharpitor footpath, but they just waved back at the two boys having fun in their boat. Inexorably, they were being driven closer to the rocks.

In the madly rocking boat, Simon found the spark plug tool, lifted the engine cover and tried to loosen the plug. It was tight.

"Hurry up, for Christ's sake," said Jack.

"I'm doing my best," snapped Simon, struggling to get the spark plug loose.

"We're drifting ashore!"

"I know!"

"We'll be killed!" Jack shouted.

"I know that too," said Simon, panic welling up in him. What could he do? He was aware of the two of them in the little boat, imagining the scene as it would appear in a film; under stress, viewing himself from outside again. Yet he was very much in the scene, and now struggling to survive.

"It won't fucking well move!" cursed Simon, now shaking with fear. Stop panicking, think! Almost unconsciously he tapped his chest twice. Don't be afraid. Yes, he could think. The screwdriver. He went back to the tools and got the big long screwdriver. He had never known why it was there, perhaps left by accident, but now his and Jack's life depended on it.

"What are you doing?" shouted a still panicking Jack.

"It's OK, we're going to be OK. I guarantee it, Jack," said Simon. He put the screwdriver into the end of the plug tool and pushed. Hard. Again. Harder. It moved! The extra leverage had done the trick. He unscrewed the spark plug and desperate not to drop it as the little boat pitched and rolled in a gut wrenching corkscrew, he saw that thread of carbon across the gap. He had been right! Wedging himself against the side of the boat, he used the gapping tool to knock the carbon out and reset the gap to 25 thou.

"How much longer?" demanded Jack, eying the approaching rocks.

"Not long, Jack," he replied with all the confidence he could summon. "You're doing a great job there holding us as straight as you can. Keep it up." Isn't that what Daniel would have said?

He replaced the plug and tightened it, reconnecting the high tension lead.

"Here we go!" he said and engaging the starting handle, gave it his usual quick upward pull. The engine chugged but failed to start. He tried again, with the same result.

"Tickle it," urged Jack, referring to bringing fuel into the carburettor.

"Don't want to flood it," said Simon.

"At this rate, we'll be flooded," said Jack tersely. But as Simon failed again to start the motor, he realised with the rocks now only yards away and *Invention* in real danger of being caught by breaking waves and smashed to matchwood and them with it, he pressed the little rod a few times until fuel just appeared in the hole. Again a sharp upward swing on the handle. The engine sprang into life.

"Home, James," shouted Simon to Jack at the tiller, relief surging through him.

"Took your time," said Jack, now grinning broadly.

Simon left Jack at the helm and turned to face the bow. He was close to tears with the emotional release and did not want Jack to see. It seemed to him that in some idiotic way, Daniel had been with him, and had saved him from the water again. Impossible, he told himself. But then he quietly wept a little for his loss and the unanswered letters. Jack steered *Invention* away from the rocks and into the estuary and calmer waters.

"You all right, Simon?" called Jack from his position at the stern.

Simon composed himself and turned to face his friend. "Yes, fine. Now," he grinned. They both knew the strain it had been and how close they had come to death.

"Well, we've done Starehole now, we don't have to do it again," said Jack.

"You're dead right there," agreed Simon heartily. "Keep away from the Wolf," he reminded Jack of Wolf Rock.

"I know," said Jack, bursting into song.

"We're riding along on the crest of a wave, and the sun is in the sky.
All of our eyes on the distant horizon,
Look out for passers by.
We'll do the hailing,
When all the ships are round us sailing,
We're riding along on the crest of a wave,
And the world is ours!"

Simon stared, so surprised he didn't join in. "How do you know that?"

"Oh, I'm a Scout. It's a scout song, but rather fits us now."

"You're such an idiot! Why didn't you say something? All these years, and I never knew you were a Scout too," said Simon, dumbfounded. And they exchanged the Scout handshake and sign.

"Nor me you," said Jack. "Never occurred to ask. Should have guessed really, you know all the knots, but I just thought that was from the sea."

As they passed South and North Sands Simon watched Jack, his best friend for two weeks each year, taken for granted and it came to him how much he liked him. He took in the blond hair, blue eyes and fair skin and was glad for the friendship. He shook off a vision of them both battered against the rocks, drowning together.

"What's the matter?" said Jack noticing his fixed look.

"Nothing," said Simon. "I was just thinking about us dying together, and I'm glad we didn't."

"Me too, Simon. Me too."

Their expedition was discovered however. *Invention* was known to the locals and they had been seen on their trip crossing the Bar. The hotel owner had spoken to Dad.

"You took the boat out over the Bar today," said Dad.

"Jack and I went to see *Herzogin Cecilie* in Starehole Bay," said Simon.

"Well, you shouldn't have done. That boat is only supposed to be used in the estuary, it's part of the conditions of hire."

"Sorry, Dad. Won't go out there again."

"What would you have done if you had got into trouble? What would it have looked like, two fifteen year old boys let loose out there. We might have had to call the lifeboat out or anything."

"It was OK, Dad, but as I say, I won't go there again. Promise."

At that Dad seemed mollified and the rest of the evening passed off well. He and Jack went into the town amid the summer crowds.

"Someone saw us out over the Bar," Simon said.

"Going out or coming back?" asked Jack.

"Don't know, but I got into bother with my Dad about it. Did you say anything to your folks?"

"I told them we'd been out, but not about breaking down. They'd have had a fit about that."

"I didn't say either," said Simon. "Let's not, eh? Might not be allowed to take the boat out at all."

So they agreed that the least said the better. They leaned on the rail on the ferry jetty looking at the passing boats and talking scouting as evening drew in.

He and Jack enjoyed the remainder of the holiday, despite the variable weather. All too soon the time to leave arrived. The usual farewells and then the long drive back to Nottingham. Phoebe was there to greet them with a lovely meal. At least it was lovely until Dad dropped the bombshell.

"So you enjoyed Salcombe, Simon?" asked Dad.

"Yes of course. Thank you very much. Fantastic."

"Well, I'm sorry, Simon, but that will have to be the last time."

Simon felt shocked. Of course he knew that it would have to end at some time, but not just yet. He knew also that he had no automatic right to be taken to Salcombe each year, but his dismay must have shown.

"I'm really sorry, Simon. But I have Phoebe to think about now and it was not fair to leave her for two weeks while we went away. I know how much it has meant to you and I had promised you last year, but things change, son. We have to move on."

"I didn't mind. I could get things done here on my own," said Phoebe.

"No, Dad's right," said Simon, trying to hide his disappointment.

"There is something else," said Dad. "I hope this doesn't come as too much of a shock. I have told Frances already."

"What?"

"Phoebe and I are going to get married soon. Next month, in fact. Nothing special, a register office. Mum knows too."

Simon fought to cope with all this change, but managed, "Oh, congratulations. Very good."

Dad smiled, so did Phoebe.

Simon got the train back to Bilthaven a couple of days later. Odd how he felt arriving back at the grand station, a feeling of homecoming as he stepped out into the street and saw the familiar city, its Bilthaven Transport buses. Lugging his bag, he got the Swiford trolley bus. There was a mishap with the collector coming off the wires right on a busy junction. This happened sometimes with the trolley buses, announced by the sound of the collector bar landing on the roof and the bus coming to an abrupt halt. The conductor then extracted a long bamboo pole from behind the downstairs seats and stood amid the traffic, lifting the collector back to the wires. The bus then resumed its journey.

Mum was pleased to see him when she came in from work and gave him a hug. She and Ken asked him about the holiday and he told them about breaking down on the way in from Starehole Bay.

"But Dad said this was the last year. You know about Phoebe?"

"Yes, we knew but didn't want to spoil the holiday by telling you beforehand."

"Are you going to the wedding?" asked Simon naively.

"No, of course not," said Mum. "I think Frances may go, but you'll be at school and it would hardly be a good thing if I turned up, now would it?"

"No, I suppose not," said Simon, realising the idiocy of his question.

The other news waiting for him was his 'O' level results. He had been away when they were published but there was a letter from the school. After their evening meal, Mum handed him the letter. Rather than open it there and then, he took it into his room. He sat at his desk, looking at it, with memories of the white envelope that had contained his entry to Hooray Henrys. Then, with butterflies in his stomach, Simon opened the envelope. Grade A for English Language, English Literature and History. The rest were B and C grades except one. Maths. With relief, Simon saw it was a Grade E. The lowest level of pass, but a pass, a palpable pass![1] He was still on course for Dartmouth!

---

[1] GCE 'O' level grades A to E later became GCSE grades A to C.

The remaining week or so of the summer holiday passed slowly for Simon. Luckily Ed Baker had a telephone so he was able to arrange a few meetings in the city centre, the favourite haunt being The Dungeon, a coffee bar that was underground just off Victoria Square. There they discussed each other's 'O' levels which were pretty similar. Both wanted History and English at 'A' level, Simon was tempted by German, Ed was keen on Economics. Otherwise, cut off from the farm and smarting from his rejection there and from Diane, he immersed himself in history, reading widely mainly about German history and modern European history, since 1789 anyway. This he knew was to be the work for A level history.

The changes that summer had shaken Simon. He had managed to forget it all while away in Salcombe, as always his annual escape from his reality. The change of fortunes at the farm affected him, just when he had become more self confident. Diane had no telephone, and while he knew roughly where she lived, he did not know her exact address. But he knew she had his phone number, and she didn't ring. Simon once more buried the hurt. Then there was the last visit to Salcombe. He was angry he had not been told, although he understood the reasons. But it had not allowed him to say goodbye to Jack properly. He doubted he would see him again. Simon thought his life seemed full of sudden breaks and insecurities. And there was the news that Dad and Phoebe were getting married. While he thought this would not affect him directly, it was another factor in the constant flux that was his life. There were the reminders of the past too. As September approached, bringing with it Daniel's birthday, Simon wrestled with his feelings. In the end he bought a card and posted it. His own birthday was a low key affair, out for a meal with Mum and Ken, a cheque from Dad, Frances phoned up from London, a few cards, including one from Ed, the only school friend to send one. Being at the end of the summer holiday, his birthday went unnoticed by school friends; it always had and Simon was used to it, but it did little to boost his self esteem. No card from Daniel. Simon wept in the night.

9. 1962/9 *Drama at sea*

The new term, a safer bus ride too. The third year boy he had helped, now fourth year of course, saw Simon as his friend and sat with him on the bus, as Martin Passmore was no longer there, and of course the Neanderthals were gone. The atmosphere on the bus was completely different. The boy's name was Charlie and was quite happy to sit and chat to Simon, now a sixth former. Simon was happy to listen; he liked the boy and was pleased he had stuck his neck out for someone likeable. There was something of Peter Holman about him, the same cheerful chirpiness. Walking round the school, if he passed Charlie, the boy would always say hello, to the amusement of Simon's sixth form friends and the amazement of Charlie's friends at him talking to a sixth former in familiar terms. Both sides knew the history of course, and Simon's stock in that respect was riding high.

At the end of September, Dad and Phoebe got married in Nottingham. Simon was not there, but Dad sent some photos, one of him and Phoebe outside the register office, Phoebe looking smart in a blue suit and white trimmed hat, Dad looking absurdly self conscious in best suit with a large buttonhole flower. He always hated his photograph being taken. Simon sent a card with congratulations.

Simon made the effort to widen his social circle. He had no friends in Swiford but he could cycle to Ed's in about forty-five minutes, and even as far as Stuart's in Cermerton in an hour and a quarter, but it was not a pleasant ride and the few times Simon did it he was on edge as he rode through the estate where the Watsons lived. Sometimes Mum would drop him off at Stuart's and Mr Miller would drive him home. So he visited Ed more than Stuart, but both once or twice made the effort to get to Swiford.

Ed was nothing like the serious Stuart. He liked pop music and was a fan of a new group, the Beatles. He had their record and *Love me do* was played all the time. Simon thought it was quite good, too. He also tried smoking.

"Try one," Ed said to Simon, offering him a cigarette.

"Try anything once," said Simon, accepting. He lit the cigarette and drew gently on it. Ed exhaled blowing smoke rings, lying back on his bed. Simon, sitting in the chair, felt the smoke in his throat and nose, it was sharp and burnt. He coughed and spluttered to Ed's laughter.

"Why do people do this?" he asked, through his coughing. He had often wondered why Mum and Dad smoked, although they had always warned him against it. That seemed hypocritical to Simon.

"You have to get used to it," said Ed.

"Why would anyone want to?"

"Go on, try again."

Simon inhaled again, the smoke coursing down into his lungs and exploding out again amid a paroxysm of coughing. Simon put the cigarette down in the ash tray.

"What's the attraction of it?" he asked.

Ed, drew and exhaled again, adopting the mannerism of some film star. "It looks good," he said, "and it calms you down."

Simon was still coughing, but managed, "If this is calm, I'll stick to rough, because that's how it feels. And I certainly don't feel as if I look good."

"You're not giving it fair chance," argued Ed.

"Perhaps it's not giving me a fair chance," said Simon. He did not pick up the cigarette.

Simon recounted this episode to Stuart.

"Why did you even try it?" asked Stuart. "It's stupid. It kills people."

"Well, lots of people do it, my parents do, they're still alive," said Simon defensively, wondering why he was defending Ed, whom Stuart did not think much of.

"At the moment," remarked Stuart dryly. "Well, I'm glad you didn't carry on. Life's uncertain enough as it is."

Simon made no comment, but secretly he agreed with Stuart, both about smoking and the uncertainty of life. He knew all about that.

Toward the end of October events took a turn that demonstrated that uncertainty and shook everybody. President Kennedy said the Russians had put nuclear missiles into Cuba and so he declared a naval blockade. Simon knew enough about naval matters to know that this was the direct path to confrontation. In the end, one ship could only stop another by force. Khrushchev showed no sign of backing down and the world held its breath as the Russian ships got closer to the American naval fleet.

It was impossible to think of anything else. Simon had grown up with the presence of the Bomb, but now there was a real possibility of an all out nuclear war.

"We only get a four minute warning," said Simon, stirring his coffee. He and Ed were sitting in the Dungeon coffee bar. It was half term, but both knew that nobody would have been going to school anyway.

"The yanks get much longer," said Ed.

"Much good that'll do them. Time to get into their nuclear shelters I suppose, but then what?"

"Got to come out sometime, and to what? And anyway, only the richest people have got nuclear shelters."

"Well, if the bomb drops now, at least we're underground," said Simon, "and with a large supply of coffee."

"Not enough ciggies, though," said Ed, lighting up a cigarette.

"If you think I'm sharing a shelter with you for months on end with you chuffing away on those things, think again!" retorted Simon.

"Go outside for some fresh air, then."

"And come back in, just glowing," smiled Simon.

"Who said we'd let you back in?" said Ed.

"I think it's all about Berlin, really," said Simon, changing tack.

"How do you work that one out? Cuba's thousands of miles from Berlin."

"It's all about power play. If Khrushchev gets away with the missiles in Cuba, he can just walk into West Berlin, knowing that he has missiles so close to the USA. It leaves the Americans very exposed."

"Well, they're both driving themselves into a corner then, and all of us with them. Does it bloody matter that much? Is it really worth killing the planet?" said Ed.

"One side will have to back down, or find a way out that makes it honours even," said Simon.

"What the heck's Cuba to him, or he to Cuba?" quoted Ed, grinning.

It took Simon a moment, but he then replied, "Always knew you were a rogue and peasant slave."

"Bravo!" said Ed, slapping Simon on the back.

"Why, what an ass am I!" said Simon, laughing now. "Time for another coffee, methinks."

"Didn't know Hamlet drank coffee," joked Ed, their sombre mood now lightened. "If you're buying, I'll have another."

"Don't push your luck," said Simon, who then went to the counter for two more coffees and biscuits.

The following days passed seemingly in slow motion. People tried to go about their daily business, but there was an air of fatalism. If it were going to happen, then it would, and there was nothing to be done about it. Most people just hoped the end would be quick.

When Khrushchev ordered the Soviet ships to turn back, the world breathed a sigh of relief.

Sixth form life was pleasant enough for Simon, but hard work. *Hamlet* was a major study as part of the English, along with *Anthony and Cleopatra* and Shakespeare's other works, the sonnets Simon liked. History was, as Simon had expected, Europe from 1789 and Simon took a special interest in Germany. He was advised that having come late to the German language, he might find the A level hard going, despite his reasonable showing at 'O' level. While his spoken German was good, there would be a lot of heavy reading. This was counterbalanced by being assured that the Economics involved some basic Mathematics, but it would be nothing he couldn't handle. But the German teacher still put Simon forward for an exchange programme the next year, when he would stay with a family in Germany. And the history course was offering a school cruise in the Mediterranean next year too, taking in Naples, Pompeii, Athens and Istanbul. Simon noted there was not much there about modern European history, but apparently it was about a broad view of history, and anyway, Simon was not going to pass up a chance like that.

Dad agreed to pay for the cruise, especially as he wasn't taking Simon to Salcombe, Mum would have to fund the trip to Germany. This led to a new change for Simon. He had been used to spending most Saturdays working at the farm, so now he would be working for money. The Saturday job was provided by Russell in one of his fish and chip shops. For £1, Simon cycled to the shop and then spent the day preparing chips. The potatoes had first to be washed. There was a machine to peel the potatoes that worked by tumbling them around in an abrasive drum, but the drum had to be cleaned periodically and also the potatoes had to be finished by hand, with the 'eyes' dug out individually. Then they were hand pressed through a chip maker, and the chips put in a large tin bath of water, along with a whitening powder that stopped them going dark before the evening trade. It was hard work, but for Simon, the hardest part was the isolation. It was lonely work because he was left in the upstairs room above the shop all day to get on with it. He had to fill four such baths before he was done which was several large sacks of potatoes. But slowly the money mounted up.

Another frustration at that time was that his fellow students were learning to drive. Simon's late birthday meant that most of his friends would be driving before he was. Ed started first, Stuart a bit later. His Saturday work also cut down on his social life, an added factor in Simon's feeling of dissatisfaction. As the cold winter took hold, there was less opportunity to get out anyway. Simon had the electric fire on in his bedroom almost continuously, and he started to use the bus to get to the chip shop as the roads were dangerously icy for a cyclist.

All through that bitter winter, Simon tried to carry on with life as normally as possible. In February, the school bus had to change its route on some days because some roads were blocked by snow. At times, the bus was driving through a canyon of snow higher than the single deck coach. Of course this weather led to snowballs being thrown, and as Simon's aim was not that good by way of retaliation, he disliked this and tried to avoid being a target. His mind wandered back to happy winter days sledging down the hill with Daniel. He thought of Daniel now less often, but when he did come to the front of Simon's thoughts, the pain was as real as ever.

One result of the harsh winter was that many driving tests were cancelled, causing considerable annoyance to some of Simon's year group who were turning seventeen before him, but Simon couldn't help feeling a little schadenfreude.

Misfortune struck Simon as the German exchange drew close. He felt unaccountably tired, became irritable and then suffered a major throat infection, fever and aches and pains. The doctor said it was probably glandular fever, and confined Simon to bed rest. So the group left for Germany without him. He started to get better after a few days, the doctor commenting that his youth and general fitness contributed to his quick recovery. This was no consolation to Simon however, who had missed his trip to Germany and was also missing his studies at school. When the group returned, Simon had to listen to all their accounts of how the German town of Fruhstadt had been taken over by them, probably an exaggeration, but it was obvious there had been a lot of fun. Better news was that the family who were to have hosted Simon had invited him for Easter, an invitation which he happily accepted, Dad deciding under the circumstances to help out with the extra travel costs.

Preparations for another major event were also taking place. Mum and Ken were getting married. This time Simon was there, and Frances too. It was also a register office do, but there was a party afterwards at some friends who had a large house and hosted this reception for them. Simon decided he liked champagne!

Ed passed his driving test and so did Stuart. Sometimes, they managed to borrow the parental car. Simon undoubtedly preferred being with Stuart, whose careful and precise nature translated into his driving; careful, competent and safe. Ed's character showed in his driving, technically competent but flamboyant and at times aggressive. Being driven by Ed was more fun, but certainly more risky.

Driving was a constant topic of conversation. One of their group, Jamie Nash, often brought his father's car to school. This was a luxury Singer Gazelle which was his father's pride and joy. This did not stop Jamie taking as many of the sixth form friends as he could cram in out at lunchtimes, a few miles along the road out into the country where there was a nice pub, The Bull. Simon too went along on these rides as often as not, Ed of course as well. Predictably, Stuart thought Jamie's driving left a lot to be desired, as proved to be the case. Jamie's theory was that one could drive faster at night because any oncoming vehicles would be betrayed by their lights. It was with some concern that the group of friends heard that Jamie was in hospital after an accident in the Singer. It was agreed that all would troop down to Bilthaven Infirmary to see him.

They arrived, with grapes, hidden bottles of beer and so on. Jamie was sitting up in bed when they eventually managed to persuade the nurse to let them in.

"Just five minutes, mind. Be gone before Matron gets back."

"Hey, Jamie, look at you!"

Jamie, heavily bandaged but with the mischievous look returning to his eye when he saw the gang, replied, "Hi. Brought any beer?"

Shielded by the group, a couple of bottles were secreted in Jamie's bedside locker.

"What happened, Jamie?" asked Ed.

"Night time wasn't it?" asked Stuart.

"That bloody cow," said Jamie. "Didn't have any lights on, did it?"

The group burst out laughing, oblivious to the suffering to the now deceased cow, or even to Jamie's injuries or the fact that the Singer was a write off.

Jamie later made a full recovery, more than could be said for the cow or the car, but he no longer had access to his father's new car.

The lower sixth continued well for Simon, and his teachers predicted excellent A level results. Simon started to hope that there was some stability in his life.

10. 1963/4 Germany

The trip to Germany was an adventure for Simon. Sixteen years old, he was to travel alone across Europe by train to Fruhstadt. On a Tuesday in early April, he set off to London, starting the Easter holiday early with the school's sanction, staying with friends of Mum for one night.

The next morning they all went to Victoria. On the station platform Simon talked to the mother of a girl who was sitting opposite him in the train. She was going to Brussels. At ten o'clock precisely, the train pulled out of Victoria. It was twenty minutes before they were clear of London. Sitting next to the girl was a man who spoke no English and Simon took him to be Flemish for some reason. After about an hour the train stopped in a station called Dover Marine. Everybody got out. It was at this point that Simon opened a conversation with the girl on the train.

"I hear you are going to Brussels", he said.

"Yes", she replied, "where are you going?"

He told her that he was going to Bavaria, and then they showed their passports to a man who just opened and shut them quickly. No attempt was made to search the bags. They all filed onto the boat, a Belgian vessel called "*Koningin Elizabeth*". They put their cases on luggage racks and tried to find somewhere to sit. They went into the bar where Simon drank the Belgian equivalent to a Coca-Cola and she drank Orange juice. But there was still nowhere to sit. In the end, they went to the café. When the boat eventually arrived in Ostend they passed through customs without any problem. Simon now had to part from the girl and find the Ostend-Vienna Express. Simon saw a big sign!

"OOSTENDE - WIEN EXPRESS"

He made for the train it indicated. The coaches were French, on the side it said,

"OOSTENDE-BRUSSEL-LIEGE-AACHEN-KÖLN,-HELMSTEDT-BERLIN-FRANKFURT/ODER-POZNAN-WARSWAZA"

He decided that somehow wasn't his train. Another carriage had a whole list of names on it including NÜRNBERG. He jumped on it with his two suitcases. Simon struck up conversation with a man who transpired to be an Italian. They had a cup of coffee. He could speak no German, so Simon had to translate for him. They talked about a wide variety of subjects, including Mussolini, Simon as ever curious about history.

It was dark by the time the train pulled up in Aachen, and the train filled with German customs officials. One asked if he had anything to declare.

"Ich habe nichts zu verzollern", Simon said. He translated for his Italian friend. There were three other men in the compartment, who it turned out were Swedish. When the passport man came along, he examined theirs and the Italian's very carefully, but he was very impressed with Simon's; he did not even look at it, but made signs to indicate that his passport was the best thing in the world. He was very polite and wishing Simon a very good journey and a safe arrival and a good stay in Germany, he clicked his heels, and backed out of the compartment. Simon looked around and found the Swedes looking at him oddly.

Eventually, the train got to Cologne. The cathedral spires stood out black and massive against a dark blue sky. The station was vast. The loudspeaker system reminded Simon of Hitler haranguing a vast audience. The Italian got off and so did the Swedes, leaving Simon in the compartment with one German passenger.

About twenty minutes after it left Cologne, the train stopped at a small, country looking station in a small town. What, he thought, is the Ostend Vienna express stopping here for? But this dingy little place was Bonn, headquarters of the Federal Republic. At Koblenz, a whole party of noisy British school children got off and peace reigned. The German put down his book, pulled down the blind on his corridor side windows, pulled out the seat and put his feet up. Simon did also but determined not to sleep lest he went past Nuremberg. The train roared on into the night.

When he woke up, the train was stopped in a vast station, with platforms as far as one could see on either side. It was half past one. It was Frankfurt /Main. He fell asleep and woke in Würzberg. After that he stayed awake, looking at the dark landscape that was Germany. It seemed so forbidding. Each practically deserted station functioned with silent efficiency. At twenty to four, the train came to Fürth and roared through the nearly empty station. He was due in Nuremberg at four o'clock. He saw the lights of the city. He got up, and took down his cases. The German looked up, got up, pushed back his seat, put the light on, let up the blind and put his jacket on. He had been lying across the door, so Simon was glad that he had got up himself, instead of having to be woken to get out.

The train pulled up in a vast station with "Nürnberg Hbt" written everywhere. Feeling slightly uncomfortable Simon got out of the train and stood on the completely empty platform. Going down some steps marked "Hauptausgang", he found himself in a draughty tunnel running at right angles to the track, with steps up to each platform. He now wanted a train to Hof. He went along through glass doors at the end of the tunnel. Hot air blew down from the ceiling. He showed his ticket to a man at the barrier and asked him,

"Wann verlasst den nächsten Zug nach Hof, bitte?"

"Sechs Uhr - Bahnsteig fünfzehn"

"Danke."

He passed out into a vast hall and noticed that the barrier through which he had come had in big red letters on this side, "Kein Eingang". He set himself to find the way back into the platforms. Suddenly, shouting arose from one end of the hall, echoing loudly up the vast space. Simon went to investigate. It was a fight. It appeared to be between some scruffily dressed black men and some very tough looking Germans in tight trousers and leather jackets.

Suddenly, police were all over the place. One looked at Simon suspiciously. He hurriedly produced his British Passport, and, waving that in one hand and flapping the other at his cases, he said,

"Ich erwarte einen Zug nach Hof"
"Britische Pass?", he said.
"Ja", Simon replied.
"Ah, verzeihen Sie!" he said and walked away.

At the far end of the hall Simon found a snack bar open, the way into the platform tunnel and a newspaper and book-stall. He suddenly remembered the British Budget and asked if they had British newspapers. He asked for the latest "Guardian" that they had and got a week-old "Manchester Guardian Weekly". He went to the snack bar and drank a cup of coffee. The sky outside was getting lighter. After looking at a stall which sold badges and cycle pennants for all over Germany and the world, but which was firmly locked up, he got out his ticket and went to the barrier. He showed the man his ticket, who made a great hole in it and said gruffly, "Bahnsteig fünfzehn."

It was now a quarter to six in the morning. Simon went through glass doors into a tunnel similar to the previous one and walked along till he came to the steps to platform fifteen. A notice on the wall at the bottom of the steps proclaimed "Hof Hbf."

Simon went up the steps onto the platform. In Germany, the same number platform goes right across from track to track, instead of calling one side one number and the other side another, as in Britain. This could mean, and did in this case, that there were two trains at the platform. He went to one and asked a uniformed figure leaning beside it, "Fährt dieser Zug nach Hof, bitte"

The man shook his head and pointing to the other train and said something so quickly Simon could not hear it. He went across to the other train and asked a young man loading mail the same question.

"Ja", he said.
"Danke"
"Bitte".

Simon got into the train and sat down. By now it was broad daylight. At six o'clock precisely, the train left Nuremberg station. Soon it was in open country. What a beautiful country it was. So perfect! The whole thing appeared to have been landscaped. It was certainly some of the most beautiful countryside Simon had ever seen. It seemed ideal. The train arrived in Bayreuth, "Wagnerstadt". Then on through idyllic countryside, past innumerable woods of spruce trees, and small German style country villages, each set in perfect surroundings.

Eventually, Simon came to Hof. Everybody got out and rapidly disappeared through the barrier into the street; he was left standing on the platform, clutching his two cases. A kiosk marked "Auskunft", stood along the platform.

He went to it, and asked, "Bitte, wann verlasst den nächsten Zug nach Fruhstadt?"

"Elf Uhr, dreiundvierzig - Bahnsteig drei"

"Danke"

That meant that, as it was now about ten past nine, he had to wait in Hof for two and a half hours. He went into the waiting room, but on the door it said in red letters

"KEIN DURCHGANG" and underneath "IIte Klasse Warterraum"

While he was deciding which to believe, a grey uniform swept by through the door into the room beyond, and he caught sight inside tables and people, obviously some of them passengers, sitting by them.

He went in and sat down. A man came and asked if he wanted to eat. He asked for a cup of coffee and paid 0.55 DM. The man growled and went away. Simon later realised that it was because he had not tipped him, as he had thought that the service was always included in Germany. Simon took out a book and read it until half-past eleven. Then he got up and with a little old woman running in front of him opening doors and saying, "Gute Reise", he went out onto the platform. On the side of a train that looked straight from the Wild West, a metal plate said,

FRUHSTADT

Simon got on it and sat down on a wooden seat. At 11:43 exactly, the train pulled out.

It rolled slowly on from station to station, stopping at all of them, through more ideal countryside. At half past twelve, the train stopped in the station. Simon got down onto the platform and began to follow the crowd across the railway lines. Then he saw Karl, recognised from the letters and photographs.

He said, "Hallo, how do you do?"

"I am very well," Simon said, which was not really true, because at that moment a wave of tiredness overcame him.

Simon was taken out through the barrier where a maroon Mercedes-Benz 190 (latest model) was waiting. His cases were put in the boot and he and Karl got in. The car drove away through a very beautiful town and then the car stopped in front of a semi-detached house. Simon got out and Karl's mother came to the door.

He went up the path, and Karl's mother said, "Herzlich willkommen in Germany."

The Mercedes, which apparently was a taxi, disappeared. Then they had a meal of liver-cheese meat, (which does not contain liver or cheese) with potatoes, and cucumber in vinegar.

Simon was shown the bedroom. It was a couch, with a cocktail cabinet beside it. The couch pulled out from underneath the cabinet.

In the afternoon Karl and Simon went into the town on Karl's motor-cycle, a Kreidler Florett 50c.c. (4.4 h.p.). They went to the post office, after having bought a postcard, and Simon wrote it and posted it to Mum. Then Karl showed him round Fruhstadt. In the Marktplatz, they met Klaus, a friend of Karl's, and waited for a wedding to come out of the Evang StadtKirche. All Simon's tiredness was now gone.

They then went back 'home' and Karl phoned Etta, his girlfriend. Later they met her from work. As they walked towards Etta's home, they talked of monarchy in Germany as opposed to republicanism. They talked also of the Weimar republic and its failure. Etta put her case in the house, (a block of flats), and then they walked to the woods and back. It was now about half past six. Etta went in, and Karl and Simon went home.

Karl's father came home from work. After a meal, Simon went upstairs and put on his suit, as they were going to the opera in Fruhstadt to watch "The Barber of Seville", in German. There Simon met some of Karl's friends. Afterwards the young ones went to a pub where Simon drank beer. He met Harald and Klaus. Harald was playing the piano very well. Simon asked if he could play any Rachmaninoff. Harald raised his eyebrows and said, "Nein".

At midnight they left the pub and started home. As they were walking home they saw a man sitting on the pavement on the other side of the street. They crossed and got him to his feet. He promptly sat down again. He was completely drunk. As the boys helped him along, a another young man came up who knew the drunk old man and where he lived. The old man was jabbering on about all the Russians he had shot in the war for the Kaiser. Karl in the end convinced him that he had been on the French front in the Great War. They arrived at his house and knocked on the door. When his wife opened it, she was furious. They took the old man upstairs and deposited him on the floor of his bedroom. All the while, his wife was telling him what she thought of him, only just remembering to thank the boys in time.

They then went straight home and to bed.

The following day, Friday, Simon woke at midday, having slept in. His continental quilt or Federbett was on the floor beside him.

At half past twelve, Karl returned from school. In the afternoon they went to Harald's where they drank champagne and ate biscuits and talked. It was very pleasant. They were there an hour until five o'clock. Then Karl and Simon went to meet Etta from work.

In the evening, after eating, the two returned to Etta's and then went for a walk. They were talking for a long while, sitting on a bench at the edge of the wood, and then they went home, by a different route and Etta kept trying to tickle Simon.

After leaving Etta, Karl and Simon went into a pub, where they met more friends. They drank beer, played German and British records on the Juke-Box, and played with the Football machine. They were singing Billy Mo. "*Ich kauf mir lieber einer Tirolerhut*".

Then they returned home, with Karl and Simon a bit "besoffen"; Karl was burping in German, English and Latin. They went to bed.

So the days passed by. On one occasion they visited Karl's grandmother where they stayed for half an hour.

After a while, the old lady, dressed in all black lace, looked at Simon and said (in German of course), "You're not from round here, are you."

"No," he answered.

"I knew that," she said, and then she announced, as though it were indisputable, "Hamburg!"

"No, a bit north and west of Hamburg," Simon said jokingly.

She frowned, and said, "There is nowhere north and west of Hamburg!"

It was then explained Simon was from England at which she did not seem very impressed. He was pleased though that his German had been good enough to make her think he was a native speaker, even if from Hamburg.

Simon was taken to the cinema, where he found his German was enough to follow the plot. They saw Etta frequently, which Simon was pleased about. There was something about her that reminded him of Diane.

He was taken on the motor cycle to see the Czech border, the Iron Curtain, which was a few miles away. Simon was warned against straying over, as the border fence was some way back from the actual border which was marked simply by white stones at ten yard intervals. But everywhere, there was a pub, and more beer.

Karl and his friends were also studying history, and the talk was often of the Nazi period, although Simon quickly learned that the older people didn't want to discuss it, the boys were quite happy to. They taught Simon the *Horst Wessel Song* and he taught them the words to *Colonel Bogey*, with its descriptions of the sexual anatomy of various Nazi leaders. This amused the Germans immensely. All said they preferred the current situation, the division of Germany, rather than a unified but Nazi Germany. Simon felt he was doing well and was accepted, even though it turned out that they were all older than he was.

Each time they met Etta, she tried to tickle Simon. He quite liked this, enjoying her closeness, but wondered what Karl was making of it. While Karl practised shot putting in a clearing in the woods, Simon learned to drive the motorcycle, and then gave Etta a ride round the clearing. She tickled him again, which made it harder to control the machine.

A week after his arrival, a letter arrived from Mum. She had received the postcard and was pleased to hear he had arrived safely. Simon met Karl's ten year old cousin who took a liking to Simon, so he set about teaching the boy English. He explained to him and Karl's parents the differences between the

United Kingdom, Great Britain and England. Democracy without a constitution seemed impossible to them, but Simon did his best to explain.

On Good Friday, Karl's father was not at work so they all went out on a day trip in the family's Volkswagen, returning in the evening to more beer with Karl's friends. Simon got rather drunk and according to Karl, fell asleep while riding pillion. Not recommended.

Simon was taken round the homes of Karl's friends, sometimes being presented with gifts, for which he was unprepared. All he could do was thank them profusely. But the evenings usually ended up in a pub, the chalk marks on the table mounting up beside Simon's seat. Much of it he could not remember! As a result Easter Sunday was spent quietly, Karl's mother providing traditional cakes and there was an Easter gift of a porcelain rabbit for Simon.

On Easter Monday, the family took Simon out into the mountains of northern Bavaria, with castles, valleys and enchanting scenery. Later they went to Nuremburg, seeing the sights of the city, the ancient Spring and the Hospital of the Holy Spirit.

The next few days were spent with the group of friends. Simon had the feeling that Karl was unhappy about the attention Etta was giving him, but Simon enjoyed it and felt there was little he could do to discourage it anyway.

By the following Wednesday, Simon and Etta were feeling close. Karl was going out for some reason and rather than just sit in the house, Simon decided to visit Etta. He knew he was missing Diane and this pushed him forward. They walked in the woods and talked. Each sensed the attraction of the other, and there was nothing he wanted more at that moment than to have sex with her. But Etta stopped short and the moment passed. Simon was left wondering what would have happened if Etta had continued. He felt regret and relief at the same time. However, he still felt guilty when back at the house with Karl.

A trip to Bayreuth followed, where Simon was granted access backstage to the great opera house, and was struck by its acoustic clarity. More scenery, the carefully matured landscape impressing as always.

The tension with Karl passed and by the time arrived for Simon to leave, all seemed well on that score.

At twelve minutes past seven in the evening on the Tuesday, the local train pulled out of Fruhstadt, bound directly for Nuremburg. Again a long wait but at two in the morning, the express left Nuremburg north bound. Simon was sharing the compartment with three girls from Liverpool who were pleased he was from Bilthaven. All the British people they had met in Germany were from London. He pooled his supply of food with theirs, the resultant debris created enough to ensure the compartment remained theirs alone for the whole twelve hours to Ostend.

They parted in London, where they eventually arrived at nine o'clock on Wednesday evening. He returned to the friends he had stayed with. His German visit was over.

11. 1963/7 Romance at sea

Soon after Simon's return to Bilthaven, one or two incidents led to a further development. He was waiting for a bus at a stop used by several routes so as soon as he saw the approaching bus was the one he wanted, he stepped forward and put out his hand. The bus came to an abrupt halt. This was a motor bus, and the driver slid back the window on his left above the engine and shouted at Simon.

"What do you think you're doing? Don't leave it so late, you're lucky I stopped."

Puzzled, Simon got on the bus and carried on with his journey. He had signalled as soon as he was sure it was the bus he wanted.

A few days later, he and Mum went to the theatre. Simon enjoyed the show from his seat in the dress circle but at the interval a notice board was put on the stage.

"That's a bit daft," said Simon. "You would think they would make the writing large enough for people to see."

Mum turned and looked at Simon, frowning. "Can't you read that, Simon?"

"No, can you?"

"Yes, easily. Perhaps we should get your eyes checked."

So Simon went to an optician in Bilthaven who said he was short sighted in both eyes, the left particularly. The spectacles were ordered. A week later after school, Simon went to collect them. He sat in the chair while the plastic frames were given final adjustments to fit. They felt strange and heavy on his face.

He stepped out into the city lights and looked along the quiet road toward the bright lights of Port Road at the end. He took out the spectacles and put them on. Jesus! Is this what other people have been seeing? Everything jumped into focus. He could read the shop signs, the blue neon Boots logo on Port Road stopped being a blue blur and became sharp. He walked along to Port Road and into Victoria Square, looking around him. It was amazing what he could see. He felt very self-conscious but nobody was giving him a second glance. Why should they? he told himself.

The next day he decided to wear the glasses all the time, which is what he had been advised to do. It had to be done so get it over with. Charlie sat next to him on the bus but never mentioned his glasses. Nobody in his tutor groups did either. It was only at morning break that Ed stopped him.

"Simon, have you got different glasses on?"

"Different from what?"

"Your old ones."

"I never had any old ones, these are the first ones I've ever had," said Simon.

Ed's reaction was just to shrug. Very little was ever said about them and Simon soon became accustomed to wearing them. And he had no more rebukes from angry bus drivers! But Simon was now worried about his ambition for a naval career.

The cruise date arrived at last. The Spring weather had banished the memories of the exceptionally harsh winter as the children all met up at Bilthaven Grand Station to catch the train to London. It was a special train just for the cruise children who were drawn from many schools in the area, including, Simon noticed, both Bilthaven Royal Grammar School and Swiford Grammar. He and Ed stayed together, Stuart was not on the cruise, so Simon did not feel he would have to choose.

The channel crossing was rough, and many of the children were sick as the ferry ploughed on into the darkening evening. The toilets stank of vomit, but Simon felt pleased with himself as he had his 'sea legs' and was not sick. He had got used to rough seas at Salcombe. He thought back to *Invention* and the time he and Jack had nearly died on the rocks under Sharpitor. But he engrossed himself in the task of looking after Ed who was having a miserable time. He persuaded him on deck, on the lee side of the ship, because the smell below was making matters worse. Ed was sick over the side instead.

At last the ship reached land and many groggy children transferred to the train that would take them to Venice. It rumbled through the night and most of the next morning. The children slept but arrived in Venice tired. They were shown round the sights of the city but could hardly take it in. At last they were taken to the ship, *MS Devonia*, specially converted for school cruises. They found their dormitories and settled in. The ship started its journey down the Adriatic Sea towards Piraeus, the port for Athens. Now the tables were turned. There was a heavy swell and the ship was slowly rising and falling and at the same time, rocking from side to side, a long, slow corkscrew that gradually affected Simon more and more until he had to rush on deck in the darkness and remembering to go to the lee side, was sea sick. Ed followed, laughing, but with him nevertheless.

"Not so cocky now, Mr Sea Legs," he laughed, as he was completely unaffected by this long slow motion, in contrast to the rougher and rapid motion in the English Channel. But Simon could not summon the willpower to make any response. When he felt he had nothing left to bring up, he, like many others affected, staggered to his bunk and collapsed onto it. Ed covered him with a blanket and left him to sleep.

The bright morning sun saw a flat calm and the children gathered on deck. To port was the coastline, bare and mountainous, of the mysterious country of

Albania, the most secretive of the communist countries. He and Ed were chatting at the rail.

"They've even fallen out with Russia," commented Ed.

"Thrown in their lot with China, instead," added Simon, looking across the few miles of sea to this brightly sunlit yet dark land. "Enver somebody, the dictator."

"Hoxha," said a voice next to them.

Simon turned to see a girl their own age. With shoulder length dark hair swept back, a high, intelligent looking forehead, and hazel eyes that were fixed on Simon. He felt that same tingle of excitement as when he had first seen Diane.

"Thank you," he said. "that's the name I couldn't quite remember. But my name's Simon."

"Ruth," said the girl. "Ruth Tickell."

"Simon Scott," he responded, and feeling a dig in his side from Ed, added, "and this is Ed Baker. We're from Cermerton Grammar School."

"I'm from Bilthaven Church High School," said Ruth and held out her hand, which Simon and then Ed shook.

So they struck up conversation. It was at first a three way conversation, she was studying English, History and Art for A level, so they had quite a lot in common. She seemed serious minded.

"I'm going to see if I can find the others," said Ed eventually. "Are you coming?"

Simon looked at Ruth; something in her expression made him say, "No, I'll stay here. See you later."

So Simon and Ruth got to know each other. She was doing the same coursework for English, *Hamlet*, *Anthony and Cleopatra* and even the William Golding Book, *Lord of the Flies*. She was not so informed about German history as Simon, but was a keen listener and paid attention as Simon talked about this. Simon enjoyed having an attentive audience, even if of only one, that listened to what he had to say.

Ruth attached herself to Simon's group for much of that cruise, but it was always understood by the others that she was there because of Simon. Naturally he got a lot of good natured teasing about this in the Cermerton boys' dormitory, but Simon was quite happy about that. He felt his stock was high and he enjoyed her company. They wandered around Piraeus together, managed to get together on the Acropolis, looked round the Blue Mosque and St Sophia in Istanbul together and as they re-crossed the Aegean Sea on a warm, moonlit night, talked by the rail of the ship, arms round each other. The conversation was about school, life in general and their ambitions.

"I planned to join the navy, but now I have to wear glasses, I'm not sure if I can."

"Won't they have you?" she asked, concerned.

"Not for the Executive Branch, those are the ones who run the ships and go to sea. Possibly on the Supply side or as an Instructor, but I wanted to go to sea."

"Well, you would be good at that," said Ruth. "Don't give up hope."

"Oh, I won't," said Simon. "I'll definitely try after A levels and see what they say."

They both turned to face each other at the same moment, their faces close, eyes meeting. Tentatively, Simon moved his lips closer to hers, she responded and they kissed by the rail in the moonlight with the white wake of the ship frothing away into the darkness, both oblivious to the perfect romantic setting of this first kiss they shared.

"You're nice, Simon," she said.

"So are you. Can we meet up when we get back? Go out together, I mean?" asked Simon, hopefully.

"I'd like that," she said, and they kissed again.

The next day they were together as the ship squeezed through the Corinth Canal, the high cliffs towering above the ship, and what seemed like barely inches either side. Simon was impressed both by the canal and the ship handling. It became recognised among both his and her groups that they were now officially 'going out'.

They 'braved' the journey between Scylla and Charybdis and on deck together they looked in the darkness at the small volcanic island of Stromboli. The ship lost speed so the passengers could have a look, but suddenly a great spout of fire and lava burst from high on the flank of the volcano. While all the kids cheered, the ship jolted forward as the Captain decided to put on full ahead to take his ship quickly away from any possible danger.

They drank coffee together in Naples and explored Pompeii, but were denied access to the erotic frescoes, much to the chagrin of most of the boys.

Simon and Ruth spent much of the train journey from Genoa back to Calais in each other's company, both suffering ribbing from their friends. But Simon took this in good part. He felt happy in Ruth's company, and wanted to spend as much time with her as he could. They made plans to meet up, exchanged addresses and phone numbers. She lived some distance away, further even than Cermerton, but they would meet up in the city.

The school year drew to a close, and despite the pressure of work, Simon felt happy. Life seemed to have reached some kind of equilibrium, his school work was going well and his teachers thought he should achieve good grades for the 'A' levels the next year. There was the worry about how his wearing glasses would affect his aim to go to Dartmouth, but Simon put that to one side, deciding not to cross that bridge before he came to it.

The school had a prefect system, but of the now large year group, just twelve prefects were chosen. Simon had hoped to be selected, but he was not. In fact none of his circle were, not Ed, not Jamie Nash, Alan Croft, not even Stuart. It was not a great loss, and some pointed out it was an advantage as the duties required of the prefects could take precious time when all attention should be on the 'A' levels. So after the summer holidays, he would have more time to spend with Ruth, he thought, and smiled to himself.

His friendship with Ruth went from strength to strength. They met every weekend on Fridays and Saturdays in Bilthaven, going to the pictures, or 'the flicks' as they sometimes called them. Or they would go to The Dungeon, sometimes meeting up with Ed and Angela, his latest girlfriend.

Ruth was interested in hearing about Simon's scouting and the church parades. She was, Simon found, a religious person and he told her about the time when Daniel had given him the wine at Communion.

"Why don't you get confirmed?" she asked.

"I might have done I expect if we hadn't moved to Bilthaven."

"So why not now?" she persisted.

"Just never carried on with church. My Mum's not specially religious. I think she believes in God, but isn't keen on the church."

"That's a shame. I wish you could come to my church."

"Sunday buses are useless," said Simon. So they kissed and cuddled, feeling close to each other. Simon already knew that despite his feeling of sexual attraction to her, there was not going to be sexual intercourse. Ruth was a practising Christian and wanted to wait for sex, believing that marriage was the only proper place for that. Yet he didn't mind, as the weeks went by and the summer holidays came, he just felt happy in her company, and maybe she would change her mind!

At last, in the summer holidays, he turned seventeen and could learn to drive. Driving lessons cost a lot of money but Mum had a friend – she knew a lot of people through the *Bilthaven Mail* – who was a recently retired police driving instructor. What terms she negotiated Simon never knew but it turned out to be one of her better investments.

On his first lesson the Saturday morning after his birthday, Simon was taken aback when the instructor arrived in his big ex-police patrol car. How would he ever handle the power and size of this car? He expected the instructor, Bernard Gough, would take the wheel, but instead Simon was put straight in the driving seat. After an explanation of how an engine needed gearing, the role of the drive chain and the clutch along with other items, Simon was told to drive the car forward. Gingerly he lifted his left foot and then the car lurched forward and stopped. Bernard had dual controls so then he helped Simon. They went to a hill outside Swiford, and stopped facing uphill. Simon was relieved as he was sweating with the mental strain of steering the big car for those few minutes.

"The clutch only operates through the thickness of a penny," said Bernard. "For most of its travel it is either engaged, that is up and driving the car, or disengaged, down and there is not drive to the rear wheels."

"It's so hard to judge," said Simon.

"You're doing fine, but before we go into Bilthaven, we need to practise the clutch. You're steering fine, so let's get the clutch done. Start the engine and hold the car on the handbrake."

Simon started the engine, first ensuring the car was in neutral.

"One tip is always to depress the clutch when starting the engine. Firstly, just in case the car is in gear, it won't jump forward so you get a second bite at the cherry, and secondly, the battery only has to turn the engine over, not the gearbox as well, so it is less strain on the battery life. Now, down with the clutch, select first gear."

Simon put the big car into first gear.

"Now release the catch on handbrake but hold it on, that is don't lower it so the car will roll back. Now slowly lift the clutch until you feel the car want to move, holding the revs steady with the gas pedal."

Carefully, Simon lifted the clutch. He felt the powerful engine start to want to move the car.

"Hold it there. Now release the handbrake."

Simon lowered the handbrake and the car moved slowly forward.

"Now slightly lower the clutch but not so much that car rolls back"

Simon did, the car balanced on the hill, stationary, allowing Simon to move it forward by small movements of the clutch. This was repeated until Simon had the feel of the clutch. They moved away and stopped several times.

"That's good," said Bernard. "Now let's go into the city centre."

Simon was shocked. When Bernard had said about going into Bilthaven, he had thought he meant in a future lesson. Bilthaven city centre on a Saturday morning! But under Bernard's guidance, he drove the big car back towards the city centre. It was very congested, but he actually drove round Victoria Square, amid the trolley buses, cars, lorries and managing to avoid cyclists and the many pedestrians. Then back out to Swiford and home.

"Well done Simon. You've done extremely well. You'll be driving in no time."

"I'm exhausted," said Simon, "there's just so much to look out for and think about. Everything happens at once."

"You'll get used to that. Most of it becomes automatic and your main concentration will be where it should be, out there on the road and other road users. Now, the method I'm going to teach you is the one the police use. It's stood the test of time and should ensure your safety and that of others."

Bernard reached into his bag and produced a blue coloured book with a picture of a police car on the front.

"This is *Roadcraft*. Read it, learn it and inwardly digest it. This is the police driving system you will be using. And this of course is the *Highway Code*," he added, giving Simon another book.

"I've already got that," said Simon, "but not this one."

"This is the latest edition. Use this one. It's the one the examiner will be using. Right, see you on Wednesday evening."

Simon spent all his spare moments studying both books. He was familiar with the *Highway Code* and although there were a few changes in the new edition, nothing he could not quickly absorb. But *Roadcraft* fascinated him, and he read it avidly.

He talked to Ruth about it. She was of course slightly older than he was (wasn't everybody in his year group?) but she wasn't learning to drive, as her parents didn't have the money. She tried to share his enthusiasm and listened while he told what he had been doing.

After his third lesson, Bernard had a surprise.

"You're going to be ready soon, Simon. You're a natural. So I am applying for your test now. We might get an early date. I know a few people," he said with a wink.

"Already?" said Simon surprised.

"By the time the test comes through you will have had at least eight lessons. You'll be fine."

And so it turned out. He had ten lessons with Bernard, some lasting as long as two hours, none less than one. He had practice in Mum's Ford with her when he could. It was very different to Bernard's car, just three gears for a start and much less powerful, but he adapted and learned a lot from Mum about road skills, reading the traffic. Mum had a pre-war 'all groups' driving licence, meaning she could drive every class of vehicle. It was her ambition to do so!

Just six weeks from his first lesson on a Friday afternoon instead of being in school, Simon took his driving test. He was nervous, especially doing the mandatory three point turn and parking manoeuvres in the big car, and then, driving along a main road in Bilthaven he came to some roadworks where the temporary traffic lights were green. But as he pulled out to go through, they changed quickly to red. Simon kept going. Had the examiner seen? He was looking down at his clipboard, making notes. That's it, thought Simon. I've failed. So in this knowledge he felt the pressure go and simply drove the rest of the course, enjoying the drive and using the car's power when applicable. Positive, assertive yet defensive, but not aggressive. They pulled up outside the test centre.

After a few basic questions on the *Highway Code*, the examiner gave Simon the news.

"Mr Scott, I am pleased to say you have reached the required standard and have passed the driving test. Congratulations."

"Passed? But I thought... " Simon stopped, not wanting to say anything that might make him change his mind.

The examiner smiled as he filled in the coveted pink pass form. "The temporary traffic lights? Yes, I did notice, but you did the right thing. They changed quickly, you were committed and the van behind you was too close. To have stopped quickly would have risked an accident. I note the van followed you through, too."

Simon just nodded. What van? he thought, but said nothing of course.

"Mum, I've passed," he said running back into the flat.
"Oh, well done, darling," said Mum, giving him a hug.
"Mum, can I borrow the car?"
"That didn't take long," remarked Ken.
"Where do you want to go?" asked Mum
"Ruth's. If that's OK."
"Oh, very well, but don't be late."

Simon went down through Russell's garage to the back lane where the little Ford Anglia was kept. It seemed so strange, driving with nobody in the passenger seat, alone in the car.

Ruth came down the steps of her house. "You've passed, then? Well done."
"Come for a ride," said Simon.

Ruth went back into her house, then returned with a jacket. "Mum says not for long. She says I should beware of boys with cars!"

They laughed at this, and he drove Ruth carefully round. They stopped for a while in a lovers' lane, but soon it was time to return.

"See you in town tomorrow?" asked Simon. "No car, I'm afraid."
"Bus suits me fine," said Ruth. Then realising what that might mean, added. "No reflection on your driving, that was good, I felt quite safe. From the driving, anyway," she joked.

"See you tomorrow," said Simon, blowing a kiss, before driving off.

Later that week he spent more time with Bernard, learning more roadcraft, driving at speed on dual carriageways and cross country as well as learning more about urban driving. Time well spent, and Simon was keen to learn from an expert, who also had a few stories to tell about his police driving career.

This was all going so well now, he thought. Simon was happy.

12. 1963/10 The Event

Simon and Ruth came out of the cinema, holding hands.
"What do you think? Decent flick?" asked Simon.
Ruth paused.
"It's good," she said, "but it's not quite the same as the book."
"Like what?" queried Simon, as they came down the steps out into the unseasonably warm night air.
"They changed some of the characters, and they missed the bit at the end where Ralph tries to tell the Navy man what had happened."

"You're right, as usual," grinned Simon. "Good we're doing the same book, isn't it?"

Ruth smiled at him.

"Yes, it's good," she agreed. "I'm going to have to catch my bus. Will you phone?"

"Not until after this," laughed Simon, drawing Ruth to one side of the cinema steps, then close to him and kissing her. She pulled him closer under the bright lights and their kiss lasted as the busy crowds coming out of the cinema swirled past them. Who would bother about a couple of teenage kids having a goodnight kiss? But they were unaware that they were being watched by malevolent eyes.

Simon watched as Ruth walked away towards where she would catch her bus and Simon then turned to walk to where Simon would catch his own bus, crossing the road.

He was then confronted by three unwelcome and familiar faces, lit by the bright lights of the cinema's large, illuminated signboard. The two Watson brothers and their friend. Simon had been very glad when they had left school. But he remembered them and they remembered him. Had Simon been a stranger to them, it is doubtful if they would have done what followed. But there was already this history of bullying, and so it was simply an escalation of what had gone before.

The dominant one, Bruce Watson, was smirking at Simon. He was about his height although he seemed to have filled out since Simon last saw him. He had a heavier muscular build, but the brown hair and hard, cold, grey eyes were the same. His friend Nev Carter was also the same height, perhaps not quite as solid, with dark curly hair. The third, Watson's younger brother David, was there too, still smaller, slighter, with fair hair and blue eyes.

"That your girlfriend?" sneered Bruce Watson.

"Yes," said Simon, with some pride, as he tried to walk away up the lane opposite the cinema, but the three blocked his way.

"I bet you like it then?" mocked Bruce Watson.

Simon gave no answer, but made to go past. Carter blocked his way. Simon stopped.

"Oh, kissy kissy," said Nev Carter.

"Bet you were you giving her some tongue," scoffed Bruce.

"Wouldn't know how," said David Watson, joining in the sport for the first time.

The other two laughed, and seeing his acceptance, David laughed too.

Each time Simon made to move, they hemmed him in.

"Oh, I don't know," said Watson, "looked a good kiss to me, eh Nev?"

"Bet that's all he can do though," said Nev.

"D'you know about the birds and bees?" demanded Bruce of Simon.

"Of course," replied Simon hotly.

"She a good fuck, eh?" said Bruce, licking his lips.

"No," said Simon, and then amid the jeers, "I mean we haven't done that."

"What's the matter, can't do it?" said Carter scornfully.

"Can't get it up!" said David.

The three were laughing now but there was added threat in the laughter.

"We'll have to show him, then," said Bruce.

"Teach him a lesson," added Nev.

The three seemed both amused and aggravated by Simon's answers.

"Oh, yes. I promised Scotty I'd teach him a lesson," said Bruce Watson, the amusement in his voice replaced by quiet menace. "I do like to keep my promises. Thought he could get the better of me, but I haven't forgotten, now it's time for him to learn who's boss."

Suddenly Bruce Watson was right in Simon's face, his left hand gripping his genitals. That sexual contact 'froze' Simon for a split second, a tiny fragment of time that would haunt him for the rest of his life. Daniel flashed through his racing mind and Simon hesitated. Had he shouted and pushed Watson away in that second, would it have been different? What if Watson had simply grabbed his arm instead? Who knows? Simon heard a click and suddenly Watson's right hand was holding a flick knife pressed against his cheek and then Carter came close and Simon could see he had produced a bicycle chain, its sharpened edges glinting in the street lights from Port Road. Now the nightmare really began.

The buildings opposite the cinema were set some fifteen or twenty feet above street level because of the steepness of the hill leading away from The Port to the city centre, above a large stone retaining wall.

"Move," said Bruce Watson, all laughter gone now, but a deadly threat in its place.

Bruce Watson and Nev Carter pushed him up some steps to a patch of ground in front of what seemed to be empty, derelict houses. Simon was very aware of that knife close to his neck, and he was quite sure that Bruce would use it to cut him. Anybody looking up from the street would see only darkness, but there was reflected light from the cinema and street lights. Simon could see there were a few shrubs and some grass, also some very large cardboard containers that had been folded flat and were scattered. Bruce Watson pushed Simon to the ground on one of these sheets, and knelt astride him, leering at him, the knife now at his throat. Simon noticed that Watson now had tattoos, a swastika motif round his wrist.

"Now you're going to be good and keep quiet," he ordered. Simon made no reply but he was trembling with fear. Bruce noticed this.

"If you do as you're told, I won't need to use this, will I?" He turned slightly.

"Get his pants off him, Nev," he said and then turned back to Simon.

"What are you going to do, Bruce?" asked Carter.

"We, Nev. What the fuck do you think we're going to do? Get on with it!"

Carter started to undo Simon's trousers, he tried to struggle but his resistance was met with more pressure from the knife. His trousers were roughly pulled down, his pants followed.

"Careful, Scotty," Bruce said. "Nev's chain can make quite a mess."

Simon felt a weight across his knees, pinning him, probably David Watson.

"Please, no. Don't do this," begged Simon. He fear was obvious in his voice and face.

"Stop, please," he said again.

His pleading for them to stop was ignored as his shoes and clothing were removed so that Simon was naked from the waist down.

Simon felt someone intimately touching him and involuntarily he felt himself becoming aroused.

"Fuck!" said Carter, "That's big!"

Bruce turned to look at Simon's now erect penis.

"That's why he can't do it," he sneered, "it's too big to get up her little cunt."

Then Watson lifted up slightly.

"Come on, Scotty, turn over," ordered Bruce, loosening his own belt.

Simon shook head his and remained still.

"Turn over!" snarled Bruce, and Simon was met with a fist full in the face knocking his glasses flying and then the sensation of the bicycle chain being dragged across his exposed thighs, its sharp edges felt even just under its own weight.

Hurting, frightened and trembling, Simon turned over onto his front. Someone stood on his hand and there was a hand in his back pressing him down. Simon felt pressure of Bruce' legs between his own, forcing them apart.

"I'm first," announced Bruce Watson. "Nev, keep watch."

Simon felt the weight on him and the entry, not with familiar gentleness but forced, unlubricated, rough, agonising, the pain too much for him to hold back the tears he had been fighting. As the thrusting continued Simon had a sensation of him ripping and tearing inside. He seemed outside himself, watching from afar. This was not him, this was another Simon Scott! But the pain mounted, Simon could see through the shrubs and the railings across to the lights of the cinema signboard opposite, now level with him, but could not cry out, fearing the blade and the chain. Watson's ejaculation brought some relief from the pain, and as he withdrew, Simon tried to turn but a vicious blow to the side of his face stunned him and Simon slumped back.

He felt Bruce Watson getting up.

"I'm next," Nev's voice said, coming closer.

"Davey, over there," ordered Bruce, telling his brother to be on lookout.

Now feeling Nev Carter take his turn, the entry this time less painful, it being eased probably by the unwelcome lubrication now present. Increasingly

Simon felt desperate and yet resigned to submit to what was being done. Carter's action was rougher than Bruce Watson's and seemed faster and deeper which just made the subjugation the more acutely felt and despite the pain from the rough treatment, Simon simply lay, focused on the lights opposite and below, and enduring the torment until it would stop.

"Oh yes! Fuck! Yer bastard!" Carter yelled obscenities as he came, and struck Simon across the back of his head as he did so. He pulled out quickly, hurting Simon more.

"Shut up, man!" said Bruce Watson to Carter.

A feeling of total helplessness and humiliation overwhelmed him and Simon simply lay on the cardboard, quietly weeping.

"Davey, come on man," said Bruce.

Simon was aware of David closer now as Nev returned to lookout duty.

"I don't know," said David, "I'm not sure."

"What you not sure about?" demanded Bruce of his brother. "You know this cretin, he's too fucking scared to complain."

"Well," began David, but was cut short.

"Just get on with it," said Bruce. "Look, we've done him, so you're gonna as well. Don't be shy. I've seen it all before, and Nev's over there."

"Hurry up," came Nev's voice from the top of the steps.

The younger one dropped his trousers and did as he was told. Simon did not offer any resistance now, all will having been driven out by fear and humiliation. It seemed that this was somehow his fate and Simon must endure it. He felt the boy's weight on him, his flesh against his own.

Perhaps numbness of the body followed numbness of the spirit, but David's assault was not as painful as the others, and he also seemed to take longer. Simon tried to imagine that this was Daniel as a way of bearing this, but it seemed a desecration of Daniel's memory and Simon tried to put him out of his mind. Then a further humiliation came over him. Maybe it was the different action, but Simon felt the young one's movement arousing him. How could this be in this brutal, unloving act? The more the boy continued, urged on by the other two, the more aroused Simon became. As David quickened toward his climax, Simon became more acutely aware of the boy hardening even more inside his body and felt his own uncontrollable release coming and suddenly waves of fire engulfed his entire being as his intense orgasm came, almost at the same time as the boy; Simon let out a moan, a mix of pleasure, pain, grief and fear. "*Fire, Fire, fire down below.*" Oh Daniel! For a moment David lay on Simon, panting, and Simon felt him lose his hardness before he withdrew.

Simon's noise alerted Bruce Watson whose face had been leering at Simon's for some of this time and now he pushed him to one side, revealing the evidence, visible enough in the light from the main road below them.

"Hey, Davey," said Bruce Watson, "you did it!"

"I know," said David, fastening his belt. "What?"

"You made him shoot his load," said Bruce. "Davey, me boy!"

Carter had come over to see. "He must be a puff," he jeered.

Bruce knelt beside Simon. He could see the slender outline of David Watson standing behind his brother, silhouetted against the backwash of lighting.

"Did you enjoy that then, puff?" asked Bruce, laughing nastily.

Simon could not answer. Somewhere the analytical part of his brain was working, wondering how he could be a puff and them not, as they had done it. But this seemed to escape the three who were greatly amused.

"Yeah, he enjoyed it, 'specially me," boasted David. And he stepped up and kicked Simon suddenly in the gut. He writhed in pain and turned back to protect his tummy.

Another kick. Bruce's voice in his ear, close and full of meaning.

"Listen, puff, you tell anyone about this and we'll find you. Get that?"

Simon lay still, only to be kicked viciously again, he cried out in pain.

"Get that?" repeated Bruce in his ear. "And if we have to, we'll tell everyone that you're a fucking queer and you enjoyed every minute."

Simon simply nodded.

"There's a good Scotty," said Bruce mockingly.

"Come on, man. Let's go," said Nev, nervously now.

"It's OK," said Bruce, "the little sugar plum fairy's going to be a good little puff. And now you'll remember what happens when someone hits me," he said close to Simon's ear. "You're lucky. I was going to cut you with my little friend here, but for old times sake, I'm being kind. Goodbye, Scotty."

Lying half naked, face down in the night, Simon was kicked several times where he lay, unable to protect himself or react in any way to the impacts, like a piece of meat, used and degraded, inertly accepting the punishment. Uttering more threats amid their contemptuous laughter, they left.

Simon simply lay there, silently crying for some time, how long is not certain. Maybe a quarter, maybe half an hour. A trolley bus hummed past, the top deck passengers visible through the bushes, but they would see only darkness had they looked out. Why had this happened? Gradually, Simon moved painfully onto his side, his bruised face and head hurting. Simon could feel no pain from his bottom, in fact Simon could feel nothing there at all. (Although that came later.) He felt with his hand and came away with unspeakable moisture, but blood as well. He wiped it on the grass. Finding his glasses and looking round, Simon feared they had taken his clothes so that he could not leave the place, but all his things were still there. With the everyday sounds of the busy night time street a few feet away below, Simon slowly and stiffly dressed himself in the dim gloom of that place and stood up, clinging onto a wooden post for support (getting a wooden splinter in his hand as a result) and then making his way down the steps again. He looked up and down the road and out onto the main road. There was no sign of the three. It was sheer ill luck they had seen him that night. Simon wept again.

13. 1963/10 Immediate Aftermath

Simon made his way slowly through the town to his own bus stop, his body aching, his face down turned. He did not want to meet anyone he knew, not now. Not ever. When the trolley bus came he sat downstairs, unusually for him. He did not want to climb the stairs. There were few other people on the bus at this time of night. He could not stop the tears rolling down his face. He realised his hands were dirty, insanitary filth staining them. Surreptitiously he tried to wipe off the worst on the side of the seat.

"Are you all right, pet?" The voice a sudden intrusion into his private hell. He turned and there were two women sitting together, looking at him intently, but kindly. He just nodded.

"Well, I don't think he's all right," said the second woman, slightly indignantly, as though she resented her friend's judgement being called into question.

"Well, he says he is." And the two fell silent, but Simon could feel their unwelcome gaze upon him. He was aware of the unpleasant odour that clung to him, he hoped the two women were far enough away not to notice. Why should he care about two women on a bus?

His stop came and he got to his feet, trying to smile at the two women for appearance's sake, and then thankfully got off the bus. It hummed away into the night. He walked slowly up his road, wondering what to say now he was home. What could he say? How could he say anything? Just where to begin? Why begin at all? What good would it do? Just lots of questions, interfering. O God, the police! No, absolutely not. Then everybody would know.

He looked up at the flat windows. There was a light in Mum's bedroom, but no other. His keys! But they were still there. He unlocked the front door and went upstairs. Entering the flat, he heard Mum calling from her bedroom.

"That you, Simon?"

"Yes," he forced.

"Get yourself some supper if you want, " she called needlessly.

"OK."

He went into his bedroom and shut the door. He locked the door and looked around him. His room. Familiar. His things just as he had left them, or rather as the other Simon had left them. He was different now, he would never be the same again. He looked at the half done history essay about Bismarck on his desk that the other Simon had done. He flung it aside. He sat on the bed and then got up again with the discomfort of his clothing. He started to undress, tossing his clothes into a heap. He realised with shame, disgust and horror that his own pants had been used by them to wipe themselves clean. He started to weep uncontrollably again, heaving sobs that convulsed his body, yet silently, silently. No noise that might attract questions.

It subsided and he put on his dressing gown and went out onto the landing. The light was still on under Mum's door.

"Going to have a bath, " he called in as normal a voice as he could manage.

"Oh, OK love," came the response through the door, with a slight note of surprise. "There should be enough hot water." He heard Ken say something and her reply, both too muffled to make out.

He made his way to the bathroom, locked the door, dropped his dressing gown and looked in the mirror. No wonder those women had looked at him. His face was dirty with tear streaks down it. Angling the mirror he tried to look at his back. Again there were filthy stains and streaks. He ran the bath and sat on the toilet. He felt the need to empty his bowel but he could not. Then it oozed out, a slippery, uncontainable stream that fell into the pan. Simon wept again with the realisation of what that was. He felt abhorrence of their seed, and found himself wishing it were Daniel's. He cleaned himself and flushed the loo without looking.

There was an inch or two of water in the bath, so he turned off the taps, climbed in and knelt down. Slowly he started to soap himself down, face, body, legs, leaving the worst part to last, unsure of what to do. But slowly and carefully he cleaned himself off with the flannel, suddenly gaining pace as he wanted to wash every last vestige of that event from his body, to erase it completely from his being as though somehow it would erase it from his mind. He rubbed the whole area so hard it hurt, but he kept rubbing. The water turned dark and he stood up to distance himself from it. When he was as satisfied as he could be he pulled out the plug and watched it disappear from around his feet. He rinsed his feet to make sure there was no part left and then ran the taps again to fill the bath with clean water. Mum had been right, there was hot water. He knelt as the bath filled around him. He let it fill and fill until the hot tap was running cold, and then slowly lay back, letting the water envelop him, its warmth a comfort to his bruised body. He was aching where the blows had fallen, but the hot water soothed it. He lay back, looking along at the now hated body, once admired for its athleticism, once loved for its own sake. Now despoiled, defiled, ruined forever. Oh Daniel! And Diane? It was not his body anymore. Yet he knew that it was, that from now on he would be forever tied to this horrible reminder, he would have to walk around in it for the rest of his days. He tried to separate his mind from his body. It was just a carriage for his brain, after all. It provided transport, nourishment and sensory input to the brain. So began a divorce between his body and brain that would be problematical for Simon in the years to come. But the horrid body kept demanding attention from the aches and pains of his beating. Gingerly he felt himself down below, something didn't feel right. There was a soft lump protruding that was yet part of him. He pushed it and it went back in, but then immediately slid out again. What the hell? Later of course he would learn about piles which would plague him from that day on, but now they were new, unknown but obviously related to what had been done. Tears tried to come again, but there were none left. He lay and soaked, trying to clear his mind. He tried to ease out the splinter under the hot water and gently managed to remove it. Another reminder gone. Good.

As he lay there, Simon started to wonder where he had gone wrong. He hated himself for not fighting, but he had been too frightened. Then he hated himself for being frightened. And he had come off! He looked at the offending parts of his body and wished them away. He wanted to slice them off, but he knew he lacked the courage to do that. He had heard of people cutting their wrists under hot water because it hurt less. Would that apply to emasculation? He toyed with the idea of going to the kitchen for the sharp knife, but lay there. He hated his body even more. He hated his weakness. On top of everything else, why had he come off? And why so intensely under those circumstances? He shuddered with the memory of it. Was it because David Watson was younger? The boast David Watson had made, "Yeah, he enjoyed it, 'specially me" kept echoing round and round in his head. Daniel kept coming into his mind, he tried to push him away, it felt a crime even to think of Daniel in any connection with this. Had he come off in some way because of his time with Daniel? He wasn't queer, he had had a good time with Diane. Oh, God, Ruth! What about Ruth? How could he face her? How could he aspire to having intimacy with her using this corrupted, violated carcass? Angry, upset, confused, the troubled teenager lay with the thoughts circling cruelly in his head, tormenting him like angry seagulls around a fishing boat.

At last, as the water cooled, he pulled the plug and climbed out. His body was red and raw, his face looked swollen on one side. He dried himself gently and then trod carefully back though the flat to his room. The light was out under Mum's door. He went into his own room, again locking the door. He picked up the Bismarck essay and put it back on his desk.

He dropped the dressing gown and looked again at himself. He hated it! He noticed his electric shaver which he had started to use, had used earlier that evening, although it had not been strictly necessary, in order to be as smooth as possible when meeting Ruth. But the desire for self mutilation was still strong, and the courage was still lacking. He picked up the shaver and ran the trimmer blade down his thigh, seeing the soft hair fall off satisfactorily, leaving a smooth track from his groin to his knee. Swiftly he ran the blade again, and then again, covering his entire leg and when that was done, he shaved the other. Next to come off was the downy teenage hair on his arms and under his arms, shaving and mutilating by proxy until only that most sensitive and hated area was left to do. Quickly he dragged the shaver across the top of his pubic bone, hair falling to the floor, then under, round until his entire body was now completely depilated from the neck down. It tingled and he rubbed himself to ease it.

Regarding himself again, with the aid of the small mirror too, he took in his new nakedness. He was a boy again. Back in that happy time when his boyish body had been loved, caressed and cared for. His skin felt smooth as it had then.

He crawled into his bed, running his hands over his new found smoothness, finding solace in the memories it brought, even in the midst of this blackness feeling arousal again. For a time he was lost in recollections of the den, Daniel's room, of those summer days in the countryside, warmth, contact and happiness in the long grass.

At last, his arousal fulfilled and abated, Simon felt suddenly very weary. He lay for a moment and turned out the bedside light. The street-lit outline of the window was visible through the curtain. Familiar yet strange. Unreal, being here back in this room, the ghost of the other Simon all round him, who had left the room just a few hours before, never to return. Fitfully he turned, wary of the pain of his divorced body, back from its dream state, demanding attention again. Why won't it shut up?

Suddenly it was happening again, he could see Bruce Watson's face, he could feel the pain, the shame, the sadness, the fear. Not again, please not again! Suddenly he woke up. Breathless, it had been a bad dream. The outline of the window was still there, it was quiet. His breathing subsided as he calmed down. The first of many nightmares for many years, never to be entirely free of them.

He fell asleep.

"Simon, are you all right?" Mum called through the bedroom door. She knocked again. "Simon?"

"Go away."

"Are you ill?"

Simon just wanted Mum to go away. Everybody to just go away. He had awoken on this Saturday morning, unwillingly. His body was wracked with pain, he hurt from his head where he had been punched and hit, down his body where he had been kicked and the unwelcome protrusion from his bottom was announcing its return with more pain. The pain in his thoughts, his feelings was as bad. Simon wanted to die. But Mum demanded an answer.

"I'll be OK," he said.

"Have you fallen out with Ruth?" came Mum's concerned inquiry.

Please Mum, just bugger off, thought Simon. "I said I'll be OK!" he snapped.

"All right. Ken and I have to go out. Get some food, won't you." It was a request rather than a question.

"Yes. Bye." said Simon back. He heard footsteps retreat and soon after, the front door downstairs as they left. He buried his head under the pillow. Can you suffocate yourself like that? He tried to pull the pillow harder over his head, in part to stop the air, in part to insulate himself from the pain of his body and the nightmare pictures and memories that would not leave him alone. He was sweating with fear again, he pulled the pillow closer. It seemed to symbolise the great black cloud that was enveloping him, crushing all thoughts from his mind except escape; escape from his pain, escape from his torment, escape from having to explain, escape from the shame, escape from the guilt – escape from life itself.

The pillow proved an ineffective suffocation tool. The body, programmed to survive, forced him to lift it as he gasped for air. He flung off the bed covers to cool himself, and lay naked on the bed. Bruised and battered, his body was still seventeen years old and it responded to this change of stimulus as seventeen year old boys do. Christ! Leave me alone! He pulled the covers over again, cooler now, but it did not quell the desire. Automatically his hand went down and as he masturbated, for a brief time it was not his Bilthaven bed he was in, but he was back, sharing Daniel's big bed; happy, being loved and valued by the one person who knew him better than anyone else in the world. But the orgasm hurt and the subsequent loss of desire left Simon feeling even more wretched, even more ashamed, hating this body that teased his brain so. Thinking of Daniel served in the end only to rekindle the pain of that loss to add to all the others. A resolve formed in his mind. He knew how he would do it. The black cloud obscuring all else apart from his intended action, which now seemed the only way out from this hell, he got out of bed and went downstairs. He had the plan in his mind, he was focused on nothing else, it was all that offered release. It mattered not to him that neighbours might have seen him crossing the small yard to the garage still naked. Once in the garage he looked around for the things he needed. The small car was there, the Jaguar was not, but it was the workbench that Simon wanted. Yes, there was the towrope. He looked around. A wooden box with some cables in. Had once been a beer crate. Tip the cables out, turn the box upside down. Thinking only now of the end, he passed one end of the towrope through the loop at the other and then cast the rope over a roof beam. How to secure the free end? The height would have to be right. He positioned the box under the rope and stood on it, placing the noose round his neck, seeing where the free end fell. The vice. That would do. He stepped out of the noose and off the box, took the free end of the rope and knotted it, round turn and two half hitches, round the large screw under the vice, then for good measure closed the vice tightly onto the rope. The bench was heavy and would not lift when the strain was put on it. Simon returned to the box and with some difficulty as the rope was now tighter, put his head through the noose. He stood on the box. Only then did it occur to him that he was still unclothed. So what. In fact his body deserved the degradation. But then, standing naked on a wooden box in a chilly garage, he felt an erection coming. Simon recoiled. Leave me alone!!

"Good bye, Daniel. I love you." He stepped off the box.

He felt his body swing free with a sharp jerk, but the PAIN! His neck was being crushed, his Adam's apple was being forced up into his skull, which was exploding with agony. He flailed around frantically as his vision started to go. His ears pounding as his head became engorged with blood. His raw lungs were screaming for air. His toes touched the floor. Gasping and tearing madly and futilely at the noose, he tottered onto tiptoe, pushing upward as hard as he could. The agony continued but the rate of collapse slowed. He was still going, but not as quickly. Think, Simon, think! The vice. Unable to see now, he reached out and found the vice handle. Which way? He couldn't think. It was too tight, he no longer had the strength. But he tried again, his muscles finding oxygen from somewhere as darkness enveloped his brain, leaving just one small spark of intelligence still working. The handle turned, the rope slackened very slightly. The noise in his head and the horrendous agony were now blotting all else out but that small spark was still there. Life. Blind and deaf, he was aware as from afar of his hands fumbling with the rope. He slackened the first half hitch. Time was running out fast. Bloody scout knots! His fingers exploring the second half hitch. Just as all consciousness left, he felt himself falling, hitting the concrete floor of the garage.

Sensation returned, and with it the pain. He could see again. He was gasping, desperately engulfing oxygen. He pulled at the noose and slipped it wide, and threw it off his head onto the concrete floor beside him. What a fucking failure! Can't even get that right! He lay panting and felt his neck. God, that hurt. He touched his Adam's apple. Torture! He couldn't swallow, the pain was so intense. Slowly, he lifted himself and sat on the wooden box, head in hands. In despairing solitude, he knew he could not try that again.

O, that this too too sullied flesh would melt,
Thaw and resolve itself into a dew!

After a while, he stood up, forcing his body, that damn body, to function. Do as you're told, his brain commanded. It's what you're for. He put the cables back in the box, and bent over to retrieve the towrope. The rush of blood to his head nearly made him pass out again. He carefully knelt, keeping his head upright, and picked the rope up, putting it away. He opened the door to the yard, now aware of his nakedness. Nothing for it, though. He walked as quickly as he could the few strides to the back door of the house that led into the common hallway. Up the stairs and into his bedroom again. Despite being filthy from the garage floor, he fell onto his bed and sobbed, each reflex swallow a fresh torment. He got up, and in his dressing gown, went to the kitchen for some water. Slowly he sipped the cooling drink, it easing the soreness of his throat. Coughing was an ordeal. He tried to speak. It hurt, but he could. His voice sounded odd, husky. Some part of that would remain with him always. But the future was of no concern to Simon now, only the present with its anguish. He returned to his bed and lay in both physical and mental hell.

But a new idea formed in Simon's mind. One that gave him purpose and motivation. Vengeance! He would find them and kill them.

Revenge his foul and most unnatural murder.

And when he had done that, he would kill himself.
Haste me to know't, that I, with wings as swift
As meditation or the thoughts of love,
May sweep to my revenge.

With that thought firing his brain, he fell asleep, a fitful, nightmarish sleep full of horrible images, the sleep that was to be his for time to come.

He woke late in the afternoon to hear Mum calling him. "Simon, are you in?"

He tried to ignore her, but he knew he could not. He tried to call out but it hurt so much. He forced himself off the bed and went onto the landing, turning up the broad collar on his dressing gown.

"Oh, there you are, Simon," said Mum from the lounge doorway. Then taking in the sight of her son, "What's the matter, darling. You look awful."

"Don't feel well," croaked Simon painfully.

"You don't sound very well. Go back to bed. I'll bring you a drink."

"Need bathroom," said Simon, carefully. Gripping and tightening the collar of his dressing gown to try to hide the marks on his neck, he walked through to the bathroom and locked the door. He dropped the dressing gown and looked again at himself, his brain regarding the despised body it was now forced to inhabit. Once again he ran some water into the bath to clean off the dirt from the garage floor, mainly dust. He had scraped his leg and arm when he fell, so he cleaned that up as best he could. That wretched protrusion was still there, defying efforts to push it back where it belonged, and it was now more painful. He felt so tired. He went back to his bedroom.

"Going back to bed," he managed with difficulty to say on his way through.

"Yes, darling, you really don't look very well," said Mum.

He lay back, in his bed this time, and tried to shut out the world, thinking of his vengeance plan. Nothing else mattered now. Their deaths followed by his, a release from all the torment of this life.

Mum brought in a drink.

"Do you want something to eat, love?" asked Mum in a worried tone. The thought of how he would eat terrified Simon, he could barely swallow his own saliva, let alone solid food. That was it, soup!

"Maybe some soup, no lumps. Sore throat."

"Simon, you sound terrible, shall I get the doctor?"

Simon's pulse raced at this. Discovery! NO!

He shook his head, and that hurt. "I'll be OK. Soup," he growled.

He managed the drink in gentle sips, and when the soup came, the heat seared through his throat, so he waited until it cooled to a tepid temperature and sipped that slowly.

He stayed in bed for days. It was half term week, time he had hoped to spend with Ruth, perhaps even using the car while Mum and Ken were at work.

All that hope, all that budding optimism for the future was now crushed. There was no future. Just triple murder and suicide. He had to get this body working properly again to carry out his final mission. He slept amid nightmares that had him waking, shaking with fear and sweating. He tried to read to take his mind off it, but he could not concentrate. It all seemed so bloody pointless now.

By mid week his voice had recovered a bit, he felt all the time he needed to clear his throat, that huskiness would not go away. It never would entirely. The bruises from his kicking turned dark and would take weeks to disappear, but the pain eased. Mostly they were hidden when he was dressed, those where he had been kicked as he lay. He felt the bruise in his hair where he had been hit about the head. His bottom hurt still which made going to the toilet a torment. But the red weal on his neck was more of a problem. Once he got dressed on the Thursday, almost a week since the attack, he wore a polo neck sweater that did the job.

"Glad you're up," said Mum when she and Ken got in on Thursday night. "Are you feeling better?"

"Not really," said Simon.

"You still sound rough. I wonder what it was you caught?" said Mum. If only you knew what I had caught, thought Simon. He said nothing. He couldn't sit in the lounge with them, it felt so artificial, normal life. He returned to his room and for the thousandth time, lay on his bed and wept, thinking only of his end once he had committed the crime he was planning. He wondered what people would say. It would certainly make headline news. What would Ruth think? She had left messages for him, which he had not answered. Would Diane wonder why he had suddenly turned into a mass murderer? It would be national news. Daniel! Oh God, what to do about that? He would have to write something down. He didn't want Ruth or Daniel to think he had gone mad. Something to do at least. He spent Friday on Mum's typewriter composing an account of what had happened. He used carbon paper so there would be a copy for Daniel and one for Ruth. It took most of the day, but it was finished. Full of typing errors but the message was clear. He took two envelopes and addressed them to Ruth and Daniel, labelled to be opened after his death and put them in his desk.

That evening Ruth phoned again.

"Hi, are you feeling better?"

Simon heard her beloved voice and it made him cry. It represented the happiness that had been stolen from him, the life that had been stolen from him.

" A little," he said.

"What have you had? Your Mam said you were really poorly."

"Not sure," lied Simon. "Some kind of flu perhaps?"

"Can you meet tonight? It's a whole week since I saw you."

A whole week! It was a week ago tonight! Simon trembled, and found himself saying, "OK. See you by the statue at 7."

At 7pm, Simon, wrapped up warm was waiting by the statue of Queen Victoria that was at the centre of the square named in her honour. And then there was Ruth, smiling at him. He tried to smile back, but could not. How could she bear to look at him? He was horrible, dirty, used, useless.

They walked about, she trying to talk to him. He could not meet her eyes, he felt so worthless. This was agony. He was torn up inside.

"Want to go to the Dungeon?" she suggested.

Simon shook his head.

"Simon, what's the matter?" There was distress in her voice. He couldn't bear it.

He turned to look at her, her pretty face, her long hair, wrapped in a woolly hat now against the cold weather. The weather had changed since the mild weather of last Friday night. Last Friday night! He could not get the pictures out of his head! He was going mad.

"Is there somebody else?" she asked, anxiety across her face. To Simon, this was a gift. He had to set her free. He knew he could never touch her again, to do so would be to contaminate her with his own defilement. So he simply nodded. Tears streamed down Ruth's face, an image that haunted him for life, and she fled. Simon never saw her again.

14. 1963/11 Rebellion

Simon spent much of the weekend in despair, rarely venturing from his bedroom, trying to get himself well enough to return to school on Monday. He did not want to, he could see little point in going now as there was not a future to work for, but he knew that not to go would raise more questions and that might lead to the discovery of his plan.

He could not wear the polo neck jumper for school, and his neck still showed the red marks of the rope, but they had faded, and he was able to blame the polo neck jumper for causing a 'rash'. Nobody looked too closely and this was accepted.

On Monday he deliberately timed his arrival at the school bus so that the would not have to wait around, so much so that he almost missed it. He got on, ignoring the one or two who greeted him and found a window seat. He stared out at the familiar scene and then felt someone sit next to him, just like when Watson had come and sat beside him. He turned, heart pounding, but it was Charlie.

"Hello, Simon," said Charlie, heaving his haversack onto his lap. Simon turned away, unwilling to start a conversation. About what? Charlie was undeterred.

"So what have you been up to at half term then?" Charlie continued happily. Apart from my rotten life being in bits, thought Simon, bitterly. But without waiting for an answer, Charlie then launched into a long description of his happy half term. Simon heard the incessant chatter hammering his brain. He felt an overwhelming resentment against Charlie. Just shut up, for God's sake. Simon realised that all his woes were Charlie's fault! If he hadn't annoyed Watson, or if he had done it further down the bus instead of right next to Simon, if he hadn't provoked Watson at all, then none of this would have happened. Simon would never have hit Watson with such dire consequences. Simon felt his anger erupt within him at this boy, the root of everything that had happened to him.

"Just fuck off, Charlie! Go and sit somewhere else."

"If that's how you feel," said Charlie in hurt tones, gathering his haversack.

"Well, I do," snapped Simon.

Charlie got up. "I don't know what I said to make you angry, Simon, but still, I'll never forget what you did for me." He took his bag and went further back in the bus.

Simon turned away and looked out of the window so that no one should see the tears rolling down his cheeks.

Back at school, he found the company of his group too much to cope with. Ed's ebullience in particular. He started to spend more time with the quieter Stuart, when he sought company at all. He knew he was tetchy and upset his friends, who started to give him a wider berth. Minor setbacks and irritations grew out of proportion, and his bad temper as a result caused comment.

Some irritations were shared and Simon, with some support, reacted aggressively to these. One was the school attempting to crackdown on the unofficial sixth form uniform that he, Ed and some others had started to wear, of plain black blazer, unbadged, black tie instead of school tie, along with white shirt and grey trousers. Quite smart really, but it did not identify them as school pupils. It had caught on and a lot of the sixth form had started wearing it. They were told to stop. What really irritated Simon and many others was that this message was carried by the school's Head Boy, rather than from the staff. Harold Vickery was OK as a person, and he and Simon had got on in the lower sixth, but since being appointed as prefect and Head Boy, Simon and others felt he had become obsessed with it and big headed too. This was coupled with the fact that he and the prefects insisted that the other sixth formers help them with their duties of supervising the rest of the school. Yet they received no legitimising of their authority and were denied access to the prefects' room. The prefects said their duties were interfering with 'A' level studies.

"I'm not doing this any more," said Simon to a disgruntled group gathered in an upstairs classroom one November Friday lunchtime.

"Nor me," said Ed. "I don't see why we should do their job with nothing to show for it. **We** have work to do as well."

"No taxation without representation," said Johnny Jobson. Another history student.

"Good point," said Ed. "Let's have a revolution, then. No more duties, and we'll wear our black jackets. Who's for it?"

A cheer went up, with cries of acclamation.

"We could get into trouble," argued Andrew Davison.

"So?" snapped Simon. "It'll work if we all stick together. But I'm doing it anyway, right?"

"I'm in," said Jamie Nash.

"OK. If you don't want to join us, leave now," said Simon.

"You're wrong," said Stuart. "You could end up in a real mess."

"Stuart, you can leave. We won't think the worse of you," said Simon.

"You might not, I will," came another comment.

"I'm going," said Stuart, "and anybody with any sense will come with me."

Simon was writing a note.

"What's that?" said Ed.

"A note to Vickery, saying we refuse to do anymore prefect duties without prefect status, and that we want recognition of the sixth form uniform."

This was greeted by a cheer from most of those present.

"Stuart, will you hand this note to Vickery?" asked Simon. "It says you're not part of it."

Stuart read the note. "All right." Stuart and a few others, including Andrew Davison and most of the girls, left.

"Right," said Ed. "Vickery will be furious when he gets that so we haven't got long. Barricade the door."

"Come on," said Simon.

The boys pulled desks across the doorway so it was impossible to open from the outside.

"What will happen when Vickery comes?" asked Johnny.

"We'll kill him," suggested Jamie.

"Don't even joke about that," said Simon, sharply.

"OK, didn't mean it literally," said Jamie indignantly.

There was an attempt to open the door, and then a loud knock. It was Percy Hunt, one of the prefects and a toady of Vickery's.

"Let me in," shouted Percy through the small pane of glass in the door.

"Does Vickery agree to our terms?" demanded Ed.

"He says you've got to go back to your duties," said Percy.

Anger welled up in Simon. He marched over to the door and shouted at Percy. "They are NOT our duties, they are yours. Tell Vickery that! Jumped up arsehole, who does he think he is?"

"I'll tell him you said that, Scott," said Percy Hunt.

"That was the plan!" retorted Simon angrily. "Fancy sending his little sidekick. Tell him to get up here himself."

Percy Hunt left.

"Hey Simon, my man!" said Jamie Nash. "That's telling him!"

"He'll be bloody furious at that," said Ed. There was a chorus of agreement. In the ensuing discussion it was agreed to remain barricaded in until Vickery agreed to their demands.

A few minutes later, Vickery was at the door. "Open this door, now!"

"Have you accepted our terms, Harold?" called Jamie.

"Of course not. Now open this door and get back to doing what you're supposed to be doing."

"No, Vickery," said Simon. "Not without either release from doing your job for you or prefect status for all upper sixth. And the uniform too."

"You ask too much, Scott," said Vickery. "I can't do those things for you anyway."

"Well, go and see Catterall, then," challenged Simon.

"Listen, he doesn't know about this yet. If I have to tell him, all hell will be let loose."

"Yes, on you as well, for allowing this to get to this stage. Good luck!" said Simon.

"Didn't want the Boss involved," said one. "It could rebound on us."

"Listen, we're in it now. You all had the chance to leave. Do you want an end to exploitation or not?" said Ed.

"Well said, Ed," added Simon. The doubters fell silent.

Soon there was another knock at the door. It was Vickery again, this time accompanied by Miss Duncan, Della Duncan they all knew, the Deputy Head. She was not liked, unlike George Catterall, the Head, who was popular. Her silver hair could be seen through the glass. Simon realised she reminded him of Miss Harvey.

"Open the door," said Vickery. "Miss Duncan's here."

"Have you agreed to our conditions?" asked Ed.

"Of course not," snapped Miss Duncan. "Now are you going to open the door?"

"Of course not," snapped Simon, in exactly the tone used by Della Duncan.

"I am ordering you to open this door!" shouted Miss Duncan. Some of the sixth formers looked anxiously at Ed and Simon. But Simon didn't care. Nothing mattered any more, least of all Della Duncan.

"No, Miss Duncan, not until we get fair treatment."

"What do you mean, fair treatment?"

"Vickery, doesn't she know what you've had us doing?" taunted Simon.

There was a hurried discussion the other side of the door, during which the bell rang for the end of lunchtime.

"Are you coming out now?" called Vickery.

"Are you going to treat us fairly and meet our terms?" countered Simon.

"We'll be back," said Vickery. He and Della Duncan disappeared.

"We're really for it now," said a chastened Jamie.

"You'll be OK, it'll be me that gets it, and that doesn't matter. If necessary, I'll say I held you here," said Simon.

"Why doesn't it matter for you?" asked Ed. "You have been odd these last few weeks."

"I probably won't be here much longer, so I'll take the blame," said Simon.

"Are you moving?" asked Ed. "Is that why you've been in such a mood since half term?"

"Moving? Sort of," said Simon. He then shook his head to deter any more questioning.

"I've got Biology now," said a voice.

"And I've got History," said Simon. "So?"

The doubter fell silent. There was a general discussion among the twenty-five or so rebels about what night happen next. Ed came over to Simon.

"Are you OK, Simon?" he asked quietly. "You've been a bit off with everyone lately and you've not been over for ages."

What could he say? How could he even begin to describe how he felt? And he mustn't jeopardise his plans by possible disclosure.

"I'm OK, a bit under the weather, that's all," he lied, he hoped convincingly.

Ed wasn't convinced. "You've broken up with Ruth, haven't you?" he guessed, not entirely inaccurately.

That was the answer, thought Simon. He simply nodded. It was true after all.

"I'm sorry, Simon," said Ed. "It's obviously really got to you. But you'll get over it."

There was a knock on the door. It was Vickery.

"Let me in," he said.

"What for?" asked Jamie.

"I've come to negotiate," said Vickery unexpectedly.

Jamie turned to look at the group. Most looked to Simon and Ed. Simon nodded, and went over to help Jamie move the desks. Vickery came in.

"You lot have got yourselves in a hell of a mess," he said. "Della's out for blood, especially yours, Simon."

Simon noted the placatory use of his first name. It had been Scott earlier.

"So what have you come to say, Harold?" replied Simon, returning the first name favour.

"You got to come out of here and go back to lessons immediately."

"And if we do?" asked Ed.

"Della and the Boss have agreed to appoint fifteen more prefects as of next Monday. Everybody here would be eligible if you stop now, except you Simon, Ed and Jamie."

"Leave Ed and Jamie out of it, Harold," said Simon. "This was my idea and I started it. I persuaded them to join in."

Ed and Jamie wisely stayed silent.

"I can't guarantee that. But they've also agreed you can wear your silly uniform, but it's not going to be made official."

"What about the upper sixth that aren't prefects? Will they still have to run round after you lot?" asked Simon.

"No," said Vickery. "That's what the expanded prefect corps is for."

Corps? Does he think he's some kind of General? thought Simon.

"That's everything we asked for," exclaimed Jamie.

"I vote we accept," said a voice.

"We'll vote when Harold has gone," said Simon sharply. "Is that it, Harold?"

"Yes, Simon. I hope you accept. It's not going to get better. Sorry about you though Simon. I think Della is really after you."

"I'm not worried about that any more," said Simon, then wished he hadn't added the 'any more' in case it prompted questions. He was actually feeling quite good. He had helped lead this revolution, along with Ed, Jamie and the others, but he knew he had been a major player. And he had helped win on behalf of his followers, just like he had led his scout patrol, putting them first.

"We'll let you know soon," Ed said. Vickery left.

"I vote for it," said one. There was a general hubbub of agreement.

"We've got what we wanted. We've won," said another.

"All in favour?" said Ed.

Every hand went up, except Simon. Ed looked at him, puzzled. Simon slowly raised his hand.

"That's it then," said Jamie. They moved all the desks away and trooped down the stairs to the bottom corridor. Vickery was there, along with Miss Duncan.

"It's a deal, Harold," said Ed.

"But not for you, Scott," said Miss Duncan. She **is** like Miss Harvey, thought Simon.

"You come with me, and you, Baker, and Nash," ordered Miss Duncan. "Vickery, I want a list of all those who were in that room."

Simon looked at Vickery. "Harold, you said the others would be all right?"

"It's OK, it's just for the record," said Vickery. Simon had to accept that. He, Ed and Jamie followed Della along to the entrance lobby where George Catterall, the Head, and Miss Duncan had their offices. Mr Catterall was there.

"So these are the rebel leaders, Miss Duncan?" he asked.

"Yes, Mr Catterall, Scott is the main one but Baker and Nash are involved as well."

"Thank you Miss Duncan, I think I'll deal with this now."

There was a look of shock on Della's face, just for a moment, but it was there long enough for Simon to see it.

"Very well," she said, turning away.

"It was all my fault, sir," said Simon. "Baker and Nash just got caught up in it."

"Very noble, Scott, I'm sure. We shall see."

They were taken into Mr Catterall's office one at a time, Simon last. It seemed that the Head had already had a full account from Della of course but also from Vickery. Jamie came out first.

"Got to be a good boy from now on," he joked as he passed Simon.

Ed came out later. "Not as bad as I thought, but no prefect badge for me. Your turn now, good luck."

Simon went in and stood before Mr Catterall. He was transported back in time, and he was standing in front of Mr West's desk, looking round for the cane. But there was no cane here.

"I have to say, Scott, I am seriously considering expulsion in your case. Such behaviour simply cannot be tolerated, whatever justification you may have had, and I've sorted that out with Vickery. All accounts point to you being the ringleader in this whole affair. But it seems totally out of character. So I am forced to wonder what is going on. Two of your teachers have commented to me in the last couple of weeks that you seem to have changed, quiet to the point of surly, uncooperative even. So what's the problem? Has something changed?"

No fool, George, thought Simon. In fact, his perception is quite admirable. But Simon's goal of terrible vengeance meant nothing could be given away. "No, sir, not really."

"Well, I am puzzled. I will of course be writing to your parents, your mother I mean, but on balance I have decided that you should stay in school to complete your 'A' levels. But be very careful from now on. And you must apologise to Miss Duncan. That's a condition of your remaining, understand?"

"Yes sir. Thank you. It was me, I persuaded the others to do it, they should not be punished."

"I'll decide about that, Scott, but your remark is noted."

Simon crossed the lobby and made his apology to Miss Duncan, which was accepted, he thought with ill grace. She it seemed had been told to accept it, just as she knew he had been told to make it. Both pretended the charade was real.

Early that evening, the news reached Britain that President Kennedy had been assassinated, and a few sixth formers arguing about badges and uniform seemed insignificant. By next Monday as events in America unfolded, the rebellion was largely forgotten.

15. 1963/11 Vengeance

Simon's mood, depression, was of course noticed at home. But in the face of his repeated denials that there was a problem, Mum put it down to adolescence hitting with a vengeance. Simon didn't care. His sole aim now was to kill the Watsons and Carter.

Revenge should know no bounds

It was a month since the attack, and time to start. It had taken him that time to steel himself, to prepare his mind. He took his scout sheath knife, a good weapon he thought, a present from Daniel and somehow appropriate, with its long, strong blade. He sharpened it until it had a razor edge, making sure the point was just as lethal.

Is but to whet thy almost blunted purpose

He knew it would have to do its work quickly and he hoped for an element of surprise. Ideally get them one by one, but he knew much would depend on the situation. He might have to shadow them until the right place was found. He thought the best plan of attack would be to strike each of them a blow with the knife quickly. To try to finish one before dealing with the next would give time for retaliation, so disable each one and then go back to kill them. Then he would go as quickly as he could to the City Bridge and fall to his death in the dark waters many feet below.

He took the trolley bus into the city, getting off in Victoria Square. Inevitably he was drawn back to Port Road and the site of the attack. He was confident that he would find them. He could not bring himself to climb those steps to look again at the site of the rape. He walked past the cinema and down to the Port. It was a rougher area especially at night, but Simon thought that this could be where they had been when they saw him that night, on their way back to Victoria Square to catch their bus perhaps. He spent the hours wandering around, looking intently at any groups of people about his age, especially if there were three. But he did not find them. Never mind, it would have been lucky to find them the first night. Not too disheartened, he went back home on a late bus.

Simon was to repeat that, taking his knife into the city to find them, night after night, wandering. He became obsessed, neglecting his homework and his studies even more, spending evening after evening pacing up and down Port Road, around the Port, back to Victoria Square, intent on his murderous quest. Except of course that Simon didn't regard it as murder. To him it was justice, vengeance. In his distorted thinking at the time, in his hatred and obsession, he did not distinguish between the two.

The weeks went by, and either the Watsons and Carter were avoiding him, or they simply weren't there. Simon grew increasingly frustrated at his failure to find them. His mood grew darker and darker. He started carrying the knife with him all the time, just in case he met them unexpectedly. He even took it to school, against the chance that somehow they would once again board the school bus. He was driven by this need that by wreaking revenge he would somehow find his own peace, and that he would at least die content.

He started to think he would never find them, his will started to fail. Some evenings he didn't go into Bilthaven, but spent the evening locked in his bedroom cursing his weakness and failure and wishing he had gone on the hunt after all.

The end of term arrived, bringing with it all the Christmas festivities. It was strange wandering around the city with murder and hate in his heart amid the Christmas lights and decorations, the huge tree in Victoria Square.

Confused, angry, depressed, he returned home. He was so very alone. That Christmas was hell. He went through the motions, taking the train to see Dad and Phoebe for a few days between Christmas and New Year; he had the knife in case he saw them at the station when leaving or arriving. Dad too noticed his mood, told him off for being rude to Phoebe and said he had to 'buck up'.

On the train home, he sat gloomily looking out of the windows at the darkening winter landscape, the closer he got to Bilthaven, the more depressed he felt, a black cloud descending on him, excluding all thoughts except his own end. He had the knife but the fire of his hatred was now an ember. Even killing them didn't seem worth the effort. He had failed in that, even.

And thus the native hue of resolution
Is sicklied over with the pale cast of thought

When the train arrived, he didn't bother to take the knife out of his bag to have it handy in case of a chance meeting. He stepped out of the station into the brightly lit streets. It was New Year's Eve but the noisy revellers were like a background to Simon as he threaded his way through them and home on the bus.

Enveloped in the deadly black cloud, he sat through the ritual *White Heather Club* on television to see in the New Year.

As midnight struck, he had had enough.

"I'm off to bed," he announced.

"Happy New Year, darling," said Mum, smiling.

"Happy New Year," said Ken.

"Yes, Happy New Year," responded Simon, as Mum gave him a hug.

Sensing all was not well, she drew back. "Are you all right, Simon?"

"He'll be tired, it's been a long journey," said Ken, kindly.

"Of course," said Mum with relief at finding a label to stick on her son's mood.

Simon nodded assent. "Good night, Mum, Ken."

He went to his room, relieved to be alone, yet fearing the loneliness that this highlighted and the nightmares of the night to come.

Next day, he was alone, again. Although New Year's Day, Mum and Ken had gone to work as the *Bilthaven Mail* was still published. Alone in the flat, he alternated between pacing around and lying on his bed, trying to still the waking nightmare going on in his head. The world's celebration of the new year only served to emphasise his despair. He would pace the length of the flat, from the kitchen at one end to his bedroom at the other. On one such lap, at random he turned into Mum's room, paced to the window and turned back. There on the bedside table were Mum's sleeping tablets. Simon stopped, frozen for a moment with the opportunity this presented. Surely less painful than his previous attempt?

How weary, stale, flat and unprofitable,
Seem to me all the uses of this world!

He hesitated, and then the decision was made. The black cloud hid any other alternative, hid the consequences for others, there was nothing except that route to oblivion. There looked to be about twenty or so tablets, the nightly dosage was one tablet. Twenty should do the job then!

He picked up the bottle, and went through to the kitchen. He stood by the sink with a glass of water, taking the tablets two at a time, sipping the water each time to help them down. The bottle was empty. Must hide the empty bottle. It would give away what he had done. He put it in the bin, burying it under the rubbish already there. Soon his pain would be over.

Back in his room, Simon undressed and climbed naked into bed and lay down to wait. He found his situation somewhat erotic. Why? He was surrendering at last, he would be free of this body, its pain and its demands, free of life and its misery. His hand went to his hardness, he was aroused by his helplessness, it was done now and he was in the power of the tablets. He started to feel light headed, but there was no pain, just the pleasure. He felt calm at last. The world seemed to rotate around him, but he was not dizzy, he just let himself go. Now, at last, the torment would be over, he would be nothing. Back to nothingness.

All that lives must die
Passing through nature to eternity

There is an unimaginable void, eternal darkness and nothingness. Then a brief spark - and oblivion returns. Such is life. It matters not. The notes were in his desk, they would be found. He thought of Ruth, and of Daniel. He felt himself going, Daniel, his beloved, was in his mind as he slipped away ...

16. 1964/1 Second failure

There was a series of explosions going on in his head. Christ! What pain! He was awake. It took a moment, and then he remembered. Oh God, he had failed again! Stop the pain, please! **Bang! Bang! Bang!** Every pulse led to an explosion of pain inside his head, crashing against and rebounding from the inside of his skull.

"Simon, are you all right?"

What was that? Who was that? Mum was there. He groaned.

"You're awake."

Simon nodded. The nuclear detonations in his head made coherent thought impossible. Yes, fuck it, I'm awake.

Mum was still talking to him. "We thought it best to leave you, you were out cold."

Why didn't you leave me then? He groaned again, covering his head with his hands. He was lying face down in his bed. Suddenly there was an external explosion, light.

"Turn the light off!" he demanded. **Bang! Bang! Bang!** Mum turned the light off again.

"What time is it?" he asked. Why did he care what time it was?

"Half past six," said Mum.

"Morning or night?"

"Half past six in the evening, Thursday evening," said Mum.

Thursday?

"You mean Wednesday?" managed Simon. New Years Day was a Wednesday, he was sure.

"No, darling, Thursday. As I say, you were out cold last night and this morning you were still asleep, so we thought we would let you catch up on your sleep."

He had been out thirty six hours, near enough. Why not forever? Now he became aware that his guts ached, but nothing compared with his head. Why won't it stop? **Bang! Bang! Bang!**

"Oh God," was all he said. He had failed again. How bloody useless could he get? He felt ill.

"I feel ill," he said. "I need the loo." He made to get out of bed. Fighting to control this worthless body, he sat up. He had to get to the bathroom. He waved Mum away. He staggered out onto the landing, shutting his eyes against the light. He made his way to the bathroom. At the sight of the toilet, he simply didn't know which end to go first. By the dimmer light of the streetlight from the back lane – he couldn't bear the bathroom light on - he emptied his intestines, from both ends until each end could give no more, but still wanted to. That bloody pile was back as well. He felt as if he wanted to expel all his internal organs that way. And still. **Bang! Bang! Bang!** He felt he could leave the loo, he rinsed his hands perfunctorily under the tap. He leaned on the wall as he went out onto the landing, destination his bed again.

"For God's sake, put some clothes on, Simon," said Ken who had happened onto the landing at the same time.

Back in bed, Mum came in and turned on the light.

"Turn it off!" commanded Simon. The light went off, downgrading the explosions from megatons to kilotons.

"I'm going to call the doctor," said Mum. "I think you've eaten something."

If only she knew.

The doctor arrived a couple of hours later, tired looking. He took Simon's temperature. Normal. He was puzzled. Of course Simon could not say what had really caused his symptoms. The doctor mused again. Sickness and diarrhoea, most likely food poisoning. Maybe a virus. A prescription for some antibiotics to help fight bacteria. Bed rest and lots to drink. He then left.

Simon simply stayed in bed, **Bang! Bang! Bang!** Reflecting on his failure, the failure to fight back when he was raped, the failure to take revenge, the failure yet again to end his life, his failure as a person. Oh God!

By Sunday the pain was easing. He could stand the light and managed to eat without it coming back. He felt drained, weak, light headed. The banging was now a dull throbbing, bearable at last. School would start on Tuesday. Another year, another term. He resigned himself to carry on.

17. *1964/1 A strange test*

Simon went through the motions, going to school, lessons, going back home. He cut himself off, listening to music trying to crush the pain. Simon played the Elgar Violin Concerto, the definitive 1932 performance played by 16 year old Yehudi Menuhin, with Elgar conducting. There was a feeling of a chaotic soul in the music which touched Simon and the violin came in like a wistful, soothing balm to quell the inner turmoil. Oh, that Simon had such a violin! How could one so young bring such depth? Simon was drawn to Elgar's music; perhaps Rachmaninoff was too painful, so many memories. It would be years before Simon could turn again to Rachmaninoff.

His friends were wary of him and generally kept a distance, but after a few weeks, Simon realised he could not go on like that. He decided his isolation was doing no good. If he had abandoned his murderous and suicidal plans, for the time being at least, he needed some human contact.

One avenue came with a new offer of a Saturday job. This was more money than he had been given at Russell's shop, and he had given that up anyway. His new job was working at a hair salon on Swiford High Street just a short walk from the flat. This was run by two young men, Roddy and Paul, and it was immediately obvious that they were queer. They were accepted by the local community as attitudes to queers were starting to change, even though it was still a crime one could be sent to prison for. Their relationship did not worry Simon of course and he felt in some way very much at ease there. He worked hard and they liked him, he joined in their banter. He spent much of his time making tea and coffee, sweeping up and replenishing stocks from the storeroom. He did learn how to trim men's hair into the still usual short back and sides. The mainly female clientele took to him, and of course the job involved constant interaction, unlike the loneliness of the upper room at the chip shop. Simon enjoyed this and began to recover some level, if not of happiness, of coming to terms with his life. The desperation and the nightmares continued, as they always would but suicide was now on hold. The dreams would involve reliving the events of that night, some very realistic. He would usually wake, sweating with fear and crying out, sometimes lashing out, as he is overpowered by the three and/or the forced penetration is re-experienced. Simon usually woke from these nightmares in a state of high sexual arousal.

He was sitting on the bus, in his usual window seat on a cold February day. Charlie was coming down the aisle with his haversack in front of him, looking for a seat. Simon caught his eye and patted the empty seat next to him. Charlie hesitated and then sat next to Simon.

"I'm sorry, Charlie," said Simon. "I was rotten to you a few weeks ago."

"So what was the matter then? Other people have said you seem to have changed."

"I can't really say. Lots of things going on in my life. But I am sorry I told you to fuck off. It wasn't your fault."

"Problems at home, then," guessed Charlie. "It's OK. I'm just glad we're friends again."

At school, Simon re-entered his group of friends, but was now closer to Stuart than Ed and the others. As the weather got better, he sometimes drove over to Stuart's at the weekend. His father was an engineer and Stuart had either inherited or learned the same practical skills. He was rebuilding an old motorcycle and Simon would watch and help, which was often simply handing Stuart the tools or holding a torch so Stuart could work.

The sudden mobility that the motorbike gave Stuart was an eye opener for Simon. If he had a bike, he would not be dependent on borrowing Mum's car or the tortuous bus journeys, all of which involved going into the city centre and then getting another bus out again towards Cermerton.

He decided to use his money from the salon to buy a motorbike. He was restricted to a smaller model as a learner, but this did not worry him. It was mobility he was after, not street cred. Stuart had now passed his test and had bought a smart eight year old maroon BSA B33, a 500cc single cylinder but with the modern swinging arm suspension. He rode pillion on the back of Stuart's bike, bringing back memories of riding Karl's Kreidler Florett. Stuart was agreeably surprised that Simon could ride pillion as it is a skill in itself, until Simon explained about the Kreidler Florett. Simon wanted to buy Stuart's old bike from him but he refused to sell it, saying he had put so much work into it. But he did help Simon find a bike, and they went to look at a BSA Bantam, 175cc two stroke with a flat out speed of about sixty miles per hour. Stuart said the bike was in reasonable condition, so Simon bought it.

It was very different to ride than the Kreidler he had ridden briefly around the forest in Germany, which had had no clutch for a start. Simon found using the clutch with the left hand was very different to using the left foot, and changing gear with his right foot took some getting used to. But it was also a light machine and more powerful than the Kreidler, so Simon was pleased. His roadcraft skills proved valuable and he soon applied for his test.

The morning of the test arrived, an early Saturday morning appointment at the Swiford test centre. When Simon went down to the garage to get the Bantam out he saw with horror that the back tyre was almost flat. And there was only about twenty minutes to his test. Using Russell's foot pump, he boosted the tyre pressure as high as he dared and set off. He arrived at the cross roads near where he caught the school bus not far from the test centre. The tyre was already noticeably softer. He pulled up on the forecourt of a garage just round the corner where he usually bought the two stroke fuel for the bike. Using the garage's airline, he again boosted the tyre and set off round the corner to the test centre.

He waited nervously in the waiting room for his allotted examiner to appear. At last he did and took Simon out to his bike. Simon glanced down at the rear tyre. The examiner was explaining the route he wanted Simon to follow. He would be observing on foot from various points but would not tell Simon in advance where these would be.

At last Simon set off, the tyre looking very flat again. As soon as he turned the corner away from the examiner, he left the route and raced to the garage, onto the forecourt at some speed to the air pump. As he was blowing up the tyre, he was aware of someone standing next to him as he knelt beside the back wheel.

"Weren't you just in here for air?"

Simon looked up. There was a boy, not much younger than Simon, brown wavy hair and blue eyes and wearing oily overalls, looking down at him.

"Yes," said Simon. "I've a slow puncture but I've got my test and it keeps going down."

"Do you want it fixed?" said the boy. "What time's your test?"

"I'm on my test now!" said Simon urgently. "I'm supposed to be riding along the High Street at the moment watched by the examiner."

The boy smiled. "That's OK," he said. "I'll stand by with the air line. You keep coming back."

"Fantastic!" said Simon, leaping onto the bike and hurtling off into the High Street, then slowing to a sedate pace for the benefit of the examiner. Simon saw him with his clipboard but he didn't stop him so he turned to continue the route. As soon as the examiner was out of sight he raced back through the side streets to the garage. The boy was standing already holding the air line and as soon as Simon stopped air was blown in without Simon having to get off the bike at all or stop the engine. Then he was off again.

This was repeated several times, the boy was always waiting and Simon was only on the forecourt for a few seconds, a pit stop a racing team would have been proud of. The examiner seemed none the wiser and the main moments of anxiety came when he stopped Simon to give him fresh instructions. Then it was back to the boy with the air line.

Back at the test centre, he waited for the examiner's verdict, his heart racing with the stress of this unusual test.

"Mr Scott, I am pleased to say you have reached the required standard and have passed the motorcycle test. Congratulations."

Simon breathed a sigh of relief. He had done it. He carefully put the coveted pink slip in his driving licence. That would be updated now to include motorcycles. It made him think of Mum's All Groups licence, and her ambition to drive every class of vehicle she was entitled to do. Having driven an electric vehicle – a trolley bus round the depot as part of a story for the paper, she only had left 'a track laying vehicle steered by its tracks'.

Then it was back round to the garage, the tyre looking very flat now. The boy was there, still waiting.

"You've been a long time," he said.

"Yes, that was the end. And I've passed, thanks to you," said Simon happily. As the boy again inflated the tyre, Simon dug in his pocket and finding a pound note, gave it to the boy. That was a lot from Simon's earnings at the salon, but he was feeling considerable gratitude to this lad who had been so ready to help him.

"Are you sure?" said the boy, now wide eyed.

"Of course," said Simon. "Without you, I wouldn't have been able to pass."

"Well, I'll only accept that if you let me fix the puncture for you."

"Done!" said Simon, enthusiastically. He wanted to hug this boy. "Can I leave it now? I need to get to work. I work Saturdays at the hair salon just along the High Street."

"What, the two queers' place?" said the boy, grinning now.

"That's the one," laughed Simon. "They're OK, actually."

So Simon got his motorcycle licence to add to the car one, and got his puncture fixed. The Bantam opened up Simon's life as he was now fully mobile and could now carry passengers. He need not depend on borrowing Mum's car, although in bad weather, he preferred that of course.

18. 1964 Kelly

Simon used his new two wheeled mobility to visit Stuart more often. He also went to see Ed, but he felt more attuned to Stuart. At school he alternated between time with the group including Ed and Jamie, and more reflective time with Stuart. And then there were the girls.

Kay Squires and Kelly Upfield were close friends and lived near each other in an affluent area called The Grange. Kay was a prefect and perhaps that was why she was a little more distant towards Simon, but Kelly was not and she was apparently keen on him, information conveyed through intermediaries.

They were talking about this at Stuart's house one Saturday afternoon after an early finish at the salon. Stuart liked Kay and decided he wanted to go out with her, but was hesitant about approaching her.

"Just tell her," urged Simon.

Stuart shook his head. "I've got to get it right, and I might make a mistake, say something wrong and lose my chance."

"Nothing ventured, nothing gained," said Simon. "Tell you what, I'll ask Kelly out and then I'll tell her that you fancy Kay."

"Ask Kelly out if you want, but don't you dare mention me and Kay. I'll do it my way, thank you," said Stuart.

"You know I just might do that," said Simon, his outward confidence covering his deep anxiety about forming another relationship. She might say no, another rejection. But what the hell! "Yes, I think I will."

"Good luck," said Stuart, "but not a word about me."

"Scouts Honour," said Simon.

"Eh?" replied Stuart.

"Never mind. So what are you going to do about Kay?"

"I think I'll write a letter."

"Write a letter?" said Simon, aghast. "What a turn off."

"No," said Stuart calmly, "that way I can say exactly what I want and take time to get it right."

"Just ask her out and then you can talk and get to know each other. That's the normal way."

"Normal for you perhaps," said Stuart, smiling. "I'll do it the way I want."

"I'll help you write the letter then," offered Simon.

"No thank you, I'll do it myself." In his own meticulous way, Stuart got out his writing material and sat at the dining table, a serious look on his face. "Now," he added, pointedly.

Simon got the message. "See you at school then. Good luck." He left and looking back through the window as he walked out to his motorcycle, he saw Stuart still sitting, deep in thought. Simon felt a pang of envy as Stuart looked forward, planning with confidence the course of his life, taking hold of his future to mould it as far as he was able to his ambition. For Simon, there was no future. Somehow that had been stolen on that October night and even his attempts to end his life had met with failure. So life was now a day to day affair, with no thought for the past, too painful, or the future, too pointless. What the hell! he thought. No letter writing for me, I'll ask Kelly direct.

What was in that letter remained forever between Stuart and Kay, but it worked, and he and Kay became a couple. But Simon eschewed the power of the written word and headed from Stuart's house over to The Grange. Kelly's parents had bought their house when The Grange was first developed, but this large estate of big houses, each set in its own grounds was where the wealthy of Bilthaven now lived.

Simon pulled up at Kelly's door, having ridden in over the gravelled drive. No doubt prompted by the noise of the two stroke, Kelly appeared first at the window and then at the door.

"Hello Simon," she said, smiling. That was a good start, he thought. But what now?

"Hello. I was just passing," he lied, "and I thought…" Actually, he didn't know what he thought. Perhaps this wasn't a good idea after all.

"Come in," said Kelly. "I was only doing homework."

"Oh, you mustn't let me stop you," said Simon dutifully.

"Sod that," she said, and grabbing him by the arm, led him into the house. A girl after my own heart, thought Simon.

"Mummy, this is Simon. He's from school. He's the one I told you about."

Mrs Upfield, smartly dressed, pearls and all, looked warily at this teenager dressed in black motorcycle clothes, but her good manners took precedence.

"Hello, Simon," she said, pleasantly enough. "Can I offer you a drink?"

Simon wondered if she were offering him a beer and looked to Kelly for guidance.

"You like tea, don't you, Simon?" Kelly asked.

Simon nodded, now aware of the ground rules. "Thank you, that would be very nice."

At Mrs Upfield's bidding, he took off his Barbour biking jacket. Luckily he was reasonably well dressed, despite not having planned this when he left Swiford. Mrs Upfield's look softened at this and at Simon's well spoken manner. He had unconsciously in response to the well heeled surroundings used his best Hooray Henrys accent. Kelly led him into the large and richly furnished lounge.

"What did you mean, the one I told you about?" asked Simon quietly, perturbed.

"I told her about what happened at school and how you beat Della Duncan and all that."

"Well, that wasn't a very good idea, was it? And it wasn't just me, others did it as well."

"No, she was all for it. For a start, I had already complained about having to spend my study time doing what the prefects were supposed to do, and she thought it was good you stood up for what you believed in. Her Mum was a suffragette, you know, and Mum was a union official."

Simon took a moment to absorb this. Somehow suffragettes, rebellion and trades unions didn't fit with the obvious affluence of this house on The Grange. Tory territory through and through.

"Oh. Right," was the best he could come up with.

"I also told her I liked you, so she's been waiting to meet you I suppose. You won't let me down, will you?"

"No of course not," said Simon, wondering what she meant by that. "You know when you said you liked me, did you mean… I mean …"

Kelly laughed. "Yes, I did mean. I'm glad you've called. Did Kay tell you?"

"Tell me what?"

"Simon, I thought you were supposed to be clever. Tell you that I fancied you."

"Oh, no she didn't."

"Well, now you know. Perhaps later we could ..."

Her remark was cut short by Mrs Upfield's entrance with a tray with teapot, china cups, a plate of cakes. In the ensuing conversation Simon tried to play down his role in the rebellion pointing out that people like Ed and Jamie had played just as big a part. It turned out she was also a Kate Drummond fan, admiring of the no nonsense, straight talking way she wrote in the *Bilthaven Mail*. Simon had the distinct impression he was being weighed up and his feelings alternated between anxiety in case the real truth about his worthless, defiled being somehow came out and defiance because it didn't matter anyway.

At last she seemed satisfied. "I'll leave you two to it, then," she said.

"Mummy, maybe Simon could help me with my homework. I'm a bit stuck on the art history and Simon is good at history."

"But I'm not doing Art," interjected Simon thoughtlessly and earning a look from Kelly.

"Fine dear," said Mrs Upfield as she left the room with the tray.

Kelly led the way upstairs to her room. Simon looked around at the artwork scattered here and there.

"Where's the art history?" he asked.

"Over there, on the table," Kelly said, indicating some opened books, but pulling Simon towards the bed. Caught by surprise, Simon allowed himself to be sat on the bed next to Kelly. They kissed, an act which released a flood of feelings in Simon. He had not kissed since that final farewell kiss with Ruth on that dreadful night. And there was Diane, all things buzzing in his head, distracting him.

"What's the matter?" asked Kelly, a hurt tone in her voice. "Was there something wrong?"

"No, nothing. I'm sorry, it's me, forget it." And he reached out and kissed her again, more prepared this time.

Simon stayed quite late, talking with Kelly. He found she was not a deep thinker like Ruth, or even Diane, and was mainly interested in things that Simon did not consider really important, such as the latest fashion, what was in the hit parade. But he went along with it because it was plain that she was interested in him, and sex. So they kissed and fondled but Simon was very cautious about anything further, partly because he felt unsure of himself and partly of course because her mother, younger sister Rowena and later father were in the house.

Simon was invited back the next day, Sunday, for 'proper tea'. Rowena's boyfriend would be there too. As he rode back to Swiford in the dark, relatively slowly because the headlight on the Bantam was not that powerful, he wondered what he was getting himself into. He knew Kelly was not soul mate material for him, but he did like her and she was keen for him. Why not?

He rode back the next day early in the afternoon. Kelly met him at the door and helped him off with his Barbour gear and helmet.

"Come into the lounge," she said. "Rowena's here with her boyfriend." Simon knew Rowena by sight for she was at Cermerton but not yet in the sixth form. He went into the lounge.

"Simon!"

"Charlie!"

"You two know each other?" asked Mrs Upfield.

"Oh yes," said Charlie, eagerly. "Simon's my hero. Remember I told you about those evil kids on the school bus ages ago and how they attacked me until someone came to my rescue? Well, here he is!"

Everybody turned to look at Simon.

"I just lost my temper, that's all."

But everybody wanted to hear all about it, and Simon was forced to listen to Charlie's retelling, with his own occasional, reluctant contributions. It was painful and Simon just wanted to be anywhere else but here. They don't know what happened afterwards, he thought. He felt his resentment against Charlie returning, but the looks everybody was giving him mollified him. He decided to play the role of reluctant hero, which after all, was the truth.

The tale of heroics, although Simon always denied such a description, made his acceptance by Kelly's family all the quicker. He started to visit more often, the bike of course affording the flexibility and mobility. Inevitably this drew him into a closer involvement with Charlie as he lived not far from Swiford. Simon would pick him up and take him on the pillion to The Grange.

One afternoon they were all talking, the weather was good and Simon suggested to Kelly they go out for a ride on the bike into the countryside.

"What about us?" said Rowena.

"I can only get one passenger on the back," said Simon.

"It's a shame you don't drive a car, Simon," said Mrs Upfield, "or you could all four go in my car."

"But you can drive, Simon, can't you?" said Kelly quickly.

"Well, yes. I passed my car test long before I started on bikes."

"Oh Mummy, can Simon take us out, please?" said Kelly.

Simon wasn't sure if Mrs Upfield would now regret her offer, but if she did, there was no trace of it. "Of course. Just be careful and come back for tea, won't you."

Mrs Upfield's car was a Morris Minor which she used as a runabout. Mr Upfield's Mercedes was of course completely out of bounds.

They all got in, Kelly in the front, Charlie and Rowena in the back.

"I'll show you the controls," said Kelly. This was the car her father was teaching her to drive in, but Simon gathered that progress was slow.

"I think I'll manage," said Simon, remembering that unlike Mum's old three speed Ford, this more modern car had four gears. Then he tripped at the first hurdle.

"Where's reverse?" he had to ask. Kelly showed him the selection of reverse gear, which turned out to be in the same place as Bernard's car, and they were then out onto the road and away.

"Where shall we go?" Simon asked.

"Anywhere. Just out into the country," came the response. So Simon drove carefully through the plush avenues of The Grange and out into the fields and woods, the hills in the distance. He took his time to get accustomed to the car, as it was more powerful than the Ford, but of course nothing like as powerful or big as Bernard's car on which he had learned. Kelly sat next to him, but in the mirror, he could see Charlie and Rowena snogging, and Simon wondered if he had got the better of the deal. They went for a careful drive round, Simon worried in case anything should happen while he had the car, especially as there might be ice on the road, through villages, past farms bringing back memories for Simon and then back to The Grange and Kelly's house.

Later that night on the way home, Charlie engaged Simon in conversation from the pillion seat. It was as might be expected a stilted conversation over his shoulder and it was frosty, but his main point was that Simon was too cautious driving the Morris, and if they do it again, they should have more fun. But Simon's mind was elsewhere. He could feel Charlie pressing close behind him, feel his thighs either side of his hips and old feelings were stirring in Simon, back to Daniel. Charlie was now almost the age Daniel had been when Simon last saw him. His feelings for Charlie were a heady mix of anger and resentment as the cause of the Watsons' attack on him, a reviving sexual attraction as he had felt with Daniel and jealousy at his confidence and assumed sexual competence in contrast to Simon's own confusion. He knew it wasn't Charlie's fault, but he was glad when he dropped him off and could continue alone to his Swiford flat and the refuge of his room.

A week or two later at school lunchtime on the Friday they broke up for Easter, Kelly suggested that Simon come over on Saturday after work – and stay all night. Her parents were going away and she and Rowena would have the run of the house.

"Yes, that would be good," said Simon enthusiastically. He was aware of course of the likely outcome of this all night stay and put his self doubt to one side.

"I'm pleased. I thought you would say yes," said Kelly. And then confirming Simon's thoughts, she added quietly, "Can you get hold of some Durex?"

This took Simon a little by surprise. It occurred to him he had no idea where to get condoms. But he wasn't going to admit this to Kelly. He had a reputation to maintain! "Yes, of course."

"Good, you'd better get some for Charlie too because I bet he won't be able to get them."

"Is Charlie going to be there as well," said Simon, annoyance welling up in him. He had imagined just him and Kelly. He hadn't given a thought to where Rowena would be.

"You don't think Rowena and him would let a chance like this go by, do you?" replied Kelly laughing, oblivious to Simon's change of mood.

Simon knew it would be no good asking Stuart, by now his closest friend, about Durex, but he knew who might know. It was just that having to ask would make him look a fool and also give away the plans. But in the end he felt his credibility with Kelly mattered more.

"Ed, can I ask you something?"

"Fire away!"

"Well since coming to Bilthaven I've never needed to get hold of any ... um .. Durex. Where would you get them?"

"What about Ruth?"

"Pardon! Why would Ruth have Durex?"

"Clot! I mean, didn't you use them with her?"

"No, I mean we didn't have sex. Not full sex anyway."

"I never had you down as the monastic type, Simon."

"I'm not. She was. So? Where?"

"Barber shops I suppose. Go and get your hair cut when they ask you if you need anything for the weekend, say yes please."

"Ed! You're a genius! The salon! I'm an idiot."

"Your words, Simon, your words," said Ed, laughing now. "Are we meeting up during the holiday? We could revise together."

Simon appreciated Ed's offer, but revising for the imminent A level exams was far from his mind. Such things just didn't seem important now, and anyway, he simply could not keep his mind on work, not even history, since the night everything changed. His concentration was non-existent.

"Maybe, I'll phone."

That Saturday, Simon chose his moment in a lull in business to speak to Roddy.

"Do we sell Durex, Roddy, only I was wondering if I could buy some?"

Roddy burst out in peals of laughter.

"What are you planning, you naughty boy?" he asked. "Paul, I think our young friend has some amorous adventures planned for tonight."

Paul came over. "Tell us all. Who's the lucky lady – or lad?" he added much to his and Roddy's amusement. Simon did not find it funny. He had sometimes come close to talking to them about Daniel, but never had.

"A girl," said Simon. "Look, do we have them or not. We do, don't we?" he asked, now remembering some discreet transactions with some of the male clientele.

"Of course," said Roddy. "We like to provide a full service for our gentlemen, but very tactfully. That's one reason why Paul or I always finish trimming off the gentlemen after you've done the basic cut. Can't have a young lad like you asking such things, can we?"

"Maybe we should now," said Paul. "Some of Dorothy's friends might buy more from Simon." They both thought this was very funny, but Simon had no idea who they were talking about.

"How many do you want?" asked Roddy, more seriously.

Simon was again unprepared. "Oh, one, I suppose," and then remembering Kelly's urging on behalf on Charlie, added quickly, "Oh, there's another lad, so two."

This caused more laughter. "They come in packs of three."

Just then the shop door opened and a lady came in for her appointment.

"With you in just a moment, Mrs Kirtley," called Paul.

Roddy beckoned Simon into the storeroom and reached up to the top shelf. He handed Simon four packets.

"Try not to use them all at once," he joked. Simon flushed with embarrassment. "So this other lad," continued Roddy, "are you and him … ?" He stopped, the question left hanging in mid air.

"Oh no," said Simon quickly. "He's going out with my girlfriend's sister. Their parents are away this weekend. How much is this? Can you take it out of my pay?"

"On the house, love," said Roddy, patting Simon on the shoulder. "Glad you've the sense to ask."

Simon had known he could rely on Roddy and Paul. He put the packets safely away.

"Now go and make Mrs Kirtley some coffee," said Roddy.

Simon ran from the salon back to the flat, he wanted to get to Kelly's as quickly as possible.

"Mum, you've remembered I'm out tonight?"

"Oh yes, Kelly's? What time will you be back?"

"I won't. It's a sort of party so some of us are sleeping there," Simon replied, trying to make it sound as though there would be lots of other people there. "I'm going to have a quick bath."

"She must be special," commented Ken, smiling. Simon chose to ignore that.

"What about tea?" asked Mum.

"No time," said Simon disappearing to his bedroom.

"I'll make you a sandwich while you're having your bath."

In the privacy of the bathroom, Simon opened one of the packets and examined the condom. He felt its slipperiness and then taking hold of himself to become aroused, he rolled the condom down his shaft as far as it would go. It felt strange and he was tempted to keep his hand going but decided he had better save himself for later. At least he had practised putting one on. He rolled it off and then faced a problem. What to do with it? He dropped it into the toilet and flushed it. It floated up and wouldn't go away! He waited for the cistern to refill and tried again, with the same result. Starting to panic, he used the toilet brush to push it down under the lip out of sight, then he flushed it again. This time it did not reappear.

After a record quick bath and a gobbled sandwich, Simon set off for The Grange, two of the four packets in his pocket, leaving the packet with just two left in his bedroom, hidden away with the other full packet. Luckily the weather was dry although chilly and the ride was completed quickly.

Kelly met him at the door, having heard the bike. He could hear Charlie's voice from the lounge. She helped him off with his bike jacket and they kissed in the hallway. He drew away, the memory of another kiss in a hallway suddenly upsetting him.

"What's wrong?" said Kelly, puzzled.

Simon thought quickly, and nodded towards the lounge door. "Them," he said.

"You are funny," Kelly said. "They've seen us kissing before."

It turned out that Charlie had already been there most of the day, and had spent most of that time revising for his GCEs with Rowena. Simon had realised that Rowena was a more serious minded and to be blunt, cleverer girl than her older sister, as well, Simon thought, as being more attractive. He envied Charlie again, and it occurred to him he had never thought about whether Charlie was especially clever at school or not. Of course he was at the grammar school.

"Mummy's left lots of food," said Kelly, "It's in the kitchen, so we can just help ourselves."

"There's beer too, Simon," said Charlie, grinning.

Simon did not particularly like beer, but went into the kitchen anyway for a glass to try to fit in. Also he did not want to get drunk just in case he had to ride the bike home after all. Charlie followed him.

"Simon," he said quietly, "Did you manage to get any Durex?"

Simon nodded and tapped his pocket, and poured some beer into the glass.

Charlie picked up a pasty, and added earnestly, "For me as well?"

"Yes, plenty. Don't worry."

"Thanks, Simon." Charlie paused. "This'll be my first time, all the way I mean, and it's thanks to you. Something else to thank you for."

"You'll be fine," said Simon, trying to sound confident.

"How old were you when you had sex for the first time?" asked Charlie, quickly followed by, "I hope you don't mind me asking."

So Charlie assumes I'm not a virgin, Simon thought; for a second he was tempted to say 'With my boyfriend when I was very young' but instantly thought better of it, and referring to Diane, said simply, "About your age."

Charlie gave Simon a dig and returned to the lounge, munching his pasty. Simon picked up his glass and a pasty and followed.

The four discussed what to do that evening. They toyed with the idea of going to a pub in the Morris, but there was some doubt as to whether they would get in, Charlie and Rowena especially, and Simon was not keen on driving anyway, so they talked, ate and watched some television, The Eurovision Song Contest, but each wondering how to make the move.

At about ten o'clock, it was Rowena who did it.

"Come on Charlie, let's go upstairs." She and Charlie got up.

"See you later," said Charlie with a Cheshire Cat grin on his face, and winking at Simon as they left the room.

Then he was straight back in.

"Simon!" he whispered urgently. "You didn't give me them!"

Simon smiled and reached into his pocket, and handed Charlie a packet. "Don't use them all at once," he joked.

"Thanks again, Simon." He left and his feet could be heard running up the stairs.

Simon looked at Kelly, wondering what to do. He wished so much that he had Charlie's youthful confidence. He felt much older than his seventeen years.

"I hope you've some left," said Kelly. "I'd better lock up."

That done they went up to Kelly's bedroom. It was as untidy as always, but that didn't matter. They lay on the bed and kissed, getting undressed in stages, until with only knickers and pants left, Kelly sat up and crawled under the covers, Simon then doing the same. She pulled his pants off as he eased her final clothing off under the sheets, their now naked bodies making close contact as they ran their hands over each other in the narrow single bed. His mind was whirling; it was almost two years now since he had sex with Diane, so much had happened since then. And it was almost four years since he had been warm in bed, naked with a lover, that last night with Daniel. Yes, so much had changed so quickly.

They kissed, his hands stroking her taut breasts, at which Kelly pulled him down for another deep kiss, the passion of which took Simon by surprise. She had hold of him, heightening his arousal, he responded by stimulating her so that she gasped with pleasure.

"Put one on," she whispered.

Simon rolled over to where his trousers lay in a heap next to the bed and found the packet in his pocket. As he opened the packet and removed the condom from its wrapper, he felt that doubt creep into his mind and his arousal fading. But he managed to get the thing on and turning back to Kelly, they kissed again. She ran her hands down his back and pulled him over between her thighs.

Lying above her, Simon's head was suddenly full of nightmarish images; of him lying beneath Watson as she was now beneath him, of that forced penetration and the pain of it, of David Watson and the humiliation of his own stunning orgasm at his doing.

And he could feel nothing now. Was it that fucking circumcision, or the latex or both? He tried to push towards her but he was no longer hard enough. He could not get that derelict garden out of his head. She tried to guide him, but it was no good. He felt as if he were going mad. And there he was, watching himself in a 'film' again. And the sense of failure swept over him. A total fucking failure! He rolled back again.

"What's the matter?" asked Kelly.

"Sorry," said Simon. "It's me. Not you."

"Are you worried in case you hurt me? It being my first time?"

Her first time? Simon had wondered but had never felt confident enough to confirm this. He felt that her virginity should give him more confidence, but instead he just felt the responsibility even more. He seemed to be always taking girls' virginity.

"Maybe. Don't worry, there's all night," he smiled, trying to sound confident.

Not even all night could mend the torture in Simon's head. A later attempt produced the same dispiriting result, made worse by the sounds from across the landing of Charlie's evident success. Guilty at not fulfilling Kelly's expectations he tried to pleasure her with his hand as he had with Diane, but not even that worked.

Eventually they fell asleep, a fitful sleep for Simon partly due the narrow confines of the single bed but mainly for the horrible nightmares that plagued him most nights and especially after his letdown on this night. The Watsons were taunting him on his failure along with the memory of their attack, David Watson in particular, taking the credit for Simon's uselessness, 'I did that,' he was boasting. He woke up with a start to find Kelly looking at him.

"Are you OK?" she asked. Simon could see her face in what he guessed was the early morning light.

"Yes, sorry, did I wake you?"

"You were dreaming I think, but it didn't seem a very nice dream," Kelly said with a note of hurt in her voice.

"It wasn't about you, nothing about you," Simon tried to reassure her. Her face relaxed a bit at that and she smiled at him.

At that moment there was a tap on the door, and Charlie's face appeared round the edge.

"I thought I heard you talking so I guessed you were awake," he said.

Kelly instinctively pulled the covers up to her neck as Charlie came into the room.

"I hope you don't mind, Simon," he said, grinning, "but have you got any more Durex?"

But it wasn't Charlie's grin that had Simon's attention. He was completely naked! Simon looked at his fit teenage body and was taken back to Daniel's room. He felt aroused, angry and jealous all at once. For a moment he could not speak and then Charlie was there right next to him. Simon wanted to reach out and touch him, but forced himself simply to say, "In my trouser pocket."

Charlie knelt down, so close to Simon and produced the single Durex.

"Thanks Simon," he said, and then leaned over and unexpectedly kissed Simon on the cheek. "I'll make it up to you." He turned and left the room.

Simon's attention was drawn back to himself and the fact that he was now very hard, which in the closeness of the bed, Kelly noticed too. She reached over him and kissed him, arousal now enveloping them both.

"You're obviously a morning person," she whispered between kisses, and pulling him closer, on top of her, opening for him, her hand guiding him.

"Christ, Charlie took the last Durex," said Simon.

Kelly's response was simply to pull him in and he felt the moist warmth of her body and then, at last, he was in. He moved so as to give Kelly as much stimulation as he could and he felt her whole body responding. But he did not feel involved in this lovemaking as he had done with Daniel, or even Diane. It was as though his brain was piloting his body, separate but commanding it, almost as if by remote control. He had to manage his thoughts to stop those horrible images taking control again. He slowed to make the pleasure last longer as she sighed with the delight of it. His hardness stayed with him and he was able to take Kelly to edge of ecstasy and then keep them both on the cusp of climax, prolonging the moment until he could stop no longer and his action quickened, Kelly's climax coming with loud cries as she pulled his buttocks down, forcing him ever deeper as she convulsed below him. Simon felt his own ejaculation coming and remembered the lack of Durex so tried to pull out. But Kelly's grip on him was too fierce as she extracted the last possible moments of her own joy, moving against him, her muscles squeezing him and then it was too late as he felt his orgasm sweeping over him, pulsing into her, fire down below, as he had with Diane, his thoughts and feelings a mix of anxiety because he did not want Kelly to be pregnant and relief that he had done it after all, and that Kelly had obviously enjoyed it.

As the fire in them both subsided, they drew apart and Simon lay back alongside Kelly. Her face was flushed and her eyes moist with feeling.

"Thank you, Simon," she said, "that was super. I knew it would be good."

"Yes, it was, wasn't it," said Simon. "It didn't hurt you?"

"Not at all," she said.

"I'm a bit worried though," said Simon. "I came in you."

"Don't worry," she replied. "It'll be fine."

Simon was not sure how Kelly would know that, but he accepted her assurance and felt content, relaxed at last that the night had not been a total disaster.

Then she spoiled it.

"We'll have to get Charlie to come in every time," she said. She was smiling, but Simon tensed.

"What do you mean?"

"Well, I saw the way you were looking at him, and then when he kissed you, that was it. There was no stopping you."

Simon felt his guts lock tight as his feelings of relaxation and contentment fled.

"As you say, I must just be a morning person," he hedged, trying to hide his fear.

"I expect so," she said. But to Simon's ears she did not sound convinced. All his doubts returned. They talked about other things until they heard noises on the landing, the bathroom.

Then Rowena called through the door, "We're going down to get some breakfast. Want some toast putting in?"

"Yes please, Ro," called Kelly.

They all ate cereal and toast and chatted, Charlie's high spirits seemed a counterpoint to Simon's reawakened fears and doubts. He simply wanted to get away; from Charlie, from Kelly, from the whole miserable situation. Once more he felt alone, the outsider, different. It was a familiar feeling, Simon realised.

He could not avoid giving Charlie a lift home on the Bantam later that Sunday morning. He was full of his success and gratitude to Simon for facilitating it. As he talked behind Simon's head, his body close to Simon, thighs against his own from the pillion seat, the image of Charlie naked kept coming into Simon's head, and he felt himself becoming aroused. Jesus! Why did Charlie arouse him more than Kelly?

He dropped Charlie off and went back to the flat. Mum and Ken were out, probably a Sunday lunchtime drink at the pub.

He lay on his bed and wrestled with the question. And then Daniel came into his head. Maybe it was just that Charlie had reminded him of Daniel. That must be it. No more than that. Memory playing tricks. But he also knew that he could not face a repeat of the humiliation of that night. There would be no more Kelly. He would have to break it off. She was not his type really anyway. Perfectly nice, but there was no real meeting of minds. Love would never take root there. Diane had held out that prospect. They had got on well, talked about serious things. But that had ended. Ruth too. Dear Ruth. The memory of her face, in tears as he had lied to her to set her free of him. He thought about his hated body, how he reviled it and how it let him down. Maybe he should just give up the idea of sex altogether. But then he thought of Daniel, his one true love, and he wept again for love lost.

He kept himself occupied during the Easter holiday. He tried to revise for the A levels, but his brain simply would not function. It kept wandering back to his humiliation that Saturday night, back to the greater humiliation of his rape the previous October. His life was a mess. He had lost the person he loved and who had loved him. Almost four years on and the pain was as strong as ever. He felt anger at his own sexual feelings, at his failure. His confusion led to depression and desperation. He passed the time by taking the trolley bus into Bilthaven and wandering round. Sometimes he took the knife with him, but he knew now in his heart of hearts it was unlikely he would use it. He no longer had the same fire for vengeance. On one occasion he walked out to the centre of the City Bridge, high above the dark and dangerous waters of the river a hundred feet below. He stood for a while, imagining his fall. Hitting the water from that height would be like hitting concrete he thought and yet that somehow seemed preferable to falling from the section of the bridge over the quayside. But the power of his imagination which enabled him to visualise such a death caused what small resolve he had to wither. He turned and walked back into the city centre and had a coffee in The Dungeon. He met one or two people he knew slightly and chatted. A brief foray into normality. The talk was of the new pirate radio station, Caroline, so when he got home he tuned in to listen.

Later that week he went to see Dad and Phoebe. He had wanted to go on his motorbike, but Mum was worried about the long journey on the small machine and so he went by train. The visit gave him the excuse he needed not to visit Kelly again, or anyone for that matter. He passed the time helping out in the studio, where he proved useful and was also paid for his efforts! Over Easter weekend, they went out and he got to drive the Austin, the same car he had ridden in down to Salcombe. Dad had never changed it and now Simon could drive it. He quickly grew to like its power and hate its gear change mounted on the steering column.

But Simon had a drive of a different kind. Russell had a boat kept at a small harbour further up the coast. This was a yacht and he and Russell had talked about sailing. Annoyingly for Russell this yacht required some major work doing which meant it would have to brought down to Bilthaven marina for work to be carried out. He asked if Simon could drive his car back down to Bilthaven while he brought the boat. Never one to pass up the chance of a drive, and knowing that the Morris estate car would be similar to drive to Mrs Upfield's Morris, he felt confident. So early on the Sunday morning he went downstairs where Russell was busy loading up what he would need in the garage. But he was loading the small luggage space at the back of the Jaguar E-type! Simon's eyes popped at the prospect of driving the Jaguar back to Bilthaven.

"We're taking the Jag?" he asked, still disbelieving.

"Yes, we need to get there as quickly as possible," said Russell. "Need to get the boat into Bilthaven and it might be a slow journey. Is that all right with you?"

Simon could only nod.

"You'll be OK with it, I'm sure," continued Russell with a smile. "Your mother tells me your police instructor fellow said you are an excellent driver."

"Did he? Good," said Simon.

Simon had been driven by Russell before in the Triumph and in the Morris, so was used to his style. He drove extremely fast, using the acceleration of the Jaguar to the full. It reminded Simon of Ed's driving, but amplified.

Just over an hour's rapid driving along the Sunday morning roads got them to the harbour. On the way Russell pointed out one or details about driving the car for Simon's benefit on the return journey. They unloaded the Jaguar onto the boat. Simon had never actually seen Russell's yacht before, and he thought it looked a very trim craft indeed, about thirty foot, Bermuda rig, but today Russell would be using the engine. He pointed out the cracks in the mainmast that needed repair before any serious sailing could be risked.

"Look after it," was all Russell said as Simon eased himself into the red leather driving seat of the E-type. He started the engine and eased the car forward. It was strange looking along that long white bonnet and getting used to steering from so far back in a car. But he soon adjusted to that and the powerful clutch and gingerly steered the car out of the village and along the minor roads to the main road back to Bilthaven. This was magical! Simon felt like the king of the road. People gave the car, and him, admiring glances. How he wished Ed could see this! And dear Daniel too. He started to get the feel of the car and its capability. He pushed the car along at 80 and 90 miles per hour where the roads allowed it. Then he came to a dual carriageway, a fairly new by pass for a market town. This was Simon's opportunity. He pushed his foot down and felt the car leap forward along the deserted road, speed climbing rapidly. Soon he was past 100 miles per hour and the car was still going, still pressing him back in his seat. It was like a fighter jet! Would he be able to get the car up to its top speed? He was now doing 135 miles per hour, the road a ribbon passing beneath him. His Roadcraft instincts told him the car was stable and going well, but then they also told him he needed to slow. Far up ahead was a group of vehicles, and there was no way that passing them at this speed would be safe. So he started to slow down. For a moment, Simon panicked. The car was not slowing, but then he looked at the speedometer and the needle was falling rapidly. It was really only when he got down to 80 miles per hour that the loss of speed was apparent. 80 felt like a crawl, but Simon knew it wasn't. By the time he caught up with the other cars and a lorry, he passed them at 60 mph, and then the dualled section was over and it was back to single carriageway roads. He thoroughly enjoyed the drive back. He resisted the temptation to take the car over to Ed's or Stuart's as Russell had not sanctioned that. It had been the drive of his life!

Back at school, the pressure was on for the A levels. Stuart and Kay were now going out together, Kelly asked why he had not been in touch. He explained he had been to see his father. She said that was OK because she was seeing someone, but she would always think of Simon as a friend. Oh, and she had had her period, so that was OK. He felt mixed feelings, relief that he was 'off the hook', annoyance at the rejection. But he could not help feeling that the real reason was his sexual inadequacy and that whoever it was she was now seeing was better than him. And that, he thought, would not be difficult for this new boy.

Both Ed and Stuart noticed the change in him, his lack of effort for the exams. This was not the Simon they had known. They both in their different ways made their concern known, which Simon appreciated, but also resented. Why could he not just get his mind sorted out?

19. *1964 Natalie*

It was the Rachmaninoff, the *C sharp minor, Opus 3, number 2*. It was being murdered, but Simon recognised it above the noise. He was at a party, friends of Mum and Ken, someone's silver wedding anniversary, but there were lots of young people there as well in this big house. Mum said it would be a break from the exams and revision. The 'A' levels were now underway, and Simon had attempted some last minute panic revision, but he could no longer concentrate the way he once had, the way Daniel had taught him. So here he was at the party, trying to forget what a mess he really was.

He had been chatting to some people who all seemed to be at Bilthaven Royal Grammar School, when he heard the familiar piece being tortuously attempted from another room. He followed the sound to the grand piano which was surrounded by guests, and a teenage boy trying to play the Rachmaninoff.

"Prelude in C sharp minor, Opus 3, number 2," said Simon. The boy stopped and looked up.

"Yes. Well, a pretty damn poor attempt at it." Simon was forced to agree in his mind, not a patch on Daniel, but he decided to be diplomatic.

"It is a very difficult piece, though," said Simon. "You're brave to try it."

"And you're kind to say so," said a girl standing next to Simon. He turned to see an attractive girl about his own age, with long dark hair streaming down over her shoulders, hazel eyes that twinkled with mischief and a nice smile that was directed at him.

He smiled back. "Well, it is. Rachmaninoff is a very challenging composer."

"Are you a pianist?" she asked as the boy resumed his attempt.

"No, sadly. I would like to have been."

"A musician though?" she continued.

"Not even that, I'm afraid. I had a friend who was, and who was a very good pianist. He liked Rachmaninoff."

The boy looked up from keyboard at that and frowned. "I say," he said, "that's a bit of a comparison! I hope he was an older chap."

"Oh be quiet, you," said the girl to him in a friendly tone, obviously she knew him. To Simon she said, "Let's get a top up."

They went to where the drinks were and filled up their glasses with punch.

"My name's Natalie," she said. "What's yours?"

"Simon. Pleased to meet you."

"Oh don't be so formal, Simon. Come on, let's talk."

So they sat down away from the noise and talked. Simon thought to himself that this was to be his new girlfriend, she was certainly different. She was unconventional in many ways, a Bohemian character and she soon fascinated Simon. She lived in a large terraced house in Bilthaven, but not too far from Swiford, her parents, who were at the party, were both university lecturers and she was at Bilthaven College studying art. Simon talked about himself and how he had come to Bilthaven. She seemed interested in Daniel, but Simon steered the conversation away from that area. She showed an interest in the cruise and when Simon said he had a slide collection of that, as well as of Salcombe and his German trip, she said she would like to see them. It was arranged that she would come to Swiford where they would watch a slide show. It was half term, so he would be at home while Mum and Ken would be at work.

On the appointed day, Simon set up his projector and screen in the lounge of the flat, and loaded the magazine with the slides he had chosen. On time, he looked out of his bedroom window to see Natalie striding up the road. He ran down to the front door to meet her.

"Hello, come in," he said. "I've got everything ready."

"I hope so," she replied, following him up the stairs. They went into the lounge where the projector was set up.

"Would you like a drink or something?" he asked.

"You're odd," she answered. "No drink, but something." With that she held his head and kissed him, her hand then exploring his body. As she held him close, he felt his belt being undone and then her hand was holding him, heightening his rapid arousal. Simon was taken by surprise by this sudden intimate contact.

"Don't you want to see the slides?" he asked, stupidly.

She laughed. "Later maybe. Where's your bedroom?"

He led the way along the landing to his room, glad that he had tidied it up. He wasn't sure what was expected, but was happy to go along with it. After a further kiss, they lay on the bed. Again her hand thrust inside his trousers and then she was sliding her hands round his buttocks, easing his trousers and pants down, which Simon willingly allowed.

"Nice and big," she said, regarding his now hard penis. Simon felt he should respond, so he started to undo the buttons on her blouse, revealing her bra. He tried to release the clips, but she stopped him and quickly took off her blouse, bra and jeans. Simon took off his shirt and shook off his trousers from around his legs, then his socks. Soon they were both naked on the bed. They kissed again and each explored the other with their hands, Simon drawing on his experience to pleasure Natalie as best he could. But Simon was unsure whether to take matters further, and so they remained, petting and caressing for some time.

"Don't you want to do more?" she asked eventually.

"Yes, but I didn't know what you …" He faltered to a stop.

"Well, come on then. Have you got any Durex?"

"Oh, yes," said Simon, remembering those he had bought before seeing Kelly. He went over to his drawers and found the packet with two left. But even as he did do he felt his arousal fading. Back on the bed, Natalie took hold to restore his hardness. But with the condom on, again he found he could feel little.

"Are you all right?" asked Natalie. "It's not your first time, is it?"

"No," said Simon. "Is it for you?" Thoughts of Diane and Kelly and their lost virginity came into his head.

"Of course not," Natalie said, smiling. "I'm not a nun!"

Her confidence seemed only to contrast with Simon's uncertainty. He moved over and pressed himself into her. But he could feel so little that even his thrusting could not fully restore his hardness, and the downward spiral of confidence and performance was set in motion. Again, those mental images of that October night haunted him. He softened despite everything until he could not continue. He withdrew and lay beside her. He didn't know what to say, so he said nothing. He felt useless and ashamed, familiar feelings to him now.

"I'm sorry," he said after a while.

"Your heart's not in it today, is it?" she said.

"I don't know why; I mean, it's not you. You're smashing."

"Look, Simon, it's just our first time together. We'll get to know each other better and then it'll be fine."

Was she just being kind? Letting him down gently? But he clutched at the proffered straw.

"That'd be good. Thanks," he said.

So they lay and talked, but there was no further attempt at intercourse. It was arranged that Simon visit Natalie a couple of days later.

He found the house in an affluent area of Bilthaven with streets of large Victorian terraced houses. He parked the Bantam and was greeted by Natalie at the front door.

"Come in, Simon," she said, smiling. That seemed a good welcome anyway, he thought. After a brief introduction to her parents, whom he just about remembered from the party, they went right up to a room at the top of the house. The ceiling sloped and there was small window. The room was untidy, and there was a wide bed, larger than a single but smaller than a double. There were paints, materials, art stuff everywhere.

"Is this your bedroom?" he asked, disbelieving.

"No, silly, that's on the next floor down. This is my den. Nobody comes in here except me."

Simon thought that was fairly clear from the condition of the room. But the bed was made up.

"So who sleeps there, then," he said, indicating the bed.

"This evening, we do," she laughed.

"Oh," said Simon, caught unawares again as she took him and kissed. He responded but then drew back.

"I don't think I can stay all night," he said. He had not been prepared for Natalie being so forward, although he thought he probably should have been, based on last time. "What about your parents?" he continued.

"That's OK. They won't come up. This is my private space."

Simon looked at her, trying to make sense of this very liberal attitude.

"Don't look at me like that," she said. "You've got soft, sensitive eyes," she added.

"It's just I wasn't expecting this, what with your parents being here, just downstairs."

"They trust me, believe me."

And then they were on the bed, she drawing him down, they undressed each other and slid naked under the bed covers.

He felt her slim figure next to him, and became very aroused. She slid down the bed and then he could feel her lips and tongue, licking and kissing him, taking him into her mouth. He had not felt that sensation since he and Daniel had explored this avenue of sexual enjoyment with each other. Thinking of Daniel made him feel sad, once more thoughts were circling in his head, confusing him. Once more the curse of the softness returned. Her head appeared on his chest.

"Didn't you like that? Most boys do."

"Yes, it felt good. Again, it's not you, it's me. Things in my head."

Natalie came and lay next to him. "You're certainly a strange one, Simon Scott," she said.

"The same could be said of you, Natalie Elliston."

She laughed at that. "We're a couple of oddballs, then." Then she reached down under the sheets. "Talking of balls..." She grasped Simon's scrotum in her hand and gently kneaded his balls. He tensed at the contact and felt his hardness returning.

"Come on then," she said, and reaching down produced a Durex condom.

Simon had been dreading this moment, dreading his past failures, dreading the failure to come. But she put it on him, and then pulled him with a fierce intensity onto her. His doubts were pecking away in his head. He tried to think of Diane and his success there, but Kelly and last time with Natalie kept coming to the fore. As he lost sensation again, and with it his erection, his self esteem nose dived. Natalie pushed him off and they lay side by side.

Again they put it down experience and decided to meet again at Natalie's house a day or two later. But sadly and to Simon's despair the next attempts at lovemaking ended in much the same way. Flagging confidence led to the same downward spiral he had felt before.

After another failure a few visits later, Natalie dropped the bombshell.

"You don't really like this, do you?"

"Sex? Of course I do."

"But not with me. Not with a girl."

Simon's gut wrenched. "What do you mean? I told you about the girl I used to meet at the farm. That was OK."

"She must have been special then. Any others?"

"A girl at The Grange I know from school."

"The Grange. Rich girl is she?"

"I suppose so."

"And did you do it with her?"

"Yes, she enjoyed it," he said thinking of their unprotected morning session after Charlie had come in for the condom.

Natalie seemed sceptical. "So what about this best friend of yours you had down south?"

Simon swallowed. Natalie was getting very close and it was very uncomfortable for him.

"What about him?"

"Just the way you were when you talked about him. Is that all you were, friends?"

"Of course!" lied Simon hotly.

Natalie had that sceptical look.

"Simon, it's in your eyes. You're a homo," she said gently.

The fear, the shame, the ostracism, the illegality!

"I'm not," he said. "Lots of boys play about a bit when they're younger. That's what they say, anyway."

"So you did play about a bit with him, then?"

Simon realised he had for the first time ever revealed that there was more to his relationship with Daniel than just friendship. He felt heartbroken that he had let Daniel down, and now was forced to deny him.

"Just usual stuff a couple of times, that's all."

"Simon, I think you're a really nice person, but you have to be honest. If he were here now, who would you rather be having sex with?"

Simon knew the answer immediately but stuffed it away. "That's silly," he said defensively. "How could he be here with us?"

Natalie nodded. "I thought so."

Simon knew that she knew. How could she, on their brief acquaintance, read him so well? She was certainly very worldly wise it seemed, in matters of sex especially.

"But I really like you," he said with feeling, and it was true. She fascinated him, her manner, her lifestyle; it was a new view on things for Simon.

"I like you, Simon. I do, honest. We've tried, haven't we? But we're going nowhere, are we?"

Should he tell her about the Watsons, about that October ordeal? Perhaps she would accept that and give him more time. He wanted more time! But he could not. He could not relive that shame, that degradation. Not even to try to save his relationship with Natalie.

"We can try again, another time," he begged.

"Let's get dressed," she said.

And that was it. He rode home to Swiford on the Bantam, weeping behind his glasses, cursing himself, cursing the Watsons, cursing his rotten life!

He vowed he would go and see Natalie, try again. But amid the 'A' levels, another legacy of October struck with a vengeance. His piles returned and he had to suffer in silence. He was not so practised at dealing with them as he became in later life, and as the wretched protrusion thrombosed, became distended and swollen, the pain became agonising, and he knew from bitter experience now that it would be at least a week before this would subside; a week of unremitting pain, a constant reminder of that night. Sitting in the exam hall for an English paper on *Hamlet*, he could hardly write. This was the one play he did know reasonably well, as much of the work had been done in lower sixth, before ... before October. He tried to get his thoughts down but the private hell of his discomfort, both physical and mental disjointed his thoughts, shattering his concentration.

Two days later, much the same in a history paper. History! His subject, his love. And yet that too fell victim to the twin daggers of his secret hell. And how could he go and see Natalie again like this? Walking was painful enough, never mind sex. The contractions that came with orgasm were sheer anguish.

An added distraction was that Mum was away, off to see the Bilthaven Regiment in Germany for the newspaper. He tried to share her glee when she got back because while with the British Army of the Rhine, she had driven a Centurion tank – a track laying vehicle steered by its tracks! A full house on her All Groups driving licence!

It was some days later that Simon at last got back on the motorbike and rode to Natalie's house. He rehearsed his conversation with Natalie, how he would say how much he felt for her, that he wanted to be with her and they should have more time. He rang the doorbell. Mr Elliston, Natalie's father, answered it.

"Hello, is Natalie in?" asked Simon.

"She doesn't want to see you," he said, and made to close the door.

"No! Please! Let me see her."

Mrs Elliston appeared in the doorway.

"It's no good, Simon. She doesn't want to see you any more," she said.

"Is she in?" pleaded Simon.

"It doesn't matter," said Mr Elliston, "she is not going to see you."

"Go away, Simon," said Mrs Elliston. "Sort your life out."

With that, Simon knew she had told them. He felt defeated, humiliated, used up. What poxy life? Before he could respond, the door was shut. He stepped back, looking up at the windows, but there was nobody, nothing. The blank windows mocked him as he stood, alone, shaking in the middle of the street. He kicked the Bantam into life and rode away.

20. *1964 Looking for Daniel*

School was finished. He and Ed had submitted their university applications months before of course, now it was a question of waiting for the A level results. Simon wanted to read history or the law. Stuart decided he would rather do a Higher National Diploma in Engineering at Bilthaven College. Simon found Stuart's company calmer and less demanding than Ed's, and the two spend much time together, apart from when Stuart was working at his summer job or was with Kay. Simon did some more work at the salon saving for a better motorbike.

No doubt because of Kay, Stuart bought a small car, a five year old Ford Anglia 105E. To do this he needed to sell his lovely maroon BSA B33, and he and Simon quickly agreed terms. This bike was in a different class to the little Bantam. It was not the fastest bike on the road by any means, the 650cc BSA Rocket was much faster, not to mention the much desired Triumph Bonneville. But its tuned 500cc engine, now fitted with Gold Star valve gear and high compression piston, gave it a respectable turn of speed, capable of reaching the magic 'ton', 100 miles per hour, and a sharp crisp exhaust note that turned heads. With about eighty miles per gallon, Simon was well pleased. This was more than local transport and he would go on long rides, exploring the hills, as far afield as the Lake District, getting back late at night.

When it was time to visit Dad and Phoebe, he overrode Mum's worries and went down on the B33. Dad seemed amused by the sight of Simon dressed in black motorcycle gear, and slightly concerned for his safety. There was room in Dad's garage to keep the bike, next to the Austin, so it worked out well.

But Simon had another reason to want the bike at Dad's; he was going to visit Daniel! On the chosen day, a fine summer's day, he announced this over breakfast.

"I'm not sure what time I'll be back," he said.

"Phoebe will need to know for supper," said Dad.

"I'll do my best, Dad."

After breakfast, Simon had a shower. He liked this and preferred it to a bath, apart from it being quicker, and he wished they had one in the Swiford flat. But he wanted to be clean when he met Daniel, just in case? He hoped so much, his optimism rose, the anticipation of seeing Daniel again. Of course, he was now almost eighteen, Daniel would be almost twenty years old; no longer a boy. Yet Simon still felt a boy. But all doubts were pushed aside. He was going to see Daniel! And then, heart singing, he was on his way.

The city hadn't changed much. Simon turned off the main road and rode up the hill. It was so quick, that hill he and Daniel used to walk up from the bus, hot in their Henrys blazers, burdened down with a heavy satchel. Don't mention the satchel. He was at the corner and he turned, stopping outside his old house. He sat on the bike and looked at it. It was the same yet changed, it had been painted, the front garden was a bit different. But this was not why he had ridden all the way from Nottingham, let alone Bilthaven. Flicking the bike into gear with his foot, he turned, noticing that the new patch of fence opposite the driveway was still discernible. He turned right at the corner and stopped outside Daniel's house. He killed the engine but then just sat. There were not many changes. There was a Ford Cortina with its funny three part rear lights parked on the driveway. Simon thought of the unanswered letters, and wondered what to do next. What's the worst that could happen? He needed answers, and he longed so much to see Daniel again. To look into those blue eyes, to see that smile, to hear that voice. Perhaps to feel that embrace, those lips, perhaps ... Maybe the loving fusion of their bodies once again would quieten the demons, override the trauma of the intrusions inflicted by the Watsons, silence and bury that nightmare. Daniel could do that, his love could do that.

He knew what he must do, or his day would be wasted, perhaps the opportunity of a lifetime discarded. He got off the bike and pulled it onto the stand, and taking his helmet off, faced the house. Tapping himself on the chest twice, he walked to the front door and knocked. Through the patterned glass he saw the outline of a figure approaching. Yes!! The door opened and there stood - a complete stranger.

"Yes?" said the middle aged woman, wary of this motorcycle suited young man on her doorstep.

Simon was taken aback by this unexpected development. "I was looking for the Gray family."

"What do you mean, grey family?"

"The surname is Gray."

"Oh I see. I'm sorry, nobody of that name here," replied the woman, starting to close the door.

"Please," said Simon, desperate. The urgency in his voice made the woman stop. "I used to live round the corner and Daniel Gray was my best friend."

"Well, we only moved in last month. We bought the house from the Markhams. I know they hadn't been here very long, but I don't know who lived here before that."

"Was there no forwarding address or anything?"

"No, I'm sorry, I really can't help. Good bye." The woman shut the door, leaving Simon standing on the doorstep. He saw the outline of her figure disappear down the hallway, that hallway where almost four years earlier, he and Daniel had their last desperate kiss and told of their love for each other. The figure disappeared, Simon knew into the kitchen. Was she going the check the Aga, Simon wondered? Images of that kitchen as he had known it flooded his mind. This was too painful. He turned and went back to his bike.

"Hello?" A woman's voice, a questioning tone. He looked. A familiar face was looking at him from the front garden next door. Daniel's kindly, elderly neighbour, wearing thick gloves and holding a pair of pruning shears. What was her name? Simon struggled to remember. Meakin. Mrs Meakin.

"Hello, Mrs Meakin," said Simon.

"Yes, it is you, it's Simon isn't it? My, how you've grown up. Never had you down as one of these Hells Angels, though."

"I'm not," said Simon, "I just use the bike to get around. I was looking for Daniel, but the woman next door knows nothing about him."

"No, they've only just moved in. It was the Markhams before that, but one of their children died. Very sad, so they moved on after only a few months."

"So what happened to Daniel's family?"

"Oh, I thought you would have known. Mr Gray got a top job in the police in London, the Metropolitan police, must be three years ago now. It was in the summer I know because we talked about the plants. All quite quick, I remember Mrs Gray saying that they had not expected it at all, and it was quite a rush getting sorted out and moving to London. Didn't you and your Mum move up north?"

"Yes we did, I am just visiting. I don't suppose you have an address for the Grays. Do you?" asked Simon, full of hope.

"No, Simon, I'm sorry. We weren't close, just good neighbours. We would sometimes chat over the fence or say hello in the street, but with me being a lot older, not much more. My family have all grown up and gone many years ago. The city's changing you know, not what it was like when I was a young girl. Too many darkies moving in."

"Oh," was all Simon could summon in response to this unexpected revelation of prejudice. London, three years ago. Is that why the letters had gone unanswered? No, not if they hadn't moved until the next summer. He had a thought.

"Mrs Meakin, are you sure it was the summer when they moved?"

"Oh yes, I remember. Mr Gray went first, but Mrs Gray stayed behind because Daniel was doing his exams. He did very well you know, she was so proud of him. He got all A grades she said. Worked like a man possessed, hardly saw him after you left. He seemed to turn very quiet, but I expect he was worrying about the exams. Then they moved straight after that I think. I remember it was a warm day because I was standing here watching while they got that piano into the van. Took about six of them. Do you remember the piano? Lovely instrument."

"Yes, I remember the piano," said Simon, fighting back the emotion. Another loss. So the letters must have been received here, it wasn't because they had moved. All A grades. That's Daniel. Probably did the same at A level too.

"I don't suppose they ever talked about me after I left?"

"Oh, I'm sure they must have, you and Daniel were always together, weren't you. But not to me. We just passed the time of day sometimes you know, that's all. Well, I must get on," said Mrs Meakin, turning back to her gardening. "Oh, the girl, Louise, she didn't go to London, she still lives here but I don't know where. She was going to get married to that young man of hers, but I don't know if she did."

Simon tried to see if that would be any help. No address for Louise. So not really. "OK, thank you, Mrs Meakin. Good bye."

He sat on the bike, putting on his helmet. He was getting hot in his bike jacket. Time to move. He started the bike and rode off, heart aching. He had pinned so much on this visit, his disappointment was a heavy weight in his chest. He had to keep blinking to keep his eyes clear of tears so he could ride the bike. He rode down past the Parade, it was just the same, he could not take the bike over the footbridge to the church so rode round, then to the church hall, that wall he had fallen over and the Scout hut behind. From there, so quickly to the junior school and into the city to Hooray Henrys. A last look. He wished he knew where Peter Holman lived. They had only ever been school friends. No, this was a now a farewell tour, not a glorious reunion. Two more places to go. He rode back out into his neighbourhood, to the spinney. Parking the bike, he walked through the spinney and along to the den. It was over grown and hard to access. Inside it was despoiled with rubbish. Just like his life. He turned away, images of happy days spent there with Daniel. He looked across the allotments. Where was Fielding these days, he wondered. Fielding was mild compared with the Watsons.

Once more, back on the bike, he followed the familiar route he and Daniel had cycled so many times. Out into the fields, to their hill, it only took about a quarter of an hour. There was the copse of trees, it looked the same. Should he leave the bike on the lane and walk up the hill? Suddenly he burst into loud, uncontrollable sobs. He had hoped for so much from today, the pain of his loss was as fierce as ever. What was the point of going up there? He knew that for whatever reason, the letters had been unanswered deliberately. The only comfort Simon could take was that perhaps they had been intercepted, the Bilthaven postmark giving away their authorship. That must be it. Daniel would have answered. Oh, but did Daniel then think that he, Simon, hadn't bothered to write? What pain that must have caused him! But then why no letters from Daniel? Even if he hadn't got Simon's, why didn't he write himself? Standing alone by his motorbike on a quiet country lane, Simon knew that this was a mystery that now would never be solved.

Sad, more lonely and desolate than ever, he started up the bike and rode as fast as he could away from it all, away from the memories, away from the city of his childhood, away from the pain – except that it was with him and however fast he rode, risking overtakes, using the power and speed of the bike reckless of his own safety, the torment stayed with him. He reached Nottingham before supper time, parking his bike in Dad's driveway.

"Hello, son, " said Dad when he went in. "Did you find your friend then?" Trust Dad not even to remember Daniel's name.

"No, they moved away the summer after we did."

"Oh. Supper's almost ready."

"Thanks, be there in a minute."

And that was it. Over.

21. *1964/8-9 College days*

Simon pushed the bike hard on the long ride back north, through variable weather, including one heavy rainstorm. His black Barbour suit kept him dry in these conditions but he was worried about water getting into the magneto or spark lead, which had happened before. Stuart had bound it up in waterproof tape and cleaned out the seals, and luckily nothing amiss happened this time. Visibility was a problem because the rain obscured his spectacles but once the weather cleared he was in bright summer sunshine and the warm light of an August early evening as he arrived back in Bilthaven, crossing the City Bridge at dusk.

He arrived home dispirited, the failure of his hopes for the trip south weighing heavily, and was met by further crushing news. The 'A' levels results were, inevitably, disastrous from Simon's point of view. Instead of the As and Bs once predicted, he scraped through with D in History, and E in each of English and Economics. Not only did Simon have to abandon his hopes of entering Dartmouth and a naval career - although he was certain that the physical damage done by the rape would cause him to fail the medical now anyway - but he had failed to reach the standard required for university entrance. He had hoped to study history or the law. The once high flyer brought low by the effects of devastating sexual degradation, the secret mental turmoil that had followed that, and would dog him for the rest of his life. Mum's disappointment was tangible which did little to help Simon.

This was made worse by the news that Ed had done well and would be going to university, where they had hoped to go together. Stuart commiserated, the friend he was, but was puzzled by Simon's poor showing. He was set to study engineering at Bilthaven College, and he and Kay were strong together by this time. Simon felt even more alone.

Simon had to think what to do. He revived his interest in trains and approached British Railways armed with his good GCEs and his 'A' levels which were at least passes. He hoped that this might grant him entry to some trainee management scheme, but all he was offered was a job as a station porter. He turned it down without hesitation.

Mum suggested he emigrate to New Zealand. Simon was taken aback. "Why New Zealand? It's miles from anywhere!"

"Exactly, my love. If there's a war, you would have the best chance of survival there. It's probably the one place where human civilisation might be able to carry on."

But Simon, aware though he was of the shadow of the bomb he had grown up under, was unwilling to leave everything he knew for the other side of the world.

By this time it was September and he was without a job and income of his own. He suggested to Mum that he train as a reporter; after all, he had good GCE English and had passed the 'A' level. For some reason he never discovered, Mum poured cold water over this idea of him following in her footsteps. She did suggest teaching, a useful stopgap she said and once qualified, he could do what he wanted, and if he found himself out of work, well, they always need teachers, don't they? She pulled strings with some of her many contacts in Bilthaven and secured Simon an interview at a teacher training college in Nusbury. This was a large town some miles from Bilthaven, but Simon had never been there and knew little of it. He went to Nusbury on the Thursday for an interview, was accepted the following Tuesday with instruction to start on Thursday, just two days later. He had a place in lodgings (digs) as all places in halls of residence had been already allocated. There was no guarantee there would be anywhere to keep the motorcycle so that was left in Russell's garage and Mum and Ken took him through in the car. The digs were within walking distance of the college buildings which was good, the other students there were second years, so he was not with anyone starting like him. But he had his own very small room, and the landlady and her husband agreed he could keep his motorbike in their garage, next to their car.

Simon opted to study history as his specialist subject of course, but he also had to study all other subjects, including maths. It was pointed out that he would have to pass the maths course to qualify, but Simon put that worry aside as being three years away. He got to know some other first year students, mainly because of a shared interest in motorcycles, there being quite a few parked under the hall of residence.

At the digs, he earned the unwelcome nickname of Groaner, this was because he could be heard in the night groaning in his sleep, a result of his recurring nightmares. He made sure from then on that his room door was kept tightly shut. A highlight of the week was a Thursday night when the landlady and husband had their night out at 'the club'. This left access to the television for the students and happily this was the night *Top of the Pops* was on which the students all watched. Sadly, the resident Afghan hound decided to join in the music and howled continuously whenever the music was played. This detracted from the enjoyment of the show, so a strategy was devised. It was found that the hound would also howl when the tomato slicer wires were plucked so as soon as the owners went out they took it turns to pluck away, the dog howling non-stop. By the time the programme started, the dog could howl no more and all that came out was a hoarse throaty whisper; and they could watch Top of the Pops undisturbed.

But such lighter moments did little to lighten Simon's mood. He was unsettled in Nusbury, did not like the course, history apart, and decided he would have no part of the extensive sexual activity in the college. His friends all found girlfriends, and one or two girls seemed to like Simon, but he did not respond and they went elsewhere. Fairly early on Stuart came over to see him, and spent a day with him and his friends, talking motorbikes and of course about girls. Stuart of course knew that Simon had been out with Diane, Ruth, Kelly and Natalie, although not about his failures, but he did jokingly make a remark that wherever Simon went, the population increased. Simon had had more girlfriends than Stuart. Once again, as when he had first arrived in Bilthaven, his reputation as a dark horse Casanova was secured, which Simon was quite happy with as it meant he would be left alone without any suspicion falling on him about any other sexual encounters he might have had. But being out in digs, he always felt something of an outsider, dependent on his friends for passing time in their rooms in hall for social interaction, which he did to the background of Bob Dylan songs like *"Mr. Tambourine Man"* and *"The Times They Are A-Changin'"*.

He made particular friends with Nicky, an ebullient Londoner who owned the fastest bike of the group, a tuned up BSA A10 650cc Rocket. They were different types but got on, partly because of the motorbikes, but Nicky found Simon's quieter, steadier ways a counterpoint to his own excesses sometimes and from Simon's viewpoint, Nicky's obvious regard for him was pleasing and helped revive a flicker of self esteem. He never confided in Nicky about his past, but was happy to take the friendship on the surface.

Most weekends, he was back on the bike on Friday night, back to Bilthaven. There he could at least be in his own space, ride along the coast in the sea air or take off into the hills. And of course there was Stuart, now his best friend, and to Simon's pleasure, that was mutual, Kay aside of course. Sometimes the three of them would go out in Stuart's Anglia, Simon in the back, but he enjoyed the company and not being in Nusbury. It was always with a certain heaviness of heart that he would return on Sunday evenings. He was not supposed to go home every weekend, in fact the colleges rules allowed for only two in each term, but his landlady was quite happy for him to; she was paid for him for seven days, so she made money on the deal.

The three years of the course dragged by, Simon spending holidays at Dad's, working much of the time, for money now, for the BBC thanks to Dad's contacts. He was able to put his earlier skills to good use and his good diction and Hooray Henrys accent, which he could still revert to from Bilthaven when required, were assets despite the huskiness and slight speech impediment residue of his suicide attempt. He learned to 'drive the panel', made short programmes, did continuity work and lost any nervousness of the microphone.

The practical parts of the teaching course were hard for Simon. There were many days spent in schools, and while he found he could get on well with the children, he found the actual teaching dull, repetitive and when issues of control arose with some of the children, very frustrating.

History was his refuge and his wide reading and willingness to do the unexpected reaped certain rewards. For example, the group were set the task of writing about an ancient civilisation, having been looking at Greece and Rome. But Simon decided to write his about China, the only student to do so, although one other had selected Egypt. There was also the option to study one country in detail, so of course Simon chose Germany. He was not the only one to do so, but one of only three. All students had to write a local history based on where they lived, so Simon, expected to do Bilthaven, produced a long and detailed illustrated history of just Swiford. The history course was run in parallel with the history degree course at Bilthaven University, one reason why Nusbury College's history course was so highly regarded. So it was especially pleasing that this local history earned him a distinction. Students also had to produce a specialist history on a topic of their own choosing. Some students came up with some very interesting topics but Simon was unique in producing one on the history of the motorcycle. Again, he was awarded a distinction for this work. Both these major works were of thesis length and standard.

Such was the workload of the history course, the same as the degree students at Bilthaven whose only concern it was, that his other studies suffered. Although his ability for concentration had returned to some extent, this was only when his interest was aroused and he still lacked the old discipline of being to apply himself to those subjects he thought dull, difficult or simply irrelevant.

The final year brought two setbacks. Firstly, Mum and Ken moved away from Bilthaven. Ken had got a new job in Whitehall and so they left Bilthaven and went to live in London. Mum got a job with the BBC there. Simon's plans to return to Bilthaven were now thrown into disarray. He knew that Mum and Ken thought he should be independent anyway and he felt he could not go to London. Also he found out that in order to gain qualified teacher status he would have to get a teaching job and teach for at least a year. This prospect filled him with dread, but not to do so would waste the three years spent at college.

22. 1967/9 Special developments

He graduated with a medium pass, except in history where he did very well. Quite how he passed the necessary Maths he was never sure, and also Physical Education, mainly based around team ball sports which he would be expected to teach, and to which Simon had rarely put in an appearance in later years. He decided for want of anything better to stay in Nusbury. He had done a teaching session during the course in a large primary school which he had liked, traditional in its ways with a firm discipline which kept the unruly elements in check. It was in a poorer part of Nusbury with declining industry, but the children were of a community and Simon had liked that about the school. So he was pleased when he was offered a job there. This would enable him to gain qualified teacher status after the first year.

He moved out of the college digs into a bedsit room in Nusbury, about a ten minute motorbike ride from the school. It turned out that the large house, once in Edwardian times a large family home, was now all bedsits and some of the tenants were less than desirable. Simon felt he could not rely on the safety of this home, and twice he came back to find his door forced and things missing.

On another occasion he came 'home' to find his door forced again, open and the young mother from across the landing in his room.

"What are you doing?" he asked.

The girl showed not the slightest flicker of disturbance. "Oh hello. I just wondered if you had any sugar coz I've run out and I need it for the babby."

"But you've broken the lock on the door!"

"Oh, don't worry about that. You don't have to fix it, that's the landlord's job. Have you got any sugar? I can't find it."

This view of things was so alien to Simon he simply opened the battered sideboard and took out his bag of sugar and poured some into an old cup and gave it to her.

"Thanks. I'll give it yer back."

"Please ask properly next time," he said by way of admonition.

But she just laughed, unmoved by Simon's request to observe what he felt were the social niceties. "Can tell you're a teacher," was all she said as she left with Simon's sugar. He wondered if it had been her the last occasions or others of his unsavoury neighbours.

Simon wedged the door closed and wept on his bed. It was his own bed from Bilthaven, from his childhood, so long ago it seemed. The different Simon, one with hope, undefiled, loved and loving. Simon did not think of Daniel so often now but in these days of despair and loneliness, he again felt the loss of his first love, his only love. He opened a tin of Irish stew and heated it on the electric ring, and ate his tea.

He had to leave his unsecured room to go to work, and remained behind in his classroom as he usually did, preparing and marking. Sometimes one or two children would stay behind to help and Simon was glad of their company, away from the formal classroom role. He was unwilling to go back to the sad solitude of the bedsit and delayed at school as long as he could. Another reason was the return of his piles. The shared toilet at the bedsit was simply revolting and his haste when using it exacerbated his problems. So he would delay at school and in the calm emptiness of the building, tolerated for this eccentricity by the cleaners, he could relax and take his time, replacing the unwelcome protrusions as best he could. He dreaded the return of the thrombosed external piles which made life impossible. When that did occur, he had to cope in silent anguish.

One morning he went down to find his BSA motorcycle lying on its side, petrol gone from the tank, acid from the under seat battery leaking out. The bike weighed several hundredweight, and only with great effort was he able to right it and get it back on the stand. There were some scratches which annoyed him. Incidents such as these increased his sense of persecution, his isolation and deepened his depression. He contemplated how he could end this misery, but memories of the agonies he had suffered before deterred him.

Lacking a base in Bilthaven, he could not go very often to see Stuart, but when he could, he travelled the miles between Nusbury and Bilthaven as quickly as possible. But he always had to return.

He would sometimes go to the pub with some of the people he had been at college with, several of whom had decided to stay in Nusbury. One of these was Nicky who was now in digs and having problems there.

They were in the pub one evening when Nicky asked, "Do you like your bedsit?"

"I hate it, you know I do," said Simon, surprised. "It's ghastly, and the neighbours are awful."

Nicky smiled. "So you wouldn't mind sharing a luxury flat with me?"

"Luxury flat? Where?"

"Not far away. It's in a private drive, converted house, an upstairs flat. Three bedrooms, lounge, kitchen."

Simon's heart leapt. "Shared toilet, though?"

"It's got its own toilet, separate from the bathroom, its own bathroom. You'd have to share the bog with me though."

"OK, you're on," said Simon.

"But you don't know how much it is or anything."

"I don't care. I'm in. Fifty-fifty?"

"Yes, of course, until we can get someone for the third bedroom, then thirds each."

"Even better," said Simon. "Here, I'll buy you another pint."

A few days later Simon left the bedsit for good. He and Nicky carried his bed through the Nusbury streets along with his odd bits of belongings. And of course the bike, now parked in the private driveway of houses, gated from the road, although in practice the gates were rarely shut.

His room was the biggest; why Nicky did not want that one he didn't know, but he wasn't going to argue. It turned out the smaller room was of course easier to heat. They acquired a television for the lounge, not colour, but 625 lines so it could receive the new BBC2 channel as well as BBC1 and ITV. The flat was furnished adequately and was also warm with gas fires, all on prepay meters. To Simon, this was heaven.

He was in Nusbury town centre one day and got chatting to a policeman, quite young, who was about his own age. It turned out that this man was not a full time policeman, but a part time volunteer, called a special constable. Simon's interest was caught by this, and he felt that perhaps this was something he could do which would give him an interest, follow his interest in the law and it appealed to his ethos of service, honed in his scouting days and to Simon exemplified by Daniel. And of course Daniel's father had been a policeman.

So Simon signed up and started the training, each Wednesday night at Nusbury's main police station. It was a large town, almost as big as Bilthaven, but had many problems which kept its police busy. He made some new friends this way. After a few months, he was kitted out in uniform and sworn in as a police officer, 'with all the powers and privileges of a constable'. Simon found that his powers were exactly the same as fulltime police officers, the regulars, except that theirs extended across all England and Wales, while his extended to his force area and neighbouring force areas only; a difference that had no practical impact.

Simon enjoyed this and it started to boost his self esteem and feeling of being worth something. He earned the respect of the regulars he worked with, to the point where unlike with some specials, they would ask him to join them. His reckless side meant that when it came to a ruckus, and there were many in the rougher parts of Nusbury, he didn't hang back, which the regulars soon appreciated. They also realised that he was an intelligent person who carried out his duties responsibly and was not going to get them into a mess. In some ways, he regarded the police as the first social service, there to protect and help the vulnerable, and his duties took him into the depths of deprivation that some people lived in. Some of the regulars found this view odd, regarding the police as a force, rather than a service, but Simon was able to make his case, which was accepted by most and actually converted one or two.

About this time he received another boost. Stuart and Kay were getting married, and he was asked to be best man. He had not expected this, although when he said as much to Stuart, the reply was, "Who else?". The wedding was held in Bilthaven of course, and one of Simon's jobs was to protect the Anglia from wedding vandalism, by providing a decoy car, actually Stuart's father's Cortina, and making it clear that it must not have things tied to it or daubs put across it. Everyone looked smart, the men in morning dress with carnation buttonholes, white, except for Stuart and Simon who wore red. The Cortina stood at the front of the reception hotel, unmarked, although Simon could see that Jamie Nash was sorely tempted. Simon warned him off. Jamie was impressed by Simon's police status, maybe that made the difference. It was good to see one or two Cermerton faces again, Kelly included, although many of the guests were people Simon didn't know, from Stuart's college days or his work. At the last second, Simon brought the Anglia round from its hiding place at the back of the hotel and Stuart and Kay set off on their honeymoon and married life together in a car devoid of embarrassing wedding paraphernalia.

At about this time, Nicky introduced Stanley into the flat. He was a student at Nicky's school, but he was their age, having entered college later. Simon was a bit annoyed that Nicky had done this without consulting him, but it meant that they had the third person and the costs were now split three ways. So Simon made the best of it, and as he got to know Stanley better, he liked him. He had a quiet yet forceful personality, which Simon found he took to.

One evening he returned in the small hours of the morning from a tour of police duty. Nicky was asleep in bed, but Stanley was still up. They sat in the lounge talking on the sofa, drinking coffee. Simon had undone his uniform tunic and removed his tie, and was feeling quite relaxed. He felt Stanley's hand on his stomach, gently pressing him backwards. Stanley's eyes met his, willing him to lie back. Simon felt that old feeling of being taken care of, of giving up control. As he lay back, Stanley felt Simon's now stiffening penis through his trousers, and then Simon felt the undoing of his belt and buttons. It was such a long time that Simon had had any sexual contact with anybody, he lay and waited as Stanley pulled his clothes down, his arousal reaching full potential as it was exposed. To Simon this was being transported into another world, back in time, and as Stanley took him and gently masturbated him, Simon was lost in his memories, thoughts of all things circling in his head. Of Daniel and the lost love but also of the Watsons, pulling his clothes off and playing with him before they did...

"Stop," said Simon, worried and confused.

"Why?" said Stanley. "You're beautiful, that's a beautiful, lovely big cock. It's hard, you're enjoying it."

"Just because it's hard doesn't mean I'm enjoying it," said Simon, thinking of that October night in Bilthaven. But he made no move to remove Stanley's hand. A thought occurred to him. "What do you mean, I'm beautiful?"

"You are," said Stanley. "You've a nice face, kind eyes, and you're fit, you've the body of an athlete. I've noticed you round the flat when you've not much on. I wanted to see the rest."

"Are you queer?" asked Simon, unnecessarily.

Stanley smiled. "Yes, I suppose I am. What about you?"

"No, I'm not," said Simon, automatically going into defence mode.

"You've never had a boyfriend?" asked Stanley in a disbelieving but friendly tone.

"Yes, but when I was a kid."

"Did he do this for you?"

"Yes, but ..."

"And you liked it then as you like it now," said Stanley, stating a fact.

Simon just nodded, emotions all over the place.

"So let me pleasure you, then."

Simon lay back, eyes closed while Stanley did just that. Simon had memories of Daniel's hand upon him, and Stanley's gentle but firm touch was so familiar yet different, arousing yet confusing. He reached his climax amid so many memories, Stanley wiping him with tissues extending the sweet thoughts of the past.

Stanley smiled at him. "For someone who's not queer, you enjoyed that."

Simon nodded. "It brought back a lot of memories."

"When did you last have sex?"

"With someone else? Years ago. Before I even came to college."

"You poor sod. Was that with him, the boyfriend?"

"No, I last saw him when I was fourteen. It was a girl."

"We'll have to put that right. I'd like to do so much more with you. And remember, my room has a double bed."

Simon nodded, knowing that despite all the pressures against it, this would happen. He looked at Stanley's shock of unruly dark hair, his hazel eyes. He was smaller than Simon by some inches, but had a strong presence that emanated from him.

"What about Nicky?" asked Simon. "He might find out."

"Why? He's out often enough."

Again, Simon nodded. There would be time.

Time there was. It became evident that Stanley found Simon attractive, who was flattered by this and it awakened his shut down emotions and sexual needs. Simon was fighting against being queer; all the social and professional pressures were against it even though homosexual acts between consenting adults in private were about to be decriminalised. He rationalised his relationship with Daniel as a growing phase; and then felt guilty about somehow demoting this most important relationship of his life. Torn as always, inner anguish between guilt and fear, of the social standards of the time and of discovery. But Stanley understood all this and there was a rapport between them, a mutual understanding that they would seek to satisfy their sexual needs as young men with each other but friendship was as far as it would go. This was not to be a love affair as with Daniel.

Partly Simon's nature, partly his lack of confidence and uncertainty allowed Stanley to take the leading role. Simon had no desire to be dominant sexually; that had resounding echoes of the force used upon him four years earlier and as it had with Kelly and Natalie, proved an insurmountable hurdle to taking the lead. So what was the alternative for Simon emerging from self inflicted celibacy apart from taking the subsidiary role with another male? It was after all the bulk of his sexual experience so far in life and one imbued in his mind with the greatest joy and happiness he had ever known. So Stanley, only slightly more experienced, took charge and treated Simon with gentleness, aware of some of his earlier trauma; with care and consideration, overcoming Simon's fears. Simon was appreciative of this but also found that his response was different. It was not like making love with Daniel, there was the legacy of that deep trauma and for Simon a certain stimulus found in subservience to this smaller man that touched on his deep feelings of inferiority, lancing and yet confirming them, the perceived degradation exciting some deep part of his post rape psyche. But Stanley too had issues and found that he had internal barriers to the relationship. Was it, as for Simon, the external pressure and condemnation that could follow? Was it simply because they could never be sure when Nicky might unexpectedly return?

Their sessions in Stanley's double bed in the flat were very tactile, sensual as well as sexual, but Simon realised that something was missing. Yes, it was sex and as such enjoyable, but it seemed that much more now was at stake than when he was younger. Exposure now would be even more life changing, and not for the better. But even more, massively, the ingredient that had made sex with Daniel so wonderful was missing; and that was love. He and Stanley liked each other, confided in each other and were friends, but Simon could not love Stanley. Tellingly, they never kissed. Gradually their sessions became fewer and eventually stopped altogether. Each knew that that for their own reasons the chemistry had not been right. They remained friends, confidants, and that lasted for life, although later separated by the ocean.

They were both sure too that Nicky was suspicious. Unreasonably he seemed to place the blame for 'corrupting' Simon squarely and exclusively on Stanley and the relationship became strained.

Simon was again obliged to turn in on himself, denying not only the unwelcome aspects of his sexuality but even his sexual needs, finding release and even more guilt in solitary pleasure.

As summer approached and the end of Simon's first year of teaching, he had a decision to make. The school, unaccountably, wanted him to stay on. Simon had found teaching unpleasant, the only lighter parts were those times when he could enjoy the company of the children outside the formal classroom structure. He had a rapport with them and most of them seemed to like him. This was a puzzle to Simon, but he accepted it.

Life in Nusbury had reached a sort of equilibrium; he enjoyed the police work, the flat was reasonable (although 'luxury' had been hyperbole) and there was a certain stability about life. He was earning reasonable money too, enough for his needs, and any alternative job would have paid less. He was offered a job as a Station Assistant in local radio which tempted him; he enjoyed his holiday work for the BBC, and had evidently impressed, but he lacked the self confidence to make the move. So, out of inertia, he stayed. He found a niche at the school for being in charge of what were then called audio-visual aids; tape recorders, radios, projectors and so on. He was innovative and brought his BBC experience to bear.

Another change that summer, as Paris erupted in riots and Robert Kennedy was murdered, was that Stuart wanted to sell the Anglia. It was now nine years old, but in good condition thanks to Stuart's care and expertise. He offered it to Simon who immediately accepted. He had found travelling to school by motorbike day in and day out over the years of his college course and his year of full time teaching a strain, especially in the winter. The car would be a step up, he could travel dry and warm and in his decent clothes, as well as carrying books and teaching aids much more easily. Stuart was buying a younger car, so Simon was glad of the opportunity. Stuart took the bike back as he had somewhere to keep it and while Simon remained its owner, Stuart would ride it for recreation and look after it. Sometimes Simon would have it back in Nusbury for a while, usually in the summer, but again only for pleasure, the car was now his transport.

Simon took the Anglia down to Nottingham but found a big increase in his petrol costs compared to the bike.

Later that summer Simon took the bike down to London to stay with Nicky at his parents' house. This was a gathering of former students and friends, some of whom had left Nusbury and had been teaching back in their home towns. The array of motorbikes outside Nicky's house was impressive.

Nicky's parents were away and so the party grew rather large. There was beer and spirits on offer and by the small hours when the bulk of local guests had left, there was the old gang with one or two others left sitting in the lounge.

They sat around talking, drinking and smoking. In this case cannabis. Simon was offered a joint by Cal, one of the London lot.

"I don't smoke," said Simon.

"It's not tobacco. Haven't you tried a joint before?"

"No. I tried smoking but I hated it."

"Try this, it's different."

So Simon took the joint. He might as well, he had nothing to lose. It was certainly different from his memory of the cigarette Ed had given him, and Simon waited for the effect of the drug to take hold. Nothing happened. The others continued to smoke and chat.

"Do you get the feeling that something is going to happen?" asked Nicky.

"Sort of," said Cal.

"Me too," said Simon, a feeling of deep foreboding now weighing heavily upon him. A feeling of unease. "Not something good."

"That's the joint," offered Cal.

"I felt a bit like this before," said Simon, who had now finished the joint. "The drug's had no effect."

Cal laughed. "If you say so."

Simon left it at that. Later they went to bed and slept, Simon's sleep being disturbed by fitful dreams and nightmares. This was commented upon in the morning. Simon felt embarrassed.

"Simon often has bad dreams," said Nicky by way of explanation. "I'm glad we have separate rooms in the flat."

Everybody chuckled at that, and just when Simon thought this would lead to questions about his nightmares, Nicky turned on the radio. The group sat still, stunned by the news that Soviet tanks had invaded Czechoslovakia, crushing the 'Prague Spring' that had seemed to offer hope for the future.

"I said something was going to happen," said Nicky, glumly. Nobody answered.

Later that day, the group dispersed, Simon crossing London to stay with Mum and Ken for a few days, before heading north, stopping with Dad and Phoebe then going up north again to Nusbury. Stuart took the bike back and Simon took the car ready for the start of the new term.

The difference in cost between the bike and the car was marked. He decided that for future visits to see Dad and Phoebe, he would find another person to share the cost. It was Stanley who came up with the solution. He was now in his final year at college.

"I'll put a notice up in the college," he offered. "There's bound to be a student who wants to get cheaply to Nottingham for the weekend and who can share the petrol."

So the notice was drafted. It was made clear to a prospective passenger that he would have to pay half the petrol and they would depart as quickly as possible on the Friday evening, returning on Sunday evening, possibly quite late. Simon hoped for a response and wondered what he would be like. But nothing happened. The days passed, and Simon resigned himself to having to bear the whole cost himself again.

He was in his room early one September evening when Nicky was shouting for him.

"Simon! You there?" Nicky came running up the stairs from where he had been tinkering with his motorcycle outside in the private road.

"What is it?" asked Simon coming out onto the landing.

"Two birds down there. They were asking for Stanley but I think it's you they want."

Puzzled, Simon went downstairs to the front door. Standing in the private road at the foot of the steps were two young women. One was taller with short, streaked blond hair, but the other, who caught Simon's attention, was small, petite even, with dark hair and deep brown eyes that seemed somehow to radiate strength and vulnerability at the same time.

"Are you the one going to Nottingham," asked the fair one.

"Yes, that's right. Are you after the lift?"

"That's me, actually," said the petite one. "Mansfield really but that's not far away."

Simon knew where Mansfield was, slightly off his route, so he was a bit disappointed, but that was outweighed by his pleasure that it was the petite one that wanted the lift.

"That's OK," said Simon. But he must not allow his stirred feelings to negate the whole purpose of the deal. "It's for half the cost of the petrol - both ways," he added hastily.

The girl nodded and agreed. "My name's Karen Turner," she said.

"I'm Nora," said the blond one. "We're in digs together not far away."

"Second years, then?" said Simon, realising that they must be at the teaching college because that was where the notice was with Stanley's name on it.

"No, first," said Karen, shyly. "But there were no places in hall left. But it's not far away."

Simon regarded her hesitancy which seemed to mirror in some way his own, and was pleased with his passenger. It had never occurred to him that a girl would turn up to share a car with an unknown man.

Such was the prosaic and uninspiring first meeting with Karen. One that was to have deep consequence for them both, sharing as they would a life together with all its triumphs and pain to come. But neither at that point had any inkling that this mercenary start was anything other than a purely financial arrangement.

That Friday evening the two set off on their journey together, one that would last for decades through the turmoil to come.

Book Three – Pandora's Box

1. *1968/9 Karen*

"Just drop me at Ollerton roundabout," said Karen, unexpectedly.

Simon thought about this as the little car sped between the trees of the forest in the darkness. "Is someone meeting you there?"

"I'll get a bus," replied Karen, but sounding a bit uncertain.

They arrived at Ollerton roundabout, well known because it was the meeting of several roads, but for little else. It was a roundabout, in the countryside. There was nothing else there and it was completely dark by this time. There were some lights perhaps a mile away. Ollerton itself perhaps? Simon pulled the car off onto the verge and stopped.

"Where's the bus stop?" he said trying to see in the light of his headlights.

"It's around here," said Karen.

"We'll wait until a bus comes then," said Simon, turning off the engine, unwilling to leave this young woman, still a teenager, on her own in darkness in the middle of the countryside. He felt the need to reach out to her, to protect her, yet fascinated by this core of determination she was showing to get home, whatever it took.

"It's not coming, is it?" he said in the end. Karen said nothing, and Simon knew then that there was no way he could just leave her there, with her bag, on the nocturnal roadside. "I'll take you," he announced.

"No, you don't have to do that," said Karen, a bit startled by this sudden offer.

"Well, I'm certainly not leaving you here, all alone," said Simon firmly, starting the engine again. He was annoyed because this was several miles out of his way, and it was already late, but he knew he could not abandon her. They drove the several miles to the town.

"You'll have to give me directions to the house," said Simon.

"No, just drop me in the market square. I'll be all right from there."

"I'll take you home, I might as well."

"No I can get a bus from here."

Simon gave in. The market square was well lit, and here there were buses in evidence. "So I'll see you on Sunday evening then, eight o'clock, back at Ollerton roundabout?" he queried.

"Yes, thank you. See you then," she said, getting out of the car.

So he dropped off this strange but single-minded girl, and set off for Dad's house. He saw Karen in his rear view mirror, walking away with her bag, unsure what to make of her, but feeling a strange affinity for her, a feeling that was familiar and yet so distant. Was it Ruth? Daniel? Diane perhaps? Certainly he felt a stirring of a sexual kind, all jumbled up with exasperation at her stubbornness, admiration for her fearless strength of mind and yet feeling the urge to shelter and care for this innocent.

After the weekend with Dad and Phoebe, Simon set off home and arrived at Ollerton roundabout at the appointed time. A white Rover was waiting, and Karen got out, along with several other people, an older woman and three men. Simon felt a moment of anxiety – was there some hostility towards him for bringing Karen alone in his car? There was no hostility, but a mixture of curiosity, inspection committee and protectiveness to Karen, the only girl among four brothers. A brief conversation with her parents Rita and Vince, and two of her brothers and Simon appeared to have passed, for the time being anyway. They bade farewell and set off on the long drive back to Nusbury.

Over the next few weeks, Simon found himself visiting Dad more often than he might normally have done. Karen was not especially enjoying college, and her digs were pretty bad; the landlady, unlike Simon's old one, was very mean, meals were the barest portions and the rain came in the bedroom so that a plastic sheet was put over the bed. So Karen was anxious to escape at every opportunity and her landlady raised few objections because, as had Simon's before, she would make on the deal. Simon accepted this because he found he wanted to see her more. They became closer and started to meet up in Nusbury, going for a drive, sometimes to a pub, just talking. He found her an enigma, vulnerable yet strong, quiet yet determined. For her part she thought Simon dependable and kind, and obviously keen on her. As a teacher he was able to offer practical advice and his student days were recent enough for him to help there, although Karen was not studying history.

Simon was wary of starting a new relationship after so many failures, but the draw of this quiet young woman was too strong. Not only did he feel a strong physical attraction but there was a meeting of minds. She was intelligent, curious and of course Simon felt flattered when she would listen to his viewpoint. But he liked it that she was always ready with hers too.

They took fish and chips up to Umbly Top, a rocky outcrop about three hundred feet high that gave a commanding view across the town. There was a track that led to the top and a place to park, so they sat with the lights of the whole town spread before them.

"I wonder how far you can see from here," said Karen.

"From this height, several miles. Probably about twenty," said Simon doing a rough calculation in his head. Having to teach mental arithmetic was improving his own! "That's probably Bilthaven over there," he added, pointing to a distant glow on the far horizon. "That's about twenty miles."

He reached across to pick up Karen's fish and chip paper and found himself close, so close to her. Their lips met and then they were kissing, Simon putting his arms round her slight frame. Then he pulled back and they looked at each other, each uncertain of the other's response.

"That's nice perfume," he said in the end. "What is it?"

"Lancôme Magi Noir," she replied.

"Very nice," said Simon, and then he kissed her again.

And so their close friendship became more and the only part of their relationship that had been missing was now in place. Simon thought it was inevitable really, they had become so close, he wondered now what had taken so long. Probably his own fears and doubts, his own underlying insecurity which was never far from the surface but which he managed to keep hidden from the world, most of the time.

Simon was not the only young teacher at the school. One day Len Buxton approached him.

"I'm thinking of arranging a trip to the Lake District with some fourth year boys[2]," Len said. "I would need another teacher and I wondered if you would like to come along."

The Lake District. Simon thought back to the childhood holidays, learning to row and climbing Great Gable.

"Yes, that would be good," he said. "Where would we stay? Camping?" he added, with doubts about catering for a group of boys and the logistics involved.

"No, youth hostels," said Len. "A roof over our heads, and hot meals."

"That sounds better," said Simon, smiling. And so the deal was done, a decision that was to have momentous consequences, one brick in the wall of Simon's eventual downfall. But for now, he was optimistic. He had Karen, his police work was going well and although teaching was still irksome, he thought that life was perhaps turning out OK.

Spring came and with it the trip to the Lake District. Len had arranged two youth hostels, and one or two walks as well as a boat ride. Nothing as ambitious as Great Gable though. But Simon enjoyed the trip, finding the company of the boys satisfying, away from the classroom grind. The relative informality appealed to him, he felt he could relate to the boys, taking him back to his scouting days. He enjoyed being 'patrol leader' again, relaxing in their friendship and evident regard for him, his self esteem rising. He was looking back to his own childhood certainly, reliving those happy times before he was severed from his early days. All that was missing was Daniel, dear Daniel. The trip became an annual event, although it was to change and become longer and more ambitious later.

While Simon and Karen kissed and explored each other, they were not in a full sexual relationship. This would be a major step for Karen and she was also terrified of getting pregnant. This had always held her back. As for Simon, he

---

[2] Now known as Year 6

was content as it meant he did not have risk more failure in that area. Also he felt that once again, he would be taking a girl's virginity, and felt unsure about the responsibility of that.

That summer, having sat enthralled like most of the planet as Neil Armstrong set foot on the moon, he travelled down to stay with Karen's family who had taken Simon under their wing. He spent a few days with Dad, also taking Karen to meet him and Phoebe. Dad seemed taken with Karen, although she was wary, as Simon had told her a little of his childhood. Then on to London to see Mum and Ken, but this time Karen went with him. He wanted Mum to meet Karen. Their relationship had evolved to where they spent as much time together as possible, when Simon was not on police duty.

Mum made them welcome, and with the correctness of her generation had allocated them separate rooms. Simon was secretly relieved at that. Karen seemed a little overawed by Mum and Ken. On their part they found her hesitant and quiet. Karen's working class, mining roots, to which she would forever remain loyal, were in contrast to Mum as a news Editor for the BBC and Ken with his senior job in Whitehall. Frances came over as well. Simon did not get to see his sister much now. She was with her boyfriend, an artist and designer, Sean. Simon did his best to reassure Karen and the visit settled down. Mum and Ken would get up early and go to work, leaving Simon and Karen to get their breakfast. One morning, when the house was quiet, he walked along the landing to Karen's room.

"Are you OK?" he asked.

Karen, still in bed, nodded. "Get in," she said. "Let's have a cuddle before we get up."

Simon climbed into the narrow bed with her. He looked into her big brown eyes and they kissed. His love for Karen demanded more and soon they were running their hands over each other, passion rising, removing each other's night wear until they were close, naked together, pressed by the confines of the single bed. He felt her love through the soft touch of her warm skin. He was now extremely aroused and wanted her more than anything. He pressed closer, Karen frowned slightly but nodded. Aware of her maidenhood, he moved above her and pressed gently.

"Haven't you got a Durex?" asked Karen.

Simon had dreaded this yet knew the wisdom of it. "Yes, wait a moment." He climbed out and ran to his room where he retrieved one from his bag. He hoped it wasn't out of date or anything. He took it back and climbed back next to Karen.

"Are you sure?" he asked her.

Karen nodded. "Yes, being in bed with you like this is amazing. I didn't know it would feel like this."

Simon had to smile at her childlike delight in the naked contact. He rolled the Durex on and still erect, he tenderly entered. With Karen he felt relaxed and this gave him confidence. He could push the nightmare thoughts away. She pulled him down and in, the pleasure on her face increasing Simon's delight and self-belief. He remembered, as always, Daniel's dictum that sex is about giving, and so used his experience recalled from many years earlier to give Karen the greatest pleasure. Her climax was stunning and instantly brought Simon to his, the mutual fire of orgasm enveloping them both. They relaxed as he withdrew and removed the Durex.

"Wow!" said Karen, with feeling.

"Was that OK?" asked Simon, perhaps unnecessarily.

"I'll say! But what about you?" asked Karen with sudden uncertainty. "You've done it before. Was it.... Was I...?"

"You were fantastic," said Simon, holding her close and kissing her. Oh, how he loved this young woman! He couldn't believe that this was his first time with a girl since Natalie, more than five years earlier. There had been Stanley of course, but Simon felt he could put that behind him now.

Back in Nusbury and the new term. He and Nicky now had the flat alone again, Stanley having finished college and left for a teaching job down south. A new class for Simon, and for Karen, a move from the rotten digs into a hall of residence, sharing a room with Nora. Their love grew and they spent as much time together as they could, sharing Simon's bed at the flat, watching the new Midnight Movie on BBC2, he offering advice and helping Karen with her college work, preparing visual aids for her, evenings in the room at the hall, until 10 pm curfew and visitors, especially male visitors, had to leave. He would walk back down to the flat, happy.

The months went by as they drew ever closer. There was no one day when it was decided they should get married. It was an understanding that evolved, was taken as a given over time. When Karen finished her college course, they would marry.

"Do you realise you've never actually proposed to me?" said Karen one evening.

"Haven't I? Must put that right then." Simon knelt on one knee next to Karen who was sitting on the sofa. She started to giggle.

"Keep a straight face, please," said Simon.

"OK," she answered, forcing her lips closed but barely able to stop smiling. Simon took hold of Karen's hand and kissed it.

"Karen Turner, will you do me the honour of marrying me and becoming my wife?"

"Of course. You can get up now." They laughed and hugged and kissed.

The announcement, when it was made, came as no surprise to anybody. The consensus from Karen's family, Simon's Mum and Dad, was, "What took you so long?"

They bought each other rings to announce their status and started saving in earnest. Then there was the question of where to live. They both decided they wanted to buy a house. Simon's Mum's advice was to buy as soon as possible as property prices always go up. "Even one brick on top of another," she said, "and then you can work your way up."

Karen took holiday jobs, as did Simon, getting paid for local radio work, and saving as much as he could out of his teaching salary. Prices in Nusbury were out of their reach, but they looked at a new estate at Hilltown just a few miles from Nusbury. Small two bedroomed houses could be just within their grasp if they could raise the deposit and get a mortgage. Then Karen's Mam Rita came out with an extraordinarily generous offer – she would pay the deposit they needed. They could now look seriously for a house to buy.

Karen was interested in the world and they talked much of politics and current affairs. Both enthused over Concorde's first supersonic flight and like most of the world, were gripped by the plight of Apollo 13. He missed her while away on the trip to the Lakes, but he and Len enjoyed it, the weather as usual in late May was kind.

Simon was busy through the election campaign with police duties and while helping police a rally in Nusbury, was surprised by how good a speaker Edward Heath was in the flesh compared with his wooden television performances. But as Karen shrewdly remarked, Clement Attlee would have won no points on television. On election night, Simon was responsible for escorting a ballot box from a polling station to the count at Nusbury College, with a double decker bus laid on to carry just it, himself and the driver. Next day Edward Heath was Prime Minister.

In the summer, Rita made another surprise announcement.

"Why wait until next summer to get married?"

"Because that's when I leave college, Mam," explained Karen. "I'll have a job then and we can afford it."

"You know Archie and his family will be gone then," countered Rita, referring to one of her brothers, Karen's uncle, who was preparing to emigrate to New Zealand. "I think you should get married around Christmas. And anyway, everything's going up in price with this government, so the sooner the better."

So it was decided. December was the date. Back in Nusbury, they found a house in Hilltown on the estate they had been looking at. It had two bedrooms, was two years old, on the end of a block of five, had central heating but no garage.

"If it's a choice between us being cold or the car, we win," said Simon. Their offer was accepted. Simon managed to arrange a mortgage through the union. It would be £24 a month, over a third of his salary, but when Karen started working, that would be easier.

Winter drew in while they waited for the house sale to go through. Simon was feeding cash to the gas fire in his bedroom constantly but it was still cold. In late November, the house was theirs. On moving day, Simon woke up in the flat to find his glass of water next to his bed was frozen. He had arranged for a van to collect his things, and he said good bye to Nicky, who was in the throes of buying the house with its two flats from the landlord, and followed the van in the car to Hilltown.

There was little furniture, but all the carpets and curtains had been left, and it was warm! Karen came over and they spent the evening in their new house. Simon's joy when getting up next morning into a heated bedroom was immense.

The next few weeks were hectic, getting the house ready. They were given a washing machine and a chair and sofa. A hired television, a second hand fridge, and a double bed! And the wedding plans continued at full speed. It was to be in Mansfield, and so Rita did most of that, and Simon was content to let her.

The wedding, just before Christmas, was on a bright, cloudless, crisp sunny day. Happy the bride! There were no rockets, but there were bells, poetry, a choir and a red carpet. When Simon saw Karen in her wedding dress, with a long train behind, he thought she looked like a princess! Stuart was best man of course, and Kay was there. Karen's train got caught on the carpeted step as she went up to the waiting priest, pulling her head back, but Simon quickly noticed this and went back to release it, to murmurs of approval. The ceremony was something of a blur to Simon, his eyes were on Karen the whole time. They signed the register – and they were man and wife!

Rita had hired a single deck bus to transport everyone from the church to the reception. This went on all afternoon, Simon and Karen changed and Stuart brought the Anglia round, with echoes of his own wedding. And then they were off. They had put so much money into the house that the honeymoon was a couple of nights in a good hotel in Malton in Yorkshire. The newspaper said the honeymoon was in Malta, and Simon saw no reason to correct that.

They were back in Hilltown before Christmas which was just as well because Karen's family were coming. It was crowded and hectic with airbeds and sleeping bags on the lounge floor but there was a turkey dinner for all and it was a real family Christmas.

In the new year, Simon was back at work, Karen back to college. Simon gave her a lift each morning into Nusbury and then went on to the school, collecting her afterwards. Her college friends, those who hadn't been at the wedding, wanted to hear all about it and about married life. But through a mix of shyness and discretion, Nora who had been at the wedding, was the only one she talked to. As for Simon, he was happy. Karen had come like a breath of fresh air into his life in his twenties and with her Simon found deep love and sexual fulfilment and the past receded into the background. The nightmares became fewer and Karen never called him 'groaner'. On those occasions when he did wake, sweating and anxious, Karen usually remained asleep next to him. He would look at her, her hair tousled lying across the pillow, her gentle breathing; he felt reassured and would drift back to sleep.

When Karen finished her course and earned her Teaching Certificate, she got a job in a primary school on the far side of Nusbury. It meant a longer drive for Simon, through the town and then back again, but now Karen was earning, they were quite comfortable.

Karen though was still deeply embedded in her family, and they travelled frequently to Mansfield. The Anglia was now really showing its age, and its lack of power was frustrating Simon, especially when he got trapped behind a lorry and could not move swiftly into a gap in the outside lane to overtake. So it was sold, and a newer Ford Escort was bought at a bargain price from a second hand dealer in Nusbury.

Rita liked to travel, cruises especially, along with the family, and now Simon was included. Now both he and Karen were earning they had the money for this. On the ship there was something for everyone and each could do what they wanted. Simon enjoyed this, he liked the sea still, and *Oriana* was a luxury ship and the food was simply superb! Karen moaned about the weight she put on and was envious of Simon who seemed to be able to eat what he wanted and remain slim. They were in Lisbon in the aftermath of the revolution that toppled the regime set up by the dictator Salazar. In Madeira they took the famous sledge ride down the mountain. Simon loved to travel and enjoyed these opportunities. Karen was less keen on the sea, never a good traveller, she suffered sea sickness. In vain, Simon pointed that Nelson had also suffered badly from this.

A more basic ship was the Romanian *Transylvania* usually used to take favoured workers of the communist state on cruises. But in an effort to earn foreign currency, this was now used to take westerners around the Black Sea. At the Bulgarian port of Varna, they were followed everywhere by men in long black coats, and the locals were reluctant to speak to the visitors. It was a very run down place. But at the Soviet naval base of Odessa, the atmosphere was much freer. Simon took many photographs, even of the warships, and of course the Potemkin Steps. He chatted to a policeman for a while who was very proud of his new car. Yalta was fascinating and Sochi too. Being back in Istanbul reminded him of being there with Ruth, and he wondered how she was. Back at Varna, it took an hour for the small airport to start all four jet engines of the Dan Air Comet.

Simon also put his radio experience to use again. The BBC local station was starting some schools programmes, and Simon got the job of presenting a kind of magazine programme aimed at junior schools. The others involved were almost all teachers as well. One later became a famous children's author.

Simon had now been teaching six years, and had been promoted within the school for his work with audio visual aids. It became apparent though that newer teachers who had the new B.Ed. degree had better promotion prospects than certificated teachers like him. So Simon signed up for a degree course, the university education that had been stolen from him a decade earlier by the

Watsons. Harold Wilson's[3] greatest legacy was the Open University which meant that Simon could continue to work and study part time. Soon this came to dominate their lives as the weekly units arrived by post. But Simon found a way of combining this with his visits, usually every other weekend, to Mansfield. The Escort, which had been as underpowered as the Anglia, and which Simon suspected of being a restored crash wreck, gave way to a brand new Ford Cortina, with a punchy two litre engine with no power problems at all. This made the regular run much more feasible. While Karen spent time with her family, Simon would retreat for much of the time upstairs and work through his units for the two weeks, leaving him much freer when at home. The second bedroom at home became a study for doing the assignments. This was a Social Sciences course, and covered sociology, psychology, politics, philosophy and linguistics as well as education. Simon found it interesting, and so did Karen. Although it was possible to take up to six years, Simon would complete the course in three and gain the degree with distinctions.

Len Buxton left the school, and Simon took over the Lake District trip himself. Because the bus cost was so great, he lengthened the trip to the whole week, rerouting through the mountains, using four hostels now, and including Great Gable. He also asked the boys to keep a diary, one boy writing after climbing Great Gable in glorious weather, "This has been the greatest day of my life". Simon still found the trip an antidote to the classroom, enjoying time with the boys, indulging in rough and tumble, setting up wide games as he had for his scout patrol. The boys loved this and many wanted to go again.

Simon had little time off school, but his piles remained a problem. Unluckily, there were times when he could not replace the protrusion, and it became swollen, thrombosed, causing Simon great pain. One day in the classroom, this was so great that he collapsed, tearful and shaking. The class were upset, but one bright lad immediately ran for help, and Mr Cooper, the headmaster came along. Simon improved enough to go to the head's office to recover. The head arranged another teacher to look after the class.

"What's the problem?" asked Mr Cooper kindly.

"It's personal," said Simon.

"Not when you collapse in front of the class like that," Mr Cooper replied. "Then it becomes my concern. And my concern for a valued colleague as well."

"It's piles," admitted Simon. "I've been plagued with them since I was seventeen."

"That's young. Do you know what brought them on?"

"Yes. Something happened," said Simon, now close to tears again with the pain and the fear of talking about the rape. Mr Cooper saw his distress.

"Well, anyway, do you get treatment?"

---

[3] Labour Prime Minister, 1964 – 1970, 1974-76

"Not really. Just ointments but when they get really bad like this, they don't work."

"My wife had them when she was expecting, but nothing like this. Please get some treatment."

"Yes, I'll see what I can do."

"I think you had better go home for today at least. Can you drive?"

"I'll manage that. It's not very far."

"If you can, let me know by tonight if you're coming in tomorrow or not."

"Yes, thank you, Mr Cooper."

Simon went to the doctor. He also spoke to Mum on the phone, who immediately got the bit between her teeth. She rang back the next day.

"When you have a problem you go to the top. I've found the top bum man in Britain, but he's here in London of course."

"I don't care if he's in Timbuktu," said Simon.

He went back to the doctor with the name and hospital. The London location raised an eyebrow, but the referral was made. So began a series of visits to London for Simon where he was given painful injections that constricted the offending veins. They worked for a while, but then they returned, and another trip to London was needed. He could usually do this in a day, catching an early train from Bilthaven and getting one back at teatime, he would be home by late evening. But this served only to revive in Simon unwelcome and unwanted memories, resurrecting his anger at the rape and all his problems stemming from that night in October 1963.

In 1974 he and Karen left the little house in Hilltown for a new build, three bedroom detached house on the outskirts of Nusbury and not far from Simon's school. This was helped by the rapid inflation, and a big 'catch up' pay rise from the new Labour government, but the new mortgage was still a lot. Karen got a transfer to a school much closer which made the long drive in the mornings unnecessary. Also that year Simon took the advanced driving test and passed, qualifying for membership of the Institute of Advanced Motorists (IAM). The examiners are all Class 1 police instructors like Bernard had been and his knowledge of *Roadcraft* stood him in good stead.

Added to this, a near neighbour was a regular police officer he knew who was now working on motor patrol, the big police cars. Specials rarely got to work traffic, but his friend used to pick Simon up when he was single crew and he would work a shift with him, operating over a much wider area and dealing with drunk drivers and traffic accidents, including one horrendous one near Hilltown where a small car with seven teenagers went out of control down a steep hill at speed and hit a bridge support. Every police vehicle available was sent to the scene, as well as ambulance and fire service of course. All seven were killed, and some cops were physically sick at the scene of carnage. There were body parts spread about and it was hard to tell what make of car they had been in. Simon managed not to be sick and did his best to help. But he didn't want to see many more like that.

2. 1976 Robert

"I want a baby," said Karen. This was said as they lay in bed one night. Simon's mind raced. He was still doing his Open University course which took up so much time. And a baby!

"We said we'd wait until I finished the degree," he said.

Karen turned to him, eyes loving and pleading. "But if we start now, it could be ages before I get pregnant, and so the baby won't be born until you finish anyway."

Simon felt a sense of panic. This was a whole new area of responsibility, was he ready for this? The self doubt surged up again. Children of his own were something he had only thought about for the future, he didn't feel the same urgency that Karen was showing.

"I'll think about it," he said, and kissed her.

"OK then, but don't just think for too long," said Karen, smiling. "It takes more than just thinking."

They kissed and turned the lights out. Lying in the darkness, Simon thought about the implications of what Karen had asked. It would be a major change and their lives would alter course for ever. If Simon had only known by how much!

But Karen's persistence won the day and contraceptive precautions were abandoned. Naturally Simon enjoyed this aspect of it.

It wasn't long before Karen said, "I'm late."

"How late?" asked Simon.

"Almost a week."

Simon knew that Karen was very regular, thirty days on the dot! So a week late was very unusual.

"We'd better go to the doctor and make sure, then," said Simon.

Simon held Karen's hand as they went in together to see the doctor.

Dr Sengupta looked at Karen, and then felt her breasts.

"Oh yes, no doubt, you're pregnant," she said.

"Don't you need more tests?" asked Simon.

"I know when a lady is pregnant," replied Dr Sengupta tartly. "When was your last period?"

"Almost six weeks ago," said Karen, smiling happily at Simon.

"So it will be early November then," said the doctor.

That summer turned out to be one of the longest and hottest on record. There was a drought and severe restrictions on water usage were imposed. But Karen was blooming. She decided that she wanted to be at home to look after the baby, so in the summer, quit her teaching job. They would be dependent on Simon's salary alone, but he had had another internal promotion and although it would be tight, they could manage.

Lying in bed one night, Karen suddenly let out a sharp little cry.

"What's the matter?" asked Simon anxiously.

"I felt the baby move!" she said, eyes shining. "It's moving round. It feels really strange." She placed her hand on her tummy. "Yes, there it is. You feel."

Simon placed his hand gently on Karen's bump. He could feel nothing. He was just about to move his hand when there was a slight rippling feeling under his hand, and then a sudden hardness.

"Ouch," said Karen. "It just kicked I think."

"Yes, I felt that," said Simon. Emotions welled up in him; this was his baby, and he had just for the first time, felt this child's physical presence.

"You are just amazing," he said to Karen, and kissed her. "It's going to be fine."

The long hot summer lasted late into the year, but it gradually cooled as winter approached. The bump was now large, and Simon would rush back from school each night to see if Karen was all right. Of course she had the school's phone number but Simon wanted to see for himself.

Simon finished his course and graduated with distinctions across the board. He was tempted to go on to a higher degree, but he realised that the imminence of fatherhood made that impractical.

November arrived and the weeks went by. It was two weeks past the due date when one evening while watching television, Karen got up and went to the bathroom. She came down again.

"What's it like when your waters break?"

"I don't know," said Simon, "and I'm never likely to. Why?"

"I think my waters have broken," she said, anxiously. "I think it's on the way."

"Right then," said Simon, "Action stations!" He phoned the hospital and explained the situation. They asked about contractions; Karen shook her head, so they were told to wait.

Simon put the phone down again – and they waited.

Next morning, there was no change, so Simon went off to work, with Karen saying she would phone as soon as there was any change. He could hardly concentrate on his work and every time there was a knock at the classroom door, he jumped in anticipation, but it was always routine.

Back home, he found Karen anxious. He made her sit on the sofa, feet up while he got the tea ready, which he often did anyway, with especial purpose now. The television was used to take their minds off it but halfway through the news, Karen said she felt the contractions.

"How often?" asked Simon, tenderly.

"Just once," said Karen, "but it was definitely there."

A short time later there was another.

"Are you sure it's not those false ones they warned us about?" asked Simon.

"Braxton Hicks," said Karen, wincing as another contraction was felt. "They seem real enough to me. Phone the hospital!"

By this time the contractions were more frequent, and hospital said to go in.

"Come on then," said Simon, picking up the bag they had packed ready, turning off the television and the lights. He took Karen out to the car.

"Is it time?" came a shouted call from a neighbour.

"Yes, we think so," replied Simon.

"Good luck then, let us know."

Simon drove carefully to the hospital and took Karen into the maternity wing. They were greeted by a harassed nurse and the place seemed very busy. Soon Karen was changed and on a trolley. A midwife nurse examined her and said everything was OK.

"But we are very busy at the moment," the midwife said. "She will need to wait here until we can find a room."

So they waited, Karen on the trolley, Simon pacing around, anxious.

"Stop pacing, Simon," said Karen, "you're making me nervous."

"Sorry, love," said Simon and stayed next to the trolley, holding Karen's hand. The midwife kept coming back and with a little ear trumpet pressed to the bump, announced that all seemed fine with the baby.

The evening wore on into night. Karen's contractions continued at the same pace but to Simon seemed to be getting more intense judging by Karen's reaction.

Later, the midwife came again. "I think we should get her into a room now." She wheeled Karen along the corridor past several rooms where women were in labour, some crying out. The crying of young babies could be heard too.

"We've managed to get a bed in here," said the midwife, drawing the trolley into a large room. There were sinks along one wall, all shining stainless steel, and some machinery. It was obvious this was not a regular birthing room.

The midwife saw the look of concern on Simon's face. "Don't worry, we have all we need, she'll be fine."

The night passed, with just fitful sleep for both of them. Breakfast was some toast and a cup of tea.

"I'll have to phone the school," said Simon and left Karen to find a phone. He spoke to Mr Cooper, who said of course he should stay, they would manage.

In the morning the doctor decided to induce the birth. Under the effect of the drug, the contractions grew more frequent as the day wore on. A new team was now on duty and the new midwife kept returning and examining Karen.

"Baby's definitely on the way," she said. Then she took an instrument with which she tried to break the waters. Karen winced.

"The waters broke before we came to the hospital," said Simon, worried.

"I don't think so," she said, and poked again. No waters came out. "I'll be back later."

By early evening, Karen was in pain and crying out with the contractions. The ear trumpet however gave no cause for concern. Simon was worried but had to place matters in the hands of the nurses.

At last, some twenty four hours after coming to hospital, the baby was really on its way. Alternately told to push, relax and breathe, the baby made its way towards the outside world. Simon watched as the crown of the baby's head appeared. There were cuts on it and evidence of bleeding. But this was a different midwife and anyway, this was not the time to complain.

"Push," the nurse urged. Karen pushed, and then the baby's head was out. Suddenly the midwife leapt forward and grasped what looked to Simon like a large grey pipe and snapped it over the baby's head, and then again.

"What was that?" asked Simon.

"The cord was round baby's neck, twice," said the midwife.

Then suddenly, the baby was out. A boy. Robert. Small and frail looking, and very dark grey in colour.

"Is that all right?" Simon asked, concerned.

"He'll soon pinken up," was the cheery reply. The baby whimpered, and then peed on the sheet.

"Well, that's working anyway," said the midwife, and she cleaned the baby, and wrapping him up, placed him in Karen's arms.

"Well done, my precious," said Simon, giving Karen a hug and a kiss on the forehead.

"We need to be in," said the midwife, indicating Simon should move away. "We need to stitch her up a bit where there's a tear."

While they dealt with the afterbirth and stitching, Simon looked at his son. What he found amazing was his son was looking back at him. And as Simon walked across the brightly lit room, wearing his white gown, the baby's eyes followed him, and appeared to be focused on this bright white moving object. The midwife said it was impossible, but Simon knew what he saw. He checked this by walking back and forth across the room, about six to eight feet from Robert. Each time, the baby's eyes tracked him, watching him. Simon wondered about imprinting, taking him back to Konrad Lorenz's work with animals in that area.

"Have you a name yet?" asked one of the nurses.

"Robert," said Simon, and Karen nodded. This had been agreed.

A few days later, Karen and Robert were ready to come home. Simon had the straps for the carry cot already installed in the Cortina. He drove to the hospital and Karen was waiting. Robert was placed in the carry cot. Simon made to pick it up.

"No. I'll carry it to the car," said the nurse. "It's our responsibility until you leave the hospital."

She put the carry cot on the ground next to the car while Simon unlocked.

"He's lovely, such a sweet little face," said the nurse, bending over to tickle Robert's chin. As she did, a pair of scissors fell from her top pocket onto Robert's face, luckily falling flat rather than points down. The nurse went pale, and quickly picked them up.

Simon lifted the carry cot on to the back seat and strapped it in, and they took Robert home.

Karen was very tired, so Simon took Robert into the bedroom, which he had decorated with Magic Roundabout characters using the overhead projector borrowed from school. And they were home.

Of course Karen's parents arrived, Rita staying for a few days. Simon was glad that Karen had the support while he went back to work.

They settled into a routine, Robert was a very quiet, placid baby at first. This made life easier, but he would not feed well. He would take two ounces and then stop, but a couple of hours later he cried for another two ounces. This became very wearing, and continued as winter turned to Spring and Robert was taken off formula milk. His problems with sleeping and feeding continued, worse if anything. Added to his 'two ounce tummy' he would often then vomit the whole lot up again, often what is called projectile vomiting, the feed being ejected with such force that it could travel several feet. He was waking up in the night, every hour or so, and when put down, cried and cried. If he did sleep, he would soon re-awake, and cry, yet still very tired. He became listless, pallid, and so did Simon and Karen!

At Easter, Simon's Mum and Ken were coming up to see Robert. Simon was getting the bedroom ready. As Robert had the larger second bedroom, Mum and Ken would have to use bunk beds in the small bedroom. But the rail would not stay in place. Simon was tired, exhausted even, from the sleepless nights looking after his son. Robert seemed unable to sleep. Now he would cry in a heart rending, whimperish way, nothing seemed to soothe him, not bottle, not nappy change, not winding. They tried to distract him but to no avail.

Simon tried to make the rail fit, and with pliers pulled at the dowel that was supposed to keep the rail in place. His hand slipped and there was an explosion of pain in his right eye. The pliers had smashed through his spectacle lens, pushing the glass into his eye.

"Karen!" he shouted, "Help me!"

Karen came running up. "What's happened?"

"The pliers slipped and now there's a load of glass in my eye! I can't see!"

"Don't rub it!" said Karen urgently.

Simon had had the sense not to rub his eye. Karen got a towel which Simon held gently to his right eye – his better eye!

He managed to get downstairs. Karen knocked on the neighbours' door for help.

"Don't worry," she said. "I'll drive him to the hospital." Karen had never passed her driving test and anyway, she had Robert to look after.

At the hospital, Simon was taken to the eye wing. Slowly the shards of glass were removed.

"Shame you still had glass lenses," said the doctor, while he worked away, Simon's head held immobile in a frame.

"What else?" asked Simon.

"Oh, lots of people have plastic these days."

"And what would have happened if I'd had those?"

"They might have been scratched. You certainly would not have had an eye full of glass."

Simon quietly cursed his glass lenses. "Will I be able to see out of it?"

"Well, light will get in, but how useful it will be remains to be seen."

So Mum and Ken spent Easter visiting Simon in hospital, with his eye bandaged against the light. It looked so odd with just his left eye, with no depth vision, and blurred, because his left had been the poorer one, and he now had no glasses.

Mum and Ken had to leave while he was still in hospital. After a week, the kind neighbour collected Simon and took him home. He now had some new glasses, with plastic lenses! But he also had a large pair of dark glasses which he wore over the top to protect his eyes from the light.

Simon's vision was now restricted which he found very stressful. He sat in the car, but lacked the confidence to try to drive it. His right eye was now like looking through patterned glass with severe distortions. Karen grew frustrated because she could not drive. While they struggled to get around, the useless car just sat there.

Robert's christening was to be in the same church in Mansfield where they had got married. A good friend who lived not far way was going and so she drove them down. Simon had been told he should still wear the dark overglasses when outside, but when he saw the photographs, he wished he had taken them off for those at least. It just added to his frustration.

Karen too was not well. She had become weepy and depressed. Simon felt as though he was carrying her burdens as well as his own, not to mention Robert, who still refused to sleep or feed as expected. Simon now walked to school, but found this awkward because he could not carry the stuff he wanted to. He started to stay behind late to get his work done, but also he realised it delayed the time when he would have to go home and try to lift Karen, and look after Robert. Yet he felt the unfairness of this.

At the hospital for a check up he asked about driving.

"It's up to you, when you feel ready," the consultant advised.

"But what about judging distances without stereoscopic vision?"

"Oh, don't worry about that," he replied. "Look, stereoscopic vision evolved so we could jump from branch to branch. It has proved very useful since from throwing spears at wildebeest to playing golf. But it only works up to about twenty feet. When you're driving, you use experience to judge distance. If a bus looks small, you know it's not a small bus up close, but a big bus some distance away, and you drive accordingly. Try it, anyway."

Tentatively, Simon took to the wheel again. It took some getting used to, but gradually his confidence returned, and he was mobile again. But one day when reversing out of a tight parking space, he misjudged the closeness to the next car and clipped the tail light. Yes, he thought, thinking back to what the consultant had said. That was a time when depth vision was needed. Luckily, he knew whose the car was, and offered to buy and fit a new tail light, which he did. He learned his limitations with regard to such matters and driving continued. After all, he reasoned, it never stopped Peter Falk!

Despite the deepening depression, both for him and Karen, Simon continued to maintain the outward appearance of normality. His nightmares returned, when he could get some sleep that is, such were Robert's sleeping habits that it was fragmented at best.

Karen was stuck in the house with a crying baby and a car on the driveway so became more and more depressed. But she found the resolve to resume driving lessons which she had abandoned before going to college. She and Simon argued when he took her out, and to Simon, this seemed only to accentuate the rift between them. But Karen passed her test and soon gained confidence in driving. She also took up teaching on supply, filling in for absent teachers, being paid by the day. This gave her an escape with flexibility and also helped the finances to the point where she bought her own little car.

The frequent trips to Mansfield continued, partly so that Simon and Karen could get some rest. Often they left Robert there in Rita's care for a few days until they could recuperate a little.

3. 1978-9 *Degradation*

Simon applied for, and to his surprise was appointed, deputy head of another primary school. It was a break after ten years with Mr Cooper in the large, perhaps old fashioned, primary school. He was pleased with the promotion, but the new school could not have been more different. It was much smaller, and it was an open plan layout. Simon immediately hated this. He had come to like the structure of his first school and he felt this lacked such structure. There was also a sharp divide among the children, with about half coming from a relatively affluent area, the others coming from a one time mining village now facing decline and deprivation. Simon liked the new head teacher, Brian Bailey, but he was very different to Mr Cooper. But as well as teaching his own class, he threw himself into the Deputy Head's role with enthusiasm, taking on the administrative and organisational tasks this involved which he felt were strengths of his. He had ideas for the school, including changing the layout in the entrance lobby to give the school clerk her own office instead of having her desk in the staffroom. But he soon found that this desire for innovation was not welcome and he overhead Mr Bailey talking about him in the staffroom as a "bloody parrot sitting on my shoulder squawking in my ear all the time". Suddenly Simon's inner fears surfaced again, he felt undermined and vulnerable. He withdrew into himself more and kept his own counsel, but this did little to lift his self esteem and depression.

One thing he did do was organise his trip to the Lake District, but as the school was too small to provide sufficient boys to go, he did this jointly with a former colleague Eric Hill who was now a deputy in another school in Nusbury. This provided an escape for Simon from home life he was finding onerous and school which he disliked. He enjoyed the rough and tumble fun fights and was in some way back in his childhood with them. The boys started to signal victory by pulling the loser's trousers down, debagging. This made Simon think of Hooray Henrys and Daniel again. On one occasion he was with his own group while Eric Hill was away with his. Simon ended up at the bottom of a heap of boys, and felt his belt being loosened, he could see, by Donald Grey. The boys were shouting encouragement, and Simon, pinned down by several, found the situation arousing.

"Get his bags off," was the cry.

"Go on then, Grey, debag 'im."

That command, with its echoes of the past, took Simon so far back. The deed was done, and Simon, his arousal now exposed, felt a mixture of elation and loathing. Some of the boys made joking comments about his size, one saying his Dad would be jealous. He dressed and made light of it, his mind a turmoil. The boys seemed to think it was a laugh and Simon thought it less likely that there would be repercussions. Despite his fear and guilt, when the boys repeated this in the dormitory later in the week, he again succumbed to the urge for degradation. Whatever was going on in his head, his inhibitions were overcome. It was like the rape, only 'safe'. Would rerunning this in 'safe mode' ease the pain? To make it safe, to make OK?

Back at work, Simon was sinking into a deep depression, but managed to keep functioning, how he knew not. Was this what the rest of his life was going to be like? He wanted to be back with Daniel, held by that strong guiding light. He felt adrift, rudderless and sinking.

As a distraction from teaching he introduced computers in to his class, the basic Sinclair ZX81 with the extra 16K RAM pack. Karen had saved up and bought him this, a huge statement of her love as it was no small amount for them. The children enjoyed this, and he taught them basic flow charting and programming in BASIC. Soon, they were writing their own short programs. Simon could see that computers would be important in the future.

He was also taking children away for shorter trips, often when Karen and Robert went to Mansfield for a break with Rita. Sometimes to the Lakes, staying perhaps one night, or even for daytrips, which meant girls could go as well because there were no dormitory issues. But the annual joint week trip remained for Simon his principal escape from the gloom of his life. The debagging was repeated and Simon found his arousal to the point where his inhibition barriers were now so weak that he crashed through them, masturbating, the humiliation somehow lancing the boil of his pain. In a distorted way he felt that in allowing them intimate knowledge of his body, the bond between them was strengthened. He was giving himself to them as he once had to Daniel – as he once had been forced to do by the Watsons. He knew this was despicable, but the self-loathing and loss of self respect only served in some way to pull him down to repeat the act.

Though I am not splenitive and rash,
Yet have I something in me dangerous.

The boys still seemed in the main to regard this as part and parcel of the fun and informality, an attitude Simon did not discourage. He was inwardly ashamed of giving way to these baser instincts with their memories of rape. Somehow Daniel was apart from that, in a special place called love.

Ironically, at this time there was pressure from government to start teaching sex education in primary schools, and Mr Bailey asked Simon to do this. This only heightened the informal talk about sex when away, and provided a context for his display.

On one occasion he was with a group on a day trip to a forest orienteering course about twenty miles from Nusbury. He sent them off in pairs, but one boy, Ben Young, was left, so he and Simon set off together round the course. He was a nice lad, a bit cheeky sometimes, but had that spark that Simon so envied. But when they stopped for a rest in the forest, Simon felt that unstoppable urge well up. Amid talk of sex, Simon again committed the sex act while Ben watched. Once more Simon seemed to be viewing himself from outside, the familiar refuge, a way of distancing his mind from the body which he hated and yet to which he was enslaved. The boy was upset and frightened which Simon at once regretted and feared. Ben threatened to report this and Simon pleaded for him not to, eventually resorting to his status as a deputy head to persuade Ben he would not be believed. As they walked back down through the forest together alone and silent, Simon was very fearful. But the incident passed, and Simon gradually relaxed, although he noticed that Ben kept his distance after that.

The school was given a full inspection which lasted a week. Simon hated this and felt under attack. He didn't think much of the manner in which this was carried out, with assumptions being made based on little evidence and without consulting the staff who could have corrected them. He was interviewed by the education authority's inspector at length, but Simon felt revulsion when it became obvious that he was being quizzed to expose any weaknesses of Brian Bailey's, trying to drive a wedge between them. Simon liked Brian Bailey and whatever differences they might have were certainly not going be discussed with this man. In the report Simon in particular was criticised for not exercising sufficient leadership in his role as deputy head and he was told by the education authority's inspector for primary schools to "Stop piss-farting about with computers! There's no future in them."

Robert's sleep pattern was still awry. The doctor prescribed those medications to get him to sleep. The advice was that he was 'foxing' and they should just leave him. Simon and Karen lay in bed, following the doctor's advice, listening to the whimpering cries from their little son next door. They tossed and turned, unable to sleep, the crying like a dagger through their hearts. By three in the morning Simon could take no more.

"I've had enough," he said to Karen, "I'm not doing this."

He got out of bed and went into Robert. This little grey faced child, cowering in the corner of the cot, tears on his face, broke Simon's heart. He wept himself as he took Robert up into his arms. How could this be? What sort of father was he? Well, not one like mine, he vowed. He took Robert back into his own bed and father and son lay close together, deriving comfort in their joint misery from each other.

At the same time it had become obvious that all was not well with Robert. His development was slow, he failed to stand unaided until eighteen months, and he would be three before he walked.

4. *1980 Harriet*

At the same time, Karen was pregnant again. She had wanted a second child, hoping for a daughter. But unlike the first pregnancy, this was terrible for Karen, with constant sickness, and a complete nervous collapse.

She went to the doctor for help. Again it was Dr Sengupta.

"Yes, you are pregnant again," she said tartly. "What are you going to do?"

"What do you mean?" asked Karen.

"You should have an abortion," said Dr Sengupta.

"What for? Is there something wrong with the baby?"

"Not the baby, you. You can't look after one baby, never mind two."

Both Simon and Karen simply sat, shocked by this. They left, Karen weeping, Simon feeling a boiling rage within. How dare she say that to Karen? What a bitch! After all Karen's efforts, with little help from the doctors apart from Phenargen, Vallergen etc., to be told of her supposed failure so bluntly and cruelly. He could see that Karen was crushed by this, felt her distress and didn't know how to help, adding to his sense of failure.

Simon now hated his life. Karen was withdrawn from him and anyway, how could he burden her with his pain when she had so much of her own? She talked of leaving and going back to her mother. Simon still loved her deeply and this thought made him distraught. Without her in his life, what would he have? He was a failure as a husband, as a parent, as a teacher. He took solace in those informal times with the children and looked forward to the week away as respite from the stress of his life.

But once more he allowed the boys to witness again his victimisation, the wound unhealed, the humiliating sex act repeated. Would the repetition of his rape, albeit in much diluted form, offer a chance to at last lay to rest the ghosts of the past? Simon knew at one level the fallibility of this specious argument, while at another clinging to the hope that somehow, even if only for a time, the deep pain of childhood would be eased by reaching out to the boys this way. He wanted them to know him in every way, as Daniel had. Why? Daniel surrogates. Such nakedness taking him back to a time when this meant being loved. The boys were those who had strong friendship bonds within their group, were self confident, intelligent and capable. As Simon said many years later, they were the boys he wished he had been. He looked at their untarnished sexual future with envy, not seeing the risk that he could tarnish theirs as his had been. There was never desire to have physical sexual contact with the boys, but it was about his own degradation with them, harking back to his own rape which, according to his psychiatrist later, "triggered something" in his psyche which in turn had its roots his in disassociation from his father. Simon would never knowingly hurt anyone, least of all a child. In his corrosive and destructive solitude with its distorted thinking at that time, such was his inner pain, he did not see himself as abusing them, rather he was abusing himself with them as witness. It appealed too to the submissive aspects of his sexuality, with its echoes of his time with Daniel. Simon was also seeking comfort in their company, harking time to the times he had felt safe and secure with Daniel and was looking in some way for emotional closeness with these boys. Were they his Scout Patrol? None of them particularly resembled Daniel and Simon was not seeking a physical type, it was more about their characters and the relationship. Using sex as a means to get close to the boy? Whatever the explanations, there were no excuses, and Simon deeply regretted his actions. His psychiatrist years later likened this to a form of self harm, analogous to hurting oneself by cutting, to damage the hated body. But Simon did not choose that route, perhaps because of the strong sexual basis of his internal pain, so it was in the form of sexual degradation that the release was obtained.

What is self esteem? Someone who has low esteem is not aware of this until it is pointed out – how do other people feel? How can one tell? It is maybe best described by its absence, a feeling of emptiness, a void, a hollowness within. But there is this memory, of that inner core of being which enabled him to go up the signal box as a confident boy and admit what had happened so as to prevent a rail crash. There was a certainty that this was right whatever the consequences, a sort of anchor. There was the confidence that had taken him to HMS Sultan in his quest for a naval career. This was taken away aged 17. It was never there again, although its elusive memory sometimes would drift teasingly past the edge of consciousness, there but just out of reach.

But at this time of huge stress, of desperation almost, where was this inner core, this underlying solidity which took him to the signal box – where was that in the hostel dormitory or out in the forest when that self belief was no longer there to stop him? Perhaps Simon had been seeking it in their company but it was never real, a phantom, insubstantial, intangible, that needed to be given substance with ever more desperate, risky measures required to make that connection, through those boys to reach back to the past, to that good time, past the rape that had robbed him, back to Daniel. But the inner substance that would surely have applied the brakes was not there and Simon was over the precipice into revolting sexual display. Yet it lanced the boil, the transitory escape of sexual release finding parallel in emotional release, satisfying the urge for disempowerment, for humiliation. Lowered and in their grasp – had they but realised it at the time. In his mind, they were in some way their future sexual selves, not their current prepubescent beings. He projected his own inner reality onto the situation in fantasy, pushing their future onto them. They would have to stand in for Daniel. It was a strong feeling but swiftly followed by fear and self repugnance for what he had done. But without that missing inner core, the need would arise again and when Simon found himself both with the drive mounting and in a possible situation, the crime would occur again, decreasing self esteem and fuelling the cycle. In his despair, desperation, depression and distortion, his view of reality was warped by the prism of his closely guarded internal misery.

Robert was still giving them sleepless nights. In desperation, they searched for information and contacted support groups, but all seemed to focus on hyperactivity. Robert was far from hyperactive, he was a gentle, placid boy – he just didn't sleep!

One evening after work, Simon and Karen were opening the post.

"Another newsletter from the hyperactive lot," said Simon. "Doubt if it's relevant."

"Let me look," said Karen. She started to read. "Simon, look at this!" She pointed to a paragraph half way down an inside page.

"If your child is listless, has a pale complexion, vomits his food, especially projectile vomiting, is always tired and finds it hard to sleep, he or she could be allergic to cows' milk."

Simon and Karen were literally speechless. This was exactly what Robert was like. Milk? It's good for you, isn't it? The adverts all said it was a natural food. But any port in a storm. With immediate effect, Robert was taken off cows' milk, and put onto soya. Within 24 hours Robert was sleeping. In fact instead of being awake for twenty hours and sleeping for four, his pattern reversed. They had to wake him up to feed him. After two weeks of this, his sleep pattern became more normal.

They reported this to the doctor, but the idea that any child could be allergic was dismissed as the writing of cranks, rubbish. But Simon and Karen knew that they were on to something.

One ray of light was the schools' doctor, Dr. Urwin. She would come and visit the school to carry out medicals. She acquired a reputation for being an oddball because she was always saying the children should not drink cows' milk. She was not believed, except by Simon. She pointed him to some books on the matter, early groundbreakers as they would prove to be, in particular the work of Dr. Richard Mackarness.

"But it is a good food source, though? Calcium especially?" he asked her one lunch break. They were sitting in his classroom talking, Simon again virtually immobile and in pain from another outbreak of his piles. He was still anxious they were doing the right thing for Robert.

"Yes, it's rich in protein and all sort of things. But our bodies are not evolved to deal with these big bovine protein molecules."

"But it's a natural food though?" queried Simon.

"If you're a calf, yes. We are the only species that drinks the breast milk of another species, and the only one that continues that after we ourselves have been weaned. So don't tell me it's natural."

"So why do some people suffer like Robert, and others don't?"

"Oh, it's inherited," Dr Urwin said as though it were obvious. "He's got this through you or your wife."

"I know of nobody on either side," said Simon.

"Ask again," said Dr Urwin. "And if it's you, you might find that coming off cows' milk will help those piles."

"I know what started those off," said Simon. In response to Dr Urwin's raised eyebrows, he continued. "When I was seventeen, I was attacked by three boys my age and then they.." Simon stopped, unable to continue.

"A sexual attack?" asked Dr Urwin gently.

Simon nodded. "All three," he said. "They took turns." And then his tears flowed. This was the first time he had told anybody at all about that dreadful night.

"Don't worry," she said. "Your secret is safe with me. But please take my advice about cows' milk, and stay on course with Robert."

That night he recounted the conversation to Karen. At least they knew they were not mad. He also mentioned the attack, but brushed over it and moved on to the milk issue.

Reading the books suggested was a eye opener. Simon phoned Mum to ask if she knew about milk allergy.

"No, love, I can drink milk. Mind you Rose has never been able to touch dairy stuff. Makes her ill. Does that help?"

"Yes, I think so," said Simon. Auntie Rose was Mum's sister. So it was in the genes then. Poor Robert had got this through him. Simon joined Robert on a milk free diet. Over the weeks the results became plain. Instead of reading himself to sleep at night, he found he could get off to sleep. He lost weight and looked fitter. His headaches that had been a nuisance stopped, his rheumatic type pains stopped, but best of all, his piles were a lot better. He would never be free of them, and would always have to be careful, but at least he could now manage them a bit better.

Telling friends about this and as something of an evangelist now about cow's milk allergy, he would say, "For years I have been swallowing things down, rubbing stuff on and shoving stuff up!" Simon always maintained that as far as piles are concerned there are two mutually exclusive groups of people; those who find piles funny – and those who have had them!

As far as the doctor was concerned, that was the last straw. Simon asked Dr Urwin if she could recommend a family doctor in Nusbury. She said she could not as that would be against professional ethics. She did say she had never had a referral regarding allergies from his current doctor. Then with a smile she said, "I do get referrals from Dr Tambling though."

Within the week, Simon had transferred to the new doctor.

In the Spring, Karen was at full term and this time there was no delay. Almost to the day, labour pains started. Robert was left with the family friend who looked after him when Karen was working – the mother of one of Simon's former pupils from Mr Cooper's days – they went back to Nusbury Hospital's maternity wing. Not much had changed in the four and a half years since Robert was born, but this time there was a proper birthing room and an electronic monitor instead of the small ear trumpet. Simon wished Robert had had such equipment. Maybe he wouldn't be.... No, don't think about that, it was painful and anyway, nothing could change it now.

He held Karen's hand as she panted and pushed. There was no delay, this baby was in a hurry to be born. But it was bigger than Robert had been and Karen had to be cut to allow the head out. And there was the baby's head, pink and with what seemed like a determined expression on its face.

"It's another boy," announced a nurse as the shoulders eased out. Probably basing her comments on the strong physique of this child. And then the rest was out. A girl! The daughter Karen had wanted! The baby cried, loud and long. She was swept up and cleaned and placed in Karen's arms, whose face was a picture of rapture.

"She's beautiful," Karen said to Simon. He smiled and hugged her and then took his daughter in his arms. She was strong and resisted, but Simon held her close.

"Does she have a name yet?" asked a nurse.

"Harriet," said Karen. This was a name in her family and it had been agreed beforehand.

He soon left the hospital to collect Robert, he had promised he would bring him to see his new sibling. He returned within the hour with Robert, who toddled in and peered through the cot at his now sleeping sister. Robert's little face lit up.

"Is that Harriet, Daddy," he asked.

"Yes, son, that's your new baby sister."

Robert was genuinely overjoyed. He hugged Karen and then father and son went home together, the bond between them, already strong, becoming stronger, a source of new strength to Simon, Robert's problems only serving to fuel this. Simon was determined to be a better father to his son than his own had been. His university studies in psychology had included some interesting work on parent child relationships and he could start to analyse what had gone wrong between him and his father.

Once home, Harriet displayed an independence that would always characterise her. Simon loved to cuddle Robert and the two would often snuggle up together, but to Simon's disappointment, Harriet did not like this and would wriggle to be free, even as a baby, she would go rigid in his arms to the point where he had to put her down again in case she fell. At least Harriet slept.

Simon was frightened of his gay sexuality and buried it deep, refusing to acknowledge it. He was determined that his fathering of Robert, and of Harriet, would be the nurturing and above all consistent model his own father had failed to provide. He knew that in some part at least, his own sexuality had been formed by the rejection by his father and amplified by his own reciprocal rejection. If the father role had anything to do with shaping his children's sexuality, Robert's especially, then he was not going to make the mistakes his Dad had made. Of course he knew that his long affair with Daniel had undoubtedly helped shape him, but he also realised that had he not had the potential within, it would have remained a platonic, normal friendship. Simon also knew, and feared, that if the potential were genetic, then he might be fighting a losing battle, but despite the uncertainty in the nature – nurture debate on sexuality, he would make sure that nothing **he** did would be responsible if his children grew up gay.

With renewed determination to set himself straight, with at least some of Robert's problems under control and Karen's return from the depths of depression Simon started to feel a little more optimistic again. Matters improved and motivation for change strengthened and so did enough of that old substance return to stop him going again over the precipice. It never stopped him wistfully looking back at the past, of missing it and seeing in the children alternative futures that might have been his, but Simon now had his own growing children, and that, with the improving situation, would be enough to prevent him from going over the line again. He was able to lift himself from his problems and face the demons of his soul and his conduct, but unable to tell anyone.

There were other pressures too. Simon had now reached the rank of inspector in the special constabulary, but had been posted to a part of Nusbury he didn't know, with many new estates and pedestrianised walkways and areas. To Simon it was a rabbit warren. He had two sergeants and about twenty constables to look after. He could spend less time actually out on duty as almost all the time he had available to give to the police was taken up with administrative work. So this too was becoming a burden rather than a relaxation and change.

Simon did find time to sit the advanced driving test again, as he needed to be sure his eye loss was not affecting his, and others', safety. Once again Simon passed easily, and when he told the examiner afterwards his reason for the retest, he said he would not have known. Simon was therefore satisfied that the accident had not affected his ability to drive and should he ever need to, could argue his case.

Simon continued his part time studies, this time Computer Science. He could see the future in computing, even if education inspectors could not. The course interested him, perhaps because it was far removed from education and was a complete change. Perhaps he was looking for a diversion to take his mind off his problems. Again Simon would graduate with distinction.

Robert's problems were highlighted even more when he started at nursery school. It was apparent that he was by no means as quick as most of the other children, although he enjoyed his time there and loved to go. The staff liked him, he was not aggressive as some small boys can be, and he was well mannered and no trouble. But he found the activities hard to cope with. His relative immaturity was there to see. As parents who were themselves academic and in what for want of a better term, were in the professional class, this was a worry and source of anxiety to Simon and Karen.

The same applied when he started school. From the start he found school a problem. He was something of a loner at times, and was always slow to make friends. The social aspects of school were difficult. Being in an open plan school on the new estate where Simon and Karen were living, he found concentration difficult, and this concerned Simon who could see open plan schools from the other side, and not favourably, especially where special needs children were concerned. Robert was slow to start reading and writing, and his number sense was non-existent. Being slow, he was picked on and called "Baby", even by some of the staff! Simon and Karen soon became worried by his lack of progress at school. But the school's only strategy seemed to be to apply more pressure. "You can't do this, so here's more of it." The failure cycle started early. The school seemed outwardly co-operative, yet things only got worse, coming to head when he was seven, with Robert totally isolated, missing every Games lesson while he was supposed to finish off work he could not do, excluded from fun activities and out of school visits for the same purpose. Failure was thus being compounded on failure. Simon found that hard to believe when he found out what had been going on. Robert never told his parents, he just accepted things fatalistically. They immediately moved him to another primary school. He was much happier there, but still no school lover.

The new school, a large fairly modern primary school, was much more tuned in to the needs of children who might have special needs. They soon flagged up Robert's problems, and the new doctor referred him to the Child Guidance Clinic at Nusbury General Hospital. He went there each Tuesday for a term, to a "school" there. They were very supportive, and their understanding did much to help Karen re-establish a belief in herself. Their diagnosis was "attention deficit", and behavioural programmes were tried, but without much success. A WISC test gave a score around average, but with a very unusual scatter. The consultant, Dr. Viking, then suggested Ritalin, 20mg dose daily. This was adopted, Robert taking this each school day only. An immediate improvement was noticed, including by the new school, who were unaware that he was taking any medication. He later transferred to Pemolin. Without it, the "switching off" effect during tasks was much more noticeable, almost like a short petit mal, a cutting out, which the consultant described as him being "in a loop", mentally.

5. 1984 Headship

At this time Brian Bailey started to talk about retiring. Some of Simon's contemporaries were getting promoted to head teacher, and there were one or two Simon was glad not to have to work for. The only way to prevent getting a new head he didn't like was to try to become a head teacher himself. He started applying, but at first got nowhere. He felt as though the adverse inspection report was counting against him in Nusbury, so he started applying outside the borough in the neighbouring county. He then got one or two unsuccessful interviews in Nusbury, and also in the county.

At last his persistence paid off and he was awarded a headship in the county town, Thirlham. The drive took about half an hour as Simon lived on the same side of Nusbury. This was Thirlham Meadows Primary School, built about twenty years earlier, and had had one head teacher since then who had now retired. Many of the teaching staff had been there since the school opened as well. They regarded this new incomer from Nusbury with suspicion. The school was like a time capsule. The furniture was old, the books were old, the teaching methodology was old. He made his case at County Hall for new furniture, not just for the children, but the worn out staffroom furniture was replaced too. Simon didn't want his teachers sitting on worn out broken chairs in their breaks.

And yet there was much of value. It was not an open plan school which Simon was glad about although he did not now have a class of his own, and it had an ethos that reminded him of Mr Cooper's school in many ways. Simon was anxious not to lose the things of value as he tried to modernise the school. The government of Margaret Thatcher was pushing change in education hard, and schools were now firmly on the political agenda, with successive Education Secretaries having to show their mettle by driving through more change.

As a result externally driven changes were now pushing schools hard and it fell to him to implement them. To the staff, it seemed as though Simon was the bringer of all this change and what they saw as disruption of their settled, and in their eyes, successful, ways. Simon felt his efforts were not appreciated by the staff. But as he was not now responsible for a class, in some ways he felt that this job suited him better. He still enjoyed the company of the children, and still continued with his annual trip to the Lake District with boys from Eric's school in Nusbury making up the numbers as before. The county asked him why he did not take girls. Simon tried to find a female staff member willing to go that would enable this, but without success. As Robert got older, he too went along on these trips, which he thoroughly enjoyed. The boys on the trips – and girls sometimes too on days out – seemed to take to him, and made a bit of a fuss of him.

Government 'initiatives' followed each other in rapid succession. The National Curriculum was introduced, with its huge number of attainment targets (later drastically reduced) that the children should achieve. Schools lost control of the curriculum as more and more was laid down centrally. At the same time local management of schools was introduced, giving schools their own budget. Fine in theory but for primary schools it took away any discretion a head teacher might have. So much of the budget went on staff costs, there was almost no leeway with what was left. No longer could Simon go to County Hall and make a case for expenditure on the school. He was now tied to his inadequate budget. He would never have got his new furniture under this regime! And now he had to deal with the maintenance of the building as well, and find out about roofing, boiler and grounds maintenance – even when to prune the roses in the flower beds outside the school. The Board of Governors was supposed to be responsible but in reality this fell on Simon. To him, there was no more classic case than when a mistake by a governor cost the school. The unpaid governor simply quit, but Simon had to deal with the consequences. He felt increasingly trapped. He had all the responsibility but not the means to change anything any more. He was running hard just to stay still.

And then he had the horrible task of making a teacher redundant. The estate around the school was maturing. The first influx of young families now had children growing older, and the number of primary age children started to fall. This meant the budget reduced. But the building and all the other costs were still there, and the only way to balance the books was to lose a teacher.

And local management meant that the county could no longer simply redeploy a teacher to a different school where there was a vacancy. Simon was now hating his job, every day was a burden; he grew to hate the sight of the postman coming, loaded down with more problems for him. The staff reduction was horrible. The teacher concerned left the profession completely after many years of loyal service, and Simon didn't blame him one bit. But Simon felt he was getting the blame from the remaining staff for this, but there was little he could do.

Robert and Harriet were now growing up fast. Harriet proved to be clever and intelligent. She shone at school, and also started to take piano lessons. Simon had bought a piano some years earlier on which he could relax, picking out tunes the way he used to in childhood. Of course it was not a grand like Daniel's, but a decent upright, iron framed and over-strung, built in London in 1910. The family went on holidays to the Lake District of course as well as visiting Karen's family in Mansfield, from where they would visit Simon's Dad and Phoebe in Nottingham, and travelling to London to stay with Simon's mother and Ken. But Simon's Mum was now afflicted with macular degeneration, a disease that causes loss of vision and to her immense frustration, she had had to give up driving. Ken didn't drive, but in London, this was less of a handicap with good public transport. Ken went to Whitehall by bus and on the underground anyway.

The miners' strike was now well underway. To Simon, this seemed to be destroying the social consensus, creating sharp divisions. This was most apparent for him in the police. Many of the regular cops he knew would be drafted away to mining areas, earning huge amounts of overtime, and he knew some even paid off their mortgages. But attitudes seemed to harden. Simon always thought that Scargill should call a ballot, also he could see the miners' case. One of Karen's brothers was on strike, but many in the Mansfield area opted to join the breakaway union and continue working. Her two brothers that carried on working supported the one that was on strike. Other families were torn apart by this. Simon was sickened by the scenes of violence shown on television, especially of police beating miners already lying on the ground. The whole thing was getting out of control, and Simon knew in his own normal police work – specials were never sent to police the strike – that the public attitude to the police was changing, with consequences in the decades to come. In Nusbury at least, the police came to be seen as Thatcher's private army.

Then came an event that really angered Simon and Karen. They were driving to Mansfield with Robert and Harriet to stay with Karen's family. A few miles from the town they came across a police roadblock. Along with others, they were pulled in, questioned and the car searched. It was obvious that they were just a family visiting relatives, but the manner of the police was authoritarian and the children got upset. Simon said it felt as though he were in Nazi Germany. They were doing nothing wrong, but they felt threatened. If

Simon, with his police experience felt this, he wondered what other people with no police connections must have felt. The police were moving back from being a service to being a force, and in Mansfield their presence was strong, it felt like an army of occupation.

Robert had now left primary school and had started to attend the local secondary school, a large comprehensive school in Nusbury. On his first day, he had to copy from the blackboard, a vertical plane, a twenty period timetable, with subject, teacher and room number in each slot to his own sheet, a horizontal plane. A timetable is of course a grid with two axes, the interpretation of which calls for complex cognitive skills. Simon and Karen had to visit the school to obtain an accurate copy, important for organising his work at secondary level. They had to start educating the new school all over again. He found the adjustment hard and Karen especially had to spend much time with him in the evenings with homework and helping him to organise himself. Because of this, his programme of patterning movements often failed to get done.

As the first term progressed, the difficulties mounted up. Robert was in the same class as a group of boys who soon made him their regular victim. One of these had tormented Robert for years at primary school, and also as he then lived near him, at home as well. Robert was separated from his one good friend. He became progressively more anxious, stressed and frightened. Karen especially made many visits to the school in a supportive way, and each time the matter was promptly dealt with, but the basic problem of Robert's vulnerability and the physical and especially mental bullying continued. As a Governor of the school, Simon tried also to be as supportive as possible. In-class support for Robert's academic problems exacerbated the social difficulties by heightening the resentment felt by those boys, only slightly more able than Robert, of the attention he received. His positive attitude to work, his home background and correct manner of speech further alienated him from the others.

But now the bullying came to the house. The boys that tormented Robert at school lived not far away, and they would sometimes besiege the house, even in the garden, with Robert unable to go and play. Simon could not bear this. His stress levels went sky high again. The bullying continued often in very subtle and devious ways difficult to pin-point, yet which gradually brought Robert to the edge of breakdown. It was apparent that the Special Needs teachers in the school had little real "clout", and were perceived by many staff as a repository for those children who were hard to handle in the classroom. Then on a cross country run at school, the bullies lay in wait for Robert and beat him with sticks. Simon had had enough. He had tried to be supportive, even serving as a governor of the school, but the school's total failure to deal with this led him and Karen to simply take Robert out of the school. This was listed as a 'cooling down' period and some work was sent home for Robert.

One day he was talking to Mavis Dobson, who was head of the lower school and of Special Needs at the comprehensive school in Thirlham near Simon's school.

"Bring him here," she said. "We'll look after him. At least until you get the situation sorted out."

"He's not going back there, over my dead body," said Simon.

"Well, let's see how it goes," said Mavis. "Don't worry, he'll be fine."

So Robert was moved to Thirlham Meadows Comprehensive School. This was about half the size of his school in Nusbury, and some of the pupils there knew Robert already through Simon, as they had moved up from Simon's school. The two schools were close together so Simon simply took Robert with him in the morning and after school, Robert would come and wait for Simon to finish his day and then the two would go home together.

The workload got heavier - Simon gave up the Special Constabulary at this time because of this. The legacy of the strike was still strong, he didn't like the air of triumphalism that now seemed to pervade so many of the regulars, and some specials too. He had become less and less happy in the police. He received visits from senior police officers asking him to stay. They would move him back to his old subdivision. They even said he was earmarked as a possible force Commandant one day! But Simon knew he could not cope with that as well as the professional and personal load he was carrying. With a heavy heart, and after over twenty years of service, he declined their offers.

Robert was now safe at school and started to settle in and even make some progress. Mrs Dobson had been at that school for many years, and as Karen remarked one day, "She walks round that school as though she owns it." Mavis Dobson would certainly have denied that but it was evident that she was excellent at her job and knew every child in the school by name. Robert called her his guardian angel and imagined her hovering above him, keeping an eye on him. He became a much happier person, and soon made a good friend.

Soon after Robert started, one boy from a higher year, known as a bit of a bully, had a go at Robert. Robert fought back, surprising even himself. The boy concerned was immediately excluded. Word seemed to get round that Robert Scott should be left alone.

But at home he was not left alone, the house continued to be a target for the local youths. Simon could stand the stress no longer, and Karen too was finding the whole situation impossible to solve and stressful. They decided to move house to Thirlham. Simon spent each day after school driving round the town, looking at certain areas. One evening he was looking round one of the desirable areas of Thirlham and drove into a cul-de-sac he had not bothered with before. One of the houses had a 'For Sale' sign. Simon immediately felt in his bones that this would be the right place.

The next day he and Karen went to have a look. Simon instantly got a good feel for the house, as he had from the outside. The garden was a safe place for

Robert and Harriet to play. It was a semi detached house, so they would give up their nice four bedroom detached house with master ensuite and double garage in Nusbury, but as it had turned out not in the best location, for a three bed semi in one of the better parts of Thirlham. As a friend pointed out to him, it's better to buy the smallest house in a good area than a big house in a poor area. How Simon now knew the truth of that! They immediately put in an offer.

Moving house is stressful at the best of times, but they found they could not find a buyer for their Nusbury home. In the meantime there were several people interested in the Thirlham house. Simon found a couple of other houses that were candidates in Thirlham but neither was up the initial find. Robert and Harriet called the houses Gold, Silver and Bronze.

At the same time, Ken was taking early retirement and on his and Mum's pensions, could no longer afford London prices. So they too were looking to move. They looked at the west country, Falmouth in particular, but were priced out. So they looked north again, along at the coast near Bilthaven. When Simon said he and Karen were moving to Thirlham, a pretty town but with good public transport links, they too were looking there.

At last a buyer came forward for the Nusbury house, a doctor. He was carefully nurtured like a tender flower, and was never told he was the only interest that had been shown. In Thirlham, there was competition for 'Gold'. Despite being a smaller house, the asking price for 'Gold' was almost twice that of the Nusbury house. Location, location, location! At last the doctor signed and the deal was done in Nusbury. In Thirlham, it had come down to sealed bids. Simon couldn't stand this and wanted to pull out just to escape the stress. But Karen held her nerve, and decided on a price she thought would do the job, and entered the sealed bid. The wait was agonising. Meanwhile they continued to show interest in 'Silver' and 'Bronze', just in case.

6. *1989 Move house*

The letter from the estate agent fell onto the mat. Harriet brought it into the kitchen, knowing what it was. The four of them sat round the table while Simon opened the letter, and read it.

"Yes!" he yelled. "Gold! We've got Gold!"

The children cheered and Simon and Karen hugged.

"Well done, love," said Simon, thinking of Karen's nerve with the sealed bid. She just smiled, happy that Simon was happy. The family cuddled in their excitement.

Later the estate agent told Karen she might have got away with a thousand pounds less, but who cared?

They went to see the house again. Mrs Tarrant let them in. Her children showed Robert and Harriet their rooms, and Robert and Harriet decided which of the two smaller bedrooms each would have. Luckily, there was no conflict, as each chose separate rooms as the one they wanted.

"I am surprised," said Mrs Tarrant. "We thought you'd lost interest."

"Why?" asked Simon.

"You never came back for another look, but all the others did, some several times."

"We didn't need to," said Simon. "We knew it was right from the very beginning."

Within a few weeks, Mum and Ken had moved to a house in the centre of Thirlham, and soon after that, Simon and family moved into 'Gold'. It was quiet and safe. Robert was already at school in Thirlham of course, and the decision was made for Harriet to attend Simon's school. He knew it was a good school and the logistics were a lot simpler than if she had gone to a primary school nearer. It was just a ten minute drive across Thirlham anyway. And now it was Karen doing the longer commute back to Nusbury where she continued to so supply and contract teaching.

They settled in at Thirlham. The change in Robert was immediate. He was much happier, could play in the garden undisturbed by bullies, and he started to grow. He had always been small for his age, which no doubt added to the bullying, but now incredibly he grew three inches in six months. It was as though a great weight had been lifted off his shoulders, literally!

Harriet was less pleased by the move, which she saw as having been forced on her by Robert's situation, and not without some cause. Simon always felt that Harriet resented Robert for the attention he got through his learning problems and all that flowed from it. And she soon moved from looking up to her big brother to the realisation that she had the legs of him academically.

Robert was also regularly taken to a specialist clinic in Chester which had been recommended to him by Dr Urwin. This involved an overnight stay and was an added expense, but the consultant here said that there was a physiological basis to Robert's learning difficulties, based on immature reflex inhibition and a degree of cerebral dysfunction, especially with vision. The patterning movement programme was designed to correct the reflex development, over a period of some two years, monitored at Chester every two months or so. This was a drain on both Simon and Karen's physical, mental and financial resources, but of course they did it. After four months, Simon and Karen noticed an appreciable amount of progress in terms of reading and writing, but recognised that Robert was still well behind his peers. He was still taking medication on school days and now working towards his GCSE exams. Simon and Karen worried about his future though.

Simon also learned to ride. It was Harriet who loved horses and she was learning. Simon was ready to have a go, and took lessons as well. He rather enjoyed it as he became more proficient. Perhaps starting late, he never caught up with Harriet, but as long as the horse was not temperamental – "preferably getting on a bit, like me," he joked – he was fine. It was something that he and Harriet shared, and Simon valued that.

They also took the children abroad, staying with friends in Germany and on a holiday to Crete. Life settled down for the family, Harriet settled in at Thirlham Meadows Primary and Simon found it strange at first when walking into assembly to see Harriet's face among all the others beaming at him.

Most Saturday afternoons, he would visit Mum and Ken in their home in Thirlham, sometimes with Karen and the kids, mostly just himself. Mum's health was frail, having had a cancerous kidney removed almost as soon as she arrived in Thirlham and she was now registered blind, white stick and all. But peering closely, she could see Simon and recognise him. But this, her kidney problems and arthritis caused this intelligent, determined woman much frustration, which Ken bore with saintly fortitude and great humour. Simon felt he should do more, but it was hard to know what, and he had his own children to look after, especially the constant worries with Robert's learning problems.

They returned to Chester after a break of a year. Robert went through some of the usual routines, and noted that almost all the reflexes were now normal, with the exception of traces of the tonic labyrinthine and Morro reflexes. They suggested some vestibular stimulation which would help the maturation of balance mechanisms, and which involved the construction of a turntable on which Robert would be rotated and contra-rotated in foetal and prone positions. It was agreed to return in the summer.

Simon was obviously interested in the children with special needs, and did his best to safeguard their interests. They had their own room at the back of the school with attached art area with sink and water. It was quiet and away from the noise of the rest of the school. He knew they needed their own safe retreat. His special needs teacher appreciated this, and Simon made a point of telling all the children that when he had been in primary school, he had needed extra help. Dear Old Miss Brown! He knew how important it was to give these children especially a sense of worth. If he could be a head teacher having needed that it gave them hope. But he felt that some of his teachers thought he should not divulge such things, but Simon saw the effect. His Special Needs teacher was not one of those of course.

But he also felt it was necessary to push the most able as well. Simon, perhaps in yet another attempt to boost his own self esteem, had sat the test for Mensa. While he knew he had a good brain, he was astonished at the result. He came out with an IQ score of 155 on the Cattell test, apparently in the best one percent. He joined Mensa as a result which led to some more social contacts. He became secretary of the local branch. At school, the spin off was the opportunity for some of the brightest kids to have a go. Several were successful and joined Mensa themselves. One boy got an incredibly high score, but Simon already knew he was perhaps the cleverest child he had ever taught and was ever likely to. Simon also knew that some of his staff were sceptical about this but Simon felt this was balanced by his evident concern for the least able, and began not to care.

But for Simon, the job pressure was relentless. He started to look for a way out, he could not face this until he had earned his full pension! He attended some seminars on early retirement, but they didn't seem to suit teachers. The county must have been aware of the pressures on head teachers, although they blamed government for it, because they ran courses for heads on things like time management. The usual quip was that they didn't have time for it! Such meetings at County Hall were a regular feature and something of a chore. Rarely was anything innovative or truly useful learned. A high degree of cynicism characterised Simon and his head teacher colleagues. One fellow head would often say that they were due for another talk about 'circles of awareness' and 'the twoness of two'. These became something of a catchphrase. There was the unfortunate speaker invited by the Director of Education to address primary head teachers. The talk was the usual jargon and the atmosphere was quite listless in the county hall committee room where the meeting was being held. But suddenly the guest speaker was talking about circles of awareness! The room suddenly, and inexplicably from his and the Director's viewpoint, collapsed in mirth, with his audience laughing out loud, a great and spontaneous release of tension. Poor man, he never knew why, and limped to the end of his presentation to a background of suppressed giggles. The Director was less than pleased, but it was a boost to the sagging morale of so many heads.

One session on time management asked heads to keep a diary of a typical day. A Wednesday was chosen and dutifully Simon managed to keep a dairy on a pad he carried with him throughout the day. This is what he wrote.

A Wednesday in March, 1992.

08:45 Arrive at school. Greet Mrs L. (parent) standing waiting outside my room. Take off hat and coat, invite her in.

08:47 Talk to Mrs L. about alleged bullying of her son Malcolm L. by Graham Ridley. Have my doubts as Malcolm L. is no angel, except in his mother' eyes.

08:52 Interrupted by phone call about a child's absence.

08:53 Resume talk with Mrs L. Promise investigation and matter dealt with.

08:58 Mrs L. leaves. Start to sort post. Part time Clerk arrives. Give her post.

08:59 Deputy Head (DHT) wants to check details of cover for a course (He is INSET Co-ordinator).

09:00 Jason B. and Debbie G. come asking for Earring disclaimer forms. Send them to clerk.

09:01 Go to check why whistle not yet blown. Goes just as I get to the yard.

09:03 Return to office. Find two kids waiting with money for my Lake District week. Take it from them and mark off on list.

09:05 Phone goes, clerk not there, I answer. Local resident complaining about broken glass outside her house. Patiently explain that we allow no glass bottles in school and unlikely to be our kids. Description then offered shows that uniform worn that of another school in area.

09:08 See mother lurking in entrance with lunch box. She does not know her child's class or teacher's name. She does manage to remember her child's name and I take the lunchbox to the class. Meet Clerk returning from kitchen. Remind her I need to talk this morning about requisitions for next year.

09:12 Grab announcement diary and hymn book and dash to hall. Assembly (child led) just beginning.

09:25 Assembly ends. Make announcements about football match result, a football practice and chess club at lunchtime. Add warning about glass bottles, just in case.

09:31 Dismiss school to classes. Remember too late that I wanted to see Graham Ridley and Malcolm L. re alleged bullying.

09:33 Monitors report overhead projector (OHP) not working correctly (used for hymns), have had to hold it together for assembly. Investigate faulty microswitch causing bulb to cut out. Bend up bar for better contact. Seems OK.

09:43 Return to office. Start opening post which is mine. Sort into categories, including a fair amount straight to the bin.

10:01 Set off round classes to take items from mail to co-ordinators etc. Also a chance to get the feel of things.

10:06 Mr. Brown asks about Support and Development Time due next day. Can't remember who is covering, will check when I get back to office.

10:17 Back at office. Phone message to ring Comprehensive school. Ring back, line engaged.

10:20 Phone call from County Hall re sibling query of Y6 pupil. Give them information.

10:23 Phone call from school nurse to fix a date for some medicals. Consult diary, agree date.

10:26 Read my post.

10:30 Break time. Shop prefect wants safe keys. Give her keys from locked cupboard.

10:32 Set off for staffroom. Met by Senior Prefect asking if he can switch jobs between two prefects. Tell him it's his decision and see me if there are problems.

10:35 Reach staffroom. Sip coffee gratefully. Talk about election campaign. Mrs Dawson wants to know why she was not told about science course Mr. Brown is going on. Can't remember offhand. Mr. Brown asks again about S.D.T. cover. Put coffee down and go to find out. Meet clerk complaining that two teachers have not put down their packed lunch numbers.

10:41 Back to staffroom, tell Mr. Brown who is covering his class for S.D.T. next day. Tell Mrs Dawson that science course came up when she was off sick weeks ago. One of the teachers who forgot packed lunch numbers is on yard duty.

10:44 Whistle blows. Mrs Phillips says photocopier not working properly. Black lines across it.

10:45 Return to office to find Malcolm L. outside, sent there for fighting. Send for prefect who sent him and other fighter. Remember Graham Ridley and send for him too. Simon P. arrives with swollen eye, having been hit by a football. Ask clerk to stick a cold compress on it. Prefect from Block 2 comes to report faulty drinking fountain. Scribble note to myself.

10:50 Prefect and Malcolm L. arrive but not Graham Ridley whose class has just left for the baths. Malcolm L. complains always being picked on, especially by Graham Ridley. Apparent that Malcolm L. has been provoking others and got a thump. Then got thumped back. Suspicions about Malcolm L. harden. Prefect confirms that Malcolm L. does this regularly. Note incident in "Black Book". Both kept in at breaks for rest of day at least.

11:02 Phone about photocopier.

11:04 Go to clerk to discuss requisitions. Cook wants to use phone, but rings before she can get to it. Comprehensive school again. Return to office to take call. Concerns next primary cluster meeting.

11:10 Return to clerk to talk about requisitions.

11:14 Mrs Tiernon arrives with money for Samuel Tiernon's Lake District trip. Daren't just stick it in pocket, so return to my office to check it off on list. Mrs Tiernon also wants advice about equipment. Give brief explanation, and remind her of parents' meeting about trip due in April.

11:21 Return to clerk to talk about requisition. Discuss aspects of this.

11:28 Need loo, but instead a phone call from parents wanting to come to look at school today. Prospective new pupil. Arrange 2-30p.m.

11:32 Loo, then continue requisition discussion.

11:44 Phone call from parents asking for homework for John K. who is off with 'flu.

11:45 Continue requisition discussion.

11:51 Mark A. appears at office having twisted ankle jumping off box in P.E. Ask clerk to put a cold compress on it. Give up idea of talking about requisition today.

11:57 Mrs H., Governor, rings up about date of Annual Parents Meeting. She's a month out. Panic, thinking I've put wrong date on draft. Scribble note to myself to phone County Hall.

12:01 Go to dining hall to eat lunch while quelling the din. Clerk goes home for day (part time only).

12:03 See Graham Ridley in dining hall, tell him I want to see him after lunch. Resume lunch.

12:06 Notice unknown well dressed lady in entrance lobby. Go to find out what she wants. She's from Harris Polls wanting to do an exit poll on April 9th. (school usually houses two polling stations). I explain I've not yet had confirmation, tell her to contact County Hall.

12:11 Resume lunch, now colder.

12:13 Approached by Geoffrey F., now a Y7 pupil from the comprehensive school with a request from their Mr. R. to use our football field on Thursday night. Tell Geoffrey F. to find Deputy Head who runs football team.

12:14 Resume lunch.

12:17 Geoffrey F. returns saying it's OK with DHT. I say it's OK too.

12:18 Resume lunch.

12:20 Return to office. Message light flashing on telephone. Call from a distant comprehensive asking advice about VAT at youth hostels, result of recent newspaper article I wrote. Call back, line engaged.

12:25 Prefect reports Malcolm L. gone outside, playing football. Send Prefect to fetch Malcolm L. Read more post.

12:26 Graham Ridley arrives. Claims Malcolm L. always "skitting" him and his family. Fed up with it. In middle of chat about the exercise of restraint when....

12:28 Malcolm L. arrives, pleading forgetfulness. Don't believe, fed up with him, extend detention.

12:30 Go out on to school field with some children to relax a bit and get some fresh air.

12:55 Whistle goes.

13:00 Return to room, collect books, depart for Room 5 where group of children are waiting for me. Phone rings as I leave room. Let machine answer.

13:02 Children there. Commence teaching.

13:24 Grounds supervisor enters room, complete with mobile phone. Wants to talk about hedging and field marking. Try politely to get rid. Commences to tell me his life story! Promise to ring up Grounds section.

13:32 Grounds supervisor departs. Resume teaching

13:50 Delivery from Barlows of goods ordered last July. Leave classroom to count boxes and sign bits of paper. Dash back to children.

13.54 Resume teaching.

14:05 End of lesson. Return to office. Message light blinking. Ignore it, retreat to staffroom. Mrs Phillips greets me with long list of concerns about Adrian W. whose behaviour is increasingly disturbed and disruptive. Promise action. Mrs Foley wants to go on science course. Fully funded so I say yes, provided cover can be found. Promise action.

14:15 Whistle goes. Lead staff out of staffroom to greet children entering building. Return to office and realise Malcolm L. not there. Collar passing Prefect and send her for Malcolm L. Extend detention further and give him letter for mother explaining it's Malcolm L.'s fault he gets hit etc. Doubt whether she'll believe me.

14:21 Listen to phone messages. Rebecca C. is to be collected at 3p.m. for appointment. Luckily find a passing prefect to delegate legwork to carrying message to Rebecca C.'s class teacher.

14:22 Phone distant school re VAT advice. Person I need is teaching. He will ring later.

14:24 Phone in about repair for drinking fountain.

14:27 Phone County Hall re Annual Meeting date. Panic over, I've put the correct date. Also ask about election closure. County Hall confirms this.

14:31 Update paperwork returns for County Hall.

14:32 Wonder where visiting parents are.

14:33 Mrs G. (parent) appears wanting some photocopies. Make copies, return to office to find unknown man and woman at door. Take money from Mrs G. and apologise for black lines.

14:34 Usher pair into office and talk about school.

14:38 Set off round school with Mr. and Mrs X, praying no disasters will happen. Quiet orderly atmosphere everywhere. Mr. and Mrs X suitably pleased.

14:55 Return to office, talk more (ignoring phone), give them brochure etc.

14:59 Mrs C. arrives. Rebecca C. not around to be collected. Direct Mrs C. to Rebecca C.'s classroom to collect her.

15:05 Mr and Mrs X leave. Listen to message. One of our volunteer helpers will be in tomorrow.

15:07 Set off to find caretaker to check no 2 pump repair and fuel stock level.

15:09 Caretaker luckily in boiler house. Bunkers have about a week's fuel left so need six tons, pump running OK so far.

15:16 On way back to office, intercepted by cook wondering why packed lunch numbers rising, school meals falling, down from 122 to 95 per day. Try to reassure her meals are fine (they are), that it's menu choice being denied to the last in the queue that causes disgruntlement, despite system designed to share this out. Resolve to check if bulge in packed lunch numbers follows class whose turn it is to be last.

15:22 Remember John K.'s homework, and stop off to tell Mrs Armitage

15:25 Return to office. Photocopier man waiting for me. Send him off to copier. Phone rings. It's teacher from distant school. Tell him about VAT in youth hostels while watching children leave school through window. (See Malcolm L. trying trip up another child. Sigh.) Remember should have done a letter about Adrian W. Scribble note to myself while talking on phone to distant school. Daughter (Y6) enters room, dumps bag on floor and departs to hall to play piano.

15:31 End phone call. Copier man appears saying we need a new drum. Expensive. We'll put up with black lines until new financial year at least. He departs to re-assemble copier.

15:34 Phone rings. It's Mrs L. about Malcolm L.'s letter. She says he's being picked on, that we've never liked him and we've got it in for him, etc. etc. He's always truthful with her and she believes what he says, and what am I going to do about it? Explain politely but somewhat curtly that the letter is true and if she doesn't like my rules, she is entitled to find another school. Put phone down and regret it.

15:37 Phone rings. Lady from Diary Council sponsoring some event wanting to use our kids to raise money. Tell her I'm allergic to all dairy produce. She decides to try elsewhere. Switch to answer machine.

15:40 Phone rings. It's Mrs L. again. Listen as she records message. Will come to see me with Malcolm L. first thing tomorrow.

15:41 Son arrives from comprehensive school nearby.

15:42 Grab bag of unfinished work, correspondence, requisition spreadsheet etc. to do on my own computer/word processor in peace at home, collect daughter from piano and DEPART!

15:45 Passing my office window on way to car, hear answer machine starting. Run to car!

Time was spent that evening doing correspondence, and trying to work out a requisition allocation on the spreadsheet based on fragmented consultation with part-time clerk. Must try to steal some more fragments later. Then started typing up this diary.

At night, sleep disturbed by dream about likely forthcoming confrontational interview with doting Mrs L. and son.

It was interesting the next morning to watch "Malcolm L." squirm as I related his life at school to his increasingly deflated mother. The little sod had told her all sorts of lies and being something of a doting dimwit, she had actually believed him. When challenged, he had no option to repeat the truthful version, much to his mother's aghast amazement, as it flatly contradicted everything he had said to her. Great!

Such a disjointed, stressful day was the norm, and of course lasted into the evening. Increasingly Simon felt himself in a vice professionally, being pressured for constant innovation and change from above, seeking to protect the staff and children from this whirlwind, with only moderate success and thus faced with resistance from below. He felt he had just become a glorified clerk, with no real control left over what was taught, and no room for manoeuvre when it came to resources. Added to which always was the memory of those crimes he had committed years earlier, and the guilt and fear was always there as an undercurrent to his life, sapping his confidence, causing his nightmares to return again and again. He would see himself in his nightmare again out of control and committing the sickening display and act, and then there was David Watson, standing there over him, as he had thirty years earlier in another life, boasting, "I did that. I screwed up your life." Why it was David rather in these dreams rather than his older brother Simon was never quite sure. Perhaps it was the memory of his taunts on that night, how he climaxed during David's rape of him, and the pride, actual pride, David Watson took in doing that.

He carried on as best he could, finding pleasure in the company of the children. For the Lakes week he thought he had at last found the female leader prepared to go, one of his dinner ladies, but then she backed out so it was back to boys only. But he enjoyed the week, kept a diary and was able to relax away from the increasingly depressing pressures of the daily grind at school.

7. *1992 New advisor*

School life continued much as before, and dominating home life as well, as more and more Simon had to work at home in order to get things done away from the interruptions of the school day. It was with some trepidation that he welcomed a new county advisor, Edna Allen, to the school. She had been head of a large primary school with the reputation of never having been there, she was on so many committees and working groups. It was also said that on her promotion, the staff threw a party – after she left! She obviously relished her role and started pressuring Simon over matters within the school. Two things came to a head. One of Simon's teachers, a quiet spoken but efficient lady called Grace, was not favoured by Edna Allen. She had come in on a temporary contract, because Simon could never guarantee that the following year the budget could afford her, but was running the netball team for the girls, and at last, had said she would go with Simon on the Lakes week. Edna Allen had been pushing for Simon to open up the trip to girls, which he was more than happy to do. This meant that Harriet, now in her first year at the comprehensive school with Robert, could go as well now, which she was desperate to do. But this did not do anything to endear Grace to Edna Allen who saw her as weak and ineffectual. But Simon could see her strengths and as with all his teachers, played to those strengths and sought to minimise the weaknesses. This became something of a bone of contention between Simon and Edna Allen. He saw why his head teacher colleagues called her 'The Ice Lady'.

Soon there was another. The nearby nursery school suffered a fire which destroyed much of the building. Arson by local youths was suspected but nobody was ever caught. The county, exemplified by Edna Allen, had a plan to close a small primary school not far away, move all those children to Simon's school and use the vacated building for the nursery, which was already attracting interest from property developers as it was in a good central location. This might have been to Simon's personal advantage financially, but when he found that if this were to happen, the school's science room, library, television room and worst of all the quiet Special Needs rooms at the back of the school would all have to become ordinary classrooms, Simon dug his heels in. He realised that in the end he would probably lose, but he felt he had to fight for children, especially the special needs children. The governors were generally supportive which was one good thing.

The stress was now telling on Simon. He set off back to school one evening for a PTA meeting, but driving through Thirlham, he started to feel dizzy and sick. This was getting rapidly worse and Simon knew he could not go on. He turned at a roundabout and managed somehow to get back home. Getting out of the car, he could hardly stand. Leaning on the car and then the house wall, he made it to the front door and got inside, and then collapsed on the hall floor. He knew he was going to be sick, but he couldn't see very well, and when he tried to stand up, he fell over again.

"Simon, what's the matter," said Karen rushing from the lounge to see what the commotion was. Robert and Harriet quickly appeared.

"Dad?" said Robert anxiously.

Simon crawled to the downstairs loo and was violently sick, beloved Karen standing over him, stroking his shoulders.

"Let's get you upstairs," said Karen. With the children, she helped him up the stairs to the bedroom. He was incapable of keeping his balance and simply fell onto the bed.

"I still feel sick," he said weakly. Harriet immediately dashed off and returned a moment later with the plastic bucket.

"Well thought of," said Karen. Robert was standing by the bed, with a look of great anxiety as he watched his father in this helpless state. Simon lay on, and later in, bed, constantly being sick even when there was nothing left.

Karen called the doctor out. Simon related the symptoms to him. The doctor seemed surprised at the rapidity at which the symptoms had appeared, their severity, and the vomiting. Simon confirmed that his hearing was normal.

"It might be Ménière's disease but I am not convinced," said the doctor. "I can give you something for the immediate symptoms, but we will need to do some more tests."

"What is that?" asked Simon.

"It's a disorder of the inner ear which affects balance. But as I say, we need some tests doing to rule other things out. I'll arrange an MRI scan, just to be certain."

"Certain of what?"

"Just to make sure there's nothing inside your head that shouldn't be there."

"Like his brain," joked Harriet.

"It would rule out there being a tumour which can cause these symptoms, but I am sure it's not," said the doctor smiling.

Karen went and got the prescribed medication immediately, and its effect was quick too. Feeling empty and weak, but able to balance by the next day, Simon rested at home.

The MRI was clear and the eventual diagnosis was labyrinthitis, and as no infection was present, stress induced. Simon continued to take the medication to keep this at bay, carrying it with him always, as he would for the rest of his life. But life returned to its normal stressful state.

The following March, Edna Allen dropped another bombshell. There was a teacher she wanted to redeploy into Simon's school. She would take this to the governors meeting the next week. For once, local management worked in Simon's favour. He had nothing against this teacher whom he didn't know, but Edna Allen's proposal was to end Grace's contract to make room. Suddenly, Daniel and the Court of Honour came into Simon's mind, how he had lobbied for Simon beforehand so that Simon became Patrol Leader. Dear Daniel, where are you now? His words, "No, idiot, before the meeting I mean. A quiet word, you know? My Dad says that all important decisions are really made before the actual meeting" came into his head. He resolved to follow in Daniel's footsteps and saw as many of the governors before the meeting as he could.

At the meeting when the matter came up, Edna Allen seemed very confident, as usual in her businesslike, arch-efficient manner. But then carefully, Simon outlined the contributions Grace had and was to make to the school. The governors were nodding approvingly, and Edna Allen's face took on a look of consternation as she realised that despite her 'belt and braces' approach, this was not going her way.

When the matter went to vote, the Chairman said, "I think we should support the head teacher on this matter." They did.

"Well, then, if that's the decision of the governors, "said Edna Allen sharply, and slammed shut her large filo-fax with a snap. "I have to leave now," she concluded. And she did.

When Simon recounted this a few days later to a head teacher colleague at another of those County Hall meetings, he said, "Be careful, Simon, she doesn't like to be crossed."

So the group of boys and girls went on the Lakes week that year. Despite all the pressure there had been on Simon for girls to go, in the event there were few takers, and as well as Harriet, Eric took his daughter and Grace hers to make up a viable female group within the party as far as dormitory accommodation was concerned. Robert was in the middle of his GCSE exams and so it was thought unwise for him to have the distraction of the week away. Simon had no idea that this would be the last such trip.

Unfortunately it rained almost continuously. Simon thought back to when he had first started the trip over a quarter of century earlier, and how the weather had been kinder. Then a simple waterproof top was all that was required. These days Simon had to recommend a proper cagoule, along with waterproof leggings or gaiters where possible. And these days if the sun shone, he now had to have high value sun block at the ready and told the children to cover the backs of their necks as for the first time, some had suffered from sunstroke and the fair skinned children could get severe sunburn. This was the same route at the same time of year over that time period, and Simon had seen the climate move to one of extremes before global climate change was even talked about outside specialist scientific circles let alone becoming a widespread concern. But sunburn was the last of Simon's problems this time. The rain was continuous and heavy, the children under orders to be in waterproofs constantly.

While the party plodded miserably along the lakeshore, Simon saw Boyd Morgan stumble slightly, and looking closer realised his blue shoulders were not his cagoule but simply a track suit top. Bringing the party to a halt, Simon, angry, berated Boyd.

"What on earth are you doing, dressed like that?" he demanded, angry with himself for not checking this earlier, but did he really have to check these kids could dress themselves? They knew the rules. "You know the rules," added Simon.

Boyd looked downcast, rain running down his face. He was shivering and pale. Dear God, thought Simon, he's on the verge of hypothermia!

"Where's your cagoule?"

"In my pack," said Boyd. Simon felt Boyd's shoulders, they were like ice.

"Best get him changed," said Eric. Simon agreed. Grace led the girls a few yards away and Simon and Eric got the boys to form a circle round Boyd. As he stripped off his wet clothes, they found he was quite literally soaked to his skin. Only his socks in his boots were dry. Even his underpants were wringing wet. Simon hesitated and decided against making him change those in front of everybody. He would have to put up with that. Dry clothes were taken out of Boyd's pack – luckily this was a day when the boys carried their own packs along Crummock Water – and he was dressed and warmed up.

Most of the children saw the seriousness of what might have been. But Nigel Mitchell thought it was all very amusing. Simon was already regretting bringing Nigel along. He did what he wanted to do, was cheeky and was never there when it was his turn to do jobs, much to the annoyance of the others. Simon remembered one of the teachers in the staffroom a couple of weeks earlier when he mentioned that Nigel would be going who commented, "Oh God, you're not taking **him** are you?"

But Simon had felt that he deserved the chance and anyway, it was then too late, and on what grounds could he have excluded him?

The week was different in another way too. The presence of the girls affected some of the boys in a way Simon had not expected from eleven year olds. They were showing off and being silly trying to create some kind of impression with the girls. They mostly ignored it, girls at that age anyway, being more mature than boys. But there was this frisson of what Simon could only describe as sexual tension which he was unsure how to do deal with. After all, there were girls at school with them. He tried to dampen it down as best he could, and Grace was good at diverting attention with indoor games in the wet evenings in the hostels. He found a rag week joke book in one hostel and would use it to entertain the children, avoiding any jokes with asterisks in them!

One evening Grace took some of the children outside the youth hostel for a ball game in a dry interlude. With alarm, Simon saw through the window one of the boys on the rickety roof of an outbuilding retrieving the ball. But he climbed down safely. Back in the hostel Simon felt he had to have a quiet word with Grace.

"Did you send that boy on the roof for the ball, Grace?"

"He said he could go up and get it, so I let him."

"That roof isn't very safe, he might have fallen."

"Yes, I see, but he seemed capable enough."

"Yes Grace, but if he had fallen and been hurt, or worse, what would that have looked like? It would be portrayed that you valued the ball above the life of a child," he said as gently as he could.

Grace looked shocked at this and just nodded. Simon got the feeling that she thought he was making too much fuss. Annoyed Simon went along to the boys' dormitory which was now the source of some noise. It went very quiet as Simon entered.

Toby Reid was lying on his bunk, grinning. "They've been telling rude jokes," he said.

"Oh for heaven's sake, just behave yourselves and stop being silly," he said to one or two now red faced boys that Toby indicated. Barnaby Davies was sitting quietly at the far end of the dormitory, looking anxious. But Simon just left and returned to the Common Room. This tension, the bad weather and the strain was beginning to tell on Simon. His piles were threatening and his old aches and pains returned brought back by the damp and cold, giving him stiff shoulders. He later mentioned this and was immediately offered a shoulder rub by Bruno Upton.

"I'm good at it," said Bruno, "I do it for my Mam."

Simon stretched his shoulders back to relive the tightness, then said, "OK, give it a go." He slipped his shirt off and sat on a chair while Bruno kneaded and rubbed. Simon had expected a bit of childish rubbing, but Bruno was surprisingly expert, and seemed to know exactly where to apply pressure and how much.

"That's very good, Bruno," said Simon. "You mother must have taught you well."

"She says I'm good at it," said Bruno, pressing away round Simon's shoulder blades.

"Well, she's right," agreed Simon. "That's excellent, thank you."

After a few minutes Bruno stopped. "I'll do it tomorrow if you like," he offered.

"Thank you, Bruno."

Then Barnaby came to tell Simon that Nigel Mitchell had been being naughty, so Simon had to go and find him who it seemed had been up to his favourite trick of leaning the full waste bin against the dormitory door so that when it was opened, all the rubbish fell out. It would be bad enough if he just did this to his own dormitory, but now he was targeting those of other hostellers as well. Simon's groups had long had a reputation of being well disciplined and well behaved. Several hostel wardens had commented that his was the one school party they didn't dread. So he was doubly annoyed with Nigel's behaviour.

Thankfully at the end of the week, the weather eased and the party were able to climb Catbells in warm weather, and play in the park in the evening. During a game of football, Nigel was roughly tackled and said the other boy had kneed his thigh. So he left his team one short and went off to play on the swings.

At least the week was ending reasonably well, thought Simon, back in the hostel and receiving a last shoulder rub from Bruno. He left the joke book in the hostel common room for others to use. He packed all the boys off into their bunks and set off downstairs for a coffee with Eric and Grace. He remembered the file he wanted to take and turned back. There in the dormitory doorway was

Nigel Mitchell, taunting members of another group. When he saw Simon reappear he fled back into the dormitory, with Simon right behind him.

"Get into bed!" Simon snapped, reaching out and catching Nigel with his hand as the boy leapt awkwardly for his top bunk, banging his thigh against the woodwork, the same thigh that had been 'deadlegged' in the park, Simon noticed with small satisfaction.

"How on earth can I bring kids away on trips like this when people like you do all you can to spoil it? You have been nothing but a constant nuisance and let down all week!"

Nigel sat silent in his bunk but with that knowing expression on his face that Simon had come to dislike intensely.

On the bus on the way home the next day, Nigel's friend, by this time pretty much his only one, came to Simon.

"Nigel is frightened you're going to tell his Dad about the bins and all that."

"Oh, forget it," said Simon, who was sitting on the back seat with Toby and Bruno where he could keep his eye on all the children.

8. *1993 Suspension*

Back at school on the Monday, Simon found a mountain of work to get on with, as well as preparing for a governors' meeting the following day, especially the financial statement. Simon worked through this carefully aware of this own mathematical weakness, but of course the computer now did the actual computation. The school was £20,000 in credit at the moment which was more than he had expected.

Edna Allen arrived early for the Governors' meeting the next day. Some governors had already gone along to the library where the meeting was to be held. She came into Simon's office.

"Will you just stay here for a moment, I have to speak to the Chairman," she said.

"I'm about ready," said Simon, picking up his papers.

"No, stay here please. I'll be back soon."

Puzzled, Simon continued to gather his things. After a few minutes Edna Allen returned.

"Sit down," she asked. Simon sat. "We have received some allegations about when you were away on your trip."

"What kind of allegations?" Simon felt as though his heart would stop.

"I can't tell you that, but there will be an investigation, in fact it's already started. In the meantime you are suspended from duty."

"Suspended?" Simon was in shock. Allegations? The old fear swept over him, he knew he was starting to shake, but tried to control it. Had his crimes of a decade and a half earlier now come to light? After all this time?

Edna Allen continued. "Of course, only the Chairman of the Governors can suspend a head teacher, but I have just spoken to him, and he has agreed."

"Does he know what these allegations are?"

"No."

"But he still suspended me?"

"Yes. I told him he had no option."

Simon sat, dumbfounded. His guts were churning and he felt faint.

"What now?" he asked.

"You go home and wait. There will be a letter. You will be on full pay of course until it's sorted out."

"How long?"

"We will get this over with as quickly as we can. Are you all right to drive?"

Simon nodded. Edna Allen, perfectly correct as always, put her hand on the folder in Simon's bookcase concerning disciplinary procedures, and coughed a deliberate cough.

"Should I take that with me?"

"I can't tell you that, it's up to you."

But Simon got the hint and picked up the file. He collected his briefcase, actually a pilot case as there was so much paperwork he took home, his coat and made his way out the car park. The children were working away in their classrooms, one or two waved and smiled as he passed. He waved back.

In the car he quickly swallowed one of his labyrinthitis tablets and drove home. He paced around the house, unsure of what to do.

When Karen got home from work, she was puzzled but tried to reassure Simon. But he was now terrified of his past catching up with him, but could not voice his real fears.

The letter arrived and it concerned him hitting Nigel Mitchell, causing extensive bruising to his leg. Simon knew that nothing he had done would have caused such bruising and that the bruises from the football and possibly the collision with the bunk were being used. The letter also outlined what was termed inappropriate behaviour and language. It all related to the week just gone, so Simon was relieved as far as that went, at least.

Then he received a phone call from the police, asking him to attend for an interview. Simon went with a solicitor the union had arranged for him. The detective inspector was friendly enough. Simon was not arrested but he cautioned Simon and took him through everything that happened with Nigel Mitchell. He explained that as far as the police were concerned, their only interest was the allegation of assault. It seemed that over the weekend, all the boys except Bruno had been interviewed and had made statements. None of the girls were questioned. Simon recounted the events as truthfully as he could. At last the tape machine was switched off. They went outside into the warm June day where Harriet was waiting to see what had happened.

The inspector shook his head. "There's nothing here for us. I'll recommend no further action."

"That's one relief, anyway," said Simon.

"Looks like a storm in a teacup to me," said the inspector.

"Well, thank you," said Simon.

"I don't know what the county council intend to do, but it's finished as far as we're concerned."

"Good bye then," said Simon, turning to go.

But as he did, the inspector spoke again. "Have you got any enemies?"

Simon stopped, surprised by this question. He thought for a moment, and replied, "None that I can think of."

The inspector shrugged and turned away.

Simon was later given a full copy of the dossier compiled by police and social services. He and his union representative picked through it. Apart from the alleged assault, the main problems seemed to be about Simon telling a crude joke of a sexual nature and allowing a boy to massage him. Simon had no knowledge of the joke in question, but of course Bruno, who was not questioned, had given him shoulder rubs on two occasions. The only statement to assert that Simon had told the crude joke in question was that of Barnaby Davies. He said it had upset him, as had seeing Bruno massage Simon's shoulders.

"It all seems to come down to this Barnaby lad," said the union rep. "What's he like?"

"He's OK, a bright lad, a bit sensitive I would guess."

"Well, their side have to prove that these things took place. I am confident we can refute their points. Don't worry. I've never lost a case yet."

Simon felt reassured by this. But the days dragged by. He phoned Edna Allen to find out what was happening.

"I am making enquiries and producing a report."

"I thought the police and social services had made all the enquiries," replied Simon.

"I have to make my own and conduct my own interviews."

"How long will that take?" he asked. It had been two weeks already, and he had been given to understand that it should only take about a week or so.

"I'm working as fast as I can," she said, "but I have other things to do as well." The phone call ended.

Simon was surprised to get a visit from the county's deputy director of education.

"I've come to offer my support," he said. "I like to visit teachers who are in trouble if I can. Try not to worry, you have the full support of the authority."

So Simon waited at home, his health suffering and he was prescribed anti-depressants by the doctor. His nightmares came back again with a vengeance, David Watson mocking in his dreams, laughing at Simon's latest misfortune. "I did that!" And not only when Simon was asleep, the images of the rape would haunt him in waking hours, alone in the house while Karen and the children were at school. He tried to shake them out of his head. One day Karen came home to find him banging his head repeatedly against the wall, trying to drive out the demons. A friend told him that Mrs Mitchell had photographs of Nigel's bruises and was showing them to anybody that would look.

Weeks went by, and Edna Allen's report arrived. The union rep was horrified by it, She had re-interviewed only those boys whose original statements had contained anything negative about Simon, and those points were amplified.

"We should ask them our own questions," said Simon. "I can explain the bruises and there were loads of witnesses to both times Nigel bruised his leg, playing football and on his bunk. But they've not been asked."

"True, so the accusations just lie there. See, here, this Boyd Morgan does not complain about when he had to change his clothes, he barely mentions it, but he does say you told jokes. But Barnaby Davies says you forced Boyd to strip almost naked in front of everybody."

"The kid was in danger from hypothermia!"

"And the jokes? Did you tell jokes?"

"I did, from a joke book I found," said Simon.

"Yes, but no child apart from Barnaby Davies says you told the sexual joke."

"Yes, but according to this, they haven't said who did."

"Well, if they did say, it's been left out."

"Toby Reid told me that some of the boys had been telling rude jokes."

"What did you do?"

"I just told them off. I hadn't heard the jokes in question."

The rep was thumbing through file. "Toby Reid doesn't mention it here."

"Was he asked?"

"Again, if he was, it's not recorded."

"This is so one sided. I know I am not supposed to make any contact with the children..."

"Child protection," interceded the rep.

"Yes, but why can't you go and ask our questions?"

"I am not allowed to. But try not to worry."

But Simon did worry. He felt right back in those dark days of 1963, when he had gone hunting for his attackers, intent on killing them before plunging from Bilthaven's City Bridge. But he received letters of support, some from parents, one or two from school staff, but not the teaching staff. He made sure they would be received by delivering them by hand to the office at County Hall.

The date of the hearing was set, the day before the end of term and the summer break at County Hall. Four of the governors were there as a panel. Simon noted all four were either employed by the county council or were married to someone who was. He pointed this out to the rep, who seemed unusually nervous.

He denied causing the bruises to Nigel Mitchell, but did not have the evidence to back up his account of how he had really got them. He denied telling the sexual joke, but did not have the evidence of who did. He accepted that Bruno had rubbed his sore shoulders, but did not have the evidence from Bruno – or his mother – that this had been perfectly innocent.

Later it was Simon's turn to defend himself, but he lacked the evidence from the children that would have supported his case. He even lacked the letters of support, the officials denying they had ever been received.

Both Mr Cooper, now retired and who had come from Scotland, and Mr Bailey were there to support Simon, but as neither had actually been there on the trip, the help they could give was limited. Brian Bailey commented that it all hung on the statement of one child and under scrutiny it just dissolved like wet tissue paper.

Edna Allen felt the criticism of her work and managed to insinuate that whatever happened in Nusbury, here in the County they had their way of doing things – implying of course that the county way was the correct way. Simon's fears came true as the allegations were put and all he could do was say it wasn't so.

The atmosphere was hostile, and when Eric came in, he could not speak for the alleged assault because he had been waiting downstairs for Simon at the time. Simon started to shake and had to take his medication during the hearing. He tried to explain the joke book, annoyed that he had not kept it. He told one of the jokes, about a canary, that he could remember, and noted that one or two of the panel had to suppress a smile. But others remained stony faced.

Then it was over. He and Karen, who had been there to support him all day, waited with him for the panel's decision.

When it came, it was a shock. The panel decided that Simon should 'no longer work at the school'. The rep was aghast. He had expected a reprimand or warning. Even Edna Allen, who had not been present while the panel debated their finding (although another officer of the county had been, to offer guidance) was surprised, and turned to look at Simon, her jaw dropped in astonishment.

Simon was shaking as they went outside, Eric was still there with them waiting. He was shaken at the news.

"I'm never taking kids away again," he vowed. But at that point, Eric's future was not Simon's concern.

"We shall appeal," said the rep.

"We don't have time, it's the end of term," said Simon. "By September it will be too late."

"Maybe that was the idea. I don't see what we can do," said the rep.

"We write a letter now," argued Simon. "After all, we're in County Hall, we can deliver by hand."

"Yes, that would do," said the rep, grabbing a sheet of paper from a nearby table and quickly writing out a note of appeal. This was hand delivered, this time with plenty of witnesses.

9. *1993 Breakdown*

Simon and Karen had to decide what to do about their summer plans. They had booked a trip to Canada. Karen had a Canadian friend Bernadette of many years who lived near Toronto and they had not met since childhood when Bernadette had visited Mansfield as a teenager. As the cost of flying came down, they had been invited over. Simon never felt less in a holiday mood, but the kids were looking forward to it and so was Karen, eager to see her friend again.

So they went. Simon tried to relax but felt his anger exploding at the check in when his frustration boiled over. Karen tried to comfort him, and he calmed down. On the plane, the children were taken on to the flight deck high above Quebec[4] to see the pilots and the instruments, as well as getting a pilots' eye view.

They picked up their hire car, Simon at first taken aback never having driven an automatic gearbox car before, but he soon got the hang of it and they set off along the Queen Elizabeth Way round Lake Ontario to find Bernadette and her husband Neil.

They enjoyed the time, visited Toronto again, up the CN Tower, went to a baseball game at the Skydome with Robert, but neither really understood the game, despite Neil's best attempts to explain things like "the bottom of the ninth" and so on. They went to Niagara Falls and the RCAF museum among other places and walked in the Shorthills. It was hot, very hot, belying Canada's cold reputation, but as Bernadette pointed out, this part of Canada has its own wine industry and is on the same latitude as northern Italy! Karen spent time with Bernadette and they also went to a lakeside resort, staying in a cottage for a few days. He and Harriet went riding, western style with much more emphasis on control through the reins and less on the leg aids which was a new experience. On the return to the stable, Simon's horse walked into a narrow gap that was a dead end.

"I'll have to lead him out," said the leader.

But Simon had already given leg and rein commands for a rein back as he would have done at home, and the horse immediately reversed out of its awkward position.

"How did you do that?" asked the leader.

"Must have European blood in him," joked Simon.

---

[4] This was not uncommon on holiday charters at that time, pre 9/11 of course.

They talked about the world, the new US President Bill Clinton, and the new Canadian Prime Minister Kim Campbell, whom Bernadette didn't rate. To Simon, this was surreal, as though his problems were of another world. But they would keep coming back, and he kept taking the antidepressants.

At one souvenir shop, run by two Asian men, he was appalled to see them openly selling swastika flags and other Nazi material. He tackled the men about it, saying they was wrong to promote this material. They became hostile.

"You leave my shop, now!"

"OK," said Simon, "but remember, you would have been one of the first into the concentration camps!"

Bernadette said she was impressed with Simon's stand on the issue. (She later wrote in a letter that the Nazi stuff had gone from that shop!)

All too soon their stay in Canada was over. Simon thought that this was the trip of a lifetime, and he had no idea if they would ever be able to return to see Bernadette and Neil again. With foreboding as the plane flew through the night back to Britain, Simon felt that black cloud descending on him again. He had kept it at bay while away, but once back home, its malevolent weight seemed to press all the harder.

He read in the paper that the County were looking for cuts in education, as they had a £2 million shortfall. He found it hard to sympathise. He found he just couldn't cope. He collapsed and was constantly weeping, unable to concentrate. The rep came to see him about the appeal. Simon did his best and wrote a more detailed account but they were still stuck without any favourable testimony from the children.

"Did you take photos of the children?"

"Yes of course. I have a slide show for the parents afterwards and they can buy slides or prints at cost afterwards. Why?"

"There has been some suggestion of inappropriate photographs."

"What!"

"So there weren't any?"

"No, absolutely not. Did any of children say there were?"

"Well, not in any of the statements we have access to. You would think if there were, that would be included." The rep was shaking his head.

"So where's that come from?" asked a shaking Simon. Even during his worst excesses years before he had never done anything like that.

"I have no idea. And what's this about money?" asked the rep.

"What money?"

"They are now talking about financial mismanagement, saying the school was wasting money and was over budget."

"What! That's not true. At the very governors' meeting when I was suspended, I was about to tell them that the school was twenty thousand pounds in credit!"

"I don't understand this," muttered the rep. shaking his head.

Simon now felt the black cloud wrapping him up. Somebody was obviously digging. What if they found out about what he had done fifteen years earlier? Of course Simon knew it had been wrong and regretted it, but he knew that would not help. It was just one more thing to haunt him.

Karen got so worried she took him to the doctor who seeing his state, arranged for him to see a psychiatrist. Dr. Yardley at the local psychiatric hospital took one look and agreed to admit him.

So Simon became a mental inpatient. Part of the therapy was to keep a diary. He was assured that this would be his property, the doctors and nurses would never read it so he could commit all his fears and thoughts down on to the paper. If he then wanted to tear it up symbolising doing away with his cares, that's fine! He kept it up for a week. This is what he wrote.

Arrived with Karen to see consultant psychiatrist at hospital. The interview lasted two hours, painfully going over the trauma of the last few weeks yet again. Then Karen went in. It was decided I should enter as an in-patient to relieve family of apparent "roster" which had been supervising me. Introduced to an Irish nurse who was to be my principal guardian angel and shown to a sparse single room (later I discovered called The Cell) containing a carpet, a bed, a chair, and a dressing table, otherwise bare. The window was covered by unbreakable glass which would not open and the lights controlled from the staff duty room opposite. I dumped my bag and lay on the bed studying ceiling with a ventilation grill, sprinkler and recessed striplight. Overheard two old dears discussing at great length whether their door should be open or closed. A kindly male nurse, whom I recognised as a former pupil of some sixteen years ago, fetched me to go to the dining room for tea. I've tasted worse spaghetti bolognese. A young lady invited me to sit next to her. Sue. I could see the scars on her wrists. She'd been in here eight weeks. She has an honours degree in classics, having "cracked up" after finals. She told me how little confidence she has. Then I told her about my Latin marks at school, and told her how I admired anybody who can study it. She also got "A" level French and German, but was so scared of meeting a French or German person and being put to the test in reality, she took classics at university. Not likely to bump into a Roman or Spartan.

After tea, had a talk with Brenda, the Irish nurse and got upset again. Karen returned for visiting, talking about the kids, currently staying with in-laws. After Karen left, watched mindless television and ate cake made by some inmates (sorry, patients) that afternoon. Very tasty.

10.00 p.m. is tablet time. I discovered that the consultant had changed my G.P.'s tranquilliser drugs for an anti-depressant, amitryptaline. I tried to turn in The Cell, and noticed a lens behind the ventilation grill. They take no chances! I realised that I had never been alone, and spent a restless night in the company of that silent eye.

Day 2, Wednesday

Having been told that breakfast was at eight if I wanted it, I woke to my watch alarm at 7.30 a.m. By eight I was in the dining room for cereal, toast and coffee, joined by Sue. I asked what happens during the day. Either talk or not much. I wandered off to my Cell again, to be intercepted by a nurse. The junior doctor wanted me. I spent the morning getting upset going over it all again. By 11.30 I was exhausted and flopped into a chair in the small, non-smokers' lounge. Lunch at midday was lamb - reasonable. I found a newspaper, in the large smokers' lounge, hitherto untouched by the old ladies who seem to make up eighty percent of the patients here. I actually had time to read it thoroughly. Just as I finished, Brenda wanted another chat - more upset. At 3.00 p.m. I went back to the Cell for a lie down. I urgently wanted some privacy. Then Karen and the kids arrived to see me - a great lift. I hugged the kids long and tightly, and talked about their concerns, it was so lovely to see them. They were going to stay with their uncle down south for a few days to give Karen a break. Eventually they had to leave, and I only cried after they'd gone.

Tea was sausage and beans and a factory mini trifle. I watched the six o'clock news and then Karen returned. I was allowed to walk in the grounds with her. In time she too had to leave again, and I returned to the television screen. The programmes were so mindless I wandered off to the patients' kitchen to find some more goodies. I made a coffee and ate some. Returned to watch a film on television. Geoffrey, sitting next to me, physically shook at each bang during a shooting scene. Speculated on his recent past.

10.00 p.m., more amitryptaline and returned for the end of the film. Turned in under watchful eye again, hoping to earn a more ordinary room for good behaviour, i.e. by still being alive!

Day 3, Thursday

The drugs must have been taking effect. I made it down for breakfast, but then returned to the Cell and slept most of the morning. I was woken for a delivery of a get well card from my mother. Lunch was an unappetising fish pie, of which I left half.

After lunch, I had a session with my consultant, the junior doctor and Florence, now my principal nurse as Brenda had gone off sick for two weeks at least. More pain at this talk, but I was moved to a new, single room, much nicer. This one has curtains at the window, and no noticeable lenses.

I spent the rest of the afternoon reading the paper and waiting anxiously for a visit from Karen Sue and Joseph were baking, earnestly putting all their attention into rolling and kneading. I watched. I got the shakes during the afternoon, brooding. The tablets were failing to calm me down, I was as anxious as ever, but this was concealed from the outside world by a shell of intense drowsiness. Not a good combination.

Karen arrived during tea and we went to the not very comfortable visitors' lounge. They would not let me show Karen my room, and when we sat a few moments on comfy chairs in the smokers' lounge, we were asked to move out. So we went outside and sat in the car, listening to one of Radio 2's witty panel shows. When we got back in, a friend phoned up with messages of support and encouragement. Then Philip, a young friend and one time former pupil at my school, arrived so we went back to the visitors lounge. The crowds of visitors had gone by this time. Soon it was time for visitors to go, and I walked with them down to the car park and waved Philip off, then Karen and I parted again. I went in and had another cry.

After that, I ate some of the cakes that Sue and Joseph had baked, and watched television through tablet time. This psychiatric hospital is an old building, arranged around a square and its stone construction, heavy Victorian windows and steeply pitched slated roofs reminded me irresistibly of Colditz Castle. And so to bed.

Day 4, Friday

I awoke to find my room door ajar. Obviously in the absence of the lens, a physical check is made during the night. My whole body felt very heavy and I had to carry myself down to the usual, short breakfast. In a drugged stupor, I returned to my room and fell on the bed, dazed. Yet inside my intellect was active and going over and over my recent trauma. But the route to the world outside my body passed through a shell of drug induced, heavy weariness. I was awoken at 10.00 a.m. by a nurse with a get-well card from two well wishers. I could do with all I could get.

At midday, I dragged myself off the bed and went down for lunch - barely edible fish and chips - and then went to read the newspaper again, the heaviness lifting slightly as the effects of last night's drugs started to wear off. Dean, a male nurse, came to have a general talk to me. I was surprised by an unexpected visitor with gifts of fruit and chocolate, a school cleaner. I know she has not much cash to spare. What a noble gesture! We talked for a short while and then I resumed my read.

The junior doctor wanted to see me and I asked for the drug treatment to be changed. She said she would arrange it.

Sue returned from a lunch out - she's allowed out now - with some college accounts to do, and so, munching apples and bananas, we talked and she did sums.

At 4.30 p.m., I had to chat with Florence, going over the same ground again, and getting upset again.

Later I saw Joseph in the smokers' lounge and congratulated him on his cake making skills. He looked very down and barely acknowledged me. I wondered whether to mention this to the staff, and thought better of it. He was obviously not having a good day though.

At tea, saw two new inmat... sorry, patients. Sitting, eyes red rimmed the evidence of their personal hell within, like us all. Did I look like that? Do I still?

It was good to see Karen after tea, but opportunities for private talk are limited, so we went out to the car. Later I watched television and took new medication at 10.00 p.m., having shaken off the effects of the amitryptaline. In bed I continued reading a biography of the Kaiser. He should be in here too!

Day 5, Saturday

Awoken at 7.30 a.m. with the information that breakfast was later at weekends and I could therefore have a lie-in. Thanks! Dozed off again and was late, but not too late, for breakfast. I noticed that Joseph was in The Cell. My medication now is in the mornings as well, and I had no trouble getting the tablet I felt I needed. I read the paper, and was then given a letter from Harriet. The love and support in it reduced me to tears again. Recovered and read some more about "Willy". Dozed off and was late for lunch, stir fry. Then I realised I hadn't shaved yet, so I went to rectify that.

Karen came at 2.30 p.m. and we went to see my mother, who, because of a recent hip replacement, cannot visit me. It was wonderful to be out - accompanied by a "responsible adult" (Karen) of course - a breath of normality, to be taking tea and biscuits in her back garden talking to her and Ken. Then we went home for a precious hour or two before returning in time for curfew to the secure supervision of my professional guardians. Someone had made a rhubarb crumble - very sweet. Sue refused any on dietary grounds. Geoffrey seemed more lively and talkative than ever before, but there was no sign of Joseph though. The old ladies potter around in the patients' kitchen, loudly discussing the merits of brown or white bread as feed for bluetits. Started carrying round my copy of Erving Goffman's "Asylums", a study of what he called "total institutions" as a sign to the staff that I knew what game they were playing. I don't think they've read it, though.

Day 6, Sunday

Breakfast at 9.00 a.m., then Sunday morning spread ahead in its emptiness. I watched an old episode of "Grange Hill" -Tucker aged eleven! Tony, Philip's older brother, turned up to see me, and I met him as I stepped out to the car park for some fresh air. He stayed two hours and we talked and talked. I took my lunch into the visitors' lounge because he was not allowed in the dining room. As he was leaving, Philip arrived to collect him.

That afternoon, I was in the corridor when I saw Elise, one of the old ladies whom Sue and I called Carrier Bag because she was never seen without one clutched tightly to her side. She had cornered one of the cleaners asking for Mary, indicating one of the staff photographs displayed on the notice board. I thought the evident confusion had arisen because there was a patient called Mary too. I helpfully offered this information. Elise glared at me.

"I know you all," she thundered in her loud, hockey mistress voice. "Don't think I don't know the intercom is listening all the time!"

I couldn't resist this, so I added, "Yes, and there's a satellite up there that's got us all on it, watching all the time."

Elise gave a look of sheer triumph and turned to the hapless cleaner. "There you are," she said. "I knew it all the time. And they think I'm the barmy one!"

Shortly after that, Karen arrived and now with her - a responsible adult - we drove out to a countryside spot and talked. Then home again and some normality. I washed the car and cut the grass, watched my choice on television.

All too soon the curfew drew near and I returned to my refuge. Sue had been visited by her mother and I felt she was upset. She also had news that Joseph was in the general hospital. Having permission to go out alone, he had bought some tablets and had a go. We patients had seen how low he was getting, why didn't the staff? Of course, nobody's perfect. That's why I'm here, for lack of perfection.

Spent time in kitchen talking to Sue, who told me there is a piano downstairs, so went down to try it out. It's badly out of tune but it was fun trying it for a while.

Back upstairs, Sue had gone to bed but I discussed calligraphy with Arthur who spent patient hours lettering dedications and verses in intricate scripts with illuminations like old monastic scrolls. Watched a video in the smokers' lounge (the VCR would be in their lounge) and went late to bed.

Day 7, Monday

Back to 8.00 a.m. breakfast. It was raining hard outside. I went back to the piano for a session and read the paper. I chanced to meet Joseph, being led in by an ambulance crew and noticed his wrist tightly bandaged.

In the afternoon I saw my consultant again and discussed the medication. Fortunately he did not insist on changing back to amitryptaline. I was also "regraded" and was now allowed out unsupervised, provided of course that I inform the staff where I'm going and for how long. Some progress anyway. It was something of a hollow blessing because I could think of nowhere to go in my unaccompanied freedom. The uncertainties of the outside world contribute to the case for my being here. So I spent the afternoon reading more about the Kaiser (up to the funeral for Queen Victoria) and actually getting interested in cricket on television.

After a tea of chicken supreme, I exercised my freedom to meet Karen and spend a couple of hours at home again. All too soon, curfew beckoned and back I went.

Sue had been to the general hospital for some treatment for a bad back and I found she had been kept in overnight. I watched television with Geoffrey and talked to Arthur about his problems. I noticed Joseph was in the smokers' lounge, but being very quiet.

After a week, I was getting used to the routine and pace of this life. Is this the thin edge of institutionalisation? I start the second week of my stay with mixed feelings.

Simon did not keep up the diary. The vestiges of his sanity were preserved by his friendship with Sue. Then one day he saw a familiar face. Anita! Another head teacher! What was she doing here? They compared notes. She too had had a hearing after investigation by Edna Allen.

"Do you know," Anita said, "I think she was actually enjoying it. She's power mad."

Simon thought back. Yes, she did seem to relish it, although Simon did think she was genuinely surprised at the verdict in his case. She had overdone it. Of course, if he were no longer there, she could no longer exercise her role with him. Was he being paranoid, he thought.

Anita was still talking about her hearing, so Simon said a bit more about his.

"Unfortunately, I had some letters of support, which I had hand delivered to make sure they got there," said Simon, "but they went and lost them."

"They lost your letters too?" exclaimed Anita.

"What do you mean, too?"

"They said they had lost mine," she replied, now putting sarcastic emphasis on the word 'lost'.

Simon's paranoia soared to new heights. But Anita was gone after a week, discharged. Simon was not deemed fit or safe enough from self harm, and although the usual maximum stay as an inpatient was three to four weeks, Simon's weeks turned into months.

The new term started without any sign of progress. Robert had left Thirlham Meadows Comprehensive for college to try his hand at BTEC. He had gained some GCSEs but not of course at high grades. But Harriet was still there and getting some hassle about Simon, despite Mavis Dobson doing her best to protect Harriet.

The school cleaner came to see him again, saying how the teachers didn't like the deputy head, now in temporary charge, who was changing things. Yet they had been told that he was still the head teacher. So they didn't know what to expect. Simon was annoyed his deputy was changing things, as though he were gone already. Edna Allen was often at the school and the cleaner thought it was she who was really calling the shots.

He got some more home leave and during one of these the union rep came to see him.

"What's happening about the appeal?" asked Simon as he gave the rep a cup of tea.

"There won't be an appeal."

"What?" Simon was stunned. What was going on? His fear leapt up and he started to shake.

"You are obviously in a bad way," the rep continued, and Karen nodded, holding Simon's hand.

"Yes, he is," said Karen. "What's happening?"

"I've been talking to the authority, and your medical certificates from the hospital say you are suffering from severe anxiety and depression, also post traumatic stress disorder. If you wanted to apply for retirement on health grounds, they would do what they can to help. And you would get some pension enhancement as well."

"Why the change of attitude?" said Simon.

"I think they are worried they might lose an appeal, and if not that, they might lose at an industrial tribunal, and that's a public hearing. They seem keen to avoid that."

"But I would win?"

"That could not be guaranteed, but they don't seem keen to take the risk."

"I don't get this," said Simon.

"Neither do I, to be honest. There's something going on but I don't know what it is. But my advice is to take their offer."

Simon thought about how he had wanted a way out, of his desperation at times with the job. But this? To go like this?

"Look, I've got the forms with me," said the rep. "Think it over, but not for too long. You're forty-eight now, with the enhancement it would be like retiring at fifty-five. Take it."

Later Simon and Karen talked it through.

"Love, you've not been happy for ages. Certainly not since you got Thirlham Meadows. I've seen the toll it's taken on you the last nine years."

"It seems like giving in," said Simon. But in his heart he knew he was going to take the offer. He no longer had the will to fight on. He was broken and he knew it. All the stresses of his life, right back to the loss of Daniel, the rape and his later crimes now were like a huge weight, crushing him.

He took the forms to Dr Yardley. "Simon, I think this is the best thing for you. You need to relax and recover. I feel there are things going on in your life that are far deeper than this present trouble. I think I need a session with you."

Simon nodded. They filled in the forms and sent them off. The session with Dr Yardley, the consultant, instead of the other doctor was painful, but slowly he teased out of Simon about Daniel, his feelings about his own sexuality but although he wanted to, he could not talk about the rape. He just hinted at something in his past. Simon noticed he wrote 'PTSD long term' on the sheet in front of him and underlined it. Simon could not tell him any more because he knew that even a doctor had a duty of disclosure where crime was concerned, but he did talk to Dr Yardley about his fears and the 'demons' within.

But this served to lengthen even more Simon's stay as his revelations had given more concern about his risk to himself.

October came and with it the thirtieth anniversary of the rape. It was a Monday rather than a Friday. It preyed on Simon's mind and deepened his depression, he withdrew to the isolation of his room and wept.

The forms came back with the agreement to Simon's retirement on grounds of mental incapacity. Cruel words, but they did the job. The rep advised him immediately to write to County Hall, resigning from his post as head teacher of Thirlham Meadows Primary School, and stating it was on health grounds alone. Simon did. During the half term he arranged to go back to the school to collect his personal possessions. He had thought just the deputy head would be there, but after he drove in along that familiar driveway, the caretaker waylaid him.

"They're all here," she whispered, and then went suddenly silent, looking over Simon's shoulder. Indeed, not only his deputy, rather his former deputy, but the Chairman of the Governors and Edna Allen. Did they think he would ransack the place? He noticed his office – his former office – had been changed round. He shrugged and took away his books and some other items. The caretaker produced a box for them, and getting a glare from the Chairman for her pains. It was intimidating and uncomfortable. And that was that. His career in teaching was over.

10. 1993 Recovery and a new life

At the same time, Simon was discharged from the mental hospital after a three month stay. But he was still cared for because although it was decided the risk of self harm had reduced, he was still deemed to be vulnerable. He was assigned a Community Psychiatric Nurse whom he spoke to every week, and he also attended the hospital to see Dr Yardley each week. He was now on a whole battery of medication to help him cope, sleep and keep the night terrors at bay. Trazodone, trifluoperazine, temazepam and the prochlorperazine he had been taking for the labyrinthitis. There was a small piece in the local paper, saying that he had retired on health grounds following complaints by parents. How much lay behind that short article, few people really knew.

Gradually Simon climbed from his depression to a level of functionality that enabled him to cope. He remained on the high levels of medication though. Over the coming years the doctor tried a reduced dose, but each time, the black cloud returned, plunging Simon into irrational despair. So the dosage was put back up and again he could appear normal as far as the outside world was concerned. Inside the turmoil remained, the nightmares and flashbacks continued, but he could manage and attain a level of normality.

He noted without much surprise that the county seemed to have solved its £2 million shortfall for that year. They sold off the damaged nursery school in its prime location to a new house building company for – £2 million. The schools were amalgamated as forecast within a year of Simon's resignation. He felt sad for the special needs children evicted from their haven, and now, according to the special needs teacher, competing for temporary space round the school.

Harriet was still suffering from bullying by a small minority of Simon's former pupils, and it was decided that she should move to another school a few miles away from Thirlham in the small town of Dirshingham. The county's chief educational psychologist came to see Simon and Karen, as Mavis Dobson had been concerned about Harriet's well being. The psychologist facilitated Harriet's move, and she said because of the circumstances, Harriet would get a bus pass to enable her to travel from Thirlham to Dirshingham.

"Are you sure about that?" asked Simon. "There are other secondary schools in Thirlham."

"Special case though, Mr Scott," she said. "Not everybody at County Hall is against you, you know."

"Glad to hear it," said Simon, with a slightly sour tone.

"My husband is a mason," she said.

Simon was puzzled. "Where does he work? Is there much call for that these days?"

She laughed. "No, I meant a freemason."

"Oh," said Simon. He wasn't sure how to react to this, he knew little about freemasons, although he had heard that a lot of senior police officers were members. Some kind of secret society with its peculiar rituals.

She now took on a more serious look. "Your Chairman of Governors is in the same lodge."

"Yes?" said Simon. "Somehow that doesn't surprise me."

"So is our assistant director of education with responsibility for finance and resources."

"The man who had to find £2 million?"

"The very one," she confirmed. Simon began to see where this might be leading.

"You know the new housing company, Thirlham Homes, that was set up to buy that land?"

"Yes, but I didn't know it was that new."

"Two of its five directors are also masons, but not in the same lodge. They know each other of course."

"What are you saying?"

"I can't say anything, but my husband is one who thinks that there is probably more than coincidence here. There are others, too."

"Are you saying it was all some kind of Masonic plot?"

"No, the Freemasons as such would not be party to such a thing, I'm sure. But it shows that there was a series of hidden links between otherwise apparently unconnected people."

"I wish my union rep had known this," said Simon.

"Ah, him. He did know. He's a member too."

"Bloody hell!" exclaimed Simon. "I'm surrounded by them! You can't trust anybody." He thought back to how the rep had been so sure the appeal would not go ahead, how he pushed Simon along the road to early retirement.

"Why are you telling me this?" Simon added.

"I felt you ought to know. I know there's nothing you can do about it."

"I'm not sure if that makes me feel better."

Dirshingham School agreed to admit Harriet. Simon went to see the head teacher, whom he knew slightly and who knew the circumstances. He was very kind and assured him that Harriet would be fine.

The next week a terse letter arrived from County Hall saying that Harriet could not have a bus pass because there was a secondary school closer to her home. Simon had expected that. So he made the commitment that he would drive Harriet to school in Dirshingham for as long as it took.

As chance would have it, Simon was allocated to a mental health rehabilitation centre in Dirshingham, so at least that fitted in. Having said he was interested in computers, they put him on a City & Guilds course on desk top publishing. Simon took to this and the instructor quickly realised that Simon's knowledge of computers was at least as good as his own. Simon took to teaching much of the course, preparing notes and exercises for the others to do, also preparing printed material for the NHS trust and other bodies. The instructor was therefore able to devote more time to the printing side of the centre. Over the coming months and few years, Simon continued to attend the centre, having passed the City & Guilds, but continuing as an 'instructor' although still a patient. Eventually the centre was sold for housing development, bringing Simon's time there to an end.

At this time, perhaps seeking a deeper solace, perhaps thinking back to Daniel and those church parades or perhaps more influenced by Karen's faith, Simon was persuaded by a friend who had taken Holy Orders a few years earlier to return to the church. Simon was guided through the process to become a full member of the church and was confirmed a few months later. Simon and Karen became quite active in their local church with the constant support of their priestly friend. Simon was overjoyed when their friend, who was curate at the church, offered Simon the role of server. Exactly what Daniel had been doing more than forty years earlier when he had offered Simon the wine!

Simon was devoted to his two growing children and Karen and Simon did their best to soften the effects of Simon's change in circumstances. Their roles changed as Karen was still teaching in Nusbury, and he was mainly at home. Simon felt guilty that his situation had affected both his children, more guilt to add to that of fifteen years earlier, but the medication helped keep him reasonably stable and he grew used to the low state of his mood until it became a sort of norm. Karen was as always loving and supportive, valuing Simon as a husband and saying he was good father. He buried his guilt and fear and tried to get on with life. He had mentioned his rape briefly to her, and she was shocked and appalled at what had been done, but Simon could not go into details with her and they didn't discuss it again for many years. Something else Simon buried away, locked in that box in his mind that dare not be opened.

11. 1995 Alzheimer's

He continued to visit his mother and Ken. They had been upset by what had happened, but were supportive.

He was sitting in their lounge one weekend chatting away.

"And how is school these days?" asked Mum, cheerfully.

Simon and Ken looked at each other, Simon surprised, Ken seemed more wary.

"Kate, Simon doesn't work at the school any more," said Ken gently.

"Oh, of course. How stupid of me. I'm so sorry darling," she said, peering at Simon, trying to see him across the small lounge.

Such incidents started to occur more often, but Mum always quickly recovered when the error was pointed out. In a private chat to Ken, Simon found that this was happening more frequently and Ken was getting a bit worried about it.

"When is it you're off to Canada?" she asked one day.

"We went last year," said Simon.

"Oh yes, so you did," Mum said, cross with herself. And the conversation moved on but about ten minutes later she asked, "You're going to Canada soon, aren't you? Are you taking the children?"

"We took them before, "said Simon, anxiously.

"How did you manage them all?"

"What do you mean, Mum?"

"All those schoolchildren on the aeroplane. They must have been a handful."

"I didn't take any schoolchildren."

"You take children away from the school don't you?" said Mum, puzzled. Simon didn't know what to say. Ken was looking quite distressed.

"Mum, I took my own children, not ones from the school. I don't teach anymore." This was painful.

"Oh yes, your two, er... um.. what're their names? I seem to have forgotten."

"Robert and Harriet."

"Of course!"

Later Ken confirmed that this was becoming more common, and sometimes she forgot who Ken was. Simon was upset she had not been able to remember her grandchildren's names. She did see them fairly often. Ken said she often forgot the names of Frances's two boys so he was not alone. It was agreed to consult the doctor.

Mum went in to see the doctor. Patient confidentiality meant that Ken could not go in with her. After a few minutes, she came out. The doctor drew Ken and Simon aside.

"Mr Thompson, your wife seems quite lucid to me. She told me about her shopping trip last week in Oxford Street, and her recent trip to Canada."

"Doctor," said Ken. "My wife hasn't been to London, let alone Oxford Street, for five years, and she has never been to Canada."

The doctor looked surprised. "Oh dear. She seemed so certain."

"I am sure that when she says it, she believes it," said Ken.

"In that case, I think I had better make a referral to a consultant in this field."

"What field?"

"Er, memory, that kind of thing," said the doctor with false nonchalance.

"You mean Alzheimer's don't you?" Ken was blunt.

"Let's not jump to conclusions just yet."

But Mum's condition got worse. Eventually the consultant confirmed a probable diagnosis of Alzheimer's disease, pointing out that the only certain diagnosis was post mortem! Ken was referred to the local branch of the National Dementia Society, where he met some wonderful people who offered support. A visitor would come to the house so Ken could go and do the shopping as now Mum's state was so uncertain that he did not want to leave her alone. Ken bore this new burden with the same quiet strength and fortitude that he had shown in the face of her blindness. Simon did what he could to help, visiting often and always at the end of the phone.

Simon felt strong enough by this time to resume his voluntary service ethos and where better than the National Dementia Society? Initially helping with their computers where Simon had some expertise, he quickly became Branch Chairman and worked hard to promote the society and cause of dementia sufferers. Over the next few years, he worked quietly away, putting his pastime of website design to good use and donating all the money raised to the Thirlham branch of the National Dementia Society, over the years into the thousands. Simon became a member of the Community Health Council among other bodies, and later the Patient Council for the mental health NHS trust where he had been an inpatient. He was elected Chairman of that as well. He found this very interesting and it gave him a new purpose, helping people with dementia and their carers, as well as those with more general mental health problems. He was still under the care of his doctor for his own mental health and still dependent on high levels of his medications, but being also a service user, as many of the patient council were, gave him extra insight.

Simon's and Karen's silver wedding was celebrated with a family meal. Karen had always liked going to see a show in London, and when they could, Simon and Karen did this, staying overnight near Piccadilly. Her family had clubbed together to get Simon and Karen a special surprise for their anniversary, but in the end they had to tell Simon. But Karen was in blissful ignorance.

At the meal it fell to Simon to make the announcement.

"Karen, my darling. You have been the most wonderful wife for twenty-five years, and I am not alone in thinking that. Your family have clubbed together to buy you – us – a special treat. You have always enjoyed going to a show, so we are off to see *Sunset Boulevard* - " and here Simon paused for effect, "- in New York!"

Karen was visibly shocked. She beamed but was completely surprised. "I thought it might be going to a show, but New York never crossed my mind!"

The family were pleased to see her reaction and final plans for the trip could be confirmed.

Harriet decided to leave school. Dirshingham School, perhaps chasing its place in the new school league tables, had pushed her hard, taking ten GCSE subjects. She did very well, earning five As, four Bs and a C. But the effect of this was burn out and after one term in sixth form, she said she had had enough. And being Harriet, now aged sixteen, there was no persuading her otherwise.

She took the opportunity to accompany Rita to New Zealand who wanted to see her last surviving brother, Harriet indulging her taste for travel.

The silver wedding trip to New York was wonderful. Apart from going to see the show on Broadway, they took a carriage ride round Central Park and a helicopter ride around Manhattan. They went to the top of the Empire State Building and visited as many galleries as they could fit in, MoMA, the Museum of Modern Art, being a favourite. Their hotel was just off Fifth Avenue, a walk from Time Square, and in their room they relaxed and made love, away from their problems in the romantic situation rediscovering their deep love for each other. Simon had no problem walking round New York city at night, carrying his video camera. He never felt threatened or uneasy. Steam poured from the vents and the yellow taxis hooted; it was just like the movies! All too soon, they flew back, back into the everyday of work, voluntary for Simon, teaching for Karen, and caring for their family.

Simon continued to visit Dad and Phoebe, often driving over from Mansfield when they were visiting Karen's family. Dad was now quite infirm, having suffered a stroke which left him with balance problems and impaired vision. He was now well into his eighties, but the sharp mind was still there and he would talk of his wartime experiences in a way he never had before, especially his beloved Mosquito. "Could turn inside a 109 you know," he would say, referring to the Mosquito's agility compared to the famous Messerschmitt. "Very useful more than once."

Phoebe cared for him patiently but her own health was not good. She still smoked and that along with the legacy of her tuberculosis was catching up with her. Dad became progressively more immobile which made him miserable. While his body was gradually packing up, his brain remained very aware. He was frightened.

Robert was now 20 and on a 'scheme', one of many as his disability preventing him from getting a job. There he met Melanie and they spent a lot of time together. Karen and Simon were distracted by family matters.

Karen's mother Rita was now in poor health. In her seventies and plagued with arthritis, she developed respiratory problems. These came to head when, undaunted, she went with Karen's dad Vince and two of her brothers on a Mediterranean cruise. There was an outbreak of some kind of infection on the ship which overwhelmed the ship's doctor. Rita was put ashore at Port Said, Vince went with her. Karen's brothers had no option but to sail off. Soon the hospital in Port Said decided to transfer her so in a rickety ambulance she was moved to a hospital in Cairo.

Vince phoned up in despair. He had managed to find a hotel and visited Rita as often as he could. Karen was worried and upset by this of course and Simon tried to comfort her. The hospital's response to her lung condition was increasing doses of oxygen, and increasing amounts on the bill!

"Bring her home," said Simon to Vince in Egypt, "in fact bring her here."

"How?" said Vince, his brain not functioning under the stress.

"Get a flight back here, to Bilthaven Airport."

"My car's at Gatwick," said Vince.

"Bugger your car, get that later."

But Vince rose to the challenge and two days later, Simon drove to Bilthaven Airport and collected Rita and Vince. She was obviously not well, and made full use of her wheelchair that Vince had had the foresight not to leave on the ship.

"It's lovely to be back home, I thought I would never see green fields again," she said as they drove back to Thirlham.

Simon put a chair and table out on the lawn at the back and took Rita out a cup of tea as she sat in the garden in the English summer sunshine.

"That's the best cup of tea I've ever tasted," she said, tears of gratitude in her eyes.

A short time later the phone rang. It was Karen's younger brother Craig.

"Simon, I'm phoning from Athens, first chance I've had to get to a phone. I've got some bad news for our Karen."

"She's about somewhere," said Simon, wondering what on earth could have happened now.

"It's Mam," said Craig. "She's in hospital in Egypt and Dad's with her."

"No," said Simon, "she's sitting in our back garden having a cup of tea and your dad and Karen are with her."

Craig was silent for a moment. "How did you do that?"

"Not me," said Simon. "Your dad got her on a plane to Bilthaven and I picked them up a couple of hours ago."

"That's a relief," said Craig. "How is she?"

"A lot better for being back home," said Simon, "but she's obviously not a well woman."

"I thought going on the cruise wasn't the best idea, but you know Mam, stubborn as they come."

Rita stayed with Simon and Karen, getting a bed downstairs and making the dining room a temporary bedroom. Vince had to go home, and to collect his car for one thing that was racking up airport parking charges.

The doctor was unhappy with Rita's lungs and she was taken to see a consultant a week later. He wanted her in hospital for tests so she went into Nusbury general hospital. Over the next three weeks, her condition declined. Simon and Karen visited very day, and as she worsened, they stayed continuously, one of them always with her twenty four hours a day. She said she wanted to be confirmed in the Church of England, and Simon was able to arrange this simply by virtue of ringing up a retired bishop of some note – some might say notoriety depending on their attitude to the legacy of Margaret Thatcher - who agreed to do this. It made Rita so happy.

"He's world famous and he came to see me," she said, full of emotion, sitting in her hospital bed after the Bishop had departed. Certainly his arrival at the hospital had caused something of a stir. And Simon who chauffeured the Bishop to and from his retirement home had a three hour one to one with one of the foremost theologians and church leaders of the day, discussing a wide range of topics, including the knotty problem of man's free will and determinism.

Craig, who now lived near London, said he would come up the next day, but he was never to see his mother alive again. She died that morning, Karen was with her, and Craig and Vince arrived a few hours later.

Simon helped with the funeral arrangements and Rita was buried where she wanted to be, in Mansfield.

There was Simon's Dad, now in a nursing home, and being turned every two hours. It was very distressing to see. Simon forgot all the antagonism of earlier years and wept to see this once proud man, world war two pilot, broadcaster, pioneering in some ways, brought low to this state.

Simon's Mum was now much worse. The phone would ring.

"Simon, is that you?"

"Yes Mum, what's the matter?"

"Come and help me. There's a man in the house."

"A man? What man? You mean Ken?"

"It's not the real Ken, it's someone pretending to be him. Come and take me home."

"Mum, you are home."

"No I want to go back home, to Mummy and Daddy."

So Simon would drive down to the house in the centre of Thirlham, try to get parked. Ken would meet him at the door, ashen and upset. They went into the lounge, where Mum was sitting in her chair.

"Oh, hello Simon. What brings you here?"

"You phoned me to come down."

"Did I? Oh well, you might as well have a cup of tea now you're here. Put the kettle on love," she finished, looking at Ken.

Sometimes Simon would be visiting when Mum would say anxiously, "Where's Simon?"

"I'm here, Mum, talking to you."

"No, the little one," she replied. "Is he home from school yet? I should be there."

Part of Simon found this interesting, in that she could simultaneously think of him as an adult and a child, each being equally real. The way Alzheimer's first destroys the chronology of memory before destroying the memories themselves. But of course it was distressing as well, and as much for Mum as Simon and Ken. In the end it was easier to go along with these false realities than constantly to try to correct them.

Then there was the time she 'got out'. Ken had gone into the kitchen to cook their supper and because he was frying fish, he shut the kitchen door against the smell spreading round the house. When he came out, Mum was nowhere to be seen. Her white stick was still leaning on her chair. Ken looked up and down the street, but she was gone. In desperation he phoned Simon who came down into Thirlham again and drove round the streets but could not find her.

They phoned the police.

"My wife has gone missing, and she has Alzheimer's disease and is registered blind," said Ken, trying to think what she had been wearing.

"Is she a small lady, grey hair, red cardigan, denim skirt?"

"Yes!" said Ken, thankful.

"She's here," said the officer at the other end of the phone. "And I'll tell you, she's keeping us all right, she'd run the place given half a chance."

Waves of relief surged through both Ken and Simon. Simon walked to the police station which was only a few hundred yards away.

"A couple out walking with their dog came across her and thought there was something amiss, so they brought here," said the desk officer.

"Hello love?" said Mum, utterly unsurprised to see Simon. "Are you working here tonight?"

"Mum, I left the police years ago. Come on back with me."

He took Mum and led her home, thanking the officers for their care.

After that her condition deteriorated rapidly. She quickly lost the power of speech and could only speak in an incoherent babble. But their years together meant that Ken could often understand what she wanted, even though Simon could not make much out.

The strain of years coping with this was telling on Ken, and she went into a nursing home to give Ken a break. She was to remain there, only occasionally leaving for visits out. She too now had arthritis and was increasingly immobile.

Simon took the chance to travel to Nottingham to see Dad. Phoebe was visiting every day, but his misery and fear was obvious. Simon didn't know which was worse. Dad, with his body giving up, trapping his still alert mind, aware of his coming end; or Mum, her mind almost gone, living solely in the moment, perhaps unaware of her true state. Simon prayed that his own end, when it came, would not be like either of these.

12. *1999 Births and deaths*

Robert meantime had decided to move in with Melanie into her council house in a run down area of a former mining village. Karen and Simon did not think the couple were well matched, but Robert was determined. They celebrated his twenty-first birthday in Thirlham, Mum was there too, but barely aware of what was going on. She seemed unaware of the celebration of her eightieth birthday some time later. Robert seemed happy enough with Melanie, no doubt, thought Simon and Karen, because of the sex. So it was no surprise when Robert announced gleefully that Melanie was pregnant. Simon and Karen just hoped it would work out. Harriet, now working in Thirlham, was very sceptical.

Then Phoebe rang to say that Dad had died. More funeral arrangements. Another funeral, in Nottingham. Simon met some old colleagues of his father's he had known in his BBC days.

That summer, Simon and Karen went off on a motoring holiday round Europe, to stay with friends in Munich and tour central Europe and the Italian Lakes. Robert and Melanie's baby was not due until September, but Harriet kept them up to date with a series of text messages.

Sitting in their friend's garden in Munich on August 11th, they waited for the sun to go out. On the television they could see the crowds gathered in Cornwall under the rain clouds and the sky darkened but sadly for them, the sun remained hidden. They tuned into Sky News and watched the eclipse over Cornwall, the UK commentators trying to make the best of the cloud and rain. Like many people in the UK, they saw the shots of the eclipse from the aircraft that every TV network seemed to have chartered to get above the clouds.

But the eclipse was coming their way, so they went into the garden where it was now warmer and dry, with blue patches in the sky. Fingers crossed! They had the foil viewers and sat on the veranda with the TV in the lounge behind them and hoping for a clear bit of sky. It cleared and then through the viewers they could see a bite taken out of the sun. It got cooler and dimmer. A strange light, unlike twilight, but best described as diluted light, Simon thought. Cooler and darker, the partially obscured sun taunted them among the clouds. It got to the point where there was just a sliver of sun left. It was in a clear patch, and Simon was looking through the viewer. He turned to check the TV, now on the local station, and saw the same image, which suddenly disappeared. He turned round and looked up, forgetting the viewer - and there was a black hole in the sky, surrounded by the corona of bright light, easily seen with the naked eye. Karen was trying to find the sun with a viewer, but Simon told her just to look. It was an eerie and awesome sight, no picture or TV image of which can properly duplicate. They could see "Bailey's beads", where tiny fragments of the sun shine through valleys on the rim of the moon. How incredible that the sizes of these two objects viewed from Earth match so exactly! Astonished and subdued they watched, oblivious of the camera lying ready for just this. The sky was a deep blue, not dark, and three or four stars were visible. Glancing down into the garden, Simon saw that there was darkness, he couldn't see the other side in shadow. It was quiet, cold and still. Blue sky, stars and clouds, but dark at ground level. Dark shapes of trees framing the deep blue sky with darkness below and around them. Distant yelps of delight from others in their gardens. The TV screen was showing totality from an aircraft above Munich. After perhaps 30 seconds, a cloud came across the face of the eclipsed sun, and they didn't see totality again, and so missed the "diamond ring" of the sun's re-appearance. But they had seen totality, which is more than many people have had the fortune to do. They all celebrated with white German sausage, a sweet mustard and beer with bretzel bread.

They moved on around their tour, bidding their friends farewell. It seemed the doctors were getting worried about the baby. Melanie smoked heavily despite all Robert's entreaties for her to stop, even just while pregnant. Simon and Karen were sitting on the terrace of their hotel in central Germany looking out across the valley and enjoying the warm evening sunshine when Simon's phone buzzed in his pocket. Another text from Harriet.

'Do you want to know the sex of the baby?'
'Yes'
'Melanie has been induced. Baby Donna is on the way.'

They waited anxiously, wondering how their lives would be affected by being grandparents.

'Mother and baby well. Donna 6lbs. Robert happy.'

They raised another glass of wine and drank a toast to Donna. They enjoyed the rest of their tour but of course wanted to get back and see their first granddaughter. Robert had painted the back bedroom of the council house as a nursery with loving care. But Melanie soon fell victim to post natal depression and kept leaving the house to spend time at her mother's house not far away. Robert was left alone in the house with Donna, he would feed and change her and a deep and close bond developed between father and daughter.

Simon went to see Mum in the nursing home. There was this incoherent, frail little woman.

"Si Si Si," she could manage, when she saw him. This woman whose powerful intellect and command of language had once been her stock in trade now unable to speak her son's name. At least she recognised him, he thought, although perhaps just as someone significant. Was she still aware of the relationship?

"Mum, you're a great grandmother," he told her. Was that a smile in response? Those once sharp blue eyes now peered blankly at him.

"Robert is going to bring Donna to see you tomorrow, she's three weeks old now." Was that a nod? He got up to leave, fighting back the tears.

"See you tomorrow, Mum. Love you."

"Love you," replied Mum with such sharp clarity it took Simon by surprise. He looked again to search those eyes for the spark of intelligence, but they seemed blank and unseeing.

In the car park, he wept until the emotion subsided. Then, abandoning his plan to visit Ken, he drove home to Karen's comforting presence.

In the morning, the phone rang. It was Ken, upset. "Simon, I'm afraid your Mum died this morning."

"Oh Ken, I am so sorry."

"Well, I lost the Kate I loved some years ago, so I don't know whether now I start mourning or stop."

"She has no more suffering now, Ken." Simon didn't know what to say. It had been expected now for so long, but even so when it came, it hurt. Simon felt odd, his father and his mother were now both gone. He was the senior generation now and it made him feel old, much older than being a grandfather had.

Simon spoke at Mum's funeral in her local church, which was well attended. The *Bilthaven Mail* carried an article about her, extolling Kate Drummond as a ground breaking journalist, which was nice of them. It was thirty five years since she left the *Bilthaven Mail*.

Harriet was now getting 'itchy feet'. She shared Simon's interest in things German and spoke it fairly well. She and a friend decided they would go and live in Berlin. A few years earlier on a family holiday, they had visited Berlin, Simon realised an ambition which was to walk through the Brandenburg Gate, which he did with Robert and Harriet each side of him. They liked the city, its busy, cosmopolitan atmosphere and its free and easy lifestyle, not to say relatively cheap. It was far from the grey city of the stereotype gleaned from wartime news and films. So the two young women set off and after a couple of weeks in a hostel soon found a flat in the Friedenau district. A new century, a new millennium and a new life.

In the Spring, Simon loaded his Ford Mondeo with all Harriet's possessions, the back seats folded flat and even the passenger seat and footwell crammed with her stuff. He crossed to Hamburg and set off on the drive to Berlin. Guided by Harriet's directions he found the flat and even managed to get parked right outside, something of a miracle according to Harriet. So the car stayed put for the week Simon stayed with them, being shown the sights. It was nice and relaxing. He met Harriet's friend Kieran whom she had met in the hostel, an intense young American who had been backpacking round Europe but had decided to stay longer in Berlin. He said this was because Harriet was in Berlin, but Simon missed the significance of that remark.

On the way back, an incident occurred which stirred his demons again. Simon was returning from Berlin by car and was looking round the ship en route from Hamburg. He found the ship had a sauna and curious, went in just to see what it was like. Suddenly he was closely surrounded by several naked teenage boys in various states of arousal. He saw their fit young bodies, some had erections and it was evident they were enjoying more than just each other's intellectual company. He backed away, but they were urging him in German to undress and join them. He felt them touching him through his clothes. Simon beat a hasty retreat but was shaking and anxious from the experience. Even once back home the ghosts would not go away and Simon sought and received further counselling via his doctor to quieten the demons again.

The church now had a new vicar. Simon and Karen continued to be active, but their friend who was curate at the church found the new vicar hard to work with. There was a silly incident when a child, who regularly helped Simon counting the wafers and dealing with the robes, got lost, only for ten minutes. But Simon was asked to help search and found the boy sitting playing by the Lych Gate. But then he got blamed for having taken the boy there in the first place, even though it had been the churchwarden who had asked Simon to help search when he was in the vestry. The vicar seemed to use this as an excuse to undermine Simon, and they soon found their position in the church impossible and withdrew from the church completely. Their friend was most upset, but could do nothing. It deepened the rift between himself and the vicar. A few months later the vicar was taken out of the parish and given a post on the bishop's staff.

Simon buried himself in his voluntary work for his various charities and committees while Karen was at school, helping Robert where he could with Donna. Robert and Melanie weren't getting on; with Melanie spending much time at her mother's, Robert seemed to carry the main bulk of caring for Donna with help from Karen and Simon. Robert was also worried about money. He was still dependent on benefits and kept getting sent on one scheme after another, but none resulted in employment. He felt that Melanie, who never shared financial information with him, was in some kind of trouble, but he didn't know what.

Simon started to grow more worried about his own health. His damaged right eye was troubling him, and he reasoned that in the decades since his accident, medical science had moved on, laser treatment perhaps. But the scarring was too bad, so he had he to continue to adjust. He was now plagued by a series of urinary infections which were painful and kept returning despite antibiotics. A scan showed his right kidney had cysts on it and it was true he often had pain from it, but the doctors didn't seem too worried.

After several months in Berlin, Harriet and her friend had been unable to find a proper job. She had done some English Conversation work, but it wasn't paying the bills and through the summer, Simon and Karen had had to move money over to bail her out, even while touring Scotland in glorious weather that summer. So Harriet came home, but immediately announced her intention of going to California to see Kieran who was now working in Silicon Valley. She didn't want to be at home any more so off she went.

Meantime Simon had undergone further tests to get to the root of his urinary problems, and they found a cancer in his bladder.

"You're lucky," said the consultant.

"Lucky? To have cancer?" said Simon.

"Well, if you're going to have cancer, this is one of the better ones. It's what we call a five year, fifty percent cancer."

"What does that mean?"

"It means that five years after diagnosis, half the patients are still alive," said the consultant brightly.

Was that meant to be comforting? thought Simon. He was still in his mid fifties and was by no means ready for this!

Harriet phoned and was given the news but she had some of her own. She and Kieran had got married! Simon was hurt she hadn't told them, but Karen accepted it. Harriet had always known what she wanted and had gone for it with a single mindedness that was admirable. Simon wished Robert had a bit more of that character trait.

The tumour was removed and Simon was told that it had been caught at an early stage and had not penetrated the bladder wall. He was lucky he had been being investigated for his kidney trouble or it might have been much worse by the time it was discovered. It had been partially blocking the tube into the bladder from his right kidney so it might have been at the root of that problem too.

All stresses of recent events pressed in on Simon; the responsibility of Donna and Robert, the strain caused by the loss in quite quick succession of Rita, his father and his mother and now his health. His depression medication was back at the maximum, and he managed to carry on.

One December day the phone rang.

"Hello?" said Simon.

"Simon? It's Mrs Palmer here – from Nottingham."

"Oh, hello Mrs Palmer," said Simon, remembering Dad and Phoebe's next door neighbour.

"It's about Phoebe. I think she's dead."

"Pardon?" said Simon, shocked.

"Well, her curtains stayed closed which is very unusual and I sometimes hear her radio through the wall and I didn't so I knocked but there was no answer. So I had the spare key and went in and she was on the floor next to her bed."

"Oh dear, have you called an ambulance?"

"Yes, and the police came too. The policeman is here, he wants to speak to you."

A man's voice, sounded quite young, Simon thought.

"Mr Scott? PC Mannion here. Are you Mrs Scott's son?"

It took a moment – he never thought of Phoebe as Mrs Scott. "No, she's my stepmother. My father married again. Is there a problem, you being there? I mean was she attacked or anything?"

"Oh no, nothing like that. But when there's a sudden death, we attend."

"Of course," said Simon, remembering. He had attended quite a few himself in his policing years.

"The doctor says it's natural causes, but there may be a post mortem."

Simon was relieved. So the next day he drove alone down to Nottingham. He spoke to Frances in London on the phone and once natural causes was confirmed, he pushed on with funeral arrangements. He decided he might as well stay in the house, although he slept in the spare room. It was odd, being alone in that house, where Dad had lived so long and Phoebe too. He started working his way through their address book, ringing up people to tell them about the funeral, Some names he knew, some he didn't. One call gave him a surprise.

He started with his usual opening. "Hello, I am Simon Scott and I am calling about Phoebe Scott, once known as Phoebe Ellis. Your name is in her address book."

"Oh yes," said this woman in Blackburn, warily.

Simon went on to break the news of her death and give details of the funeral. "Will you be coming? So I have an idea of numbers for catering."

"No, I won't come. I haven't seen Phoebe for forty years or more. I'll send some flowers though. After all, she was my sister."

Sister! Simon was speechless. Phoebe had never talked about her family and it had never occurred to Simon to ask. A sister she hadn't seen for forty years, but who was only a hundred miles away, perhaps a three hour drive? Simon could not absorb this. The conversation ended and Simon needed time to recover, musing on the strangeness of life and relationships before resuming his phone calls.

Another funeral.

Then in February without warning – to Robert anyway – he and Melanie were evicted from the council house for rent arrears. Robert was on a scheme so Simon drove to the house to find bailiffs throwing stuff out. It was heartbreaking to see Donna's toys out in the snow, their pathetic sticks of furniture being dumped in the street. Robert was distraught. Melanie said little, having been found out as not managing the money. She had been hiding all the bills and ignoring them.

Melanie took Donna back to her mother's, Robert came back home. To ease the burden, Karen agreed with Melanie's mother, who had other daughters living at home, that they would have Donna at the weekends, so Robert could keep contact with his daughter. But Robert missed Donna so much that when Melanie got another house, he went back to try to mend their relationship. Robert tried hard, and he said Melanie did too, but Simon and Karen's fears that they were not well matched proved well founded. They parted once more, but Melanie was now pregnant again. Robert and Melanie stayed friends and Donna still came to be with her Daddy at weekends, an added strain though for Simon and Karen, however much they loved little Donna – it was hard work and they were not as young as they had been when struggling through their own children's childhoods. This was a tremendous strain as Karen was having a very hard time at work with her unsympathetic head teacher. Looking after young babies is something that young people have the mental and physical resources to do, so it took its toll on Simon and Karen. Melanie was extremely hostile. But Simon and Karen kept negotiating and putting in resources for the sake of the baby, and an outright break was avoided - just. Melanie was very suspicious of Simon and Karen, by her own later admission, and thought they were trying to take her children away from her. A turning point came when after one of her family reported her to Social Services for abusing Donna (a total fabrication), Robert was extremely supportive of her and was very angry. His support impressed the investigators and also Melanie. Robert and Melanie became a bit more friendly after that, and she started to want Robert back again. Maybe she realised what a caring and gentle man she had lost, but it was too late.

At one of his cancer checks every three months, an unpleasant procedure with a camera inserted into the bladder via the obvious route, the cancer had returned. Simon could see this now on the monitor, a weird feeling looking at the inside of his own bladder, but it took his mind off the pain of the insertion. Quite soon the second tumour was removed and during the same operation, the tube from the right kidney into the bladder was widened to ease the strain on the cystic kidney, a procedure called a uretetic meatotomy which Simon liked saying because of the way it rolled off the tongue.

That summer, Simon and Karen decided to celebrate Harriet's wedding. The actual ceremony in California had apparently been very small, but the wedding reception was to be anything but. He and Karen decided to push the boat out. As Simon remarked, they had just the one daughter, and only Harriet could have the wedding one year on one continent and the reception another year on another continent!

A medieval castle, now a luxury hotel, was chosen as the venue. Friends and family came, some former colleagues such as Brian Bailey, Melanie, now heavily pregnant – in fact Simon wondered if the baby might be born during the meal. Kieran and many of his friends came over from America, mostly from Ohio, his home state, staying at the hotel, one friend, Trent Liddell, remarking, "I'm sleeping in a room that's older than my country!" Bernadette and Neil came too. It was a real gathering. While the excellent gourmet meal was being served, Donna sat in her high chair, nonplussed by the food around her.

"Chips!" she called.[5]

There were no chips. Simon went to the hotel kitchen.

"Any chance of a plate of chips?"

"For the young lady, sir?" came the response with a smile.

"Yes, she has not yet had time to acquire a taste for the finer things."

"Certainly, sir, no trouble at all."

---

[5] What are known as chips in Britain are French Fries in America but are usually fatter than the fast food variety.

So everybody, including Donna, ate to their satisfaction.

After the partying was over, most of the young Americans took advantage of their visit to Britain to see something of the country. Most had never left the USA before, some had never left Ohio. Bernadette and Neil stayed a few days with Simon and Karen, Harriet and Kieran jetting off home.

On the Tuesday ten days later, Simon took Bernadette and Neil to Bilthaven Airport to catch their flight to Amsterdam, from where they would fly to Toronto. He was due for a cancer check that afternoon, but then they got the news that Melanie had gone into labour, so she and Simon ended up in the hospital at the same time, on different floors of Thirlham's brand new modern hospital.

Simon was laid on the table, exposed and bracing himself as they prepared to insert the camera tube. He was used to this by now and had got over being self conscious.

A nurse came into the room carrying some equipment.

"You'll never believe it," she said. "There's been another one."

"Two?" said the doctor, camera stopped in mid air.

"Yes, can hardly believe it."

Simon couldn't stand this. "Two what?" he asked.

"Two aeroplanes," said the nurse. "One flew into a skyscraper in New York, but now there's another."

"The pilots must have been asleep," said Simon, imagining a couple of light aircraft with private pilots at the controls.

"They're saying it must be deliberate, it's all on the TV now."

"That's a complicated way of committing suicide," said the doctor, no doubt under the same illusion as Simon. "Now keep still, it hurts less that way. Try to relax."

Simon gritted his teeth as the tube was pushed in.

But the nurse was still talking. "No, not like that. And there's all those passengers as well."

The doctor stopped pushing. "Passengers? You mean airliners? Commercial jets?"

"Yes, Boeing somethings. Both of them I think."

"Good God!" said the doctor.

Simon was at that point more interested in the half inserted camera!

"Oi!" he said.

"Oh, sorry, Mr Scott," he said. After a few moments Simon was again looking at the scar on his bladder wall and the hole where his kidney drained. Some twists and turns to survey the rest of the bladder.

"Excellent," said the doctor. "Healed up well. See you in three months," he added, withdrawing the camera much to Simon's relief.

After a short recovery time, he made his way to the maternity floor.

Robert was there, beaming. "It's another girl, Dad!"

Simon went in to see Melanie. One of her sisters was there and tried to stop him and Robert, saying it was now none of their business now that Robert had left Melanie. Simon was not disposed to argue and they went back in anyway. Melanie made them welcome and the sister departed.

She was holding the baby and Donna was there, regarding her baby sister, now called Florence. Robert picked her up and held her, showing her to Donna, childlike joy all over his face.

That evening, they watched with horror the images from New York. It seemed scarcely credible that any human being could deliberately wreak such death and destruction on fellow men.

Robert said straight away, "It's that same man again, Bin whatsisname." Robert was of course right, and the infamous name of Osama Bin Laden would not be forgotten.

Bernadette phoned from Amsterdam. They were stuck there because no planes were crossing the Atlantic. They had been put in a hotel some miles from the airport, but found that flights were being given out to people who could board at short notice, so after that like many others she and Neil camped out in the concourses at Schiphol. Days went by and when she could Bernadette phoned up. She was finding the strain hard.

"Come back, then," said Karen. "Get a flight back to Bilthaven and stay here until it settles down."

"Karen, we'll give it one more night and if there's no sign of anything, we will. Thank you so much."

Nothing else was heard until three days later when Bernadette rang from her home in Canada. They had heard of a flight leaving Amsterdam for Memphis. Neil had said they should take it, at least it was on the right continent! Once they did, they managed to get a flight to Buffalo NY. Not even flights into Canada from the USA were permitted yet. From Buffalo they managed to get a taxi across the Peace Bridge into Canada and then home. The American taxi driver, a Moslem of Asian extraction, was terrified he would not be able to re-enter the USA. But by that time all Bernadette and Neil could do was wish him luck. They were home! Their bags arrived weeks later. Neil said he would never fly transatlantic again.

Donna continued to stay at weekends, but Florence didn't, as having a baby as well as a two year old was too much for Karen weighed down with work under an unappreciative and bullying head teacher, while Simon's precarious mental health was never far from the edge of depression. Meanwhile, Robert, on yet another scheme, met Fiona Webb. He found he could talk to her and poured out all his troubles to her. Slowly they became close. Melanie took a dim view of this and was initially hostile to Fiona, believing wrongly that she was the reason Robert had left her.

Life settled into a routine, Simon was still working hard for his charities, but limiting himself to one meeting or event a day, as that was as much he could handle before becoming over stressed. His threshold was still low. But it kept him busy, and he would lose himself in his computer, trying out some programming and website building.

In the end, Karen had enough of the head teacher she was working for. She resigned, to the head's astonishment who thought she had Karen where she wanted. But Simon said he would support Karen whatever action she took, which made her decision to quit the easier.

Robert and Fiona said they wanted to be together and they took a rented house near Hilltown. At weekends he came back to Thirlham to be with Donna while Fiona went back to her home. Their Hilltown house was in a poor state. It had a solid fuel boiler that didn't work so they had no heating or hot water. Repeated attempts to the large property company handling it fell on deaf ears. Luckily it was the summer and they managed by boiling water in the kettle. Simon described it as a brick tent.

Karen went with Robert to the council office in Hilltown, which came under Nusbury council now, to sort out his housing benefit. Karen was telling the official about the house and the poor state it was in.

"Mrs Scott," she said quietly. "You seem to have a bit about you. Why don't you buy a house, let it to your son and his housing benefit could cover the mortgage."

"You can't do that, can you?" said Karen. "He's my son. Can you let a house to your own son?"

"Yes, of course," said the official. "As long as it's genuine and not what we call a contrived tenancy, in other words a fraud. Your son would be living there?"

"Yes, of course he would," said Karen, trying to digest this information and its implications.

Robert's six month lease was due to expire in September. But quickly Karen saw a house for sale in Hilltown that seemed just right. Small, cheap to run, with three bedrooms. Space for the girls if they came to stay, thought Robert. Simon used the money his Dad had left him as a deposit. They made it in time and Robert and Fiona moved into their house in Hilltown. By default, Simon and Karen had become buy-to-let landlords. Now the girls went to stay at Hilltown with Robert and Fiona at weekends. Simon and Karen were always on hand to offer support, both practical and financial, which was much needed.

The new term had now started and Karen was snapped up by a small school in Nusbury that was actually much nearer to Thirlham, being on the same side of Nusbury as Thirlham and Hilltown. The difference was immediate. The new head did nothing but praise Karen's work and quickly got her on to the higher pay scale, which her previous head had been blocking.

Simon was at his desk one day when the phone rang.
"Hello?" said Simon.

"Hello, is that Simon Scott?"

"Yes, who am I speaking to?"

"My name is George Arthur. If you are the right Simon Scott, I think you were in my year at King Henry VII School....."

"Hooray Henrys!" interrupted Simon.

"Yes, so it is you. I am involved with Patient Councils and found your name on the national website and tracked you from there."

"Well done," said Simon. "What can I do for you after all this time?"

"I'm organising a reunion for our year group and I'm ringing round people I can find. I've got a lot already because many stayed put or came back after university. But you left early, didn't you?"

"Yes, we moved up to Bilthaven in 1960."

"That's right," said George. "I remember now."

"Do you remember Daniel Gray?" asked Simon hopefully.

"Daniel Gray," repeated George thoughtfully. "No. Oh wait, he was the year above us wasn't he? Pianist?"

"Yes, that's right. Are you in contact with him?"

"No, as I say, it's for our year."

"What about Peter Holman," asked Simon, still hopeful.

"Oh, yes. Him. Sad. Hanged himself when he was eighteen. Had issues with his sexuality or something."

Simon felt as though a knife had been driven through him. Peter! Poor Peter! Tears of grief flooded out from him. Happy, cheerful, chirpy Peter! Why hadn't I been there for him? thought Simon. If only I had stayed.

"Hello? You still there?" George was querying down the phone.

Simon forced his voice to sound normal. "Yes. It was something of a shock. We were friends, I knew he was gay, he came out to me at Hooray Henrys."

"I hope not that kind of friend," joked George.

If you only knew, thought Simon. And why not that kind of friend? Nothing wrong with being gay! Hadn't even been a crime for decades. But George was still talking, he gave the date of the proposed reunion. With mixed feelings Simon noted it clashed with one of his cancer check days. But George's attitude was putting him off anyway, and he was still trying to absorb the shock of Peter's suicide. He explained he could not come and why. George wished him luck and rang off, probably keen to dial the next number on his list.

Simon sat and wept for Peter. Dead all these years! How cruel, to be driven to that for loving someone of the same sex. It's just love! Why is that so wrong? Simon felt a resurgence of his own feelings. That box in his mind was straining at its seams and hinges to burst open. He knew this was a reaction to George's apparent indifference to Peter's death, almost as though it didn't matter because was Peter was gay. Well it did matter! It did bloody well matter! Maybe he was doing George an injustice, but Simon felt a wave of anger at the bigots who had driven Peter to suicide. God! What a way to go! Simon remembered the excruciating agony of his own hanging. He cried out loud as he realised that poor Peter must have died in agony at the end of his rope.

Karen came in. "What's the matter love? I thought I heard you cry? Who was on the phone?"

"Someone from the past, organising a school reunion from Hooray Henrys. But he told me a friend of mine had committed suicide aged just eighteen because he was gay."

Karen put her arms round Simon, aware of his distress. "That's terrible, poor boy. That wasn't your friend who was the swimmer and played the piano?"

"No," said Simon, "it was a friend at school."

Karen went back to what she had been doing. Simon had a sudden terrible thought. What about Daniel? If Peter had been driven to suicide, had the same fate befallen his dear Daniel? He tried to think. He knew Daniel had moved to London in the summer of 1962, so he was alive then! Simon had already searched the internet fruitlessly for Daniel. Google threw up millions of results and he spent hours working his way through page after page, but none of them were his Daniel. He just had to hope that Daniel was still alive. Maybe one day they would meet again?

Karen's eldest brother was ill and as it turned out, terminally so. A lifetime of smoking was paid back with cancer and heart disease. She was upset and they made several trips to Mansfield to see him in hospital, and then there was another funeral. He was a widower but had not made a will and had stepchildren. This led to some acrimony and Karen was left to sort it out. Simon was with her, helping and supporting as best he could, using his aptitude for planning and administration to good effect. This lasted months, and was then complicated by the illness and death of her next brother just a year later. Another funeral, which Simon helped to arrange, along with cemetery fees and the headstone. Simon had designed Rita's headstone, and he did the same now. Harriet drew a design of colliery headstocks which was incorporated. All Karen's older brothers were miners, her younger brother, Craig, worked with computers. The two estates got intermingled and it took a lot of negotiation and work to get it resolved. The brothers were buried near their mother.

Melanie had moved into a rented house with Donna and Florence. This was managed by the same property company that Robert and Fiona had used. They hadn't improved. There was mould all over the bathroom and the girls were bathed in front of the fire in a metal bath, like something from a previous century. Simon and Karen subsidised Melanie for the sake of the girls, and Robert too was supportive. He would not hear anything said against Melanie. When social services carried out a review of how Melanie was managing the girls, Robert spoke up for her.

But Simon and Karen could not see their granddaughters living in such conditions. They used the rest of their savings as deposit on a small house in

Dirshingham which Melanie liked because she could get to her mother's easily. The fact that her mother moved house frequently didn't seem to matter. The buy-to-let 'empire' doubled in size. The girls settled in there with their mammy and Donna started school in Dirshingham.

Then came the news that Harriet and Kieran were splitting up. After 9/11, Kieran's Silicon Valley job had been finished and they had moved back to his roots in Ohio. When Simon and Karen had visited them, both in California and Ohio, Karen especially was aware of some undercurrent, a tension, but Harriet had insisted all was well and it was quite plain that she didn't want her parents' involvement. The marriage had lasted three years. Simon and Karen hoped that Harriet would come home, or at least back to Britain, but she moved in with a friend for a while, but she was moving away. Trent Liddell offered a house share to Harriet. He was renting a house by himself, so the arrangement suited them both. Harriet was working in Ohio and could just about support herself. Later she and Trent became 'an item' and bought a house together. It seemed to Simon and Karen that their daughter was putting down roots again in America. Harriet insisted she would always remain British, she would never take US citizenship, but she had the 'green card' so she could live and work there. She set up a business, working from home, preparing kits for quilt making which she sold over the internet. She also indulged her love of animals with a dog, and then fostered another dog. She was asked to 'fill in' for the dog trainer at the local animal hospital and it soon became a long term job. She took courses in dog training, but her own instincts and rapport with animals were her main assets and helped her make a success of this.

Donna and Florence now had a baby half brother. Melanie had given birth to a boy, Kyle. The father immediately vanished literally leaving Melanie holding the baby. This made the little house Simon and Karen had bought cramped, but the girls had one little bedroom and Melanie and Kyle slept in the other.

Simon's sixtieth birthday came, and Karen decided to celebrate it in style. She and Harriet had bought Simon a flying lesson in, of course, a Tiger Moth. He flew this aircraft that Mum had flown in her youth, over the hills and did the 'Dam Busters' run along Ladybower reservoir. Simon was amazed at how light the plane was to control. Of course there was a real pilot in the other seat!

For his actual birthday, Harriet came over although Trent had to work. Karen arranged a splendid birthday week. They invited friends for a celebration meal at a local hotel and at the weekend held a garden party, complete with a bouncy castle. In the years that they had lived in Thirlham, the nature of their small street had changed, from Robert and Harriet being the only children when they first moved in, to being a street with several families. Donna and Florence knew and played with the local children when they visited which was most Sundays, and so they all enjoyed the bouncy castle. So did some of the adults! It was such a warm time and Simon felt he was genuinely liked by his friends and neighbours which was a new feeling for him. He never doubted Karen's love of course, and his love and closeness to her remained as strong as ever. He knew that she was his anchor and that without her, he would be adrift, heading for the rocks as he and Jack had been so many years before.

Whether it was the change in social attitudes, a tendency as one gets older to look back more or thinking of the loss not just of Daniel, but of Peter and the manner of his death, Simon started to think more about the gay aspects of his make up. His relationship with Karen remained as deep and true as ever, but the hidden bomb in his mind was threatening to explode. There was this side of him that would always make him feel isolated to some extent. He started to chat on-line with gay men and found he was far from alone in being a happily married man with a gay past and gay feelings. He met up with a couple of men similar to him for a coffee and it was interesting to talk. He also met a young man, James, for a drink, by which he meant a cup of tea. He lived on a council estate with his mother and brothers in Cliffport, not far from Thirlham and as the name implied, on the coast. Simon had often taken Robert and Harriet there for a walk on the beach below the cliffs and now took Donna and Florence.

There was something about James that attracted Simon. Yes, he had dark brown hair and blue eyes, but unlike Daniel's eyes, these were pale, sad eyes. He was a good looking, gay man in his mid twenties but they got on and talked. He had been left by his partner, but Simon felt there was a deeper sadness. He talked about Daniel which he liked. He had never talked to Karen in detail about him, and to chat to someone who could relate emotionally and sexually to Simon's relationship with Daniel was a wonderful feeling. They met once or twice for a lunchtime cuppa. Simon felt that this was a safety valve for his gay feelings.

That summer, he and Karen went to visit Harriet in Ohio to see her new home and Bernadette and Neil in Canada. They flew charter from Bilthaven to Toronto and drove in torrential rain along the now familiar QEW to Bernadette's. They all went for meal out at a good restaurant overlooking the Niagara River to celebrate Simon's sixtieth. Bernadette taught philosophy at a local university and Simon especially liked to discuss ideas with her. He woke up one morning thinking about Kant and how the application of the Categorical Imperative was related to the distribution of power in a society. Bernadette was still working but she was unconvinced by his hypothesis. She argued that there are moral and ethical absolutes, he argued that as products of human thought, they are essentially social constructs, i.e. for a relativistic view. The extreme case of torturing babies for fun was the core of her case which would be regarded as immoral in any society. Simon argued that this might not always be the case to which she replied that such a society would not have a moral code at all! He cited exactly that situation at Auschwitz. Karen said he was just being perverse. She and Bernadette spent time together, lifelong friends, catching up and just being with each other, girl talk. After all, Karen had known Bernadette longer than she had Simon.

Then they drove off into the United States on the long drive down to Ohio. They had a SatNav now which after several hours guided them right to Harriet's door. They spent time together, following Harriet shopping and getting to know the dogs. At night, Simon would lie in bed, hearing in the distance the familiar, distinctive sound of American locomotives sounding their warnings as long freight trains rumbled through the Ohio night.

They had a phone call to say Florence was not well. The girls were with Robert and Fiona it being the school holidays. Advice was offered. Simon got also an email saying he was to receive an award from the National Dementia Society for voluntary service. At first he thought this was either a joke or a scam of some kind, but it turned out to be true! A later phone call said Florence now had medication from the doctor and was on the mend.

Karen and Simon went out for a walk round the neighbourhood. They found the local primary school which looked well equipped. Then Simon started getting text messages. It turned out that a brick had been thrown through Melanie's front window in Dirshingham while she was staying with her mother. So he had to spend some time talking to Melanie, her mother, Robert and Fiona about this and care for the girls, send an email to the letting agent to arrange repair. The neighbour had reported it to the police and it had been boarded up.

Harriet had arranged a barbeque in her garden, or yard as she called it, that evening as a farewell before Simon and Karen returned to Canada.

Simon was chatting to some of the guests. One young woman was interested in their travel from Canada.

"I've never been to Canada," she said. "What's it like up there?"

"Outwardly, very like here, but it does has a different feel to it."

"Oh, in what way?"

"Well, the British often say how like America it is, but many Americans say how British it seems. Maybe because of the Queen," ended Simon jokingly.

The young woman looked puzzled. "You mean the Queen of England?"

Simon wondered why Americans always referred to her as the 'Queen of England'. "She's Queen of Canada as well."

Astonishment came over her face. "Is that right? I guess I don't know much about Canada. I suppose we kind of protect them, don't we."

"Protect Canada?" said Simon. "Who from?"

The young woman looked taken aback, obviously unsure now.

Simon continued, "There is only one country in the world where the military have a contingency plan to attack and invade Canada."

There was a moment of blankness on her face before the truth dawned on her. "Oh, I'm sure we would never do that," she said in the end.

"So am I," added Simon, placatory.

They drove north again, worried about events in Dirshingham. They spent a couple more days with Bernadette before catching their night flight back, air travel chaos breaking out in the UK while they were blissfully unaware over the mid Atlantic. At Bilthaven Airport, Robert rang to ask if they were all right.

"Why not? The flight was fine, we're tired that's all."

"Dad, there's a big terrorist alert on. Something about bombs made of liquid. You can't take anything on board any more."

Simon couldn't take this in, both he and Karen already suffering the effects of jet lag, always worse on the return, west to east, journey. And they knew they were coming back to dealing with the problems of Melanie and the Dirshingham house. Melanie was now saying she was too frightened to return to the house where she and the girls had lived for three years. This was the longest that Melanie had lived anywhere in her life. It seemed she had fallen foul of loan sharks, which explained why Simon would have to top up her gas and electricity meters when he took the girls back home on a Sunday evening, and the lack of food in the cupboards for her and the three children. Simon and Karen knew the girls needed stability, but as Melanie was homeless and living with her mother, she could not have the girls back. So they stayed with Robert in Hilltown and as term started, Simon drove from Thirlham to Hilltown, collected the girls and took them to school in Dirshingham, then back to Thirlham, a twenty mile round trip. But he had done a similar thing for Harriet, so he would do it for Donna and Florence. It became another routine.

Robert had been seeing a psychologist about his learning problems with his previous diagnoses of 'attention deficit' which Simon had always argued was purely descriptive rather than diagnostic but was the best they had. But the psychologist now referred him to one of the country's top neuro-psychiatrists who just happened to be in Bilthaven. Simon went through with Robert. He watched while his son was put through a battery of tests that Simon found fascinating. Some, he could see what they were aiming at, others were a mystery. Robert and Simon were asked to wait for the results.

They were asked back in. "Well, I have the results. They are interesting."

"Yes?" said Simon.

"I can confirm what you have thought all along, that Robert suffered oxygen starvation at birth because of the cord which caused some brain injury."

"What we thought then," said Simon.

"Not only that, but I can tell you exactly where in Robert's brain the injury is."

The relief at getting a proper diagnosis after twenty-five years of battle and struggle to get services and help for Robert was immense. Simon felt he could kiss this man! He didn't. It was explained that the injury was in the area of the brain that acted like a telephone exchange, enabling the different parts of the brain to communicate. This explained why he could do so many things well, and score well on some tests but zero on others, Simon remembered the puzzlement at the wide scatter of Robert's childhood test scores. To compensate for this, Robert's brain had to work extra hard.

"I expect he finds concentration for long very hard, and tires quickly. He cannot complete tasks, often forgets things, has problems organising."

Robert was nodding at this accurate description of himself and his difficulties. Simon was amazed.

"That's him," he said.

"The bad news is that there is no cure, Robert will have to find strategies that work for him so he can cope with the demands of life. He's actually doing very well. You should be proud of him."

Simon looked at his son, who was grinning back at him. "Oh I am, believe me, I am."

A week later, Simon and Karen journeyed south for Simon to attend the annual dinner and receive his voluntary service award. Simon always said that others did far more than him, but that recognition boosted his self esteem. He had had a good sixtieth, now the confirmation after decades of struggle of Robert's diagnosis. 2006 was being a good year and Simon felt as though things were coming together at last, at long last.

13. *2006 Retribution*

Simon was at his desk, the phone rang.
"Hello?"
A woman's voice. "Is that Mr Scott, Simon Scott?"
"Yes," answered Simon.
"This is Detective Constable Teresa Charlton." Simon wondered what developments there had been in Melanie's problems to prompt this.
"Yes?" said Simon.
"We would like you to come in for interview. We have received some allegations about you relating to about thirty years ago when you were teaching in Nusbury."

Simon froze. Oh Jesus, not after all this time, surely?

O my prophetic soul

He started to shake but managed to answer.
"When?"
"Perhaps the day after tomorrow? 10 am?"
"Yes," said Simon. The call ended. Karen came in.
"What's the matter, love? Who was that on the phone? You seem upset."

Simon recounted the content of the phone call to her. He did not say more, although of course he had a good idea what it was about as he remembered his horrible displays in the dormitory.

"You must have a solicitor," said Karen sensibly. Simon contacted his union of which he was a retired member. They arranged for him to be met at the police station by a solicitor from a big legal firm in Bilthaven.

Simon couldn't sleep, he was still on the highest medication level and dare not take more.

Karen took the day off work to be with Simon. They met the solicitor, Carl Irving, who seemed very businesslike. The heavy door into the entrance lobby opened. A young woman appeared.

"Mr Scott?" Simon nodded. "DC Charlton. Come this way, please."

"I'll wait," said Karen. Simon nodded again. He was dosed up with tranquillizers but was still shaking. Simon and Mr Irving followed her into a passageway, the large door thudding shut behind him. As they walked along, DC Charlton spoke.

"Simon Scott, I am arresting you on suspicion of gross indecency with a child under 14. You do not have to say anything but it may harm your defence if you do not mention when questioned something you later rely on in court. Anything you say may be given in evidence."

"What!" Simon was shocked. Gross indecency meant rape, sexual assault, didn't it? Whatever he did, Simon knew he had never hurt a child in that way. They were shown into a small room.

"Here is the summary, I'll leave you to discuss it. Knock on the door when you're ready," said DC Charlton. She had a look of supreme self confidence on her face that Simon instantly disliked. She handed Carl Irving a folder containing a sheet of paper and left, closing the door.

"Can they hear what we're saying?" asked Simon.

"No, and even if they could, they couldn't use it in evidence," he replied. They read the sheet. It was a summary by a Benjamin D Young; occupation, police officer; saying that thirty years ago Simon had taken him into a forest and had exposed himself and masturbated in front of him, aged ten at the time. Simon's mind was a blank, he had been expecting it to be about the dormitory at the youth hostel. He struggled to remember. It was so along ago and so much had happened.

"I don't remember this," he said to Mr Irving, head in hands.

"In that case you simply say No Comment to each question," he advised.

The interview lasted what seemed like an eternity to Simon. He found it hard to think, to focus. He did so at the best of times since his breakdown fifteen years earlier, but under this stress he knew he wasn't thinking well. So he took refuge in Carl Irving's advice and simply replied "No Comment." Once or twice, he did answer questions, such as did he remember Ben Young. His name said like that brought back the image into Simon's mind of the chirpy lad he had once taught. Yes, he said, he did remember him, a sort of cheeky chappy. But Simon struggled to remember this incident in the forest, even when they read Ben Young's full statement to him. It seemed he had seen Simon in the street and it had reminded him and he decided to report him. DC Charlton and her silent colleague who sat in did not seem satisfied.

The interview ended after about three hours. Simon was shaking so much he could hardly stand.

"We will be making further enquiries," DC Charlton said.

"You will grant my client bail in view of the historic nature of these allegations," said Carl Irving. It wasn't a question, it was a statement.

"Yes, no problem. First though come us with us," she said. Simon was photographed, fingerprinted and had a DNA swab taken from his mouth. That took another half hour. Then he was bailed pending further enquiries.

Once out past that door and into the fresh air, Simon felt some relief.

"Will that DNA swab show up anything?" asked Mr Irving.

"What do you mean?" asked Simon.

"They will be checking it against DNA recovered from crime scenes, especially sex crimes. Will they find a match? Best say so now if that's the case."

"Christ no!" said Simon, "Nothing like that."

Mr Irving seemed to relax a bit.

"Very well, Simon," he said. "As soon as you hear from them, get in touch."

"I will, and thank you."

Simon looked round for Karen. She was sitting in her car waiting for him.

"You've been a long time," she said as he got in and sat next to her. "What's it about?"

Simon bit the bullet. "About thirty years ago when was at Brian Bailey's school I masturbated in front of the boys while away in the Lakes."

Karen sat, silent. Simon could not look at her. He could feel her shock. This wonderful woman whom he loved so much, who had rescued his poxy life and made it good, to whom he owed so much. What must she think of him now?

"When's the divorce?" he asked.

"I don't want to talk about it now," said Karen, tight lipped, fighting back her emotions. Fear, anger, astonishment. She didn't know what to think. Could this be the Simon that had been her rescuer, her rock and mainstay through all these years? Perhaps she didn't know him at all. She started the engine and they drove home.

That night, Simon's nightmares returned, he woke sweating. As before over many years, they were related to the rape. This involved Simon walking along somewhere, a city street, a country path. He realised that he was being shadowed by three individuals on a parallel path, they turn out to be the Watsons and Carter, yet sometimes although it was them, it was at the same time not them but others. Teenage youths. When they realised he had seen them, they started towards him intent on attacking him. He would wake up, sweating and fearful.

He was in the spare room, that had been Harriet's room once. Her things were still there, her pictures on the wall. Images of him and Ben the forest slowly came back to him, of the boy's fear and how Simon fought to stop him telling his parents what he had done. How utterly vile, he thought. How could I have done that?

The next day, they put on a pretence as they were taking Robert, Fiona and the girls to *Joseph and the Amazing Technicolour Dreamcoat* in Bilthaven. Simon looked at them, his son and his two granddaughters he loved so much. It was hard to appear 'normal' but he managed. Two days later it was Robert's thirtieth birthday and he and Karen went to Hilltown for a birthday tea that Fiona had prepared. Simon did his best and the girls remained unaware. But Robert knew his Dad.

"Mum, is Dad all right?" he asked Karen. "It's not the cancer again, is it?"

"No, nothing like that," said Karen. "We'll talk tomorrow."

The next day, Karen called in on her way home from work, and while girls were in their rooms, she told Robert and Fiona the outline of what was happening. That evening, Simon received a text message.

Hi Dad. You are not fighting it on your own. I am here for you. Your here for me the way you always have been. I love you and that cant change. Robert (your son)

That made Simon cry. A knock at the door produced a police officer and two social workers. They had a long talk, mainly with Karen. They seemed satisfied that she had known nothing about it, and they were concerned for the safety of the girls. But it was agreed that Simon could continue to do the normal things but in everybody's interest, he should never be alone with them. So Karen, Robert and Fiona made sure that was the case, with Simon's full cooperation of course. The girls never realised they were being constantly chaperoned. Melanie was present at the meeting with social services. Her remark when agreeing to this was, "That's fine by me, after all he's done for me!"

Simon became a recluse, he stayed with Ken for some weeks, returning home in the day time when Karen was out to catch up with his jobs. Karen knew whatever the cost, she had to protect the girls, not from Simon because she knew he would never harm or do anything amiss to them, but to safeguard their position with Robert and so that all measures could be seen to be taken. The girls now went some weekends to see their Mammy, Melanie was still living with her mother but now had another child, a boy, from a man who had vanished as soon as she was pregnant. It made the house very crowded, and Melanie's family were as yet unaware of the situation.

Christmas came and went, a strange charade for the girls' sake, with more interviews. The police now had four statements from boys – now men of course – who had been witness to Simon's crimes. Three of them were now serving police officers – one even said Simon's police role all those years ago had inspired him. They said he had been a brilliant teacher or a fantastic teacher. Not Simon's own recollection of his teaching years, but it only served to confuse him, such praise coming from his accusers. One wrote, "I feel I am betraying him". Simon had no idea that he had been regarded in this way which made the loss of credibility and reputation all the more painful and poignant. The police had also gone back to the people who had complained in 1993, but no offences were disclosed then.

Then into the New Year and Simon took the decision to resign from all his charitable work. He did not say why in his letters of resignation, but he realised that it would come out eventually. They replied with great concern, and like his neighbours, wondered if he were fighting the cancer again.

The dreams continued. In one, Simon was in bed at night and he went downstairs into the kitchen. Either he turned on the lights or they were on, but near the sink he saw a pool of red wine on the floor. He moved towards this past the table to see that it was not red wine but blood, it was his blood. He was lying naked on the floor, apparently dead, his red flesh exposed from some kind of traumatic, bloody wound.

In another, he was out, in woodland or sometimes in a cityscape. There was a serpent, entwining itself through trees or round street furniture. But Daniel was with him so he was safe. The serpent then turned towards them intent on attack. It was huge, many feet long and perhaps three feet in diameter. It went for Daniel but he punched it hard on the nose and it retreated. Suddenly though, Daniel was not there, Simon was alone and the serpent came for him, huge with fierce eyes and its mouth agape displaying sharp teeth, opening wider as it came right up to him to consume him. He was terrified and woke up screaming.

He and Karen decided that they had better tell their neighbours with children what was going on, be open about it. Karen did the talking, explained what had happened, said something about the strain they had been under at that time but did not offer any excuses, and even offered to move away. Their neighbours were shocked as it seemed so unlike the Simon they knew. They had noted how Simon had been out so little and had thought it was the cancer back again. Simon was amazed how understanding they were. They could not condone the deed, but knew that to do such things, Simon must have been under incredible stress.

As one commented, "We're free thinkers here, we'll make our own minds up. And whatever you did in the past, however reprehensible, that's not you now. The past should stay in the past, especially after thirty years."

It was a great relief to Simon and Karen.

Soon he had to appear at the magistrates court. Carl Irving advised him to withhold plea.

"I should plead guilty, after all I did do it," said Simon.

"Yes, but not here, not yet."

"Because of DC Charlton?"

"Not particularly. Although she does have a triumphalist attitude which I don't much like."

"Cocky, you mean," said Simon.

"You might call it that," said Carl Irving, with a slight smile.

So Simon withheld his plea and the case was adjourned. The press were in court so Simon expected it to be in the papers. They were in suspense for a few days, but there was nothing. But Ken was now anxious about Simon staying with him, so he left and went to London for a few days to stay with Frances. She knew what was happening and they talked about it when Sean was at work, as she had not told him or her two sons, who of course were no longer at home but who were in touch. She talked of her memories of Simon's childhood and how Dad had abused him. She remembered things that Simon had long forgotten and felt that at least some of the explanation of Simon's problems lay there. Simon felt closer to his sister than he had for many years. But he went back north and moved to a hotel on the edge of Thirlham. It was now four months since he was arrested and charged, and the hotel was a huge drain on their resources so Karen said he might as well come home.

The house in Dirshingham was still empty and needed a lot of work doing so Simon filled his time with that. He met James a couple of times which was a lift, although in their talks, Simon didn't mention his impending prosecution. But he was good to be with, and Simon found he could relax in his company.

He and Karen had bought tickets to see *Guys and Dolls* at Bilthaven Theatre, so they went and enjoyed an evening together which they thought they might not have been able to have. Simon expected that he would serve a jail term when the time came so he made arrangements so that Karen could deal with the banking, which Simon did on-line, as well as setting other affairs in order to make things easier for her.

He met Carl Irving at the magistrates' court for the next appearance. Mr Irving said they had some problem because it seemed that the police officers who were his accusers were reluctant to give evidence. Why, he wasn't sure, but he thought that although they were allowed anonymity as far as the press was concerned being the victims, their colleagues would inevitably find out. This apparently they didn't want.

Simon noted that Brian Bailey had made a statement and said he would willingly give evidence against Simon. Of course he had not been there so Simon wondered what he could say about the actual offences, but he knew that Brian must be feeling so betrayed and he felt really sorry about that, Brian who had been his friend and defender years before. His sense of betrayal must have been huge, as well of course as other colleagues and those who had put their trust in him. So again, under instruction, Simon withheld plea and it was adjourned for a month.

Simon's doctor refused to increase the dosage of his medication any more; he had been at the maximum for so long now which he needed to manage his depression. He was referred back to the mental hospital as an out patient. Dr Yardley was long gone, so he was now under the care of Dr Norman. Mr Irving cautioned Simon about saying too much as he would have a duty of disclosure.

"But I'm going to plead guilty anyway," said Simon.

"Yes, but we don't want to hand it to them just yet. Wait until Crown Court," advised Mr Irving.

"Yes, I see that."

"I must say," said Mr Irving, "you seem to be taking it on the chin."

Simon looked at him. "What else can I do?"

"I've seen men go to pieces facing less than you do."

"Ah," said Simon, "that's the tablets." But he also knew it was Karen's continued love and that of his family that was bearing him up. So he tried to keep busy. At least his cancer check, annual now, was clear again, the beast held in remission. Given the stress he was now under, that was a surprise in some ways. And as always, Karen, confused, confounded, upset and angry, was there for him. He tried to explain, but it was so hard.

They - Karen was with him of course - had a very hard interview with his barrister who pushed Simon hard to the point of tears. But this was his way of assessing Simon, and his parting words were, "I'll do my best for you, Mr Scott. See you in Crown Court."

Simon started to see Dr. Norman but bearing in mind Carl Irving's advice, steered clear of the prosecution. But he did talk about his childhood, his father and Daniel. But not the rape – not yet. It was a long slow process.

In August, ten months since his arrest, Simon appeared at Thirlham Crown Court. Standing in the glass walled dock, he felt the shame of his downfall. But then he had lived with shame all his life in one form or another; Dad and his outbursts that alienated him from most of the neighbourhood kids, Daniel and the fear of their love and its sexual nature being exposed, the rape and his failure to fight back and of his orgasm as David Watson sodomised him, his gay feelings and his guilt for Karen's sake, his crimes and the wrong he had done to those boys and now eventual exposure, thirty years later, and his public humiliation.

How is it that the clouds still hang on you?

He had brought an overnight bag with the things he thought he might be allowed in prison, having read the Prisoner's Handbook on-line. So he stood in the dock while the charges were read out, citing seven incidents in total. He couldn't hear what the clerk of the court was saying because of the glass screen, he tried to stand with his ear in line with the small gap but each time the clerk stopped, he said as clearly as he could muster, "Guilty." He was and he knew it and he would have to take whatever came. Mr Irving had said that he would not be sentenced but there was a chance he could be remanded to prison to wait for reports and the sentence hearing.

And where the offence is let the great axe fall.

But the judge listened to his barrister's case for bail to be extended. The judge addressed Simon, who could only hear bits of it but he said that because of the historic nature of the charges, the fact that he appeared not have reoffended since that time, he would allow continued unconditional bail, but that should not be taken that he would not face a custodial sentence. He was to sign the sex offenders' register immediately.

Relieved, shaking, Simon stepped down from the dock. Karen was waiting for him as always. They went straight to the police station to sign the register; get it over with, thought Simon. He was back in that detached zone, as he had been when young and now since his arrest, viewing as though from outside, seeing himself as an actor in some drama. Perhaps this was a psychological defence, he had used it in 1963 to protect himself, that divorce between body and brain which he still felt after all those years, even with Karen, his love and light. Now they had to steel themselves for the press – but again, it didn't come. Did they think it was an old story? Mr Irving however cautioned Simon saying that they would probably report it after the sentencing hearing, at which details of his offences would be read out.

Sitting at home, he and Karen reviewed their long years married, all the troubles they had come through together, for better for worse, in sickness and in health. They had been lucky in many ways. They had lived in a beautiful, good country in a time of great prosperity since the second world war, with cheap food, cheap energy, a welfare state that took care of Robert with his brain injury and helped him, a National Health Service that cured Simon's cancer and took care of his mental health needs.

"You know," said Simon, "I think people will look back on the lives of the post war baby boomers, which we are, and regard it as a golden age."

"True," said Karen. "It's certainly changing now, ever since Thatcher and the destruction of the social consensus. With all its faults, it was a country that at heart was caring and at one with itself. Apart from the idiots of course."

"Yes, and Blair has failed to bring that back," said Simon.

"We are lucky to have lived when we have," said Karen.

"Well," said Simon smiling, "basically, we're born, we spawn and we're gorne!"

"Hopefully we do a bit more than that," replied Karen.

Simon was interviewed by a probation officer, Naomi Mills and a police officer from the public protection unit. They were preparing a pre-sentence report for the court. His mind was still a haze but he tried to answer as honestly as he could.

His neighbours offered statements of support which of course Simon accepted. Frances also sent a letter in which she described some of the trauma of his early life.

In September, ten months after his arrest he returned to the Crown Court. Karen, taking the day off, and Ken were with him. He had his bag packed with him again, as he felt certain that he would be in a cell that night.

Till the foul crimes done in my days of nature
Are burnt and purged away.

It was a different courtroom, this one had no glass walls round the dock. It was a different judge, Simon noticed. He stood, with security guards either side of him now. He felt cold and weak. Again a lot of what was said passed over him.

The prosecution barrister started reading out the accounts of what Simon had done on each of the occasions. Simon had to stand and listen, watching the reporters scribbling their notes. He wanted to die there and then. He felt now there was nothing left for him. He was visibly shaking, one of the guards quietly said, "Are you all right?" Simon nodded.

The judge suddenly interrupted the prosecution barrister halfway through the third charge.

"I think that's enough, I've read the case file."

The barrister stopped. He seemed put out at this, but of course obeyed the judge. Simon was pleased, it had been so hard to listen to it all. There followed some discussion between the two barristers and the judge. The prosecution was arguing for a custodial sentence long enough to enable a remedial programme to be completed in prison, the defence was saying that these were historic offences and of their kind, relatively minor, and that Simon now constituted no threat. He would be able to complete a programme outside prison and remain able to support his wife and son, who because of his disability, was dependent on Simon. Karen's statement that Simon was the lynchpin of the system of care for Robert and the girls was referred to. Simon looked round at where Karen and Ken were sitting in the public seats, she was listening intently to what was being said.

Then the judge handed down the sentence. Simon was to serve a community sentence, being on probation for three years during which time he must attend the sex offenders' programme and he must remain on the sex offenders' register for five years.

"You are forbidden to work with children in future – although I doubt if you will be seeking employment again," said the judge suddenly remembering Simon's age.

It took a moment for Simon to register that he was not going to be locked up.

The prosecution then asked for a sexual offences prevention order, known as a SOPO.

"No, that's not necessary in this case," said the judge. The prosecutor again stopped.

The prosecution then made an application for costs. The judge asked if any damages were being sought, but the prosecutor said no, it was solely about justice being done not personal gain for the victims. When the prosecution costs of several hundred pounds were mentioned, Simon's barrister immediately asked if that could be paid at one hundred pounds per month, looking round at Simon for confirmation. He nodded and said, "Yes."

The judge then addressed Simon. "Mr Scott, you have been a silly and foolish man. I don't think you are a paedophile, but you went over that line, fortunately you had the sense to step back again. If you had not, you would have been going to prison. Also I've taken into account that it is thirty years since these offences and I've read the letters of support. You seem to have led a worthy life since then. Go away and get on with your life. You may step down."

"Thank you, sir," said Simon, quietly, still trying to grapple with what had happened. The guard ushered him out of the dock, where Simon picked up his bag and then out of the court. Karen and Ken were there in the foyer, waiting. A wave of relief came over Simon. Carl Irving and his barrister came out.

"Thank you so much," said Simon.

"That's the result we were hoping for," said his barrister.

"Yes, thank you."

"I think it's fair, all things considered," said Carl Irving.

Simon could only agree.

As he, Karen and Ken left the court, he saw some movement in the car park and looked across. As he did he saw a photographer with a telephoto lens resting it on the roof of a car. Simon saw the shutter go, and swiftly the man ducked into his car and drove out.

"Don't worry," said Karen, noticing Simon's anxiety level rising because of this. "We can't do anything about that now."

"Come round for some lunch," said Ken, thinking to celebrate Simon's freedom. But Simon was now suffering a reaction and was shaking and in distress. He managed to take one of his trifluoperazine tablets, and while waiting for it to take effect, sat on a seat in the street.

"Thanks, Ken, but I really don't feel up to it."

The following day, the *Nusbury News* carried his story with banner headlines across the front page and the photograph which had been taken outside the court. It was not a kind article and made the most of the sleazy sexual side of the story. In contrast the *Bilthaven Mail* and the local free paper, the *Thirlham Gazette* carried articles which were much more factual, also reporting the judge's comments about his later 'worthy' life, and no doubt drawing on their archives, said that Simon had done much charity work in recent years, listing the charities he had chaired or helped. Perhaps in deference to the judge's words, none of the press reports, not even the Nusbury one, used the word paedophile or the press favourite, pervert. Simon was glad they no longer lived in Nusbury. He was worried about vigilantism, both for him and Robert in Hilltown, and he again became a virtual recluse. As time passed there was none, and the neighbours they had spoken to remained supportive, saying that the press will do what they have to do to sell papers, one calling the *Nusbury News* a 'rag'. Some other neighbours remained distant, but that did not worry Simon over much, that was their right. They did not take it out on Karen or the girls, whom they continued to accept, so Simon was grateful for that. It was obvious that Karen's colleagues at her school in Nusbury had read the *Nusbury News* article – they could hardly miss it – but nothing was said apart from her head teacher offering her support, and it moved into the background. Karen thought that the head had had a word with the staff about it.

The lack of a SOPO meant that he could be normal with the girls again, no longer needing to be chaperoned, and this was confirmed by social services. Soon he was in the routine of weekly visits to his probation officer Naomi, and sooner than expected was given a date to start the Sex Offenders Rehabilitation Programme, SORP. He met James again for a chat and a cuppa. They had a pub lunch together and talked, but Simon felt he could not mention his conviction, and James seemed not to have seen it in the paper. He had lost weight although slim enough already and seemed preoccupied, which Simon attributed to him still feeling the loss of his ex boyfriend.

14. *2007-8 Rehabilitation*

Dr Norman was a different character to Dr Yardley, more deliberate, choosing his words carefully. Now of course, Simon could be much more open in his sessions with him. He talked more about Daniel, his early life, he managed to mention the rape but skirted round it. That was still taboo. Dr Norman seemed interested in the content of Simon's nightmares. He recounted those he could remember, but there were many times when after waking in a panicking sweat, the nightmare was a vague memory that faded quickly. Others though remained clear and sharp. One had Simon in a building, there were children there who were in his charge. There was a problem with the toilet so he went in to sort it out. But it was not the toilet, it was a small office and in there were three masked youths robbing it. They attacked him. He woke up.

Another had Simon on board a ship which was sinking. He was inside the heavily listing vessel trying to find a way out before it went under. He was chest deep in water which was rising fast. He arrived at a passageway upwards but because of the list was unable to reach it unaided. Three teenage males were higher up and he asked them for a helping hand. They turned towards him. It was the Watson three. They laughed and left him to drown. He was panicking as the water rose over him. He woke up.

In the one he called the octopus, his naked body was somehow suspended or floating free face down, either under water or in mid air, it was not clear. But he could breathe. A large octopus or giant squid type of creature was wrapping its tentacles around him, encircling him and gripping him like a series of snakes. He felt them sliding over his back, round his neck, over his shoulders and round his body, wrapping round his thighs until he was held helpless. Then one of the tentacles probed him and started to penetrate him, going incredibly deep until he was in such pain - he woke up, sweating and screaming, Karen next to him wakened and desperately trying to comfort him.

Not all the dreams were based in the past, 'The Gun' being an example. Simon was aware of three faces, but it was the middle one that had his attention. It was Bruce Watson, he was older, now Simon's age, but those cold, grey eyes were the same. He had come to finish the job. He raised an automatic pistol, looking along it at Simon. It was aimed at Simon's own eyes. Watson's eyes were fixed on Simon, holding him in their grip. He fired the gun. Simon woke up, shaking and fearful, sweating profusely.

Dr Norman made copious notes about these nightmares, but in response to Simon's request to be a 'Joseph' and interpret them, he was non-committal. Simon was often frightened to go to sleep. He also started to see a counsellor, Denise. Again he mentioned the rape but she said early on that she was not a specialist in rape counselling, and perhaps he should try to obtain that. But Simon quickly found that wherever he turned for help and counselling for his own trauma, as soon as he revealed that he had a conviction for a sexual offence, they broke contact. So Simon continued to carry the burden without specialist help, relying on Denise and the regular but more widely spaced meetings with Dr Norman.

Before starting SORP, Simon underwent psychometric testing. This was done on a day that Simon called a 'black cloud' day so he was far from his best. Some of the scenarios seemed ludicrous to him, but he guessed they must be based on real life occurrences. It was hard to try to imagine himself in a position he would never have been in, for example with regard to the ill treatment of women. When it came to children, he didn't know whether to answer with respect to his victims or his own grandchildren. Very confusing, and Simon was sure his answers were too.

SORP was to be in four blocks of eight or nine weeks, one full day per week, with breaks between the blocks. In December he drove for the first session to Gerdlington, about a half hour drive from Thirlham. This was not a town he knew well, but his SatNav guided him. Nervously he went in, to find a group of about eight men drinking coffee. One offered to make him one, which was a welcoming note. Most of the chat was about football. Once the session started with two probation officers running it the rules were devised by the group. This was done in two teams. Being non-judgemental, confidentiality, regarding all offences equally, not talking over each other, respecting the other person's view, referring to victims by their first names (to personalise them yet protect their identity), no physical contact among group members, not associating with each other outside the group etc. were the kind of things. It was also pointed out that all sessions would be videoed but they were assured that this was to monitor the officers to ensure SORP was delivered the same across the country. That assurance was met with some scepticism by the members.

They had to say what they felt their risk level of reoffending was. All the others put themselves at low risk, but Simon was so confused, his head was in such a state, so much stirred up in the last year, that he felt he bridged the gap between medium and low. He could not see that he would ever offend again, especially after thirty years, but until he had done more of the course and achieved a greater understanding of his motivation (so hard to remember and feel again decades later) he felt that his own assessment of his risk was inevitably biased.

Then each person had to say what their offences were. Simon felt sick at this, he started to shake again. There was rape, touching various female parts, voyeurism and harassment. Simon realised with mounting fear that his were the only offences involving boys rather than girls. He found himself getting increasingly upset as the afternoon went on. He went to get some water and had a few tears before he went back in. He took some medication to calm himself. Simon was led through the brief outline of his crimes, how long ago, the age and gender of the victims, and the fact he was a teacher at the time. Simon focused on the officer, he felt he could not meet the gaze of the others. He was shaking back in his seat.

At the end of the day, the others left like racehorses from the starting blocks. Simon couldn't get out of his seat. He was drained, weepy and once the others had gone, tears flowed. The officers came and sat with him for almost half an hour while he wept and went through some of the issues. He started to recover. Simon was also aware that they would have work to do before they could go home, and felt bad about taking more of their time than he was entitled to. He drove home slowly, content in the slow moving traffic stream from Gerdlington to Thirlham.

Karen was already home, and anxious to hear how the first session had gone. He talked to her, his best friend, his soul mate, always there for him as he had tried to be for her over so many years. Each week he would meet Naomi who had received feedback from the SORP officers, and would go over it with him. More pain. But as Simon kept telling himself, it beat prison by a long way.

The next week back to Gerdlington, a bit less anxious perhaps. It was explained that each offender had to produce a piece of personal work in each block. So Simon had to prepare 'My Offence'. Others in the group who were on later blocks were preparing other work, having already done 'My Offence' in their Block 1. It was hard to know when or where to start, how much to include and where to end. There was so much to it, it was hard to encapsulate this onto a flip chart, double spaced. The fact that he had already done a lot of writing and talking about it in his one-to-one sessions with Denise and Dr Norman helped and he was able to overcome writer's block to get the basics down. The next week, Simon was relieved he was not presenting, but watched others present their work for later blocks. Other members were encouraged to question and comment on the one presenting. Simon did his best to make positive comments and to participate as much as he could. He could not help, thinking back to his psychology course many years before, what good case studies some of these men would have made. But then he would as well, he realised; that brought him up with a jolt.

Christmas was a little more normal. Now that the threat of imprisonment was removed and the restrictions on Simon with regard to Donna and Florence also, it was a happier time. Robert, Fiona and the girls came over, as well as Melanie and her little boy, for Christmas lunch. They took the girls to the pantomime and taxied them to friends' parties. During the holiday, Simon and Karen took them out to interesting places in Nusbury, Bilthaven and beyond. The girls remained unaware of Simon's conviction and he knew how fortunate he was.

It was a new year, there was a financial crisis as banks ran into trouble, but SORP continued. At the first session, Simon had to present his 'My Offence' to the group. He was acutely aware that his offences were the only ones involving boys with the overtones of homosexuality. But he had to get on with it, which started with reading out the account of what he did, where and when. Then he was asked questions about what he had written to fill in more detail. The factual ones were straightforward, questions about the trips, how they started, the 27 years he took the long trip and details of the shorter trips, mainly the day trips to go orienteering. He was asked about the showers and he explained that these varied from one hostel to another, one having an open shower area with three shower heads. He explained that on occasion he had to go in while the boys were showering to quell the noise etc. There was discussion of accommodation arrangements and how the offences took place when colleagues would not come in, after 'lights out' etc. He was asked why he chose certain boys, and he explained they were the able, self-confident ones with strong peer group ties.

Much harder were the questions about motivation, justification. Simon talked about his domestic situation at that time, the problems they were having with Robert, his depression, his eye loss and his sense of inadequacy, frustration and isolation. He was disconcerted when an officer used his surname in front of the group as it had seemed a rule that the group identified themselves as well as the victims by forenames only. He also had to talk about the need for humiliation with sexual overtones – but could not talk about the origin of this - , his need for the boys' company etc. - all things he was familiar with from his one to one sessions, but disclosing these in front of the group was much harder. Simon tried to get across the sense of being driven and the compulsion he felt at the time, but not altogether successfully, maybe because he was unable to discuss his childhood events especially the gang rape, never mind brain chemistry! He sensed one member's contempt which meant perhaps he was unable to be as forthcoming as he might have been. Other group members' questions were searching but supportive. Simon mentioned his childhood experiences, good and bad, but he was unable to go further into that for which he was grateful. He didn't think he could have done so. It was very intense and after an hour and a half (fifteen minutes over the allotted time) he was still only half way down the sheet. The officer called a halt at that point for which he was very glad as he was feeling the stress.

Simon sat, trembling but relieved the ordeal was over for the time being. The rest of the session was taken up with various activities designed to look at the motivations of group members at the time of their offences. Simon was the only one with offences so long ago. One member had on his sheet was "This was a risk I had to take". That struck a chord with Simon. He also explained that he had hoped the boys liking him and would be loyal to feel that he would not be reported. But he also pointed out that even after thirty years, the past could catch up.

The weeks went slowly by, and Simon gradually became more accustomed to the demands of SORP. It was never easy and he frequently left in a state of high emotion and upset. Simon became very dependent on his counsellor Denise to counteract the shattering effect of some of the work carried out there, which affected his self esteem and reawakened old nightmares. His psychiatrist commented that Simon had been suffering from an undiagnosed post traumatic stress disorder since the age of 17. Not only was Simon confronting his crimes of thirty years earlier, but also having to confront his real sexuality. This caused Karen much pain and uncertainty which again fed back into his distress and eroding self esteem.

They had to draw a lifeline, with the highs and lows. Simon's was twice as long as everybody else's, but he pointed out he was twice as old as anybody else there. He was relieved when the officer said that events one did not wish to talk about could be just left as a red mark. The officers knew a little of Simon's rape of course and seemed sensitive to his difficulty talking about it in front of the group. When it came to presenting the lifeline to the group the following week, Simon came unstuck.

It said much for Simon's state of mind that he had missed off his graduations (good), his cancer and kidney problems (bad). The officer asked about Karen as the most positive thing that had happened to him, and asked why this was.

"Because she is the most amazing, wonderful person," Simon replied.
"Is there nothing positive about yourself?" asked the officer.
"What do you mean?"
"Positive things about your own nature."

Simon was stopped by this. He realised just how low his self esteem really was now and despite the officer being as positive as she could be about all the good things, Simon could only come up with one thing.

"I think I have been a good father," he said, tamely.

"Say more about that," replied the other officer. There were always two in each session. Simon thought that this male officer had some issues about his own father, based on or two comments he had made and on his knowledge of psychology and his recent reading.

"I was determined not to be like my own father," Simon said. "Not like he was to me." Simon was aware of the theory behind this from his own studies which reinforced his approach to fatherhood.

"You know giving up is not a solution?" said the female officer. Simon took that as a euphemism for suicide, which she knew he had attempted, and was there beneath the surface, sometimes shallow like that week; when times were a bit better, it sank deeper away from possible enactment. But he acknowledged that "me topping myself" would not help Karen, Robert and the girls, nor Harriet for that matter. He wondered if this opening of Pandora's box and going over everything in the group was the best therapy. His own strategies for coping developed over decades since the offences and which had successfully stopped his reoffending for almost thirty years were now in tatters and he just didn't know where he stood. Simon was sure he would never reoffend but it certainly raised issues about his own sexuality.

The questioning continued, and Simon realised he would have to live with the fact that his actions caused harm, albeit psychological rather than physical, to those boys, Ben Young in particular, which pained him because he always liked children and wanted to do good by them. But the worst punishment for him was not that, nor the SORP course, probation or the register, but that he had hurt Karen and now could not visit Harriet in America because of US rules on entry by people with criminal records. Canada too was now closed to him. Those **really** hurt him. He was asked about his ambition for the future. He said he wanted to live long enough to see the girls into adulthood, but he was thinking of his cancer and own mental frailty. He lost control of his emotions and ran outside. He was sitting on the bench when the female officer came out and offered to get his coat, but he had recovered enough to go back in for the break.

Simon tried to get involved in the others' timelines. What a series of tragic lives, of neglect, of being abused themselves as children. Sexually, physically and emotionally. One particularly sad and quiet group member said he had touched a girl sexually, because he thought it would be the only chance of sex he would ever get. Simon thought that was one of the saddest things he had ever heard. All said the same, that when they had tried to get help for their own abuse, the door was slammed in their faces. And yet, reasoned Simon, from a public protection point of view, these people, himself even, need such help as much as any other. As he had read, the victim – victimiser cycle was well documented.

The weeks passed by. One exercise was to write a letter of apology to the victims. Simon was glad of this because he had wanted to do this from very early on. But then he was told that it was purely an exercise and the letters must not be sent. He said that he had offered via his solicitor, his barrister, the judge and his probation officer to apologise to the victims, in person should they wish it, but he was unsure whether this had ever been passed on to them. His letter to Ben Young – Simon had chosen him as the one who had reported him - was analysed by the group, and he was asked how he thought Ben Young might react if he got the letter. Suddenly Simon thought how he would react if he got a letter from the Watsons and Carter. He started to shake as those nightmarish images flashed through his head. Luckily at that point, the officer called a halt.

They were shown videos such as the infamous Gallienne child abuse case from Canada. Simon found this in particular disturbing, with echoes of his own offences but also of his own rape once more. He had to resort again to medication to keep stable. In that state, he then had to reassess his own risk as the first block ended. He repeated his medium risk, but was asked what might move him toward low and no risk. Simon could see no end to this torment in his lifetime and was also thinking of his cancer check soon, so before he could stop himself, he said, "Death."

That produced a stunned silence, broken by one member who said, "That's a bit drastic". The rest was a blur but Simon was relieved to go back to his seat.

He was asked to stay behind at the end of the group to talk to the two officers. One said he felt Simon was holding back, that he had a public face and a private face. Simon agreed, saying how hard he found the group. He told them that his work with his counsellor Denise had led him to recognise that he was at least bisexual, how uncertain he was about this, how the attack on him had affected his sexuality, which he had always 'blamed' for his sexual confusion. Simon then told them about his work with Denise over his relationship as a boy with Daniel, which he had had always regarded as a positive aspect of his childhood. Simon read to them some notes he had written about Daniel from his PDA[6]. He said how hard he found it to regard that relationship as abusive and thinking about it in that way was like a betrayal of the love they had fifty years earlier. The officers said that half hour had achieved more than the whole block so far in that Simon had disclosed these. He said he had discussed his sexuality with Naomi so disclosure was not the issue, the group was. He was not really ready to talk about Daniel yet as he was still working through this with Denise, but felt bounced into it. The officers said that he would have protection from

---

[6] Personal Digital Assistant; a small pocket computer, used as a diary, for holding contacts and other information.

any adverse reaction to his sexuality. Weary and shaken Simon left for home, the first block over.

The second block started a couple of weeks later. Only two members of the previous block were still there, as the rest had finished. The new group was a couple of people starting Block 1, and some others who had been on a parallel course elsewhere. This time Simon felt less isolated in that two other members of the group of ten had male victims or had looked at young males online. At the end one officer asked Simon how he felt, and he said the more diverse nature of the group had helped. He asked how he had got on with the activities that day, and was told it was "fine". Simon felt that his sessions with Denise were helping with SORP more now.

As the work progressed Simon sat through the others' personal work, varying depending on the block they were on. Simon's Block 2 work was 'My Cycle', focussing on how the offence was set up, the thoughts and feelings at the time and how one justified it to oneself afterwards. When it was his turn to present later on, he had prepared a full flip chart sheet. He described the anguish over Robert going on at the time, describing the time he and Karen had left Robert to cry, but had eventually gone in, ignoring the doctor's advice. That moved one member to tears. Simon then started to talk about Daniel, and once started, wanted to keep talking about him. It was as though sharing Daniel with the group in some way made him seem close again. He disclosed their later sexual relationship and that his first orgasm had been with Daniel and the effect this seemed to have had in adding to his sexual confusion. Simon's feelings for Daniel and how that contrasted and perhaps compensated for his problems with his father were talked about. He talked of the warmth, closeness and feeling protected, and described the Scouts and Daniel's role in that.

As with everybody else who had presented so far, there was discussion about the level of interest boys of that age have in sex. This led again to talk of whether the boys had been upset or felt abused at the time. Simon said he had recently re-read Ben's statement and it was obvious that he had been, but he said others less so. He said that he had not felt he was being abused by Daniel although some would now regard it as abuse. The female officer immediately and predictably pointed out that Daniel was only two years older than him while he had been an adult in charge of the boys. Of course Simon accepted that, but the point he was trying to make was that although a victim may not feel abused at the time, there may still be long term effects, as there obviously had been in his case.

It was said that the sudden move north aged 14 was the marker that separated him now from the comment on the sheet, "How he once was". Simon replied, "No, that came later." But when asked to say more, his determination deserted him and he came to a dead stop, simply unable to bring out the multiple rape in 1963. After a pause, they continued, by simply 'going round' that event, although he felt that group members thereby missed a major factor in what had made him. He said he was addressing his sexuality, and he was at least bisexual. He had used the boys to work out his feelings of inadequacy and low self-esteem. His fantasies did not involve boys, but sometimes his nightmares did, though usually older ones.

The block continued, with role play scenarios and personal work presentations by the others, as well as exercises on sexual attitudes, mood management and problem solving. During a video about a Shropshire boarding school case which included one quite graphic description by a teenage boy of being raped, he had to fight to keep himself in check and stop himself from shaking. He felt tears coming, anger welling up in him, both at their pain and the memory of his own at about their age. He felt the whole session was messing with his head in a dangerous and unpredictable way, he felt bludgeoned. Simon sat, tightly controlled, feeling literally suicidal once again. He thought of taking a time out and going outside but that would break the rigid control and he wasn't sure where that would lead. He remembered Dr Norman had said he was in effect suffering from untreated Post Traumatic Stress Disorder for 44 years. This was poking the wound with a big stick. One member noticed his distress and said something to the female officer. But at the lunch break, after a discussion about the video in which he could take no part and which seemed to last an eternity, he went away and found a corner and wept. For the boys, for himself – Simon didn't know. When he had recovered a bit, he went back in and the female officer asked if he was OK. He said not really but what else could he say?

An event that May had a profound effect on Simon. He was outside the house, washing his car when one of the local children in the street came past on his way home from school.

"Hi Simon," said Tim, stopping.

"Oh, hello, Tim," said Simon, dropping his sponge into the bucket. Tim looked hot in his school uniform, carrying his bag over his shoulder. Simon was transported back to walking back up the hill with Daniel, hot in the summer heat with their Hooray Henrys blazers on. But Tim was still at primary school. "Had a good day at school?" Simon enquired.

"Oh, we're doing SATs," said Tim wearily.

"Are you Year 6 now?" asked Simon, slightly surprised, forgetting how quickly children grow up.

"Yes," said Tim. Simon stood, looking down at Tim. It was May and Tim was the age of the boys he had taken off on his Lake District trips many years before. Simon thought that he might have been taking Tim away on his trip, and when he was talking to Tim it came to him how young the boy really was. The thought that he might have offended against Tim or people like him shocked him as he saw him afresh, as a child. He actually felt sick and said he had to get on washing the car. So Tim said "See ya" and carried on home. Simon called that his 'Tim Moment'. Also around that time he found some photographs taken on one of his Lake District trips. Looking at them, Simon realised the children seemed so small. Yet when he been working with them, spending the greater part of every working day with them they had seemed bigger. The perspective of time helped him now see them as they really were, young children. He felt fresh disgust for his actions so long ago. So overall, what with Tim, SORP, Denise his counsellor and family support, the love of Karen, Robert and the girls, Simon felt perhaps his own assessment of his risk was lessening. He could see why others had placed him as low risk in a new way.

In June, Block 3 started. One or two new members, one or two gone. Simon recounted the 'Tim Moment' but refrained from mentioning the dream in the group. He did discuss it with Karen of course, as well as Denise and Dr Norman. He had to again describe his offences for the new members. There was a review of the four blocks' personal work, for Simon this time it would be 'Risk Factors'. Increasingly he felt more comfortable in the group, and he brought his own knowledge of psychology to bear as well as his reading about sexual offending and its treatment. He introduced the sociological concept of a personal construction of reality to the group, pointing out that this could enable distortions in thinking to appear real. The officer said that was a useful idea, but they had to stick to the script! There were still times of high stress and tears.

In a later session he had to present again. This time 'Risk Factors'. He was feeling more anxious but nothing like as bad as before. He decided to start with Feelings, because he thought that this was where it all started. He talked more about Daniel. He talked about the significance of the age 14 to him, and how he was drawn to the bright, confident boys. He explained how he tried to project characteristics onto those boys to make them older and more like Daniel. They were the nearest available. A member asked about his relationship with his mother; he said he was close to her, but she had had her own troubles and sometimes couldn't cope with his clinginess. Of course that would make him cling all the more. Another member asked about feelings of sexual inadequacy. Simon tried to respond but without going into the details of the rape and how this affected his attitude to physical intimacy, it was not a good answer. He simply said that there had been some unsatisfactory relationships with girls. He could not go into details. There was discussion about the risk to him of losing his family support system, especially his wife, and it was agreed that this could be a big risk were it to happen. An officer asked how he would cope, and he said he would run for help. The officer said this was a very positive answer and showed he recognised the risks. There was a long discussion about his point under Thoughts of 'failing to acknowledge the risk'. He said that he had kept a lot of things screwed down for thirty years but now the box was open and his feelings were again in tumult, but this time he was coming to an understanding of the reasons. He said the risk would diminish, he hoped so anyway, but this was why at the moment he put himself still at medium risk. He likened it to the frog that only jumps half the distance across the pond, his jumps get shorter and shorter but he never actually reaches the other side. That analogy seemed to be accepted. Inappropriate fantasy involving boys was raised. The female officer seemed to imply that this was working for him, but he said that it was a big turn off for him because of his fear of his own feelings. The female officer then asked if so, why he indulged in such fantasies, but he said that it was Daniel as he remembered him, aged sixteen, who was only ever the subject of such fantasy. Was that a fantasy or a memory, Simon asked.

The officer pursued the risk Simon had written of 'loss of mental capacity'. He said he had worked with people with dementia, such as Alzheimer's (he nearly launched into a detailed lecture on the different types of dementia) and that inappropriate sexual desire was not uncommon. He quoted one case he knew of in particular. No charges in that case had been brought because of dementia onset, but he wondered if he would get a sympathetic hearing because of his record should he ever suffer loss of mental capacity and lapse. The officer asked him to separate that item from the others because it was more of an external factor rather than a Thought, which he did. He was expecting questions about his 'desire to recapture youth' item, but none came. Perhaps he had said enough about Daniel. On the Behaviours there was little discussion, the officer queried an item on alcohol; he said it was not currently a problem but it was not beyond the realms of possibility. He was at pains to point out that all this was about what might happen and the risk flowing from that, not what was going to happen or even likely to happen. At last he sat down.

One member said he thought he had done well, he had been on the programme with him since he had started and he had seen a change. The female officer agreed with that. Both she and her colleague said it was an excellent piece of work and he had made some very good points, especially his acknowledgement of his feelings about the 14 year old. Simon thought that seemed to have ticked a box for them.

In the final round up session, he said how different this group was from his Block 1 group, that he had felt hostility when he did his first presentation of "My Offence", but this was very different and it was down to the group support. The female officer chided him for not taking the credit for himself, so he did. He said various factors fed into this, his counsellor, psychiatrist, the group and his own research. The officers acknowledged that his own efforts were paying off.

Of course while all this was going on, life at home continued. He did his best to support Karen at work, and there was always the need to help Robert and Fiona look after the girls. Simon was getting up early every morning, driving to Hilltown, collecting Donna and Florence also Robert or Fiona, driving to Dirshingham where he would park away from the school. He had been advised by Naomi not to go near the school since he had been all over the papers, so Robert or Fiona would take them into the school's breakfast club, which of course Simon and Karen were paying for. Then he would either drive back to

Hilltown to drop off Robert and/or Fiona (unless they were staying in Dirshingham shopping and then getting the bus back) before going back home, by which time Karen had left for work. Then he would work on his computer or of course, some days he had places to go, Gerdlington for SORP, meetings with Naomi etc.

Topics in that block included work on sexual fantasy, and what was appropriate or not. Simon felt confident enough to challenge this on the grounds that appropriate was a subjective judgement, and that the test should be illegality, as the whole course was about offending.

There is nothing either good or bad, but thinking makes it so

Other members then challenged Simon about this which led to an interesting discussion which Simon quite enjoyed. Various strategies to control fantasy were discussed as well.

A later session saw a return to the victim apology letter. Simon was on edge the entire time leading up to this. Throughout the discussion the thought kept coming into his head of how he would feel if he suddenly got a letter from the Watsons. How would he have reacted if he had got that when he was say 18? He thought he would probably have killed them, literally, as at that time he had been totally uncaring about his own future. That had been his intention. And if he had got it five years ago? Probably he would have just accepted it as closing a part of his distant past. Glad perhaps of their repentance. But now? He was not sure, because so much was going on in his head. This was with him throughout the discussion. He sometimes wondered how Ben's distress at witnessing his crime compared with his own from a much more vicious, violent and demeaning crime. Simon remembered as a teenager being 'touched up' by the school bus driver, Ted Johnson. He had hardly given it a thought since. He still felt a sense of unresolved injustice about the Watsons which manifested as anger, buried for decades but now resurrected in full force. It did little to suppress his stress levels.

Then it was his turn after the sandwich lunch to present his new version victim letter. He chose Ben Young because he had seemed the most affected and it was he who reported him in 2006.

Dear Mr Y-----

I want to apologise to you for the offence I committed against you when you were a boy. Whatever reasons motivated my actions, there are no excuses. I was an adult in whom you placed your trust and I betrayed that trust.

I am very sorry that you were upset and frightened by my actions. I have received, and am still receiving, professional help with my problems.

I let you down, also your parents and my own colleagues in the broken trust they placed in me.

I hope that you can now *try to* move on and that the disclosure of my offences offers you some closure and that you can put those painful memories behind you.

I cannot undo the past but I have learned a lot about myself and my offences *in order to prevent reoffending* and I am deeply sorry.

The parts in italics are those that he added while at the flipchart board. One member wanted the *try to* and the female officer wanted the *in order to prevent reoffending* inserted. So he did. The long time lapse was mentioned and that Ben now had a good job as a police officer and a family. Otherwise the officers thought it was a good letter and there was comparatively little discussion of it.

The next week produced another eye-opener for Simon. It was a role play, about Simon's offence against Ben Young in the forest, but Simon was a spectator while other group members took the roles of himself and Ben Young. The thoughts and feelings of himself and Ben Young were drawn up as the day trip progressed, the role playing members putting in how they thought it must have felt. The member playing Simon would occasionally give him a questioning look, and Simon had to admit to himself that it was pretty close so he just nodded. It was very stressful going through it again. A watching member suggested that Simon had not set out with the intention of committing any offence, but the female officer challenged him and said he could not know what Simon had been thinking. Only one person knew what he had been thinking. Simon commented that even he was not sure after this long gap, but it was true that he had wanted to be with the children and enjoy their company. The female officer reminded him that Simon had said in previous work each time, "never again". Simon reminded her that many trips had taken place when no offence was committed.

But what struck him like a thunderbolt was "Ben"'s suggestion that Ben might have feared for his own physical and sexual safety, possibly rape. Of course Simon knew that he had never had the intention of assaulting him, and that had blinded him to the possibility that Ben might have feared sexual assault. Simon knew from the context they meant rape, although the term sexual assault was used in the group. What astonished, confused and upset him was that, with his history especially, this fear that Ben had possibly felt, even if not explicit, had simply never occurred to him! Why had Simon never thought of that?

The play's the thing
Wherein I'll catch the conscience of the king

Simon's conscience was well and truly caught by this revelation! As before he was upset that Ben had been frightened, but this took it to a whole new level. So he felt really low. What a frightening yet pathetic sight it must have been! The group was supportive, and as they broke up, several had a quiet word of support for him.

It was now into the school's summer holiday. It had been two years since Karen had seen Harriet and she had always vowed she would never leave it as long as that. So Karen set off for Canada to stay with Bernadette and then travel down to Ohio to see Harriet. Simon was on his own. He was anxious, wondering what Karen and Harriet would say, and he wept again for the loss of his right of entry to the USA and Canada.

But there was one more SORP session in the third block. There was a discussion about sexual awareness and at what age children have sexual feelings. The 'script' said from birth, but quite how a new born could be asked, Simon wasn't sure. They also talked about how sex drive was affected by age. They said they had had this question before, and their answer was pretty much the same. The guidance said that frequency may decline but intensity does not. After break it was the end of block Risk Assessment. Last time Simon had placed himself across the medium to low risk boundary, 20% medium, 80% low. He said he would not change that. Although he had learned a lot on this block, especially in the Risk Factors exercise, the realisation the previous week of Ben's possible fear of rape had been very much on his mind, and Simon was feeling very unsettled about it. Simon had thought he had victim empathy in spades, so this was making him question himself again.

Be all my sins remembered

This was not enough to push him to higher risk, but had halted his progress toward lower risk. The member who had been with him from Block 1 said Simon was being too hard on himself. The female officer said it was positive that Simon was recognising this and sharing it with the group. It showed Simon was giving matters a lot of thought.

The officers said there would be new people on the next block, which would start in September. One of the female officers that Simon and others liked then said that this was her last session as she would not be on the next block. That's a shame, he thought she was the most empathetic of all the facilitators, without sacrificing any professionalism. She seemed to see the whole person rather than just the offender, which had been a major factor in his own ability to open up in the group, added of course to the much more friendly composition of this group compared with the Block 1 group. Simon drove home in the rain.

He spoke to Karen most evenings, bearing in mind the five hour time difference. It preyed on his mind what she and Bernadette might be saying about him, never mind she and Harriet but there was nothing he could do about it. Karen was away three weeks. He did jobs, tried to keep busy, was seeing Naomi, painted the outside of the house and of course spent a lot of time with Robert, Fiona and the two girls. They never questioned why Simon had not gone with Grandma to see Harriet. They accepted that they could only afford one air fare, which had the merit of some truth! They bought some furniture from IKEA for Robert's house which Simon spent some time putting together. He found that if you had solid doors on the bottom units of the Billys, you could not have glass doors on the top as they overlapped. So Simon drilled new holes and repositioned the doors so you could! He also took the girls to visit places, to a book centre in Bilthaven which they loved, and showed them the house in Swiford where he had lived in the flat in Bilthaven many years before. They said it was very nice. The street had hardly changed in forty years. The house was obviously no longer flats though. Russell no longer lived there, he was very old now but was still in touch with Ken, the two would meet up now and then for lunch, sometimes in Thirlham, other times in Bilthaven. He drove to Cermerton and showed them the school, now looking a bit tattered. The separate grammar and secondary were gone, it seemed to be a separate school and the old grammar school was now a sixth form college. There was a lot of building work going on.

He was still seeing Denise and this helped him. Karen seemed distant on the phone which worried Simon. Denise encouraged Simon to write things down – well, on the computer – which he did, starting to assemble the bits of his life which he regarded as milestones. He wrote a piece about Daniel and then slowly and painfully, a little about the rape. With Karen away, he could work until late at night or even into the small hours, which suited him. He took the girls to the small market town of Biltham, twenty miles up river from Bilthaven. There was a market there and a church dating back to Saxon times which fascinated them.

Late August and with some fear, Simon drove to Bilthaven Airport in the morning to meet Karen. The previous evening, Karen had phoned him and said she had come to a decision. But she would not say what it was. Simon had hardly slept. She was going to leave him, he knew it. He parked the car and with a heavy heart, on the edge of tears, waited in the concourse. The board said her Airbus A310 had landed and the wait seemed interminable. Passengers came out through the doors, to be greeted with glee by families, others, often men in suits pulling wheeled cases, simply walked passed looking for a taxi. But these were not Karen's flight.

Then he saw some arrivals were carrying bags with the Maple Leaf of Canada on them. Canadian luggage tags and duty free bags from Toronto. His pulse started to race, wondering what was going to happen.

There she was, tired looking after the night flight, she hadn't seen him. She looked solemn. He could hardly bear this.

"Karen!" he called. She turned and saw him. Her face transformed as she smiled at him. Relief swept over him.

"Hello, love," she said as they hugged like so many others. God, how he had missed her! He couldn't help it, his eyes watered.

"What's the matter?" she asked, concerned.

"I thought you were going to leave me," he said, as he wheeled her suitcase out of the concourse and towards the car park.

"Why? Why think that?"

"You said you had reached a decision," said Simon. "My mind has been going mad, and you sounded so distant on the phone."

"No, love, nothing like that. You silly, silly man. I love you, warts and all. I'm just tired, that's all."

They hugged again beside the car. "So what's this decision then?" he asked, heaving her case up.

"You thought that was it, that somehow Harriet had persuaded me to leave you?"

"Yes, I know she is angry with me about it all. And you talk to Bernadette too."

"I think Harriet is angry with you, but over there, she's out of it. She doesn't see what's happening here so she sees everything from a strange perspective. Like the wrong end of a telescope. But she still loves you, she's still your daughter. And that's my decision; not to leave it so long again before I see her."

A huge weight lifted from his shoulder, they drove home, Karen falling asleep on the way as jet lag took hold.

15. *2008/08 Lunch at the Lighthouse*

He walked along to the Lighthouse, the bar cum restaurant by the harbour. The tables outside were in the full heat of the sun. Simon felt he needed the shade now, so he went inside. He glanced at the bottled beers in the cool cabinets behind the bar, seeking wheat beer.

"Can I help you?"

The barman was in front of him.

"I was looking for wheat beer, German."

"We have Hoegaarden."

"Is that wheat beer?" said Simon. It was a new one to him. The barman pulled a small amount into a glass. Simon tasted it. It was lighter than the Bavarian stuff, but very pleasant and on this hot day, hit the spot. He decided to try it. Holding his beer, he went up the steps to the diners' area. An attractive waitress came up, apologising for not having seen him there. She was shapely with fair hair and strange blue eyes that looked almost artificial, as if they were impenetrable blue plates that hid whatever was behind them. Were they coloured contact lenses? He found them a little disconcerting. But their owner showed him to a table by the windows, overlooking the harbour. He looked at the menu and decided to go for a salad. A salmon salad looked good from its description.

A tall young waiter with tousled brown hair which made him quite boyish appeared.

"Would you like to order now?" He had dimples in his cheeks which added to the boyishness. Simon ordered the salad and sat back with his beer and indulged in some people watching. It was a mainly young clientele, some stripped to the waist in the heat showing off their tanned skin. The river sparkled in the sunshine, so different from the dangerous waters of his youth. Then, immersion meant an immediate tetanus injection. Now it was apparently one of the leading salmon rivers of England, a sure sign of a healthy river. The salad when it came was superb, an unusual mix of salads and herbs with the fresh salmon, but probably not from the river in front of him. When he finished he sat watching the young people, sipping his wheat beer and watching the young waiter as he moved gracefully around, wiping and resetting tables. He thought of Harriet, who used to visit the Lighthouse when she was in Bilthaven, one of her haunts. Depressed and with the thought of cancer never far from his mind, he suddenly felt like Dirk Bogarde's Gustav von Aschenbach in "Death in Venice". Why is life so bloody brutal?

Then he was there.

"Would you like to see the dessert menu?"

Simon felt the need for a positive response.

"Certainly, but I'm not promising."

The waiter smiled, a beautiful smile that accentuated the dimples in his cheeks. He left the menu.

Simon looked at it. He had intended to be good, to stick to the salad so that those few extra pounds would be the more easily lost. The summer pudding with Cornish clotted cream looked enticing. But too many calories by far.

Suddenly a new face was by his side, a different waiter, young also with an open, intelligent face but with dark, almost black hair, but the eyes! Deep blue with feeling in them that seemed to go back forever. Daniel! But of course it wasn't.

"Are you ready to order, sir? And then a smile. It seemed genuine. Simon's resolve melted instantly like ice cream in the hot sun outside.

"Summer pudding please."

He smiled again and took the dessert menu away.

A moment later Simon saw the dark haired waiter moving among the outside tables, deftly collecting plates and glasses. Simon watched.

The summer pudding arrived and it was delicious. Simon ate it slowly, relishing each mouthful.

Just as he finished, his mobile phone stirred in his pocket. A message from America on the home phone. He found Harriet's number and placed the call.

She answered immediately.

"Are you psychic?" he asked. "I was thinking about you."

"Oh?"

"I am at the Lighthouse Bar. Just finished a lovely summer pudding."

"Oh great."

"I love you," said Simon, suddenly feeling the loss of his travel rights to her. "I miss you. I'm sorry."

"What for?"

"Everything." He felt the tears coming, and he knew it could be heard in his voice. "I'll talk to you later," he ended, lamely.

"Sure," she said, her tone puzzled yet aware of his mood. The call ended.

"Is everything all right?" The dark haired waiter was there. Was he really concerned about Simon's distress? But the tone was the automatic one used by waiters when the last thing they want is a negative answer. Simon turned toward him, aware of the tears in his eyes. He nodded. The waiter left a plate with the bill.

Simon was suddenly aware of the white ensign, the flag of the Royal Navy, flying at the reserve base across the harbour. Oh, what might have been different! Those raping bastards! He wiped the tears away.

He looked at the bill. The dark haired waiter's name was Dan according to the printout. Of course, he got a tip.

16. 2008-9 James

September and Simon was to start SORP block 4. At the beginning it had seemed a mountain to climb but now here he was. He drove to Gerdlington and walked to the office. He went in to be met by one of the female officers.

"Hello Simon," she said as they went into the lobby where they gathered before each session. "We have some new people starting, so I know you will help them."

But Simon couldn't speak. There, sitting on a bench looking very nervous, was James!

But the officer was still talking. "Simon, this is James, he's starting Block 1."

Simon could see recognition starting on James's face once he had overcome his surprise! As James opened his mouth to speak, Simon quickly grabbed his hand and shook it, saying, "Hello James, I'm Simon. How do you do?"

The officer didn't seem to notice the breach of the 'no physical contact' rule and James, catching on quickly said with a slightly puzzled look, "Hi, Simon. Pleased to meet you."

As the group were ushered through into the meeting room along the corridor, Simon managed to whisper to James, "We're not supposed to know each other." James nodded. Once in the meeting room, James sat next to him. Simon thought he looked terrible. It had been a while since they had met, and now James was thin, drawn and grey in pallor. Simon drew comfort from his presence, and James drew comfort from Simon's. So in the icebreaker where they had to introduce the person next to them, he introduced James to the group, aged 27 from Cliffport, which was a small port about fifteen miles along the coast from Bilthaven. It was quite a journey from Cliffport to Gerdlington by bus. When the group split into two for some work, Simon and James were together.

After that it was the Risk Assessment again. They had to say what their offences were and give their risk own assessment. Being a 'senior' member now, Simon went first. He stood in front of the group as so many times before. He saw James looking at him with great curiosity. Simon had got used to recounting his offence, but now James was there. What would he think? But then Simon didn't yet know why James was on SORP.

So he started. "Thirty years ago when I was a teacher and was in charge of boys on field trips. While there, I exposed myself and masturbated in their presence. Two years ago I was recognised by one of the boys, now a police officer, who reported me. I pleaded guilty. I got three years probation, five years on the register and SORP. When I started I put myself at medium risk, and had thought about moving to low risk but what I have learned since then has made me reconsider."

Simon again put himself at medium 20% and low 80%. He sat down and stared straight ahead, not wanting to meet James's eyes. Why did he feel such shame anew, more than normal? James. He felt a touch on his elbow, James surreptitiously. He turned, James smiled at him. Suddenly Simon felt better. Then the new members had to state their offence and place themselves. Of course they found this hard, none more than James.

He stood shakily in front of the group. He fixed his eyes on Simon, who tried to beam encouragement and confidence back to him. "Last year I was depressed because my boyfriend had left me – I'm gay," he added looking warily around the group. "Someone came round for a drink and we looked at some porn on the computer. Twinks, which are men that look a lot younger than their actual age. He wanted to have sex with me but I wouldn't. The man then reported me and I was arrested and my computer taken by the police."

So that explained the loss of online contact and the use of text messaging, thought Simon.

James continued. "They found eleven level one images - that's the lowest level - in the temporary internet files folder. I got six months in prison, suspended for two years, two years probation, five years on the register and an order saying what I must do if I have a computer again."

The officer asked, "Where do you place yourself on the risk scale, James?"

"Low risk," he replied. So, like all the new ones, he put himself as low risk.

Back in his seat next to him, Simon risked a pat on the arm. James looked at him and smiled. How his face changes when he smiles, thought Simon. Simon was relieved to hear James's offence. He had imagined all sorts of things, from male rape downwards. Simon was so frightened that James, his friend, had done that. How would he have coped? But what I did was far worse than what James had done, thought Simon.

They managed to have a quick chat at lunchtime over the sandwiches. They agreed to meet outside at the end of the day. Simon told himself that because this was a pre-existing friendship, it could not be covered by the no associating rule. But he also knew it would be better not to advertise it.

Simon got embroiled in an argument that afternoon. There was a discussion of sexual attitudes. A new format, a statement was to be read out and they had to go to one end of the room depending on whether they agreed or disagreed, or they could stay in the middle. The first statement was "Most women don't report rape because they enjoy it." Everybody went to the Disagree end. Simon was inwardly angry about this because it ignored male rape – again!

"It's not just women that get raped," he said tartly.

The officers knew why he said this. "Yes, but the question is about women."

"Why? Why is male victimisation seen as less important than female?"

"Well, it's not of course."

"So why doesn't the question read, 'Most **people** don't report rape because they enjoy it', or ' Most **victims** don't report rape because they enjoy it'?"

"That's what's on the sheet we have."

Simon shook his head. Then another thought occurred to him. "Who says that they enjoy it anyway? Being raped enjoyable? I can't think of anything worse."

"Simon, that's the question," said the officer.

"No it's not," retorted Simon, angrily. "It's about whether they fail to report it because they enjoy it. It presupposes that they have enjoyed it!"

At this point the other officer stepped in. "Simon, I think we have to leave it there. Your points have been noted, but we must follow the guidelines to ensure that SORP is the same everywhere."

Simon knew he wasn't going to get any further, so he let it go. James was grinning at him which made him feel better.

But the next statement was "When a woman says No, she sometimes means Yes." Most went to the Disagree end but two stayed in the middle. This led to a prolonged discussion. It was really a disagreement about the precise terms of the statement rather than any fundamental feelings about it.

One member intervened. "What if it's role play and a scenario of bondage where the submissive might be saying 'No', but within the role play?"

"Say more?" said the female officer, one of their favourite ploys to draw members out. "How would they know when 'no' really meant 'no' in that case?"

"They would have a safe word," the member answered.

"What do you mean?" asked the female officer.

"The submissive can say 'no' as long as they want but the dominant won't stop unless the submissive says the safe word," explained Simon.

"Why not just have 'no' as the safe word then?" asked the puzzled female officer.

"Because that would spoil the fun," said Simon. "In a scenario, it would be the safe word that would really be 'No', even if it the actual word was 'fish'n'chips'. The word 'No' would be part of the role play."

The male officer understood, but the female officer took some time to grasp what Simon meant. Simon was trying to get to the semantics of 'No' rather than the literal word.

At the coffee break, several of the senior group members said "Well done" to Simon. He wasn't sure what the new ones thought about it, but as Simon said, they were told to be open and honest, so they couldn't complain when he was.

At the end of the day, Simon went out to find James, who had gone ahead, waiting.

"Five minutes, and now I've just missed my bus," he complained. "There's not another to Cliffport for another hour."

"Come on then," said Simon, "we'll catch the bus up." They walked quickly to where Simon had parked and tried to follow the bus route, but it must have made good time. They ended up leaving Gerdlington entirely.

"I need a cuppa," said James. "And some tabs." Smoking was something Simon had never bothered with and didn't like it that James smoked. Added to which James was asthmatic and smoking didn't help that either.

"Don't smoke in the car," he said to James, whose response was to wind the window down and hang his head out. It made Simon laugh. They stopped at a garage where James bought ten cigarettes, and there was a Macdonald's there, so they had a cup of tea and sat down in a quiet corner.

"How do you think it went today?" asked Simon.

"All right, I suppose," said James. "Hated standing there, saying about it."

"I know, that's horrible."

"You seemed OK."

"That's because you get used to it."

"I'll never get used to it."

"You will," said Simon.

"You kicked off a bit, didn't you?"

"When?"

"About rape?"

"That's a sensitive subject for me."

"Why?"

Simon's heart started to pound. James was looking at him, curiously, expectantly. Simon thought, maybe I can talk to about it to James. He took a deep breath. "I was raped by three lads when I was seventeen. They had a knife and a chain. They took turns." Tears started to flow. Luckily they were in a corner away from others.

"Don't cry," said James, unsure how to deal with this. But then he put his arm round Simon and hugged him. Simon felt that warmth and affection, it made him feel better. Slowly, James teased the facts from Simon. Simon suddenly found himself talking about it, as though James had in some way smashed the dam of fear and shame that had held him back from speaking of that night for so many years. This was the first time he had gone into any detail with anybody. Simon felt as though a weight had been lifted from him.

"Not sure if it makes you feel better, but I was raped too," offered James.

"When?"

"When I was a kid." James stopped.

"You can tell me," said Simon. "I always thought there was more going on with you than the boyfriend leaving."

Simon looked now at his friend, those pale, sad blue eyes now watering, a single tear rolled down James's cheek.

"There was this man, Colin Duncan, supposed to be our friend. Lived next door but was always in our house."

"When was this?" asked Simon gently.

"When I was six."

"Six!"

"Yes and it carried on until I was fifteen, when we moved to our present house."

"What!"

"I hate him!" said James vehemently.

Simon sat, shocked. "How often?"

"Two, three times a week."

"What!"

"Stop saying 'what'," said James irritably.

"For nine years?"

"Yes. Leave it now. I don't want to talk about it."

"Didn't you report it?"

"No. Did you?"

"No."

"Well then."

"You poor thing," said Simon, and put his arm round James, but James brushed him off.

"Don't do that," said James. "I don't like being touched by older men. Now you know why. So just leave it. I'm going outside for a smoke. You coming?"

So they stood outside in the September sunshine while James smoked. Simon looked at him. He had always sensed some inner sadness. Poor James. Nine years of hell made his one hour of torment pale into insignificance.

Simon drove to Cliffport and dropped James off and went back to Thirlham, his mind still buzzing with his own revelations and what James had told him.

He managed to have some time with Donna and Florence who had two more days off school before the term began. They were excited and a little nervous about their new teachers, but it was fine in the end and they both liked them.

The next week back in Gerdlington, he made a point of sitting next to James. Simon noticed straight away that he was due to present his block 4 work, "What's Changed". Luckily Simon had brought his preparation notes with him, but he still felt anxious about doing it. It was to be the last session of the day.

Then the officers introduced the four pieces of personal work which would be done throughout the four blocks, one per block. Block 1 people do "My Offence", block 2 "My Cycle", block 3 "My Risk Factors" and block 4, which applied to him, "What's Changed". Simon was asked to describe what was the purpose behind "My Offence" to which he replied it was about accepting and taking responsibility for the offence(s). Simon said that the female officer had used the word 'challenge' in respect of the questions that would be put by other group members, which might sound threatening, but Simon said it would be supportive, and questioning the actions, not the person.

The officers then ran though some scenarios for each item of personal work, with the male officer playing the role of 'John' who had indecently assaulted his three young nephews. These were of necessity much shorter and less detailed than the real thing; it was to familiarise the new members especially with the structure of the programme. These took up the rest of the morning.

After lunch they had a session to prepare their personal work. The officers were stretched helping new members. James needed help because he had forgotten his glasses, Simon offered but then another member said that as he was not presenting his block 4 work this week, he would. So Simon spread his flipchart sheet out on the floor and copied up his draft from his notes.

As the time for the presentation came nearer his anxiety level started to go up and up. Simon took a trifluoperazine tablet, went to the loo twice and still hot and bothered, took off his sweatshirt.

Before Simon was called out to the front, he was asked what he expected to get out of the exercise. Simon said to get it over with. But also that it drew together the work of the other three blocks and was in a sense an assessment of what had changed in his thinking over the blocks, thus the name, and was a way forward, rather than a way of looking backward to the offences. There was discussion of "Old Me" and "New Me". Simon said that was OK as far as it went, but there was only one him, and Simon was still him, the person who had committed the offences, although thirty years ago. Simon commented on what the female officer had said before, that the programme was not about cure but control.

Then Simon went out to the front with the female officer facilitating, and started to work though the various sections of the "What Changed" sheet.

The female officer questioned him about boundaries. Simon said this was obviously a weakness of his and it had been a topic of discussion with Karen.

Simon had to explain the projection of false realities, which was his projecting onto the boys his own scenario. He was asked about rebuilding his relationship with Karen, and Simon said that she had known nothing of the offences and it had come as a great shock to her. She was finding adjusting to this new reality hard, but they were still close and it would take time. He said that in some respects she had married "a pig in a poke". The female officer had not heard of this expression so Simon had to explain it. Simon said there was a forty year shared history and they needed each other, they were still each other's favourite person and best friend. They also needed each other to help look after Robert and the girls. They were parenting again as well as grandparenting and Simon said it was virtually a 24/7 job.

Simon was also asked about relationships with boys. He recounted the "Tim Moment" again, and said that he was now simply a friendly neighbour to the kids on the street rather than as he had been then, thirty years ago, trying to be a pal to the boys. The female officer said that recognising that was a great step. He thought he would be asked to expand on inversion, but after Simon said it was a psychological process in childhood by which a man could become fixated on children, nobody asked for more. A new member was interested in the part about rebuilding his relationship with his wife, because he was going through the same process. Simon said that this was a benefit of the programme because other members' experiences could be applied to one's own.

He said it had been a long process of readjustment and that he now reluctantly had to recognise he was bisexual at least. James floored him by asking, if now that he had admitted that to himself as much as anything, Simon now felt stronger. He stopped and thought, trying to look into himself. How perceptive James could be, he thought. So he had to say that overall, yes he did. Simon no longer had to hide his sexuality, which had taken a psychological toll over fifty years. He said he wasn't going to start telling all and sundry or anything, but Simon no longer felt as if it had to be hidden and suppressed.

An older member said very encouraging words, saying Simon was too hard on himself, and that he had done a great deal in his life, and the offending was a tiny part. He reminded him how Simon had said this to a previous member, about wearing sackcloth and ashes. So now Simon was hoist with his own petard.

> For 'tis the sport to have the engineer
> Hoist with his own petard

He was asked about activities in the future and his aims in life. He said that his aim was to live long enough to see the girls into adulthood. He said his voluntary work had all stopped, but that perhaps in the future there might be something he could do. He was asked what he did purely for himself rather than for others, and he couldn't think of anything.

He was exhausted when at last he sat down. The group gave positive feedback, saying Simon had been open and honest, that he had obviously found it hard but had delivered a good piece of work.

After the group dispersed, later than usual, Simon sat and recovered for a few moments. The female officer spoke to him with some encouraging words.

Simon went and sat in the car for a while, but as soon as James came after a quick smoke, then he wanted to get away, so he drove out of Gerdlington but didn't feel ready to go home, so they stopped for a coffee on the way. Tea for James. Simon found this quite relaxing, and realised how much better he felt in James's company.

"You didn't like that bit about being gay, did you?" asked James.

"I'm not sure what to think about it. But you were right when you said that recognising it makes me stronger. How did you know that?"

"I'm gay," said James. "In this country, you quickly learn you have to be strong."

Simon's mind suddenly went back to Daniel, that last night, when Daniel had said, "Maybe one day this bloody country will wake up to the truth." It was certainly taking its time.

"What's the matter?" asked James, aware of the change in Simon's mood.

"Just thinking of something Daniel once said. I loved him, you know."

"You still do, my friend," said James. Simon once more realised that James seemed to know him better than he knew himself, in some ways anyway. But then James reached out and hugged Simon and to his astonishment, kissed him lightly on the cheek.

"I thought you didn't like older men?" said Simon.

James laughed. "Don't build your hopes up, Simon. I may be gay, but I don't fancy you."

"I fancy you," said Simon, before he could stop himself, before he even realised that he did.

"So you're gay?" said James, smiling.

"No," said Simon with the automatic response of a lifetime. "Oh, I don't know."

"Nobody in their right mind would choose to be gay," said James.

"You are."

"Yes, but I didn't choose it. But it's what I am, I can't change it. Neither can you change what you are."

"Am I changing?"

"No, you are learning bit by bit what you really are. A bit late, like," James finished smiling. "And I'm sorry, you might fancy me, but it's not gonna happen. We're friends though, eh?"

"Yes, friends," said Simon.

They drove to Cliffport and then Simon went home, his mind buzzing with the SORP day but mainly because of his conversation with James. He was relieved in a way that James didn't fancy him. That removed temptation to which he might have succumbed and that would have been terrible for Karen, his life partner, best friend and, as he thought about it, the person who mattered most to him in the whole world. He felt happy and more content than he had for many months.

Simon could relax more now, he had done his final piece of work for SORP and while there were hard parts, it was made better for him by James being there. They sought each other out and enjoyed their company, going for days out when Karen was at work. Simon always looked forward to Karen being home, but now he had a friend, a true male friend. Maybe the age gap mattered for James with regard to sex, but it didn't seem to matter to either of them with regard to friendship. Talking things through with James gradually enabled Simon to accept himself. They talked much about sexuality and being gay, what it meant. James helped Simon through this process. And Simon was able to take James to places he had never thought of going, away from that Cliffport council estate.

The weeks passed and Simon and James supported each other in SORP as best they could. The new ones started doing "My Offence" which they were nervous about. Simon said it would get better as the blocks went on because now it was known to all the group. James said he was nervous about doing his own "My Offence" whenever that would be, but he did feel a bit better about it now. He said he would rethink his own draft in the light of what he had learned watching the three presentations so far. An older member reminded the group of Simon's comment two weeks before when he said he was optimistic about this being a good group, which he said had been true and he was positive about this block.

That evening Simon looked at James's draft of "My Offence". He thought it was lacking in detail, and said so.

"Now that I've seen the others, that's why I'm going to do it again," said James. So they sat and worked through it, Simon using his experience of SORP to draw more out of James until they had a draft that Simon thought was a big improvement. Certainly he thought fuller than his own Block 1 piece.

James was anxious about the next week, but he was not called to present. Others did their various block work, and Simon tried to be supportive. He noticed that James was more relaxed and was starting to take more of a role in the group. He was pleased for his friend.

Simon got involved in an argument with one elderly member who was presenting Block 2, "My Cycle". He had invited boys to his home and had followed one into the bathroom and masturbated there. The member strenuously denied any homosexual feelings but Simon probed this vigorously and the member said he had become aroused with the boys, that when they were around he got a sexual buzz. He also said he had taken them to the swimming baths, choosing one at Gerdlington where there was an open changing room, where the males all got changed together. Simon said that he had been forced to look again at his own sexuality, and the member should think about his own feelings. But the member said he was not gay at all, despite a series of offences involving boys. A senior member just sat there shaking his head, and the newer members asked equally probing questions, tripping the elderly member up in inconsistencies. Simon said there was a lot of dissonance in the member's account, a word which the female officer used when summing up.

The group feedback was all along the lines that the elderly member needed to be more open with the group. Simon said that he realised that the elderly member had found that very hard, how difficult it was for men of their generation (the elderly member was 75) to admit to gay feelings and that the group had been quite hard on him but that it was intended to be supportive and help him. This was echoed by others, the member who had earlier been shaking his head in particular.

In Round Up, Simon praised all three presenters that day. He ended by saying that the elderly member needed to be more honest with himself before he could be more honest with the group. The female officer said that was a good note on which to end a very full day.

"You were a bit heavy today," said James in the car later.

"Why? I mean in what way?"

"You were pushing him too hard. He's even older than you by quite a bit. And look how long it's taken – sorry, taking – you to admit you're gay."

"We're supposed to challenge," countered Simon.

"Yes, but not that hard."

So they drove to Cliffport and to the run down council estate where James lived with his widowed mother and brothers, James commented he hoped his older brother hadn't been drinking. Simon knew the older brother was nice enough but unreliable, who when he got drunk assaulted James for being gay. He got drunk frequently. His younger brother, Liam, was severely physically and mentally handicapped and James helped his mother look after him as the older brother was too unreliable. What a way to live!

At his meeting with Naomi that week, Simon was told he had been confrontational in the group. Naomi said there was a line between supportive challenging and confrontation and Simon had crossed it. So James had been right then.

When they met up for a chat and a cuppa, Simon told James what Naomi had said.

"I thought you said your probation officer was OK," said James.

"She is, but even you said I went too far."

"True," grinned James. Then his expression changed. "I wish I had your officer. Mine hates me." James had talked of his probation officer, Ruby Simmons, before.

"Why should she hate you?"

"Well I don't know. Maybe coz I'm gay. I've met yours, Naomi. She's nice."

"She's just doing her job, I expect."

"She never believes anything I say. She doesn't even believe I was abused by Colin Duncan. She turned round and said I'm making it up. How can I trust her?"

Simon kept his thoughts to himself, although he could see how if Ruby dismissed one of the most critical formative influences on James as a lie, the relationship was never going to work. James often said how two faced Ruby was, nice when other people were around but when they were alone, a "right bitch". Simon wondered how much James's view was coloured by his own anger at the world and his life. Abused for so many years in the most horrendous way. Simon wondered why James was as sensible as he sometimes could be. But he was quick tempered, which Simon had soon discovered and had been on the wrong of it once or twice. But James always apologised and told Simon that he was his friend. Despite the friendship of neighbours and others who had stood by him, Simon felt that outside the family James was his one true friend. He knew he could be completely open with James and he with him. He hadn't felt this since Daniel. Karen, try as she might – and she did – could never identify with his feelings of that deep visceral male to male love that Simon was now recognising in himself and that this distressed young man had awoken.

The next week at SORP turned out to be hard. There was debate about Simon's questioning of the elderly member the previous week, saying Simon had been trying to force his experience onto him. The female officer, a different one that week, gave him the chance to respond immediately. The feedback from the previous week Naomi had given him had said that Simon had been confrontational, so this was a further confirmation. Simon apologised to the group and to the elderly member, and said his questioning had not been intended to force the elderly member to say he was gay, but only that he should look again at his own sexual preferences in the light of his offences. The elderly member then launched into a monologue about a time when he was younger when someone had arrived at work driving a pink 2CV and the elderly member said he was gay because of that. He said that to him, gay people (and he then went into a long discourse into the word gay and its changed meaning) was 'limp wristed' people. Simon noticed James, who was sitting between him and the elderly member and who had made no secret of the fact that he was gay in the group, looking decidedly uncomfortable. The female officer said that this was a stereotype and that gay people were of all sorts. In his eventual response Simon said again that the elderly member was not being forced to follow his path but that he was only being asked to look again. Simon used the word stereotype to hint that the elderly member's monologue indicated that perhaps he was afraid to look at this aspect of his make up. He thought the point was not lost on most of the group.

The day was spent with new members presenting "My Offence". Later it was James's turn. He said that since seeing another member's two weeks ago he realised his own prepared account was not full enough and had rewritten it. He said that after breaking up with his boyfriend he had been lonely and depressed and had starting using drink and drugs. He asked an older man round for a chat, but not sex, and when there they looked for gay porn. They looked for "twinks", males that appear younger than they really are. They looked at eleven images of teenage looking males in various erotic poses although James said he thought their actual age was over eighteen. James refused to have sex with the man who then left. He later reported James to the police.

Under questioning, especially searching questions from the female officer, James said his drug habit had been very intense when younger and that at one time he had been spending most of his money on drugs. He now regretted this. The female officer pressed him on the search terms used to find the websites. James said he had searched on twinks, but then added "teen porn". The female officer said she knew what search terms he had used because of the case files and the police had recovered them from his computer, hinting at "boy love" to which James agreed. He was put to some hard questioning from both the female officer and from one or two group members.

Simon hung back a bit for fear of being considered confrontational, but then asked, "Did you pay to access this website?"

"No," replied James, looking shaky standing at the front by the flip chart.

"Did that make you think anything about whether the images were legal or not?"

"Yes, I thought they would be over 18 because we didn't pay to look at them."

The female officer then demanded, "What happened later on, James?"

"The man left when I said I wouldn't have sex with him."

"And after that?" she asked.

"He came back."

"Why did he come back?"

"He still wanted sex with me."

"What did you do?"

"We looked at the websites again, and he was still pestering me for sex."

"Why didn't you have sex with him?"

Simon felt the female officer was pushing James hard and could detect distress in him. James was flustered and flushing, wondering how he could explain his anxiety about older men.

At this point the other officer said, "But you did look at websites again?"

James was obviously grateful for the no doubt intentional change of direction and simply nodded.

Simon saw a chance to get back in. "Did the police tell you how old the boys were?"

"They said they were aged fifteen to seventeen," answered James.

"Did you think they were?"

"No, I thought they would be eighteen, but that they looked younger. People often think I'm younger than I am." Simon knew the truth of that.

"So did the police trace the models then to find out how old they were?"

The female officer came straight in. "Simon, they were not models! They were abused children, victims! Your use of the word model is not appropriate and I find your use of the word disturbing!"

There was a moment's silence in the room. Simon felt upset as he thought she was overreacting.

"The word has already been used in the discussion, and I was simply using it as a convenient term to ask the question."

The other officer then said, "No, the victims were not traced, they could have been anywhere in the world. But they looked under eighteen and that is an absolute offence in law."

"So James," continued Simon, trying to conceal his anger, "this man came round, you looked at the website ...."

"We had a few beers as well," interjected James.

"OK, and then you refused to have sex with him and he left."

"Yes," confirmed James.

"But later he came back to look at more images with you and press you for sex again?"

"Yes, but I wouldn't have sex with him."

"Was he angry that you wouldn't?"

"Yes," said James. "He turned round and said I was leading him on and teasing him."

"Were you?" asked Simon.

"No," said James. "He knew right from the start I wouldn't have sex with him."

"So he left annoyed and later reported you to the police?"

"Yes," said James, simply.

The female officer had grown more agitated throughout this exchange and then said in a vehement tone, "Well thank goodness he was a public spirited citizen who reported this child abuse!"

That was met with another silence as everybody in the room was now aware that the informant had gone round to James's house with a view to sex, and himself willingly viewed the images of teenage boys, had voluntarily returned later to view more and press James for sex and when James had refused, had then reported him. Simon also wanted to make the point that these were the only images on James's computer and they were in cache, not saved. There was no store of pictures and no suggestion that James had tried to save them permanently or distribute them to others. But the officers moved on and Simon could not elaborate further on James's behalf.

Simon remained quiet after that, seething, especially when one member was praised for his earlier questioning of a new member using his own experience, the very thing Simon felt he had been criticised for doing with the elderly member the week before.

Simon was asked for feedback for James. Simon said he deserved credit for having seen the poor quality of his first draft and on his own initiative producing a much longer and more detailed one. Simon said he had obviously found it difficult but that he had done very well, in fact much better than he had when presenting his Block 1. He said that this group was very good, compared to the group when he had been on Block 1; he looked to the female officer for some sign of confirmation, but she appeared stony faced, although she had agreed this was the case on previous occasions. He said that James probably had more to get off his chest, but it was an excellent start. Other group members gave very similar feedback.

James was subdued in the car going back.

"I did my best to help you get your point across," said Simon.

"I know, but I think she hates me," said James, referring to the female officer. "I bet she's a friend of Ruby's."

Simon tried to be positive. "Look, it was a good piece of work, I think, and so did the other group members."

But James was depressed and felt he was being got at. They met for a talk during the week but James's mood was low.

He talked to Karen about the progress on SORP. She listened attentively and offered support. Simon knew how lucky he was to have her. And there was the pleasure of seeing Donna and Florence as well.

James looked ill when they met up in Gerdlington the next week. The plan for the day involved Life Time Lines. Simon had done this before in his block 1. It turned out he was the only one to have done this, because his Block 1 had been done before the two groups had been amalgamated. The male officer led the group through the creation of a fictitious Life Time Line about 'Bob' showing how the ups and downs of his life were laid out along the line. They then had some time to prepare their own chart. Simon wondered whether simply to re-use his original one from his folder with minor additions, but the female officer – the usual one this week - said he should do it again. Simon had the A4 size original draft so he pinned his flipchart sheet on the wall, and set to creating the time line. Simon had spoken about Daniel to the group before so there was no problem there, but this time instead of putting a big red X for the rape, he put deep in the negative zone, 'Raped'. Otherwise it was much as before, but Simon added in some positives from later on, his various academic studies later in life, and of course the support he had received from Karen and his family.

As Simon suspected, because he was the only person to have done this work before, the female officer asked him to go first. He was happy to because he was determined to be open now about everything, rape included, and Simon thought this would give a lead to the other group members and also set the tone for the others. It would allow him to get this off his chest, which he had previously baulked at. After the usual preliminary questions (What do you want to get out of this work? How would like other group members to respond? etc.) Simon took his chart to the front. He was feeling shaky but he had committed himself by writing 'raped' on the chart. He started off by describing his early years, his fear of and poor relationship with his father, ameliorated by his friendship with Daniel, two years older than him, which became a sexual relationship. Simon recounted overhearing his father forcing himself on his mother and his feelings at that time, which was swiftly followed by their sudden move north, his isolation, the bullying by the Watson gang, his sexual relationships and the loss of his virginity, with a girl Simon added to differentiate that from his loss of virginity with Daniel. Then the rape, how he went off the rails, trying alone to come to terms with it, his failure to get to university, reluctant entry to teaching, meeting Karen, which took the line up high again, but Robert's birth, his problems and the virtual collapse of the marriage (separate but parallel Simon described it as), his eye accident, the new job Simon disliked, all contributing to huge stress, a sense of abject failure as a husband, parent, teacher. The line plunged low. This was the period when Simon offended. Harriet's birth, the improvement in the marriage and the rebuilding with Karen based on their underlying love which had never stopped, led to improvements, then his early retirement, the birth of Donna and Florence and then the arrest and prosecution. The line went up and down over the time axis in response to these events.

The group remained quiet throughout this, in fact they were transfixed, and obviously taking it all in. James, despite his illness, had listened intently. Afterwards, the female officer asked him to include the fact of his sexual relationship with Daniel, which she said occurred at the end. Simon pointed out that his first orgasm aged eleven was with him, so this was a long term sexual affair. He was asked what he saw as the pivotal events in his life. Simon said the move north and the loss of Daniel, the rape and its aftermath and the low time after Robert's birth. Simon talked of his suicide attempts aged seventeen, which seemed to shock the female officer a bit, and said that once that black cloud descends, it blots out all else except the desire to end everything.

How weary, stale, flat and unprofitable seem to me all the uses of this world

Simon had to take action in future before the cloud got too close. He talked a bit about the rape. More than before but not in the level of detail he had told James. The female officer said he had done extremely well to be open about that which she knew he would have found very difficult. Simon put it down to the supportive nature of the group which enabled him to feel confident about revealing this. The female officer said again that it was not just the group, but his own courage to do this which deserved credit. She said it showed how much progress he had made through the course.

"You are obviously a very intelligent person," asked one member, "and yet you committed the offences which you knew were wrong."

"Well, yes, apparently I have a very high IQ," said Simon, "but that shows that having an IQ through the roof doesn't necessarily make you a better person. Other character traits are at least, if not more, important."

Man's wit doth surmount all, but man himself.

"I think you are being too hard on yourself," commented the male officer.

Simon said he was also receiving counselling and psychiatric help which all played a part. One member asked whether his wife was the best counsellor. Simon said they talked very frankly now, but she was involved, and a good independent counsellor was well worth trying, aware that the member was trying to rebuild his own marriage. When Simon sat down, the feedback from the group was very positive, from all sides.

Other members then went through their life stories; there was drink, drugs, chaotic lives, sexual abuse and depression. Simon thought once more of the victim – victimiser cycle.

In Round Up at the end, one senior member singled Simon's presentation out as the most courageous and best piece of work he had seen on all the course so far, to the accompaniment of nods from other group members. Simon thanked him for that and the support of the group. He singled out a young member's work saying that he was so young and yet there was an underlying maturity there which would stand him in good stead. The youth positively beamed with pleasure at that and said it made him feel really good. He had thought this group would be horrible but now he looked forward to coming and it was a group of friends he met each week. Other group members said they felt the same. James, looking and feeling ill, said nothing.

As the group broke up, the female officer made a point of coming to him to say how well she thought Simon had done and again praising his courage.

With this positive feedback, Simon was feeling upbeat and persuaded James they stop on the way back to Cliffport for something to eat. James's mood seemed to lighten when the two were alone together, which pleased Simon.

James presented his life time line the next week, outlining the abuse he had suffered as a child, his work as a Butlins Redcoat, modelling and some acting work. The loss of his father to cancer affected him deeply and then his boyfriend left. Simon asked most of the follow up questions, asking about his family, whom of course Simon knew. James said his mother knew he was gay if only because the boyfriend had lived with them for over two years, but he couldn't talk to her about his sexuality or his offences. Simon was exploring especially the effect of early sexualisation, drawing on his own experience. While Simon could never regard Daniel as having been abusive and obviously Colin Duncan had gravely abused James, he put it to James that this had coloured his attitude to sex. The male officer said that this was a useful avenue and that perhaps it had helped reduce inhibitions so that James could commit the offences. Simon said it was likely in his case too. It turned out that both Simon and James had suffered head injuries when young, Simon's when he fell over the wall, James's in a car accident aged eleven. James remarked that since that accident he had been unable to swim. Simon said from his research there was a link between frontal lobe injury and inhibition reduction.

James agreed with Simon's suggestion that the adulation he felt he was getting as a Redcoat and model was a compensation for the feelings of low esteem stemming from the abuse. Simon said he could see many parallels with his own situation, in his case the reaction to rape, and his compensation was in the 'adulation' one receives as a teacher. This was perhaps why he was able to remain in a job which in many ways he did not like, but this all broke down at the time of his offences.

Simon said he thought James had had done very well, and apologised to the group for asking most of the questions but so much of what James said had struck a chord with him.

Simon was now nearing the end of SORP. It had been a long haul, but then he was told that after SORP there was another course called 'Looking Forward' which would last a further twelve weeks. Simon accepted this philosophically, he wanted to co-operate and it was a lot better than prison!

He continued taking Donna and Florence to school (with Robert or Fiona of course) and helping Karen with school work. She followed his progress through SORP closely and they would talk in detail about each session when he got home. She was concerned about Simon and the toll the course was taking on him and so was glad it was drawing to a close. His weekly feedback from Naomi was usually good and Simon felt he was managing to hold things together.

He spent time with James, picking him up from Cliffport and going for days out. James was anxious about being in Cliffport since his case was reported in the *Nusbury News* in the lurid terms usual for that paper and would only leave the house in company. That usually meant Simon. The two became closer and Simon realised with some confusion that he loved James. This took nothing away from Karen, it was a different kind of love, but James offered him something in his psyche that Karen, with the best will in the world, could not supply. The analytical part of Simon's brain found this interesting because he realised that being gay wasn't just about sex. Just as well, because James did not want sex with Simon, but it was about a male to male bond that was apart from sex. Perhaps this was why some men could have gay sex under pressure of circumstance; prison, long sea voyages etc. as a purely sexual release, yet still deny they were gay and revert to solely heterosexual relationships when they could. So being gay was as much a state of mind as a sexual preference. What he was finding with James, through long hours of talk, was that this state of mind was part of him. He had buried it for so many years, battened down the hatch and refused to admit this. But Ben Young had opened Pandora's box releasing this whirlwind and Simon knew there was no putting it all back. James helped him and supported him through this.

17. 2008-10 City Bridge

But James was still suffering the untreated torment of many years of abuse. He was also feeling the pressure of SORP. This all came to a head one October day. The two had been on a lovely day out, by train this time and were travelling back to Bilthaven. He started to talk about how rotten his life was, how everybody let him down. Simon could not help remembering the 'poor me' thinking they talked about on SORP.

"You'll find someone one day," said Simon.

"Well there was this lad who wanted to meet me. I liked him and he liked me but I had no way of meeting him."

"If he likes you that much, he'll meet another time."

"He's gone away now."

"He'll come back," said Simon.

"It doesn't matter. I'll just fucking be single for ever, I'm a fucking loser anyway."

"You won't. You're not. This shows there are lads out there who like you. Contact him again when he gets back, or keep in touch while he's away."

"This SORP is really getting to me. Ever since I started it I'm starting to get attracted to boys coz of it," said James, his anxiety level visibly rising.

"Yes. It heightens everything. My gayness for a start! Since I met you a couple of years ago, I have become more aware of things. It has raised my gay sexuality after many years of suppression."

"Well, it's raised things I didn't want raising."

"But I don't think it puts anything there that wasn't there already. It just raises ghosts you were rather kept quiet," explained Simon.

"I might tell my doctor coz for me I think that if somewhere is making you worse and liking boys then you shouldn't go."

"You can try, but it won't work. The first blocks are the hardest. If you are attracted to teenage boys, then you need to admit that to yourself, and then deal with it. I will help you."

"I know you will," said James. "But everybody gets this wrong. I don't want to do anything with them, I just like being with them."

"The pictures?"

"Look, I'm gay. I admire the male form and I like good looking young guys. That doesn't mean I'm gonna have sex with them. But I enjoy their company."

"You're trying to recapture your stolen youth, to relive your lost childhood. I can identify with that."

James thought a moment. "Yes, I think that's true. My childhood was shit. Didn't have one really, so, yes, I like being around lads, looking at them. But that's all."

"James, I think that's great progress. You are starting to look and yourself more and understand yourself. That's really good. I'm proud of you."

He seemed to calm down after that. The train was delayed getting back to Bilthaven and James had missed the train to Cliffport. There were frequent Thirlham trains because trains between Bilthaven and London usually stopped there.

"Don't go yet," said James. "Let's have a drink. You're not driving." So they went to a gay bar in Bilthaven. James seemed at ease in these surroundings. Simon was worried about the time, he wanted to get back for Karen.

"I'll have to go, James," he said. "Karen will be wondering where I am, probably got the tea ready by now."

"You go home for tea," said James. "I think I'll stay on here. I'm enjoying myself."

"OK, but make sure you get the 8:30 train. That's the last to Cliffport."

"I'll come and see you off," said James. Simon was slightly surprised by that, but they walked back to the Grand Station.

Simon's train was waiting. On the platform, James gave Simon a hug. He was smiling.

"I do love you, Simon," he said unexpectedly. "You're my one true friend. I'll always love you for that." He then kissed Simon on the cheek. Simon boarded the train and found a seat. James was on the platform smiling through the window. As the train moved off, James waved and then turned and walked away.

Back home, Karen was there. She talked of her day at school and Simon offered one or two ideas about a project she was doing. Watching television later Simon noticed it was nine o'clock. James should be home by now he thought. He decided to check and rang James's mobile phone.

"Hi, you home yet?"

"No."

"Why not, did you miss the train?"

"Yes, I knew I was going to."

Simon realised that James was crying. "What's the matter, what's going on? Where are you?"

"Still in the gay bar. It doesn't matter now. I'm not going home."

"Why not?"

"Look, I've had a great day, a lovely last day."

"Last day?"

"It's not your fault, nothing is your fault. You've shown me nothing but love, and I love you in my way. But I can't go on."

"No, James, no!"

James was really crying now, Simon could hear the sobs. "Nothing good's ever happened to me, I've had twenty one years of hell, all those years of Colin Duncan, and I can't do it any more."

"Please, James. O God! Please don't," pleaded Simon, fighting back the tears himself. "I love you, you know I do. I'll help you."

"If I'd turned round and said something about Colin Duncan, maybe he wouldn't have abused my sister as well. I can't take this guilt any more."

"Please don't, James."

"I've made up my mind, Simon. I love you, but it's time to end it. You've been the best friend I could have had. Good bye." The phone went dead. Simon tried to redial but either James's phone was off or he rejected the calls.

"What's the matter?" asked Karen, concerned by Simon's upset.

"James. He's in Bilthaven and he's going to kill himself. Thank God I phoned him. I have to go."

Karen looked shocked. She was worried about Simon and James, wondering where it might lead. She too was aware that Pandora's box was blown wide open and was very unsettled.

Simon drove to Bilthaven as fast he safely could. He found a parking spot in a street not far from the gay bar and ran there, hoping he wasn't too late.

With relief he saw James was there, sitting at a table with some other men, crying and upset. When he saw Simon, he became distraught.

"What are you doing here? You shouldn't have come!"

Two of the men came up to Simon. "You should be ashamed of yourself, what you did to this man. You're coming outside with us."

"What are you talking about?" said Simon, shaking off one of the men.

"No," said James. "That's not him, he's my friend."

"Is this the bastard that abused you, James?" asked the other man, still gripping Simon's arm.

"No!" said James again. "Let go of him. He's my friend." The man let go of Simon, rather reluctantly, perhaps not quite believing James. Simon sat next to the weeping James, putting his arm round him for comfort. But James got up.

"Why have you come back?" James demanded. "You shouldn't have. You're not going to stop me."

"I'll take you home," said Simon, again trying to comfort him. But James shook him off and ran out of the bar, Simon trying to keep up. James fell to the ground on his knees in the plaza, curled up, head in hands, howling with his distress and anguish. But as soon as he felt Simon's touch, he was up and off again.

"Please stop, James. Where are you going?"

"The City Bridge, and then that's it," said James, striding ahead. Simon thought of his own plans many years earlier to fall to his death from the City Bridge. But he couldn't let James do this, he just could not, whatever it took. As they got close to the bridge arguing, oblivious of passers by, Simon grabbed James to stop him, pleading with him. James broke free, and again Simon fought him, encircling him with his arms, pinning James's own arms to his side.

"What going on?" A man was next to them, demanding to know. They stopped, Simon still pinning James's arms. The man showed a warrant card. "I'm a police officer," he added.

Simon took an instant decision, try to pass it off so the cop would go away? No, then he would be no further forward. Simon knew what he had to do, even though it would expose their relationship and whatever would follow from that.

"This young man is intent on taking his own life."

James gave Simon a look of sheer fury and hatred. But by this time the cop was calling for backup. The die was cast. A van arrived quickly and they were both taken to the police station. There was paperwork of course. They took down James's details. They didn't seem especially interested in Simon and didn't note his details which was a relief. Then they were both taken in a police car to the Bilthaven Infirmary. More waiting and more paperwork.

"You shouldn't have come back," said James again, when they were in a room at the hospital waiting for a doctor.

"And where would you be now if I hadn't?"

"Dead. In the river."

"Well, now you're not."

"Listen. I'm gonna get locked up. And that's thanks to you. I can't face that, I'd rather be dead."

"Thanks for that, James. What else could I do? You'd be dead now if I hadn't told that cop. I could not let that happen. I care too much about you."

"Which is why you shouldn't have come back."

"What about your Mam? Think of the distress for her if you killed yourself."

"She knows, I phoned her."

"What! She must be out of her mind worrying." Simon turned to the cop at the other end of the room. "Can I go outside to make a phone call?"

"You can. He can't."

Simon went outside. It was a cold night now and Simon realised it was two in the morning! But he knew Elaine, James's mother, would be frantic.

The phone was answered quickly.

"Hello?" Elaine sounded frightened.

"Elaine, it's Simon. James has just told me he phoned you earlier. He's OK."

"Are you with him? He said you'd gone home. I've been so worried. I thought it was the police phoning."

"I went back. James is with me, but he's in police custody and we're at the hospital. He was going to do it, Elaine, but a police officer came up and I had to tell him what James was planning."

"Thank God, is he hurt?"

"No, he's OK. Very upset of course and angry with me for stopping him."

"Don't worry about that. Thank God, he's so lucky to have you, Simon."

"I'll keep you informed of what happens."

Simon also phoned Karen and told her. She was quiet on the phone, subdued. Simon knew there would be talking when he got back, he knew Karen well enough for that. But he was committed and could not leave James now.

Later a doctor arrived and talked at length to James. After signing James over, the police left, their job done, a great relief to both James and Simon. James started to relax a bit.

"Have you somewhere to go?" the doctor asked James. James hesitated.

"If you let him out, I'll take him home," said Simon.

"Who is there?"

"His mother and brothers."

"I think as long as he is with you, I can let him go. The crisis team will call in the morning, later today I should say, and they will take over James's care."

So James was released into Simon's care. They stepped out into the beginning of dawn's light.

The morn, in russet mantle clad, walks o'er the dew of yon high eastern hill
In the car they talked.

"I'm sorry I was angry with you," said James. "Is Karen OK?"

"I don't think she's very happy," said Simon.

"Sorry. You're the best friend ever. I'm sorry if this has caused trouble with you and Karen. Life's shit, everything I touch turns to shit, now I've ruined you."

"Let me deal with that," said Simon. "I don't regret what I did tonight. Neither do I regret a single day we've spent together."

They arrived back in Cliffport as it was getting light.

"Just drop me off," said James.

"No, I'm coming in to speak to your Mam."

"She'll be asleep."

"I doubt it."

Elaine appeared at the door. "Oh thank God," she said. "Simon, I don't know how to thank you."

"Mam, it's all right," said James.

Simon told Elaine briefly what had happened and that the crisis team would be calling later.

He and James parted with a hug and a few tears. Simon drove home to Thirlham, exhausted.

18. 2008-10 An end and a setback

The next session of SORP was Simon's last as his Block 4 and James's block 1 ended. James recounted that a few days earlier he had been feeling suicidal, and a friend had stopped him jumping from the City Bridge by involving the police who took him to the hospital. He had since been seen by a Mental Health team and hoped to get proper help to deal with his history of abuse for the first time. He did not divulge the identity of the friend.

In the following activity, a discussion around human sexuality, one question was about the causes of differing sexual orientation. Of course they said in the end nobody knows but there were a lot of theories. At one point a member said he thought homosexuality was 'disgusting'. James, who was sitting next to Simon as usual, stiffened at this but said nothing. The facilitators didn't pick up on it, so before they moved on Simon pointed out that this had been said, and that it could cause offence to some in the group. The female officer said she had not heard the comment but that Simon was right to raise the issue and it was not in keeping with the group rules. As the morning ended, they did the risk assessment again. The female officer was taking this, the elderly member as ever taking a long time. When it was James's turn, he said he knew he would do his My Offence work again, but was then told that he would have to repeat all block 1. He was visibly distressed at this as he had thought he would do this as part of his block 2. Simon tried to have a word with James during the lunch break but James's anger and hurt was too strong, he withdrew into himself.

Back in the Risk Swamp, Simon at last placed himself in the low risk zone, saying that as a result of his work with his counsellor, psychiatrist and on the group that he was getting a closer understanding of himself and the gay side of his sexuality. The female officer asked him how he would cope with these needs that might have to be met, and Simon replied that the world was very different from thirty years ago, and that it would not involve children. If it were to happen, it would be adult males, but Simon was hoping to work things through with Karen. Any future sexual activity would be within the law.

Simon knew that at the end of each block there was a positives exercise where they had to write something positive about each group member, so Simon had prepared this in advance, as had other experienced group members. But the exercise was different, they had to say something positive about themselves! Simon remembered the question James had asked him earlier in the block about whether admitting to his gay side had made him stronger, so Simon said that this was true and that in some ways Simon was a stronger person because of this self knowledge.

In Round Up, Simon said the group had done well, and advised the members to set the ethos for the new members coming in to the next block so that the supportive and cooperative nature of the group would continue.

James was morose in the car going back. Simon didn't know what to say. He felt that James didn't warrant such a setback which was serving only to make him more hostile to the whole SORP process just when he had started to accept it and do well.

"I bet Ruby had something to do with this," said James, bitterly.

"You can't know that," said Simon, "and anyway, why should she influence that, even if she could?"

"Of course she can," said James. "They talk to each other don't they?"

"Bloody idiot!" said Simon.

"Why am I an idiot?" demanded James.

"Not you, the prat in the Nissan Micra."

"Oh," said James, smiling at last. The driving habits of Micra drivers were a standing joke between them.

"OK, so they talk. But why should Ruby want you to repeat the block?"

"Because she's a two faced cow?" suggested James.

Simon knew he was never going to get James to see reason, so he let the matter drop.

Back home Karen was waiting to see how the final SORP session had gone.

"I never thought I'd see this day," said Simon. "It seemed to stretch ahead forever when I started, but here I am!"

"Well done, love," said Karen, as they hugged.

"James has to start again though," said Simon, and he explained what had happened. Karen sympathised but her attitude to James was ambivalent at best and she was more interested in Simon.

In the run up to Christmas, Simon tried to lift James's mood. They spent days out, visiting local attractions and even went into Bilthaven Cathedral. Simon tried to show James some of the interesting features of this ancient church but the highlight was when they climbed the tower. James made this climb slowly with frequent stops and use of his inhaler. They were rewarded with superb views across the city and James's mood seemed to lighten.

As they emerged back into the cathedral at the foot of the tower, they were approached by an usher.

"There's a communion service about to start if you would wish to partake," the elderly lady said.

Simon looked at James who to his surprise nodded. As they walked through the great church, Simon said, "I didn't realise you were religious or a church member."

"I'm not specially, but I know you are from when you told me about Daniel. I'm actually a catholic but haven't been to church for as long as I can remember. Will that matter?"

"The Church of England is much more accepting, and anyway, it's up to God, not a priest, whether he accepts your communion."

"I'm not sure what to do."

"I'll guide you through it."

So for the first time for many months, Simon took Holy Communion. Having James next to him as they knelt at the rail and received the wafer and wine made it extra fulfilling for Simon with memories of Daniel. He felt suffused with contentment as he had so many years before. He was aware of James's nervousness and touched his arm briefly in reassurance.

"How did you feel about that?" Simon asked James afterwards.

"It was all right," said James, non committal. "I know it meant more to you though."

"Yes, especially because you were with me."

"I knew that," said James. "That's why I did it, coz I knew it was important to you."

Simon was touched at that. "Thank you, James. That was kind. I do love you."

"I know you do," said James, smiling. "I love you too."

The following week James received more bad news. Because of his fear of leaving the house in Cliffport, Simon would pick him up and drive him for his weekly meetings with Ruby. Simon would drop him near the probation office about a fifteen minute drive from Cliffport as he knew they could not be seen together. He emerged from one meeting, angry.

"I'm not going back to SORP at all," he announced as he got in the car.

"Why not? You have to, don't you?"

"Ruby wants me to herself. She turned round and said I'm gonna have to do all of it one-to-one with her. Weeks of it. I think I'd rather be back on SORP. Either way it's without you there."

"I'm sorry, James. You just have to get through it."

"I can't face thirty six weeks of her. No way!"

"James, you have no option."

"Just drive," ordered James. So they drove back to Cliffport in silence.

Just before Christmas Simon went with Robert and Donna to the hospital in Nusbury for refitting of her ear grommets. Donna had started to shout at everybody, a sure sign that her glue ear was returning which the consultant had confirmed. It was an anxious day, with Robert pacing back and forth the whole time his precious Donna was in the operating theatre.

"I'm glad you're here, Dad," he said. "I'd find it hard to cope on my own."

"Of course I'm here," said Simon.

A drowsy Donna emerged from the operating theatre and was wheeled up to the ward. She soon perked up and after her twenty-four hour fast, tucked greedily into the meal Simon bought for them in the hospital restaurant. They went home the same night, Robert relieved and meeting an equally relieved Florence and Fiona. Donna phoned Melanie and said she was back home and wished everybody would stop talking so loudly!

James became more depressed and on some days simply refused to emerge from his room. When he did, Simon took him out away from Cliffport and according to Elaine, it always did him good because he returned home happy. Simon never lingered at James's home because of the risk of a surprise visit from Ruby which had been known. He gave James a lift each week to Ruby's office, the intensive one-to-one was due to start after Christmas so these were mercifully short visits.

Simon spent Christmas with Karen and Robert, Fiona and the girls of course. Donna and Florence went to stay with Melanie and her boyfriend which also gave them time with their little brother. But they were back in time for Christmas Day lunch with the Scott family.

19. 2009/01 Looking Forward

Simon's first meeting with Naomi of 2009 was partly in preparation for the 'Looking Forward' course Simon was due to start. Fortunately, Simon's appointments with Naomi never clashed with James's appointments with Ruby. Naomi pointed out that Simon was lucky in that a 'Looking Forward' course was about to start and he had been allocated a place. Some people had to wait months after SORP or release from prison to join 'Looking Forward'. Simon was surprised that some of the course members would have been in prison and completed the equivalent of SORP inside.

The new term started and Karen was back at work, Simon was back with James. They resumed their routine. James was upbeat because Ruby was off work having some minor operation in hospital which meant both that his dreaded sessions were delayed and he was seeing other officers, including Naomi, whom he liked.

"Why can't I have an officer like that?" he moaned.

But Simon was now going to the 'Looking Forward' course, held in the same room at the office in Gerdlington. He found there were four other group members he knew from SORP, some had finished SORP before him and had had a longer wait. But familiar faces helped Simon settle in. The others had done a SORP style course in prison but for one member, this was his first such work. The core of the work was the "Wheel of Life". This was in eight segments each covering a different aspect of life. The idea was that each of these areas should be in balance with the other to achieve a life balance. One member remarked, "I can't believe it's not Buddha!" This raised a laugh of course with its reference to a TV advert for a margarine type of spread.

Brevity is the soul of wit

The officers explained the wheel by example and they picked Ozzy Osbourne, as being someone well known to everybody. Simon knew little about him other than he had been a member of Black Sabbath. (Noisy with little melody.) However, this was to be a group exercise, so his lack of knowledge of this person's intimate life, which had apparently been all over reality TV, was not such a hindrance. They were marking him highly on Inner Peace, so Simon said, "Everything I have heard about him so far today screams of a man desperate for attention, deeply unhappy and looking for something he couldn't find." That brought the officers to a halt. She looked at her notes while the male officer looked at him and admitted he had not thought of it that way.

Then they had to go through the eight areas listing the obstacles he might face in achieving a high level in them. Back on drink and drugs featured in several areas, the loss of relationship etc. They seemed to think that only inner peace could enhance creativity, so Simon mentioned Tchaikovsky and Alan Turing. They did not ask who Turing was. The female officer said that when they did their obstacles, they should think of risk factors.

At the end they were each given a an A1 sheet with a wheel drawn on it, so they could do their homework; define their own Wheel of Life and also say what obstacles they might face. The group then broke up. The traffic was horrible and it was strange driving home without James.

The next week Elaine phoned Simon early in the morning.

"Simon, James is in hospital."

"Why, what happened?"

"He started to panic in the night, he got out of bed and couldn't stand up and he was shaking and couldn't move. Simon, he was so frightened he asked me to call an ambulance."

"Which hospital is he in?"

"Nusbury General."

"Did you go with him?" asked Simon, remembering Liam, James's younger disabled brother.

"I couldn't, I had to stay here for Liam."

"Of course. Elaine, you should have called me. James should not be alone going through that."

"What else could I do?"

"Don't worry, I'll come through to Cliffport as soon as I can."

Luckily it was not a Naomi or course day so Simon drive over to Cliffport. Liam was now at the day centre so he and Elaine headed for the hospital.

James was lying in bed, asleep. Simon watched him, love for him in his heart and gently stroked his hair. James stirred and pushed Simon off.

"I'm OK," he grunted.

"I'm sorry I couldn't be there for you, James, but I only found out this morning."

"I didn't want to put you out," said Elaine.

"Got anything to eat?" asked James. This was regarded as a good sign.

The doctor said he thought it was an extreme stress reaction which had led to the fit-like symptoms. But all the signs were now normal and James could go home. Simon drove James and Elaine back to Cliffport, relieved that he was not more seriously ill. James stayed in bed the next day, missing an appointment with Ruby. Elaine phoned to say he was ill.

The next day he got a letter from Ruby saying he was in breach of his probation and would be taken to court unless he could supply documentary evidence he had been ill. Luckily James had a discharge letter from the hospital which he had not yet sent to his own doctor, so Ruby was sent that instead and the threat of court was lifted.

"See what she's like?" complained James. "Would your officer have done that without so much as a by your leave?"

Simon was forced to agree that he doubted that Naomi would have taken such action with out at least making contact first. It seemed that for whatever reason, James had little credibility with Ruby, or her with him.

Simon was also still seeing Denise, his counsellor. The appointments were not as frequent as before but Simon still found it helpful to keep contact and review his life. He talked about his feelings for James and how Karen regarded this with some fear. Denise tried to explain how Karen might be seeing it which corresponded well with Simon's own assessment, however much he tried to calm Karen's fears.

The next week there was an incident that would have been comical had it not been so potentially serious. Simon was unwell and Elaine had promised to see James safely on to his bus to meet Ruby. Simon was in the house when his mobile phone rang.

"Simon, I need you to come and help me." It was James.

"What's the matter?"

"I'm on the bus on my way to see Ruby and it's broken down. I need you to come and get me. If I'm late she'll breach me again. The cow wants me in prison, I know it."

"Calm down," urged Simon. "If the bus has broken down, that's a valid reason."

"Not for her it's not. I've phoned her and she turned round and said she doesn't believe me. She's gonna breach me again."

"Where are you?"

James explained where the bus was, halfway from Cliffport to the town where James's probation office was.

Simon drove over but could not find the bus. He phoned James.

"I can't find it."

"I was just about to phone you. Another bus has come and I'm now on that. I'll still be late though."

"Try to get a note, anything, at the bus station to say the bus broke down," advised Simon. "I'll come and find you when you come out."

So Simon drove the rest of the way and waited in the usual car park. His phone rang.

"She's not here," said James. "Guess where she is."

"Tell me."

"She and the copper have gone to find the broken down bus. I said they don't believe me. If she didn't believe me about Colin Duncan, she's never going believe anything I say."

"So what's happening?"

"I'm being seen by someone else, they just said I had attended on time and it was OK, I can go. I'm on my way to you now."

When James arrived at the car, they had to laugh at the image of Ruby and the police officer standing by the broken down bus, which apparently they had found, in the knowledge that James had been telling the truth. And James had the brief note on a bus company compliment slip, saying the bus had "experienced engineering problems."

"Why can't they just say it broke down," laughed James, relieved.

Simon had a very unsatisfactory next session on the course. The day was to be devoted the Offence Cycle. This was a rerun of the Block 2 work, My Cycle. The plan was each person would have about a quarter of an hour to go through their offence and its cycle with either the male officer or the female officer.

It didn't quite work out that way. Simon had thought he might be called early on but as time went on, it became apparent that like on Block 1, he was the only person whose offences involved males. Some people took over half an hour to go through it, but there was no group participation at all, they were a passive audience. Simon got progressively more and more anxious, to the point where he was taking his trifluoperazine tablets to calm his nerves.

In the end he was called second last by which time he was very stressed, and very aware that he was the only offender against boys.

After he outlined his offences, the male officer took him quickly through the parts of the cycle. Simon mentioned that at the time he was very stressed, at a low point in his life with his marriage under strain, having lost an eye, feeling a failure as a parent, husband and teacher, and missing Daniel badly. He talked quickly about his feelings of revulsion at the time, about the degradation which he said harked back to 'something else' in his life, how he planned the trips, but not specifically to carry out the offences and about the boys and what drew him to them; their peer group bonding, intelligence, outgoing personalities; not a physical type, although he did mention that Daniel had dark hair and blue eyes, a weakness of his since. But none of the boys looked like him. Simon talked quickly about wanted him back, about the scouts and the camaraderie he felt then and had wanted to feel again.

The male officer asked him about masturbation and whether Simon thought about the boys. He said no, he often did think of Daniel. He asked at what age, and Simon said sixteen, the age he was when he last saw him. Simon said that was a memory, not a fantasy.

Then Simon sat down. It had taken seven minutes. He felt angry about this.

In Open Space at the end, they had to say how they felt when they arrived and now at the end of the day. Simon said he had felt good when he arrived, and now he felt stressed, anxious and annoyed. He asked what had been the point of the day. He said this was supposed to be about group work but there had been no group work, it was like watching the Jeremy Kyle Show, with each person being put in the pillory, with no chance for the group to contribute. Simon also said he now felt like the 'only gay in the village' and at a disadvantage because of that.

The officers seemed taken aback by the strength of his criticism, and the male officer said he had made some valid points, but it was important for the group to get to know each other this way, and it had been a valuable way of showing that they had taken on board the lesson of My Cycle because they had all done this without reference to previous work, so the lessons were still in their heads. At this Simon said that his at least had been so superficial, seven minutes, as to be meaningless. The male officer offered to see him individually the next morning at the Thirlham office if Simon still felt the same way.

The next morning Simon went to see the male officer in Thirlham to talk through his problems with the day. This went well, and the officer offered him the chance to defer 'Looking Forward' so that a later group might include more gay men. Emphasis on might! Simon declined the offer; after all he knew four members and the others seemed OK. He did say that Simon had made some valid points and they felt that the exercise should take place over two days to allow for more time and group work, but the 'powers that be' had not so far responded.

The weeks went by and Simon settled down into 'Looking Forward', developing his Wheel of Life. Karen was as supportive as ever and he in his turn helped her with the mountain of paperwork it now seemed to take to teach a class of primary school children. She was never really happy using a computer and Simon was able to be of real assistance to her in this field as well as contributing ideas.

"I'd be lost without you," said Karen.

"No you wouldn't," said Simon. "You'd find a way, you always do. Improvisation is your key strength."

"Not where computers are involved," said Karen ruefully.

"Well, I'd be lost without you too. We've always been a good team, haven't we?"

"I couldn't manage Robert and the girls without you," said Karen.

"Well, I couldn't without you, either. Why do you think that it has to be you that has my help? I need your help to do it as well." Simon took Karen in his arms and they hugged and kissed, each other's best friend and soulmate.

James had another run-in with Ruby over a missed appointment. He started to talk more about Colin Duncan. He showed Simon a song he had written:

Damaged
Verse 1
I cant believe what you did to me,
I'm down on my knees and I'm
Trying to break free,
I don't know why I can't feel inside,
I'm tryin' to make it, but I just seem to hide.
(Chorus)
I just want to get away,
Saving all your lies for another Day,
Walking around trying to find somewhere,
Had enough of being damaged.
Verse 2
I close my eyes to take it all in,
I don't need nobody tryin' to make me over,
I just want to live simple and free,
Seems like nothing's going my way lately.
(Repeat Chorus x1)
Bridge
Sorry if I ain't perfect, sorry if I don't give a damn,
Sorry if I talk my mind, sorry for doing what I want,
I will keep my head up and stay strong.
(Repeat Chorus x2)
Bridge x1 (end)

Simon could see in those words all James's pain from the years of abuse he had suffered, knowing exactly what it was about but he emphasised the final line as hope for the future and when James was depressed, he would quote it to him, "Keep your head up and stay strong." He and James talked about their pasts, trying to work things through, effectively counselling each other. James talked more to Simon about Colin Duncan. They wept together for their broken childhoods.

Simon knew it was good for him to talk, but it also caused a reaction in James, deepening his depression. James suffered an asthma attack and simply stayed in bed taking his medication until it passed. Elaine rang Ruby to explain. She demanded a medical certificate. James did not have one, he had simply self medicated until the attack subsided. But Ruby threatened again to breach James. Simon went over the next day and took James to the doctor. The doctor would not give James a certificate for the previous day because she had not seen him then. Eventually Simon paid for a private certificate stating that James had suffered from asthma since childhood and suffered periodic attacks. But nothing specific to the day in question. They had to hope it would do.

Ruby made him another appointment but this fell on a day when Simon had to be in Gerdlington. Simon drove over early to Cliffport to find James depressed and unwilling for another session with Ruby.

"I'm not going," he said, stubbornly.

"James, you have to," said Simon. "She'll breach you and you'll end up in prison."

"That'd be better than being with her!"

"That's silly."

"It's not. And anyway, I'm not well, my chest hurts again."

"I don't think she'll accept that, even with the note. Not twice in quick succession."

"I don't care."

"James, it's not just Ruby. Behind her is the probation service, the police and all the power of the state. Right up to parliament and the Queen."

"So?"

"James, you can't buck the power of the state."

"Oh for fuck's sake, Simon, just shut up."

"Look, I'll take you. I can drop you off on my way to Gerdlington. I can't bring you back but at least she won't have reason to breach you."

"I'm not going. I can't come back by myself."

Simon, running out of time, ran out of answers. After a final plea, he left and went to Gerdlington. He had a one hundred percent record of compliance with his order and did not wish to jeopardise that.

The highlight of the day was a discussion on the Spirituality segment of the wheel. The comment "was there a God?" drew some comment from another older member and this led to a theological discussion about the role of a Creator, determinism as against free will etc. The male officer was listening with interest until he decided they had better get back on the topic!

James received the expected breach letter. When he went to the police station (Simon waited outside) he was charged with the breach and also twelve further low level images on his computer, which the police still had. James vehemently denied this. He was bailed until May.

"I need a better lawyer," said James. "My last one was useless."

"He kept you out of prison," countered Simon.

"Well, I'm not going back to him." James was clearly distressed. Simon looked at him, this man he loved, and could feel his torment and inner anguish. So much pain, so many years.

"We'll go and see Carl Irving," said Simon.

A few days later they were in Bilthaven at Carl Irving's office. Simon had emailed Carl and asked him to help James.

"Hello Simon," said Carl. "I must say I didn't expect to see you again."

"Nor I you," said Simon, "but I am very grateful to you for agreeing to help James."

"He hasn't exactly helped himself," said Carl, turning to look at James. He looked terrible, thought Simon. Drawn again and ill looking. James said nothing, leaving the talking to Simon as he often did when dealing with authority. He trusted Simon absolutely, even to managing his bank account. So this was an extension of that care.

Carl agreed to represent James, but warned against being too optimistic.

"He seems good," said James as they left.

"Worked for me, and his reputation is very high. I have googled him you know."

The week's discussion at Gerdlington was interesting on four risk domains:

1. Sexual Interests: sexual preoccupation, sexual preference for children, sexualised violence, other offence related sexual interests

2. Distorted attitudes: adversarial sexual beliefs, sexual entitlement, child abuse supportive beliefs

3. Management of Relationships: inadequacy, distorted intimacy balance, grievance thinking, lack of emotional intimacy with adults

4. Self Management: lifestyle impulsiveness, poor problem solving, poor management of emotions.

Simon said that his psychiatrist had told him that there were probably many people out there who harboured sexual fantasies involving children which if enacted would break the law. The question was why they didn't act on them while Simon and other offenders did. His point about loss of mental capacity caused a discussion. Simon said he had experience of people with dementia showing inappropriate sexual behaviour as a result of disinhibition, and that now Simon would be vulnerable to people not putting this down to mental loss but to deliberate behaviour. He said that his mother, who would have been 91 now, had suffered from Alzheimer's. He said he didn't drink much but that should he turn to the bottle in the future, that would be a risk. He also pointed out that he didn't have a sexual preference for children, they had simply been the unfortunate vehicles for his own self degradation.

Carl emailed to say could James go to see a barrister, Charles Nicholson, in Bilthaven. He also thought it better if Simon let James go in alone so as not to endanger their relationship. So Simon picked James up and drove him to Bilthaven and waited for James to come back. It was a long wait. James appeared and got in the car.

"Well, there's good news and bad news," he said.

"Well?" said Simon.

"The good news is that you and I should be able to see each other openly. Because we have a close and loving relationship, it's human rights. Everybody has the right to a personal and private life. That's us."

"It's not as though we have a civil partnership or anything," said Simon.

"No, but we love each other, and we can say we do more than we do."

"I do love you, James, but I won't lie to a court."

"Well, just make it sound like it then," James retorted irritably.

"Ok so what's the bad news?"

"It looks like I might have to go to prison."

"Oh shit!"

"He says he will do his best to keep it as short as possible."

"James, I'm sorry." Simon reached out and gripped James's hand. James did not pull away, needing the comfort.

"Let's go," said James. Simon drove back to Cliffport and then home.

Simon tried to immerse himself in the everyday. Florence had to dress up as an Edwardian child to celebrate the school's centenary and Karen borrowed a smock from a neighbour that with one of Karen's old berets made her really look the part.

The course continued, one interesting discussion concerned informed consent during a session around whether young boys could enjoy sexual feelings. Simon made the point that he had no idea whether his young victims had been sexually aroused or not. This came back to informed consent and he said that he had consented to his sexual relationship with Daniel and had enjoyed it. But as he had been so young, it would not be informed consent. Asked by the female officer why informed consent was important Simon said early sexualisation could damage a person later on. The female officer asked if that was his case and Simon said he was not the best person to judge. The male officer asked who was then? Simon said his psychiatrist probably, which drew a smile from the male officer. The female officer said there a was need for emotional content, not just sex. Simon came straight back and said that Daniel and he had been very close, they grew up together and he was a great help and support to him when he was having a difficult time and that sex was a part of their friendship. The female officer pulled a face but said nothing. At last it was someone else's turn and Simon sat quiet, trying to recover. The weeks passed and they talked through the four domains, relating them to the eight segments of the Wheel of Life.

Simon tried to take James's mind off his situation, continuing his days out, helping him sort out his benefits, going to a benefits appeal hearing with him, which they won, trying to show James that he could take control of his life instead of being a piece of flotsam at the mercy of others. But of course James felt he was at the mercy of Ruby and what he described as her vendetta against him.

Simon also tried to get James counselling for his childhood abuse. As he had found, every organisation he tried, charitable or statutory, slammed the door as soon as it was revealed that there was a history of sexual offending, even as in Simon's case, thirty years earlier. But at one place in Bilthaven, a gay centre that offered counselling, they seemed to offer a "don't ask, don't tell" policy. Simon took the hint and never actually pointed out James's conviction. A first counselling session for James was booked for early May.

Eventually, 'Looking Forward' came to an end as had SORP before it. But there was an interesting finale. The local probation service was being inspected and the group members were invited to remain behind after the last session to talk, in confidence, to Her Majesty's Inspectors with no officers present. Some people left, but Simon and three others, all SORP veterans, remained to meet the inspectors. They were assured the camera was off and it was completely confidential and anonymous. Simon ended up having to explain what 'Looking Forward' was and how it followed either SORP or its prison equivalent. He wondered why the inspectors didn't know this basic stuff to start with. One member was aggrieved that often he felt he was being told what to think. Simon said the fact that so many on the course were themselves victims of child sexual abuse was not addressed, but could be crucial to the cause of an offender's behaviour and therefore important for future prevention and public protection. Simon said no help was available to offender victims. He also highlighted the situation where an offender's relationship with his probation officer had broken down and how if a request for a change was put in it might lead to repercussions; also that in any dispute the probation officer held all the cards. It was quite a wide discussion but shorter than expected. Simon drove home in the sunshine.

There was a striking dream that came to Simon one night. He was in bed, restless and unable to sleep. The only light was that of the street lamp through the curtains. He became aware of more light, rapidly brightening until it was an intense white radiance, bathing his naked body in light. Despite the immense power of the light it was not dazzling and the rest of the room was still dark, the focus was entirely on him. Something within the light communicated with Simon, perhaps a 'voice', perhaps directly into his thoughts. The message was nebulous, a feeling rather than actual words. It concerned his sexuality and that he could at last safely release his gay side, and be who he really was. It was a warm, safe feeling, reassuring. The light then smoothly and quickly faded until the only light was that of the street lamp through the curtains. Karen was still asleep beside him. Now calm, Simon drifted off to sleep. Was it a dream? Was it real? Simon would never be quite certain.

There was the problem of the court case at the end of April at Bilthaven Crown Court.

"Please come with me," begged James.

"I can't," said Simon, "you know that. If we're seen together, we're both in more trouble."

"Please, I need you. I can't do this on my own," James repeated, in clear distress, adding, "Ruby doesn't know you, so why should anyone find out? Please?"

So Simon weakened, worried that without his support, James might even fail to turn up which would be disastrous.

They drove to Bilthaven, James smart in his dark suit, Simon more casually dressed. They found the court he was due to appear in and waited on the seats outside.

James nudged Simon. "Ruby," he said, indicating a middle aged woman coming towards them, along with another man.

"Hello, James," said Ruby smiling. "This is my colleague from the police public protection unit who is with me today."

James nodded. Ruby paid no attention to Simon at all, but the police officer was looking at him. His face seemed vaguely familiar to Simon but he could not place it.

Ruby was still talking to James. "Now there's nothing to worry about, James. And I'm glad you have someone here to support you," she smiled, rubbing her hands. She then moved away with the police officer.

"She seems OK," said Simon.

"Just you wait," said James, shaking his head.

They went in for a meeting with Charles Nicholson. He had the medical certificate about asthma that Simon had paid for and the compliment slip from the bus company.

"I am hoping the judge will see reason, although I've no doubt that Mrs Simmons will do her usual."

"What's that?" asked Simon.

"Let's just say I've had run ins with Ruby Simmons before. So has the judge, so I think he has the measure of her."

They were called into the modern court room, Judge Edwards QC presiding. Simon sat in the public seating, James was led to the dock. Seeing James standing there, isolated, frightened, alone, Simon wanted to call out to him.

But break, my heart; for I must hold my tongue.

As Ruby started to speak, Simon's jaw dropped. The chameleon had shifted colour as she proceeded to demolish James, saying he had failed to "engage" with the system, had broken appointments, was uncooperative, had failed to take the opportunity offered by SORP and so on. It was a complete hatchet job! But it became apparent that the judge wanted to give James more time, and as the discussion between the lawyers came round to adjourning, especially as the evidence about the extra images was not prepared, Ruby seemed to get more agitated. Simon was reminded of Violet Elizabeth from the "*Just William*" books.

In the end it was adjourned for six weeks to allow time for James to show he could 'engage' and for the question of the twelve extra low level images to be resolved.

James and Simon were reunited outside the court.

"Well, I told you what she was like. She turned round and tried to get me locked up. Now do you believe me?" asked James.

"I would never have believed it, James," said Simon, still reeling from Ruby's duplicity. "What an absolute cow." He thought too that James's speech mannerism of "turned round" was in this case particularly apt.

"Let's get a drink," said James. "Celebrate liberty." They went to the Lighthouse Bar not far away and sat in the Spring sunshine, sharing their relief at James's freedom. Simon revelled in his company, he felt his body and mind coming together again, a strange feeling of unity, oneness within himself that he hadn't felt since childhood.

Two days later, Naomi phoned Simon, who was at home, Karen at work. "We need to come and see you, myself and the police liaison. Are you available in an hour?"

"Yes," said Simon, anxiously. "What's the problem?"

"James Phillips," said Naomi. "We'll see you within the hour." She rang off.

Simon's heart sank. He had obviously been recognised. Fear gripped him. He tried James's mobile but got no reply. That made him more anxious. He took trifluoperazine to calm himself.

The doorbell rang. Naomi, stony faced, and the female cop, in ordinary clothes, came in. Simon led them into the lounge.

"How long have you known James Phillips?" asked Naomi.

"About three years," said Simon, thinking back to those first on-line contacts.

"You realise that you are both on the sex offenders register?"

"Yes, but neither of us were when we met."

"But you must have realised that when you met on SORP."

"Yes, but we already knew each other."

"What kind of relationship do you have with James?"

"We're close friends," said Simon.

"Is that all it is?" demanded Naomi.

The police officer spoke. "If it's a sexual relationship, that's actually none of our business, as you are both adult. Our concern is two offenders associating."

More honoured in the breach than the observance.

"We've done nothing illegal, we just spend time together. I try to help and support him."

"And what does he do for you?" asked Naomi tersely.

"He has helped me to come to terms with myself," said Simon, thinking how denying his homosexuality for so long was like being in a prison, until James set him free. He again thought back to Hamlet:

This above all: to thine own self be true,
And it must follow, as the night the day,
Thou canst not then be false to any man.

But Naomi was talking. "James has already been spoken to. There must be no further contact."

Simon was shaking. "None?"

"None. We will be seeking to vary James's prevention order and take one out against you. You have deceived me, Simon."

"I never wanted to," he replied.

"Why didn't you tell me?"

"What would you have said?"

"What I just have. To break all contact with James Phillips."

"Will you be seeing James?" Simon asked the police officer.

"As you know, Naomi is not James's probation officer, but I will see him," she replied.

"It's just I have his birthday card. If you could give it to him?"

She seemed to hesitate, but Naomi shook her head. "Sorry, as Naomi says, no contact means just that. You obviously have a deep emotional attachment to James, but you have to get over that."

"I'll see you as arranged next week," said Naomi, getting up to leave.

After they had gone, Simon wept. Another loss.

Simon tried to settle down to a life without James. He focussed on Robert and the girls. Karen was sympathetic, knowing what a break it was for Simon.

He had to try to find himself and with Karen's acquiescence went to a big weekend gay party in Blackpool in May. He found it interesting but felt out of place. It just made him miss James all the more. And the town seemed a shadow of its former self, a bit run down and tacky – a metaphor for himself perhaps. He made friends with a group but also found time to take some photographs at the pleasure beach for Karen to help in a school project. He mused about his position, amid the gaiety and the drag queens, wondering why he felt so low. Low self esteem – was it because he was always two years behind Daniel, never as good as Daniel, that he grew up expecting to be second best in some way?

Back home he recounted the weekend to Karen. She could not relate well to Simon's awakened sexuality but he felt the constancy of her love and was so grateful for it. He knew many women would not have shown such generosity, but then he had always known that Karen was not any woman!

She tried to adjust to the situation. "I am not going to throw the baby out with the bathwater," she said as they talked things through. "I still love you. I wouldn't have been a teacher with out you, I know that. You have always been there for me."

"And you have always been there for me, supported me. Why can't you see that? I've needed you just as much as you've needed me."

"I feel all at sea, lost. But I want you to be yourself. It's so cruel, you were never allowed to be who you really are."

"Karen, I am the man who has loved you for forty years. I still love you. You are still my number one, always will be. You are my anchor, without you, I'd be nothing."

"I just feel so unsettled, unsure. I thought I knew the future, our future together."

"I still want that future, to be with you," insisted Simon. "But I can't close Pandora's box now. I can't go back to the days of suppression before all this blew up. At least with James, it wasn't a sexual affair."

"It's not that that worries me, it's the emotional attachment. You love him."

"Yes, but it's different. It's not the same sort of deep love I have for you."

And so the conversations would go on, repeated in different forms many times as they tried to negotiate a new settlement between them.

They decided that relationship counselling might help, so they arranged this and attended a number of sessions together. Maureen the counsellor talked to them both at length, teasing out the stresses and as an impartial yet sympathetic observer, feeding back how she saw the situation. Everything was discussed. One interesting exercise for Simon was that he should write letters, one to his father and one to Daniel – what he would write if he really could. The emotions and feelings that these letters generated in Simon surprised him.

He wrote first to Daniel:
Dear Daniel,

Where are you now? Why did you never reply to my letters, or write one yourself? Did they stop you after we were found out? That must have been terrible for you. God knows what went on after I left. I remember your parents as being kind and loving, so proud of you and your many achievements. When they found out, was there an equal and opposite reaction? Did the strength of their love and pride for you lead to an equally strong condemnation?

I try to imagine what you are like now. My memory of you is of this beautiful and wonderful teenager, the love of my life, my refuge in times of trouble, always kind, always loving, always my strength and support. I like to think you are still that kind of person, and whoever you have shared your life with, that person is one of the luckiest on this planet. But I have been so fortunate too. Although some terrible things happened to me after we parted, I later met and then married a wonderful woman, Karen, who really loves me as much as you did, and values me as much as you did. Perhaps that was part of the attraction, but she has been a wonderful wife, best friend and life partner.

Were there any more boyfriends after me? Was I a one-off in your life? I think that is probable. I bet you got married and had those two boys and two girls you talked of once. I hope you have been as lucky as I have been with my wife.

Have you thought of me over the years? Remembered the good times we had, scouts, Hooray Henrys, and of course sex, in the den, on the hill, your bedroom? You have always been in my mind, for many years at the back, a comforting memory. But now you are very much to the fore. I was talking to a close, gay friend a while back about you, and said how much I loved you when I was young. With great insight, he told me I still loved you, and I realised that I still do, and always will. Who do I love? Daniel at 16? Daniel as I imagine him at 64?

The other night I had a dream:

The doorbell rings, and Karen, who is alone in the house, answers it. On the doorstep is a man of about my own age, tall with grey hair and deep blue eyes.

"I am looking for Simon Scott," he says, " Is this where he lives?"

"Yes, but he's not in at the moment," says Karen. "I can give him a message. Who shall I say called?" But somewhere deep in Karen's mind, she knows who this is, and he confirms it.

"My name is Daniel Gray. Simon and I were friends way back, in childhood."

"Daniel," says Karen, the shock hitting her as her fear is made real. Her face shows this.

"Oh, I see he's told you about me," says Daniel, concern on his face.

At that point, a car pulls onto the driveway.

I turn the corner into the cul-de-sac, seeing the almost new Audi parked outside my house and feeling a moment of fear at who this might be. But as I pull onto the drive, I see Karen at the door talking to a man. He turns to look as the car comes onto the drive. I do not recognise him, who is this? I get quickly out of the car and walk to the front door. As I get closer to the man, the stranger smiles, a wonderful smile that radiates from those amazing blue eyes, and instantly I know who it is. Daniel! My precious Daniel! After all these years! I burst into tears at the sheer emotion, we hug on the doorstep.

We are sitting in the lounge talking over a cup of tea, the three of us. He decided to find me and found me on Google. But far from putting him off, that had made him all the more determined to find me. He knew that I must have been under some terrible strain to do such things. Karen is worried and anxious about what this development means. I try to reassure her, so does Daniel. He too has a family, a life. But the spark is still there, and Daniel and I go off to his hotel. He holds me, kisses me as he makes love to me. It is wonderful.

But we each have to return to our lives, but this time knowing that the other is there, still loving, and promising to meet regularly, never to be permanently parted again.

Wishful thinking? Dream fulfilment? A need for 'closure', and happy ending? But it shows, my love, how much you still mean to me, and always will. I think it is interesting that even in a dream, there is a reality. We do not go off into the sunset together, we each want that with our own wives, we each love our wives and are desperate not to hurt them. But we are together again.

I hope you are well, and happy. Have you found me on Google? Did you turn away in disgust? Or am I for you just a distant memory from childhood? I would so love to know....

The letter to his father was in some ways not easy:
Dear Dad,
Where did it go wrong? As a child I felt frightened of you, rejected by you. I felt as though somehow I could never be in some way what you wanted me to be. You saw me as a let down. Was it because I wasn't sporty, hated rugger? No, it goes back before that, back to before I can remember.

So I grew up feeling as though somehow I could never 'make the grade' and this spread from you to a more general feeling of inadequacy and inferiority. Your language and behaviour alienated me from many of the local kids, some of whom were told not to play with me because of your sometimes public swearing and temper. Luckily I had a counterweight, someone who genuinely loved me and told me I was not inferior or inadequate. But despite his love and encouragement, when my own father is capricious and inconsistent, these negative feelings became a heavy burden which to some extent I carry to this day.

So why? I know you recognised this in later life and wrote a letter to me apologising. Sadly that letter no longer exists. Reading it provoked such an angry reaction in me that I destroyed it. Now I wish I hadn't. But as I remember it did nothing to explain why you treated me in this way. What had I done?

Yet you could be loving, and you told me sometimes you loved me, you used to sing that "You are my Sunshine" to me. You've no idea how I hate that song. If I was your sunshine, then why the temper, the slipper, the feeling that somehow I just wasn't up to the mark?

Many questions, no answers.

The relationship counselling did help, Simon and Karen knew that whatever, they still loved each other deeply and both were desperate to make it work in this new landscape with Pandora's winds rushing over it.

Simon and Karen spent time together, often just watching television in quiet communion, watching *Midsomer Murders* laying bets as to how many bodies there would be before the inept Barnaby recognised the killer; probably the only person in Midsomer Sleepy Hollow left alive!

Simon felt the weight of depression again. He talked to Denise about Karen, James and the black cloud. Why these depressions came, he knew not.

There seemed no obvious link with the events of the day. The black cloud has a mind of its own.

Again he went back over his life, trying to understand; who he was, why he was, why he had done the bad things he had done, he talked to Karen about Daniel, about his father – whom Karen had always been a bit wary of – and about the rape.

"It's all right," she said, her arms around him as he wept yet again with the memories of the October evening in 1963.

"How could they? How could they do that?" he sobbed.

"Because they could," said Karen. "It wasn't about sex, it was about power, domination." She felt the strength of his pain and felt helpless to soothe it.

"I didn't want to be gay. James said that nobody would choose to be gay."

"I'm not sure if that's true," said Karen. "but you have to be true to yourself. Why don't you try to find Daniel?"

Simon looked up, astonished at this suggestion coming from Karen. "I've tried searching, but no luck. And I'm not sure I want to find him. What of his life now? I don't want him to know what's happened. And if we met now we might just fall into each other's arms, so dangerous. If he asked me to go and live with him, I just might."

"If not him, someone else. You are very loving. You could meet someone and fall in love."

"I won't. I haven't in forty years."

"What about James. James, you love James."

"Yes, but we can't see each other, and anyway, I was never going to go off and live with him. We'd drive each other round the twist. I want him to find the boyfriend he yearns for and be happy."

"But you would be jealous."

"Maybe, but I want him to be happy, just as I want us to be happy."

"I don't want to lose you, Simon."

"You'll never lose me," said Simon.

They decided to continue seeing the relationship counsellor and spent several sessions with Maureen which they found helpful in clarifying the issues and getting past the haze of hurt and emotion.

20. *2009/6 Inversion*

Simon found a place in the hospital car park quite easily, it was rather late in the day. He had Dr. Norman's final appointment. He made himself known at the reception:

"Hello Simon."

"Hello Clare, how are you?"

"Fine thanks. Take a seat, he shouldn't be long."

Simon glanced at the board where it showed how late the consultants' appointments were running. There was nothing showing for Dr Norman. He sat and stared out of the window at the town below.

"Simon?" He turned and it was Clare peering out of the reception window. "You can go along now."

Simon walked along to the familiar consulting room.

"Come in, have a seat, Mr Scott," said Dr. Norman. Simon sat down while Dr. Norman leafed through the now bulky file that pertained to him.

"How are you?" asked Dr. Norman, cautiously.

"OK," said Simon. "Well, actually, no. Sometimes I feel pretty desperate. I get very low."

"You're taking the medication?"

"Oh yes, that's what gets me to sleep at night."

"You still have the emergency card I gave you?"

Simon's hand moved unconsciously to where his wallet was in his jeans pocket. He nodded.

"Don't hesitate to ring if you feel so bad," urged Dr. Norman. Simon nodded again.

Dr. Norman continued, "We were talking last time about your mother and this boy you knew when you were young, er...?"

"Daniel," said Simon

"Yes. Daniel," he paused. Conversing with Dr. Norman was sometimes a slow process, as he often stopped to gather his thoughts, careful of what he said to a patient who was at some risk of self harm. "The ... er... Oedipal stage can be very difficult when there are some ... some ... problems with the father."

"I'll go along with that," said Simon, with feeling.

"Yes ... you see ... a boy who has undergone ... er ... sexual inversion of some kind ...

"It's OK," said Simon, "you can say paedophile, I won't explode."

"Well, yes, "said Dr. Norman. "That is a term many would use, although I think not strictly accurate in your case. Ephebophilia or even hebephilia some would argue ...

"Because of Daniel?" offered Simon.

"Yes, Daniel." Dr. Norman confirmed. "And of course that implies nothing illegal," he added hastily.

"But I did break the law," Simon pointed out. "Never mind any moral considerations. Although the judge did say, for what it's worth, that I am not paedophile, but I had stepped over the line and then stepped back."

"Many people out there, consciously or unconsciously, have paedophilic thoughts and desires, or ephebophilic or hebephilic even," he said with a smile. "That might lie behind much of the current demonisation, people not liking what they see reflected in themselves."

"You mean, 'methinks he does protest too much'?"

"Exactly."

"I think I know why people hold prejudiced views."

"Yes?" queried Dr. Norman.

"It is a defence mechanism. They feel under attack by whatever it is they are faced with, their own self esteem endangered; it threatens to undermine their own world view they have acquired over many years, mainly no doubt from their own upbringing. This could undermine the way they have always seen the world, and they either lack the ability, or the courage, to reorder their whole world."

"Probably pretty close to the mark. I forget you studied psychology. However, what we are looking at is why you acted on your thoughts and feelings when most people don't."

"The loss of control," said Simon.

"Yes," said Dr. Norman, "and we have talked about the stress you were under at that time, and the possibility of your head injury affecting frontal lobe restraining functions which .. "

"Which offer no excuse," interjected Simon.

"Well, we're looking at reasons. Whether they are used as excuses is another matter."

"I don't," said Simon, "but I do want to understand reasons."

"Remind me, you lost consciousness when you had the fall?"

"Yes, for some time apparently, although to me at the time, it was seamless. But when I came round, the ambulance was there and so was my mother."

"Possibly a quarter or even half an hour, then. But no fracture?"

"No. They said I had a thick skull. I actually think they meant that literally, but I got teased about it of course. But I was kept in overnight."

"I am wondering if there was ...er ..injury or disruption to the brain tissue. As I was saying, there is some evidence that frontal lobe damage can affect control mechanisms, especially where deeper or ... er ... stronger impulses are concerned."

"Like sex?"

"Certainly. That is one of the strongest impulses where control would be factor. These days I am sure you would be given a scan. You've never had one I suppose?"

Simon shook his head. "No." The scan he had years earlier for labyrinthitis slipped his mind.

"And there's no certainty that any injury or scarring in the brain tissue would show anyway, especially after this time. So let's look back at the beginning. I have been thinking about this inversion aspect, and your case is unusual."

"I never fit the norm," said Simon. He noticed that Dr. Norman was now less hesitant, thankfully, as he warmed to his theme.

"It's a bit of a double whammy actually," continued Dr. Norman. "Your emotional attachment to your mother was very strong, perhaps in compensation for your father's attitude. But if you felt that your mother's love was not returned ..."

"I know she loved me, but I think she had her own problems, in fact, I now know she did."

"Exactly. You know **now** she did, but not then. And you felt that she was unable to protect you from your father?"

"Possibly. I think sometimes she found my strong need for her a bit cloying. I did sometimes feel as though I were being swatted off like an annoying fly."

"Hmmm. Of course that would tend to make you cling all the more."

"Well, my father professed to love me, and I think in some way he did, but at the same time he subjected me to physical and emotional abuse."

"Yes, we've talked about that, haven't we," said Dr. Norman, attempting to leaf back through the thick folder of papers, and then giving up. "Given your ... er ... poor, even disastrous relationship with your father, you would have faced a particularly difficult problem at the Oedipal stage. Quite difficult for you."

"Isn't all this Freudian stuff a bit old hat now?"

"Well, it's ... er ...shall I say ... still current. The fact that it's still widely used and applied ... its longevity ... people wouldn't use it if they didn't think it was valid. I think it has proved itself by still being around, it has credibility."

"OK. So this Oedipal stage then. This is at - how old?"

"Oh, quite young. You see, male children realise that the father is there and that there is a rival for the mother's love. So it's really quite young, when you first become aware of the father figure. The boy then has to work out – at a deeply subconscious level of course – what to do about this. The usual tack to take is for the boy to identify with the father, crossing the bridge some have said, and so learn from the father how to retain the mother's love, and ... er... by extension, earn the love of a woman, or women, in later life."

"So what happens to the boy who is frightened of the father, who doesn't want to cross that bridge?"

"Well, the boy cannot then identify with the father so he is left stranded to some extent. Of course many boys find another role model, some sons of single mothers for example, although some would argue that they are at greater risk of problems later on."

"So we're back to Daniel?" posed Simon.

"What often happens is that the stranded boy turns back on himself as the only reliable love object available."

"Ah, this is where Narcissus comes in," said Simon.

"Well, yes. The name is taken from the ... er ... Greek legend of course but it's not an exact parallel I would say. But the boy becomes fixated on himself at this young age even as he gets older. This is obviously absurd, so the boy then projects this on to others, boys at the sort of age he was at the time of this Narcissistic inversion."

"Young, prepubescent boys," confirmed Simon.

"Yes, precisely. That's the classic ... er ... er ... paedophile," finished Dr. Norman, remembering the 'permission' to use the word. "For attraction to young boys, anyway."

"But I don't feel sexual attraction to young boys," said Simon. "I like them, well, some of them, anyway. But sexually, no."

"The boys involved in your ... er ... offences were... ?"

"Ten, eleven," admitted Simon, with a heave. "They were there. A substitute."

"Ah yes, I think now we can explore that better. This is where ... er ..." glancing down at the file "er ... Daniel comes in."

"Yes?" said Simon.

"You knew him from quite a young age?"

"About seven," said Simon, "although he was – is, I expect – two years older than me."

"Well, the hypothesis is – and it really can never be much more than that you understand – that Daniel – er .. you said how much you looked up to him?"

Simon just nodded, his mind full of Daniel, Daniel the teenage friend, his first love, his first lover. Simon felt that warmth and yet sense of loss he always did when thinking of him.

"So you avoided the Narcissistic inversion, to a large extent anyway, because you were able to adopt Daniel as a male role model, you agree?"

"Yes, I think so," said Simon. "He was talented, clever, sporty, good looking ..."

"Interesting," interposed Dr. Norman. "Go on."

"Well, he was just the boy everyone wanted to be. Not just me, but I know other boys sort of hero worshipped him as well, just thinking of the Scouts for example. But he was popular at school as well."

"But in your case it er ... evolved into something more?"

"Yes, as we got older it developed into a sexual relationship."

"Do you think on his part this was exclusively with you?"

"How do you mean?"

"Did he ... um ... have other friends with whom he was ...erm..."

"Oh no," said Simon with certainty. "It was just us. There was nobody else on either side. I am certain of that."

"And the emotional content was ... er ...?"

"Sorry?"

"Well, many boys indulge in some ... um ... same sex ... um ... play in puberty, and I ..."

"No," said Simon. "I know what you mean. This was not a quick wank behind the bike sheds. We were, I suppose, lovers. He was my first love, and I his."

"You were both sexually active then?"

"Yes." Simon paused. "My first orgasm came with him. It was, to be honest, wonderful, and I think it had a huge effect on me, more than I have realised for a long time. I was very emotional when it happened, and he just held me close. Of course, **he** had been sexually capable before that, but that was **my** first time."

"How did feel you about that? Having sex with another boy."

"It felt good. We enjoyed each other's nakedness, which actually preceded sexual maturity."

"Do you think you came to associate being naked with a boy, or boys, with the pleasure and security you felt then?"

Simon had to stop and think for a moment. "Yes, I think I must have done. That's interesting. Yes. I am pretty sure that will have been a factor in my later actions. My offending."

"Say more?"

"I think now, based on what I have learned in the last few years both about sexuality in general and my own in particular, that shared male nakedness at some level symbolised shared love, such nakedness becoming associated with love, emotional closeness. So at a very low point in my life, I tried to reach back, to feel that again, those unfortunate boys being the vehicle."

"So you loved Daniel and enjoyed each other's bodies, but outwardly, this was just a friendship between two boys."

"Yes. I knew that it would have to be kept secret, which I did for many, many years. But to me it felt right. I did not think it was wrong, we loved each other. We used to go to his house after school – we were both 'latch key kids' - and have sex. It was a great way to relieve the stress of the day."

"So sex became associated with stress relief? More than what one might called ordinarily."

"Perhaps. Some people turn to drink, cigarettes or drugs. For me, sex does the trick. Maybe why I've never been a smoker, or much of a drinker and never bothered with drugs."

"And at the time of your offending, you were under stress?"

"Hugely. I felt everything was falling apart. The learned habit of stress release through sexual release may well have played a part."

"Learned?"

"Yes, in my time with Daniel. It was more than sex of course. We loved each other."

"And in terms of your sexual orientation?"

"I don't think I thought about it in those terms at that time. I felt no guilt or shame inside myself, although as I say, I was aware that society at large would condemn our relationship."

"And later? Before the ... er ...attack on you?"

"I was happy with my sexuality. I was happy that I had had a sexual relationship with Daniel, although I missed him desperately, I was happy that I had enjoyed sex with Diane. I was enjoying my sexuality in whatever form it took. But I don't think I sat down and thought, I'm bisexual or homosexual or whatever. I was a teenager enjoying a varied sex life."

"How did the attack affect this?"

"Oh, hugely I think. The gay aspect was crushed after that, repressed and held down, locked away. I felt that it had in some way despoiled my love for Daniel, and I hated it, them and myself for that. The only way I could protect Daniel in my heart was to lock it away and somehow separate him from what had been done to me. I suppose that meant denying myself any future gay expression of my sexuality. It was just too dangerous. Never mind the legal and social pressures of the time."

"Dangerous?"

"Yes, in terms of letting anything get near Daniel."

"How do you regard your sexuality now?"

"You mean gay or straight or whatever?"

"Well, it's how you define yourself, not what others define you as."

"I'm pretty sure that there are those out there who would define my sexuality in the most simplistic and brutal terms."

"But it's not they who matter, is it? Of course there will be people who have just read the papers or who see things in very simplistic terms. They will define you in their own limited frame of reference. They don't know you, or well enough anyway, to make an informed judgement. No, it's about how you see yourself now. You've kept a lot repressed, I think."

"Oh yes, I'm sure of that," said Simon. "I know now I'm gay or maybe bisexual. I am attracted to women, some anyway, and some men. But I don't think I am wholly gay, or straight for that matter. But this is all new to me and I am still struggling with it. But I have gay fingers," Simon smiling at this last comment.

"Fingers?"

"Yes, isn't there some research that shows that gay men much more than straight men have a ring finger shorter than the index finger, while straight men have longer ring fingers than index fingers?"

"Ah, this is supposed to be related to the level of testosterone while the boy is in the womb. Some evidence that it is linked to the state of the mother's immune system during the pregnancy, but the jury is still out on that."

"Well, my pregnancy nearly killed my mother, I'm told."

"It's a theory," said Dr. Norman. "So you had, what? You've mentioned Daniel and loving him. A loving, sexual relationship with him?"

"Yes, over several years," said Simon. "I loved him." Simon fought back a tide of emotion. "I think I still do."

"Have you contacted him?"

"No. I tried Googling him, but no luck. It's quite a common name. But now I think I don't want to find him. I mean, I'd like to think he's OK, but I don't want to meet him. After all, he's still two years older than me, but my memory is of him as a teenager. And to be honest, I'm too ashamed. I'd hate him to know about this. If he remembers me, let it be as I was then, too. Also, I'm married and I love my wife very much. Suppose the old flame reignited? God knows where that might lead. No. Let it go."

"He was the leader in your relationship?"

"Oh yes. He was a very self assured personality. He had a very physical presence. But he looked after me. I have never considered this relationship abusive of me, although I now realise that many today would say it was. To me at the time it was intense, loving and caring and the most important relationship in my life in many ways."

"Why do say it was not abusive? He was two years older than you."

"Because I know he loved me. He helped me. I might well not have passed the eleven plus without him."

"But he introduced you to sex at a very early age?"

"Yes, I suppose so."

"And as you say, this was not just a quick ... um ... fling behind the bike sheds or wherever. This was a long standing, very close, intensely sexual relationship."

"Sex was a part of it. We were just so close in so many ways. We just knew each other so well."

"But you were having sex together well before you were even a teenager?"

"True."

"And you don't think that, as an older boy, he was not abusing you?"

"No, I won't have that. It's so hard to explain. It simply wasn't like that."

"Well, abusive or not, and I accept that you didn't feel abused at the time, such early sexualisation will have left its mark, don't you think?"

"I still don't feel I was abused by Daniel, only by those three ..." Simon stopped. "Yes, without placing any blame on Daniel, or me, I agree that having such a relationship at such a young age, and for so long, probably skewed my sexual development."

"I think that's progress. You obviously still feel deeply about Daniel, and I don't want to spoil that for you. But I am glad that you recognise the effect it has probably had."

"Yes, it had an effect, but the relationship was not abusive."

"Right, let's leave that issue there. But it came to an end," said Dr. Norman.

"Yes, my mother brought us away, quite suddenly. It was a very traumatic parting for me. I was removed at short notice from everything I knew aged fourteen and a half, and especially from Daniel."

"You mean the actual parting or the loss?"

"Both, but the parting itself was traumatic."

"Why particularly traumatic for you?"

"We were having a last fling the night before I left and were discovered *In flagrante delicto* by his mother. She wasn't very happy. Turns out his sister had guessed long before, but not his mother. So there was a row, but it did show each of us how much we loved each other. We told each other for the first – and last – time that night." Simon paused as he tried to fight back tears at the memory of that terrible night. "That sudden, brutal separation had a much greater effect that I've previously realised. There was no time for adjustment, a mere fortnight and the axe fell. No wonder I have spent so much of my life trying to recover from that, to go back by proxy to make it right. It's a bereavement of sorts."

Dr. Norman waited a moment, before moving on. "You've talked before about your sense of isolation when you moved north, away from the Midlands. Lonely, and because your school was some distance away, isolated."

"Yes, and falling prey to bullies as well."

"How did this make you feel?"

"Pretty awful. I missed Daniel terribly. I wrote, but never got an answer. I suppose now, looking back, his parents prevented him."

"But this was a rejection in your mind?"

"Absolutely. I felt deserted."

"Would you say that then, aged fourteen, you turned in on yourself?"

"Very much so."

"You see, there might be some mileage in the idea that at this stage you took a 'time out' with regard to development, and that like the small boy deprived of the father's love, you lacked that as well as now your, as you described him, first love's care and affection. So like the young child who undergoes narcissistic inversion, you, again at a … um … subconscious level, you look at yourself aged 14, not long into puberty, as the love object."

Simon thought about this for a moment. Fall in love with himself?

"I don't think I loved myself," he said.

"Only at a very deep, primeval level. Of course, as we said before, it is absurd, so what happens?"

"Oh, you mean projection?"

"Exactly. So you look to other teenage boys to recapture the lost … er … Daniel."

"Possibly," said Simon, "but that would only apply then, not now. I have real issues with teenage boys as you know."

"Well this goes back to our discussions about ephebophilia and hebephilia. After the ... er ... thing that happened ..."

"You mean after I was raped," said Simon sharply. "It's OK now, you can say it. I can say that word now."

"That's good, that's progress," said Dr. Norman. "but yes, after that any normal development of these same sex feeling was frozen. Your identification with teenage boys became overlaid with extreme fear and anxiety of older teenagers, suppressing it, refusing to allow this to follow you to adulthood and develop into an attraction for adult males which at least would have been legal after ... um ... 1967. When did it happen?"

"1963," said Simon.

"Quite. So instead, it was reduced to the younger teenage boy, the 14 to 16 year old being an ideal?"

"I have to agree with that. At least, that's how it feels. But I had had girlfriends, and by 1963 I was not a virgin, with girls I mean, never mind Daniel, if you count that."

"But the rape changed that."

"Yes, everything was different after that."

"So you turned back to the teenage ideal?"

Simon thought for a moment. A bird was twittering annoyingly in the tree outside the window.

"Except I wasn't with teenagers, they were a bit younger. So they substituted. Yes. I was - am – envious of them. There was this need to be a part of them, for them to know me intimately, maybe going back to Daniel?"

"Envious in what way?"

"Sexually I suppose, if I'm really honest. I saw them as my psychosexual betters in some way, with a sexual future that I felt was denied to me."

"I can see that. I think ..."

At that moment there was a knock on the door. Clare came in.

"Dr. Norman, I'm leaving now." She looked at Simon, and back to Dr. Norman. "It's past time."

"Thank you, Clare," Dr. Norman said. "I shan't be a lot longer." Clare left, closing the door.

"Do you want to continue?" asked Dr. Norman. "I feel as if we are getting to the crux of things today."

"If you are OK to carry on?" said Simon.

"Good. So there you are, stranded in a sense, in your adolescence, unable to get past your loss of Daniel, blocked by the .. er ... rape from developing sexually further. But you did get married." It was not quite a question, more a statement that looked for confirmation.

"Yes, later. I thought I was coping, that the past was put away, locked away tightly. I love my wife deeply. I wanted to protect her and look after her.

After all, I had had a good teacher, being loved and protected in a sexual relationship. So now I took that role model and applied it to her."

"Hmm. That could work. So Daniel was the male role model instead of your father. But of course most fathers do not have sex with their sons. To put it another way, most boys do not have a sexual relationship with their male role model."

"True. No wonder I'm so screwed up," said Simon.

"So you were talking about being married."

"I am so sorry that I hurt her. I think in time as the memory of the rape trauma became more manageable, was I able to move on sexually, and by-pass the older teenager, developing a sexual attraction to adults, female and as I now realise, male as well. Though I think the rape thing made me suppress any idea of being gay or bisexual. That side of me was barred after the rape, suppressed. And of course it was a very different world then. It might have been all flower power and free love in San Francisco or a trendy set in London, but it certainly bypassed me. OK, I was having sex, but it wasn't 'free love', more like furtive love. But I think my wife was a major factor in me being to put it all away. She's my rock, my foundation. She enabled me try to lead what I thought was a normal life. And it was really. I mean, we've got two kids."

"So think back to when you did the ... er ..."

"Crimes?" said Simon.

"Well, ... er ... yes. In the light of our discussion today and previously, do you think this sheds any light on that? What were your feelings at that time?"

"I thought my life was falling apart," said Simon. "I was unhappy in the job, I had lost one eye in accident, I had a child whose disability was extremely hard to take and to cope with, my wife was at her wit's end. My rock and foundation wasn't there at that time, and in some sense I was lost. We were simply surviving. I was pretty desperate. Then too. . "

"But the boys?"

"Oh God. I feel so ashamed about all that." Simon paused as the wave of emotion swept over him, his eyes watering.

"Take your time," said Dr. Norman. "You're doing very well, and it's not easy."

"It's so despicable," said Simon. "Those kids looked up to me. I think they liked me, most of them anyway. In fact some of their statements say just that. I never felt it at the time though. I just felt I was a walking failure, bluffing my way through the job, through my being a parent, husband, everything." Simon reached out for a tissue from the box on the desk, wiping his eyes. "And there they were, these clever, confident boys. I wanted to be them again, I suppose. To go back."

"But why the sex offences?"

"I wish I knew," said Simon. "It was like a suppressed need that oozed up when all other defences were down. I thought in some distorted way that it would make me close to them. Although it was not really them I wanted. I wanted Daniel. I wanted him to be masturbating me. But he wasn't there, they were."

"Did they masturbate you?"

"No, thank God. I'm glad they never did. In some part of my mind, the barrier was still there. It's just as though it had been pushed back allowing more to happen before the boundary was reached. Of course, the boundary should have been much further forward, if you see what I mean."

"Yes, that is possible. It is a problem with boundaries. Thinking back to the frontal lobe possibility. We know that children will push their behaviour often to the boundary to find where it is. If they don't find it they keep pushing."

"The spoiled child? I don't think of myself as having been spoiled."

"No, I would say not, but you see … er … as a child in a sexual sense, your boundaries were already well back after your relationship with Daniel. Being naked with a boy, a sexual relationship with another boy – this was to some extent already part of your psyche. So you went into adulthood with your ethical boundaries intact except in this one crucial area, where your boundaries were much further back than most people would regard as the norm."

"Sort of anything goes?"

"I hesitate to put it as strong as that. That would imply an almost psychopathic, ruthless attitude to others' sexual needs. But taken along with other factors from your early years, this … er … weakness in your defences was … er … made you vulnerable to going too far."

"To take the analogy further, "said Simon, "the boundary was there but it wasn't strong enough. Think of it as elastic, and when I was so driven to debase myself I was able to push it back to allow myself to do those things."

"Do you think the boys saw it as you debasing yourself?"

"No. At the time I felt it though. I was simply using their presence to enhance my fantasy."

"I am right in saying you never intended harm to the boys?"

"Oh God no. After what happened to me, the rape especially, I could never mean that. I could never force myself sexually onto another person. But you see, I didn't see them as victims, then I mean. They were just part of my scenario I was fantasising in my head. *I* was still the victim. The rape, the loss of Daniel, my son's disability. I was the victim, not them. Sounds pathetic and self pitying, doesn't it?"

"Well, don't worry about that. It's how you felt. Leave value judgements to others."

"But I can't put the blame onto anyone else. In the end, it was down to me. It was my choice, I made the decision to do those acts. I have to live with that."

"You never had any help with the … er … rape and its effects?"

"No. I mean I can't blame anybody for that either. I couldn't tell anyone."

"You have mentioned suicide attempts at that time before, which as you realise, means you are at a higher than normal risk."

"Yes."

"Did you feel suicidal at the time of your offences?"

"Maybe. Nothing like after the rape though. Or now."

"But you have a lot to live for now, despite everything."

Simon felt suddenly angry. "You've never been there. It's like a great darkness pressing all around you. It's no good saying think of the family, think of those you leave behind. When that darkness presses down, none of those thoughts are visible anymore, there's only crushing blackness, but with one small point of light, one small escape, and that's oblivion."

"That's very graphic, and I am concerned about you. You seem to have gone back somewhat. Has something changed?"

"Well, yes. You remember I spoke about James, the young gay man I know?"

"Yes, I remember you spoke very positively about him, how helpful he had been to you."

"Well, now our friendship has been found out and I can no longer see him."

"Because you both have convictions for sexual offences?"

"Yes. I had probation and police descend on me a few weeks ago and was told in no uncertain terms. They told James as well, apparently."

"You felt very strongly about him, I recall."

"I love him. And I'm missing him like hell. I had no idea that it would hurt like this."

"Is this what is behind your drop in mood, do you think? The new suicidal thoughts?"

Simon nodded, he could not speak now.

"I fear this is something you just may have to get over," continued Dr Norman. "But now you are getting help, which you didn't after your ... um ... rape."

"I suppose I will have to, but it's so hard. As for 1963, I didn't tell anybody why I was so 'off it' then, so how could I get help? And rape of a male wasn't even recognised in law then. Added to which, I had all this guilt about it because I had 'enjoyed' it, and gay sex was illegal then. I think a part of me thought it might be me that ended up in prison, not them."

"I would think that unlikely."

"So do I – now. But not a seventeen year old in 1963."

"Different times."

"Very different, despite all the hype we hear now about the Sixties," said Simon. "I have always thought that the rape was the single factor in forming my peculiar sexuality, but being prosecuted and all that has followed from that, I now believe that while it was crucial, my relationship with Daniel had a far deeper effect than I had ever realised. As I say, I have now come to identify myself as bisexual at least. Probably gay. And that's not easy."

"Why is that? Some might argue that you can have the best of both worlds."

"Oh no, it's not like that. It's not like having a sex drive that can be satisfied with either a man or a woman. Bisexual I think is an accurate description. It's like having two sexualities, both of which demand expression. Dual sexuality, perhaps."

"Interesting. So no amount of sexual … um … satisfaction with a woman would quell the homosexual side, and presumably vice versa? Is that what you mean?"

"Yes, I think that's right. Which makes it bloody difficult. Far from having the best of both worlds, it's a curse. Let's face it, nobody would choose to be gay if they had a meaningful choice, would they?"

"Some gay men might dispute that."

"No doubt, but they don't have a choice. This is one of the things I have talked about with James. However it's caused or determined, once one's sexual orientation is fixed, presumably either by genetics or by programming from an early age, you're stuck and just have to make the best of it. So of course they're going to say that. I bet though that if they could be given a real choice – impossible of course – they would opt for being straight. James agrees with that."

"It's a point of view. And as you say, it's not one that can ever be meaningfully tested."

"No. Shame. I would certainly not choose to be gay. I've tried to keep a lid on it all these years, but now it's out of the box and can never go back."

"What's your attitude to boys now?"

"I'm scared stiff of them to be honest. There are boys that age, ten, eleven I mean, living near me. I look at them, they are just kids. The thought of doing what I did back then again with these kids horrifies me. It actually makes me feel physically sick at the thought of it."

"Older boys? Fourteen year olds?"

"Know what I think? I believe it's not young teenagers in general, but one in particular, Daniel, at some deep level needing to go back to age fourteen, pick up those broken threads and move on. But of course Daniel is not a teenager any more, but that's the memory I have of him and will probably have for the rest of my days. I now have to learn to recognise that I will never 'find' him."

"I think that that's significant progress. You've come a long way, not least today. It's obvious you've been thinking about all this."

"Oh yes. Of course I talk to Denise, my counsellor, and then there's the programme as well. It's all fed in, and each one has helped the other."

"You are coping with the programme?"

"It's finished now, thank God. But, yes, I think so. It was bloody hard at times, but I suppose it's the least I deserve."

"Don't be so ready to put yourself down. You've achieved a lot in your life, and done a lot. Helped a lot of people, not least people with dementia and those with mental health problems. I've no doubt that you helped a great many children too in the course of your teaching career, even some of those who gave statements in your case said you were a good teacher. And you were a special constable for many years. You've done more than most to serve the community. And you've looked after your family, helped your son in particular. Still are doing. So look at the whole picture."

"That's nice. But you know what the hardest part is?"

"Of what?"

"Of the sentence, the punishment. And it's nothing the judge ordered, not probation, not the sex register or the programme." Simon stopped to gather himself. "No, the greatest pain, the most painful thing of all is that now I cannot visit my daughter in America, see her or her children if they come, my grandchildren from her."

"Oh?" queried Dr. Norman.

"I can't get a visa now, and of course with a criminal record, I am not eligible for their visa waiver scheme, you know, that little green card you get. So I can't go there again. That really, really hurts, above all else. And then there's James, being parted from him." Simon felt the emotion again, and wiped a tear away.

"And you're still seeing Denise? You talk to her about James as well?"

"Yes," said Simon. "It all helps."

"Good," said Dr. Norman. "I think you should do. If she needs me to write to the health trust about funding it, let me know. The PCT might take a bit of notice."

"Thank you. I'll mention it. It's not been an issue so far."

"How are you feeling now?"

"Exhausted, but in some way, surprisingly better," said Simon. "I don't think I'll ever be the way I was before, but maybe I'll find a new equilibrium. I know myself a lot better, and in some way, I feel better admitting my real sexuality and all that comes from that. I'm not suppressing it any more. James was helping me through that."

"Well, that can only be good. It's a valid hypothesis, what we've discussed today. No-one can ever say for sure of course, but it's coherent, and it works for you. That's what matters."

Simon nodded.

"Go home and have a relaxing evening, "advised Dr. Norman. "You've worked hard today."

"I feel shattered," admitted Simon, relaxing as the interview drew to a close. "I'm sorry to have kept you."

"Not at all, it is quite interesting from a professional standpoint as well, you know," smiled Dr. Norman.

"I've never fitted a stereotype," said Simon. "Always the unusual one."

"It would be a dull world indeed if everybody stuck to stereotypes. I think a month? Unless of course you need it. I take on board what you said about James and the darkness, but try to be positive. You have the card. That's what we're here for. Use it if you need to."

"Thank you."

"I'll get Clare to send out a new appointment."

The two stood up and shook hands.

"Mind how you go," said Dr. Norman.

Simon went out into the now near deserted car park, and sat in the car. Without warning tears flowed. Not self pity, but a release. A recognition of the intricate web of events and interactions that had led him to do those despicable things thirty years earlier, that had haunted him since, of his own self being. Perhaps, not too late in life, in his sixties, he could at last be who he really should have been. And incredibly he had Karen's loving support. It was liberating! If only he could share it with James.

21. 2009/7 Reunion and Separation

Simon tried to take Dr Norman's advice. And of course he had Karen. They had a couple of weekends away, to Norfolk and another to the Peak District, first visiting Mansfield Cemetery to tend the graves, Rita and Karen's brothers. They didn't linger, as Karen now had no close family in Mansfield, so went to Derbyshire. They talked, as always then, about recent events and what they might mean for the future, but came to no conclusion. Back in the room, helped by the red wine no doubt, they relaxed watching television.

They decided after a later than planned and large "full English" breakfast to drive to Lyme Park, the large house, palace almost, used as "Pemberley" in the BBC's *"Pride and Prejudice"*. They started on this fine but breezy day with the grounds, including of course the lake out of which Colin Firth as D'Arcy famously emerged. They also saw that Miss Elizabeth Bennett could not have driven up to the house as shown - unless horse and carriage had descended several flights of stone steps. The tricks they play with camera angles and the power of suggestion! In the Orangery, they managed to identify a couple of plants from their garden which had long been a puzzle. They enjoyed a long walk in the sunshine before looking around the house. The interior was not used in the drama, but had many items of interest, including some priceless Chinese porcelain.

They also visited Kedleston Hall, another stately home. This had been used in a film on which James had worked as an extra. Simon wandered round, wondering if he were stepping in James's footsteps. Karen of course was aware of this connection and let Simon work through this, her love and understanding a great support. The day was marred by an upsurge of that old reminder of past trauma as his piles returned. He slept badly with his nightmares plaguing him. He wept quietly so Karen would not know. He used temazepam to get back to sleep. And took more trifluoperazine. Chemical coshes to get by.

Back home, life resumed. Simon was at his desk when the phone rang.
"Hello?"
"Simon, it's Carl Irving."
Simon was surprised, and also worried. "Oh, hello Carl."
"Do you know where James is?"
"James? No. Why?"
"He's failed to turn up to court today. It was the magistrates' court, just to rebail him, but if he doesn't go, they'll arrest him and he'll be locked up."
"I'm not supposed to contact him."
"Is there any way you can get a message to him? He must go, even late, as long as he gets there today."
"OK, I'll see what I can do."

Part of Simon was relieved to have the 'excuse' to contact James, but he was frightened, both for James's state of mind that had led him to not go to court and what the consequences of contacting him might be. But he knew that he must try to keep James from being locked up. He dialled the number.

"Hello!" James's voice.
"Where are you?"
"In the house."
"James, I've had Carl Irving on the phone. If you don't get to court, they'll arrest you."
"I can't do it without you."
"James, you have to. It's just to rebail you. Please go. Take a taxi, whatever. Carl says as long as you get there today, it'll be OK. Please."

There was a long silence. Simon could hear James breathing, he could feel the stress.

"OK. I'll go. But I need to see you. We have to meet."

Simon knew that to keep James on track, he would have to agree. If he said no, James would almost certainly retract his decision to go to court. "Yes, we'll meet. I've missed you, too. But go to court."

James went and made it in time. He was rebailed to appear at Bilthaven Crown Court in August.

Simon sat waiting in the gay bar in Bilthaven. He sat at the back. The place was practically empty this Tuesday lunchtime. And then, there he was, looking around. For a few seconds, Simon didn't move, just watching James. Emotions welled up in him. He stood up and James saw him. He came across, smiling. Simon threw his arms around him and hugged him so tightly.

"OK, OK," said James, disentangling himself. "I knew you'd be like this," he smiled.

"I've missed you. How are you?"

"Crap. Looks like Ruby's gonna get her way. Charles says I should plead guilty. Get a shorter sentence. Also coz I help Mam look after Liam. He might have to go into care if my Mam can't cope without me."

"That would mean prison?"

"Yes. But I don't get it. The cops have had my computer for over a year now. How come they've just found these new images."

"But didn't you get it back?"

"Yeah, but for two weeks, and it was a year ago they took it again. I just don't get it, why are they saying about these extra ones?"

"What kind are they?"

"They say like before, the least serious kind, but still illegal, according to them. But I didn't look at them."

"To be honest, James, I don't care whether you did or didn't. Either time. I love you and I know you won't any more. That's what important to me. The future."

The two friends talked over lunch, about James's plight, about life. Simon told him about visiting Kedleston Hall, which led James into some anecdotes about the film he had been working on and the stars that had the leading roles.

"Will you meet me again?" asked James.

"Like this, very carefully, now and again," agreed Simon. "It's so good to see you."

The two left separately, with a hug and kiss.

They met again a week or two later, James more anxious about his court appearance.

"I wish you could come with me."

"I wish I could, but you know I can't. But I'll be there, in your head. Remember how I told you that Daniel was with me?" Simon tapped his chest twice. "Like that."

James smiled. "Yeah, OK. But I want you to be really there."

Simon reached across and tapped James's chest twice. "That's the best I can offer."

Simon got on with life, helping Robert and the girls, going out with them, spending time with Karen. But on the day of the court case, he was fretting and anxious. He had a meeting with Naomi that morning and tried to appear calm and normal. He knew that Elaine was going with James. Liam was at the day centre. At least James was not facing it alone.

Later his phone rang, Elaine's number.

"Simon, I'm on the bus going back to Cliffport."

"One, or two of you?" Simon asked, apprehensively.

"Just me."

"Oh God! How long?"

"Six months for breach of his probation, but if he's good, he'll be out after three."

"How was he?"

"Simon, he was devastated, I'm so worried about him. He was talking about suicide again."

"Try to be strong. I was talking to James last time we met. I said he had an inner strength and that would see him through."

"I hope so, Simon, I really do. I don't know what I will do now. I need James's help with Liam, and his older brother just isn't reliable, especially when he's had a drink."

"Take each day at a time," advised Simon. There was little else he could say.

The *Nusbury News* carried the case, couched in its usual sensational terms, branding James a pervert in the headline, ignoring that this was a grievously damaged young man after years of horrendous childhood abuse and who had been in deep distress after the loss of his partner whom he had loved but who turned out to be using him, and bringing in things that were not relevant to the case but which made James sound far worse.

Simon buried himself in building shelves for the girls, helping Robert revamp the girls' bedrooms at the Hilltown house.

Elaine was on the phone. "They didn't say you and I can't meet, did they?" she said. So Simon drove over to Cliffport and met Elaine at the shopping centre, away from the house. They talked and Simon tried to be encouraging and sympathetic. But it was obvious that Elaine was in for a hard time without James's support and help.

The weeks went by. Every time Simon drove near the prison, which was on the far side of Thirlham on his route to Hilltown, he thought of James, locked away, of his spirit and how he would be desperate. Also the prison was not far from Ken's house, whom Simon visited every Sunday to see how he was as he had when Mum was alive, to see if the aging Ken needed anything. Simon would walk close to the tall, forbidding walls and shout encouragement over the wall, just in case James could hear them. In fact he thought of James far more than usual. What was happening? Was he all right? How was he being treated? Was he being abused? He thought of James's smooth, slim body - would that be a target for some unscrupulous and vicious prisoner?

The girls spent time with Melanie; Simon and Karen had family to stay, all welcome distractions. Karen was aware of Simon's distress at James's incarceration and his fears for his safety and well-being. As always with Karen, Simon found great comfort in their mutual love and the deep, unshakable bond between them, over forty years in the forging.

Simon had an appointment at the eye clinic to investigate the possibility of laser surgery to his damaged eye. Perhaps he would be able to see again if the cornea could be repaired! But examination showed the scarring was too deep, his brain would have to continue to ignore the useless information coming from his right eye as it had for over thirty years. But the news added to his frustration and accentuated his depression brought about by his worries about James. The tablets allowed him to function, outwardly normal.

As term approached he and Karen took the girls to Bilthaven to buy new shoes and boots for the coming school term. Robert and Fiona could not afford all the things Donna and Florence needed, so Simon and Karen made up the difference so that their granddaughters would not be at a disadvantage. Florence's gymnastics and guitar lessons, Donna's school trips etc. fell into the same category.

Elaine phoned to say she had received a letter from James. They met and Simon read it. It was not good reading. His depression and misery infused every word. It was a distressing letter, with talk of killing himself. He was thinking about his home, his Mam and Simon, although the reference to Simon was a coded one. Together, Simon and Elaine wrote a reply, as cheerful as they could make it with lots of encouragement, and with coded messages of love from Simon. Elaine also received a Visiting Order and went to see him. Simon wished he could go too. When Elaine reported back, she was upset. He was just like the letter, he was having a hard time, although he had not suffered physically, or as Simon had dreaded, sexually. Elaine spoke to the prison staff, urging them to keep an extra eye on James for his own safety.

Carl Irving contacted Simon.

"Simon, Carl Irving here."

"Hello, Carl. What can I do for you? Is it about James?"

"Yes, it is. James has launched an action under the Human Rights Act about you."

"From inside prison?"

"Yes. He is claiming the right to a 'personal and private' life with you which is anybody's entitlement under the act. His barrister, Charles Nicholson, wants a statement from you to support James's claim."

"Can James do that?"

"Yes, this is everybody's entitlement under law. It should start with saying something about you, your own offences, then describe your relationship with and feelings for James, and end with how you see the effect on James and yourself if the prohibition on your relationship continues."

"OK, I'll do that, of course I will."

"Let me have that when you drafted it, email it to me," said Carl.

"Yes, I will. And I'll try not to make too long," Simon smiled, aware of Carl's advice that judges don't like reading very long documents when a short one would do.

Carl was suddenly serious. "Simon, how far are you prepared to go with this?"

"All the way, if need be," said Simon. "European Court, if that's what it takes."

"It might generate more publicity," warned Carl.

"I hope not," said Simon, "but if it does, then it does. I won't abandon him now."

Simon's statement was accepted after some initial editing at Carl's suggestion. Then it was waiting, the anticipated hearing about this kept being postponed. There was a triumph when on the seafront at Cliffport, which was the nearest coastal point to Thirlham, not just Donna, but Florence as well, finally mastered the art of riding a bicycle. After that, when they were in Thirlham, it was hard to get them off their bikes, which were kept at Thirlham as the Hilltown house had nowhere to store them.

Simon supported Karen in her schoolwork, especially where the computer was concerned, kept in touch with Elaine, and through her, sent James postal orders so he could pay for some small permitted extras in prison. A later letter was a bit more optimistic, James had got a job as a trusted cleaner which gave him the run of the prison so he spent less time in his cell and could mingle more with other prisoners. But the underlying depression was still there.

The issue of Donna's secondary school was now on the agenda as she was now top juniors and would be moving on in 2010. So time was spent by Robert, with support mainly from Karen, assessing Donna's needs and looking at secondary schools.

November arrived and at last, on the day before he was due to be released, the hearing at Bilthaven Crown Court was scheduled in front of Judge Edwards again, to set the terms of James's prevention order which would include the prohibition on their friendship. Simon met Charles Nicholson before the hearing. He asked much the same questions as had Carl, and Simon re-affirmed his commitment to James, whatever it took. Charles said that Simon could go in and sit in the public seating. The press seats were empty – it was five o'clock already.

Then the door at the back of the court was opened and James was led in. He looked better than Simon had expected. It was so wonderful to see him again! Their eyes met across the courtroom and in that moment of contact Simon knew that their mutual love was as strong as ever. But then James looked away and although Simon hardly took his eyes off him, James looked straight ahead, while his relationship with an 'older gentleman' – Simon was not named, but it was obvious it was he - was described; except at one point when the Crown barrister tried to imply that Simon and James had deliberately sought out children at a fund raising event they had planned to attend, saying it was a family event and for children's charities.

Simon could contain himself no more. Almost unconsciously tapping himself on the chest twice, he was on his feet. "Arthritis Research!" he blurted out as he and James looked at each other in indignation.

"SShh," said the clerk of the court to Simon.

"It's a gross distortion," muttered Simon, but quite audibly.

At this the judge looked at Simon, aware of course who he was, and gestured with his hand that Simon should be quiet. But there was a slight smile on his face for an instant.

"I apologise, Your Honour," Simon said, sitting down.

The Crown barrister, disconcerted by this, and perhaps realising that she may have over egged the pudding, said, "In fairness, I should point out that the gentleman concerned did attend the event with his wife and grandchildren, although of course Mr Phillips did not attend."

From that point, things seemed to move James's way more. To Simon's surprise, James would still be allowed to own and use a computer, under certain safeguards, his period on the register was extended to seven years, automatic after having been in prison. This was because his offences were no more serious; in the judge's words, "There was no further escalation."

But then there was the issue of Simon. To their huge relief, the judge refused the Crown's petition to ban the friendship.

"It seems to me to be a very loving and supportive relationship," commented the judge.

Then the hearing was over. Before he could look again at Simon, James was led out and was gone.

Simon was elated as he met Charles outside the courtroom.

"I can meet him out of prison tomorrow morning," he enthused.

"No you can't," said Charles. "This may seem crazy, but while James now can associate with you, you can't with him. So if you see him, he faces no sanction, but you still would."

Simon could hardly believe his ears. "What? But I thought ... "

"I'm sorry, but what you now have to do is launch your own action."

"When can we do that?"

"It would take months," said Charles.

"Months!" Simon's elation vanished into a pool of despair. He had pinned so much on this day. He drove home, desperate. He knew James would now be expecting him outside the prison gates in the morning.

Sure enough, the phone rang next morning.

"Where are you?" said James. Carefully, Simon explained the legal tangle and mess they were still in. Like Simon the previous evening, James could not believe it, his hopes dashed too.

"How will I get home?"

"You have money?"

"Yes, some. It's all I have. Got no benefits now."

"I'm sorry, you'll have to use that."

Later that week, Simon was back in Bilthaven at Carl Irving's office to discuss the situation. He gave Simon a list of questions to put to Naomi.

The next day at his regular meeting with her, after the usual discussion of what he was doing, news of the family and his activities, Simon said, "I've been to see my solicitor to talk about me and James."

"Your solicitor? He would need to know the facts from James's solicitor, I would think."

"No problem, it's the same solicitor," said Simon, at which Naomi raised an eyebrow. Simon described events at the court a couple of days earlier, which Naomi didn't know about, and then took a breath. "On what legal basis do you prevent me from seeing James? Also, what would be the sanction if I did?"

Naomi paused. "There is no legal reason why you cannot see James. It's just that we have concerns about two offenders associating. It was of course a condition of SORP that you could not associate, and at that time, there would have been sanctions. But neither of you are now on SORP."

"So I can see him?"

"Let me run this by some colleagues first, Simon. I'll see you next week, but until then I would ask you to maintain distance from James."

Simon did not wish to endanger the progress made so he agreed he would not see James. But on the phone he described what had happened and urged James to be patient. James had news of his own. Because he had been in prison, he was now only subject to the prevention order, not even on probation any more. No more Ruby!

At the meeting next week at Simon's home, Naomi and the police were there – not a good sign thought Simon. Naomi repeated what she had said the previous week and both she and the police officer again spoke of their concern but affirmed that no sanction would follow.

"Then I shall see him. I love him and I want him in my life."

"And Karen?" queried Naomi.

"Karen is my wife, she is my number one and both she and James know it. But there is room for him, and now, after all that has happened, I need him. And I think he needs me."

"More probably the latter," commented Naomi.

"I understand your concerns in general terms, but in this case it is not a problem. We are not seeking to do anything illegal. Just be together. I know there will be supervision, but now we have nothing to hide."

Naomi did not seem pleased with Simon's decision, but could see his determination and the strength of his commitment. She would have to trust him but keep an eye on him. "You would have been on monthly visits at this stage of your order, Simon, but I am putting you back on weekly. Come and see me next week."

Simon nodded, it was what he expected. As soon as they left, he drove to Cliffport.

"We're legal!" he said to a surprised James when he walked in. James smiled but then his mood sank again.

"Look," he said. Simon then noticed the boarded up, smashed windows, egg stains on the remainder.

"The fucking *Nusbury News* is to blame for this," he said angrily. Elaine was quiet, obviously tense. "That article was crap, half of it was nothing to do with it," James continued.

Simon didn't know what to say. After all James had been through, Colin Duncan, his loss of his father, his boyfriend, prosecution and prison, and now this, mindless idiots following the herd.

James was still ranting. "The family aren't speaking to me, not even my cousin, one brother won't, the other can't. My aunt and my Nanna are not speaking to me. I was better off in fucking prison."

"I'm here, James," said Simon.

"Yes, you and my Mam. That's it! I'd be better off dead."

"James, please don't talk that way," said Elaine.

"It's true," snapped James.

Simon stayed and talked as James calmed down a bit and they drank tea in his room. "Why didn't you look at me in court?" he asked; this had been on his mind. "I was looking at you the whole time."

"I know," said James, "I could see that. But I knew if I looked at you, I'd probably start crying or something daft. That wouldn't have looked very good," James added with a smile.

Simon smiled and gave James a quick hug. But James would not leave the house now, such was his fear and anxiety, not even with Simon. So eventually he left.

He talked it through with Denise that week. She was pleased that at least the stress of the fear of discovery had been lifted from Simon, but had little advice to offer with regard to the vandalism at Cliffport. She again suggested he put his thoughts on paper as a way of organising them in his mind, a technique she had suggested to Simon before about Daniel, the rape and his offences of so long ago.

The next week, Simon was able to coax James out. His mood seemed to improve while they were out, and the two could at least enjoy time together without worrying about bumping into Naomi, Ruby or anybody else. But the vandalism continued sporadically, with Elaine alternatively depressed and defiant.

A major step was that James decided to act about his past, which Simon had been urging him to do for many months.

"I'm going to report Colin Duncan," he said. "My sister is too, so I'm going to make a statement."

"Well done, James," said Simon, genuinely proud of him for doing this. It took courage, Simon knew. Courage he had never had.

22. 2009/11 *On the Edge*

Simon drove over to Cliffport. Elaine was there, and James, who seemed unsettled. The police officer was due to interview James about Colin Duncan.

"You mustn't hang back," advised Simon. "Say exactly what he did, no half measures. If you show any doubt and it goes to court, the defence will tear you apart."

"Ok, don't tell me what I already know," snapped James, his nerves evident.

"I'll stay in if you want me to," offered Simon.

"No, I'd rather do it myself," said James, adding, "Thanks though."

The female police officer arrived at just after ten o'clock. Simon was introduced as James's friend.

"You can stay if you like, if James would like that," she said after a brief chat in which she ascertained that Simon knew all that was going on James's life.

James said, "I'll do it myself."

So Simon left the room, and later took Elaine to the shops in Cliffport while the interview went on. Simon had assumed it might take an hour, but time dragged by. He started to get anxious. At three in the afternoon he sent James a text, "How long?" The reply came back "30 minutes". Simon arrived back at the house to find them still at it so he waited in James's bedroom off the lounge while they finished.

Then he heard raised voices from the lounge. It was James's grandmother Delia, who lived opposite, pouring a torrent of vitriolic hatred at James, blaming him for all that had happened, saying he was not welcome and should leave, that nobody would forgive him, nobody wanted him. He was useless, always had been, was no good to anybody. The police officer tried to explain that James had paid the penalty for his wrongdoing and that he should be left alone.

"Nobody round here will leave him alone while he's here, he should just bugger off," shouted Delia. Elaine had often said how her mother-in-law was two faced, nice to your face, bad mouthing you when your back was turned, and Delia was obviously unaware that Simon was behind the door listening to this bile. Simon wondered whether to go out and confront her but decided that it might make matters worse. He heard Delia leave, and he went into the lounge. James looked shaken.

"That *is* your grandmother, isn't it?" questioned Simon.

James nodded.

"I mean, not by remarriage or anything, but your blood relative grandmother?" he asked again, just to make sure because of the complexities of James's family.

"Yes, she is," said James.

"I don't know what to make of your family, James," said Simon.

"Well, we're finished now," said the police officer. "It's been a long haul but it's all done now. Thirty one pages of your statement, but it should mean I won't have to keep coming back to check things when we interview Colin Duncan."

"You have an address for him?" asked Simon.

"Yes, and we think it's genuine, but we haven't interviewed him yet. Well, I must get away back to Thirlham and get on with the job. Thank you James." She left.

"That was a marathon. I am really proud of you, James," said Simon.

"Let's get away," said James. So they drove swiftly out of the town. They went to Bilthaven and Simon parked the car. They enjoyed a nice late lunch at an American style restaurant. James liked the young manager there, wishing he could know him better. They both agreed he was gay. He made up a special cocktail for James that he had done on previous visits.

"I bet he's got a boyfriend," said James.

"Probably," said Simon, who could certainly see what James saw in the young man.

"He's young to be manager," said James.

"I'd guess mid twenties."

"Younger," said James with certainty.

At the bar James took the direct route. "Can I ask, how old are you?"

"Twenty-one," said the manager, smiling.

"You've done well, to be manager at twenty-one," said Simon.

"Thank you," came the smiling response. He then went off to serve other customers.

They decided – or rather James decided – to go bowling. It was cheap before six o'clock and it was now five. Simon edged in to the lead on the first game, and then gained a huge lead in the second. James was becoming more frustrated. Simon knew it wasn't the bowling or even the young restaurant manager. His mood seemed darker and he was wasting his shots, hammering them down the lane without a care, more often than not going into the gutter. Simon won the game by a huge margin. The third game was the same, and they abandoned it half way through. Simon was worried about James, but he seemed to recover.

"Let's go for a drink," he said.

"OK, but one, I need to get back to Karen."

"Two?"

"Maybe two," said Simon.

They walked through the city to a bar and while Simon stuck to orange juice and the like, James was buying cheap bottles of booze. He was obviously deeply unhappy. Simon tried to talk to him, to reason with him, but he would not listen. He wanted to go from bar to bar, desperately trying to drown his inner anguish.

"I just wanna have a good time," James argued when Simon urged restraint. They met a man in a bar, a white South African now living in Bilthaven. He seemed educated and interesting to talk to, clearly gay, which he confirmed. More drink. Then the man started trotting out conspiracy theories, saying that global warming was a myth by the 'world government' to levy more taxes but the most ludicrous being that Barack Obama was a plant, he had not grown up in Hawaii but was really Nigerian and a secret Muslim, pointing out his middle name was Hussein (a very common Muslim name, Simon pointed out) and that Obama was really a code for Osama. Simon just wanted to get away, James wanted to go with the man to meet his friends, but the man left.

So they moved to another bar. Simon kept protesting and wanted to leave, but he knew that James was in no state to be left. Simon did not want a repeat of the previous October. So he stayed with his friend, past midnight and into the small hours.

Outside another bar they met a young man struggling with his cigarettes. There is a bond among smokers which Simon of course did not share. This man, Kevin, was already the worse for wear, but James gave him a light and he gave James a cigarette. They went into the bar for more drink and then out onto a smokers' roof terrace.

"Why don't you come with me?" slurred Kevin.

"Why?" asked Simon, cautiously. He seemed a nice enough man, who had phoned his girlfriend to say he was out and had met this young gay man and his older friend.

"Have a good time," said Kevin.

"James, I need to get home."

"You go home then, I'll be OK."

"I'm worried about you."

"Don't be."

They went back into the bar from the roof terrace, at least it was warmer, if a lot noisier. James and Kevin went to the bar, Simon following. He saw James was looking at him intently, he said something that Simon couldn't hear for the loud music.

"What?" he called.

"I love you," said James more clearly.

"He'll be OK with me," shouted Kevin in Simon's ear. "We'll have drink or two, get a kebab and he can go back to my place. You pick him up in the morning."

Simon's will to resist was weakening. He was tired, having been up since half past six the previous day.

He beckoned James closer. "Will you phone me if you feel at all unsure?" he said into James's ear.

"Yes, I will. Go home to Karen."

So with a heavy heart, Simon left and drove home to Thirlham. He took the bed in the spare room to avoid disturbing Karen. He dare not take a tablet so did not sleep but lay and turned over in the bed.

At four o'clock his phone rang next to the bed, it was James.

"He's buggered off, I don't know where he is," said James. "Can you come and get me."

"I'm in bed," said Simon.

"Please?"

"OK, where?"

"Meet me at the bus station."

Simon quickly dressed and drove rapidly back to Bilthaven along empty roads. It wasn't frosty so he didn't have that to worry about.

At the bus station, there was no sign of James. Each time he tried James's phone, he got put to voicemail. Repeated attempts had the same result. He sent James a text, "Please answer the phone, I am in Bilthaven. Where are you?" There was no reply so Simon drove round the empty city centre. Now terrified he drove to the City Bridge, it was deserted. He drove slowly over, looking all round.

Then a text. "I luv u and Mam." Simon's heart sank. His anxiety level was now sky high. Not again, please not again. He parked up and tried James again. He answered! At least he was alive!

"Where are you?"

"On the edge."

"Edge of what?" It was windy where James was and it was hard to hear.

"Edge of my life."

"Please James, let me come and get you."

"I had everything I wanted before, home, friends, family. Now I have nothing. Just you and my Mam, and I'm not even sure about her."

"She loves you James. I love you. Please, where are you?"

"It's too late. I love you, Simon."

The phone went dead. Simon was screaming in the parked car, he felt so helpless. The man he loved was going to die and he could do nothing. Perhaps he was already dead. "No! No!" he screamed. But there was no-one to hear. Just then a police van and a car, blue lights blazing, went tearing past toward the City Bridge. "Oh God, no!" Simon knew in his gut it was James. He followed them to the bridge and to his horror they pulled up on the right where a police officer was leaning over the heavy wrought iron rails looking into the water far below. Simon pulled up behind the police van and rushed to the side where the PC was.

"What's going on?" he called. But as he did so he saw James, sitting on the outside of the rail with his back to the roadway, low down on a tiny ledge, nothing between him and the dark waters a hundred feet below, staring at the oblivion. "James, I'm here for you. Please!" he called. He could only see the back of James's head, but he moved his head in such a way that Simon knew he had been heard.

The police officer waved him back, but now at least was armed with James's name. Another cop came up to Simon. "Let the officer do his job."

Simon stepped back. Another officer was talking to a young man who was saying how he and his girlfriend had been walking cross the bridge when they heard a voice saying he how he had once had all he wanted and now he had nothing and his life was over. Puzzled they looked over the rail and had seen James sitting precariously above the river. They dialled 999. Lucky, they said, he had been on the phone talking or they would never have seen him. Simon recognised his own conversation with James a few minutes earlier. Thank God for his timing.

The officer continued to talk to James while Simon, shaking, unable to contain his terror, could only watch, his eyes fixed on the back of James's head low through rail in case it was the last sight he would ever have of his love alive. Officers took his details and he also gave them James's details and a brief resumé of his troubles. Simon knew that James's life was on a knife edge, the waiting was agony. All James had to do was slightly straighten his thighs and he would slip off into eternity. Simon knew he would be unable to bear this. To steady himself, he was shaking now, he took one of his blue trifluoperazine tablets he always carried. If only James could see how valued and loved he was. Simon thought of the great gift James had given him, that of self acceptance, to cease fighting his sexuality and accept himself. He thought of the shining light dream – had that been James? Simon prayed for James's life on that cold empty bridge with only the police vehicles and his own car there.

Suddenly James was standing up and turned to face the waiting police officers, the first officer holding James's arm. Other officers started forward but James put his hand up to stop them, which they did. He could still fall backward, Simon was holding his breath, praying. James looked at Simon, their eyes met briefly. He spoke to the officer holding his arm and then, to Simon's immense relief, swung his right leg up and over the parapet, then his left and he was safe, surrounded by officers. At that moment, Simon's phone went, it was Elaine, distraught.

"What's happening? Deirdre's had a text from James saying he was going to jump!"

"Elaine, it's OK, he's safe. I'll call you back."

Simon rushed forward, putting his arm on James's shoulder. "It'll be OK, James. I'll help you, you know I will."

James appeared frightened as he was ushered to the police van. "What happens now?" he asked.

"We'll take you to the police station and a doctor will see you," said the officer who had been with James; PC Hunter, Simon could read his name tag now.

"Is he being arrested?" asked Simon as James was placed in the van.

"No, it's for his own safety."

"Can I go with him?"

"No, he is in police custody now, he'll be taken to the police station."

"I was able to stay with him last time."

"Sorry, you can come to the police station yourself but you won't be able to see him."

The door of the van shut and Simon lost sight of James. He did follow the van to the police station but had to find somewhere to park. He waited in the front office.

Later PC Hunter took Simon into an interview room.

"Thank you so much, you deserve a commendation."

"It's nice to get thanks for a change," smiled PC Hunter. "Actually, I'm glad you turned up. I felt a change in James after he knew you were there. It was a turning point. You're obviously very close."

"We love each other. I wish I could help him more."

In the interview, Simon filled in many details about James, confirming PC Hunter's assessment that James was gay, placing that night's actions in the context of James's overall trauma.

"Will I be able to see him at all?"

"No, he's in the custody suite. You'd better go home. He's got to get the alcohol out of his system first."

"Tell him I love him, won't you?"

PC Hunter smiled. "Of course I will."

Next afternoon, later that same day in fact, Elaine phoned to say James had just been brought home. Simon was shocked. He knew James needed help, and had expected a transfer to hospital for a time. He drove over. James was lying in bed, looking very tired. Simon gave him a hug and a kiss.

"James, I am so glad you're here. I really thought I'd lost you."

"Still here worse luck."

"I'll help you. I told you before it'd be tough and not quick, but stay with me, and I'll do whatever I can."

"I know you will. Thanks. I never knew real love until I met you. Everybody else has just used me. You're a mint friend."

"So are you."

"I don't do much for you, except give you grief."

"James, you have taught me self acceptance, to understand male-male love, you have given me the most wonderful gift. And it was by talking to you that I was able to talk about when I was raped. You helped me confront my past. I will always love you for it."

Later at home, Simon wrote a letter to the Chief Constable praising PC Hunter for his expertise and professionalism.

23. 2009 Wedding and a set up

Simon and Karen were sitting in the lounge of the Hilltown house with Robert and Fiona.

"Mum? Dad?" said Robert.

"What is it Robert?" asked Simon.

"Fiona and I have something to tell you."

"Yes?"

"We want to get married," said Fiona when Robert seemed to be having trouble finding the right words. Robert beamed expectantly at his parents, but with a hint of nervousness.

"Well, you've been together now for eight years, so it's about time you made an honest woman of her, Robert," said Simon. Robert's face lit up at his Dad's endorsement of their plans. Fiona sat, smiling.

"Yes, why not," said Karen, sealing the approval.

This did of course involve Karen and Simon in another round of arrangements to be made, never mind the cost. But as Simon pointed out, Harriet's wedding had been a big event and the marriage had only lasted three years. Robert and Fiona had already been together eight years, so they could hardly do less for him.

James meantime had become a prisoner in his own home, fearful of going out because of the idiots. Attacks on the house continued and the council installed CCTV which helped. James would only leave the house with Simon who parked at the side and they left through a back door. Then they would drive out of Cliffport and James could relax a bit. They resumed going to the cinema in the afternoons, visits to Nusbury or Bilthaven. Some family members started to talk to James again, the most important being his cousin to whom James was close. His mood lifted which was a great relief to Simon.

It was a Sunday morning and Simon woke first. Karen was asleep next to him. He looked at her, the way her hair was tousled after the night's sleep on the pillow. Such love. She opened her eyes, saw him looking at her and smiled. He kissed her, feeling her warmth next to him and then as arousal took hold, took her into his arms as they re-affirmed their longstanding love for each other.

It had been a good Christmas, despite the appalling weather. The snow had prevented the girls getting to Melanie and for over a week, Simon had been unable even to get his car out of the street. The snow was still lying but at least he could get the car in and out, albeit with some difficulty. He needed to as well, because there was a lot of catching up to do with wedding plans and of course, helping James. It was a great relief when the snow cleared.

He went with Robert to the hospital in Nusbury when Donna needed her grommets refitting. A routine operation but general anaesthesia is never wholly without risk. So it was a relief later when Donna started telling everybody to be quiet and stop slamming doors!

Since coming out of prison, James had been without a computer and Simon was checking his email account periodically. But at the end of January, James decided to get one which he would use within the limits set by the judge, and he told his supervising police officer this. Simon arranged the purchase of a reconditioned but quite powerful computer. But while this was in hand, Simon noticed unusual activity on James's email account, several emails apparently sent to himself. He knew James had no internet access or computer so curious, he opened these to have a look. His heart practically stopped. There were several pictures of teenage boys, one with four of them on a bed, naked, others in naked poses. Simon felt cold inside. How could this be? He froze while he thought what to do. He knew he would have confront James with this, but how? He printed out the images, and then using a special scrubbing program, removed them entirely from his own hard disk.

Stony faced, he walked into James's room.

"Hi Simon," said James.

Simon laid out the pictures on James's desk, ironically where his computer was due to be. James's face was one of shock.

"What are those?" he asked.

"Don't you know?"

"No. Why should I?"

"They were in your email account, sent from you to you."

"I haven't been in my email since coming out of prison, you know that."

"So how did they get there then?"

"Well, I don't fucking know, Simon. You're the only person who looks at it. And why would I send them to myself?"

Simon had to agree it didn't make sense. "I don't know, James, but don't accuse me. I didn't put them there."

"Well, there's only you and me know the password. And it wasn't me. I haven't even got a fucking computer yet." James paused. "Oh fuck!" he said quietly. His face was now even more ashen.

"What's the matter?"

"Ruby. Fucking Ruby demanded to know my password."

"When?"

"Ages ago. After I got done the first time."

"So Ruby could access your email account?"

"Yes, and I've just told the cop I'm getting a computer and I bet she told Ruby. The bitch!"

"So Ruby thinks you already have a computer. And she's logged in to plant these images on it. Jesus!"

"I told you she hates me! And I bet that's how the second ones got there that I went down for. She always wanted me in prison! Now we've got her!"

"No James, we haven't. It's bloody obvious I know, but there's no proof. There's only these printouts, and they are going on the fire right now."

"What about your computer?"

"James, don't be silly. Do you think I left them there? They've gone; thirty five Gutman passes, a full scrub, cluster tips, free space, a full boot time defrag, the lot."

"So she gets away with it, sending me to prison and fucking up my life, everything."

Simon didn't know what to say. He remembered how James had always vehemently denied the second group of images were anything to do with him. And now there had been an attempt to plant a third batch on him. He sat and watched as James raged in his anger and frustration. Eventually he seemed to calm down.

"The first thing to do is change the password," said Simon eventually.

"Yes, do that," said James.

A few days later Simon collected the computer intended for James, and took it to his house. He installed a basic set of programs, mail client, extra browser, paint software, office software. He invited the police to come and check it before he took it to James. This way they would know James had not yet touched it, and that it was clean, days after the attempted image planting. The computer was given the all clear, and James at last had a computer again, running within the terms of his court order. Simon would dearly have loved to have been able to get Ruby prosecuted and this might have meant James's conviction being overturned, but he had not been able to see a way of doing this without retaining the images on his own computer and putting himself at risk of prosecution. So as James bitterly said, Ruby got away with it.

Simon and Karen's Winter and Spring were dominated by wedding preparations. It was to be a church wedding in the village where Fiona had grown up and where many of her large extended family lived, followed by a reception at a country hotel not far from Hilltown for about a hundred and twenty guests! It all had to be booked, banns read, catering, drinks, cake, dresses to be organised, suits to hire, flowers, music, photographer – and the rings of course! Simon took out wedding insurance, just in case! The financial burden fell almost all on Simon and Karen as Fiona's mother didn't have the means. But they were determined that Robert should have a good wedding. And Donna and Florence were looking forward to being bridesmaids.

The week leading up to the wedding was very wet and windy, but they all resolved to make the most of it whatever happened.

Simon continued to see James, and at Robert's insistence, James took part in Robert's stag night out at a posh restaurant in Bilthaven. In deference to Karen's sensibilities James was not coming to the actual wedding. Simon hated having to explain this to him, but he understood.

Three days before the wedding, Simon went to Bilthaven airport to meet Harriet. He was anxious about this, he had not seen her for four years and he wondered how she would 'be' with him after all that had happened in those years. As he waited by the Arrivals gate, he wondered if the parking machines took card payments. He wandered over to check but as he did so, he saw a familiar face. Was it Eric Hill? He hadn't seen him for many years. As he got closer he was sure it was but then he saw Eric looking straight through him. So that's the way he wants it, thought Simon. So he said nothing. Simon checked the parking payment machine and it did take cards. When he turned round, Eric Hill and his little group had moved away to below the large departures and arrivals board. Just then the gates opened and Simon saw people walking out. A small, slight young woman was looking at him, smiling, pulling her luggage behind her. Harriet! It took him a moment to realise it was her. They hugged. Simon didn't mention Eric Hill, and it wasn't relevant anyway. He was glad to have his daughter with him. Harriet was very chatty as they drove back to Thirlham, pleased to be back in Britain. She said how much she missed Britain, its ways, the culture, just the whole British ambience.

Robert and the girls were happy to see Harriet again. Robert had chosen her to be his Best Man. He reasoned that had he had a brother, he would have been his Best Man, so why not his sister? Simon had drawn a detailed plan of the wedding weekend, so everybody knew where they had to be at what times, who was ferrying who to hair appointments, flower collections etc. He had a chart with the key players' lines colour coded – he called it the 'tube map'[7]. All lines converged on the church!

The day of the wedding at the end of March dawned bright and sunny. It was cold and breezy but the sun shone out of a clear blue sky. The service was lovely and both Robert and Fiona said all their lines without error. After milling around outside in the sunshine while photographs were taken, the whole group set off, many on a bus hired for the purpose, to the hotel, following the Rolls Royce and Bentley carrying the happy couple and the bridesmaids. Fiona's mother wanted Fiona's uncle to make the speech but he handed over quickly to Simon, who had a speech prepared just in case. Then Robert, with some

---

[7] A reference to the coloured map of the London Underground, since copied by other underground rail networks. Londoners refer to the Underground as the 'Tube'.

trepidation, stood up for his speech. Working from notes and with Harriet in close support he made an excellent short speech, remembering all the important points. Simon and Karen felt so proud of him. Then Harriet made her 'Best Man' speech, which everybody agreed was outstanding. So it all went well, the food was plentiful and of high quality and in the evening there was a disco. As invited, Melanie arrived for this along with Kyle, now six, and they danced with Donna and Florence. Everybody agreed the wedding had been a great success. In Fiona's large family, weddings came round fairly often, but many said this was the best yet. Simon and Karen were happy that it had all gone off well. The day next the rain came down again – they had got the one fine day in a spell of poor weather. Most people gave gifts of money toward the honeymoon, when Robert, Fiona and the girls would go to see Harriet in America and take in Niagara Falls, an ambition of Fiona's.

24. 2010 Honeymoon and Holiday

As the time of the trip to North America drew closer, Simon tried to help as best he could. It was decided that Karen would go too, to help Robert and Fiona with the girls, and also to see Bernadette, however briefly and of course to see Harriet again. Simon knew he could not go now and tried to be philosophical about it, but it hurt.

"Would you mind if I went away while you're in America?" Simon asked Karen.

"No, of course not," said Karen. "Where would you go?"

"I thought I might get away for a few days with James. Try to get a late deal cheap." Simon could sense Karen's uncertainty, but amazing and generous woman she was, she readily agreed.

Simon and James were in Nusbury and tried a couple of travel agents. In one, they found that prices on a Mediterranean cruise leaving at the right time, just three weeks away, had been slashed. The two decided to go for it and started making arrangements; luckily James had a passport.

So in August, Simon took Robert and Donna to Bilthaven Airport, while Karen drove her car with Fiona and Florence. She would leave her car in the long stay car park. Simon waved his whole family off through security and drove to Cliffport to check if James was ready. At 4 a.m. next morning he and James were back at Bilthaven Airport for their flight to Palma to join the ship.

James took the window seat.

"This is the first time I've flown," he told Simon.

Simon was surprised. "What, ever?"

"Yes. I've never had a holiday before. Well, I did once spend a night at a caravan site when my aunt was there, but that's all. This is the first time I've had a proper holiday."

James's happiness was evident, he spent the flight looking at the ground or commenting on the shapes of the clouds. "That one looks like a ship" or "See that one, it looks like a face."

Their two berth inside cabin was clean and comfortable with all the amenities required. As they cruised the Mediterranean, going ashore at their various ports of call, Simon watched his friend's enjoyment and took pleasure in that, as well as being in James's company the whole time. Text messaging allowed him to keep in touch with Karen. They could not afford most of the shore excursions so found their own way round when ashore, which was more exciting anyway, Simon's French enough when English wouldn't do. Palermo was busy and noisy, and with a lot of graffiti. They did though in Naples take the trip to Pompeii and up the volcano Vesuvius. They had to climb the last thousand feet on foot to the crater's edge, but James coped, using his inhaler and stopping a couple of times.

In Ajaccio they shopped and drank in street cafés. They got on the wrong bus in Toulon but the driver dropped them for no fare at the correct stop for their number 40 bus to Mt Faron. They wondered how many bus drivers at home would do that. They took the cable car to the top and admired the view. Later James was sketched by a street artist.

In Barcelona they went to Sagrada Família but the queues to get in were far too long.

"It's certainly different," commented James. Then they went on to 'Camp Nou', the home of Barcelona FC which James wanted to see, and rode the cable car across the harbour, going right over their ship.

The week passed all too quickly and James wanted to stay on the ship for its next cruise which some passengers were doing, but necessity – and finance – prevailed and they flew home. Both were pulled aside at Bilthaven Airport and questioned about where they had been and who they were with. This was because they both had records.

James started to get defensive but Simon calmed him down. "It's a small price to pay," he said.

The immigration officer that interviewed Simon was po-faced.

"Where have you flown in from?"

"Palma."

"How long have you been away?"

"One week."

"Who with?"

"James Phillips."

"Where is he now?"

Simon pointed at James a few feet away. "There he is."

"Have you been anywhere else?"

"Yes. Palermo, Naples, Ajaccio, Toulon, Barcelona."

"In a week?

"Yes."

"How did you travel. By car, taxi?"

Simon was taken aback by this stupid question and was himself now getting annoyed by the contemptuous and hostile tone the officer seemed to have. Bilthaven Airport was not a big one and it was a holiday flight from the cruise ship. "It would have to be one that floats," he retorted.

"Why?"

"Geography not a strong point then?"

"No need to be like that," said the immigration officer, handing Simon back his passport.

"See what I mean?" said James as they went to collect their bags from the carousel.

When Simon recounted this to Naomi at his meeting a few days later, she laughed. "They seem to be stopping everybody these days," she said.

A week later, Simon was back at the airport to greet excited Donna and Florence who were full of their time in Canada, where Bernadette had laid on a BBQ, and of course their time with Harriet, including among many other things, a trip to Pittsburgh to watch the Steelers play. That had its own drama as the game had to be halted for a violent thunderstorm.

Life resumed its routine, with Donna starting secondary school in Dirshingham, the same one Harriet had attended. Harriet's favourite English teacher was now the Head Teacher. Simon took a picture of Donna in the uniform standing by the old brick wall outside the school and emailed it to Harriet.

"It's very odd seeing Donna wearing my school uniform, and I recognise that wall," was her emailed reply.

In September another milestone passed. Simon's three year community order, probation, expired. He had a last interview with Naomi and that was that. He was still on the sex offenders' register for another two years which meant he would still see his police supervisor Gemma.

"At this point in your order I would normally see you every six months in your case," said Gemma, "but because you are with James, I will see you every two months. His supervisor Lindsey will see him more often as well."

"Fair enough," said Simon.

Simon was soon back at the airport, this time in October with Karen. It was half term and as part of their Ruby Wedding, they flew to Nice for a few days. Their hotel was near the sea front, the *Promenade des Anglais*. They relaxed, and talked, walked and did some shopping. One day they spend one Euro each on the bus fare to Monte Carlo. The bus was hot and crowded, and took about forty minutes, but then there they were, in this playground of the rich and famous. But much of it was tacky, not what they had expected. Also half the streets were being dug up which led to traffic chaos. But Simon wandered down to where a row of gleaming white, large motor yachts were moored, and looked at the opulence on show. Then he noticed that all except one was flying the red ensign, the British merchant marine flag. All these yachts were British owned. This while the coalition government back at home was planning to cut services and benefits for the poor.

He saw a middle aged man in working clothes, washing out a small boat that belonged to one of the yachts.

"Hello," said Simon.

"Hello," replied the man in good English. In fact, Simon wondered if he were English.

"Who owns all these yachts?" asked Simon.

"Some are chartered," said the man, "but most are owned by city people – bankers," he added by way of explanation, and then spat into the water.

Simon walked on and rejoined Karen. They got the bus back to Nice and decided that Monte Carlo was not what it was cracked up to be.

They enjoyed their relaxing few days, looking round Nice, visiting the Matisse Museum, seeing the sights. They were tired when they got back home but it had been so good to get away together.

25.   2010 Trial and Rejection

It was a year since James had made his statement to the police about Colin Duncan and had then that night gone to the City Bridge, unable to bear the pain any longer. And now, after several delays, the trial was due at Thirlham Crown Court. James had been told to wait until he got a phone call, but Simon drove to Cliffport to wait with him. Mid morning and the phone rang, could James be there in half an hour? Difficult but they would try. Simon drove to Thirlham with James and Elaine, and managed to get parked near the Crown Court.

They waited in the witness room. The case officer who had taken James's long statement a year before came in and took James into a side room to read his statement. At just after midday, James was called.

"Good luck," called Simon. He wanted to go in the public gallery but the police said he was too close to James and might talk to other family members due to give evidence about what James had said – or the defence could allege that anyway. So Simon played safe and waited. After half an hour James came back as the court had adjourned for lunch.

"Colin Duncan still looks as scruffy as ever," he said. He was tense and snappy, Simon recognised the mood. They went out to a pub for food, about which James complained as it was not to his taste. The pub changed it, but he still left much of it.

That afternoon, James resumed his evidence, while Elaine and Simon waited, fingers crossed. He tried to imagine what was going on. He remembered the courtroom well, James said it was the one without the glass dock.

At last, James came back. "I'm finished now."

"How did it go?" asked Simon.

"When I saw him there, I just wanted to jump over and smash him," said James, clenching his fist.

"Did the defence bring up your own record?"

"That's all they talked about," snapped James. "Come on, let's go."

Simon swallowed, his heart heavy. If James's anger had come across to the jury, it would not do him any good. But Elaine and James's aunt were still due to give evidence, mainly that James had talked of this for years, he had not just made it up. Also his sister was due to give evidence.

The next day, Simon again waited at Cliffport. James's sister was not sent for and neither was anyone else. Simon felt in his bones that the case had been curtailed. He stayed on but eventually left and went home.

He had been home an hour when his phone rang. It was James's supervising police officer; Lindsey, not the case officer.

"Simon, are you with James?"

"No, I was earlier."

"The verdict is in and it's not good, for James that is."

"Not guilty?"

"Yes, I'm afraid so. We were worried about him. We don't want him going off a bridge or anything and we thought you were the best person to offer him support."

"I feared this," said Simon. "Thanks for letting me know."

Simon phoned James.

"I know," said James before Simon could say anything. "I'm OK."

"I'll come through."

"You don't need to."

But after they hung up, Simon knew he had to go anyway. When he walked into James's room, James looked up, surprised.

"James, I couldn't not come," said Simon, squeezing James's shoulder. James smiled.

But his face saddened. "Shit happens. And it always happens to me."

"I believe you, James. Remember that. So do lots of other people."

"Just leave it," said James.

Simon stayed with his friend for a few hours until he was sure James's mood was not too dark. He drove home puzzled and angry at the way the prosecution had been handled and that James had been put through all that, almost losing his life off the City Bridge – and for what?

26. *2010 Unorthodox Nuptials*

Despite unusual November and December blizzards that brought a repeat of February's disruption and paralysis, the year ended on a more cheerful note for Simon and Karen, if somewhat unconventionally. Simon got an email from Harriet shortly before Christmas saying that while she and Trent has been putting up the decorations, he had asked her to marry him. She had accepted of course.

"I wondered how long it would take," said Karen. "I had a feeling when we were there that it might happen."

"For this, I will crawl on bended knee to the American embassy for permission to enter," said Simon. "My daughter's wedding has to be a good reason?"

"I hope so," said Karen, "but I'll go. First we need to find out when it is."

Engagement cards were bought and posted, both from Simon and Karen but also from Robert, Fiona and the girls. Ken too was quick to send a card. The Christmas post probably meant they would not arrive until the New Year, but it's the thought that counts.

Simon was dumbfounded a few days later, just before Christmas, to receive another email from Harriet announcing that she and Trent were now married! They had done this in a simple civil ceremony in Ohio – and called at the supermarket for washing powder on the way home!

"Only Harriet could do that," commented Simon. "Always her own person, bless her."

"Now we have to send wedding cards, hot on the heels of the engagement cards," said Karen.

"It does mean that we've seen both our kids married in the same year," said Simon. The details were fleshed out later in a long phone call with Harriet, and Trent of course.

27. *2011 Full Circle*

A new year, an uncertain future. But Robert and Harriet were now both married, Donna and Florence were doing well at school and James was trying to come to terms with the acquittal of Colin Duncan.

Simon doubted if he would ever be free of medication, but perhaps, he felt, there would be some kind of stability in the closing years of his life. Nevertheless he felt the need to set out the past, although where to turn? He sat and thought about what Denise had once said about how writing was his best medium. Perhaps a more imaginative account would help, rather than the bald, purely factual accounts he had devised so far for the benefit of all the agencies that had a piece of him. But how, what? It had been hard enough building up the factual document.

But maybe another account would allow him to explain more about the role of others in his life, Daniel especially, his first love, who for so long had been hoarded like a secret treasure in the recesses of his mind. Daniel, who was now on his mind so much, the subject of his fantasies and memories. But Daniel as he was then, not the pensioner he would be now. The thought of his beautiful boy as a pensioner was quickly put out of his mind.

And Karen, the amazing, wonderful Karen, who had come into his life at such a crucial time and had lifted him from the depths of despair. Together they had lived a good life; yes, with many ups and downs but their love had survived all the traumas and disasters and together they had enjoyed the triumphs that life can bring. Karen was the great love of his life. Simon knew that without her steadying influence over more than forty years his life might have been very different, tragic possibly, with hope for a future banished, like James.

And yes, James. Simon knew he would do whatever he could to give James that hope for his future; there but for the grace of God. So different, yet so much in common. James who had given him the great gift of self acceptance; James, the third love of his life.

So where to start. He would need to peel back the layers of his soul, to lay bare the forces that had driven his life, both good and bad actions, to try to understand what it was that had made him. He sat, staring at the computer, head resting on his hands, elbows propped on the desk by the keyboard, lost in a reverie. He would have peel back the layers of the years, going further and back; his mind wandered back, right back. Mummy. Those little shorts he used to wear. Fancy remembering those now! Then he began to type:

Simon felt the increasing panic well up in him. He knew that he was not going to make it in time. He ran up the stairs, nearly tripping over a loose stair rod that was failing to keep the worn, rough, red stair carpet in place. The bathroom door was closed, and Simon reached up for the handle struggling to turn it. Perhaps it was the way his small body had to stretch up, but he knew then that he had lost. ...

www.ingramcontent.com/pod-product-compliance
Lightning Source LLC
Chambersburg PA
CBHW060909300426
44112CB00011B/1400